PREGNANCY LAW IN SOUTH AFRICA

BETWEEN REPRODUCTIVE AUTONOMY AND FOETAL INTERESTS

PREGNANCY LAW IN SOUTH AFRICA

BETWEEN REPRODUCTIVE AUTONOMY AND FOETAL INTERESTS

Camilla Pickles
LLB LLM LLD (University of Pretoria)

JUTA

First Published 2017

First Floor,
Sunclare Building,
21 Dreyer Street,
Claremont 7708

ISBN 9781 4851 1954 8

SET IN 11 ON 12 POINT TIMES ROMAN BY HELANNA TYPESETTERS

PREFACE AND ACKNOWLEDGMENTS

Nearly every woman or girl of reproductive age faces the potential for pregnancy for a large portion of her life, and many will come to experience pregnancy more than once during that time. Despite this almost ever-present potential for, or experience of, pregnancy the South African law remains relatively silent and legal commentary is generally rather scarce too. Aside from legislating and commenting on parenthood avoidance and conception issues, there is little available on the theme of pregnancy continuation and the application of the law and human rights to the various situations that may arise when pregnancies are continued to the moment of birth. Some scholars have recognised this gap and have highlighted select issues in the area of pregnancy and law. These include how to protect the unborn from liberal termination-of-pregnancy laws or third-party violence which terminates pregnancies without pregnant women's consent. They also support the notion of foetal personhood and prenatal substance abuse as a form of child abuse against the unborn. Those publishing on these select areas suggest law reform measures that are directed at legal recognition of the unborn and they all emphasise the need to extend legal protection to the unborn as individual entities. In their quest to secure optimal foetal development and live birth, the proposals directly or indirectly side-line women and overlook women's role in relation to their pregnancies and how proposals for law reform may impact women as legal subjects with human rights.

Thus, while there are attempts to address gaps in the law in relation to specifi issues in pregnancy, favouring the individual protection of the unborn at the expense of pregnant women's agency and rights gives rise to a tension between female reproductive autonomy and foetal interests. This approach to law reform will be ineffective because it fails to recognise that there is more to pregnancy than just the unborn, and the relationship between pregnant women and the unborn is not necessarily an adversarial one. I fin the possible implications of these scholarly pieces troubling, and I was inspired to ask whether it is possible to regard pregnancy in law as embodying both women and the unborn and whether the pregnancy can be construed in a way that it does not come to be framed as an adversarial relationship. These questions are particularly important questions to ask and answer because there are very few perspectives available on pregnancy in law and a one-sided perspective is not enough. It is not enough if the ultimate aim is to ensure that the law is able to meaningfully navigate the complexities of pregnancy and thereby serve as an authoritative tool to help promote and ensure healthy pregnancies and healthy pregnancy outcomes. To this end, current perspectives on how to develop the law and remedy gaps must be countered by informed, women-centred and women-advancing arguments.

These concerns motivated me to write a doctoral thesis, upon which this book is based. When looking at the concerns of prenatal substance abuse, termination of pregnancy, violence that terminates a pregnancy, and the extension of legal personhood to the unborn, I found that pregnancy-related issues will never be adequately resolved unless the potential for an adversarial pregnancy relationship is removed. In response, I propose a relational approach to pregnancy, centred on fostering relationships, in order to eliminate the potential for tension. This approach is framed as the not-one-but-not-two approach to pregnancy and it recognises that a pregnant woman and her foetus are two separate entities but inseparably linked through pregnancy. It focuses on the embodied connection that pregnancy represents and the contextual realities in which pregnancy exists. When applying this approach to the focus areas of this book, I found that a relational approach encourages imaginative and constructive possibilities for law reform efforts without sacrificin women's reproductive autonomy and rights or the recognition of the unborn.

This book attempts to encourage thinking about reproductive rights during pregnancy and it aims to lay the foundation for the development of pregnancy law without invoking the polarised notion of foetal rights. It is hoped that this book provides a sound theoretical approach to pregnancy in law and that the recommendations herein help achieve healthy, rights-affirming pregnancies.

I owe a great deal of gratitude to many people who have encouraged, supported, inspired and challenged me: my supervisor, Professor Ann Skelton, Carika Keulder, Professor Karin van Marle, Professor Rebecca Cook, Professor Jackie Heaton, Jessica Farmer, Emile Zitzke, all the librarians at the OR Tambo Law Library, Professor Jeanne Flavin, Lynn Paltrow, Farah Diaz-Tello, Sarah Ainsworth, Kylee Sunderlin, Kebe, Jess Cochrane, Joss Taylor and everyone else from National Advocates for Pregnant Women. I was very fortunate to be able to study as a full-time doctoral student in the Department of Private Law, University of Pretoria and this was made possible by the Faculty of Law's Structured Programme and the DAAD-NRF Joint Scholarship Programme. I am grateful to the team at Juta and Company, especially Linda van de Vijver. I thank my family for their constant support and reassurance. Most importantly, I am lovingly thankful for my husband, Bryan Pickles and daughter, Charlotte Pickles: their love and unwavering encouragement kept me motivated and strong.

Camilla Pickles
March 2017

CONTENTS

TABLE OF CASES AND RELATED DOCUMENTATION

South Africa

Other case law

AMICI CURIAE BRIEFS

Amici curiae brief of the Alabama Women's Resource Network, American Academy of Addiction Psychiatry, American Society of Addiction Medicine et al in the matter of *Akron v State* 2011 WL 3781258 (Ala Crim App)

Amici curiae brief of American Academy of Addiction Psychiatry, American College of Obstetrics and Gynecologists, American Psychiatric Association et al in the matter of *Ex parte Ankrom* 2013 WL 135748 (Ala)

Amici curiae brief of American Academy of Addiction Psychiatry, American College of Obstetricians and Gynecologists, American Psychiatric Association et al in the matter of *Ex parte Kimbrough* 2013 WL 135748 (Ala)

Amici curiae brief of American Association of Suicidology, American College of Obstetricians and Gynecologists, American Congress of Obstetricians and Gynecologists et al in the matter of *Shuai v State* 966 NE 2d 619 (Ind App 2012)

Amici curiae brief of American Public Health Association, National Association of Social Workers, Alabama Women's Resource Network et al in the matter of *Kimbrough v State of Alabama* in the Court of Criminal Appeals of Alabama, criminal appeals number CR-09-0485 (2010)

Amici curiae brief of American Public Health Association, American Nurses Association, American Psychiatric Association et al in the matter of *McKnight v South Carolina* 540 US 819 (2003)

Amici curiae brief of American Public Health Association, American Nurses Association, American Psychiatric Association et al in the matter of *State v McKnight* 576 SE 2d 168 (SC 2003)

Amici curiae brief of Legal Voice and Perinatal Loss Support Organizations and Experts in the matter of *Shuai v State* NE 2d 619 (Ind App 2012)

Amici curiae brief of the National Association of Alcoholism and Drug Abuse Counselors, South Carolina Association of Alcoholism and Drug Abuse Counselors, American College of Obstetricians and Gynecologists et al in the matter of *Whitner v State* 492 SE 2d 777 (SC 1997)

Amici curiae brief of Pegasus Legal Services for Children, New Mexico Section of the American College of Obstetricians and Gynecologists, New Mexico Public Health Association et al in the matter of *State v Martinez* 141 NM 763 (NM 2007)

Amici curiae brief of South Carolina Medical Association, South Carolina Nurses Association, South Carolina Association of Alcoholism and Drug Abuse Counselors et al in the matter of *McKnight v State* 661 SE 2d 354 (SC 2008)

BIBLIOGRAPHY

Books, Chapters in Books, Journal Articles and Related Publications

L Ackermann *Human Dignity: Lodestar for Equality in South Africa* (Juta, Claremont 2012)

C Albertyn, L Artz, H Combrinck, S Mills & L Wolhunter 'Women's freedom and security of the person' in E Bonthuys & C Albertyn (eds) *Gender, Law and Justice* (Juta, Cape Town 2007) 295

C Albertyn 'Equality' in E Bonthuys & C Albertyn (eds) *Gender, Law and Justice* (Juta, Cape Town 2007) 82

C Albertyn & B Goldblatt 'Equality' in S Woolman & M Bishop (eds) *Constitutional Law of South Africa* 2 ed (Original Service 3) 35-1

C Albertyn 'Claiming and defending abortion rights in South Africa' (2015) 11(2) *Revista Direito Getulio Vargas* 429

NN Aljalian 'Fourteenth Amendment personhood: Fact or fiction? (1999) 73(2) *St John's Law Review* 495

American Society of Addiction Medicine 'Survey find lower rates of substance use by pregnant women, but rapid resumption of use after pregnancy' (2009) 24(4) *American Society of Addiction Medication News* 16

MB Arthur 'Early Greece: The origins of the Western attitude toward women' (1973) 6 *Arethusa* 7

BH Arzuaga & BH Lee 'Limits of human viability in the United States: A medicolegal review' (2011) 128(6) *Pediatrics* 1047

S Basu, J Andrews, S Kishore, R Panjabi & D Stuckler 'Comparative performance of private and public healthcare systems in low- and middle-income countries: A systemic review' (2012) 9(6) *Public Library of Science Medicine* e10001244

B Becker-Cantarino '"Feminist consciousness" and "wicked witches": Recent studies on women in early modern Europe' (1994) 20 *Signs* 152

VE Beetly 'Mississippi Initiative 26: Personhood and the criminalization of intentional and unintentional acts by pregnant women' (2011) 81 *Supra* 55

B Bekink *Principles of South African Constitutional Law* (LexisNexis, Durban 2012)

JL Bermúdez 'The moral significanc of birth' (1996) 106(2) *Ethics* 378

D Bilchitz 'Health' in S Woolman & M Bishop (eds) *Constitutional Law of South Africa* 2 ed (Revised Service 4 2012) 56-1

PPA Biller 'Birth-control in the West in the thirteenth and early fourteenth centuries' (1982) 94 *Past and Present* 3

B Bird 'Fetal personhood laws as limits to maternal personhood at any stage of pregnancy: Balancing fetal and maternal interests at post-viability among fetal pain and fetal homicide laws' (2014) 25 *Hastings Women's Law Journal* 39

J Birenbaum 'Contextualising choice: Abortion, equality and the right to make decisions concerning reproduction' (1996) 12(3) *South African Journal on Human Rights* 485

M Bishop & S Woolman 'Freedom and security of the person' in S Woolman & M Bishop (eds) *Constitutional Law of South Africa* 2 ed (Original Service 6 2008) 40-1

RH Bloch 'Medieval misogyny: Women as riot' (1987) 20 *Representations* 1

T Boezaart 'Child law, the child and South African private law' in T Boezaart (ed) *Child Law in South Africa* (Juta, Claremont 2009) 3

T Boezaart *Law of Persons* 5 ed (Juta, Claremont 2010)

T Boezaart '"Wrongful life"—The Constitutional Court paved the way for law reform' (2015) 26 *Stellenbosch Law Review* 399

JP Boley 'The history of caesarean section. 1935' (1991) 145(4) *The Canadian Medical Association Journal* 319

E Bonthuys 'Gender and work' in E Bonthuys & C Albertyn (eds) *Gender, Law and Justice* (Juta, Cape Town 2007) 244

D Boonin *A Defense of Abortion* (Cambridge University Press, Cambridge 2003)

JE Boswell '*Expositio* and *oblatio*: The abandonment of children and the ancient and medieval family' (1984) 89 *The American Historical Review* 10

C Botha *Statutory Interpretation: An introduction for Students* 5 ed (Juta, Cape Town 2012)

K Boyd 'The impossibility of informed consent?' (2015) 41 *Journal of Medical Ethics* 44

D Brand 'Judicial deference and democracy in socio-economic rights cases in South Africa' (2011) 3 *Stellenbosch Law Review* 614

K Brennan 'Evidence of infanticide and exposure in antiquity: Tolerated social practice, uncontrolled phenomenon or regulated custom?' (2002) 2 *University College Dublin Law Review* 92

G Brown 'Bei Bei Shuai: Pregnancy, murder, and mayhem in Indiana' (2014) 17 *The Journal of Gender, Race & Justice* 221

FG Buckstaff 'Married women's property in Anglo-Saxon and Anglo-Norman law and the origin of the common-law dower' (1893) 4 *The Annals of the American Academy of Political and Social Science* 33

VL Bullough 'Medieval concepts of adultery' (1997) 7 *Arthuriana* 5

J Burchell *Principles of Criminal Law* 3 ed (Juta, Lansdowne 2005)

BA Burkstrand-Reid 'The invisible woman: Availability and culpability in reproductive health jurisprudence' (2010) 81 *University of Colorado Law Review* 97

BA Burkstrand-Reid 'From sex for pleasure to sex for parenthood: How the law manufactures mothers' (2013) 65 *Hastings Law Journal* 211

W Burnham *Introduction to the Law and Legal System of the United States* (West Publishing Group, Minnesota 1995)

MC Buthelezi & M Reddi 'Killing with impunity: The story of an unborn child' (2008) 41 *De Jure* 429

SM Butler 'Abortion by assault: Violence against pregnant women in the thirteenth-and fourteenth-century England' (2005) 17(4) *Journal of Women's History* 9

SM Butler 'A case of indifference? Child murder in later medieval England' (2007) 19(4) *Journal of Women's History* 59

SM Butler 'Abortion medieval style? Assaults on pregnant women in later medieval England' (2011) 40 *Women's Studies* 778

E Cantarella *Pandora's Daughters: The Role and Status of Women in Greek and Roman Society* (Johns Hopkins University Press, Baltimore 1987)

P Carstens & R Du Plessis 'Medico-legal aspects pertaining to children' in T Boezaart (ed) *Child Law in South Africa* (Juta, Claremont 2009) 587

P Carstens & D Pearmain *Foundational Principles of South African Medical Law* (LexisNexis, Durban 2007)

MJ Casper 'Operation to the rescue: Feminist encounters with fetal surgery' in LM Morgan & MW Michaels (eds) *Fetal Subjects, Feminist Positions* (University of Pennsylvania Press, Philadelphia 1999) 101

R Castro & J Erviti 'Violations of reproductive rights during hospital births in Mexico' (2003) 7 *Health and Human Rights* 90

RJ Chadwick 'Obstetric violence in South Africa' (2016) 106(5) *South African Medical Journal* 423

RJ Chadwick, D Cooper & J Harries 'Narratives of distress about birth in South African public maternity settings: A qualitative study' (2014) 30 *Midwifery* 862

IJ Chasnoff, WJ Burns, SH Schnoll & KA Burns 'Cocaine use in pregnancy' (1985) 313 (11) *The New England Journal of Medicine* 666

J Christman 'Relational autonomy, liberal individualism, and the social constitution of selves' (2004) 117 *Philosophical Studies* 143

A Christoffersen-Deb 'Viability: A cultural calculus of personhood at the beginning of life' (2012) 26(4) *Medical Anthropology Quarterly* 575

G Clark 'Roman women' (1981) 28(2) *Greece & Rome* 193

IG Cohen & S Sayeed 'Fetal pain, abortion, viability, and the Constitution' (2011) 39 *Journal of Law, Medicine & Ethics* 235

E Coleman 'Infanticide in the early Middle Ages' in SM Stuard (ed) *Women in Medieval Society* (University of Pennsylvania Press, Philadelphia 1976) 47

J Coleman 'An introduction to feminisms in a postfeminist age' (2009) 23(2) *Women's Studies Journal* 3

LR Collins & SL Crockin 'Fighting "personhood" initiatives in the United States' (2012) 24(7) *Reproductive BioMedicine Online* 689

RJ Cook & BM Dickens 'Dilemmas in intimate partner violence' (2009) 106 *International Journal of Gynecology and Obstetrics* 72

RJ Cook & BM Dickens 'The injustice of unsafe motherhood' (2002) 2 *Developing World Bioethics* 64

CR Daniels 'Fathers, mothers, and fetal harm: Rethinking gender difference and reproductive responsibility' in LM Morgan & MW Michaels (eds) *Fetal Subjects, Feminist Positions* (University of Pennsylvania Press, Philadelphia 1999) 83

SA de Freitas & GA Myburgh 'The relevance of science for the protection of the unborn' (2009) 45 *Journal for Christian Scholarship* 61

S de Freitas 'The South African Constitutional Court and the unborn' (2012) 5(2) *International Journal for Religious Freedom* 51

DL Dell & BW O'Brien 'Suicide in pregnancy' (2003) 102(6) *Obstetrics & Gynecology* 1306

BM Dickens & RJ Cook 'The legal effects of fetal monitoring guidelines' (2010) 108 *International Journal of Gynecology and Obstetrics* 170

BM Dickens & RJ Cook 'Legal and ethical issues in fetal surgery' (2011) 115 *International Journal of Gynecology and Obstetrics* 80

BM Dickens 'Legal aspects of the beginning of human life' in KF Beller & RF Weir (eds) *The Beginning of Human Life* (Springer Science & Business Media, Dordrecht 2013) 35

BM Dickens & RJ Cook 'Types of consent in reproductive health care' (2015) 128 *International Journal of Gynecology and Obstetrics* 181

SK Dickison 'Abortion in antiquity' (1973) 6 *Arethusa* 159

AFPL d'Oliveria, SG Diniz & LB Schraiber 'Violence against women in health-care institutions: An emerging problem' (2002) 359 *The Lancet* 1681

J Donovan *Feminist Theory: The Intellectual Traditions* 4 ed (Continuum International Publishing, New York 2012)

DA Dombrowski 'St. Augustine, abortion, and Libido Crudelis' (1988) 49 *Journal of the History of Ideas* 151

G Douglas *Law, Fertility and Reproduction* (Sweet and Maxwell, London 1991)

J Downie & J Llewellyn 'Relational theory and health law policy' (2008) Special Edition *Health Law Journal* 193

GA du Plessis 'Feticide: Creating a statutory crime in South African law' (2013) 24 *Stellenbosch Law Review* 73

B Duden 'The fetus on the "farther shore": Toward a history of the unborn' in LM Morgan & MW Michaels (eds) *Fetal Subjects, Feminist Positions* (University of Pennsylvania Press, Philadelphia 1999) 13

DJ Dudley, R Goldenberg, D Conway, RM Silver, GR Saade, W Varner, H Pinar, D Coustan, R Bukowski, B Stoll, MA Koch, CB Parker & UM Reddy 'A new system for determining the causes of stillbirth' (2011) 116(2) *Obstetrics & Gynecology* 254

RM Dworkin *Life's Dominion: An Argument about Abortion, Euthanasia, and Individual Freedom* (Alfred A Knopf, New York 1993)

B Ehrenreich & D English *Witches, Midwives & Nurses: A History of Women Healers* 2 ed (The Feminist Press, New York 2010)

BL Epstein 'The successes and failures of feminism' (2002) 14 *Journal of Women's History* 118

D Fagundes 'What we talk about when we talk about persons: The language of a legal fiction (2001) 114 *Harvard Law Review* 1745

E Falk *Privacy, Due Process, and Morality: A Legal Analysis of Federal Fetal Personhood* (unpublished Honours Capstone, American University 2013)

EA Farnsworth *An Introduction to the Legal System of the United States* 4 ed (Oxford University Press, Oxford 2010)

RH Feen 'Abortion and exposure in ancient Greece: Assessing the status of the fetus and "newborn" from classical sources' in WB Bondeson, HT Engelhardt, SF Spicker & DH Winship (eds) *Abortion and the Status of the Fetus* (D. Reidel Publishing Company, Dordrecht 1983) 283

MA Fineman 'Feminist legal theory' (2005) 13 *Journal of Gender, Social Policy & the Law* 13

M Fitzpatrick 'Fetal personhood after the Unborn Victims of Violence Act' (2006) 58 *Rugters Law Review* 553

J Flavin *Our Bodies, Our Crimes: The Policing of Women's Reproduction in America* (New York University Press, New York 2009)

J Flavin & LM Paltrow 'Punishing pregnant drug-using women: Defying law, medicine, and common sense' (2010) 29 *Journal of Addictive Diseases* 231

NM Ford *When did I Begin? Conception of the Human Individual in History, Philosophy and Science* (Cambridge University Press, Cambridge 1988)

M Ford 'Nothing and not-nothing: Law's ambivalent response to transformation and transgression at the beginning of life' in SW Smith & R Deazley (eds) *The Legal, Medical and Cultural Regulation of the Body: Transformation and Transgression* (Ashgate, Surrey 2009) 21

R Forst 'How (not) to speak about identity: The concept of the person in a theory of justice' (1992) 18 *Philosophy and Social Criticism* 293

CD Forsythe 'Homicide of the unborn child: The born alive rule and other legal anachronisms' (1987) 21 *Valparaiso University Law Review* 563

L Foxhall 'Household, gender and property in classical Athens' (1989) 39 *The Classical Quarterly* 22

S Fredman 'Engendering social and economic rights' in B Goldblatt & K McLean (eds) *Women's Social and Economic Rights: Developments in South Africa* (Juta, Claremont 2011) 4

EB Freedman *No Turning Back: The History of Feminism and the Future of Women* (Ballantine Books, New York 2002)

M Friedman, J Metelerkamp & R Posel 'What is feminism? And what kind of feminist am I?' (1987) 1 *Agenda* 3

SA Gambaudo 'French feminism vs Anglo-American feminism: A reconstruction' (2007) 14(2) *European Journal of Women's Studies* 93

JF Gardner *Women in Roman Law and Society* (Croom Helm, London 1986)

A Giubilini & F Minerva 'After-birth abortion: Why should the baby live?' (2013) 39 *Journal of Medical Ethics* 261

T Glennon 'Regulation of reproductive decision-making' in SD Sclater, F Ebtehaj, E Jackson & M Richards (eds) *Regulating Autonomy: Sex, Reproduction and Family* (Hart Publishing, Oxford 2009) 149

M Goodwin 'Prosecuting the womb' (2008) 76(5) *The Georgia Washington Law Review* 1657

M Green 'Women's medical practice and health care in medieval Europe' (1989) 14 *Signs* 434

L Greenhouse & RB Siegel '*Casey* and the clinic closings: When "protecting health" obstructs choice' (2016) 125 *The Yale Law Journal* 1428

P Groarke 'The legal concept of the person: A relational account' (2010) 51*The Heythrop Journal* 298

D Grossman, D Constant, N Lince, M Alblas, K Blanchard & J Harries 'Surgical and medical second trimester abortion in South Africa: Across-sectional study' (2011) 11 *BioMed Central Health Services Research* 224

GR Gunstan 'The moral status of the human embryo: A tradition recalled' (1984) 1 *Journal of Medical Ethics* 38

BW Häefele 'An explorative study on the impact of prenatal methamphetamine (TIK) abuse on early child and school behaviour' (2012) 1 *Acta Criminologica* 56

HR Hahlo & E Khan *The South African Legal System and its Background* (Juta, Cape Town 1973)

J Haldane & P Lee 'Aquinas on human ensoulment, abortion and the value of life' (2003) 78 *Philosophy* 255

J Harries, P Orner, M Gabriel & E Mitchell 'Delays in seeking an abortion until the second trimester: A qualitative study in South Africa' (2007) 4 *Reproductive Health* 13

J Harries, K Stinson & P Orner 'Health care providers' attitudes towards termination of pregnancy: A qualitative study in South Africa' (2009) 9 *BioMed Central Public Health* 296

J Harries, N Lince, D Constant, A Hargey & D Grossman 'The challenges of offering public second trimester abortion services in South Africa: Health care providers' perspectives' (2012) 44 *Journal of Biosocial Science* 197

J Harris *The Value of Life: An Introduction to Medical Ethics* (Routledge, London 1985)

WV Harris 'Child-exposure in the Roman Empire' (1994) 84 *The Journal of Roman Studies* 1

LH Harris 'Rethinking maternal-fetal conflict Gender and equality in perinatal ethics' (2000) 96(5) *Obstetrics & Gynecology* 786

LH Harris, A Arbor & L Paltrow 'The status of pregnant women and fetuses in US criminal law' (2003) 289(13) *Journal of the American Medical Association* 1697

P Harris 'Compelled medical treatment of pregnant women: The balancing of maternal and fetal rights' (2001) 49 *Cleveland State Law Review* 133

F Harris-Stoertz 'Pregnancy and childbirth in the twelfth- and thirteenth-century French and English law' (2012) 21 *Journal of the History of Sexuality* 263

HI Hartmann 'The unhappy marriage of Marxism and feminism: Towards a more progressive union' (1979) 3 *Capital & Class* 165

M Hayden 'Women in the Middle Ages' (1913) 3 *The Irish Review* 282

J Herring 'Relational autonomy and rape' in SD Sclater, F Ebtehaj, E Jackson & M Richards (eds) *Regulating Autonomy: Sex, Reproduction and Family* (Hart Publishing, Oxford 2009) 53

J Herring & PL Chau 'My body, your body, our bodies' (2007) 15 *Medical Law Review* 34

MB Hickcox-Howard 'The case for pro-choice participation in drafting fetal homicide laws' (2008) 17 *Texas Journal of Women and the Law* 317

S Hoctor 'Specifi crimes' (2008) 21 *South African Journal of Criminal Justice* 99

R Hodes 'The culture of illegal abortion in South Africa' (2016) 42 *Journal of Southern Africa Studies* 79

S Honikman, S Fawcus & I Meintjes 'Abuse in South African maternity settings is a disgrace: Potential solutions to the problem' (2015) 105 (4) *South African Medical Journal* 284

K Hopkins 'Contraception in the Roman Empire' (1965) 8 *Comparative Studies in Society and History* 124

M Horn 'Mothers versus babies: Constitutional and policy problems with prosecutions for prenatal maternal substance abuse' (2008) 14 *William and Mary Journal of Women and the Law* 635

RJ Horsley & RA Horsley 'On the trail of the "witches:" Wise women, midwives and the European witch hunts' (1987) 3 *Women in German Yearbook* 1

R Hursthouse *Beginning Lives* (Basil Blackwell, New York 1987)

RJ Huser *The Crime of Abortion in Canon Law: An Historical Synopsis and Commentary* (unpublished DCL dissertation, Catholic University of America, 1942)

LC Ikemoto 'Furthering the inquiry: Race, class, and culture in the forced medical treatment of pregnant women' (1992) 59 *Tennessee Law Review* 487

E Jackson *Regulating Reproduction: Law, Technology and Autonomy* (Hart Publishing, Oxford 2001)

CR Jeffery 'The development of crime in early English society' (1957) 47 *The Journal of Criminal Law, Criminology, and Police Science* 647

R Jewkes, N Abrahams & Z Mvo 'Why do nurses abuse patients? Reflection from South African obstetric services' (1998) 47 *Social Science & Medicine* 1781

R Jewkes & L Penn-Kekana 'Mistreatment of women in childbirth: Time for action on this important dimension of violence against women' (2015) 12 *Public Library of Science Medicine* e1001849

D Johnsen 'Shared interests: Promoting healthy births without sacrificin women's liberty' (1992) 43 *Hastings Law Journal* 569

S Johnstone 'Women, property, and surveillance in classical Athens' (2003) 22 *Classical Antiquity* 247

L Jordaan 'The legal validity of an advance refusal of medical treatment in South African law (part 1)' (2011) 44 *De Jure* 32

L Jordaan 'The legal validity of an advance refusal of medical treatment in South African law (part 2)' (2011) 44 *De Jure* 259

TS Jost 'Rights of embryo and foetus in private law' (2002) 50 *The American Journal of Comparative Law* 633

C Kaczor *The Ethics of Abortion: Women's Rights, Human Life, and the Question of Justice* (Routledge, New York 2010)

M Kaplan '"A special class of persons": Pregnant women's right to refuse medical treatment after *Gonzales v. Carhart*' (2010) 13 *University of Pennsylvania Journal of Constitutional Law* 145

C Kaposy 'Improving abortion access in Canada' (2010) 18 *Health Care Analysis* 17

PS Karlan & DR Ortiz 'In a different voice: Relational feminism, abortion rights, and the feminist legal agenda' (1993) 87 *Northwestern University Law Review* 858

AJ Karnein *A Theory of Unborn Life: From Abortion to Genetic Manipulation* (Oxford University Press, Oxford 2012)

I Karpin 'Legislating the female body: Reproductive technology and the reconstructed woman' (1992) 3 *Columbia Journal of Gender and Law* 325

RM Karras 'Invisible women' (2005) 39 *Medieval Feminist Forum* 15

M Katz 'Ideology and "the status of women" in ancient Greece' (1992) 31 *History and Theory* 70

MW Kaufman 'Spare ribs: The conception of woman in the Middle Ages and the Renaissance' (1973) 56 *Soundings* 139

KA Kellett 'Miscarriage of justice: Prenatal substance abusers need treatment, not confinemen under chemical endangerment laws' (2014) 40 *New England Journal on Crime & Civil Confinement* 455

J Kelly 'Early feminist theory and the *Querelle des Femmes*, 1400-1789' (1982) 8 *Signs* 4

O Kiefer *Sexual Life in Ancient Rome* (Abbey Library, London 1934)

PM Koch 'Ambiguous interests: Material desires and fetal interests' (2016) 16(2) *The American Journal of Bioethics* 31

DP Kommers, JE Finn & GJ Jacobsohn *American Constitutional Law: Essays, Cases, and Comparative Notes* 3 ed (Rowman & Littlefiel Publishers, Lanham 2009)

M Kowaleski & JM Bennett 'Crafts, gilds, and women in the Middle Ages: Fifty years after Marian K. Dale' (1989) 14 *Signs* 474

H Kruger & A Skelton (eds) *The Law of Persons in South Africa* (Oxford University Press Southern Africa, Cape Town 2010)

LM Kruger & C Schoombee 'The other side of caring: Abuse in a South African maternity ward' (2010) 28 *Journal of Reproductive and Infant Psychology* 84

HJ Kruuse 'Fetal "rights"? The need for a unifie approach to the fetus in the context of feticide' (2009) 72 *Tydskrif vir Hedensdaagse Romeins-Hollandse Reg* 126

JG Landels 'An ancient account of reproduction' (1979) 44 *Biology and Human Affairs* 94

P Laufer-Ukeles 'Reproductive choices and informed consent: Fetal interests, women's identity, and relational autonomy' (2011) 37 *American Journal of Law & Medicine* 567

EJ Lee 'The abortion debate today' in K Horsey & H Biggs (eds) *Human Fertilisation and Embryology: Reproducing Regulation* (Routledge-Cavendish Publishing, London 2007) 231

SJ Lee, HJP Ralston, EA Drey, JC Partridge & MA Rosen 'Fetal pain: A systematic multidisciplinary review of the evidence' (2005) 294(8) *Journal of the American Medical Association* 947

N Levy 'The moral significanc of being born' (2013) 39 *Journal of Medical Ethics* 326

N Lince-Deroche, D Constant, J Harries, K Blanchard, E Sinanovic & D Grossman 'The costs of accessing abortion in South Africa: Women's cost associated with second-trimester abortion services in Western Cape province' (2015) 92 *Contraception* 339

PB Linton 'A fool's errand: State "personhood" proposals' (2009) 35 *Human Life Review* 61

PB Linton 'The legal status of the unborn child under state law' (2011) 6 *University of St Thomas Journal of Law & Public Policy* 141

BB Little, LM Snell, TT Van Beveren, RB Crowell, S Trayler & WL Johnston 'Treatment of substance abuse during pregnancy and infant outcome' (2003) 20(5) *American Journal of Perinatology* 255

JS Loengard 'Legal history and the medieval Englishwoman: A fragmented view' (1986) 4 *Law and History Review* 161

CC Lougee 'Modern European history' (1977) 2 *Signs* 628

D Lupton *The Social Worlds of the Unborn* (Palgrave Macmillan, Hampshire 2013)

S Lurie 'The changing motives of cesarean section: From the ancient world to the twenty-firs century' (2005) 271 *Archives of Gynecology and Obstetrics* 281

S Lutchman 'Insufficient access to substance abuse treatment centres for illicit drug users and its potential effect on a foetus: A breach of the right to access to health care services' (2015) 19 *Law, Development & Democracy* 65

C MacIntosh 'Conceiving fetal abuse' (1998) 15 *Canadian Journal of Family Law* 178

CA MacKinnon 'Reflection on sex equality under law' (1991) 100(5) *The Yale Law Journal* 1281

CA MacKinnon *Sex Equality* 2 ed (Foundation Press, New York 2007)

R Macklin 'Dignity is a useless concept: It means no more than respect for persons or their autonomy' (2003) 327 *British Medical Journal* 1419

WD Malcolm 'The Unborn Victims of Violence Act: Addressing moral intuition and the right to choose' (2004) 1(2) *Tennessee Journal of Law & Policy* 277

P Mali & L Cheng 'Concise review: Human cell engineering: Cellular reprogramming and genome editing' (2012) 30 *Stem Cells* 75

M Manian 'Lessons from personhood's defeat: Abortion restrictions and side effects on women's health' (2013) 74 *Ohio State Law Journa*l 75

SA Mann & DJ Huffman 'The decentering of second wave feminism and the rise of the third wave' (2005) 69 *Science & Society* 56

BA Manninen 'The value of choice and the choice to value: Expanding the discussion about fetal life with in prochoice advocacy' (2013) 28(3) *Hypatia* 663

C McCann 'Fertility control and society in medieval Europe' (2009) 40 *Comitatus* 45

JJ McCartney 'Some Roman Catholic concepts of persons and their implications for the ontological status of the unborn' in WB Bondeson, HT Engelhardt, S Spicker & D Winship (eds) *Abortion and the Status of the Fetus* (D. Reidel Publishing Company, Dordrecht 1983) 313

JE McConnell 'Relational and liberal feminism: The "ethic of care," fetal personhood and autonomy' (1996) 99 *West Virginia Law Review* 291

CJ McDonough 'Motherhood and feminism: Lessons from the Titanic' (2006) 8 *Journal of the Association for Research and Mothering* 123

A McLaren *A History of Contraception: From Antiquity to the Present Day* (Blackwell Publishers, Oxford 1990)

S McLean 'Women, rights and reproduction' in S McLean (ed) *Legal Issues in Human Reproduction* (Gower Publishing, Aldershot 1989) 213

D McQuoid-Mason 'Privacy' in S Woolman & M Bishop (eds) *Constitutional Law of South Africa* 2 ed (Original Service 12 2003) 38-1

C Megone 'Potentiality and persons: An Aristotelian perspective' in MG Kuczewski & R Polansky (eds) *Bioethics: Ancient Themes in Contemporary Issues* (MIT Press, London 2002) 155

S Meredith *Policing Pregnancy: The Law and Ethics of Obstetric Conflict* (Ashgate, Aldershot 2005)

D Meyerson 'Abortion: The constitutional issues' (1999) 116 *The South African Law Journal* 50

MW Michaels & LM Morgan 'Introduction: The fetal imperative' in LM Morgan & MW Michaels (eds) *Fetal Subjects, Feminist Positions* (University of Pennsylvania Press, Philadelphia 1999) 1

BDH Miller '"She who hath drunk any potion"...' (1962) 31 *Medium Aevum* 188

MK Miller 'Refusal to undergo a cesarean section: A woman's right or a criminal act?' (2005) 15 *Health Matrix* 383

JRL Milton *South African Criminal Law and Procedure: Volume 2: Common-Law Crimes* 3 ed (Juta & Co, Cape Town 1996)

S Mohapatra 'Unshackling addiction: A public health approach to drug use during pregnancy' (2011) 26 *Wisconsin Journal of Law, Gender & Society* 241

LM Morgan 'Fetal relationality in feminist philosophy: An anthropological critique' (1996) 11(3) *Hypatia* 47

AB Morrison (ed) *Fundamentals of American Law* (Oxford University Press, Oxford 1996)

C Morroni & J Moodley 'Characteristics of women booking for firs and second trimester abortions at public sector clinics in Cape Town' (2006) 12 *South African Journal of Obstetrics and Gynaecology* 81

D Moster, RT Lie & T Markestad 'Long-term medical and social consequences of preterm birth' (2008) 359(3) *The New England Journal of Medicine* 262

E Munro 'Feminism: A fourth wave?' (2013) 4 *Political Insight* 22

TF Murphy 'Adoption first The disposition of human embryos' (2014) 40(6) *Journal of Medical Ethics* 392

AS Murphy 'A survey of state fetal homicide laws and their potential applicability to pregnant women who harm their own fetuses' (2014) 89 *Indiana Law Journal* 847

GA Myburgh *Humanity and the Protection of the Unborn: A Jurisprudential Rationale for the Furtherance of the Anthropological Paradigm of International Law* (unpublished LLM dissertation, University of the Free State, 2008)

J Nedelsky 'Reconceiving autonomy: Sources, thoughts and possibilities' (1989) 1 *Yale Journal of Law and Feminism* 7

J Nedelsky 'Property in potential life? A relational approach to choosing legal categories' (1993) 6 *Canadian Journal of Law and Jurisprudence* 343

J Nedelsky *Law's Relations: A Relational Theory of Self, Autonomy, and Law* (Oxford University Press, Oxford 2011)

C Neel 'The origins of the Beguines' (1989) 14 *Signs* 321

E Nelson 'Reconceiving pregnancy: Expressive choice and legal reasoning' (2004) 49 *McGill Law Journal* 593

E Nelson *Law, Policy and Reproductive Autonomy* (Hart Publishing, Oxford 2013)

C Ngwena 'Accessing abortion services under the Choice on Termination of Pregnancy Act: Realising substantive equality' (2000) 25 *Journal for Juridical Science* 19

C Ngwena 'An appraisal of abortion laws in southern Africa from a reproductive health rights perspective' (2004) 32(4) *Journal of Law, Medicine & Ethics* 708

CG Ngwena 'Inscribing abortion as a human right: Significanc of the protocol on the rights of women in Africa' (2010) 32 *Human Rights Quarterly* 783

JT Noonan 'Marriage in the Middle Ages: Power to choose' (1973) 4 *Viator* 419

JT Noonan 'Christian tradition and the control of human reproduction' (1984) 4 *Journal of Christian Jurisprudence* 1

S Noonan 'Theorizing connection' (1992) 30(3) *Alberta Law Review* 719

M O'Sullivan 'Reproductive rights' in S Woolman & M Bishop (eds) *Constitutional Law of South Africa* 2 ed (Original Service 12 2005) 37-1

A Oakley *The Captured Womb: A History of Medical Care of Pregnant Women* (Basil Blackwell Publishing, Oxford 1986)

K Offen 'On the French origin of the words feminism and feminist' (1988) 8 *Feminist Issues* 45.

K Offen 'Definin feminism: A comparative historical approach' (1988) 14 *Signs* 119

S Oluwele 'Africa' in AM Jaggar & IM Young (eds) *A Companion to Feminist Philosophy* (Blackwell Publishers, Oxford 2000) 96

E Ordolis 'Maternal substance abuse and the limits of law: A relational challenge' (2008) 46 *Alberta Law Review* 119

M Ovens 'Maternal substance abuse in South Africa: An area for concern?' (2008) 1 *Acta Criminologica* 77

M Ovens 'A criminological perspective on the prenatal abuse of substances during pregnancy and the link to child abuse in South Africa' (2009) 179(4) *Journal of Early Child Development and Care* 503

M Ovens 'A criminological perspective on the prenatal abuse of substances during pregnancy and the link to child abuse in South Africa' (2010) 11 *Child Abuse Research in South Africa* 38

O Oyewùmí 'The white woman's burden: African women in Western feminist discourse' in O Oyewùmí (ed) *African Women & Feminism: Reflecting on the Politics of Sisterhood* (Africa World Press, Trenton 2003) 25

D Page 'The homicide by child abuse conviction of Regina McKnight' (2003) 46 *Howard Law Journal* 363

CL Palladino, V Singh, J Campbell, H Flynn & K Gold 'Homicide and suicide during the perinatal period: Findings from the National Violent Death Reporting System' (2011) 118(5) *Obstetrics & Gynecology* 1056

J Palmer 'Seeing and knowing: Ultrasound images in the contemporary abortion debate' (2009) 10(2) *Feminist Theory* 173

LM Paltrow '*Roe v Wade* and the New Jane Crow: Reproductive rights in the age of mass incarceration' (2013) 103 *American Journal of Public Health* 17

LM Paltrow & J Flavin 'Arrests of and forced interventions on pregnant women in the United States, 1973-2005: Implications for women's legal status and public health' (2013) 38(2) *Journal of Health Politics, Policy and Law* 299

L Paltrow & K Jack 'Pregnant women, junk science, and zealous defense' (2010) *The Champion* 2

L Paterson 'Gender negotiations in France during the central Middle Ages: The literary evidence' in P Linehan & JL Nelson (eds) *The Medieval World* (Routledge, London 2003) 246

C Patterson ' "Not worth the rearing": The causes of infant exposure in ancient Greece' (1985) 115 *Transactions of the American Philological Association* 103

MS Paulsen 'The plausibility of personhood' (2012) 74 *Ohio State Law Journal* 13

JH Perlow & H Lesmes 'Homicide and suicide during the perinatal period: Findings from the national violent death reporting system: To the editor' (2012) 119(6) *Obstetrics & Gynecology* 1275

C Pickles *S v Mshumpa: A Time for Law Reform* (unpublished LLM dissertation, University of Pretoria, 2010)

C Pickles 'The introduction of a statutory crime to address third-party foetal violence' (2011) 74 *Tydskrif vir Hedensdaagse Romeins-Hollandse Reg* 546

C Pickles 'Termination-of-pregnancy rights and foetal interests in continued existence in South Africa: The Choice on Termination of Pregnancy Act 92 of 1996' (2012) 15(5) *Potchefstroom Elektronies Regsblad* 403

C Pickles 'Lived experiences of the Choice on Termination of Pregnancy Act 92 of 1996: Bridging the gap for women in need' (2013) 29 *South African Journal on Human Rights* 515

C Pickles 'Personhood: Proving the significanc of the born-alive rule with reference to medical knowledge of foetal viability' (2013) 24 *Stellenbosch Law Review* 146

C Pickles & D Labuschagne *Pregnancy, foetal individuation, and claims to another's body: Some relational issues in a South African context* (2014) unpublished paper presented at a conference of the Society of Law Teachers of Southern Africa hosted by the Oliver Schreiner Law School at the University of Witwatersrand 15 January 2014

C Pickles 'Approaches to pregnancy under the law: A relational response to the current South African position and recent academic trends' (2014) 47 *De Jure* 20

C Pickles 'Eliminating abusive "care": A criminal law response to obstetric violence in South Africa' (2015) 54 *South African Crime Quarterly* 5

M Pieterse 'Legislative and executive translation of the right to have access to health care services' (2010) 14 *Law, Democracy & Development* 1

M Pieterse *Can Rights Cure? The Impact of Human Rights Litigation on South Africa's Health System* (Pretoria University Law Press, Pretoria 2014)

MS Pignotti & G Donzelli 'Perinatal care at the threshold of viability: An international comparison of practical guidelines for the treatment of extremely preterm births' (2008) 121 *Pediatrics* e193

R Pillay 'The beginning of human personhood: Is South African law outdated?' (2010) 21(2) *Stellenbosch Law Review* 230

TL Powell, L Parker, CF Dedrick, CM Barrera, DD Salvo, F Erdman, SP Huff & M Saunders 'Decisions and dilemmas related to resuscitation of infants born on the verge of viability' (2012) 12 *Newborn & Infant Nursing Reviews* 27

K Proehl 'Pregnancy crimes: New worries to expect when you're expecting' (2013) 53 *Santa Clara Law Review* 661

G Quinot & S Liebenberg 'Narrowing the band: Reasonableness review in administrative justice and socio-economic rights jurisprudence in South Africa' (2011) 22(3) *Stellenbosch Law Review* 639

R Rebouché 'The limits of reproductive rights in improving women's health' (2011) 63 *Alabama Law Review* 1

CJ Reid 'Marriage in its procreative dimension: The meaning of the institution of marriage throughout the ages' (2009) 6 *University of St Thomas Law Journal* 454

NK Rhoden 'Trimesters and technology: Revamping *Roe v. Wade*' (1986) 95(4) *The Yale Law Journal* 639

GA Richardson, SC Hamel, L Goldschmidt & NL Day 'Growth of infants prenatally exposed to cocaine/crack: Comparison of a prenatal care and a no prenatal care sample' (1999) 104(2) *Pediatrics* 18

L Riley & A Furedi 'Autonomy and the UK's law on abortion: Current problems and future prospects' in SD Sclater, F Ebtehaj, E Jackson & M Richards (eds) *Regulating Autonomy: Sex, Reproduction and Family* (Hart Publishing, Oxford 2009) 239

SCM Roberts & C Pies 'Complex calculations: How drug use during pregnancy becomes a barrier to prenatal care' (2011) 15 *Maternal and Child Health Journal* 333

OF Robinson, TD Fergus & WM Gordon *An Introduction to European Legal History* (Professional Books Limited, Abingdon 1985)

R Roth *Making Women Pay: The Hidden Costs of Fetal Rights* (Cornell University Press, Ithaca 2000)

LM Sagrestano & R Finerman 'Pregnancy and prenatal care: A reproductive justice perspective' in JC Chrisler (ed) *Reproductive Justice: A Global Concern* (Praeger, California 2012) 201

LE Saltzman, CH Johnson, BC Gilbert & MM Goodwin 'Physical abuse around the time of pregnancy: An examination of prevalence and risk factors in 16 states' (2003) 7 *Maternal and Child Health Journal* 31

J Sarkin-Hughes 'A perspective on abortion legislation in South Africa's bill of rights era' (1993) 56 *Tydskrif vir Hedensdaagse Romeins-Hollandse Reg* 83

DM Schaps 'What was free about a free Athenian woman?' (1998) 128 *Transactions of the American Philological Association* 161

JR Schroedel, P Fiber & BD Snyder 'Women's rights and fetal personhood in criminal law' (2000) 7 *Duke Journal of Gender Law & Policy* 89

M Schulman *The Nasciturus Non-Fiction, The Libby Gonen Story: Contemporary Reflections on the Status of the Nascitural Personhood in South African Law* (unpublished LLM dissertation, University of the Witwatersrand, 2014)

TJ Scott 'Why state personhood amendments should be part of the profil agenda' (2011) 6 *University of St Thomas Journal of Law & Public Policy* 222

I Seri & J Evans 'Limits of viability: Definitio of the grey zone' (2008) 28 *Journal of Perinatology* 4

J Seymour *Childbirth and the Law* (Oxford University Press, Oxford 2000)

S Shamu, N Abrahams, M Temerman, A Musekiwa & C Zarowsky 'A systematic review of African studies on intimate partner violence against pregnant women: Prevalence and risk factors' (2011) 6(3*) Public Library of Science ONE* e17591

L Shanner 'Procreation' in AM Jaggar & IM Young (eds) *A Companion to Feminist Philosophy* (Blackwell Publishers, Oxford 2000) 429

BD Shaw 'The family in late antiquity: The experience of Augustine' (1987) 115 *Past and Present* 3

BD Shaw 'Raising and killing children: Two Roman myths' (2001) 54 *Mnemosyne* 31

JA Shields & S Serna 'The demise of feminist communitarianism' (2011) 40 *Perspectives on Political Science* 9

E Shorter *A History of Women's Bodies* (Basic Books, New York 1984)

RB Siegel 'Dignity and the duty to protect unborn life' in C McCrudden (ed) *Understanding Human Dignity* (Oxford University Press, Oxford 2013) 30

A Skelton 'Girls' social and economic rights in South Africa' in B Goldblatt & K McLean (eds) *Women's Social and Economic Rights: Developments in South Africa* (Juta, Claremont 2011) 58

S Smith 'Criminalising prenatal substance abuse: Hurting women and their unborn children' (2012) 6 *Health Law Outlook* 14

SE Smith 'No safe harbors: Examining the shift from voluntary treatment options to criminalization of maternal drug use in Tennessee' (2015) 46 *The University of Memphis Law Review* 203

CR Snyman *Criminal Law* 5 ed (LexisNexis, Durban 2008)

RA Spence 'Abandoning women to their rights: What happens when feminist jurisprudence ignores birthing rights' (2012) 19 *Cardozo Journal of Law & Gender* 75

R Solinger *Reproductive Politics: What Everyone Needs to Know* (Oxford University Press, Oxford 2013)

C Stansell *The Feminist Promise: 1792 to the Present* (The Modern Library, New York 2010)

B Steinbock *Life before Birth: The Moral and Legal Status of Embryos and Fetuses* 2 ed (Oxford University Press, New York 2011)

A Stoner 'Sisters between: Gender and the medieval Beguines' (1995) 4 *Ex Post Facto* 29

A Strode, S Mthembu & Z Essack '"She made up a choice for me": 22 HIV-positive women's experiences of involuntary sterilization in two South African provinces' (2012) 20 *Reproductive Health Matters* 61

K Sunderlin & L Huss 'The mythology of "addicted babies": Challenging media distortions, laws, and policies that fracture communities' (2014) 86 *Different Takes* 1

R Suppé 'Pregnancy on trial: The Alabama Supreme Court's erroneous application of Alabama's Chemical Endangerment Law in *Ex Parte Ankrom*' (2014) 7(2) *Health Law & Policy Brief* 49

B Taylor 'Feminism and the enlightenment 1650-1850' (1999) 47 *History Workshop Journal* 261

The Stillbirth Collaborative Research Network Writing Group 'Association between stillbirth and risk factors known at pregnancy confirmation (2011) 306(22) *Journal of the American Medical Association* 2469

The Stillbirth Collaborative Research Network Writing Group 'Causes of death among stillbirths' (2011) 306(22) *Journal of the American Medical Association* 2459

JJ Thomson 'A defense of abortion' (1971) 1 *Philosophy & Public Affairs* 47

M Tooley 'Personhood' in H Kuhse & P Singer (eds) *A Companion to Bioethics* (Blackwell, Oxford 2001) 117

A Tsao 'Fetal homicide laws: Shield against domestic violence or sword to pierce abortion rights?' (1998) 25 *Hastings Constitutional Law Quarterly* 457

LJ van Bogaert 'Rights of and duties to non-consenting patients—informed refusal in the developing world' (2006) 6 *Developing World Bioethics* 13

K van Marle & E Bonthuys 'Feminist theories and concepts' in E Bonthuys & C Albertyn (eds) *Gender, Law and Justice* (Juta, Cape Town 2007) 15

F van Oosten 'The Choice on Termination of Pregnancy Act: Some comments' (1999) 116 *The South African Law Journal* 60

A van Parys, A Verhamme, M Temmerman & H Verstraelen 'Intimate partner violence and pregnancy: A systematic review of interventions' (2014) 9 *Public Library of Science ONE* e85084

AA Veleda & TE Gerardt 'About humanly giving birth: The insertion of the nursing in the humanization of birth movement in Brazil' (2014) 1 *Journal of Nursing and Socioenvironmental Health* 47

S Visser 'Prosecuting women for participating in illegal abortions: Undermining gender equality and the effectiveness of state police power' (2011) 13 *Journal of Law & Family Studies* 171

JJ Volpe 'Effect of cocaine use on the fetus' (1992) 327(6) *The New England Journal of Medicine* 399

ME Wallace, D Hoyert, C Williams & P Mendola 'Pregnancy-associated homicide and suicide in 37 US states with enhanced pregnancy surveillance' (2016) 215(3) *American Journal of Obstetrics & Gynecology* 364.e1

M Warren 'Abortion' in H Kuhse & P Singer (eds) *A Companion to Bioethics* (Blackwell, Oxford 2001) 127

MA Warren 'The moral significanc of birth' (1989) 4 *Hypatia* 46

R West 'Jurisprudence and gender' (1988) 55 *The University of Chicago Law Review* 1

R West 'Theories of addiction' (2001) 96 *Addiction* 3

M Wiesner-Hanks 'World history and the history of women, gender, and sexuality' (2007) 18 *Journal of World History* 53

JF Will 'Beyond abortion: Why the personhood movement implicates reproductive choice' (2013) 39(4) *American Journal of Law & Medicine* 573

G Williams 'The foetus and the "right to life"' (1994) 53 *Cambridge Law Journal* 71

JC Williams & SL Shames 'Mothers' dreams: Abortion and the high price of motherhood' (2004) 6 *University of Pennsylvania Journal of Constitutional Law* 818

I Wilmut, AE Schnieke, J McWhir, AJ Kind & KHS Campbell 'Viable offspring derived from fetal and adult mammalian cells' (2007) 9 *Cloning and Stem Cells* 3

S Wilson & J Dugard 'Taking poverty seriously: The South African constitutional court and socio-economic rights' (2011) 22(3) *Stellenbosch Law Review* 664

S Woolman 'Dignity' in S Woolman & M Bishop (eds) *Constitutional Law of South Africa* 2 ed (Revised Service 3 2005) 36-1

Electronic Sources

American Civil Liberties Union 'Tenn. Governor singles out pregnant women for discrimination' (29 April 2014) *American Civil Liberties Union* available at <https://www.aclu.org/reproductive-freedom-womens-rights/tenn-governor-singles-out-pregnant-women-discrimination> (accessed on 23 June 2016)

American Society of Addiction Medicine 'Public policy statement: Definitio of addiction' *American Society of Addiction* 19 April 2011 available at <http://www.asam.org/quality-practice/definition-of-addiction (accessed on 23 June 2016)

Amnesty International 'Struggle for maternal health: Barriers to antenatal care in South Africa' available at <https://www.health-e.org.za/wp-content/uploads/2014/10/Struggle-for-Maternal-Health-.pdf> (accessed on 1 April 2016).

Angry Black Women Watch 'ABWW Signal Boost: Tennessee's pregnancy criminalization law will hit black women the hardest' (18 April 2014) *Angry Black Women Watch* available at <https://abww.wordpress.com/tag/sb-1391/> (accessed on 23 June 2016)

A Armstrong & D Hsieh 'The "personhood" movement is anti-life: Why it matters that rights begin at birth, not conception' (31 August 2010) *Coalition for Secular Government* available at <http://www.seculargovernment.us/docs/a62.pdf> (accessed on 10 May 2016)

Begin before Birth 'Fetal development' *Begin before Birth* available at <http://www.beginbeforebirth.org/in-the-womb/fetal-development> (accessed on 19 May 2016)

R Chadwick & M Stevens 'Confronting birth violence in South Africa' available at <http://mothersandbirthmatter.co.za/Confronting-Obstetric-Violence-in-South-Africa.php> (accessed on 31 March 2016)

R Chadwick 'Obstetric violence—starting a conversation' (6 March 2016) available at <http://mothersandbirthmatter.co.za/Obstetric-Violence-Starting-A-Conversation.php> (accessed on 31 March 2016)

G Casey 'Born alive: The legal status of the unborn child in England and the U.S.A' (2005) available at <http://researchrepository.ucd.ie/bitstream/handle/10197/5546/Born_Alive.pdf?sequence=1> (accessed on 18 November 2016)

Center for Reproductive Rights 'Punishing women for their behavior during pregnancy: An approach that undermines women's health and children's interests' (September 2000) *Centre for Reproductive Health* available at <http://reproductiverights.org/sites/default/files/documents/pub_bp_punishing women.pdf> (accessed on 23 June 2016)

Center for Reproductive Rights 'Whose right to life? Women's rights and prenatal protections under human rights comparative law' (20 March 2012) *Center for Reproductive Rights* available at <http://reproductiverights.org/sites/crr.civicactions.net/files/documents/ TL_3%2014%2012.pdf> (accessed on 3 July 2014)

Center for Reproductive Rights 'Whole Women's Health v Hellerstedt' available at <http://www.reproductiverights.org/case/whole-womans-health-v-hellerstedt> (accessed on 10 May 2016)

R Cohen 'Will Tennessee legalize the New Jane Crow?' *SocialistWorler.Org* (23 April 2014) available at <https://socialistworker.org/2014/04/23/will-tennessee-legalize-new-jane-crow> (accessed on 23 June 2016)

BM Dennis 'Love: Another aspect of Roman marriage' (2006) available at <http://www.brandonmdennis.com/pdfs/Non%20Fiction%20-%20Love%20-%20Another%20Aspect%20of%20Roman%20Marriage.pdf> (accessed on 21 January 2016)

D DeMarco 'The Roman Catholic Church and abortion: An historical perspective part 1' *CatholicCulture.Org* available at <http://www.catholicculture.org/culture/library/view.cfm?id=3361> (accessed on 11 May 2016)

D DeMarco 'The Roman Catholic Church and abortion: An historical perspective part 2' *CatholicCulture.Org* available at <http://www.catholicculture.org/culture/library/view.cfm?recnum=3362> (accessed on 11 May 2016)

D Fleming 'Timeline of Greek & Roman antiquity' available at <http://people.umass.edu/dfleming/english704-timeline.html (accessed on 11 May 2016)

Govtrack.US 'H.R. 23 (113th): Sanctity of Human Life Act' available at <https://www.govtrack.us/congress/bills/113/hr23/> *Govetrack.US* (accessed on 10 May 2016)

Guttmacher Institute 'State laws and policies: An overview of abortion laws' *Guttmacher Institute* (1 April 2014) available at <https://www.guttmacher-.org/state-policy/explore/overview-abortion-laws> (accessed on 10 May 2016)

Guttmacher Institute 'State laws and policies: Substance abuse during pregnancy' (1 March 2016) *Guttmacher Institute available at* <http://www.guttmacher-.org/statecenter/spibs/spib_SADP.pdf> (accessed on 23 June 2016)

Health Systems Trust 'TOPs by Gestational Age' *Health Systems Trust* available at <http://indicators.hst.org.za/healthstats/88/data/gedo> (accessed on 13 April 2016)

Human Rights Watch 'Stop making excuses: accountability for maternal health care in South Africa' *Human Rights Watch* (2011) available at <http://www.hrw.org/reports/2011/08/08/stop-making-excuses-0> (accessed on 23 March 2016)

Z Ives 'Feticide and criminal law: Is there an acceptable approach?' (1998) available at <http://repository.unm.edu/bitstream/handle/1928/2402/IvesZachary.pdf?sequence=1&isAllowed=y> (accessed on 9 May 2016)

Legi Scan 'Tennessee Senate Bill 1391' *Legi Scan* available at <http://legiscan.com/TN/bill/SB1391/2013> (accessed on 23 June 2016)

B Lester 'Another "drug baby" media scare?' (12 March 2005) *Common Sense for Drug Policy* available at <http://www.csdp.org/publicservice/dejavumeth.htm> (accessed on 20 June 2014)

National Advocates for Pregnant Women 'Prenatal exposure to illegal drugs and alcohol: Media hype and enduring myths are not supported by science' (24 March 2010) *National Advocates for Pregnant Women* available at

<http://advocatesforpregnantwomen.org/2010%20drugmyth%20factsheet%20v3.pdf> (accessed on 23 June 2016)

National Advocates for Pregnant Women 'NAPW documentation State v. Greywind' (14 April 2012) *National Advocates for Pregnant Women* available at <http://advocatesforpregnantwomen.org/issues/criminal_cases_and_issues/napw_documentation_state_v_greywind.php> (accessed on 24 June 2016)

National Advocates for Pregnant Women 'Lessons from the U.S. experience with unborn victims of violence laws' (13 January 2004) available at <http://www.arcc-cdac.ca/action/LessonsfromUS.pdf> (accessed on 23 May 2016).

National Conference of State Legislation 'Fetal homicide state laws' (March 2015) *National Conference of State Legislation* available at <http://www.ncsl.org/research/health/fetal-homicide-state-laws.aspx> (accessed on 14 July 2016)

National Institute on Drug Abuse 'Topics in brief: Prenatal exposure to drugs of abuse' (May 2011) *National Institute on Drug Abuse,* available at <http://www.drugabuse.gov/sites/default/files/prenatal.pdf (accessed on 23 June 2016)

S Newman 'Timeline of the Middle Ages' *The Finer Times* available at <http://www.thefinertimes.com/Middle-Ages/timeline-of-the-middle ages.html> (accessed on 21 January 2016)

LM Paltrow 'How Indiana is making it possible to jail women for having abortions' *Political Research Associates* (29 March 2015) available at <http://www.politicalresearch.org/2015/03/29/how-indiana-is-making-it-possible-to-jail-women-for-having-abortions/#sthash.9lp9ETVr.dpbs> (accessed on 11 May 2016)

Personhood USA 'North Dakota Measure 1' *Personhood USA* available at <http://www.personhoodusa.com/campaigns/north-dakota-measure-1-2014> (accessed on 22 April 2014)

Personhood USA 'About us' available at <http://www.personhood.com/about> (accessed on 11 May 2016).

Personhood USA 'Education' available at <http://www.personhood.com/education> (accessed on 11 May 2016).

Personhood USA 'Become a citizen co-sponsor of the Life at Conception Act' available at <http://www.personhood.com/become_a_citizen_co_sponsor_of_the_life_at_conception_act> (accessed on 11 May 2016).

JM Pieklo 'Plea deal reached in Bei Bei Shuai prosecution' *Rewire* (2 August 2013) available at <http://rhrealitycheck.org/article/2013/08/02/plea-deal-reached-in-bei-bei-shuai-prosecution/> (accessed on 19 May 2016)

K Pollitt 'Protect pregnant women: Free Bei Bei Shuai' *The Nation* (7 March 2012) available at <http://www.thenation.com/article/166664/protect-pregnant-women-free-bei-bei-shuai> (accessed 19 May 2016)

Resolve 'Personhood legislation Personhood bills and ballot initiatives' available at <http://www.resolve.org/get-involved/the-center-for-infertility-justice/personhood-legislation/?referrer=https://www.google.co.za/> (accessed on 11 May 2016)

South African National Aids Council 'The people living with HIV stigma index: South Africa 2014: Summary report' (May 2015) *South African National Aids Council,* available at <http://www.stigmaindex.org/sites/default/files reports/Summary-Booklet-on-Stigma-Index-Survey%20South%20Africa.pdf> (accessed on 28 January 2016)

South African Press Association 'Foetus theft may have been to keep boyfriend, court hears' *news24* (26 August 2014) <http://www.news24.com/SouthAfrica/News/Alleged-foetus-thief-says-murder-was-to-keep-boyfriend-20140826> (accessed 28 August 2014)

South African Press Association 'Man in court for murderous rage' *IOL News* (28 August 2014) <http://www.iol.co.za/news/crime-courts/man-in-court-for-murderous-rage-1.1742716#.U_OB8WIBXs> (accessed 20 June 2016)

Statistics South Africa 'Minimum development goals: Country Report 2015' available at <http://www.statssa.gov.za/MDG/MDG_Country%20Report_Final30Sep2015.pdf> (accessed on 31 March 2016)

C Steele 'DA to begin prosecution of mothers who use drugs' (1 October 2012) *NorthJersey.com* available at <http://newsok.com/article/feed/441574> (accessed on 26 June 2016)

Substance Abuse and Mental Health Service Administration 'Methadone treatment for pregnant women' (March 2009) available at <http://store.samhsa.gov/shin/content/SMA14-4124/SMA14-4124.pdf> (accessed on 23 June 2016)

The American College of Obstetricians and Gynecologists 'Information about methamphetamine use in pregnancy' *American College of Obstetricians & Gynecologists* (2006), available at <http://vanilla47.com/Methamphetamine%20Pharmacology/Information%20about%20Methamphetamine%20Use%20in%20Pregnancy.pdf> (accessed on 23 June 2016)

United Nations 'Sustainable development goals: 17 goals to transform our world' available at <http://www.un.org/sustainabledevelopment/sustainable-development-goals/> (accessed on 4 April 2016)

World Health Organization 'Information fact sheet: Intimate partner violence during pregnancy' (2011) *World Health Organization* available at <http://apps.who.int/iris/bitstream/10665/70764/1/WHO_RHR_11.35_eng.pdf?ua=1> (accessed on 30 June 2016)

World Health Organization 'Unsafe abortion: Global and regional estimates of the incidence of unsafe abortion and associated mortality in 2008' 6 ed (2011) *World Health Organization* available at <http://whqlibdoc.who.int/publications/2011/9789241501118_eng.pdf?ua=1> (accessed on 1 April 2016)

World Health Organization 'Understanding and addressing violence against women: intimate partner violence: Intimate partner violence' (2012) *World Health Organization* available at <http://apps.who.int/iris/bitstream/10665/77432/1/WHO_RHR_12.36_eng.pdf?ua=1> (accessed on 30 June 2016)

Chapter 1

INTRODUCTION

Pregnancy, the unborn and the pregnancy relationship shared between the unborn and pregnant women are poorly formulated in law.[1] MacKinnon aptly demonstrates this concern.[2] She argues that we have failed to formulate an adequate articulation of pregnancy, pregnant women, the unborn and their relationship because our methodology in law is to proceed on the basis of analogy and distinction.[3] When faced with a pregnancy, we almost always attempt to slot the maternal/foetal relationship into legal spaces allocated to other existing relationships recognised in law.[4] She argues that had women (being those who experience pregnancy) participated equally in formulating laws, we might have ended up comparing other relationships to the maternal/foetal relationship (as the norm or benchmark) rather than comparing the maternal/foetal relationship to other existing relationships.[5] This process has 'othered' pregnancy in law. According to MacKinnon, 'the fetus has no concept of its own, but must be like something men have or are: a body part to the Left, a person to the Right. Nowhere in law is the fetus a fetus.'[6] In relation to pregnant women and the pregnancy relationship, she asserts that '[i]n a legal system that views the individual as a unitary self, and that self as a bundle of rights, it is no wonder that the pregnant woman has eluded legal grasp, and her fetus with her'.[7]

This book is dedicated to developing sound legal concepts of pregnancy and the pregnancy relationship, and meaningful legal responses to pregnancy-related issues. It does this by focusing on and dismantling the tension, or the potential for tension, between women's and girls' reproductive autonomy and foetal interests[8]

[1] According to a recent decision of the Inter-American Court of Human Rights in *Case of Artavia Murillo et al ('in vitro fertilization') v Costa Rica* (2012) (*Case of Artavia Murillo et al*) (para 187), 'pregnancy' concerns that stage in procreation when a fertilised egg, known as a zygote, implants into a woman's uterus. Thus, the mere process of fertilisation, being the process that takes place when male and female gametes fuse, does not give rise to a pregnancy but allows for a potential pregnancy and potential development. Without implantation (also termed conception), the fertilised egg does not have access to maternal nutrients and cannot develop further into a blastocyst, embryo and later into a foetus (para 186). However, the judgment does not conceptualise the occurrence of pregnancy in law per se, it merely provides an indication of when the law might accept that a woman is pregnant.

[2] CA MacKinnon 'Reflection on sex equality under law' (1991) 100 *Yale LJ* 1281.

[3] MacKinnon (1991) *Yale LJ* 1314.

[4] MacKinnon (1991) *Yale LJ* 1314. Some of these relationships include the employer and employee, termites in the ground and tumours in bodies.

[5] MacKinnon (1991) *Yale LJ* 1314.

[6] MacKinnon (1991) *Yale LJ* 1314.

[7] MacKinnon (1991) *Yale LJ* 1316.

[8] The concept of 'foetal interests' is used purposefully to denote the fact that the unborn do not have rights and also should not have rights. Reference to foetal interests in the context of this book

during pregnancy in four specifi areas: foetal personhood, violence against pregnant women that terminates pregnancies, substance abuse during pregnancy and termination of pregnancy.

At the core of the tension between women's autonomy rights and foetal interests is the issue of personhood or legal subjectivity and the consequence of being considered a legal subject in law. In South Africa, legal subjectivity vests once a person is born alive.[9] Upon the occurrence of live birth, a person is vested with all constitutional rights and duties found in the Constitution of the Republic of South Africa, 1996.[10]

Several constitutional rights provide the space for women to exist as autonomous, self-determining agents. In *Christian Lawyers Association v Minister of Health*,[11] the court stated that the right to self-determination is a constitutional imperative and identifie the following rights as those rights that vest women with the capacity for self-determination: s 12(2)*(a)* and *(b)* provide that everyone has the right to bodily and psychological integrity, which includes the right to make decisions concerning reproduction and security in and control over their body; s 27(1)*(a)* offers everyone the right to access reproductive health care; s 10 states that everyone has inherent dignity and the right to have their dignity respected and protected; and, in terms of s 14, everyone has the right to privacy.[12] A foetus has very limited, if any, recognition as legal subjectivity vests only once a person is born alive.[13] Until live birth, a foetus does not hold constitutional rights or duties.[14]

This position has been challenged in court to a limited degree and in each case the position of a pregnant woman and her foetus has merely been confirmed For instance, the Eastern Cape Division in *S v Mshumpa*[15] found that one could not murder a foetus, since the victim of murder must have been a living person and until birth a foetus is not a living person.[16] The court described the existence of a pregnancy as a 'unique togetherness' and said that the wonder of pregnancy is not in the separateness of the pregnant woman and the foetus but rather in their

specificall refers to implied foetal interests in continued existence, allowing for uninterrupted development until live birth or general foetal welfare. These interests are determined with reference to the biological drive for survivability inherent in all things living. For a critique of the use of interests in relation to the unborn, see PM Koch 'Ambiguous interests: Maternal desires and fetal interests' (2016) 16 *American Journal of Bioethics* 31.

[9] T Boezaart 'Child law, the child and South African private law' in T Boezaart (ed) *Child Law in South Africa* (2009) 4–5 and H Kruger & A Skelton (eds) *The Law of Persons in South Africa* (2010) 13.

[10] Boezaart 'Child law, the child and South African private law' 4–5 and Kruger & Skelton (eds) *The Law of Persons in South Africa* (2010) 13.

[11] 2005 (1) SA 509 (T) (*Christian Lawyers* (2005)) 518B–E. This decision is briefl discussed below.

[12] Also see generally M O'Sullivan 'Reproductive rights' in S Woolman & M Bishop (eds) *Constitutional Law of South Africa* 2 ed (Original Service 2) 37.

[13] Boezaart 'Child law, the child and South African private law' 4–5.

[14] Boezaart 'Child law, the child and South African private law' 4–5.

[15] 2008 (1) SACR 126 (E) (*Mshumpa*).

[16] *Mshumpa* 149E–F.

closeness.[17] Thus, it was found to be unnecessary to devise a separate offence for harm caused to the unborn.

There are further examples in which the legal positions of the unborn and pregnant women have been confirme by courts. In *Christian Lawyers Association of SA v Minister of Health,*[18] the court found that a foetus does not have the right to life in terms of s 11 of the Constitution, and recognised that, if an unborn were granted that right, there would be 'far-reaching and anomalous consequences' for women.[19] Later, in *Christian Lawyers* (2005) the court found that the right to individual self-determination lies at the heart of the right to terminate a pregnancy.[20] However, this right is not absolute, it may be limited once a foetus is viable (which was found to occur more or less at the end of the second trimester), but the limitation on women's rights may not constitute an outright limitation when it comes to terminating pregnancies.[21]

Further, in *Christian League of Southern Africa v Rall,*[22] the court found that the application of the *nasciturus* fictio did not vest a foetus with legal personality but rather held benefit in suspension until the foetus was born alive.[23] Consequently the application of the *nasciturus* fictio cannot protect a foetus against conduct that terminates prenatal life, as there is no possibility of live birth in the context of termination of pregnancy.[24] More recently, the Constitutional Court in *H v Fetal Assessment Centre*, in the context of wrongful life claims, confirme that constitutional rights only apply after birth.[25]

Some South African academics have begun to question the validity of viewing a pregnant woman and her foetus as a single entity, and recommendations are being made that foetal interests should receive increased and more direct protection in law.

Pillay[26] argues that the born-alive rule has no further purpose in law, as advancements in medical technology have developed to the point where we can now prove the presence of life at the point of foetal viability.[27] Based on this argument, Pillay asserts that personhood should be extended to a viable foetus.[28]

---

[17] *Mshumpa* 151H.

[18] 1998 (4) SA 1113 (T) (*Christian Lawyers* (1998)).

[19] *Christian Lawyers* (1998) 1122E.

[20] *Christian Lawyers* (2005) 518A.

[21] *Christian Lawyers* (2005) 522F–I; 527E.

[22] 1981 (2) SA 821 (O) (*Rall*).

[23] *Rall* 822H.

[24] *Rall* 823E.

[25] *H v Fetal Assessment Centre* 2015 (2) SA 193 (CC) para 50.

[26] R Pillay 'The beginning of human personhood: Is South African law outdated?' (2010) 21 *Stell LR* 230.

[27] Foetal viability indicates the point in foetal development where a foetus is capable of independent survival if born. At this point in development, all the vital organs are present and able to perform their functions sufficiently. See generally IG Cohen & S Sayeed 'Fetal pain, abortion, viability, and the Constitution' (2011) 39 *Journal of Law, Medicine & Ethics* 235 and C Pickles 'Personhood: Proving the significanc of the born-alive rule with reference to medical knowledge of foetal viability' (2013) 24 *Stell LR* 146.

[28] Pillay (2010) *Stell LR* 230.

Kruuse[29] and Du Plessis[30] call for feticide laws to be enacted that would allow a foetus to be a victim of criminal conduct despite it not yet being vested with constitutional rights. On the topic of maternal substance abuse, Ovens[31] argues that prenatal substance abuse should constitute the crime of child abuse, so that a pregnant woman could be held criminally liable. Myburgh[32] takes the position that, when women electively terminate their pregnancies, they are exercising their reproductive rights irresponsibly and criticises the fact that women's interests are always considered when discussing foetal interests. De Freitas supports her view,[33] and both De Freitas and Myburgh have argued that the unborn should have better protection from termination of pregnancies.[34]

In South Africa, there is clearly a call for a shift from viewing the foetus and the pregnant woman as a single entity to viewing a pregnant woman and her foetus as two separate entities.[35] The most alarming feature in these recommendations is that very little consideration is given to the implications of adopting these recommendations, particularly when it comes to the effects on the experience and outcomes of pregnancy generally. Some of the implications of adopting this approach can be gleaned from the United States' experience; it has adopted the view that pregnancy constitutes two separate entities for quite some time. One of the glaring consequences of this approach is the fact that a tension arises between women's rights and foetal interests, and this results in one 'party's' interests being subordinated for the benefi of the other 'party's' interests.

The tension between women and the unborn they carry is found to occur in many instances but only four of these will be explored,[36] namely, in the

[29] HJ Kruuse 'Fetal "rights"? The need for a unifie approach to the fetus in the context of feticide' (2009) 72 *THRHR* 126.

[30] GA Du Plessis 'Feticide: Creating a statutory crime in South African law' (2013) 24 *Stell LR* 73.

[31] M Ovens 'Maternal substance abuse in South Africa: An area for concern?' (2008) 1 *Acta Criminologica* 77 and M Ovens 'A criminological perspective on the prenatal abuse of substances during pregnancy and the link to child abuse in South Africa' (2010) 11 *Child Abuse Research in South Africa* 38.

[32] GA Myburgh *Humanity and the Protection of the Unborn: A Jurisprudential Rationale for the Furtherance of the Anthropological Paradigm of International Law* (unpublished LLM dissertation, University of the Free State, 2008) 58–60.

[33] S De Freitas 'The South African Constitutional Court and the unborn' (2012) 5 *International Journal of Religious Freedom* 51.

[34] SA De Freitas & GA Myburgh 'The relevance of science for the protection of the unborn' (2009) 45 *Journal for Christian Scholarship* 61.

[35] *Mshumpa* (151H) is the most recent decision that has confirme that South Africa follows a single-entity approach. The court described this approach in terms of the 'unique togetherness' shared between a pregnant woman and her foetus.

[36] A number of other areas have been identifie where a tension between female autonomy rights and foetal interests persists, such as advocating forced medical interventions for the benefi of the unborn. See L Jordaan 'The legal validity of an advance refusal of medical treatment in South African law (part 1)' (2011) 44 *De Jure* 32 and L Jordaan 'The legal validity of an advance refusal of medical treatment in South African law (part 2)' (2011) 44 *De Jure* 259. In the case of advance medical directives, Jordaan argues that the interests of a viable foetus should be considered and balanced against the interests of an incompetent pregnant woman who has made an advance medical directive refusing medical treatment. In the medical realm, the tension generally occurs in cases where medical intervention is deemed necessary in order to secure the live birth of a foetus and the

application of termination-of-pregnancy laws; the extension of legal status to the unborn; violence against pregnant women; and in the case of women inflictin self-harm during pregnancy. Current attempts at addressing these areas of concern usually end with women being in an adversarial position in relation to the unborn they carry.

The conflic that arises during a termination of pregnancy procedure generally does so in cases of elective terminations,[37] as therapeutic termination procedures (based on sound clinical judgements) can be justifie by necessity.[38] The defence of necessity is relevant because continued pregnancy poses a risk to the woman or is a result of unlawful conduct, such as rape or incest.[39] The general argument is that legislation that permits termination of pregnancies on demand or for socio-economic reasons is said to be arbitrary and contrary to foetal interests,[40] pitting female reproductive autonomy and foetal interests against each other.

---

pregnant woman refuses to consent to treatment or acts contrary to the instructions of her attending physician. Medical interventions range from hospitalised birth, caesarean-section deliveries or blood transfusions. In these cases, the attending physician approaches the courts to obtain an order to compel compliance with his or her medical advice on the basis that non-compliance with the medical advice will result in irreversible harm to the foetus or stillbirth. Under these circumstances female autonomy is diminished in order to ensure medical treatment. (See generally S Meredith *Policing Pregnancy: The Law and Ethics of Obstetric Conflict* (2005) and P Harris 'Compelled medical treatment of pregnant women: The balancing of maternal and fetal rights' (2001) 49 *Cleveland State LR* 133.) The foetus is considered to be a second 'patient' to whom the doctor owes a duty of care. This topic has received considerable attention in the United States. For more on this issue see LC Ikemoto 'Furthering the inquiry: Race, class, and culture in the forced medical treatment of pregnant women' (1992) 59 *Tennessee LR* 487; E Nelson 'Reconceiving pregnancy: Expressive choice and legal reasoning' (2004) 49 *McGill LJ* 593; MK Miller 'Refusal to undergo a cesarean section: A woman's right or a criminal act' (2005) 15 *Health Matrix* 383; M Kaplan '"A special class of persons" – pregnant women's right to refuse medical treatment after *Gonzales v Carhart*' (2010) 13 *University of Pennsylvania Journal of Constitutional Law* 145; BM Dickens & RJ Cook 'The legal effects of fetal monitoring guidelines' (2010) 108 *International Journal of Gynecology & Obstetrics* 170; and P Laufer-Ukeles 'Reproductive choices and informed consent: Fetal interests, women's identity, and relational autonomy' (2011) 37 *American Journal of Law & Medicine* 567. Also, holding attending health care professionals criminally liable for negligently causing stillbirth. For instance, see generally M Schulman *The Nasciturus Non-Fiction, The Libby Gonen Story: Contemporary Reflections on the Status of the Nascitural Personhood in South African Law* (unpublished LLM dissertation, University of the Witwatersrand, 2014). Schulman argues for the protection of foetal interests during birth. He presents the unborn as separate entities deserving of laws' protective reach. The concerns with this approach are the same as discussed in relation to medical treatment of pregnant women.

[37] Elective termination of pregnancy refers to those circumstances where a woman terminates her pregnancy for non-therapeutic reasons, namely on demand or for socio-economic reasons.

[38] According to Snyman, necessity covers the circumstances where a person acts out of necessity to protect his or her or somebody else's life, bodily integrity, property or other legally recognised interest, which is endangered by a threat of harm which has commenced or is imminent and which cannot be averted in another way. CR Snyman *Criminal Law* 5 ed (2008) 115.

[39] C Ngwena 'An appraisal of abortion laws in Southern Africa from a reproductive health rights perspective' (2004) 32 *Journal of Law, Medicine & Ethics* 708 711.

[40] Myburgh (*Humanity and the Protection of the Unborn* 48) considers the use of elective termination procedures as irresponsible, an abuse of female reproductive rights and an insult to our sense of humanity.

In the case of criminal law, the tension arises where a third party or the pregnant woman herself acts contrary to the interests of the foetus, thereby injuring the foetus or terminating the pregnancy outside of the bounds of the Choice on Termination of Pregnancy Act[41] (the Choice Act). The tension usually arises in cases of violence against pregnant women[42] and prenatal substance abuse.[43] In these scenarios either the legislature or the judiciary embarks on a process of attempting to resolve the tension, which usually results in female reproductive autonomy being diminished in favour of foetal interests.[44]

How each scenario is currently dealt with depends on the approach taken. On the one hand, the foetus and the pregnant woman can be regarded as a single entity and the foetus acquires a legal status and independent protection only once born alive. On the other hand, the foetus and the pregnant woman can be regarded as two separate entities, each with their own sphere of existence and each independently considered in law.[45]

In essence, the single-entity approach is based on the 'oneness' of the pregnant woman and foetus, as the foetus is wholly subsumed (embodied) in and dependent on the woman's body; the unborn are something akin to a bodily organ. In the case of the separate-entities approach, the foetus is viewed as more than an organ; it is seen as a human being[46] and therefore it is argued that the foetus should be granted status as a person in law. Characteristically, the single-entity approach applies the

---

[41] Act 92 of 1996.

[42] For example, see C Pickles 'The introduction of a statutory crime to address third-party foetal violence' (2011) 74 *THRHR* 546.

[43] For example, see E Ordolis 'Maternal substance abuse and the limits of law: A relational challenge' (2008) 46 *Alberta LR* 119.

[44] Meredith *Policing Pregnancy* 187.

[45] See M Ford 'Nothing and not-nothing: Law's ambivalent response to transformation and transgression at the beginning of life' in SW Smith & R Deazley (eds) *The Legal, Medical and Cultural Regulation of the Body: Transformation and Transgression* (2009) 24–30. Ford states that the law's response to a foetus is to grant it special status which has been justifie in numerous ways. Special status has been based on 'potentiality' which suggests that the fact that a foetus holds the potential to become something else is a reason to attribute value to foetal life. Special status has been granted out of respect for interests, which follows the position that a foetus has interests of some sort that should be respected. Here, 'interests' refers to the ability of a foetus to feel pain or pleasure, which would require us to refrain from causing a foetus any unnecessary pain. Special status has also been justifie with reference to relationships. This ground of justificatio requires one to go beyond 'rights and interests' arguments and look at the underlying relationships. Finally, special status has been granted on the grounds of dignity. Ford argues that the special status of the foetus is not founded on interests of the foetus but on the wider societal interest in preserving the dignity of human life generally. A more comprehensive discussion of the different theories will follow in Chapter Three and a revised application of special status will be forwarded in Chapter Ten.

[46] According to Dickens, at common law to be a human being suggests that one is a human *in* being and thus one who is born alive. See BM Dickens 'Legal aspects of the beginning of human life' in KF Beller & RF Weir (eds) *The Beginning of Human Life* (1994) 35. It seems that contemporary discourse has moved away from this definin feature; this will be revealed as the book works through the different debates concerning legal protection of the unborn. It seems that the unborn are viewed as human beings because developments in medical technology support that view—the unborn look like those who are already born and share the same genetic make-up. See Chapter Three in this regard. This book recognises that the common law requires a human to be in being before he or she will constitute a human being, but goes on to engage the more contemporary positions that the

born-alive rule,[47] while the separate-entities approach rejects this rule or supports the development of legal principles beyond the rule, because medical technology has advanced enough to prove life prior to actual live birth.[48]

Supporters of termination-of-pregnancy laws tend to follow the single-entity approach, while those that advocate foetal rights or who are 'pro-life' supporters are likely to follow the separate-entities approach. Supporters of the separate-entities approach also accept unauthorised intervention to ensure continued foetal development or live birth, since a foetus is perceived to be a person in need of treatment or enhanced legal consideration.[49] The single-entity approach find that unauthorised interventions are a violation of female autonomy rights and that being pregnant is not a justifiabl limitation of women's rights.[50] In the case of criminal issues, the single-entity approach will not permit a foetus to be considered a victim of criminal conduct and pregnant women are not obligated to protect the foetus from harm. The separate-entities approach generally supports the possibility that a foetus can be the victim of criminal conduct[51] and, if the approach is applied to extremes, women might also have the duty to conduct themselves according to the best interests of the foetus, ensuring proper development and live birth.[52]

A tension is clearly present in each area of law and there have been attempts to resolve the issue by approaching courts or advancing arguments supporting the enactment of legislation. When recognising the unique relationship that develops through the biological fact of pregnancy, South African court decisions usually end with an individualised conception that interprets the pregnancy relationship in terms of the pregnant woman's autonomy rights.[53] These sorts of decisions do not reflec a capacity to address the shared needs of the pregnant woman and the foetus she carries.[54] In contrast, those United States decisions or legislative provisions that embrace the separate-entities approach reject the values of connection and present the view that a woman is a foetal container whose autonomy and bodily

---

unborn are human beings from a genetic perspective and attempts to tackle the implications of that view in law.

[47] This rule requires that a person must firs be born alive in order to qualify as a legal subject; see Pillay (2010) *Stell LR* 230.

[48] Pillay (2010) *Stell LR* 230.

[49] Jordaan (part 1) (2011) *De Jure* 32 and Jordaan (part 2) (2011) *De Jure* 259.

[50] See generally Meredith *Policing Pregnancy*.

[51] Kruuse (2009) *THRHR* 126.

[52] See Meredith *Policing Pregnancy* 130–62. As an overview, Meredith discusses the maternal duty to act in the best interests of the foetus with reference to circumstances where pregnant women have been incarcerated for the duration of their pregnancies in order to curb their drug dependent activities, where women have been charged or convicted with child neglect based on conduct prior to the birth of their children, and in some instances where women have faced charges of dealing drugs to a minor where their babies have tested positive for narcotics or alcohol at birth. Going even further, harmful conduct during pregnancy has at times been used as a ground to justify the removal of a child from the care of his or her mother. The author has linked the criminalisation of third-party foetal violence to maternal liability (139).

[53] Ordolis (2008) *Alberta LR* 134.

[54] Ordolis (2008) *Alberta LR* 134.

integrity may be violated through state- or court-sanctioned intervention.[55] However, this approach also undermines the interests of both pregnant women and the unborn they carry.[56] In each case an adversarial environment is created. This approach is not conducive to the fact that women bear the constraints of pregnancy and that the unborn are innately reliant on women for live birth. There needs to be a sense of cooperation for the further good of both, namely healthy pregnancies and healthy pregnancy outcomes.[57]

In a steadfast rejection of the single-entity and separate-entities approaches, this book focuses on the shared connection between a pregnant woman and the foetus for the duration of the pregnancy, and thus recommends a relational approach to pregnancy. This recommendation draws on the work of Nedelsky.[58] She rejects a liberal construction of autonomy which views individuals as being atomistic and calls for a definitio of autonomy that recognises people as inherently social in nature. She argues that autonomy is made possible by constructive relationships; this includes intimate, cultural, institutional, national, global relations, all of which are in a constant state of interaction.[59] This approach recognises that human existence and the experience of autonomy is characterised by the presence of relationships and interaction with others.[60] 'Relationships are central to people's lives—to who we are, to the capacities we are able to develop, to what we value, what we suffer, and what we are able to enjoy.'[61] She emphasises that the centrality of relationships in our inherently social existence indicates the

[55] Ordolis (2008) *Alberta LR* 134.

[56] Ordolis (2008) *Alberta LR* 134.

[57] Generally third-party intervention during a pregnancy is justifie by the fact that these individuals or institutions have an interest in securing the live birth of the foetus. Intervention can result in forced medical treatment, criminal liability and/or the incarceration of pregnant women. This is a very narrow construction of a 'healthy pregnancy outcome', as it is clearly one-dimensional in that it focuses only on the unborn individually and fails to consider pregnant women beyond being mere foetal carriers. For purposes of this book, a 'healthy pregnancy' is a pregnancy that progresses without unauthorised third-party intervention, where pregnant women progress though their pregnancies without having their rights violated in order to serve the interests that others may have in the unborn they carry. This construction recognises that, in order to maintain a healthy pregnancy, pregnant women will inevitably come into contact with health-care providers for prenatal care, indicating that there will be a certain degree of dependency on others for securing a healthy pregnancy. However, what determines a healthy pregnancy under these circumstances is that the compounded needs of both the pregnant woman and foetus are addressed in a relational fashion. Thus, violating the autonomy of a pregnant woman will not advance the interests of the foetus, who has an intricate link with the pregnant woman. The idea of a 'healthy pregnancy outcome' moves beyond merely securing the live birth of a foetus, and looks also to securing the autonomy and bodily and psychological integrity of the pregnant woman concerned. Further, a 'healthy pregnancy outcome' aims to protect the wellbeing of existing relations (and possibly her future relation to her new child, if the woman has decided against adoption), namely, protecting her family unit and placing in the community. Securing the live birth of a foetus is an important aim, but it should not end with a woman being separated from who she is beyond her pregnancy.

[58] J Nedelsky 'Reconceiving autonomy: Sources, thoughts and possibilities' (1989) 1 *Yale Journal of Law & Feminism* 7 and J Nedelsky *Law's Relations: A Relational Theory of Self, Autonomy, and Law* (2011).

[59] Nedelsky *Law's Relations* 118

[60] Nedelsky *Law's Relations* 119.

[61] Nedelsky *Law's Relations* 3.

constitutive nature of the various relationships one might share with others. This accentuates the reality that a person's experience of themselves and their core capacities[62] are influence by the relationships he or she engages in at all levels of existence.

A relational approach serves as both an investigative and transformative tool.[63] It helps to identify who the participants are in a particular relationship. Further, it assists in determining the quality of that relationship; that is, whether the structure of the relationship secures or undermines core capacities.[64] When a destructive relationship arises it is arguably because the law has structured the relationship in that way, and this indicates the necessity of reforming laws to allow for an improved structured relationship.[65] With a contextualised perspective in place, such as one that focuses on relationships and those aspects that influenc relationships, it is easier to identify how to restructure or transform relationships so as to allow for more constructive, capacity-building connections between relating parties.[66]

It is through the process of centralising focus on relationships that more imaginative solutions come to the fore. This view ensures individuals' unique core capacities are secured and realisable even though they might be wound in webs of relationships characterised by varying degrees of dependency.[67] Focusing on the centrality of relationships helps to distinguish between those relationships that foster autonomy and those that undermine it; this understanding will guide the transformation of destructive relationships into ones that foster autonomy.[68]

In the context of this book, Nedelsky's relational approach to autonomy helps to develop a more contextual understanding of pregnant women within the four areas of focus. It assists in demonstrating that pregnant women are not purely isolated individuals free from external influences This approach offers the opportunity to create the space to consider context and recognise that there are numerous relationships that influenc the experience of pregnancy and which inevitably determine whether healthy pregnancies and healthy pregnancy outcomes can be achieved. When approaching a particular area of law relevant to pregnancy one needs to have a contextual understanding of pregnant women having regard to their social setting and the actual presence of a pregnancy and the unborn in order to meaningfully resolve the issue, and Nedelsky demonstrates how this can be achieved through a relational approach.

This relational approach requires one to consider the pregnant woman in relation to the foetus rather than in an adversarial confrontation with the foetus,

[62] Such as our dignity, equality and autonomy, to name a few.

[63] Nedelsky *Law's Relations* 67.

[64] Nedelsky *Law's Relations* 133.

[65] Nedelsky *Law's Relations* 67.

[66] Nedelsky *Law's Relations* 67.

[67] This approach might create an absolute tension with regard to the requirement that like cases be treated alike in order for justice to be achieved. By focusing on the individuality of each person there is a risk that one will no longer be able to predict certain outcomes in law because uniqueness would require case by case reactions, thus diminishing predictability of justice and causing like cases to be treated differently instead of alike.

[68] Nedelsky *Law's Relations* 122.

both united with mutual needs. Contrary to the single-entity approach, the proposed relational approach recognises the presence of foetal life which is explicitly included as something necessary to consider since the pregnant woman shares a connection to the foetus. Contrary to the separate-entities approach, the proposed relational approach does not consider the foetus as entirely independent of the pregnant woman because of the relational link shared between the foetus and the pregnant woman.

Ultimately, Nedelsky's work provides the basis for the solution to pregnancy adversarialism, particularly because her work demonstrates *how* to include the consideration of context in a constructive, forward-looking manner. Nedelsky's writing provides a theoretical backing for the way forward regarding pregnancy in law and demonstrates how to create the space to consider the unborn and achieve this end without compromising autonomy.

It is very important to illuminate concerns about the way the law frames female reproductive autonomy, pregnancy and the connection between pregnant women and the foetus. Without these issues being properly framed, pregnancy-related concerns will never be meaningfully addressed and healthy pregnancies and pregnancy outcomes may never be fully realised.

Female autonomy and foetal interests are currently seen as conflictin notions in most factual scenarios considered by the law, whether in terms of criminal law or private law. The approach assumed by the law prevents legal systems from recognising foetal interests without being confronted with the force of female autonomy or without undermining female autonomy. The moment an opportunity arises to advance foetal interests an impression is created that foetal interests have a heightened value and this too would establish a ground for justifying the limitation of female autonomy beyond the current limitations imposed by laws.[69]

For instance, in South Africa, where intentional harm is inflicte against a pregnant woman which causes the termination of her wanted or intentionally continued pregnancy, the harm to the 'extra-ness' that her pregnancy represents cannot be addressed by the courts since female autonomy (expressed through termination of pregnancy) prohibits the consideration of foetal interests.[70] There is a concern that if the unborn are recognised, women's rights will have to be severely limited for the unborn's benefit Ultimately, the notion of self-determination which provides women with autonomous freedom is the very notion that prevents the law from taking decisions favourable to foetal interests. This should not be the case, because some women want to continue pregnancies and have that process of continuation protected.[71]

It is not the purpose of this book to redefin constitutional principles relevant to the right to life. The book is also not aimed at discovering new ways and means of developing opportunities to grant a foetus constitutional rights, since it is quite

[69] Limitations such as those found in the Choice Act which increasingly limit women's access to pregnancy termination as the pregnancy progresses closer to birth.

[70] These were the facts that the court had to decide on in *Mshumpa*.

[71] For instance, see BA Manninen 'The value of choice and the choice to value: Explaining the discussion about fetal life within prochoice advocacy' (2013) 28 *Hypatia* 663 and Schulman *The Nasciturus Non-Fiction*.

clear that female autonomy also needs to be advanced through the recognition of foetal interests, rather than be limited any further in favour of a foetus.

Recognising that a foetus is not a person in law and acknowledging that female reproductive autonomy is important to the dignity and equality of all women and girls, the book establishes a third, relational approach to taking foetal interests into account without narrowing the boundaries of the law as it currently stands for women. This approach questions the validity of the single-entity and separate-entities approaches, since one fails to acknowledge the unborn while the other is adversarial in nature and automatically places foetal interests and female autonomy at loggerheads with one another. Pregnant women need to be considered contextually, having regard to their relational ties to the unborn they carry, to the society in which they live and the availability of support structures to assist women during the course of their pregnancies.

Ultimately, we need to ask whether the value of connection can resolve the tension between women's reproductive autonomy rights and foetal interests, thereby avoiding an adversarial approach, and allowing for coexistence of legally recognised foetal interests and female autonomy.

This book constitutes four parts. Part One seeks to determine what factors give rise to an adversarial pregnancy environment. Chapter Two provides a very broad historical overview, which contemplates the social position of women in relation to the unborn in order to determine whether the two were ever in opposition to one another. A historical study considers the development of female reproductive autonomy and foetal interests. The chapter helps highlight trends and changes that occurred over time to the present day. Chapter Three takes up the historical theme and explores the rise and waves of feminism (as a leading social movement aimed at emancipating women) as a response to women's oppression discussed in Chapter Two. Chapter Three further contemplates the role of scientifi advancements in prenatal care, the eventual individuation of the unborn and the development of theories concerning why the unborn are entities of value and worthy of separate or individuated attention.

Part Two looks at the current position of South African law regarding pregnant women and the unborn. Chapter Four deliberates on the legal status of pregnant women and determines the extent of their reproductive rights during pregnancy. Chapter Five focuses on the unborn and establishes that South Africa currently subscribes to the single-entity approach and the not-one-but-not-two approach (not-one/not-two approach) to the unborn and explores the implication of these approaches. Chapter Six considers the various arguments advanced by South African scholars for changes to South African law. It further contemplates the quality of their arguments against the backdrop of advancing foetal interests and reproductive autonomy. Furthermore, the chapter critically considers whether these suggestions for reform will secure healthy pregnancies and healthy pregnancy outcomes.

In Chapter Six it is demonstrated that South African scholars advocate for a separate-entities approach to pregnancy in order to better protect the unborn and Part Three tests the credibility of the claim. Part Three focuses on the United States and current developments taking place in relation to pregnancy in the law. The United States is a useful jurisdiction to consider because it is an example of a country that has accommodated the call for protecting foetal interests and adopts the separate-entities approach.[72] This can be gathered from the fact that certain states have introduced legislation which moves beyond the born-alive rule given that a foetus can be the victim[73] of criminal conduct. In certain instances, there is also a duty on pregnant women to protect the unborn from harm. This is the case despite the fact that women have a right to terminate their pregnancies.[74] Ultimately, the comparative analysis reveals the effectiveness of the United States' separatist laws in realising healthy pregnancies and healthy pregnancy outcomes in those areas identifie by South African scholars as being in need of reform. It also assists with demonstrating how the persistence of the tension between female autonomy rights and foetal interests hampers effective law reform.

Part Three begins with Chapter Seven, which discusses the legal status of pregnant women and the unborn and establishes that the unborn are vested with a form of legal status in the United States. It further demonstrates that granting legal status to the unborn does not necessarily result in better protection of the unborn and this findin is supported by research stemming from Chapters Eight and Nine. Chapters Eight and Nine critically delve into the themes of third-party violence that terminates prenatal life and prenatal substance abuse as constituting child abuse. Part Three establishes that if the aim of law reform is to secure healthy pregnancies and pregnancy outcomes, the separate-entities approach is a poor method of achieving that end.

Part Four suggests a way forward. Chapter Ten advances an alternative view of pregnancy based on relational feminism and the not-one/not-two approach, and it further advances a unique form of status for the unborn in law. The chapter thereafter applies this revised view of pregnancy to the identifie areas in need of reform, namely, to termination-of-pregnancy laws, prenatal substance abuse, violence against pregnant women and personhood of the unborn. Chapter Eleven concludes the book and reflect on some of the key findings

---

[72] See generally BA Burkstrand-Reid 'The invisible woman: Availability and culpability in reproductive health jurisprudence' (2010) 81 *University of Colorado LR* 97.

[73] Legislation is in place at both state level and federal level (Unborn Victims of Violence Act, 2004) that confronts third-party foetal violence that results in the termination of a pregnancy. At state level, 38 states have foetal homicide laws in place: see National Conference of State Legislators 'Fetal homicide state laws' available at http://www.ncsl.org/research/health/fetal-homicide-state-laws.aspx (accessed on 14 July 2016). This approach leaves the applicability of the born-alive rule in a questionable position.

[74] *Roe v Wade* 93 S Ct 705 (1973). It was found that the right to terminate a pregnancy lies in women's constitutional right to privacy, however as a pregnancy progresses to the point of viability (approximately the second trimester) the state has sufficient interest in foetal life to limit the right to terminate a pregnancy.

PART ONE

THE DEVELOPMENT OF AN ADVERSARIAL PREGNANCY ENVIRONMENT

Chapter 2

WOMEN AND THE UNBORN IN PRE-MODERN SOCIETIES

2.1 INTRODUCTION

This chapter considers the social status of women[1] and the unborn in pre-modern times. In this respect, it provides a general overview of the position of the unborn, the regulation of female sexuality, and women's economic, political and cultural roles in antiquity and the Middle Ages, and demonstrates that there is no historical account of an adversarial pregnancy environment. While gaining a true account of pregnant women's social experiences may be a challenge,[2] the chapter does

---

[1] It is mostly the lives of free women that will be considered. A free woman was one who did not have a master and did not have to live to serve a master; see DM Schaps 'What was free about a free Athenian woman?' (1998) 128 *Transactions of the American Philological Association* 161 163; 165 and JF Gardner *Women in Roman Law and Society* (1986) 205–31.

[2] There are a number of methodological shortcomings inherent in a historical study of this nature. First, secondary sources are the primary generators of information and this is problematic because these texts are interpretive in nature. Also, not all historical texts survived the ages. Those texts that did survive may not have survived intact. Consequently, one may be left with an incomplete picture of a particular topic. For those texts that have survived, it should be noted that the texts were drafted in foreign languages and the process of translation creates the risk of losing an understanding of the context and tone of the source. Additional issues arise when evaluating the content of ancient or mediaeval texts. A number of authors have alluded to the fact that existing texts are notoriously empty of the lived experiences of different social classes, particularly women and children within these classes. In this respect, see M Wiesner-Hanks 'World history and the history of women, gender, and sexuality' (2007) 18 *Journal of World History* 53; R Karras 'Invisible women' (2005) 39 *Medieval Feminist Forum* 15; and JS Loengard 'Legal history and the medieval Englishwoman: A fragmented view' (1986) 4 *Law & History Review* 161. For those texts that do mention the 'invisible' portions of ancient populations, the texts mainly represent the views and experiences of wealthy, educated men. For instance, see MW Kaufman 'Spare ribs: The conception of women in the Middle Ages and the Renaissance' (1973) 56 *Soundings* 139 140–1. Kaufman, in the context of literary works, argues that our image of the Middle Ages is informed by literature which is subject to the artist's personal, unconscious prejudices and conscious distortions, all meshed together through the prism of the artist's imagination. He states further (140–1) that mediaeval literature was mainly produced by aristocratic men representing a very small portion of the total mediaeval population; however, contemporary scholars and authors rarely question the validity of the depiction of women presented by these historical personalities. Kaufman's (140) arguments can also be applied to non-literary texts and to those texts originating from ancient Greece and Rome since literacy (for purposes of record keeping and legislative drafting) was a skill reserved for privileged men. Consequently, it is important to recognise that women's lived experiences were not widely documented and where there was documentation it was very rarely done by women themselves. We are left with a distorted and incomplete view of women, pregnancy and the unborn in antiquity and the Middle Ages which impacts on the quality of the information presented in this chapter. Also see generally Wiesner-Hanks (2007) *Journal of World History* 53; Karras (2005) *Medieval Feminist Forum* 15; and Loengard (1986) *Law & History Review* 161 who also allude to these concerns.

provide a measure of insight into the evolution of the status of women and the unborn and demonstrates how perceptions undermined or advanced the needs of either the unborn or women.

This chapter contrasts the roles of Christianity and the state in the ancient Greek, Roman and mediaeval European societies,[3] and contemplates how each institution influence the lives of women and the independent (but non-scientific recognition of the unborn. It becomes apparent that women's subsidiary and under-valued position is maintained in both secular law and the Christian teachings developed later, while the unborn receive increasing consideration and protection as societies move towards Christian ethics. It is important to note the role of Christian ethics, because, although the Church and state developed and functioned independently of each other, secular law came to rely on the moral code of the Church in areas concerning marriage, sexual practices and morality, and property rights.[4] Further, the notion of crime contains the moral issue of sin, for which punishment is required.[5] Here, the state was viewed as an agent of God and its purpose was to control sinful individuals on earth.[6]

While there is no obvious historical account of an adversarial pregnancy environment, the merger of the state and religion does show that an adversarial environment begins to take root. The undercurrents of this situation prove unfortunate for women, who are held fast in a position of subservience in religion and the law, both with socially far-reaching scope. The unborn are elevated in God's name, which is later secured in law. This creates an ideal environment for adversarialism.

[3] The West is an important focus area because the historical foundations of the South African and American legal systems can be traced back to the Western development of European law. Ancient Greek laws influence Roman law, which infiltrate Europe after the fall of the Western Roman Empire. The spread of Roman law in Europe led to the wide-reaching reception of Roman law principles in Europe, including the German Reich, with Holland as one of its feudal dependencies. The reception of Roman law in Holland gave rise to a united Roman-Dutch law. This legal system was brought to the shores of South Africa in 1652, when the Cape of Good Hope was occupied by the Netherlands, spearheaded by Jan van Riebeeck from the Dutch East Indian Company. England was mostly exempt from the European reception of Roman law, developing instead its own common legal system. This law was received into the United States and South Africa. See HR Hahlo & E Khan *The South African Legal System and Its Background* (1973) 484–5; 504–9; 514–17; 525; 567; 575–8; OF Robinson, TD Fergus & WM Gordon *An Introduction to European Legal History* (1985) 205–56; AB Morrison (ed) *Fundamentals of American Law* (1996) 9–14; and W Burnham *Introduction to the Law and Legal System of the United States* (1995) 1–2; 39; 42. In line with these linkages, this chapter will trace the Western development and evolution of women and the unborn, spanning from ancient Greece, through Rome and into Western European societies.

[4] CR Jeffery 'The development of crime in early English society' (1957) 47 *Journal of Criminal Law, Criminology, and Police Science* 647 664. Also see Robinson, Fergus & Gordon *An Introduction to European Legal History* 123.

[5] Jeffery (1957) 47 *Journal of Criminal Law, Criminology, and Police Science* 664. Jeffery (652) states that the concept of crime developed as it did as a result of the interaction between the state and the Church.

[6] Jeffery (1957) *Journal of Criminal Law, Criminology, and Police Science* 652.

2.2 WOMEN AND THE UNBORN IN ANCIENT GREECE

The position that women enjoyed in ancient Greek society is a matter of much debate.[7] However, research indicates that, with the introduction of fifth-centur urban city states (oligarchies), women faced increased chastity and seclusion.[8] These states were characteristically governed by a small group of people (free men who were citizens) and were merely a federation of households (*oikoi*) under the power of individual patriarchs.[9] According to Foxhall, a household was considered a fundamental building block of ancient Greek society, as it was the primary space for the expression of age and sex roles, affinity, socialisation and economic cooperation.[10] A household included not only a wife and children but also slaves and property.[11]

McLaren states that it was under this system of households that women became domesticated.[12] Without referring to any authority, he asserts that Greek laws held that women had no life outside the household.[13] However, Arthur demystifie this position, stating that the concept of 'household' (*oikos*) itself was a legal principle that define all aspects of a woman's position:

> The state was conceived as a union of *oikoi*, each of which was an association of husband, wife, children and slaves, together with property which supported them and whose growth their association was designed to promote.[14]

Greek society is said to have made a very clear division between public and private life. Women's lives were secluded from men and it seems their roles were played out in the private world of the household, where they were responsible for its efficient operation.[15] A woman fell under the head of the household[16] (that being her husband or father) and he made all the decisions.[17] Only men could operate in the public world (beyond the boundaries of the household) and Foxhall

---

[7] A McLaren *A History of Contraception: From Antiquity to the Present Day* (1990) 14. Also see M Katz 'Ideology and "the status of women" in ancient Greece' (1992) 31 *History and Theory* 70 72–82 where the author gives an overview of the divergent interpretations of the status of ancient Greek women.

[8] McLaren *History of Contraception* 15.

[9] McLaren *History of Contraception* 15.

[10] L Foxhall 'Household, gender and property in classical Athens' (1989) 39 *The Classical Quarterly* 22.

[11] McLaren *History of Contraception* 15.

[12] McLaren *History of Contraception* 15.

[13] McLaren *History of Contraception* 15. Oddly, McLaren does not refer to any such laws.

[14] MB Arthur 'Early Greece: The origins of the Western attitude toward women' (1973) 6 *Arethusa* 7 31–2.

[15] Foxhall (1989) *The Classical Quarterly* 30.

[16] Emphasising the effect of different classes, Schaps ((1998) *Transactions of the American Philological Association* 164; 167–77) explains that belonging to the head of a household must be distinguished from being a master's slave. He states that free Athenian women were subordinated to free Athenian men and the relationship was one of affection. This was not the case for the relationship shared between a master and slaves. Generally, free women had more independence than a slave since they could not merely be sold, detained or beaten; they were entitled to have and express an opinion. Free women sometimes had their own slaves and could even divorce their husbands. However, their independence was always subject to the head of the household.

[17] Foxhall (1989) *The Classical Quarterly* 30. Arthur (1973) *Arethusa* 33 states that upon marriage, a woman was technically only 'loaned out' to another family for the purpose of producing a legitimate heir.

asserts that the head of the household worked on behalf of his household or in consensus with it.[18]

A woman could not legally represent herself or her interests, but had to be represented by the head of the household (her *kyrios,* meaning representative or guardian).[19] This impacted on women's ability to own or control property.[20] At most, women were vested with 'informal' powers to transact or deal with property, but only to the extent that their *kyrios* made provision for this to happen.[21] This construction left women dependent on men at two levels, intimately within the household and formally within the public sphere, as a woman's relations with her *kyrios* were instrumental in advancing her interests.[22] Arthur argues that, as long as women continued to be associated with the private spheres of life, they would appear to be 'a sub-species of humanity', a mere aspect of men's existence.[23] She argues further that the social and legal structure of this ancient Greek state factually endorsed and prescribed the subservience of women and this took away their existence in their own right.[24]

McLaren asserts that marriage played a fundamental role in Greek society. The purpose of marriage was to produce heirs and only males were recognised heirs.[25] The ideal household was self-sufficient, with a fertile wife, who produced children, and could assist in maintaining the property.[26] Although the wife's fertility was honoured in the household, it was just as important to avoid producing too many heirs, because then the family's wealth would have to be divided among too many claimants.[27] According to McLaren, the ideal familial structure would consist of one son to maintain the family name and one daughter to fortify an alliance with another family through marriage.[28]

This notion of the ideal Greek household and city state could be successfully achieved only if reproduction was controlled.[29] Consequently, while it was important to have a family, the ancient Greeks did not view the arrival of every

[18] Foxhall (1989) *The Classical Quarterly* 31.

[19] S Johnstone 'Women, property, and surveillance in classical Athens' (2003) 22 *Classical Antiquity* 247.

[20] Johnstone (2003) *Classical Antiquity* 247.

[21] Johnstone (2003) *Classical Antiquity* 248. Johnstone states that this 'informal' power has been interpreted as 'freedom' for women. For instance, see generally Foxhall ((1989) *The Classical Quarterly* 22) who argues that a woman's dowry gave her leverage in her relationship with her husband, because if she was unhappy she could divorce her husband and take her dowry with her (39). However, Johnstone ((2003) *Classical Antiquity* 269) points out that if her husband resisted returning the dowry, the woman would have to get her father to litigate on her behalf. This demonstrates that a woman's attempt to gain control is ultimately dependant on a man.

[22] Johnstone (2003) *Classical Antiquity* 269.

[23] Arthur (1973) *Arethusa* 36.

[24] Arthur (1973) *Arethusa* 36.

[25] McLaren *History of Contraception* 16.

[26] McLaren *History of Contraception* 17. The wife was tasked with directing the domestic slaves and at times enjoyed temporary power when her husband was away.

[27] McLaren *History of Contraception* 17.

[28] McLaren *History of Contraception* 17.

[29] McLaren *History of Contraception* 17.

child as a blessing.[30] There were several fertility control methods available: divorce, remarriage and adoption for the purposes of gaining an heir; and contraception, termination of pregnancy and exposure for the purposes of decreasing potential heirs.[31]

It is noteworthy that fertility control was primarily a woman's business based on 'female knowledge'.[32] The presence of this 'knowledge' indicates that women saw themselves as having active control over their fate and it indicates a serious intention to gain control over procreation.[33] Fertility control practices varied and included breastfeeding, herbal potions, obscure barrier methods and vaginal suppositories.[34] In case of all attempts to curb fertility failing, women believed they could remedy the problem with magic in the form of protective amulets and talismans.[35]

Should conception occur despite adopting the above methods of fertility control, women had access to termination-of-pregnancy procedures. In fact, there is evidence that Greek philosophers advocated this as a method of population control.[36] For instance, Aristotle called for the employment of termination of pregnancies to regulate fertility and he described a termination of pregnancy as 'to have a miscarriage induced before sense and life had begun in the embryo'.[37] However, terminating a pregnancy was not the preferred method of fertility control, because it usually required the use of violence and further required 'outside' assistance or instruction, especially in cases where there were complications.[38]

Although ancient medical texts described the termination of pregnancy as being practised in secret, there is no evidence that there were any laws against it.[39] The absence of laws on the topic did not mean that women were free to terminate pregnancies as they wished; they had to obtain permission from their husbands (if

---

[30] McLaren *History of Contraception* 17.

[31] McLaren *History of Contraception* 17.

[32] McLaren *History of Contraception* 26; 28.

[33] McLaren *History of Contraception* 28.

[34] McLaren *History of Contraception* 26; 27.

[35] McLaren *History of Contraception* 28. For instance, McLaren (28) refers to the work of Pedanius Dioscorides (40–90 AD) who authored a five-volum encyclopaedia on herbal medicine and who asserted that an asparagus root amulet will ensure infertility.

[36] McLaren *History of Contraception* 18 and RH Feen 'Abortion and exposure in ancient Greece: Assessing the status of the fetus and "newborn" from classical sources' in WB Bondeson, HT Engelhardt, S Spicker et al (eds) *Abortion and the Status of the Fetus* (1983) 289.

[37] McLaren *History of Contraception* 18. The issue of 'sense and life' will be discussed below.

[38] McLaren *History of Contraception* 28. Other contraceptive methods fell within the intimate sphere of a woman's life. In the case where termination of pregnancy was required she had to move beyond her intimate 'female knowledge'.

[39] McLaren *History of Contraception* 29. Also see SK Dickison 'Abortion in antiquity' (1973) 6 *Arethusa* 159. Reviewing the work of Professor Nardi (E Nardi *Procurato Abortio Nel Mondo Greco Romano* (1971)) she agrees with Nardi's findin that there is no demonstrable evidence of the existence of any laws whatsoever against termination of pregnancy; all that is mentioned in the available sources is that women terminated their pregnancies even though it placed their health at great risk.

married) or fathers (if unmarried).[40] McLaren and Feen state that terminating a pregnancy was only ever considered wrong if it was done without the permission of the husband or father.[41] The heads of households were the only people recognised as competent to adequately judge the issue as to whether or not a pregnancy should be terminated.[42] Further, a husband's permission was required because the termination of a pregnancy denied him heirs; it cheated him of hopes and the continuity of his name.[43] McLaren states that if a woman terminated her pregnancy without her husband's or father's permission, she could be condemned to death.[44]

Public tolerance of the termination of pregnancy is understandable when placed in the context of the exposure of children. According to Dickison, exposure was a relatively common practice.[45] Only the father of the child had the right to expose the child because he was not obliged by duty to accept his children.[46]

If termination of pregnancy and exposure were allowed only by the head of a household, it leaves one questioning how the unborn were perceived in ancient Greek society. Feen states that the concept of life revolved around the principle of 'ensoulment' being a metaphysical speculation rather than a biological process.[47] Accordingly, a soul was the source or cause of life.[48] The Greeks believed that there was a variety of souls: nutritive souls for plants; sensitive souls for animals and rational souls for humans.[49] Feen states that some Greeks believed that the unborn would go through an entire transformation of souls as it developed, from the nutritive soul of a plant, to the sensitive soul of an animal and eventually a human rational soul.[50] According to Gunstan, it was believed that the soul was what gave a substance or organism its characteristic form.[51]

It is not clear when an unborn was vested with a rational soul, but, according to McLaren[52] and Feen,[53] it was believed that a male unborn was not endowed with a

---

[40] McLaren *History of Contraception* 32 and Feen 'Abortion and exposure in ancient Greece' 291. In the case of a divorced woman, she had the option of exposing the child if the father did not recognise the child, see McLaren *History of Contraception* 33.

[41] McLaren *History of Contraception* 32.

[42] McLaren *History of Contraception* 32.

[43] McLaren *History of Contraception* 32.

[44] McLaren *History of Contraception* 32. He states that the fact that there were sanctions imposed against women who did not have their husband's permission presupposes that women did act on their own.

[45] Dickison (1973) *Arethusa* 166; C Patterson '"Not worth the rearing": The causes of infant exposure in ancient Greece' (1985) 115 *Transactions of the American Philological Association* 103. For more on exposure, see Feen 'Abortion and exposure in ancient Greece' 115; 118.

[46] McLaren *History of Contraception* 34 and Feen 'Abortion and exposure in ancient Greece' 285. McLaren (33) states that the extent to which exposure was adopted is not clear and he suggests that it was unlikely that the elite practised exposure.

[47] Feen 'Abortion and exposure in ancient Greece' 293.

[48] Feen 'Abortion and exposure in ancient Greece' 293.

[49] McLaren *History of Contraception* 31 and Feen 'Abortion and exposure in ancient Greece' 293.

[50] Feen 'Abortion and exposure in ancient Greece' 293.

[51] GR Gunstan 'The moral status of the human embryo: A tradition recalled' (1984) 1 *Journal of Medical Ethics* 38 39.

[52] McLaren *History of Contraception* 31.

[53] Feen 'Abortion and exposure in ancient Greece' 294.

rational soul until 30 days (Hippocrates) or 40 days (Aristotle) after conception. A female unborn was ensouled with rationality only 80 days (Hippocrates) or 90 days (Aristotle) after conception.[54] Aristotle did believe that the unborn were alive from a very early stage but only in the same way as a vegetable was.[55]

It must be remembered that, according to Aristotle, the termination of a pregnancy could take place only before 'sense and life had begun in the embryo'.[56] In this context 'sense' is synonymous with movement and 'life' with ensoulment. Feen states that 'ensoulment' or 'life' refers to the sensitive soul of an animal and he cautions that it would be a mistake to associate the rational soul of a human being to foetal movement.[57] A rational soul was required for thought processes.[58] Therefore Feen argues that Aristotle probably viewed an embryo with 'sense and life' as a potential human life with a potentially rational soul, and a pregnancy should not be terminated at this point because of what the embryo might become, rather than what it had become.[59] Contrary to Feen's assertions, Gunstan has interpreted Aristotle's work as endowing a formed foetus (being one that is recognisably human) with a rational soul.[60] Feen states that it is not clear what the ancient Greeks held to be the most plausible approach to ensoulment, but evidence seems to indicate that it was generally accepted that rationality occurred at birth with the newborn's firs breath.[61]

Aristotle's approach distinguishes between a 'formed' and an 'unformed' unborn: An 'unformed' foetus was one that did not hold 'sense' and 'life'.[62] The sex of the foetus and foetal movement indicated the presence of life and sensation.[63] The sex of a foetus was determined by referring to the position of the foetus in the uterus.[64] Further, it was believed that the female unborn began to move at four months after conception, while the male unborn moved three months after conception.[65] Dickison argues that it was Aristotle who was the firs to ever make this distinction and attach significanc to it.[66] In fact, Aristotle's distinction regarding foetal development is historically significant It is the sole contribution by Greek thought to later ecclesiastical legislation regarding termination of pregnancies and thus played a fundamental role in Roman law on the termination

[54] McLaren *History of Contraception* 31. It was believed that females took longer to be 'ensouled' because females were 'thinner' so it took some time for them to coagulate.

[55] McLaren *History of Contraception* 31. For more on Aristotle's theory see NM Ford *When Did I Begin? Conception of the Human Individual in History, Philosophy and Science* (1991) 19–36.

[56] McLaren *History of Contraception* 18.

[57] Feen 'Abortion and exposure in ancient Greece' 294.

[58] Feen 'Abortion and exposure in ancient Greece' 294.

[59] Feen 'Abortion and exposure in ancient Greece' 294.

[60] Gunstan (1984) *Journal of Medical Ethics* 39 and Ford *When Did I Begin?* 38.

[61] Feen 'Abortion and exposure in ancient Greece' 295.

[62] Dickison (1973) *Arethusa* 165.

[63] Dickison (1973) *Arethusa* 165.

[64] McLaren *History of Contraception* 21.

[65] McLaren *History of Contraception* 31. For more on ancient theories of reproduction see JG Landels 'An ancient account of reproduction' (1979) 44 *Biology and Human Affairs* 94.

[66] Dickison (1973) *Arethusa* 165.

of pregnancies.[67] According to Ford, Aristotle's theory dominated the fiel of reproduction for 2 000 years because no one was able to challenge his position with any popular support from the masses; his theory held its ground well into the eighteenth century.[68]

Despite the Greeks' position on ensoulment, it seems the unborn was no more than a potential human being and was regarded as part of the pregnant woman's body until birth.[69]

With an understanding of beliefs on ensoulment, one would naturally think that birth would hold significan meaning, as at that point the foetus was separated from the mother's body and could breathe and was thus worthy of protection. This was not the case. It was only once a newborn infant had been named and accepted into the family by the head of the household (through a public naming ceremony) that it could be said that the infant had entered a meaningful and recognised life.[70] Consequently, there was a distinction between the murder of a newly born child named and recognised as a member of a family and the exposure of an infant in the firs few days of birth.[71] The difference does not lie in the nature of the action taken but rather in the status of the 'victim'. Patterson stresses that exposure was a limited and a specifi act affecting a newborn that had no place in the family unit, whereas murder could only be committed against a child that had been named and accepted into the household.[72] Patterson argues that 'child-murder' was legally prohibited but not exposure.[73]

During the period spanning 320–30 BC (the Hellenistic period), women's status changed. Although they were still excluded from political life and still subordinate, Cantarella asserts that this period saw a growing respect for women. There were increased opportunities for women to participate in social life, and their legal capacities were extended.[74]

Despite the continued requirement of a guardian's consent, women were able to personally buy and sell goods and property; mortgage their property; give and obtain loans; draft wills; be heirs; and inherit legacies.[75] Widows or women who were not legally married were vested with fairly broad powers over their daughters, as these women were entitled to expose their daughters, place them in

---

[67] RJ Huser *The Crime of Abortion in Canon Law: An Historical Synopsis and Commentary* (unpublished DCL dissertation, Catholic University of America, 1942) 5.

[68] Ford *When Did I Begin?* 36.

[69] McLaren *History of Contraception* 31.

[70] Patterson (1985) *Transactions of the American Philological Association* 106–7.

[71] Patterson (1985) *Transactions of the American Philological Association* 105.

[72] Patterson (1985) *Transactions of the American Philological Association* 105. See also Feen 'Abortion and exposure in ancient Greece' 287.

[73] Patterson (1985) *Transactions of the American Philological Association* 106. Patterson justifie this statement with reference to Solon's laws, which declared that selling one's children into slavery was unlawful; thus Patterson concludes that killing one's named and accepted child was also unlawful.

[74] E Cantarella *Pandora's Daughters: The Role and Status of Women in Greek and Roman Society* (1987) 90. She points out that it is not clear what caused this change but theorises that contributing factors may include the fact that the city-state was replaced by monarchs and the influence of these political systems or it may simply be the fact that classical values crumbled in the new system.

[75] Cantarella *Pandora's Daughters* 91.

an apprenticeship or even arrange for their marriage.[76] Cantarella[77] also provides evidence of women exercising political power.[78] However, she states that these women achieved this power as representatives of a dead sovereign or they would manage to assume those sorts of positions through the use of abuse and violence.

According to Cantarella, it was in this era that the dignity of the individual woman began to be recognised.[79] She argues that women rebelled against subordination to male power on the grounds of autonomy.[80]

In the context of ancient Greek history, the literature considered portrays both women and the unborn as agents employed to advance the needs of a male-dominated society. At this point in history an adversarial pregnancy environment was not even on the horizon, as there was no clear tension between the interests of women and the unborn, at least not to the extent experienced today, when pregnant women and the unborn are being pitted against each other.

2.3 WOMEN AND THE UNBORN IN ANCIENT ROME

From its earliest days,[81] Roman law reflecte a deeply patriarchal society where male citizens qualifie as heads of family (*paterfamilias*)·and only men were vested with full rights.[82] A family (*familia*) included a *paterfamilias*, a wife, biological children, slaves, wet nurses, tutors and foster children.[83] All the family members were subject to the *paterfamilias*,[84] who was declared to have complete power over both married and unmarried children until his death.[85] Some hold the view that in the early Republic a father's powers went so far as to vest him with the right to kill those belonging to his household.[86] However, others have asserted

[76] Cantarella *Pandora's Daughters* 91.

[77] Cantarella *Pandora's Daughters* 92.

[78] For instance, Cantarella (92) refers to Olympias (mother of Alexander the Great) who played an influentia role in the Macedonian court and exercised governmental power while Alexander the Great was away fightin the Persians.

[79] Cantarella *Pandora's Daughters* 97.

[80] Cantarella *Pandora's Daughters* 91. Cantarella refers to a Hellenistic law that empowered a father to interrupt his daughter's marriage. This was challenged in the second century by a daughter arguing against her father's powers stating that a father cannot remove a daughter from a marriage without her 'will'.

[81] Ancient Roman history began with the rise of the Republic in 753 BC which existed until 30 BC. The Republic is subdivided by early Republic (510–270 BC); middle Republic (270–120 BC); and late Republic (120–30 BC). The Roman Empire emerged during 30 BC–410 AD. It was during the early Republic that the Romans became involved in the affairs of Greek provinces and eventually Greece became a Roman province in 146 BC. Consequently, there was a lot of Greek influenc in Roman culture and this will be evident from the discussion that follows since it covers the years before and after the Roman takeover of Greece. See D Fleming 'Timeline of Greek & Roman antiquity' available at http://people.umass.edu/dfleming/english704-timeline.htm (accessed on 11 May 2016).

[82] Cantarella *Pandora's Daughters* 113.

[83] McLaren *History of Contraception* 43.

[84] McLaren *History of Contraception* 43.

[85] McLaren *History of Contraception* 43. It was only once the *paterfamilias* died that his direct descendants were liberated, see Cantarella *Pandora's Daughters* 115.

[86] McLaren *History of Contraception* 43 and Cantarella *Pandora's Daughters* 109.

that this is merely a rhetorical assertion of the immense power men held in the household.[87]

According to McLaren the idea behind having a family was to maintain prestige and wealth, and marriage was a method of achieving this.[88] Marriage ensured children and children conserved the household, maintained the estate, carried the family name and forged important family alliances.[89] Heirs were considered integral to the household and there are reports that wives were sometimes shared.[90]

Roman women[91] were believed to be 'freer' than Greek women, because they were not segregated from the men; they dined with their husbands and were not forbidden to venture out in the streets.[92] However, according to Shaw, married Roman women were guarded to see that they did not stray from the realm of their husband's authority and neighbours and friends were regularly called on to maintain surveillance over absent husbands' wives.[93]

Women generally played a domestic role and Cantarella asserts that their lives were meticulously planned for the primary purpose of reproduction.[94] Women did not possess individual names; generally a woman was named after her origin in relation to a group of families to which her family belonged and her individual family name or the feminine form of her father's name.[95] Cantarella interprets this

---

[87] See BD Shaw 'Raising and killing children: Two Roman myths' (2001) 54 *Mnemosyne* 31 56–76. Shaw covers this topic extensively but his various assertions will not be discussed; the point being made is that there is some doubt whether a *paterfamilias* truly held the power of life and death.

[88] McLaren *History of Contraception* 43. There were two laws that confirme the importance of marriage and marriage ethics in Rome: *Lex Lulia de Maritandis Ordinibus* (18 BC) and *Lex Papia Poppaea Nuptialis* (9 BC). These two laws were later merged into the *Lex Lulia et Papaia.* Essentially these laws stipulated that one could only marry another from an appropriate age group and that a marriage had to be fertile. In the case where a couple procreated, they were granted certain rewards and sanctions were imposed on those who had no children. In this regard, see Cantarella *Pandora's Daughters* 122.

[89] McLaren *History of Contraception* 46. Also see BD Shaw 'The family in late antiquity: The experience of Augustine' (1987) 115 *Past & Present* 3 12. However, there are contrary views concerning this construction of marriage. For instance, see BM Dennis 'Love: Another aspect of Roman marriage' available at http://www.brandonmdennis.com/pdfs/Non%20Fiction%20-%20Love%20-%20Another%20Aspect%20of%20Roman%20Marriage.pdf (accessed on 21 January 2016); O Kiefer *Sexual Life in Ancient Rome* (1934) 178; and CJ Reid 'Marriage in its procreative dimension: The meaning of the institution of marriage throughout the ages' (2008) 6 *University of St Thomas Law Journal* 454.

[90] McLaren *History of Contraception* 47.

[91] According to Cantarella (*Pandora's Daughters* 114) female slaves were mere objects rather than subjects of law. Female slaves were responsible for household chores and they had to make themselves available to male members of the family for sexual gratification Female slaves could not marry but merely engage in relationships which could be interrupted at any time and they also held no right over their children. For a general overview of female slaves, see Gardner *Women in Roman Law and Society* 205–31.

[92] McLaren *History of Contraception* 45 and Cantarella *Pandora's Daughters* 134.

[93] Shaw (1987) *Past & Present* 30–1.

[94] Cantarella *Pandora's Daughters* 109.

[95] Cantarella *Pandora's Daughters* 124.

practice as indicating how women were perceived: they were a fraction of a family, anonymous and passive.[96] Further, Shaw describes married Roman women as 'a species of domestic property'.[97]

A woman did not enjoy any political rights, and civil rights could be exercised only with the consent of her formally appointed male guardian.[98] In the fift century BC, Roman women could inherit, own and bequeath property, but only to the extent that they were formally represented by their guardian.[99] Women were placed under guardianship for life, as it was believed that they were unable to take care of themselves as a result of the 'frivolity of their spirit'.[100] Cantarella views guardianship as a means of nullifying women's legal capacities.[101]

Despite the implementation of a guardianship system there were mechanisms available to women for escaping this imposition through the *ius Liberorum*. Roman authorities actively sought to encourage population growth.[102] Roman culture praised and rewarded fertility; motherhood was a means of enhancing a woman's social status.[103] On this basis, the *ius Liberorum* established that once a free woman had three children she would be freed from guardianship.[104] The *ius Liberorum* included a rather cynical undertone: Women were held under guardianship in order to gain advantage from their reproductive capacities to achieve the Roman goal of population growth. This suggests a measure of coercion to perform the 'public duty' of procreation and it seems to imply that, without the guidance of a guardian, they could not be trusted to perform this duty voluntarily. Despite the potential 'advantage' the *ius Liberorum* offered, there was a compelling need to limit the number of children per household.[105] Romans understood that having too many children could potentially threaten the household; and McLaren explains that even one child was thought to be a strain. To have three or more children was considered the exception rather than the norm.[106]

Fertility control was a very important consideration for the household, even though it was viewed as a 'female problem'.[107] Numerous methods were adopted

---

[96] Cantarella *Pandora's Daughters* 126.

[97] Shaw (1987) *Past & Present* 30.

[98] Cantarella *Pandora's Daughters* 113.

[99] McLaren *History of Contraception* 45.

[100] Cantarella *Pandora's Daughters* 122. Concerning the issue of guardianship, only males were considered capable of managing themselves and remained under guardianship until they reached 14 years of age.

[101] Cantarella *Pandora's Daughters* 122. For a general overview and a descriptive account of the lives of Roman women, see G Clark 'Roman women' (1981) 28 *Greece & Rome* 193.

[102] McLaren *History of Contraception* 42.

[103] McLaren *History of Contraception* 47. Fertility was very important; the groom's family were known to send midwives to examine the prospective wife's uterus in order to determine whether she was deemed fertile or not (49).

[104] Cantarella *Pandora's Daughters* 123.

[105] McLaren *History of Contraception* 50.

[106] McLaren *History of Contraception* 51.

[107] McLaren *History of Contraception* 47. Midwives performed termination of pregnancies and doctors were only ever involved with the procedure if it was believed that a pregnant woman's life was in danger. See McLaren *History of Contraception* 62.

to curb fertility and prevent unwanted pregnancies. Women (incorrectly) employed the rhythm method, drank herbal teas and used cedar gum as a barrier method.[108] Evidence suggests that they used pessaries, suppositories, plugs and douches made of olive oil and white lead or alum.[109] Women also wore amulets and talismans.[110]

When contraceptive methods failed, women could attempt to terminate their pregnancies provided it was with the consent of the *paterfamilias*.[111] McLaren asserts that it was considered insubordination if a woman terminated a pregnancy for her own purposes, as she was perceived to be motivated by self-centredness.[112]

During the Republican period there were no laws against the termination of pregnancies.[113] During this period and in the early centuries of the Roman Empire, a foetus did not have an independent existence until birth.[114] Feen states that this approach was drawn from the work of the Stoics (an ancient Greek philosophical school that held much influenc during the period of the Roman Empire) who believed that a soul existed in the body of the unborn in a 'potential' form and that once a newborn breathed after birth, the air actualised the potential through a cooling process.[115] At most, the unborn held a *spes animantis*, being a hope of living or being ensouled.[116] Until birth, the unborn were considered to form part of pregnant women's bodies, similar to fruit from a tree.[117] Consequently, McLaren points out that if a *paterfamilias* opposed a pregnancy termination it was probably because it was contrary to his own interests and not because he was defending the life of the unborn as a valued entity.[118]

McLaren argues that, generally, fertility control was limited to the 'practical solution' of killing, selling or exposing excess children.[119] As with the Greeks, live birth was not a significan occurrence for the Romans. Roman infants were worse off than Greek infants, since all Roman children were subject to the power of life and death that the *paterfamilias* held in his household.[120] This power endowed a

---

[108] Roman women believed that it was necessary to avoid sex during the days that immediately followed menstruation, see McLaren *History of Contraception* 57 and K Hopkins 'Contraception in the Roman Empire' (1965) 8 *Comparative Studies in Society and History* 124 140.

[109] McLaren *History of Contraception* 58 and Hopkins (1965) *Comparative Studies in Society and History* 134.

[110] McLaren *History of Contraception* 59 and Hopkins (1965) *Comparative Studies in Society and History* 124. McLaren (54) states that upper-class Roman women had good reason to employ contraceptive methods because they were married off earlier, they did not breastfeed and by restricting their fertility these women were able to secure substantial inheritances for already existing children.

[111] McLaren *History of Contraception* 61.

[112] McLaren *History of Contraception* 61.

[113] McLaren *History of Contraception* 62.

[114] McLaren *History of Contraception* 61.

[115] Feen 'Abortion and exposure in ancient Greece' 295.

[116] McLaren *History of Contraception* 82.

[117] Feen 'Abortion and exposure in ancient Greece' 295.

[118] McLaren *History of Contraception* 61.

[119] McLaren *History of Contraception* 52.

[120] K Brennan 'Evidence of infanticide and exposure in antiquity: Tolerated social practice, uncontrolled phenomenon or regulated custom?' (2002) 2 *University College Dublin LR* 92 104.

father with the right to put his child to death, even after he recognised the child as part of the *familia*.[121]

According to Harris, exposure was commonly relied on because, unlike contraception and termination of pregnancies, it permitted the *paterfamilias* to choose the sex of his children.[122] The family's interests, as interpreted by the *paterfamilias*, dictated whether or not a newborn would be accepted or not.[123] The *paterfamilias* held the right to sell any child, grandchild and any other descendent if it was considered necessary.[124] Exposure was also used to avoid extreme social embarrassment in cases where an infant was born to an unmarried woman.[125] Further, some slave women were known to expose their children because they were not prepared to bring them up into slavery and some divorced pregnant women were also known to make use of exposure.[126] This indicates that without the security and support of a household, a woman's reproductive capacity could be the source of great hardship, which may have encouraged the abandonment of unwanted children.

Roman adherence to the concept that the *paterfamilias* held far-reaching power over his family effectively limited the state's ability to interfere in aspects pertaining to marriage, exposure, contraception and termination of pregnancy.[127] However, during the Roman Empire (30 BC–410 AD), under Augustus (30 BC–14 AD), the powers of a *paterfamilias* were curbed to the extent that he could no longer sell his children into slavery or send them to their death.[128] Justinian (527–565 AD) later declared that killing a child was the same as homicide.[129]

Cantarella argues that Roman women were freer and more aware of themselves during the early stages of the Empire.[130] Marriage was no longer a means of 'transferring' a woman into another's family but progressively became an equal relationship based on the will of both parties involved.[131] Men and women had the same right to divorce.[132] In the last centuries of the Republic, lifetime guardianship laws changed and a woman was able to replace the chosen guardian with one of her choice, one whom she trusted.[133] Later, under Claudius (14–68 AD), the guardianship of free-born women was abolished and under Constantine (274–337 AD) guardianship disappeared altogether.[134] Widows were granted the

[121] Brennan (2002) *University College Dublin LR* 104. According to Brennan (105), this power could not be exercised arbitrarily and the *paterfamilias* was required to consult with kinsmen of the child before he was permitted to make a decision concerning the fate of the child.
[122] WV Harris 'Child-exposure in the Roman Empire' (1994) 84 *Journal of Roman Studies* 1 11.
[123] McLaren *History of Contraception* 52.
[124] Cantarella *Pandora's Daughters* 116.
[125] Cantarella *Pandora's Daughters* 12–13.
[126] Cantarella *Pandora's Daughters* 14.
[127] McLaren *History of Contraception* 42.
[128] Cantarella *Pandora's Daughters* 136.
[129] Cantarella *Pandora's Daughters* 136.
[130] Cantarella *Pandora's Daughters* 135.
[131] Cantarella *Pandora's Daughters* 136–7.
[132] Cantarella *Pandora's Daughters* 137. Where the intention to marry no longer existed, the parties were automatically divorced.
[133] Cantarella *Pandora's Daughters* 139.
[134] Cantarella *Pandora's Daughters* 139.

right to be guardians of their children, and this right later extended to natural mothers too.[135] Women could also gain custody over their children when their husbands acted shamefully and women could inherit from their children and vice versa.[136]

In the firs centuries of the Empire, women experienced wide-ranging emancipation to the extent that they enjoyed sexual freedom, developed intellectual interests, freely married and divorced, openly used contraceptives and terminated pregnancies, educated themselves and began to live outside the context of matrimony.[137] However, it seems that emancipation was enjoyed only by the aristocracy.[138]

Cantarella asserts that men thought very poorly of emancipated women because they behaved contrary to the old rule of subordination and family morality.[139] She refers to a number of Roman texts in which men complained that wives had left their husbands for younger men. Others were using their slaves to place their husbands under surveillance but refusing to be placed under surveillance themselves; wives also wanted to 'make love and not babies'; wives were asking for consent to have lovers or were engaging in affairs with doctors.[140] Some of the liberties enjoyed by women were viewed as a sign of lack of self-control, selfishnes and luxury.[141] The occurrence of these sorts of complaints indicates that women were not mere passive recipients of assigned reproductive expectations but were actively asserting and engaging their sense of autonomy in various ways.

In the firs and second century AD, the termination of pregnancies was vehemently opposed in cases where a woman terminated a pregnancy against her husband's wishes, since it interfered with a husband's interests.[142] Initially, when a woman behaved contrary to her husband's wishes it was considered a 'matrimonial offence' but was not illegal per se.[143] However, under the reign of Severus (193–211 AD), who was succeeded by his son Caracalla (198–217 AD), the termination of pregnancies without a husband's consent was criminalised for the firs time in Roman history and it became a public concern.[144] The termination of a pregnancy was believed to have catastrophic consequences for the family and as family morality was increasingly a public issue, the termination of pregnancies could no longer constitute a private affair.[145] The firs public sanction for termination of pregnancy without a husband's consent was exile.[146] Under these

[135] Cantarella *Pandora's Daughters* 140.
[136] Cantarella *Pandora's Daughters* 140.
[137] Cantarella *Pandora's Daughters* 140–1.
[138] Cantarella *Pandora's Daughters* 142. Very little is known about other women who did not fall within that social class.
[139] Cantarella *Pandora's Daughters* 144.
[140] Cantarella *Pandora's Daughters* 144.
[141] Cantarella *Pandora's Daughters* 150.
[142] McLaren *History of Contraception* 62.
[143] Cantarella *Pandora's Daughters* 148–50.
[144] Cantarella *Pandora's Daughters* 165.
[145] Cantarella *Pandora's Daughters* 165.
[146] Cantarella *Pandora's Daughters* 165 and Feen 'Abortion and exposure in ancient Greece' 291.

circumstances, it was not the termination of a pregnancy that was being punished but rather a woman's defiance

Further, according to Cantarella, the second century AD saw, for the firs time, judicial 'custody of the womb' for the benefi of a husband.[147] During the joint reign of Marcus Aurelius (161–180 AD) and Lucius Verus (161–169 AD), Rutilius Severus asked the emperors to resolve a problem he faced with his ex-wife.[148] He claimed she was pregnant (presumably with his child) and she denied the existence of a pregnancy.[149] The emperors decided that the woman should be examined by three midwives and, if she were found to be pregnant, she should be guarded to ensure that she did not terminate the pregnancy.[150] Cantarella understands this to imply that emancipated women were women who could not be trusted.[151]

Under Constantine's reign (303–337 AD) Christians were granted religious freedom[152] and under Theodosius (379–385 AD) Christianity was declared the state religion.[153] The introduction of Christianity saw further changes to relationships between men and women.[154] Marriage became monogamous[155] and permanent and it was preached that men and women had equal standing in a marriage.[156] Despite their equality in marriage, Christian teachings contradicted this notion by explicitly referring to male superiority within the household and so the theme of comprehensive subordination of women returned to Rome again.[157] Eventually, Christianity became male dominated and hierarchical, calling for women to be increasingly conservative and return to their 'natural' role.[158]

Chastity was also robustly enforced, since chastity was nearer to God than marriage. Chastity was a superior state of holy living to which Romans were encouraged to aspire (even in marriage).[159] Sexual intercourse was only for those

[147] Cantarella *Pandora's Daughters* 149.
[148] Cantarella *Pandora's Daughters* 148.
[149] Cantarella *Pandora's Daughters* 149.
[150] Cantarella *Pandora's Daughters* 149. Cantarella does not mention the reason why Rutilius sought to protect the pregnancy from being terminated; it may be that he did not have any heirs and wanted a son. However, the point remains that, regardless of his reasons, his actions can be perceived as indicating that only men could legitimately decide whether a pregnancy should be terminated and Cantarella argues that this implies that women who do terminate pregnancies did so for immoral reasons or to hide immoral reasons or to hide the 'fruits of illicit relations'.
[151] Cantarella *Pandora's Daughters* 149.
[152] Cantarella *Pandora's Daughters* 157.
[153] McLaren *History of Contraception* 76.
[154] Cantarella *Pandora's Daughters* 157.
[155] Under Constantine and Constans, in 339 AD, it was established that adulterers should be condemned to death by being burnt at the stake and in 506 AD a husband was granted the power to kill his wife. Under Justinian (526–565 AD) adulterers would face the penalty of detention. This was the firs time in Roman history that punishment involved a complete limitation of a person's liberty and adultery was the firs crime to ever be punished by the sanction of detention. See Cantarella *Pandora's Daughters* 163–4.
[156] Cantarella *Pandora's Daughters* 157.
[157] Cantarella *Pandora's Daughters* 158.
[158] McLaren *History of Contraception* 94.
[159] Cantarella *Pandora's Daughters* 167.

who were married and could be used only for the purposes of procreation.[160] McLaren explains that if one engaged in sexual relations for pleasure and not procreation, it was regarded as unnatural and perverse.[161] It was the drive towards chastity that led to the 'demonizing' of women (except for the Virgin Mary) by Church fathers, as women represented 'fles and passions'.[162] Under Augustine (354–430 AD), one of the great fathers of the early Christian Church, Christianity reached its peak of misogyny and women were regarded as temptation and 'instruments of evil and sin' and according to Cantarella, women's purpose was to bear children.[163]

Another significan development under the influenc of Christianity was the shift in the approach to the life of the unborn and the reasoning for criminalising the termination of pregnancies and contraceptive practices.[164] Christians were concerned with the interests of the unborn and viewed the foetus as a living human being and on these grounds the criminalisation of termination of pregnancies was justified [165] The basis of humanity also justifie the position that exposure and infanticide constituted murder.[166]

This approach to foetal life can be traced back to the third century BC when the Old Testament was firs translated into Greek.[167] According to the Greek version of the Exodus text (21: 22–23), if an unformed foetus is dislodged from a woman's uterus as a result of a blow, that person who inflicte the blow is liable to pay compensation.[168] In the case where the foetus was formed, the party had to 'give life for life' and thus be sentenced to death.[169] Huser points out that Greek and Latin translations of the Exodus text differ.[170] According to the Latin translation, compensation[171] had to be paid by the person who accidentally caused the

[160] McLaren *History of Contraception* 78.

[161] McLaren *History of Contraception* 79–80.

[162] Cantarella *Pandora's Daughters* 169. Cantarella (169) considers some Christian writings of the time and refers to texts that describe women rather poorly. According to Turtullian (an early Christian theologian from 160–240 AD) women were the 'gate of the devil'. John Chrysostom (a Church father) described women as having 'infantile' minds. Clement of Alexandria (a Christian theologian from 150–215 AD) wrote that 'women must seek wisdom, like men, even if men are superior and have firs place in every field at least if they are not too effeminate'.

[163] Cantarella *Pandora's Daughters* 170. McLaren (*History of Contraception* 79) states that Augustine asserted that a marriage could be defended if it produced children, fidelit and continence. Love was considered to be a destructive passion and dangerous if involved in a marriage. Further, sex was symbolised as the fall from grace and the source of disorder; impotency, frigidity and erections were all uncontrolled and demonstrated a man's enslavement to lust.

[164] McLaren *History of Contraception* 73. The author states: 'If stop signs imply the existence of traffic, the clergy's ongoing condemnations of abortion and contraception can at the very least be taken as evidence of the continued employment of such practices.'

[165] McLaren *History of Contraception* 73 and Cantarella *Pandora's Daughters* 148.

[166] McLaren *History of Contraception* 81.

[167] McLaren *History of Contraception* 82.

[168] Huser *The Crime of Abortion in Canon Law* 6.

[169] Huser *The Crime of Abortion in Canon Law* 6.

[170] Huser *The Crime of Abortion in Canon Law* 6.

[171] According to McLaren (*History of Contraception* 82), compensation was determined with reference to the stage of foetal development.

termination of the pregnancy and, if the pregnant woman died as a result of the accidental conduct, that person would be sentenced to death.[172]

McLaren points out that, in the Greek translation, there is a clear shift of focus from that on the life of a woman to the 'life' of the foetus.[173] According to Huser, the Greek translation elevated the status of a formed unborn to that of a human being.[174] Of further significance Huser states that it is the Greek translation that was broadcast throughout the Roman world and it proved to be a great influenc on Roman laws and moral doctrines.[175] In Rome, Christianity introduced the moral view that termination of pregnancy was a serious sin and a heinous crime since it caused the death of a human person even though unborn.[176] The Church condemned the termination of pregnancy as a violation against the unborn itself.[177]

Religious teachings each had their own contributions to make concerning these translations. Philo of Alexandria (a Jewish biblical philosopher during the period 20 BC–50 AD) followed Aristotle's assertion that a foetus gained 'sense and life' after 40 days, but he also adopted the Stoic position that the foetus was part of a woman's body until birth; however, he condemned exposure and the termination of a pregnancy in the case of a formed foetus.[178] Augustine did not believe that a foetus was fully formed at the moment of conception and he maintained that only once a foetus became fully formed and 'endowed with sensation' could one speak of a 'soul living in the body'.[179] Thus Augustine asserted that a woman who terminated a pregnancy of an unformed foetus was guilty of 'perversion', but if the foetus was formed, she was guilty of homicide.[180]

On the other hand, conciliar legislation stemming from various Christian councils ignored the distinction between formed and unformed foetuses and simply combined termination of pregnancies with infanticide.[181] According to Huser, the Council of Elvira (305 AD) was the firs council to enact legislation to punish termination of pregnancies by refusing the woman Holy Communion for life (even on the pregnant woman's deathbed).[182] Huser states that the council's position was very influentia in the centuries to follow, to the extent that it served

[172] Huser *The Crime of Abortion in Canon Law* 6. It is noteworthy that there is no mention of intentionally terminating a pregnancy by a third party or by the pregnant woman herself. Huser argues that use of 'accidental' indicates that voluntary termination of pregnancies was not a prevalent practice among the Jewish and their immediate neighbours.

[173] McLaren *History of Contraception* 82.

[174] Huser *The Crime of Abortion in Canon Law* 6.

[175] Huser *The Crime of Abortion in Canon Law* 8.

[176] Huser *The Crime of Abortion in Canon Law* 12.

[177] Huser *The Crime of Abortion in Canon Law* 12.

[178] McLaren *History of Contraception* 82.

[179] McLaren *History of Contraception* 83.

[180] McLaren *History of Contraception* 83.

[181] McLaren *History of Contraception* 83–4.

[182] This is in terms of canon 63 of their conciliar legislation, see Huser *The Crime of Abortion in Canon Law* 17.

as the basis for the majority of ecclesiastical enactments against the termination of pregnancies into the Middle Ages.[183]

On the topic of Christian opposition to contraception, in antiquity, the distinction between fertility control and termination of pregnancies was rarely made; in fact, the same medicines were prescribed as contraceptives and abortifacients.[184] For instance, McLaren[185] and Hopkins[186] refer to the work of Soranus, a Greek physician practising in Rome during the firs or second century AD who stressed that contraception prevented conception, while the termination of pregnancies destroyed what had been conceived. At that time, these assertions were rare and were considered insignificant[187] Hopkins states that there was a general lack of clarity on the concept of 'contraception', even among the most educated, and he argues that this may have stemmed from the fact that doctors were unable to tell when a pregnancy began, nor were they able to agree about the length of gestation.[188] It was for this reason that Christians did not distinguish between the termination of pregnancies and contraceptive methods.[189]

It must be mentioned that although the Church always held that it was a serious sin to terminate a pregnancy at any stage of development, at various times it accepted a distinction between the shades of meaning of 'formed' for purposes of determining appropriate penalties.[190] In other words, the termination of pregnancies at any stage was generally offensive, but the penalties for such conduct were graded according to the distinction of whether the foetus was formed or not.[191] In effect, canon law followed Augustine's position.[192] McLaren argues that condemnations of termination of pregnancies were based on the fact that the termination of a pregnancy was a 'non-procreative act' rather than on the argument that life was present at conception.[193] In line with McLaren's assertion, McCartney points out that it is not the official teaching of the Church that a new human being exists from the moment of conception, but the leadership of the Roman Catholic Church sought to maintain a link between sexual activity and procreation.[194] Thus it

[183] Huser *The Crime of Abortion in Canon Law* 21; for more on later conciliar legislation see 22–9.
[184] McLaren *History of Contraception* 84 and Hopkins (1965) *Comparative Studies in Society and History* 136.
[185] McLaren *History of Contraception* 61.
[186] Hopkins (1965) *Comparative Studies in Society and History* 136–7.
[187] McLaren *History of Contraception* 61.
[188] Hopkins (1965) *Comparative Studies in Society and History* 138.
[189] McLaren *History of Contraception* 84.
[190] Huser *The Crime of Abortion in Canon Law* 1.
[191] Gunstan (1984) *Journal of Medical Ethics* 39.
[192] McLaren *History of Contraception* 84; Gunstan (1984) *Journal of Medical Ethics* 40; and see generally DA Dombrowski 'St. Augustine, abortion, and Libido Crudelis' (1988) 49 *Journal of the History of Ideas* 151.
[193] McLaren *History of Contraception* 84.
[194] JJ McCartney 'Some Roman Catholic concepts of persons and their implications for the ontological status of the unborn' in WB Bondeson, HT Engelhardt, S Spicker et al (eds) *Abortion and the Status of the Fetus* (1983) 313. In fact, Gunstan ((1984) *Journal of Medical Ethics* 38) asserts it was only in the late nineteenth century that protection was granted from the moment of conception.

follows that, even if foetuses are not human beings, the termination of pregnancies would still be 'illegal'.[195]

Though the Church acknowledged that marriage and childbearing were burdensome for women, it nevertheless insisted on holding women accountable for engaging in the 'sinful undertakings' of fertility control.[196] This attitude was maintained despite the fact that controlling reproductive capacity was for the benefi and wellbeing of the entire household.[197] In the case where economic considerations were advanced for justifying the use of fertility control, the Christian fathers stressed that abstinence from sexual intercourse was the only permissible tactic.[198] In fact, McLaren states that the Church fathers played down the 'economic' argument because it implicated men in the issue.[199] Thus, Christianity placed the spotlight on women as those to blame for the need for fertility control because they were portrayed as being driven by lust.[200]

In spite of the Church's position women were still attracted to Christianity because it offered them a 'legitimate alternative' to the extent that Christian teaching stressed celibacy and thus offered women the option of avoiding marriage and childbearing.[201] Further, McLaren states that there was a genuine desire to overcome and redefin sex roles.[202] Traditionally, marriage and childbearing were policed by men in order to serve their own interests whereas Christianity brought with it an alternative way of life away from marriage altogether, since virginity was holier than marriage.[203]

At the end of the Roman Empire there is a clear change in the dynamics concerning women's lives in relation to unborn life. Women's subordination was confirme in Christianity but the life of the unborn was elevated in an independent worth and was seen to be deserving of protection. This indicates that the foetus receives individualised consideration, as something separate from the body of the pregnant woman. Although there was no obvious direct tension between pregnant women and foetuses at this point, this heralded the beginnings of a change in thinking processes where the needs of the unborn were being elevated above the needs of women.

2.4 WOMEN AND THE UNBORN IN THE MIDDLE AGES

During the early Middle Ages,[204] Western barbarian states emerged and civilisation was characterised by small clusters of rural societies which were

---

[195] McCartney 'Some Roman Catholic concepts of persons' 313.
[196] McLaren *History of Contraception* 90.
[197] McLaren *History of Contraception* 90.
[198] McLaren *History of Contraception* 90.
[199] McLaren *History of Contraception* 90.
[200] McLaren *History of Contraception* 90.
[201] McLaren *History of Contraception* 88.
[202] McLaren *History of Contraception* 88.
[203] McLaren *History of Contraception* 88.
[204] Generally, the Middle Ages (also referred to as mediaeval times or Dark Ages) spans from the fall of the Western Roman Empire in 476 until the end of the fifteent century. This timeframe can be subdivided into the early Middle Ages (476–999); the high Middle Ages (1000–1299); and the late Middle Ages (1300–1499). See S Newman 'Timeline of the Middle Ages' *The Finer Times* available

violent, pagan or Arian Christian.[205] The sophisticated development of reproductive knowledge of the Greeks and Romans was lost, due mainly to mass illiteracy, and the Church was left to take on the role of keeper of Western culture whereby Romans and Franks were the major role players.[206]

The older Roman-style families disappeared and were replaced by a new system of balanced households.[207] In this context, women fell below men (husband, father or brother) and a number of scholars assert that they basically formed part of the man's property.[208] Paterson describes a mediaeval woman as a

> transparent object of exchange between men: often virtually invisible, she functions as a trophy or reward for valorous service, as a status symbol, a channel of noble blood and property, or a means by which a man may avenge himself on another man (by seducing or raping that man's wife).[209]

Hayden states that women had very little say about whom they married, and polygamy and abduction were common practices.[210] Marriage was viewed as a means to an end, and was generally driven by the need for property.[211] A marriage was sealed by the exchange of property and sexual intercourse; once those actions had taken place, the wife 'belonged' to her new husband.[212] Kaufman states that courtly love was a 'fanciful rebelliousness', since women were generally denied the satisfaction of romantic fulfilment[213] Noonan claims that during the high Middle Ages the Church required both man and woman to willingly consent to a

---

at http://www.thefinertimes.com/Middle-Ages/timeline-of-the-middle-ages.htm (accessed on 21 January 2016).

205 McLaren *History of Contraception* 101.

206 McLaren *History of Contraception* 102.

207 McLaren *History of Contraception* 102.

208 For instance, see VL Bullough 'Medieval concepts of adultery' (1997) 7 *Arthuriana* 5 and FG Buckstaff 'Married women's property in Anglo-Saxon and Anglo-Norman law and the origin of the common-law dower' (1893) 4 *Annals of the American Academy of Political and Social Science* 33 34; 41.

209 L Paterson 'Gender negotiations in France during the central Middle Ages: The literary evidence' in P Linehan & JL Nelson (eds) *The Medieval World* (2003) 246 255. Paterson (259) points out that rape falls under *raptus* (meaning abduction), which comprised of the violation of another man's right over a woman's sexuality. Worst of all, a woman's interest in pursuing her attacker would be put aside if her husband or father felt that enforcing his rights would be an inconvenience to existing relations between himself and the attacker. This gives a good indication of the position women held in mediaeval society. However, Kaufman ((1973) *Soundings* 139) argues that the popular conclusion that mediaeval women were subjugated is partially as a result of what he calls 'masculine historical rationalization'. This assumes that modern women are much better off when compared to mediaeval women and its corollary, the 'male argument from progress' which concludes that men are much more enlightened in modern days compared with the barbaric positions they held in mediaeval times. Kaufman (140) asserts that the 'more we get ourselves to believe the sexual injustices of the "Dark Ages," the more we are able to persuade ourselves of our own evolutionary progress'. Consequently, we should recognise 'female subordination' statements cautiously.

210 M Hayden 'Women in the Middle Ages' (1913) 3 *The Irish Review* 282 285. On polygamy see McLaren *History of Contraception* 103.

211 McLaren *History of Contraception* 103 and Kaufman (1973) *Soundings* 145.

212 McLaren *History of Contraception* 103.

213 Kaufman (1973) *Soundings* 145.

marriage.[214] Nevertheless, even he concedes that the tension between the moral ideal and actual practice, and between legal norm and social practice, inevitably caused different approaches in different societies.[215]

Husbands held great authority over their wives, and women rarely questioned this.[216] Divorce was readily available to men, even for the most frivolous of reasons.[217] According to Hayden, a husband could sell or punish his wife or even bequeath her to a friend upon his death.[218]

Kaufman argues that the above described position of women should be accepted as the position of wealthier, upper class mediaeval society.[219] Accordingly, he argues that, when one looks at lower social classes, where prestige and power were not real possibilities, one find a structure of close-knit extended kinship based on communal relations, which were supported and allowed for sustenance.[220] The socio-economic conditions of the poor demanded that women be regarded as companions, and spouses lived on an equal footing.[221] Kaufman asserts that it was in this class division that women experienced autonomy in free labour, because they played a real social and economic part in their society.[222] On the other hand, aristocratic society forged an extensive land-holding economy and developed a system that maximised and profite from the sexual division of labour.[223]

Despite the subordinate role women faced at home they are found to have enjoyed more freedom than Roman women did.[224] Women mingled freely in public among men and openly shared in their husbands' sorrows and triumphs.[225]

---

[214] See generally JT Noonan 'Marriage in the Middle Ages: Power to choose' (1973) 4 *Viator* 419. He states that the Church had a vested interest in introducing consent as a requirement since the institution wanted to prevent compulsion being used as a ground for divorce.

[215] Noonan (1973) *Viator* 431.

[216] Hayden (1913) *The Irish Review* 285.

[217] Hayden (1913) *The Irish Review* 285.

[218] Hayden (1913) *The Irish Review* 285. Hayden (286) points out that there are many reports of women being brutally punished by their husbands but just as many reports of wives being treated with respect and confidence Also see SM Butler 'Abortion by assault: Violence against pregnant women in thirteenth- and fourteenth-century England' (2005) 17 *Journal of Women's History* 9 22.

[219] Kaufman (1973) *Soundings* 147.

[220] Kaufman (1973) *Soundings* 147.

[221] Kaufman (1973) *Soundings* 147.

[222] Generally, Western European working-class women enjoyed limited economic independence and were publically active. Women's work was characteristically unskilled work (or was at least considered such) and included domestic services, petty retailers, midwifery and prostitution. Some women were members of various guilds but were never considered full members, and were generally excluded from any benefit associated with membership to a particular guild. Guilds were formed in order to bring people together who specialise in the same trade or craft for mutual social, religious and economic benefi and were notoriously male dominated. In fact, most guilds operated out of household workshops and women were incorporated as members of the household rather than as workers in the guild. The exclusion of women from full participation in guilds severely restricted their ability to pursue autonomous economic benefit especially since by the fourteenth century most urban trades were organised and regulated by the guilds. See McLaren *History of Contraception* 106–7 and M Kowaleski & JM Bennett 'Crafts, gilds, and women in the Middle Ages: Fifty years after Marian K Dale' (1989) 14 *Signs* 474 475; 477–79.

[223] Kaufman (1973) *Soundings* 147.

[224] McLaren *History of Contraception* 104.

[225] Hayden (1913) *The Irish Review* 286.

Loengard states that thirteenth-century records demonstrate that a small minority of unmarried adult women enjoyed property rights similar to those of men, but, for purposes of inheritance, women were disadvantaged, as property usually passed exclusively to male heirs.[226] She argues that the real distinction concerning property rights lies in that between men and single women on the one hand and men and married women on the other.[227] In this regard Buckstaff states that, according to Germanic tribes and later English tradition, only once a woman was married did she acquire a legal right to certain property in her own name, which Buckstaff indicates was a clear break from the experiences of women in antiquity.[228] Nevertheless, when it came to management and control of a woman's income, her rights were generally suspended during her husband's life.[229] Hayden points out that, 'free' as women were, in the background, husbands retained control.[230]

At this point in history there are records of increased alternatives available to women. Christianity brought in a different dimension to women's lives, which went beyond marriage. These alternatives either offered women a substitute for married life or it offered them other principles to live by while married.[231] Women could turn to the Church in order to legitimately protect their interests. The attraction to religion was fuelled by the Church's preaching of monogamy and its hostility to divorce.[232] To women who did not want to marry, the Church offered the opportunity of living a life of celibacy in a nunnery.[233] However, not all women accepted the Church; Kaufman states that women were also attracted to mystical movements such as the Beguines.[234] Stoner accepts the Beguines as one of the firs feminist movements, as these women rejected the Church's define roles for women as either nuns or wives, and developed a unique freedom of movement, female religious expression, and economic independence.[235] Kaufman[236] describes the Beguines as threatening to the developed masculine ecclesiastic hierarchies and Stoner[237] points out that this was the cause of their downfall.[238]

---

226 Loengard (1986) *Law & History Review* 167.

227 Loengard (1986) *Law & History Review* 167.

228 Buckstaff (1893) *Annals of the American Academy of Political and Social Science* 39.

229 Buckstaff (1893) *Annals of the American Academy of Political and Social Science* 39.

230 Hayden (1913) *The Irish Review* 284.

231 Hayden (1913) *The Irish Review* 289 and McLaren *History of Contraception* 104.

232 McLaren *History of Contraception* 104.

233 Hayden (1913) *The Irish Review* 288.

234 Kaufman (1973) *Soundings* 143. Beguines were groups of celibate laywomen who prayed and worshipped together but who took no permanent vows and followed no prescribed rules. See A Stoner 'Sisters between: Gender and the medieval Beguines' (1995) 4 *Ex Post Facto* 29.

235 Stoner (1995) *Ex Post Facto* 29.

236 Kaufman (1973) *Soundings* 143.

237 Stoner (1995) 4 *Ex Post Facto* 29; 34–6.

238 Also see generally C Neel 'The origins of the Beguines' (1989) 14 *Signs* 321.

Mediaeval communities were interested in large families, which led to an 'obsession' with procreation.[239] McLaren asserts that a good wife was a fertile wife, and wives who bore many children were honouring their husbands.[240] Doctors asserted that sexual intercourse was essential for women's good health and the public actively approved of vigorous marital sexuality.[241]

The drive for large families also encouraged community surveillance of women of reproductive age.[242] Men's concern about and fear of women's reproductive power fed misogyny during the Middle Ages.[243] The Church presented female sexuality as dangerous and it was asserted that sex, if not deadly, could drive a man to early retirement or cause him to contract leprosy.[244] Sadly, the Church did not recognise pregnancy as a potential threat to women's health; rather, the Church found that women were a risk to men's health.[245] McLaren argues that ultimately, the Church aimed to protect men from female domination (through their sexuality) and the Church called for women to be trained in submissiveness.[246]

Most fertility control mechanisms were aimed at increasing conception rather than preventing pregnancies or live births.[247] However, even with the drive for large families, in reality, family sizes were modest as a result of late marriages, the high infant mortality rate and economic strain.[248] A number of scholars understand that smaller family sizes also indicate that women were limiting pregnancies.[249] Procreative control was deemed a woman's concern.[250] Besides facing economic pressures, women had a vested interest in limiting pregnancies in order to protect their health.[251] Pregnancies were limited by periodic sexual self-restraint (as

---

[239] McLaren *History of Contraception* 109. In this regard, see F Harris-Stoertz 'Pregnancy and childbirth in the twelfth- and thirteenth-century French and English law' (2012) 21 *Journal of the History of Sexuality* 263 267. The author discusses the payment of *wergeld* which was a system of compensation where a money payment had to be made to a family group if a member of that family were killed or injured. In this respect substantial sums of money had to be paid over if a person caused the death of a fertile or pregnant woman, or injured a pregnant woman causing the termination of her pregnancy. Harris-Stoertz argues that prescribed amounts payable are an indication of the seriousness of the crimes committed against a family. For a general discussion of *wergeld* see CR Jeffery 'The development of crime in early English society' (1957) 47 *Journal of Criminal Law, Criminology, and Police Science* 647 655.

[240] McLaren *History of Contraception* 109.

[241] McLaren *History of Contraception* 110.

[242] McLaren *History of Contraception* 110.

[243] McLaren *History of Contraception* 111. For some examples, see generally RH Bloch 'Medieval misogyny: Women as riot' (1987) 20 *Representations* 1.

[244] McLaren *History of Contraception* 112.

[245] McLaren *History of Contraception* 111.

[246] McLaren *History of Contraception* 112.

[247] McLaren *History of Contraception* 110.

[248] C McCann 'Fertility control and society in medieval Europe' (2009) 40 *Comitatus* 45 47 and McLaren *History of Contraception* 113.

[249] McCann (2009) *Comitatus* 47; McLaren *History of Contraception* 113; and BDH Miller ' "She who hath drunk any potion" . . .' (1962) 31 *Medium Aevum* 188 190–3. Also see generally, PPA Biller 'Birth-control in the West in the thirteenth and early fourteenth centuries' (1982) 94 *Past & Present* 3.

[250] McLaren *History of Contraception* 115.

[251] McCann (2009) *Comitatus* 47 and McLaren *History of Contraception* 115.

advocated by the Church)[252] and through the use of contraceptive mechanisms.[253] Contraceptive methods included herbal and magical potions, pessaries, amulets, suppositories, anal intercourse and *coitus interruptus*.[254]

Where contraceptive efforts failed, women could terminate pregnancies by using potions, pessaries or violent blows to the uterus.[255] Early termination of pregnancies (prior to ensoulment) held an ambiguous moral standing; on the one hand, some doctors prescribed therapeutic terminations, while others saw the termination of a pregnancy as a crime committed against the husband.[256] In the case where termination of pregnancy was a crime against the husband, he was entitled to divorce his wife on the grounds that she terminated her pregnancy.[257]

The Church, on the other hand, with its task of policing morality, condemned termination of pregnancies, as it was an act against procreation and was thus sinful.[258] The issue of ensoulment came to the forefront once again and it was believed that an unborn became human once it had received its soul from God.[259] The prominent Dominican priest and philosopher Thomas Aquinas (1225–1274), relying on Aristotle's work, asserted that the unborn progressed through various souls (firs vegetative and then sensitive) until the unborn took the form of a recognisably human body, which occurred at 40 days for males and 90 days for females.[260] At this point, the unborn was ensouled with a rational soul.[261] According to Haldane and Lee, Aquinas posited that, at the very least, the unborn must have the beginnings of organs (not necessarily fully developed organs that were immediately functional) in order for ensoulment to occur.[262] Thus it must hold the potential for human life. However, there were other positions as well. McLaren[263] refers to a text exploring foetal development titled *Anatomia Ricardi Anglici* in which an author argues that, based on his observations of terminated pregnancies at various points of development, the unborn takes on a complete

[252] McLaren *History of Contraception* 116. However, the Church was more concerned with the immorality associated with non-procreative sex than with fertility control. To that extent the Church also condemned women from 'mounting' men, and oral and anal sex since all these practices frustrated procreation (121).

[253] McLaren *History of Contraception* 116.

[254] McCann (2009) *Comitatus* 51–2 and McLaren *History of Contraception* 119.

[255] McLaren *History of Contraception* 124. On the use of violence to terminate a pregnancy see SM Butler 'Abortion medieval style? Assaults on pregnant women in later medieval England' (2011) 40 *Women's Studies* 778. For more on potions that women took in order to terminate pregnancies see Miller (1962) *Medium Aevum* 190–3.

[256] McLaren *History of Contraception* 125.

[257] McLaren *History of Contraception* 125.

[258] McLaren *History of Contraception* 125. The extent of the prescribed punishment depended on whether the unborn was formed or not; see Gunstan (1984) *Journal of Medical Ethics* 39.

[259] See generally J Haldane & P Lee 'Aquinas on human ensoulment, abortion and the value of life' (2003) 78 *Philosophy* 255.

[260] Harris-Stoertz (2012) *Journal of the History of Sexuality* 266.

[261] Harris-Stoertz (2012) *Journal of the History of Sexuality* 266.

[262] Harris-Stoertz (2012) *Journal of the History of Sexuality* 266.

[263] McLaren *History of Contraception* 126. However, Aquinas' position held its place in Christian history against termination of pregnancies. According to Haldane & Lee ((2003) *Philosophy* 261) the Catholic Church itself has made reference to his views and referred to his position as the position informing the Church's stance on termination of pregnancy in the past.

human form 30 days after intercourse. According to this text, 'vitality' could only be detected at 60–70 days.[264]

This understanding of ensoulment informed the Mediaeval Church in its position against the termination of pregnancies, but this distinction was used only for purposes of classifying and distinguishing penalties.[265] To cause the termination of a pregnancy prior to ensoulment was still considered a sin in the eyes of the Church, but it would be equal to a lesser sin, such as that of using contraceptives.[266] However, if a termination of pregnancy occurred after ensoulment, it would be considered homicide.[267] Noonan points out that the act of terminating a pregnancy was a crime against God, as it destroyed what He created, and an offence against love of one's neighbour, because it was a *type* of killing.[268] This is a continuation of the Roman position where the woman's husband was removed as the victim of the act of terminating a pregnancy. As a result of the poor understanding of foetal development, the concept of ensoulment was vague, to say the least, but accepting a delay in ensoulment helped justify leniency towards the early termination of pregnancies.[269]

On the issue of the therapeutic termination of pregnancies, Haldane and Lee refer to the work of the Archbishop of Florence, Antoninus (1389–1453), who held that a pregnancy may not be terminated after ensoulment, even in the case of a pregnant woman's life being at stake.[270] Further, Antoninus asserted that a pregnant woman may not bring on her own death in order to save the 'life' of an ensouled unborn.[271] It seems that in this sort of scenario it was left to God (as the Creator) to determine the outcome of a pregnancy, as it was argued by both Aquinas and Antoninus that one could not commit homicide in order to avoid another evil.[272]

---

[264] McLaren *History of Contraception* 126.

[265] D DeMarco 'The Roman Catholic Church and abortion: An historical perspective part 1' at 4, available at http://www.catholicculture.org/culture/library/view.cfm?id=3361 (accessed on 11 May 2016). Also see D DeMarco 'The Roman Catholic Church and abortion: An historical perspective part 2' available at http://www.catholicculture.org/culture/library/view.cfm?recnum=3362 (accessed on 11 May 2016).

[266] Haldane & Lee (2003) *Philosophy* 261.

[267] Haldane & Lee (2003) *Philosophy* 262. It must be noted that the Church's condemnations were merely based on morality and it was only in 1917 that the termination of a pregnancy prior to ensoulment was considered homicide. See McLaren *History of Contraception* 126.

[268] JT Noonan 'Christian tradition and the control of human reproduction' (1984) 4 *Journal of Christian Jurisprudence* 1 8–9.

[269] Butler (2005) *Journal of Women's History* 9; Haldane & Lee (2003) *Philosophy* 261 and McLaren *History of Contraception* 126.

[270] Haldane & Lee (2003) *Philosophy* 262. Antoninus took his lead from Aquinas.

[271] Haldane & Lee (2003) *Philosophy* 262. Research indicates that post-mortem caesarean deliveries were being practised from as early as 600 BC. One of the earliest Kings of Rome enacted the *Lex Regia* which required the removal of the unborn before the burial of its mother. The purpose of this law is not clear since it cannot be ascertained whether this was done in an attempt to save the life of the unborn or whether it represented a burial practice; see JP Boley 'The history of caesarean section. 1935' (1991) 145 *Canadian Medical Association Journal* 319.

[272] Haldane & Lee (2003) *Philosophy* 262 and S Lurie 'The changing motives of cesarean section: From the ancient world to the twenty-firs century' (2005) 271 *Archives of Gynecology and Obstetrics* 281.

This is not to say that there were no practices or policies in place to save the lives of the unborn in cases where pregnant women passed away during labour. In the case of a pregnant woman dying during labour, the Church imposed obligatory post-mortem caesarean-section delivery in a bid to save the soul of the unborn by removing it from the woman's body in order to save its life and to baptise the child once successfully delivered.[273] In the Middle Ages, caesarean deliveries were never performed on living women since it was not considered a medical procedure that could save her life, but was rather something that would hasten her death.[274] Thus, according to Lurie, caesarean-section delivery was more of a cultural event[275] that was guarded by the Church because it was preferred that the mother and foetus were buried separately.[276]

Exposure was also practised by women seeking to limit family sizes. According to Boswell, there were no secular laws preventing the exposure of newly born infants.[277] It was mainly women who exposed infants, but according to McLaren, this was usually done in accordance with their husbands' direction.[278] Roman, German and Scandinavian fathers retained the right to expose their children; this occurred in cases where the father refused to accept the child into the family.[279] In fact, it is widely supported that exposure was commonly practised.[280] Despite this, during the Middle Ages, secular laws emerged which were aimed at protecting the life and interests of the unborn.

Third-party assaults on pregnant women and self-induced pregnancy terminations were classifie as homicide if the unborn 'died' as a result of this conduct.[281] All the focus was placed on the loss of prenatal life rather than on the harm caused to a pregnant woman in the case of assault.[282] However, the confusing theoretical basis concerning ensoulment tainted any legal efforts in this regard. McLaren refers to the early thirteenth-century treatise, the Fleta, which was the firs English

[273] Lurie (2005) *Archives of Gynecology and Obstetrics* 282–3.
[274] Lurie (2005) *Archives of Gynecology and Obstetrics* 282–3.
[275] It was viewed as a cultural event because caesarean-section deliveries very rarely saved lives. According to Lurie, it was only during the Renaissance era that caesarean-section deliveries became medical procedures. See Lurie (2005) *Archives of Gynecology and Obstetrics* 282–3.
[276] Lurie (2005) *Archives of Gynecology and Obstetrics* 282–3.
[277] JE Boswell '*Expositio* and *oblatio*: The abandonment of children and the ancient and medieval family' (1984) 89 *American Historical Review* 10 24. In fact, Boswell (28) argues that the only perceived problem with exposure was the fact that parents might unknowingly have sexual intercourse with one of their abandoned children (in the case where the child is found and made to work as a prostitute) and Christians were concerned by the fact that the abandoned child is an indication that a couple engaged in sexual relations for pleasure rather than for procreative purposes.
[278] McLaren *History of Contraception* 127.
[279] Hayden (1913) *The Irish Review* 284 and McLaren *History of Contraception* 127. Hayden asserts that it was only newly born females that were subject to this practice and not males. However, McLaren does not make a distinction.
[280] McLaren *History of Contraception* 127. For more on exposure see SM Butler 'A case of indifference? Child murder in later medieval England' (2007) 19 *Journal of Women's History* 59 69–70; Boswell (1984) *American Historical Review* 23; and E Coleman 'Infanticide in the early Middle Ages' in BM Bolton (ed) *Women in Medieval Society* (1976) 47.
[281] Harris-Stoertz (2012) *Journal of the History of Sexuality* 269.
[282] Harris-Stoertz (2012) *Journal of the History of Sexuality* 269.

legal commentator's writings on termination of pregnancy.[283] McLaren quotes the Fleta as stating the following:[284]

> He, too, in strictness is a homicide who has pressed upon a pregnant woman or has given her poison or has struck her in order to procure an abortion or to prevent contraception, if the foetus was already formed and quickened, and similarly he who has given or accepted poison with the intention of preventing procreation or conception. A woman also commits homicide if, by potion or the like, she destroys a quickened child in the womb.

According to this text, it was argued that the termination of a pregnancy after ensoulment was as serious a crime as the use of contraception.[285] The effectiveness of this legal treatise to address concerns for the wellbeing of the unborn is questionable. McLaren suggests that this law remained in place because it was so rarely relied upon and thus never really critically questioned.[286] One can infer from this that the intention of protecting prenatal life was clearly present, but since there was a lack of knowledge of foetal development this intention could not be realised effectively.

The secular position moved towards a more practical approach at the end of the Middle Ages and required live birth for the crime of homicide. The most influentia statement depicting this shift is that of Sir Edward Coke (1552–1634), who stated:[287]

> If a woman be quick with childe, and by a Potion or otherwise killeth it in her wombe, or if a man beat her, whereby the childe dyeth in her body, and she is delivered a dead childe, it is a great misprision and no murder, but if the childe be born alive and dyeth of the Potion, Battery, or other cause, this is murder, for in law it is accounted as a reasonable creature, in rerum natura, when it is born alive.

Casey[288] and Forsyth[289] argue that legal authorities are concerned with the evidentiary difficulties associated with proving the cause of a termination of pregnancy in the case where violence is inflicte on pregnant women or in cases where women terminated their pregnancies.[290] The live birth of a 'quick childe' was required for purposes of murder,[291] thus quickening (or formation, according to Aristotle's approach) became an important point as it indicated proof of prenatal

---

[283] McLaren *History of Contraception* 126.

[284] McLaren *History of Contraception* 125.

[285] McLaren *History of Contraception* 126.

[286] Butler (2005) *Journal of Women's History* 12 and McLaren *History of Contraception* 126. This legal treatise is distinguishable from the Church's position. As mentioned earlier the Church considered the termination of a pregnancy after ensoulment to amount to murder while engaging in contraceptive practices was considered a lesser sin; see Harris-Stoertz (2012) *Journal of the History of Sexuality* 270.

[287] As quoted in G Casey *Born Alive: The legal status of the unborn child in England and the U.S.A.* (2005) at 16, available at http://researchrepository.ucd.ie/bitstream/handle/10197/5546/Born_Alive-.pdf?sequence=1 (accessed on 18 November 2016).

[288] Casey *Born Alive* 17.

[289] CD Forsythe 'Homicide of the unborn child: The born alive rule and other legal anachronisms' (1987) 21 *Valparaiso University LR* 563.

[290] It must be noted that there are conflictin views as to whether this quote serves as an evidentiary rule or a substantive rule of law.

[291] Casey *Born Alive* 16.

life in law and no longer only in religion.[292] Also, according to Forsythe, this rule informs the law on the termination of pregnancies, namely that a pregnancy should not be terminated after quickening.[293] This is the position that informed the law as it developed from the Middle Ages to the present day and takes the form of what we now understand as being the born-alive rule.[294]

Even though women faced certain risks during pregnancy and childbirth and there was a need to limit the heirs within a family, there was still a very strong drive to ensure at least one legitimate heir to continue the family line (for nobility) and maintain access to land (for the less wealthy).[295] As a result of this increased interest in obtaining a legitimate heir, pregnant women were treated with great suspicion, and, according to Harris-Stoertz, this is reflecte in the secular English law of the high Middle Ages.[296] For instance, men had an interest in the 'women only' birthing chamber because English law prescribed that the birth of an heir did not count if it was born dead, was never heard crying or was born a 'monster'.[297] This law proved problematic, because women were not considered acceptable witnesses (they could not have direct access to court) and men were not allowed into the birthing room to witness the birth.[298] The man had to stand outside and wait to hear a wailing child, as not even the women present to assist during labour were trusted to convey this critical information concerning an heir.[299]

Not only had Church and secular law began to act for the individual interests of the unborn but Harris-Stoertz sees the above example (along with others)[300] as an indication that men had begun to assert control over other issues that were primarily 'womanly concerns'.[301] However, there are far more extreme instances of male-centred interventions in the realms of 'womanly concerns'. During the Middle Ages, both the Church and the state widely condemned the practice of witchcraft, which resulted in unprecedented numbers of women being accused in court of practising witchcraft.[302] Those accused of and tortured into confessing

[292] Forsythe (1987) *Valparaiso University LR* 568. Forsythe (573) refers to this as the 'quickening doctrine'.

[293] Forsythe (1987) *Valparaiso University LR* 574.

[294] See generally Casey *Born Alive* and Forsythe (1987) *Valparaiso University LR* 563.

[295] Harris-Stoertz (2012) *Journal of the History of Sexuality* 275.

[296] Harris-Stoertz (2012) *Journal of the History of Sexuality* 275. This is particularly interesting because marriage and sexuality usually fell within the jurisdiction of the Church.

[297] Harris-Stoertz (2012) *Journal of the History of Sexuality* 276. Being born a 'monster' indicates that the neonate is born with a disability.

[298] Harris-Stoertz (2012) *Journal of the History of Sexuality* 276.

[299] Harris-Stoertz (2012) *Journal of the History of Sexuality* 276.

[300] In an example where the needs of the unborn were recognised, Harris-Stoertz refers to the mediaeval English and French custom of suspending death sentences or physical punishment (mutilation and torture) when the convicted person was a pregnant woman. Once the woman gave birth or it was proven that she was not pregnant, her punishment would commence. Here the object of concern was prenatal life alone as the pregnant woman's punishment was merely postponed. See Harris-Stoertz (2012) *Journal of the History of Sexuality* 271

[301] Harris-Stoertz (2012) *Journal of the History of Sexuality* 264.

[302] RJ Horsley & RH Horsley 'On the trail of the "witches": Wise women, midwives and the European witch hunts' (1987) 3 *Women in German Yearbook* 1 12.

have been identifie as including peasant healers, wise women and midwives.[303] Typically, these women had not been formally trained at universities and their knowledge was derived from centuries of practical experience in caring for women in relation to womanly concerns.[304] Shorter also explains that, with regard to midwifery, midwives closely guarded their knowledge from formally trained physicians and even the women they attended to.[305] Furthermore, apart from attending to womanly concerns in particular, they also cared for members of the broader community.[306]

Witch hunts simultaneously occurred with the increased state and Church regulation of health care.[307] On the one hand, the Catholic Church is cited as stating that no one does more harm to the Church than midwives.[308] Horsley and Horsley suggest that this is because of the secrecy surrounding birth and because midwives were known to use charms, spells and incantations to assist women giving birth.[309] The Church therefore required midwives to be examined by a bishop for the purposes of admittance and to take an oath that they would not use sorcery or spells while assisting birthing women.[310] The state co-operated with the Church and began to regulate and control midwives' practices.[311] The practice of medicine was increasingly limited to those who were formally trained, thereby excluding female practitioners whose knowledge base derived from centuries of practice outside of formal institutions.[312] For instance, in a parliamentary statute in Edinburgh, anyone who was not approved by the 'surgeons' was not allowed to practise the art of surgery and the Act explicitly threatened women that, if caught doing so, they would be prosecuted under the relevant witchcraft legislation.[313]

This systematic suppression and characterisation of women healers as witches led to a recognisable decline in the development and passage of and access to 'women's knowledge' and its benefits[314] It also meant that, in addition to women being excluded from the economy and relegated to the domestic sphere, their traditional knowledge about women's reproductive health and its roots were also now lost to male control. This rendered nearly every facet of their lives subject to male domination and this took place in an environment where society and law were increasingly acting for the benefi of the unborn to the exclusion of the women carrying them.

[303] See Horsley & Horsley (1987) *Women in German Yearbook* 1; B Ehrenreich & D English *Witches, Midwives & Nurses: A History of Women Healers* 2 ed (2010) 7–24; and M Green 'Women's medical practice and health care in medieval Europe' (1989) 14 *Signs* 434.

[304] E Shorter *A History of Women's Bodies* (1984) 38.

[305] Shorter *A History of Women's Bodies* 39.

[306] Green (1989) *Signs* 434.

[307] Horsley & Horsley (1987) *Women in German Yearbook* 1.

[308] Ehrenreich & English *Witches, Midwives & Nurses* 18.

[309] Horsley & Horsley (1987) *Women in German Yearbook* 9–10.

[310] Horsley & Horsley (1987) *Women in German Yearbook* 10.

[311] Horsley & Horsley (1987) *Women in German Yearbook* 10.

[312] Horsley & Horsley (1987) *Women in German Yearbook* 19.

[313] Horsley & Horsley (1987) *Women in German Yearbook* 19.

[314] Ehrenreich & English *Witches, Midwives & Nurses* 21.

2.5 CONCLUDING REMARKS

Prior to the introduction of Christianity, both women and the unborn existed on a level playing field under the authority of the head of the household, both valued in so far as each could advance the needs of the head of the household. However, as Christianity was accepted and incorporated into society's moral order, the life of the unborn gained an independent value protected by the Church in the name of God. Consequently, the platform for tension between the needs of women and the foetus began to take form.

Throughout history there is a dominant and reoccurring theme of female subordination. However, the true extent of subordination is questionable, as authors vary in their account of female subordination. On the extreme end of the scale, women are presented as being wholly subordinate to men and they are portrayed as lacking the capacity to live a life beyond the domestic sphere. However, it would be incorrect to perceive women as absolutely passive recipients of this designated and over-regulated role.

There are a number of subtle indications that some women actively exercised autonomy. The existence of regulations may be a signal of activity in a particular area, which called for the regulation of certain conduct. Consequently, the constant calls for training women in submissiveness, private seclusion, and condemnations of fertility control and terminations of pregnancies all possibly indicate that women were not 'adequately' submissive and did exist in the public sphere. They may also indicate that women continued to exert control over their bodies on a wide scale. Further, McLaren's[315] reference to 'female knowledge' of fertility control and termination-of-pregnancy procedures indicate that, despite the fact that women lacked access to the public arena, they still functioned in their space as human beings, and developed their own means of sharing important knowledge among themselves in order to care for and advance themselves free from the constraints of male regulation.[316] This is particularly apparent when one considers the prevalent role of midwives and female healers and the perceived threat they posed to the state and Church. Further, Cantarella's description of Roman women engaging in sexual relations outside of marriage for non-procreative purposes also suggests that women did not simply accept nominated husbands and exist on a purely procreative level but were also driven by desire and the need for intimate relations. Another indication of women asserting their autonomy is the public participation in mystical cults described by Kaufman,[317] Stoner[318] and Neel.[319] In this respect, women did not accept the male-dominated Church or marriage as their only options; instead they carved out a spiritual course on their own terms.

[315] McLaren *History of Contraception* 26; 28.

[316] Reference to 'women's knowledge' also demonstrates that this knowledge is passed on from one woman to the next which can be interpreted as the existence of unwritten women's history. Thus, it would be logically unsound to accept the available written texts as the only historical account of women.

[317] Kaufman (1973) *Soundings* 143.

[318] Stoner (1995) *Ex Post Facto* 29.

[319] Neel (1989) *Signs* 321.

The regulation of women in ancient Greece, particularly their reproductive capacity, was not done in order to advance the interests of the unborn but rather to advance the interests of the head of the household. Although Aristotle advocated a limitation on when a pregnancy could be terminated, the fact that there were no identifie laws imposing some form of sanction for non-compliance suggests that a late termination of pregnancy may not have been an issue of great social concern. Further, when a husband withheld permission to terminate a pregnancy it was because the birth held the potential benefi of advancing the man's patrimonial goals and not necessarily because the unborn had some intrinsic value as an individual. Consequently, there do not seem to be any areas where a potential tension between the needs of pregnant women and foetal interests could have arisen in ancient Greek history. This may stem from the fact that neither women nor the unborn had any legally recognised interests to advance. Reproductive autonomy was apparently an unrecognised concept, as were foetal interests. What can be seen is that women and the unborn seem to have been positioned on the same level in a system of domination.

However, this position changes in Roman history, particularly with reference to the rise of Christianity and the ideological shift it encouraged. The Church introduced a new moral and social philosophy: Humans were weak and immoral, born into original sin as a result of their fall in Eden, and the purpose of life on Earth was salvation, which could be found in the Church.[320] Women were offered refuge from a life of marriage and the Church claimed to accept sexual equality but, according to Church teachings, women's sexuality needed to be controlled. Cantarella states that, even though the political, social, and economic conditions changed from those of Greece, the essential issues surrounding women were the same.[321] Misogyny, although founded on new assumptions, was merely reconfirme in Christian ideologies[322] and the fact that these ideologies came from a higher spiritual source solidifie women's perceived inferior position. Thus, as religion spread, the status of women declined.[323]

Christianity not only maintained the notion of female subordination but also introduced an additional restriction on women. It held that all pregnancies, including unwanted ones, held some form of value, based on a distorted understanding of foetal development as espoused by Aristotle. In this regard, it was believed that the life of the unborn had a value that originated from beyond the household and power of the *paterfamilias*. This position resulted in women's needs being held in abeyance not only for the benefi of her household and the *paterfamilias* but now also for the unborn. These are the firs indications of the interests of the unborn beginning to be elevated above the needs of women. The Church's position of subordinating women and valuing the unborn continued into the Middle Ages.

While the advancement of women's interests remained somewhat static, a new paradigm emerged, holding that that an unborn holds a value independent of that

[320] Jeffery (1957) *Journal of Criminal Law, Criminology, and Police Science* 652.

[321] Cantarella *Pandora's Daughters* 170.

[322] Cantarella *Pandora's Daughters* 170.

[323] McLaren *History of Contraception* 63.

of a pregnant woman. In Roman history we fin vague examples of women being placed under various forms of surveillance in order to ensure the wellbeing of the unborn and later the mediaeval Church actively repudiated the notion of the therapeutic termination of 'ensouled' pregnancies. Adding to the undercurrents of the situation, however 'rebellious' women's individual actions were, women of these times did not consciously come together and bring about wide spread social change, consequently weakening their ability to change their position in reproduction. This added to the power of Church's teachings and the law's approach to the value of prenatal life. Here one find the beginnings of an environment that had the potential to foster a relationship where tensions may arise.

Chapter 3

MODERN SOCIETIES AND PREGNANCY ADVERSARIALISM

3.1 INTRODUCTION

Early modern history reveals a hive of activity concerning, among other issues, the creation of an adversarial pregnancy environment.

With the influenc of the Renaissance, women began to self-construct a platform for open, collective expression of will, female perspective and rejection of male-driven and define practices. Women began and continued the process of changing the face of their traditional position to the extent that it did not suit their inner direction and experience of equality. These efforts were reflecte in the feminisation of the law aimed at addressing issues particular to women and removing the masculine as the 'norm' or yardstick. Feminists contributed to opening the door for equality with respect to decisions concerning marriage, reproduction, education and professionalism. Relevant to the notion of pregnancy adversarialism, it was their call for reproductive freedom that contributed to the development of an adversarialist pregnancy environment, since this sort of freedom is primarily concerned with women's interests as the foremost concern rather than focusing purely on prenatal value and advancement.

During the process of feminising laws, reproductive technologies developed and provided first-han access to gestating foetuses, objectively displaying 'life' before birth. Medical professionals and the broader public were able to relate to, 'care' for and experience the unborn as individuated patients or members of society independent of pregnant women. These third-party experiences of pregnancy elicited theories on how to frame the status of the unborn and the significanc of birth became an issue. Eventually the unborn were 'disembodied' from the pregnant women carrying them. This development not only removed women as conveyers of pregnancy or gestational knowledge but also rendered them vulnerable to society's demands to act for the benefi of individuated gestating life.

This chapter discusses feminism, its three 'waves'[1] and women's collective call for equality and reproductive freedom (as a means of achieving equality). It also considers how the unborn became known to third parties (medical professionals, society and the state) and independent entities and reveals the consequences of this new found knowledge.

This chapter establishes that women's historical position of subordination, the feminist drive for equality and the identificatio of and acting for the benefi of

[1] There is discussion that a fourth wave of feminism is emerging. See J Donovan *Feminist Theory: The Intellectual Traditions* 4 ed (2012) xiii–xiv and E Munro 'Feminism: A fourth wave?' (2013) 4 *Political Insight* 22.

the unborn as separate entities readies the ground for an adversarial pregnancy environment. This is particularly because women aim to secure reproductive freedom, while third parties who have a vested interest[2] in the unborn use the unborn's 'proven' individuality as leverage for justifying intervention in female reproductive freedom which ultimately undermines their equality.

3.2 THE RISE OF FEMALE CONSCIOUSNESS AND FEMINISM

Lougee states that, despite the fact that the Renaissance is well known for its advances in culture and the material conditions of life, this period also brought with it increasing inequalities in social powers between men and women.[3] However, Becker-Cantarino argues that women, in their own capacity, enter history in the early modern period, because there was a marked rise in feminist consciousness during this time.[4] At this point, women became aware that they belonged to a subordinated group and as a result of being classifie as part of this group, they had suffered wrongs.[5] Further, women progressively became aware that their suffering was not imposed on them by nature but was the result of societal structures.[6] This awareness developed into a sense of connectedness, and women began to develop an autonomous definitio of goals and strategies to change their 'unnatural' position.[7] Essentially, women developed alternative ideas or visions for their future.[8] These ideas took different although not mutually exclusive paths in order to address the wrongs suffered. Stansell refers to these as 'cracks' in the social order and states that, where cracks begin to appear, it inevitably comes to the attention of individuals who examine that particular area and widen the distance between what is supposed to be and what is.[9] Before looking at the actions women embarked on to agitate the cracks that appeared in the social order of the time, it is necessary to firs contemplate the term 'feminism'.

The term was firs devised by the French in the 1880s as '*féminisme*', '*femme*' meaning 'woman', and '*isme*' referring to a social movement or political ideology.[10] However, Offen argues that the exact origins of the term are unknown, but it was widely used during the early 1890s and by 1894–95, the term had found

[2] A father-to-be will have an interest in the unborn as will medical professionals, in relation to their aims to promote healthy pregnancies, optimal foetal development and safe birth, and the state on the basis that it bears responsibility for the welfare of all citizens.

[3] CC Lougee 'Modern European history' (1977) 2 *Signs* 628 633.

[4] B Becker-Cantarino '"Feminist consciousness" and "wicked witches": Recent studies on women in early modern Europe' (1994) 20 *Signs* 152 154; 156.

[5] Becker-Cantarino (1994) *Signs* 156.

[6] Becker-Cantarino (1994) *Signs* 156.

[7] Becker-Cantarino (1994) *Signs* 156.

[8] Becker-Cantarino (1994) *Signs* 156.

[9] C Stansell *The Feminist Promise: 1792 to the Present* (2010) 6. Although Stansell is referring to women's activities in the 1700s, her comment is equally applicable to women's activities that date back as far as the 1400s. In this respect, see J Kelly 'Early feminist theory and the *Querelle des Femmes*, 1400–1789' (1982) 8 *Signs* 4.

[10] EB Freedman *No Turning Back: The History of Feminism and the Future of Women* (2002) 3.

its way into publications in England, Belgium, France, Spain, Italy, Germany, Greece and Russia.[11]

Offen[12] describes feminism as being pro-women and as encompassing both an ideology and a movement for socio-political change founded on the critical analysis of male privilege and female subordination. Historically, feminism was founded on, and was in tension with, male domination of both the political and intellectual spheres of societies.[13] However, Offen states that more recent feminist developments have now surpassed this original manifestation of feminism.[14] She asserts that feminism has a wide historical range, which varies between cultural traditions and female experiences.[15] Nevertheless, a common value underlies all the diverse feminist perspectives: feminism uses gender (that is, the different social constructions of the behaviour of the sexes) as the basis for analysis.[16] In this context, feminism critically engages topics such as the personal autonomy of women, the social organisation of the family and the state, the unequal distribution of political, social and economic power between the sexes, patriarchal thought and various institutional and social control mechanisms.[17] Offen states that feminism seeks to terminate the masculine hierarchy but not necessarily 'sexual dualism'.[18]

---

[11] K Offen 'Definin feminism: A comparative historical approach' (1988) 14 *Signs* 119 126 and K Offen 'On the French origin of the words "feminism" and "feminist" ' (1988) 8 *Feminist Issues* 45. According to Taylor the term 'feminism' firs featured in the context of the international suffrage campaigns which were advanced by female suffragists. Nevertheless, she points out that what has become clear is that most of the ideas that fell under the term 'feminism' had already existed for well over a century under other descriptions. Taylor argues further that it was the collection of these ideas under one term that indicates a level of political self-awareness that was not present in earlier periods. Thus, prior to the emergence of the suffrage movement, there already existed a body of views on women who identifie themselves as taking a particular position, and on this premise Taylor asserts that is necessary and justifiabl to consider these views as feminist views. See B Taylor 'Feminism and the Enlightenment 1650–1850' (1999) 47 *History Workshop Journal* 261 264. However, Offen ((1988) *Signs* 131) points out that some authors describe these earlier views and activities associated with those views as 'precursors' or 'forerunners' of feminism, or of 'proto-feminists'. Offen (131) is critical of this approach because it fails to firs describe what 'feminism' is, and one is left with many different and sometimes conflictin ideas of feminism. On that note, both Taylor ((1999) *History Workshop Journal* 264) and Offen ((1988) *Signs* 132) state that when considering these early feminist views, the subject must be approached in their own terms and must be considered within the cultural context in which early feminist views were written because the concept of feminism is not static.

[12] Offen (1988) *Signs* 150–2.

[13] Offen (1988) *Signs* 150–2.

[14] Offen (1988) *Signs* 150–2.

[15] In this respect, Freedman (*No Turning Back* 8) states that feminism must recognise the overlapping identities of women as members of classes, races, and nations. This requires the acknowledgement that there is no universal idea of woman that can be projected onto all women in various societies, cultures and traditions since gender has developed differently through time and place.

[16] Offen (1988) *Signs* 150–2.

[17] Offen (1988) *Signs* 150–2.

[18] Offen (1988) *Signs* 150–2.

Thus, according to Offen, feminists seek to create a balance between men and women on the basis of their shared humanity and respect for difference.[19]

What also becomes apparent, and what makes definin feminism difficult, is that the term 'feminism' on its own does not identify all the possible different perspectives by women with different female experiences linked to their existence in different cultures, races, classes, and societies.[20] Freedman[21] states that feminism asks two questions: first what about women (meaning what difference does gender make)? Secondly, which women (which essentially asks, what difference do ideas about race, class, or nationality make)?[22] Consequently, it is necessary to qualify the term 'feminism' with additional descriptive terms such as socialist feminism, black feminism or ecofeminism (to name a few).[23] Van Marle and Bonthuys[24] stress that there is no single correct feminist approach and that feminism has evolved as a result of internal feminist debates about feminism itself. At times, different feminist perspectives can be contradictory and overlap or intersect with one another, depending on the area of focus.[25] However, Freedman states that they should all explicitly address justice for women as their primary concern.[26] Feminist theories can be positioned historically according to the 'three waves of feminism'.[27]

First-wave feminists, such as liberal feminists, aimed to achieve equal treatment of men and women and called for the development of neutral standards.[28] These feminists wanted to vote and gain access to the public domain, which was typically reserved for men. They argued that women's differences as far as biology, psychology and intelligence went were not disqualifying factors for entry into the public world.[29] According Van Marle and Bonthuys,[30] liberal feminists

[19] Also see Freedman's (*No Turning Back* 7–8) working definitio of feminism where she identifie equal worth, privilege, social movements, and social hierarchies as four critical components in the definitio of feminism.

[20] Freedman *No Turning Back* 6.

[21] Freedman *No Turning Back* 8.

[22] For instance, Offen ((1988) *Signs* 123) points out that at the start of the suffragette movement some women in England and the United States linked the notion of feminism with the idea of equality with men (liberal feminism), while other women in Europe focused on sexual difference (cultural or relational feminism) rather than on the sameness of men and women.

[23] Freedman *No Turning Back* 6. Van Marle and Bonthuys point out that these differences in theories relate to what different feminists identify as evidence of subordination, how they defin and frame subordination and the remedies they suggest to overcome subordination and secure liberation; see K Van Marle & E Bonthuys 'Feminist theories and concepts' in E Bonthuys & C Albertyn (eds) *Gender, Law and Justice* (2007) 16.

[24] Van Marle & Bonthuys 'Feminist theories and concepts' 15.

[25] Van Marle & Bonthuys 'Feminist theories and concepts' 15.

[26] Freedman *No Turning Back* 8.

[27] However, Van Marle and Bonthuys warn that the various forms of feminism as discussed in the context of a particular wave are not purely historical terms, seeing that a number of contemporary feminists are currently adopting first or second- wave approaches. See Van Marle & Bonthuys 'Feminist theories and concepts' 17.

[28] Van Marle & Bonthuys 'Feminist theories and concepts' 17.

[29] Van Marle & Bonthuys 'Feminist theories and concepts' 17.

[30] 'Feminist theories and concepts' 17; 31. Also see M Friedman, J Metelerkamp & R Posel 'What is feminism? And what kind of feminist am I?' (1987) 1 *Agenda* 3 5–6

argue that women's emancipation lies in the assertion that men and women are equal, have an equal claim to rights, and are equally free to participate in the public spheres of various professions and politics. Liberal feminists' initial figh for equality assisted in securing women's right to vote.[31] Further, their efforts resulted in the liberalisation of divorce laws through newly enacted legislation – married women could protect their property, which meant that they could establish themselves economically, thus giving divorced women better leverage in child custody cases.[32] Women got increased access to higher education and a number of professions.[33] Nevertheless, liberal feminism also left many 'women issues' untouched. Van Marle and Bonthuys point out that these beneficia advances did not extend to working class and black women.[34]

From the 1960s to the 1980s, second-wave feminists emerged in the West.[35] Second-wave feminism included radical feminism,[36] relational feminism[37] and socialist feminism.[38] Van Marle and Bonthuys maintain that, after first-wav

[31] Freedman *No Turning Back* 372 tabulates the year when women were granted the right to vote. During 1890–1910, the firs three countries to grant women voting rights were New Zealand, Australia, and Finland. During 1910–1940, women in the United Kingdom, Canada, the United States, Russia, and the Netherlands (to name a few) were granted voting rights. The majority of countries extended voting rights during 1940–1960, with South Africa being among the last to extend voting rights to women of all races in 1994.

[32] Donovan *Feminist Theory* 26 and Freedman *No Turning Back* 55.

[33] Donovan *Feminist Theory* 26 and Freedman *No Turning Back* 55.

[34] Van Marle & Bonthuys 'Feminist theories and concepts' 32.

[35] BL Epstein 'The successes and failures of feminism' (2002) 14 *Journal of Women's History* 118.

[36] Radical feminists sought to establish the original cause of female oppression and went further to establish that female oppression was the cause of all other forms of oppression and domination. These feminists argued that patriarchal control (as a social system of male-define values) oppressed women, and was thus also the cause of all the other forms of oppression (for instance racism and economic exploitation). They focused on relations between men and women, especially the fact that men dominated women in their personal relationships. Radical feminists argued that the experience of oppression that occurred in the private area of personal relationships (family, marriage, and the bedroom) should not be conceived and limited to being a woman's individual (private) problem, but should be widened and understood as a broader social and political issue. See Friedman, Metelerkamp & Posel (1987) *Agenda* 8; Van Marle & Bonthuys 'Feminist theories and concepts' 34; and MA Fineman 'Feminist legal theory' (2005) 13 *Journal of Gender, Social Policy & the Law* 13 20.

[37] Relational feminists emphasised that there is a difference between men and women; women can be define according to their relationships with others, and feminine qualities are actually a source of strength and pride, which can contribute positively to public regeneration. These feminists saw value in being a woman, and they celebrated the perceived differences that women had from men. Relational feminists sought 'equality in difference'. They accepted that women were more emotional than men and that rationality was not any greater in value than emotion; consequently they rejected the imposed hierarchical status of the oppositional qualities applicable to men and women. See Donovan *Feminist Theory* 31–2; Van Marle & Bonthuys 'Feminist theories and concepts' 35; and Offen (1988) *Signs* 139.

[38] Socialist feminism, in its wide-ranging formulations, generally sought to address gender and class oppression in order to liberate women. In essence, it created a 'dual system theory' recognising that patriarchy creates gender oppression and that class systems create class oppression and work alienation for most women. See Van Marle & Bonthuys 'Feminist theories and concepts' 33–4 and HI Hartmann 'The unhappy marriage of Marxism and feminism: Towards a more progressive union' (1979) 3 *Capital & Class* 165.

feminists had secured women's access to the public sphere, second-wave feminists faced a number of practical difficulties in the context of formal equality.[39] Formal equality proved particularly problematic with respect to pregnancy, childcare, housework and sexual harassment, all of which are essentially women's issues that are not experienced by men.[40] According to Gambaudo, second-wave feminists rejected the 'equal to man' argument because being equal to man meant being the same as man, and this approach denied women's visibility and recognition.[41] In this context second-wave feminists drew on the differences between men and women, highlighted the consequences of these differences and worked towards countering existing negative effects associated with difference.[42]

Radical feminists successfully brought public and legal attention to issues of domestic violence and pushed for the recognition of sexual harassment as a 'gendered legal harm'.[43] Epstein[44] credits radical feminists with the accomplishment of affirmative action in the United States. Generally, relational feminists were concerned with 'protective legislation' aimed at protecting and advancing women's differentness.[45] In this respect they fought for a welfare state that would regulate the food and drug industries and labour conditions, as well as aiding access to education and health care.[46] They also called for 'voluntary motherhood'[47] and subsidies for childrearing.[48] Fineman states that relational feminist activities led to the deconstruction of the traditional male perspective in law and feminised the law to the extent that our stance on sexual assault, domestic violence, family laws, sexual harassment and battered women's syndrome was transformed.[49] Donovan[50] also credits relational feminists with the realisation of protected maternity leave. Socialist feminists called for day-care facilities, paid maternity leave, sick leave, affirmative action, waged housework, guaranteed annual income, contraception and termination-of-pregnancy rights, equal participation in the labour force and fair pay, and encouraged the development of and participation in trade unions.[51]

---

39 Van Marle & Bonthuys 'Feminist theories and concepts' 17.

40 Van Marle & Bonthuys 'Feminist theories and concepts' 17.

41 SA Gambaudo 'French feminism vs Anglo-American feminism: A reconstruction' (2007) 14 *European Journal of Women's Studies* 93 95. In this respect, Gambaudo (95) argues that second-wave feminists faced up to patriarchy and define themselves as different to men, 'with different needs, different sensitivity, different modes of expression, etc. than those man had define for her'. Also see Epstein (2002) *Journal of Women's History* 121.

42 Van Marle & Bonthuys 'Feminist theories and concepts' 17.

43 Van Marle & Bonthuys 'Feminist theories and concepts' 34–5.

44 (2002) *Journal of Women's History* 121–122.

45 Donovan *Feminist Theory* 60.

46 Donovan *Feminist Theory* 59.

47 'Voluntary motherhood' in the context of the earlier feminist movement refers to a wife's right to refuse to have marital sex in order to avoid a pregnancy. This later turned to a call for contraception. See Freedman *No Turning Back* 232.

48 Donovan *Feminist Theory* 56.

49 Fineman (2005) *Journal of Gender, Social Policy & the Law* 17.

50 *Feminist Theory* 62.

51 Donovan *Feminist Theory* 79 and Friedman, Metelerkamp & Posel (1987) *Agenda* 16–19.

Third-wave feminism came to the fore in response to what Donovan[52] calls the 'tyranny of monolithic concepts that became the central concern in feminist theory at the end of the twentieth century'. Van Marle and Bonthuys[53] identify three major third-wave feminist views: postmodern feminism,[54] postcolonial feminism[55] and critical race feminism.[56] Third-wave feminism rejects many aspects of second-wave feminism.[57] It focuses on differences between women (as opposed to differences between men and 'universal woman') and deconstructs the essentialism of the second wave.[58] It calls for an understanding of women's context (in terms of race, sexual orientation, colonisation, religion, culture and class) in addition to gender[59] thus acknowledging individuality.

Characteristically, feminism houses numerous female perspectives, assertions and critiques all stemming from the individuality of women's lived experiences

---

52 *Feminist Theory* 183.

53 'Feminist theories and concepts' 17.

54 Postmodern feminism focuses on the local and contextual realities of subjects. It looks at the difference between men and women and differences between women. Postmodern feminists stress that individuals are not vested with a fixe inherent identity, so identity is always subject to alteration, depending on context and discourse. Postmodern feminists aim to deconstruct dominant principles by considering counter-marginal principles and bringing multiple meanings and contexts to the fore. This strand of feminism strongly resists any form of generalisation, coherence and universality and, by avoiding generalisations, they are able to deconstruct the essential conditions required for authority (or dominant principle). See Donovan *Feminist Theory* 184; 197; 204; Van Marle & Bonthuys 'Feminist theories and concepts' 37–8; and SA Mann & DJ Huffman 'The decentering of second wave feminism and the rise of the third wave' (2005) 69 *Science & Society* 56 63; 56.

55 Postcolonial feminism (also known as global feminism) focuses on non-Western women, and links the history of colonialism to the current position of women, looking at how former colonial powers continue to dominate in ways other than through the traditional construction of colonisation. Postcolonial feminists examine and address issues of race, class and sexuality, and, by focusing on the marginalised, look to displace dominant discourses of unity such as 'third world woman'; 'black woman'; and 'white woman'. In this respect, all those who were 'othered' (by exclusion from the dominant discourse of the West and colonial encounters) will fin inclusion. See Mann & Huffman (2005) *Science & Society* 56; Donovan *Feminist Theory* 166; 184; and Van Marle & Bonthuys 'Feminist theories and concepts' 38–40.

56 Their focus is on working-class black women and calls for increased attention to the gendered subordination of black women and their racialised experiences. As a result of colonisation and capitalism, black women experience harms that are not always adequately considered by Western feminist scholarship. For instance, critical race feminists found that conventional feminism excluded the experiences of black women by developing a feminism based on white, middle-class academic experience, and the issues addressed by these feminists have very little benefi for black women. Critical race feminists call for issues of race, class and gender to be addressed simultaneously. See Van Marle & Bonthuys 'Feminist theories and concepts' 40–1 and O Oyewùmí 'The white woman's burden: African women in Western feminist discourse' in O Oyewùmí (ed) *African Women & Feminism: Reflecting on the Politics of Sisterhood* (2003) 25–43.

57 J Coleman 'An introduction to feminisms in a postfeminist age' (2009) 23 *Women's Studies Journal* 3 10. Second-wave feminism is considered to be 'essentialist' to the extent that a single feminist narrative or truth was being presented as the narrative for all women during the course of second-wave feminism, consequently marginalising those women that did not fi into that narrative or truth. See Van Marle & Bonthuys 'Feminist theories and concepts' 38.

58 Mann & Huffman (2005) *Science & Society* 57.

59 Van Marle & Bonthuys 'Feminist theories and concepts' 17.

which are located in their varying social, cultural, and racial contexts. It successfully mobilised women on a collective scale. Despite some of the divergent constructs, a unifying thread can be identifie among these diverse perspectives—women's call for equality in both the private and the public spheres.[60] It is the call for equality, but more specificall , equality in the context of reproduction, that is relevant to the notion of pregnancy adversarialism.

3.3 FEMINIST CALLS FOR EQUALITY AND PREGNANCY ADVERSARIALISM

MacKinnon find that the claim to equality is based on being human.[61] However, MacKinnon states that, currently, what it means to be 'human' is constructed according to men's standards and she understands this to mean that women (who cannot reach that standard) are seen as something below being human (second-class citizens).[62] As a result of their 'second-class status', women are denied respect, dignity, resources, protection and power.[63] She then goes on to question whether the existing standard of 'human' should be feminised, thus enabling women to be understood as human and therefore equal.[64]

MacKinnon's work is focused on achieving equality between men and women by comparing women's 'humanness' with that of men. However, Ackermann is sceptical of this approach.[65] He argues that stating that 'person A "is equal" to person B is on its own meaningless'. He requires one to ask, in what respect are people equal? While MacKinnon uses being human as the standard, she does not elaborate on what it is about being human that makes people's claims for equality legitimate or what kind of 'human' would be feminised enough to make the concept sufficient to include women. Ackermann answers this by stating that people are, or should be, equal with regard to their human dignity.[66]

Ackermann understands human dignity to be synonymous with 'inestimable' human worth and he argues that a number of inherent human traits vest in all

[60] C Albertyn 'Equality' in E Bonthuys & C Albertyn (eds) *Gender, Law and Justice* (2007) 82. Albertyn (83–90) explains that feminist demands for equality have evolved through the years from demands for formal equality (equal treatment to men) to demands for substantive equality (recognising differences between the sexes, context and disadvantage). Further, Albertyn (94–5) explains that substantive equality should be both backward- and forward-looking in that it should remove past disadvantages and put mechanisms in place to secure future equality. This approach to equality can be seen as transformative equality. Substantive equality is the form of equality currently in place in South Africa, whereas the United States and Canada have adopted a formal approach to equality; for more on equality see C Albertyn & B Goldblatt 'Equality' in S Woolman & M Bishop (eds) *Constitutional Law of South Africa* 2 ed (Original Service 3) 35–5 to 35–7.

[61] CA MacKinnon *Sex Equality* 2 ed (2007) 3.

[62] MacKinnon *Sex Equality* 3.

[63] MacKinnon *Sex Equality* 2.

[64] MacKinnon *Sex Equality* 3.

[65] L Ackermann *Human Dignity: Lodestar for Equality in South Africa* (2012) 23.

[66] Ackermann *Human Dignity* 23. However, see Albertyn & Goldblatt 'Equality' 35–5. The authors ask the same question but come to a different answer. They answer the question by stating that at the very least there should be equality in respect of outcomes and opportunities. The authors contend that understanding equality in these terms assists in addressing areas of material disadvantage.

persons, based on the fact that they form part of the human race.[67] Ackermann requires human worth to be understood as:[68]

> [T]he capacity for and the right to respect as a human being. This arises from all those aspects of the human personality that flo from human intellectual and moral capacity; which in turn separate humans from the impersonality of nature, enables them to exercise their own judgment, to have self-awareness and a sense of self-worth, to exercise self-determination, to shape themselves and nature, to develop their personalities and to strive for self-fulfilmen in their lives. It also arises from the capacity of human beings to enter into meaningful relationships with others and thereby achieve self-fulfilmen at least in part.

Placing Ackermann's work in the context of contemporary feminist aims for equality, it can be understood that women seek equality in human worth regardless of sex or gender,[69] to secure the space for self-awareness, develop their sense of self-worth, freely exercise self-determination and shape themselves in terms of their inner direction in order to secure self-fulfilment Further, in cases where women do enter into relationships in order to achieve self-fulfilment such relationships should result in legitimising and reinforcing their 'sense and experience' of human worth.[70] In a situation where a person, institution or the state unjustifiabl interferes with or refrains from positive enforcement of these aims,

[67] Ackermann *Human Dignity* 4; 52. He does not qualify the attribution of human worth by requiring a minimum level of mental capacity. Further it is implicit that sex or gender will not qualify a person's human worth either. Woolman offers a different construction of dignity. See S Woolman 'Dignity' in S Woolman & M Bishop (eds) *Constitutional Law of South Africa* 2 ed (Revised Service 3) 36–6 to 36–19. Working off the Constitutional Court of South Africa's jurisprudence, Woolman identifie fiv definition of dignity. First, every individual is an end in themselves. This means that an individual cannot be treated as a mere instrument towards achieving others' aims or desires. Secondly, dignity can be define as 'equal concern and equal respect'. This definitio houses a negative obligation not to treat a person merely as a means but to also see them as able autonomous agents. Third, dignity can be define as self-actualisation. This definitio follows on from the notion that due to the fact that people have the capacity to create inner meaning they are also entitled to respect for the meaning that they pursue. Fourth, dignity can be define as self-governance. Woolman explains that since we house the capacity to formulate our own ends that give our lives meaning, we should also be entitled to collective decision-making that determines the ends of our community (that is, democratic existence). Finally, Woolman identifie 'collective responsibility for the material conditions for agency' as the fift definitio of dignity. This definitio of dignity recognises collective dignity as being that which brings the community together, and he states that collective dignity can only occur under conditions of mutual recognition of one another's ends in a community unit.

[68] Ackermann *Human Dignity* 86.

[69] They are not merely seeking equality with men in respect of what men may fin suitable parameters of what it might mean to be human. If we were to accept that women only seek equality with men, then we will be left with having to redefin what it means to be human or at least look to see which sex offers the most inclusive definitio of 'human'. This forms a side show and detracts from the issues at hand.

[70] Ackermann *Human Dignity* 25. Ackermann refers to this requirement of human dignity as the '"relationality" aspect of human dignity'. This portion of dignity recognises that certain rights cannot be achieved in isolation and therefore people are required to enter into relationships in order to gain access to these rights and enjoy them. These sorts of rights are called 'associational individual rights'.

they will be infringing on women's human worth and therefore negatively impacting on their experience of equality among others.[71]

Narrowing the focus of equality to the context of reproduction, O'Sullivan states that reproductive freedom is a 'precondition' for the sexual and social equality of women.[72] Reproductive freedom is the freedom for women to decide with whom they would like to procreate and whether or not they would like to become parents, bear children, how many to bear and the preferred spacing between children.[73] Going further, reproductive freedom should be seen to include decisions on how to progress through pregnancy and birth. In reaching these sorts of decisions, reproductive freedom also includes autonomous decision-making in respect of desired methods of contraception, conception and birthing techniques. This construction of reproductive freedom engages the notion that, despite the fact that it is only women who hold the capacity to gestate the unborn and give birth, there is no obligation on them to become parents and therefore reproductive freedom is also the freedom not to reproduce.[74]

Women's biological capacity to procreate functions beyond their intentions concerning whether they would like to be parents or not, and if this capacity is left to run its natural course, sexually involved[75] women of reproductive age could very easily be held in a cyclic state of pregnancy, birth and childrearing.[76] Therefore, it is essential to secure a safe environment in which to make

[71] Under a constitutional regime this type of interference would then require the consideration of whether one is dealing with sex and gender discrimination.

[72] M O'Sullivan 'Reproductive rights' in S Woolman & M Bishop (eds) *Constitutional Law of South Africa* 2 ed (Original Service 2) 37–13.

[73] See the Beijing Declaration and Platform for Action endorsed by the Fourth World Conference on Women (4–15 September 1995) paras 94–7 and United Nations Programme of Action adopted at the International Conference on Population and Development (Cairo, 3–15 September) Chapter Seven.

[74] See generally L Shanner 'Procreation' in AM Jaggar & IM Young (eds) *A Companion to Feminist Philosophy* (2000) 429–35. Shanner explains various feminist positions on reproductive freedom. For instance, liberalists require little intervention in women's reproductive decisions and therefore they argue that termination of pregnancies, genetic diagnosis and selection, gestational services and high-tech fertilisation technologies should be freely available to women on demand. Socialist feminists, however, focus more on restructuring social and cultural institutions to suit women's reproductive lives thereby allowing women to gain economic independence while still engaging in family life if they so choose. They see gestational contracts and marketing of *in vitro* fertilisation as a means of exploiting women, particularly the young and impoverished. Shanner points out that radical feminists understand reproductive freedom as a means to remove women as 'procreative objects' and generally reject any form of outsider intervention. It is necessary to recognise that reproductive freedom can be and has been translated into a number of rights. For instance, see C Albertyn, L Artz, H Combrink et al 'Women's freedom and security of the person' in E Bonthuys & C Albertyn (eds) *Gender, Law and Justice* (2007) 364; O'Sullivan 'Reproductive rights'; and G Douglas *Law, Fertility and Reproduction* (1991) 17–25. Specificall , reproductive freedom is based on the rights to self-determination and bodily integrity. However, O'Sullivan dedicates an entire chapter to explaining how the rights in the South African Bill of Rights give meaning to women's reproductive freedom.

[75] 'Sexually involved' should be seen to include consensual acts of sexual engagement and also non-consensual acts such as rape and coercive sex practices and relations such as forced marriages and sexual slavery.

[76] This obviously depends on the circumstances of the women concerned and whether they are in a position to refuse sexual advances. Albertyn, Artz, Combrink et al ('Women's freedom and security

reproductive decisions concerning sex, contraception, conception, pregnancy continuation and birth in order to remove this vulnerability. The importance of this becomes apparent when one considers the cultural, social and physical implications of bearing and rearing children, because these are disproportionately burdensome for women.[77]

While some women may fin parenthood positively life-definin and rewarding, other women may experience parenthood as perpetuating existing inequalities to varying degrees.[78] At times, the presence of a pregnancy may itself be a manifestation of human rights violations such as in the case of child marriage, rape or coercive sexual relationships. O'Sullivan[79] and MacKinnon[80] explain that the consequences of pregnancy and parenthood can include job loss, being overlooked for promotion, inadequately paid or unpaid maternity leave, lack of affordable or adequate health care and later childcare, and interrupted and sometimes abandoned careers and education.[81] Further, pregnancy, childbirth and rearing children can be physically taxing for women and at times life-threatening.[82] Adding to the encumbrances described here, not all pregnancies are intended or wanted,[83] and if women's reproductive freedom is lacking, those not wanting to continue with a pregnancy would face forced pregnancy and birth experiences and parenthood in cases where adoption is not opted for or is not an option.[84] These issues are increasingly problematic for young girls[85] and

---

of the person' 364) point to this concern, namely that women are 'not equal in choosing to fall pregnant'.

[77] See O'Sullivan 'Reproductive rights' 37–13; MacKinnon *Sex Equality* 1074; and Albertyn, Artz, Combrink et al 'Women's freedom and security of the person' 364.

[78] MacKinnon *Sex Equality* 1074–5.

[79] 'Reproductive rights' 37–13.

[80] *Sex Equality* 1074–5.

[81] Also see E Bonthuys 'Gender and work' in E Bonthuys & C Albertyn (eds) *Gender, Law and Justice* (2007) 170–5; CJ McDonough 'Motherhood and feminism: Lessons from the Titanic' (2006) 8 *Journal of the Association for Research and Mothering* 123; and JC Williams & SL Shames 'Mothers' dreams: Abortion and the high price of motherhood' (2004) 6 *University of Pennsylvania Journal of Constitutional Law* 818.

[82] MacKinnon *Sex Equality* 1076 and RJ Cook & BM Dickens 'The injustice of unsafe motherhood' (2002) 2 *Developing World Bioethics* 64.

[83] Cook & Dickens ((2002) *Developing World Bioethics* 75; 79) provide a number of examples that would explain the phenomenon of unwanted pregnancies. The authors associate unwanted pregnancies with laws and practices that prevent access to reproductive health mechanisms such as contraceptives, elective sterilisation procedures and family planning services. In some instances, oppressive laws make women economically dependent on men which can expose the vulnerabilities of sexual and other forms of violence. Also, women are susceptible to being involved in unsafe sex relationships where they are not in the position to deny sexual advances, demand the use of condoms, or access contraception. Furthermore, inadequate sex and family planning education can lead to increased experiences of unwanted pregnancies.

[84] See generally Cook & Dickens *Developing World Bioethics* 64.

[85] While the focus of this discussion has mainly been on women's experiences, young girls cannot be excluded because most girls reach reproductive age before reaching adulthood. Therefore, reproductive freedom must extend to girls too. Regarding girls' biological vulnerabilities, reproductive health and social support structures in South Africa for young married girls and mothers, see A Skelton 'Girls' social and economic rights in South Africa' in B Goldblatt & KS McLean (eds) *Women's Social and Economic Rights: Developments in South Africa* (2011) 67–75.

women[86] living in poverty, whose social support structures are inadequate or non-existent in terms of health care services, education and childcare facilities.

O'Sullivan understands that pregnancy has the potential to seriously curb women's ability to participate as citizens.[87] In line with that, MacKinnon argues that 'social structures, economic organization, and cultural attitudes do not tend to support most women in being, or being seen as "good mothers" and full citizens too'.[88] Evidently, it is important that women are free to make reproductive decisions, because the cultural, social and physical implications of procreation and the associated experiences are far-reaching and long-lasting.

From the above description of women's unique reproductive experiences, it is clear that reproductive freedom is not an already possessed freedom for all women and girls, but rather a goal that must be achieved.[89] Jackson states that reproductive freedom is not synonymous with unregulated reproduction or the absence of external constraints.[90] In order for women to be able to gain the benefit of reproductive freedom external constraints must be addressed and regulations need to be in place to ensure safe sexual freedom and equitable access to satisfactory reproductive health-care services. A number of institutions bear this responsibility, and include the state and state action in respect of acceptable population control policies, laws pertaining to the realisation of reproductive freedom, rights and health, the health-care industry in the administration of health-care services and family members, friends or wider society in their position to offer personal support to women making reproductive decisions.[91]

With the above in mind, reproductive freedom should be understood as relational in that women cannot act on a reproductive decision without relying on external sources of support.[92] Some examples of the relational underpinnings of reproductive freedom are worthy of consideration. Where a woman decides not to conceive a child, she will need external assistance in order to gain access to birth-control mechanisms or to undergo a sterilization procedure. The relational nature of reproductive freedom holds true even for those women who decide to avoid parenthood through abstinence. Here, it can be argued that a woman relies on others to respect her decision and not force themselves or their desires onto her. Respecting women's freedom to make and live by that decision contributes to their enjoyment of reproductive freedom. Another example is the case where a woman seeks to legally terminate an unwanted pregnancy; this end result cannot be

---

[86] Williams & Shames (2004) *University of Pennsylvania Journal of Constitutional Law* 827–29 and Cook & Dickens *Developing World Bioethics* 64.

[87] 'Reproductive rights' 37–14.

[88] *Sex Equality* 1075.

[89] E Jackson *Regulating Reproduction: Law, Technology and Autonomy* (2001) 318.

[90] Jackson *Regulating Reproduction* 318.

[91] See O'Sullivan 'Reproductive rights' 37–12 to 37–13; 37–23 to 37–24. Also see Jackson (*Regulating Reproduction* 11–160) who in her three chapters on birth control, termination of pregnancy and pregnancy and childbirth goes into pronounced detail on how the various identifie institutions play off one another in the context of either assisting women to realise their reproductive aims or act as inhibitors to realising their decided reproductive path.

[92] Jackson *Regulating Reproduction* 115.

achieved by her acting on her own and she needs the assistance of a regulated system that secures access to safe termination-of-pregnancy services and health-care professionals to perform the procedure. Further, the relational underpinnings of reproductive freedom are also present in cases in which women plan to continue with their pregnancies. They will need prenatal and postnatal care, assistance during birth and social support during maternity leave.

It is the relational nature of reproductive freedom that contributes to the development of an adversarial pregnancy environment, which fosters the potential for tensions to arise during pregnancy. This is especially so when women rely on third parties who are drawn to realising foetal interests in continued existence rather than securing pregnant women's equality. Relevant relationships include those where third parties (being the state, the medical profession and the judiciary) engage with pregnant women and attempt to derail their self-define direction solely for positive foetal-related outcomes and not for purposes of advancing women's sense and experience of equality in human worth. Examples of this playing out include restrictive termination-of-pregnancy laws and the use of coercive legal interventions to secure 'proper' management of pregnancies that ensures optimal foetal development and positive foetal outcomes. These sorts of interventions infringe on women's equality both during and after a pregnancy. They impact on their equality during pregnancy, because third-party intervention may go against how some women plan to experience their pregnancies and possible births, and directly remove pregnant women as able, autonomous decision-makers. Further, women's experience of equality will also be impeded after birth in cases where there are restrictive termination-of-pregnancy laws because pregnancy will be forced, thus resulting in unwanted parenthood and all the above-described social and cultural consequences. Ultimately, women are treated as a means to an end, which is to secure desired foetal outcomes in spite of women's chosen ends, thereby devaluing them as human beings and intruding on their sense and experience of dignity or human worth which results in unequal human existence.

This discussion demonstrates that female reproductive freedom, as a fundamental precursor for sexual and social equality, is not primarily concerned with foetal interests as an individual concern.[93] Rather, reproductive freedom concerns women's interests in the broader context of self-actualisation and assists in achieving desired ends that characteristically move beyond a purely procreative position. However, the relational foundation of reproductive freedom may place some women in a vulnerable position whereby they rely on third-party support systems whose intentions are not aligned with women's rights but rather with foetal interests. Therefore, women's drive for reproductive freedom backed by feminism's calls for equality can be seen to contribute to developing pregnancy

[93] Manninen explains that at the start, feminism was primarily concerned with detaching women from the unborn since reproduction was one of the primary sources of women's subordination. However, feminism is slowly adjusting its position on the unborn but this is more of a contemporary occurrence and still not a very popular position. See BA Manninen 'The value of choice and the choice to value: Explaining the discussion about fetal life within prochoice advocacy' (2013) 28 *Hypatia* 663.

adversarialism, but only in so far as a woman's ends are not aligned with third-parties' ends.

3.4 UNVEILING PRENATAL LIFE

Lupton, writing on the social worlds of the unborn, points out that as the women's movement came to the fore, so did the 'foetal citizen', through foetal identity and individuation.[94] Through the use of technology, pregnant women's bodies have been 'opened up' enabling one to gain visual access to the unborn, track its growth and development, and even offer direct therapeutic services. These developments are seen as indisputable evidence of biological life, albeit unborn non-legal life. Visual aids like ultrasonography and foetal medicine identify prenatal life and individuate it from the living condition of pregnant women's bodies and lives.

Duden explains that the unborn 'we live with today were firs conceived not in the womb but in visualizing technologies'.[95] Prior to technological contributions in medicine, during the 300 years prior to the firs depiction of 'fetuses without mothers' in 1799, the unborn were represented as fully grown miniature persons dancing in pregnant women's uteruses, presenting the 'child hoped for'.[96] Pregnancy was understood as a female-based bodily experience.[97] Thus, getting to 'know' the unborn was based on fairly rudimentary processes in comparison with the amenities of today's medical practices.[98] Most information obtained on the

[94] D Lupton *The Social Worlds of the Unborn* (2013) 105.

[95] B Duden 'The fetus on the "farther shore": Toward a history of the unborn' in LM Morgan & MW Michaels (eds) *Fetal Subjects, Feminist Positions* (1999) 16.

[96] Duden 'The fetus on the "farther shore"' 18–19. A Frankfurt physician, Dr Soemmerring, was the firs to present the representations of the unborn as entities progressing through gradual development. However, Duden (23) explains that his method of representing the unborn was such that the images were not real representations but rather a blueprint for the 'evolution of general fetal development'. Thus, the representations do not have an umbilical cord, or any biological connections to the pregnant woman and appear out of context. According to Duden, this representation casts the unborn in a space that makes them untouchable, a form of 'disconnected visibility' yet their lifelike representations suggest a very real closeness. Duden (23–4) argues that it is Soemmerring's depictions of the unborn that led to the notion that the foetus we know today is the product of mechanically produced records (biomedical measurements) rather than the bodily experience of pregnancy. A 'disembodied' or acontextual foetus comes to the fore again in the late 1900s; this is discussed below.

[97] Duden 'The fetus on the "farther shore"' 20. A pregnancy was only ever 'confirmed by a woman's experience of quickening, being the time when a woman firs feels the unborn stir in her uterus. Even in this case, the unborn was not considered a 'child' but rather a 'child-to-be'. If there was premature delivery, the product of conception was not considered a child but rather a 'mole', 'Mooncalf', or a 'misshapen thing'; see Duden 'The fetus on the "farther shore"' 20.

[98] A Oakley *The Captured Womb: A History of the Medical Care of Pregnant Women* (1986) 25. Oakley states that the firs foetal heartbeat was accidentally heard in 1818 when a physician was attempting to listen for foetal movements through a woman's corset. In the 1800s and early 1900s, abdominal palpitation was the only method available that could assist in determining the position of the foetus for the purposes of labour. Internal examinations and examination of vaginal discharge also assisted in determining the onset of early pregnancy. In 1928, after the discovery of pregnancy hormones, the firs urine pregnancy test was performed. While these elementary practices (some more than others) had various advantages, none of them provided information about the condition of developmental life within the uterus. See Oakley *The Captured Womb* 25; 26–7; 96; 155.

unborn was collected from experiments on miscarried or aborted foetuses.[99] However, when it came to understanding how the unborn existed and 'lived' within women's bodies, the medical profession had very little to go by and had to rely on the descriptions provided by pregnant women. Physicians' knowledge could only go as far as pregnant women were able to describe and articulate their experiences and essentially physicians could only observe from the outside.[100] Aside from the hazardous practice of x-raying pregnant women,[101] it was only in the late 1940s that ultrasonography was introduced into antenatal care.[102] After a series of mechanical refinement and developing two-dimensional foetal images (as opposed to early one-dimensional images), having an ultrasound became routine practice at some clinics in the United Kingdom.[103]

Oakley states that ultrasonography gave third parties 'real-time' scans which showed 'life' in the uterus, the real activity behind women's abdominal walls.[104] New information came to light which included the observation of foetal breathing motions, eye movements, and foetal hiccups, and physicians also discovered that the unborn empty their bladders a certain number of times per day.[105] Further, ultrasonography enabled physicians to determine what could be considered normal growth patterns and facilitated the identificatio of a number of different congenital abnormalities.[106] Ultrasonography made it possible for third parties to have direct access to the unborn and opened up the opportunity to gather detailed information about the unborn prior to birth.[107] Then, terms such as 'fetal patienthood' and foetal 'personality' began to permeate the discussion of pregnancy.[108]

---

[99] Jackson *Regulating Reproduction* 126 and Lupton *Social Worlds of the Unborn* 4. Further, Lupton points out that the vast majority did not have access to newly discovered information.

[100] Oakley *The Captured Womb* 155.

[101] Getting actual visuals of the unborn inside the uterus originally took place in 1896 through the use of x-rays. In this instance an x-ray was performed on a pregnant woman, who at the time had miscarried but had not yet expelled the foetus. In 1899 the firs living foetus was x-rayed and by 1910, x-rays were considered a medical norm in antenatal care in certain areas of the United Kingdom. While this practice assisted with detecting certain pregnancy complications and foetal abnormalities, it eventually became apparent that there were serious risks associated with the practice and it was discontinued. See Oakley *The Captured Womb* 28; 98; 100; 102; 105.

[102] Oakley *The Captured Womb* 157.

[103] Oakley *The Captured Womb* 146.

[104] Oakley *The Captured Womb* 156.

[105] Oakley *The Captured Womb* 167.

[106] Oakley *The Captured Womb* 167–8. Oakley (171–4) points out that other methods of foetal visualisation were developed, such as fetoscopy and amnioscopy whereby an endoscope (optical instrument) is inserted directly into the amniotic cavity in order to view the unborn directly. More recently, embryoscopy has made its way into clinical practice and this enables one to view a four-week embryo; see Jackson *Regulating Reproduction* 127.

[107] Oakley *The Captured Womb* 155.

[108] Oakley *The Captured Womb* 155; 189 and Lupton *Social Worlds of the Unborn* 3. Jackson (*Regulating Reproduction* 129) rightly points out that the terms 'fetal patienthood' and the more contemporary term, 'fetal medicine' pose a problem since they are not morally neutral descriptions of clinical practice. She explains that these terms draw attention away from pregnant women and their rights as patients themselves. The terms tend to side line women's right to refuse treatment as patients, thus preventing the physician from treating the unborn as a patient or practising foetal medicine.

These gradual obstetric developments created an authoritative space for obstetricians to claim a knowledge superior to that of the pregnant women themselves in terms of their bodily experiences of pregnancy.[109] Ultrasonography enabled the medical profession to 'dispense with mothers as intermediaries, as necessary informants on fetal status and life-style'.[110] It should be noted that these developments do not take place in a vacuum; they are founded on a history of female subordination, increased surveillance of pregnant women, active appropriation of women's reproductive health-care knowledge, and increasing secular and religious interest in the unborn.

There is a very clear, steady move from identifying the unborn towards individuating them as having separate living needs from those of the women carrying them. Roth argues that the firs sign of 'separating'[111] the foetus from the pregnant woman was found in 1941 (during the hype of x-raying and scanning pregnant women), when a doctor justifie preventing natural birth on the grounds of 'fetal distress' rather than referring to the conditions that originated with the pregnant woman herself.[112] However, Shorter looks earlier than that and suggests that from 1901 'fetal indications' were beginning to be accepted for the purposes of obstetric intervention during birth.[113] After examining a number of medical texts, he notes that, from around the 1930s, shaving pubic hair, birthing positions, routine episiotomies, the use of forceps and caesarean deliveries were all increasingly justifie for the purposes of securing positive foetal outcomes.[114] Shorter argues that this meant that obstetricians were prepared to intervene in the birthing process, despite the fact that the pregnant woman concerned was not in a compromised position.[115]

Further, stemming from the initial visuals of the unborn, increasingly refine technological developments in medicine also enabled foetal monitoring and surgery, which tends to emphasise the foetus as a patient in need of individualised

---

[109] Oakley *The Captured Womb* 98.

[110] Oakley *The Captured Womb* 155.

[111] The process of separation should be interpreted as an indication that people are acting on the new found identity of the unborn.

[112] R Roth *Making Women Pay: The Hidden Costs of Fetal Rights* (2000) 33. In this respect Roth refers to the work of WR Arney *Power and the Profession of Obstetrics* (1982).

[113] E Shorter *A History of Women's Bodies* (1984) 166. Jackson (*Regulating Reproduction* 128) confirm that this trend continues to persist, stating that the yardstick for successful obstetric practice is foetal health and wellbeing; consequently medical textbooks are increasingly devoted to treating the unborn, and less dedicated to the care of pregnant women.

[114] Shorter *A History of Women's Bodies* 164–76. In this respect women were expected to be clean-shaven in order to secure a sanitised birthing area (167) and women were expected to deliver on their backs in order for the attending physician to have sufficient access to the uterus to accurately monitor foetal heart rates (169). Episiotomies were routinely performed in order to 'spare the child a prolonged expulsive stage of labour' (172). Assisted deliveries in terms of forceps and caesarean-section deliveries also increased for purposes of ensuring healthy foetal outcomes (174–5). On the topic of forceps delivery Shorter (174) quotes the proceedings at a White House Conference in 1933: 'Until comparatively recently forceps were used infrequently and then only when the mother was unable to deliver herself, fetal indications were not recognized.'

[115] Shorter *A History of Women's Bodies* 166; 176. Rather dramatically, Shorter interprets this as meaning that medicine has 'stanched from women's hands whatever hopes of autonomy and control' they wished for.

medical attention.[116] Casper states that once ultrasonography had been integrated into obstetric care, clinical attention turned to foetal surgery.[117] This is because ultrasonography revealed a range of structural problems, thus creating the need for a surgical solution to remedy identifie foetus-related complications.[118]

Also, in earlier writings[119] it was argued that advancements in medical technology were continually improving its ability to ensure the survivability of a premature foetus earlier in gestation, thus giving the *impression* that the limit of foetal viability[120] was being pushed back to earlier points in gestation.[121] However, it should be noted that no matter how far medicine develops, the benefit of technology are limited in cases where the unborn is too underdeveloped to sustain life.[122] Nevertheless, the position of increased survival rates of premature neonates also feeds the view of 'foetal patienthood', since doctors are cited as arguing that, if a 23-week-gestated neonate can be successfully treated after birth, then a foetus of the same gestational age deserves care too.[123] Jackson states:

> [G]iven the increasing range of technological innovations that allow the fetus to be seen, monitored, diagnosed and treated while still *in utero*, it is probably unsurprising

[116] Jackson (*Regulating Reproduction* 127) explains that if any anomalies are detected in a foetus, it can now receive treatment while still in a woman's uterus. She states that blood transfusions can be performed via the umbilical cord. In some cases, the foetus can be removed from the uterus, operated on, and then returned to the uterus for later birth (127 fn 66). Also see BM Dickens & RJ Cook 'Legal and ethical issues in fetal surgery' (2011) 115 *International Journal of Gynecology & Obstetrics* 80.

[117] MJ Casper 'Operation to the rescue: Feminist encounters with fetal surgery' in LM Morgan & MW Michaels (eds) *Fetal Subjects, Feminist Positions* (1999) 106.

[118] Casper 'Operation to the rescue' 106.

[119] For instance, see S McLean 'Women, rights and reproduction' in S McLean (ed) *Legal Issues in Human Reproduction* (1989) 219.

[120] Foetal viability refers to the point in foetal development where a foetus will be capable of independent survival if it were to be delivered. In this respect gestational age, organ development, sex and attending health-care facilities all contribute to the survivability of the foetus. For a detailed definitio of clinical foetal viability see C Pickles 'Personhood: Proving the significanc of the born-alive rule with reference to medical knowledge of foetal viability' (2013) 24 *Stell LR* 146 155–60.

[121] It has come to light that the viability line is not pushed back but rather there is an increased incidence of survival for those neonates born at the point of viability. See J Sarkin-Hughes 'A perspective on abortion legislation in South Africa's Bill of Rights era' (1993) 56 *THRHR* 83 89.

[122] See EJ Lee 'The abortion debate today' in K Horsey & H Biggs (eds) *Human Fertilisation and Embryology: Reproducing Regulation* (2007) 288 and Sarkin-Hughes (1993) *THRHR* 89. These authors explain that without sufficient development (representing an 'anatomical threshold') extremely premature neonates will not be able to survive because their bodies will be too underdeveloped to sustain basic life. For more on the limiting role of viability in a clinical setting see Pickles (2013) *Stell LR* 146; TL Powell, L Parker, CF Dedrick et al 'Decisions and dilemmas related to resuscitation of infants born on the verge of viability' (2012) *Newborn and Infant Nursing Reviews* 27; BH Arzuaga & BH Lee 'Limits of human viability in the United States: A medicolegal review' (2011) 128 *Pediatrics* 1047; and I Seri & J Evans 'Limits of viability: Definitio of the grey zone' (2008) 28 *Journal of Perinatology* S4.

[123] Jackson *Regulating Reproduction* 128.

that some doctors consider birth to be an arbitrary point at which to recognise the fetus as a patient in its own right.[124]

Thus, as technology improves, it moves from foetal identificatio towards fortifying individuation by third parties in the medical field However, the process of identifying and individuating the unborn is not only found in the context of the medical treatment of pregnant women. As technology advances, its finding become more accessible to the public and thus attract wider public attention. In this respect, access to the unborn is no longer limited to attending physicians but expands to include other members of the public. Michaels and Morgan state that, as the unborn move into the public arena, the notion of 'foetal personhood' enters the public sphere.[125] Lupton argues that this process has led to 'infantilising of the unborn'.[126]

According to Palmer the introduction of three- and four-dimensional ultrasonography scans is the cause of increased third-party foetal visibility beyond the clinical setting.[127] This is owing to the fact that three- and four-dimensional ultrasound scans are far clearer, and one no longer needs a medically trained eye to interpret the image, as is required for two-dimensional images.[128] These images present a clear picture, in real time, of the unborn engaging in human behaviour, which elicits a sense of familiarity on the part of the viewer.[129] To the untrained eye, these multi-dimensional scans are also perceived to portray foetal consciousness with regard to reactions to stimuli and detailed facial expressions.[130] That is,

[124] Jackson *Regulating Reproduction* 127. This proves particularly problematic for pregnant women because, as Lupton (*Social Worlds of the Unborn* 22) points out: 'Once a foetus becomes designated as a "patient", the maternal body in which it is developing tends to be viewed as an "environment" or even an "incubator" for the nourishment and protection of the unborn.' This may very well lead the sidelining of women's wellbeing and health since the unborn will be the primary focus of the medical attention.

[125] MW Michaels & LM Morgan 'Introduction: The fetal imperative' in LM Morgan & MW Michaels (eds) *Fetal Subjects, Feminist Positions* (1999) 2–3.

[126] Lupton *Social Worlds of the Unborn* 3.

[127] J Palmer 'Seeing and knowing: Ultrasound images in the contemporary abortion debate' (2009) 10 *Feminist Theory* 173 177. Palmer (175) explains that three-dimensional scans are a series of two-dimensional scans recorded and reconstructed into three-dimensional data based on geometric information gathered through the two-dimensional scan process. Four-dimensional scans are really just updating these scans at short intervals to create the impression of movement. Interestingly, Palmer (175) points out that three- and four-dimensional scans are not frequently used for clinical purposes because the technology used to obtain two-dimensional scans is of a superior quality for purposes of obtaining clinical data. Lee explains that these scans do not offer any additional information about foetal development and thus have limited value in a clinical context; see Lee 'The abortion debate today' 238. Lupton (*Social Worlds of the Unborn* 4) describes the scans as being used for purposes of prenatal bonding.

[128] Palmer (2009) *Feminist Theory* 175.

[129] Palmer (2009) *Feminist Theory* 175.

[130] Palmer (2009) *Feminist Theory* 184–5. Palmer (185) points out that, in medicine, reactions to stimuli and facial movements are reflexe rather than conscious movements or expressions of emotions. Also see Lee 'The abortion debate today' 238–9, in which Lee puts forward the same argument. This shows that ultrasound images tend to undergo cultural interpretations that are at odds with medical practice and knowledge. More about the ability to feel pain or express emotion will be discussed below when considering the interest approach to valuing foetal life.

the scans are used to argue that the unborn feel pain and, as they have been recorded 'smiling', they must also be consciously experiencing happiness.[131]

As a result of removing the need for clinical interpretation of the image, these images have moved into the public domain via newspapers, television broadcasts and advertisements, pregnancy books and magazines, and documentaries, and have begun to play a role in the wider debates concerning reproductive rights.[132] More often than not, these images are presented a contextually and detached from the social and political contexts of pregnancy.[133] The unborn are presented as floatin in space, which suggests the 'disembodied subjectivity' of the unborn, or a form of 'foetal autonomy'.[134] Lupton also explains that the maternal 'nine-month-long work' and the 'interembodied' nature of gestation have disappeared and the extent of maternal erasure has even gone so far as to exclude women from representations of the birthing process.[135] Additionally, increased media coverage of foetal surgery, presented as 'rescue operations', embeds in the public's mind the notion that the unborn are separate patients in need of individualised medical attention.[136]

Lupton understands the development the foetal citizen as a contributor towards an environment characterised by adversarialism.[137] While technology gives third parties access to pregnancies, Roth argues that it is not technology itself that creates an adversarial pregnancy environment but rather the social and political relations of technology.[138] She stresses that scans do not speak for themselves, but have to be interpreted by the viewer: '[T]echnology alone does not tell a story.'[139] Roth's cautionary note rings true when one considers Palmer's discussion of how foetal reflexe in response to stimuli have numerous interpretations, depending on who is interpreting, their context and underlying motives. For instance, non-medical individuals understand those reflexe to be an indication of the experience of pain and emotions, while medically trained individuals understand those reflexe to be part of a complex neurological system but still involuntary and

[131] Palmer (2009) *Feminist Theory* 184–5.

[132] Palmer (2009) *Feminist Theory* 175. For instance, Lupton (*Social Worlds of the Unborn* 47–8) shows how these technologies informed the pro-life stance against termination of pregnancies and how they used this technology to advocate for law reform.

[133] Lupton *Social Worlds of the Unborn* 40 and Palmer (2009) *Feminist Theory* 176–7.

[134] Palmer (2009) *Feminist Theory* 176–7 and Roth *Making Women Pay* 33. Palmer (177) notes that some feminists have questioned the presentation of these images as 'reality' since the images do not include the pregnant woman's body. They have called on viewers to be critical of the 'reality' these images are perceived to represent and argue that more attention should be given to who produces the images and who sees the images. This is an important task because 'ways of seeing are recognised as socially embedded'. Also see Lee 'The abortion debate today' 288, who shares the same view.

[135] Lupton *Social Worlds of the Unborn* 40.

[136] Casper 'Operation to the rescue' 107. Casper explains that while pregnant women generally, out of the need to secure healthy birth outcomes, accept foetal surgery, maternal health is sidelined for the benefi of the unborn. This is also clear when one considers the history of the development of foetal surgery, where fatality risks were so high but physicians pushed through because the positive foetal outcomes urged them on. In this respect, see Casper 'Operation to the rescue' 106–7.

[137] Lupton *Social Worlds of the Unborn* 105.

[138] Roth *Making Women Pay* 32. For instance, in the United States politics revolving around women and reproduction has led to foetal-rights sympathisers using advances in medical technology to justify their calls to extend full legal status to the unborn.

[139] Roth *Making Women Pay* 33.

without any conscious appreciation.[140] One interpretation is driven by the underlying social construction of 'child' and emotional reactions to what is seen (developing moving foetus), while the other is influence by a 'scientifi approach' in the context of the uncertain.[141] Regardless, both views tend to focus on the individuality of the foetus.

Michaels and Morgan state that currently foetal representations 'converge with prevailing norms about the nature of subjectivity and personhood . . . fetuses are sexed, named, "photographed," surgically altered, spoken to and about, and even speak themselves, Hollywood style'.[142] Roth argues that as interpretations continue to provide the unborn independent status, women begin to be erased as important social beings.[143] An adversarial pregnancy environment will certainly come to the forefront when the process of assigning independent subjecthood to the unborn takes place in an active women's-rights arena.

3.5 'SPECIAL STATUS' OF THE UNBORN

These technological advancements have allowed the public to biologically and socially 'know' the unborn and thus have fuelled the development of a number of theories on prenatal life and where the value of such life lies. Theories that have been developed on the foundation of medical science are presented as objectively legitimate, since they stem from scientifi technological advancements and observations that provide universally applicable evidence of 'life' before birth and proof of the humanness of the unborn.[144] These theories are then used to question the appropriateness of the law in so far as it does not protect the 'person' that a foetus has come to represent.

Tooley points out that, beyond law, the term 'personhood' can be interpreted in a number of ways.[145] Personhood can either denote a purely biological connection to the human species, or it can indicate a type of 'mental life'[146] found in adult

[140] Palmer (2009) *Feminist Theory* 184–5.

[141] Palmer (2009) *Feminist Theory* 182–5. Here Palmer (182) is considering a debate that took place on a parliamentary level, about whether four-dimensional ultrasound scans should be used as evidence of foetal consciousness in the context of termination of pregnancies. It was found by the committee that the scans are not helpful with respect to understanding the scientifi neurobiological development of the unborn. In one of the public comments (183), a participant called on the panel to view the unborn as a developing child from as early as 18 weeks' gestation, and he based this call on the evidence of what was seen via four-dimensional scans. The panel (183–4) agreed that what was viewed was memorable and elicited emotions but went on to separate scientifi knowledge about pregnancy and emotion, and made their decision from a scientifi position.

[142] Michaels & Morgan 'Introduction: The fetal imperative' 6.

[143] Roth *Making Women Pay* 34.

[144] This is opposed to the theories found in early history based on somewhat flawe observations, divine principles, or myths, none of which could be tested or disproved without adequate access to technology and advanced knowledge systems. See Casper 'Operation to the rescue' 105; Palmer (2009) *Feminist Theory* 177; and Lupton *Social Worlds of the Unborn* 2.

[145] M Tooley 'Personhood' in H Kuhse & P Singer (eds) *A Companion to Bioethics* (2001) 117.

[146] See J Harris *The Value of Life: An Introduction to Medical Ethics* (1985) 14–9 for an example of definin personhood in relation to mental capacities. For a recent example of the implications of adopting this approach, see A Giubilini & F Minerva 'After-birth abortion: Why should the baby live?' (2013) 39 *Journal of Medical Ethics* 261.

human beings. He emphasises that it is important from an ethical perspective to determine what a person[147] is, because the designation of 'personhood' demands moral status, making it morally and possibly legally wrong to destroy it or interfere with its proper development.[148] The position in respect of law, particularly South African law, is that prior to birth the unborn lacks personhood, even though it is part of the human species. Once born, the newborn is a person and is vested with legal subjectivity and rights as a person, regardless of its ability to act rationally, be self-aware or display any other form of 'mental life'.[149]

The above legal description of personhood does not clarify why it can be ethically wrong to terminate late pregnancies or experiment with biological products linked to human reproduction. Science has visibly demonstrated unborn life and their medical and social individuality, but now one is left to determine what should be done with prenatal life. In this respect, a number of theories attempt to explain why we should value prenatal life in some instances, but shy away from valuing it in other situations. According to Ford, this process of valuing[150] and/or devaluing[151] prenatal life is really a process of assigning 'special status' to the unborn.[152] Here 'special status' refers to the fact that although the unborn are not assigned the legal status of personhood, they still represent something that holds distinctive and intrinsic value and are worthy of our consideration or even protection.[153]

It must be noted that some of the theories considered here and the manner in which they are used to justify special status are not the only ways these theories can be, or have been adopted. For instance, Boonin discusses some of the same theories as they have been applied by 'abortion critics' to extend the right to life to the unborn at varying stages of development.[154] Boonin's work demonstrates that numerous theories can be stretched in an attempt to extend the right to life to the unborn. While Boonin goes into great detail to convincingly discredit these theories as an 'abortion defender', he does not consider the theories in a more nuanced fashion and his conclusions all seem to end with demonstrating how the right to life cannot be justifiabl extended to the unborn. His approach does not

[147] As opposed to non-humans such as animals, machines or a simple group of cells; see Harris *The Value of Life* 14.

[148] Tooley 'Personhood' 117.

[149] T Boezaart 'Child law, the child and South African private law' in T Boezaart (ed) *Child Law in South Africa* (2009) 4–5.

[150] Here, 'value' indicates a demand for a certain measure of respect close or equal to that demanded by personhood.

[151] Being something 'less' than personhood.

[152] M Ford 'Nothing and not-nothing: Law's ambivalent response to transformation and transgression at the beginning of life' in SW Smith & R Deazley (eds) *The Legal, Medical and Cultural Regulation of the Body: Transformation and Transgression* (2009) 22.

[153] Ford 'Nothing and not-nothing' 22. Here, the moral status of the unborn can be seen to inform law's granting of special status to the unborn. Steinbock explains the difference between 'moral standing' and 'moral status'; see B Steinbock *Life before Birth: The Moral and Legal Status of Embryos and Fetuses* 2 ed (2011) 1. 'Moral standing' indicates to us whether a particular entity's interests or existence counts, and 'moral status' tells us *how much* its interests or existence counts.

[154] D Boonin *A Defense of Abortion* (2003) 19–132.

extract any further uses for these theories.[155] A particular theory seems to 'stand or fall' by its ability to extend the right to life to the unborn. Conversely, in this chapter, these theories are used in a more balanced fashion, namely, to show that, although the unborn are not vested with full status, they are still accorded special status. Understanding these theories as conferring special status on the unborn, specifi attention is given to the grounds used to limit the value of prenatal life so as to avoid merely extending legal subjectivity to the unborn.

3.5.1 Potentiality

Potentiality is grounded on the premise that because an entity has the potential to become something more complete and meaningful, it is worthy of respect or assigned special status.[156] Applying this approach, the unborn is valued as a developing human being, since it holds the potential (complete genetic make-up) to become a unique individual human being with full moral status, or a complete and independent person.[157]

Ford raises a number of criticisms against this method of conferring special status on the unborn. First, she states that not all unborn actually hold the potential to become persons, as some have severe deformities and may not survive until birth.[158] Secondly, she cautions that not only the unborn hold the potential to become fully fledge persons, because the potential can also be found in sex gametes, requiring special status to be conferred on those entities too.[159] Thirdly, Ford succinctly states:[160]

> In our dealings with entities in the here-and-now, it could be argued, we should accord them the status appropriate to what they currently are, rather than to what they may one day be. We should focus, for example, on the appropriate way to value the embryo/foetus as an *actual embryo/foetus*, rather than a potential something else. (Emphasis in the original.)

In this respect, Ford points out that we are merely valuing a human characteristic that the unborn does not actually have, and the author find this a

[155] The portion of Boonin's work that discredits these theories projects a sense of an 'all or nothing' situation which does not help develop an understanding of why unborn life is sometimes protected, while other times it is not.

[156] Ford 'Nothing and not-nothing' 24.

[157] Ford 'Nothing and not-nothing' 24; M Warren 'Abortion' in H Kuhse & P Singer (eds) *A Companion to Bioethics* (2001) 127 131; R Hursthouse *Beginning Lives* (1987) 72; and Harris *The Value of Life* 11. Megone offers a different approach to potentiality; see generally C Megone 'Potentiality and persons: An Aristotelian perspective' in MG Kuczewski & R Polansky (eds) *Bioethics: Ancient Themes in Contemporary Issues* (2002) 155.

[158] Ford 'Nothing and not-nothing' 24–5.

[159] Ford 'Nothing and not-nothing' 24–5. Ford relies on Harris's work; see Harris *The Value of Life* 11–12. However, Ford does acknowledge that there have been some qualifying restraints applied to potentiality arguments, for instance, the argument that potential is limited to those entities that can, in their natural state, develop into humans. This qualificatio will exclude individual ovum and sperm from being afforded special status since in their natural state (without fusion) they cannot develop into a human being.

[160] Ford 'Nothing and not-nothing' 25.

little perplexing.[161] Dworkin is a critic too, as he rejects the notion of 'future possibilities' and offers a 'frustration thesis' instead.[162] Dworkin views unborn life as a continuing process, which is of worth because there is a certain degree of 'natural investment' in that developmental process, meaning that, as unborn life continues to develop, there is increased investment in its natural progression through 'life'.[163] Consequently, as foetal development continues, it makes any loss of life increasingly significan owing to increased natural investment.[164] That is, through the premature loss of prenatal life, we have frustrated certain investments in a particular life's journey.[165]

3.5.2 Human dignity and species membership

Tooley states that some authors have rejected the notions that potentiality or personhood are grounds for valuing the unborn; rather, some have suggested that, since the unborn belongs to the human species it arguably deserves special status.[166] Here, speciesism and human dignity (denoting human worth) are relevant.

Retired Constitutional Court Justice Ackermann understands dignity as expressing inherent human worth; in fact, human dignity is presented as being synonymous with human worth.[167] Ackermann stresses that by the mere fact of being part and parcel of humanity, our worth is demanded, and he states:[168]

---

[161] Ford 'Nothing and not-nothing' 25. Additionally, Ford (25; 27), relying on Hursthouse, points out that this approach holds very little value in terms of practical application, especially since Hursthouse (*Beginning Life* 73) emphasises that the potentiality argument can either be applied very conservatively or liberally. In this respect Hursthouse (73) explains that the potential seen in unborn life can be ranked very low (moving away from humanness) by liberalists or it can be ranked very high (moving closer towards humanness) by conservatives. Consequently, Ford (25; 27) argues that this approach is weakened, since its application depends on whatever normative context the holder's foregoing ethical outlooks are. Warren ('Abortion' 131) refers to a fittin example: 'It is true that potential human beings are often highly valued, particularly by persons who wish to have children. If a pregnancy is wanted, then the fetus will be valued for its human potential. But if the pregnancy is unwanted or medically dangerous, or the fetus is found to be severely abnormal, then its value as a potential human being may be outweighed by the needs of actual human beings.' Lupton's work in *Social Worlds of the Unborn* also alludes to the same issues.

[162] RM Dworkin *Life's Dominion: An Argument about Abortion, Euthanasia, and Individual Freedom* (1993) 87; 89. In the context of loss of life, he states that the loss is not sad because of what can or may happen in the future, but rather what has already happened: it 'frustrates' the redemption or realisation of natural and human investments made in terms of that life.

[163] Dworkin *Life's Dominion* 87–9.

[164] Dworkin *Life's Dominion* 87–9. Dworkin (88) explains that the depth of feelings of loss (or frustration) is determined by the stage of life when that life is lost because 'frustration is greater if it takes place after rather than before the person has made a significan personal investment in his [or her] own life, and less if it occurs after any investment has been substantially fulfilled'

[165] This approach also find application under 'interest theory', namely that prenatal life is valued because the unborn has an interest (investment) in its own natural progression towards a journey through life. This denotes a process of natural investment within its own biological development.

[166] Tooley 'Personhood' 123.

[167] Ackermann *Human Dignity* 4. Ackermann points out that 'worth' connotes infinit and is something that cannot be qualifie with a pricetag or replaced by something else. Further, he (52) asserts the 'human worth' is the secular flipsid to the religious position that individuals are created in the image of God.

[168] Ackermann *Human Dignity* 51. Also see Ford 'Nothing and not-nothing' 29.

> The dignity accruing to any person does not depend on the fact that this person is able to exercise a particular degree of reason or *any reason at all*. All that is required is membership of the human species. In order to protect the dignity of all members of the species, it is necessary that protection be given (not necessarily absolute protection) in certain circumstances to a member even before birth and even after death. (Emphasis in the original.)

Ackermann acknowledges that he is advancing a 'species argument', and goes on to explain that absolute worth extends to the individual within the species and to the entire species of that individual.[169] In this respect, he asserts that the act of conception (despite the intention of individuals participating in sexual relations) can inevitably lead to the production of a member of a species and, through that process, the products of conception join in on the worth of the species.[170] This value accrues to the unborn, regardless of whether it develops as a perfect specimen of our species; thus his construction of human worth also includes those with the 'barest minimum of intellect and emotion'.[171] Despite emphasising the inherent value of unborn members of our species, Ackermann qualifie this value by stating: 'I would also argue that *certain aspects* of human dignity pre-date birth and survive death.'[172] (Emphasis added.)

Considering Ackermann's quoted work mentioned above (former and latter), one can extract two (albeit vague) limiting factors to the inherent worth in the context of the unborn. First, *certain circumstances* will determine whether the protection of dignity will extend to the unborn. Secondly, only *certain aspects* of human dignity exist prior to birth. Ackermann does not indicate what the 'certain circumstances' may be, nor does he clarify what those 'certain aspects' are.[173] Rather, he places this issue in the hands of the 'interpreter of the Constitution',

[169] Ackermann *Human Dignity* 52.

[170] Ackermann *Human Dignity* 52.

[171] Ackermann *Human Dignity* 52. Also see Dworkin *Life's Dominion* 70, whose position falls in line with Ackermann's approach.

[172] Ackermann *Human Dignity* 52. Ackermann's assertions correlate with Dworkin's earlier work on the intrinsic worth of the unborn. Dworkin (*Life's Dominion* 71–4) states that something's intrinsic value exists independently, beyond what others enjoy, want, or need. In respect of that value, we fin the need to protect it because it is important within itself and not merely because others fin value through their enjoyment of it. In the context of human life, Dworkin states that human life is inviolable (or sacred) and the hallmark feature of this characteristic is the fact that it is intrinsically inviolable because it exists. In its existence, it represents human life and once human life has begun it should flouris rather than be destroyed. Here, destruction can be seen as an act of dishonour, since human life demands honour.

[173] However, something that may indicate 'certain aspects' can be ascertainable from Ackermann's (23–4) suggested meaning of human worth:

> '*[T]he human worth (dignity) of each and every person is the capacity for and the right to respect as a human being. This arises from all those aspects of the human personality that flow from human intellectual and moral capacity; which in turn separate humans from the impersonality of nature, enables them to exercise their own judgment, to have self-awareness and a sense of self-worth, to exercise self-determination, to shape themselves and nature, to develop their personalities and to strive for self-fulfilment in their lives. It also derives from the capacity of human beings to enter into meaningful relationships with others and thereby achieve self-fulfilment at least in part.*' (Emphasis in original.)

Clearly, certain elements of this construction of human worth cannot be enjoyed by the unborn.

who, with access to developments in science, will be better positioned to determine where various aspects of dignity begin or end.[174]

The search for some indicators that could be used to clarify Ackermann's 'certain circumstances' or 'certain aspects' leads to Harris and Dworkin respectively. Harris suggests that the unborn are part and parcel of humanity; however, they are not 'persons', since they lack certain characteristics, such as the capacity for pain and pleasure, a sense of self and time, and rationality.[175] Thus, while we value the unborn for being part of our species, the fact that they are not persons justifie our treating them differently from already-born individuals.[176] However, Dworkin, in the context of the termination of pregnancies, states that human life should not be irresponsibly wasted and one should have sufficient 'justificatio of appropriate importance' in order to tamper with human life.[177] Here, 'appropriate importance' refers to, among other circumstances, the contextual setting in which women fin themselves when confronted with whether to continue with a pregnancy or not, and can include life-threatening pregnancies, foetal abnormalities, detrimental social and economic circumstances, age and issues linked with familial responsibilities.[178] These decisions are seen to go beyond the arbitrary waste of human life.

While Ackermann himself does not provide complete clarity on the extent of dignity in respect of or in the unborn,[179] he does articulate the grounds for justifying the valuing of unborn life, namely that it forms part of humanity and, as such, it deserves consideration and value, or special status. Further, to leave the interpretation of the value open to the 'interpreter of the Constitution' salvages the value of dignity to the extent that it is not cast in stone but enables the inclusion of future and unpredicted developments in our understanding of the value. This approach makes the value of dignity more amenable to changing circumstances, and ensures that it is socially and contextually informed.

---

[174] Ackermann *Human Dignity* 52.

[175] Harris *The Value of Life* 7–27. Also see Jackson *Regulating Reproduction* 228–9, who approvingly raised the same argument.

[176] Harris *The Value of Life* 7–27. However, it must be noted that the characteristics or essential traits that constitute a 'person' are the topic of endless debate. For instance, see Tooley 'Personhood' 117–26. Also see Megone 'Potentiality and persons' 155 and JL Bermúdez 'The moral significanc of birth' (1996) 106 *Ethics* 378 381–2 for a critique of Harris.

[177] Dworkin *Life's Dominion* 58.

[178] Dworkin *Life's Dominion* 50–60. Worthy of notice is the fact that it has been advanced that since the unborn are recognised as human beings and science shows life in even the simplest form of human life, then the unborn must be seen to have the same rights as those already born, particularly the right to life. See Warren 'Abortion' 129–31. However, this claim must be recognised as being far too extreme and Warren notes this position to be highly ambiguous and empirically unsound for a number of reasons; for these reasons; see 130–1. Also see Jackson *Regulating Reproduction* 226–7 for biological justification for denouncing this position. Since this approach extends full legal status and therefore implicitly denies special status of the unborn, it will not be considered any further.

[179] A further example of Ackermann's elusive reference to the unborn is found where he (52) goes on to state that 'I am not for one moment suggesting that the mother of the *conceptus* does not have rights which are to be weighed up against the dignity rights of the *conceptus*, and which in particular circumstances, would prevail.' It needs to be mentioned that here again is another issue that leaves one perplexed because Ackermann uses 'dignity *rights*' (emphasis added) of the unborn.

Critical of human dignity as a ground for valuing foetal life, Ford considers this approach to be flawed since it simply assumes that the human species is something special, without justifying what is special about being human in comparison with other species.[180] In this respect, Dworkin offers a plausible explanation. He states that we value our species more because we see ourselves as the highest-ranking species in terms of evolution and that without humanity, all knowledge, art and culture would disappear.[181] Ford further advances that speciesism could lead to extreme results, namely, justifying race preference on the grounds that those that form part of a particular race share in their distinct human relationships.[182] However, it is asserted that racism, as opposed to the inclusion of the basis of humanity, cannot be practically justifie in a constitutionally informed legal system.

3.5.3 Respect for interests

Steinbock,[183] an avid proponent of the interests approach, explains that this approach recognises that those entities that have the ability to care for their own welfare have 'interests',[184] and thus have moral status and require things to be done for their own sake. The interest approach requires one to consider the entity itself, in other words, what may be important to it rather than considering what makes the entity significan to others.[185] In this context, 'interests' denotes a claim the entity has against others to act or refrain from acting in certain ways, and it also encompasses a claim for attention or concern.[186] Having the 'ability to care' for one's own welfare requires a certain level of consciousness, because, without awareness, the entity will be unable to care about anything that happens to it, or even whether it is wholly destroyed.[187] That is not to say that those living entities without consciousness (and thus no interests of their own) do not matter, as there may be reasons to preserve them, but this will derive from the value others attach to the entity rather than from the value the entity has in itself.[188]

---

[180] Ford 'Nothing and not-nothing' 29.

[181] Dworkin *Life's Dominion* 77; 82. Dworkin (82–3) links humanity's value to value in natural creation (as mentioned in the text) and in the form of deliberative human creation. Deliberative human creation emphasises that all individuals, in their unique spheres, develop certain interests, ambitions, personality traits, and that in itself is an expression of 'human creative intelligence' which also find links to genetics and culture.

[182] Ford 'Nothing and not-nothing' 29.

[183] Steinbock *Life before Birth* XIV.

[184] For instance, they have a 'stake' in their comfort, being the need to avoid pain and discomfort, and experience pleasure or happiness.

[185] Steinbock *Life before Birth* 2.

[186] Steinbock *Life before Birth* 2.

[187] Steinbock *Life before Birth* 5. Steinbock states that 'interested beings' can be made happy or sad, they can feel pleasure or pain, but they do not always have to know what will make them happy or sad. Further, she (7–15) points out that the requirement for consciousness is an issue in dispute with some authors arguing against the necessity of consciousness and others arguing that consciousness on its own is not enough for purposes of interests.

[188] Steinbock *Life before Birth* 6. Steinbock explains that these organic entities do not have a stake in their own preservation, but we may still have an obligation to preserve them. She (7) states: 'We can have obligations *regarding* mere things, but these obligations are not *to them*.' (Emphasis in the original.) With respect to embryos as non-sentient, and thus non-interested beings, Steinbock

Steinbock's approach to interests does not adopt an 'all or nothing' position, since she asserts that even the most rudimentary of interests (for instance, pain, discomfort, pleasure) count as being relevant interests, and this standpoint opens up the interests approach for the inclusion of 'marginal cases'.[189] Marginal cases represent those entities that are not 'persons' (being legal subjects) and also those that do not merely constitute 'things', such as rocks or sand.[190] The unborn can be classed as 'marginal cases', because they are neither persons nor mere things.

In the context of the special status of the unborn, the respect for interests falls on the notion that the unborn have interests of some sort and those ought to be respected.[191] Steinbock argues that, once a foetus becomes sentient, it gains interests and therefore acquires special status.[192] She points out that it is not the ability to experience pain that is significant what is significan is the fact that the ability to feel pain is an indication of conscious experience in its most primitive form.[193] Relying on the scientifi evidence of foetal development, Steinbock states that the foetal nervous system is in place between 20–24 weeks of gestation and she concludes that the foetus may be capable of feeling pain at that point.[194] However, it must be noted that no one is able to provide any definitiv answers as to when or even if a foetus can feel pain, because the foetus cannot be asked. However, Steinbock stresses that scientifi evidence places a duty on us to err on the side of caution.[195]

Despite the fact that a foetus may be sentient, ability on its own will not be sufficient for the purposes of extending legal status to the unborn. Steinbock turns to 'time-relative interests' to justify only extending special status to a sentient foetus instead of legal status (or the right to life).[196] The term 'time-relative interests' refers to the fact that:[197]

> [O]ne's interest in staying alive is not simply determined by the amount of good in one's future but also by the degree of psychological connectedness between oneself now and

(270–8) admits that her interest approach does not extend to embryos but she goes on to call for the development of a third category for moral consideration to be developed based on respect. Here she emphasises that respect does not have to be an 'all or nothing' factor but can be granted in degrees relative to the entity in question. Due to the fact that the embryo is a potential person and a symbol of human existence it will demand more respect than an animal or plant. She states that the respect accorded does not remove the ability to experiment with embryos provided that the sorts of experiments embarked upon advance the greater good of humanity. Her approach is significan here because it indicates that different theories can be used for explaining special status at different points in gestation.

189 Steinbock *Life before Birth* 2.

190 Steinbock *Life before Birth* 2.

191 Ford 'Nothing and not-nothing' 27.

192 Steinbock *Life before Birth* 40. She (1; 40) states that an embryo and 'pre-sentient' foetus do not have moral standing, meaning that their existence does not have a claim to our moral attention.

193 Steinbock *Life before Birth* 46.

194 Steinbock *Life before Birth* 46–7. For more on the ability to feel pain see IG Cohen & S Sayeed 'Fetal pain, abortion, viability, and the Constitution' (2011) 39 *Journal of Law, Medicine & Ethics* 235 and SJ Lee, HJ Ralston, EA Drey et al 'Fetal pain: A systematic multidisciplinary review of the evidence' (2005) 294 *Journal of the American Medical Association* 947.

195 Steinbock *Life before Birth* 47–8.

196 Steinbock *Life before Birth* 77.

197 Steinbock *Life before Birth* 73.

oneself in the future. Psychological connectedness is a matter of both the richness of the subject's mental life and the number of internal connections within a subject's narrative, including memories of past experiences, anticipation of future experiences, plans, intentions, and goals.

Steinbock explains that time-related interests require some form of psychological unity, being a psychological investment in a possible future, in order for there to be a stake in one's continued life.[198] Accordingly, she asserts that sentience alone cannot afford a foetus the right to life; it can however extend special status, as it has interests (albeit rudimentary).[199] In this form, the sentient foetus's claim to life is 'weak' and the termination of a pregnancy is still a harm to it.[200] As psychological connectedness increases, the greater the harm the pregnancy termination will be because the foetus will have stronger time-relative interests in continued life.[201] Steinbock argues that a late-term foetus will have both consciousness and psychological connectedness, but the right to life cannot be extended to it because of the fact that the foetus exists within a woman's body and it may be impossible to give effect to that right without violating the rights of the pregnant woman.[202]

While Steinbock's approach offers a very attractive explanation as to why prenatal life holds value, there are a number of drawbacks to her line of argument. For Steinbock, sentience is understood to signify a definitiv line in foetal development that makes a foetus more like a neonate.[203] However, basing the initiation of special status of a foetus on a disputable fact, such as foetal sentience, is seen to leave her theory vulnerable. Further, the fact that Steinbock rejects foetal viability as morally significan is viewed as further weakening her argument.[204] Both issues will be discussed here.

To start, at most, sentience can only be understood as a 'possible' attribute of prenatal life. Steinbock herself cites authority for the fact that it cannot be said with any certainty when sentience begins during prenatal development,[205] but that 'it seems unlikely that foetuses have experiences of any kind before mid-gestation'.[206] Later, Steinbock states that a 'late-gestation' foetus *is* conscious

[198] Steinbock *Life before Birth* 77. Steinbock refers to an example where a few people and a dog are stranded on a boat at sea and someone must be sacrifice to prevent the boat from sinking. In these sorts of circumstances there is general agreement that the dog should be sacrifice and that it would be wrong to sacrific human life. Steinbock states that it is the time-relative interest that explains this response: 'The difference between the human being and the dog is that the human being is much more psychologically invested in and connected to her possible future than the dog is to hers. A human being has a well-developed, nuanced sense of herself as a protagonist in a life story—a narrative—that dogs do not have.'

[199] Steinbock *Life before Birth* 81.

[200] Steinbock *Life before Birth* 81.

[201] Steinbock *Life before Birth* 81.

[202] Steinbock *Life before Birth* 81. However, earlier in her work (55–9), Steinbock seems to suggest that conceptually a late-gestation foetus is the same as a neonate and that there is no conceptual bar (as opposed to a physiological bar) that prevents extending the right to life to the a later-term foetus.

[203] Steinbock *Life before Birth* 101.

[204] *Life before Birth* 99–101.

[205] Steinbock *Life before Birth* 46–50.

[206] Steinbock *Life before Birth* 34.

and sentient.[207] It is not very clear when a foetus is a late-gestation foetus. This approach is somewhat unreliable, because her protested definitiv line in foetal development becomes slightly blurred.

Cohen and Sayeed[208] and Lee, Ralston, Drey et al[209] also deal with the quandary of foetal pain. In summary the authors explain that there are two elements involved in the ability to feel pain—psychological and physiological. Physiologically speaking, nociception is the physical response to noxious stimuli which involves reflexivel moving the limbs away from stimulation. Generally, nociceptors develop prior to those structures required for the conscious awareness or perception of pain (that is, thalamocortical pathways). The authors state that nociception must be distinguished from the personal experience of pain. Nociceptors merely allow for a physical response to pain, but not for a conscious response to it. Psychologically, pain is recognised as a subjective and emotional experience. It requires the presence of consciousness, which allows one to recognise that a particular stimulus is unpleasant. Since pain is linked to the emotional psyche, arguably, it is something that needs to be learned through life experience. Pain can only be consciously experienced with the aid of the thalamocortical pathways which are believed to develop in the third trimester at 29–30 weeks' gestation.

Conversely, there is authority that pain is something that cannot be experienced until *after* birth. Lee[210] cites a number of clinically related sources which indicate that the 'true pain experience' can only be developed after birth; since the complex emotional experience of pain can only develop once the neonate is exposed to the world beyond a uterus, it has to learn to recognise pain. The feeling of pain is seen to be something that develops after birth along with memory, anxiety and other cognitive brain functionalities.

The anomaly of foetal pain does seem to leave Steinbock's approach in murky waters. If foetal sentience is questionable and one's approach is premised on that notion, it will lead to questionably extending special status to the unborn. This anomaly could be partly remedied by the inclusion of foetal viability in the equation of according special status, because research indicates that foetal viability is an inevitable development and it sets in prior to the possible experience of sentience. While the possibility of conscious experience calls for special status of the unborn, viable foetuses should be included in the equation of when the benefit of special status vest, even if the inclusion of viability would lead to a weaker claim to protection compared with the claim for protection demanded by the presence of sentience. However, Steinbock does not agree.

Steinbock[211] is critical of the moral significanc of foetal viability and while most of the critiques relate to the judicial construction of foetal viability,[212] one

[207] Steinbock *Life before Birth* 58.

[208] Cohen & Sayeed (2011) *Journal of Law, Medicine & Ethics* 235.

[209] Lee, Ralston, Drey et al (2005) *Journal of the American Medical Association* 947.

[210] Lee 'The abortion debate today' 238–9.

[211] *Life before Birth* 99–101.

[212] Most of the sources Steinbock relies on in her critique of foetal viability refer to the judicial construction of foetal viability rather than the clinical construction of viability. This is a valid

critique is linked to the technical interpretation of the term of viability which will be considered here. According to Steinbock, it is argued: if the moral significanc of independent survivability of a foetus is attached to the clinical point of viability, and clinical viability is influence by technological advances, developments such as 'external womb technology' will effectively pull the threshold of viability to the point of conception.[213] It is argued that this is because the unborn, through improved technology, can 'survive' *ex utero* at early points in gestation.[214] Consequently, more weighty special status will have to vest extremely early in gestation, and one implication would be that access to termination-of-pregnancy services could be severely impeded.

Admittedly, this argument has some merit *if* clinical viability is understood to denote mere 'external survival'. However, it is asserted that it would be inappropriate to interpret 'clinical viability' as so widely construed that it supposes that any possible form of *ex utero* existence at any point in gestation is 'foetal viability'. It is offered that the correct interpretation of clinical foetal viability is one that is narrowly construed. In this respect, Christoffersen-Deb refers to medical texts and explains that viability is described as the 'lower limit of fetal maturation compatible with extrauterine (sic) survival' which aids in determining whether the a foetus is 'sufficiently mature, such that not initiating resuscitation is

concern; see Pickles (2013) *Stell LR* 146. In this article a comparative study was conducted between the United States and South Africa and it was determined that, according to the legal construction of foetal viability, a foetus may be viable at any time from 19–20 weeks' gestation. Rhoden, in her critique of how *Roe v Wade* 93 S Ct 705 (1973) has been interpreted by the legislature and later judicial decisions, offers an explanation as to why different accepted stages of viability may be found. Decisions rely on medical technology as it stands at the time of a particular decision, thus what was the point of survivability when *Roe* was decided in 1978 is no longer the point of survivability today because medical technology is constantly improved upon. See, generally, NK Rhoden 'Trimesters and technology: Revamping *Roe v. Wade*' (1986) 95 *Yale LJ* 639. Therefore, the judicial construction of viability is incomplete and ambiguous and should not be used for purposes of extending special status. The clinical definitio of foetal viability is preferred for purposes of extending special status. Clinical foetal viability is understood in terms of being a grey zone for survivability, and does not indicate an 'on-off switch' as generally depicted in law. Gestational age, weight, antenatal exposure to corticosteroids, foetal sex, presence or absence of deformities, whether the pregnancy involves single or multiple gestations, resource availability, and socio-cultural factors all play a role in determining foetal survivability. Though foetal survivability is a medically informed estimation that can only be confirme upon physical examination after birth, it still represents an inevitable point in foetal development that will occur, unless of course the pregnancy is terminated or miscarried. In this regard see generally Pickles (2013) *Stell LR* 146.

[213] Steinbock *Life before Birth* 99–101 and Rhoden (1986) *Yale LJ* 655–73.

[214] Steinbock *Life before Birth* 99–101 and Rhoden (1986) *Yale LJ* 655–73. Rhoden (671) formulates two constructions of viability when discussing the implications of *Roe*'s reliance of viability. Viability$_1$ refers to the technical construction of viability, that is, the purely clinical notion of independent survival, while Viability$_2$ refers to the normative concept of survivability which encompasses the notion that a viable foetus is so 'substantially developed that it has a claim to societal protection'. She states that when *Roe* was decided, viability was estimated to occur at 28 weeks' gestation. Rhoden then argues that the court has been misinterpreted as applying a purely technical construction of viability (Viability$_1$). Instead, since viability was understood to occur in tandem with 'substantial' foetal development the court was actually referring to the 'value laden' Viability$_2$. This discussion focuses on Rhoden's notion of Viability$_1$.

unacceptable'.[215] First, this highlights that foetal viability is centred on a certain degree of foetal development, that is, the most basic necessities for life must be in place before one can begin to discuss the notion of 'viability'. Secondly, only when that degree of development is in place can technological support assist in sustaining life after birth. Accordingly, the foetus must have developed all essential bodily functions that place it in the position to sustain life with the assistance of technology. Here, technology is not creating human life, as the wide construction of viability presupposes, but rather aids in supporting already existing viable life.[216] The term 'viable' in this instance is not linked to technology's ability to create life but to the foetus's physical ability to live.

With this understanding in mind, the significanc of viability becomes more apparent. The significanc of viability lies in the fact that from the point of viability the foetus is no longer undergoing the process of rudimentary development of a body that can sustain its life.[217] Rather, at this point, all the necessary functionalities are in place and as the foetus progresses through later gestation, it goes through the perfecting and strengthening process of bodily organs and functionalities.[218] The fact is that everything is in place for the purpose of sustaining life, but for the foetus's location within a woman's body, it cannot sustain independent life. It offers the firs point in foetal development that the foetus has a 'fightin chance' for independent life if born at that point. Thus a viable foetus is developing stronger connections with its eventual birth and this development then moves from a biologically significan development to also being a socially significan event.[219] Foetal viability thus can be seen as bolstering the foetus's worth in respect of securing special status.

On more general grounds, Dworkin rejects the notion that the unborn may have interests of their own.[220] Earlier in his chapter titled 'What is sacred?' Dworkin discards the notion of valuing prenatal life on the basis that the unborn may possibly be sentient at some point during gestation.[221] He states that individuals still object to pregnancy termination despite the absence of sentience, thus indicating that there are far more significan reasons for objecting to terminating

---

[215] A Christoffersen-Deb 'Viability: A cultural calculus of personhood at the beginning of life' (2012) 26 *Medical Anthropology Quarterly* 576.

[216] In fact, even prenatal life created through technological advancements, like 'external womb technology', will not make an embryo or very under-developed foetus viable until the essential degree of physical development is in place which originates from the unborn's body itself.

[217] However, see Rhoden (1986) *Yale LJ* 655–73. She approvingly cites a number of pro-choice authors who argue against the biological significanc of foetal viability. Their argument is that viability lacks significanc because to them, consciousness is understood to be significan and not merely the ability for independent survival.

[218] In this respect, see Christoffersen-Deb (2012) *Medical Anthropology Quarterly* 575. Christoffersen-Deb (584–5) explains that in the case of imminent pre-term delivery, foetal viability is the dividing line between terminating the pregnancy or getting ready for a caesarean-section delivery and facilitating neonatal intensive care. He (585) indicates that increased gestation after viability will increase the chances for positive foetal outcomes.

[219] See generally D Meyerson 'Abortion: The constitutional issues' (1999) 116 *SALJ* 50.

[220] Dworkin *Life's Dominion* 98.

[221] Dworkin *Life's Dominion* 89.

prenatal life.[222] Ford also objects to a 'respect for interests' approach, because it is not clear how to determine these interests, and she stresses that on a practical level these sorts of indeterminable interests cannot be wholly respected, especially when considering pregnant women's interests.[223] Harris points out that the issue of sentience is flawed as pain can easily be curbed with anaesthesia, thus the reason for special status (or non-interference) runs deeper than the concern that the unborn may feel pain.[224] However, Harris' position fails to show that sentience is an indication of foetal consciousness, and it is not sentience itself that is significant

3.5.4 Special status based on relationality

Relational feminism is driven by an ethic of care and by virtue of adopting the approach the unborn are viewed as subjects worthy of value.[225] Morgan[226] states that 'fetal relationality' is a feminist-based response to foetal individuation which attempts to construct a form of status that is consistent with pro-choice narratives.[227] In this approach, the existence in relationships is an essential characteristic of personhood or status.[228] Ford explains that using relationships as the foundation for special status requires a move beyond rights and interests discourse and brings focus on the relationships that exist in terms of a pregnancy.[229] This approach calls for a contextual understanding in which rights and interests exist.[230]

Morgan, having considered a number of relational feminist works on this topic, summarises that a relational approach views the unborn as 'moving through' pregnant women, and thus the unborn cannot form relationships with others independently and nor can others form relationships with them.[231] However, a unique and intimate relationship exists with pregnant women, and any relationships with others are indirect and facilitated through pregnant women.[232] On this

222 Dworkin *Life's Dominion* 89.

223 Ford 'Nothing and not-nothing' 28.

224 Harris *The Value of Life* 118.

225 See JA Shields & S Serna 'The demise of feminist communitarianism' (2011) 40 *Perspectives on Political Science* 9. According to Shields and Serna, this position cost relational feminists their leading role in early feminism in the United States.

226 LM Morgan 'Fetal relationality in feminist philosophy: An anthropological critique' (1996) 11 *Hypatia* 47 48.

227 Feminism was primarily concerned with detaching women from the unborn since reproduction was one of the primary sources of women's subordination. However, feminism is slowly adjusting its position on the unborn, but this is more of a contemporary occurrence and still not a very popular position. See Manninen (2013) *Hypatia* 663. Morgan explains that this adjusted position is deemed necessary because feminism can no longer continue to deny increasing moral and social status of the unborn since it would result in 'anti-mothers' or 'child-killers' type of feminism and this would lead to denying the significanc of many women's experiences linked to pregnancy and childbearing. See Morgan (1996) *Hypatia* 48.

228 See generally, P Groarke 'The legal concept of the person: A relational account' (2010) 51 *The Heythrop Journal* 298 and N Levy 'The moral significanc of being born' (2013) 39 *Journal of Medical Ethics* 326.

229 Ford 'Nothing and not-nothing' 28.

230 Ford 'Nothing and not-nothing' 28.

231 Morgan (1996) *Hypatia* 52.

232 Morgan (1996) *Hypatia* 52.

ground, because the unborn cannot relate independently, but exist in a relationship of dependence in respect of pregnant women, they cannot be granted full status.[233]

Morgan states that a relational approach is founded on biological and psychological relations.[234] The fact that the unborn are physically found within and wholly dependent on women's bodies emphasises an understanding of biological unity during a pregnancy.[235] The unique physical position of the unborn calls for special social status, and this approach empowers a pregnant woman to determine the status and value of the foetus she carries.[236] Morgan accepts biological connections as a ground that informs foetal relationality, but warns that a biological approach is insufficient on its own because relationships need to be reciprocally experienced.[237]

Concerning the psychological grounds, Morgan emphasises that the very nature of a relationship is reciprocity between individuals connoting a bond, and asks the question: On whom does the onus for the experience of relations rest?[238] There are two schools of thought in this respect. Some feminists place the onus on the unborn and, since the unborn lack certain mental and physical characteristics equal to those of full legal subjects, the unborn lack full legal status.[239] This approach then provides a justificatio for the right to terminate pregnancies because the unborn are 'ineffectual relational agents'.[240] Another school of feminist thought places the onus on pregnant women, and state relationships are characterised by interdependence and an awareness of the existence of interdependence.[241] These feminists assert that even if the awareness of interconnectedness turns out to be one-sided, that is, the pregnant woman is aware of the interdependence of the unborn, a relationship can still exist.[242] Pregnant women's awareness of their relationship with the unborn is seen as a process of forming a person, thereby not extending full status to the unborn.[243]

Although Ford accepts the importance of relationships in the context of important human bonds, she is critical of this approach because the unborn cannot experience relationships in any direct or meaningful way.[244] The relationships experienced during pregnancy (in terms of the unborn and woman) are one-sided, with the unborn being the object of relations or 'passive recipients of the ethical behaviour of others'.[245] This brings into question whether this approach has any value as a universal application for the purposes of special status.

Morgan is also critical of the above relational construction to the extent that Western feminists fail to adequately encompass one of the true aspects of

[233] Morgan (1996) *Hypatia* 52.
[234] Morgan (1996) *Hypatia* 52–3.
[235] Morgan (1996) *Hypatia* 52.
[236] Morgan (1996) *Hypatia* 52.
[237] Morgan (1996) *Hypatia* 52.
[238] Morgan (1996) *Hypatia* 53.
[239] Morgan (1996) *Hypatia* 53.
[240] Morgan (1996) *Hypatia* 53.
[241] Morgan (1996) *Hypatia* 53.
[242] Morgan (1996) *Hypatia* 53.
[243] Morgan (1996) *Hypatia* 53.
[244] Ford 'Nothing and not-nothing' 29.
[245] Ford 'Nothing and not-nothing' 29.

relationality: the attribute of social existence.[246] Turning to non-Western traditions, she calls for a 'culture-bound' understanding of relationality which recognises that the body is socially constructed in both the physical and the psychological sense.[247] Consequently, a body or a person is valued because it is seen as the product of specifi social interactions.[248] Since the person is socially constructed, and communities engage in 'psychological nurturance' to create persons, communities are seen to hold collective responsibility for bringing persons into existence.[249] In this respect the unborn is seen as a mixture of a number of different kinds of social influence that facilitate its condition.[250] Thus, the unborn should be viewed as socially constituted. Relevant social influence can include failed contraception; promotion into a better paying job; the personality traits of those involved with the unborn's constitution; exposure to substances such as prenatal vitamins; or the daily intake of various foods.[251]

Although Morgan does not expressly state as much, this approach places value in the unborn because of the fact that it represents a portion of a culture, a society and social influenc which all contribute to its creation and continued development. Morgan explains that the decision to terminate a pregnancy is framed as a decision to interrupt the social process of making a person.[252] However, this approach comes at a price. Morgan admits that in cases where non-Western societies formulate prenatal life in this fashion, it is very rare that termination of pregnancies will be performed under the 'free choice' of the pregnant woman concerned, and it usually involves social decision-making.[253]

3.5.5 'Personhood Dependent Principle'

Karnein construes personhood as being founded on primary and secondary considerations.[254] First, she argues that those that are capable of moral agency[255] are accorded personhood. However, she understands that, in many instances, human beings may lack moral agency (such as neonates, young children, the infir or those with mental disabilities) but still demand the protection generally afforded to moral agents. On this basis, she argues that there are secondary

---

[246] Morgan (1996) *Hypatia* 56. She argues that these feminists prefer to understand relationality in respect of inherent properties of the unborn and the pregnancy, or in the pregnant women themselves, or both. Morgan explains that 'they are reluctant to let relationality "leak out" into a pregnant woman's social world (eg, father, parents, friends, or government agencies) because shared relationality might provide justificatio for undercutting her sovereign control over the fate of her pregnancy'.

[247] Morgan (1996) *Hypatia* 56.

[248] Morgan (1996) *Hypatia* 56.

[249] Morgan (1996) *Hypatia* 56–7. Morgan points out that non-Western 'nurturing' is not associated to the Western construction of nurturing, in that it does not demand female selflessnes but rather it is a quality found within communities' equality distributed between men and women.

[250] Morgan (1996) *Hypatia* 57.

[251] Morgan (1996) *Hypatia* 57.

[252] Morgan (1996) *Hypatia* 57.

[253] Morgan (1996) *Hypatia* 57–8.

[254] AJ Karnein *A Theory of Unborn Life: From Abortion to Genetic Manipulation* (2012) 4; 19.

[255] She (19) define moral agents as subjects of morality who are receptive to morality's demands and who are capable of acting accordingly.

considerations that inform whether personhood attaches to an entity or not, in this case these entities should form part of the human species and form 'intimate parts of our social universe'.[256] She understands that being endowed with personhood demands respect and a commitment to protection.[257]

Karnein excludes the unborn from personhood, arguing that personhood only attaches at birth.[258] Despite the fact that a human embryo or foetus is of human descent and can be subject to the social universe of other human beings,[259] to Karnein, foetal dependency ('symbiotic attachment') is a qualifying factor to extending personhood to a foetus.[260] She argues that in order to be a person the 'entity in question must not inevitably rely for its continued existence on life support of a kind that can always be denied'.[261] She understands and respects the notion that pregnant women have the right to terminate their pregnancies and this then counts as a detriment to the status of the unborn.[262] Thus, it is the unborn's special kind of structural reliance on one specifi and irreplaceable person that serves as the grounds for denying the unborn personhood and the related protection.[263] Thus, while Karnein does not explicitly acknowledge this, her construction of personhood is effectively made up of four elements: capacity for moral agency, being of human descent, partaking in the social universe of moral agents, and being capable of independent survival (meaning that the entity cannot rely on only one specifi person for maintaining independent life).

While the above-described criteria deny the unborn full status, Karnein suggests that there are reasons why we should value some of them. Her reason lies in the fact that we all derive from embryos, consequently already born persons have 'backward-orientated interests' in the wellbeing of the embryo from which they developed.[264] Since we owe certain obligations to persons, such as to refrain from harming them, we have a reason to treat the unborn that develop into persons in anticipation of the persons they ultimately become.[265] The special status that we extend to these embryos requires us to refrain from altering or removing features

[256] Karnein *A Theory of Unborn Life* 4; 22.
[257] Karnein *A Theory of Unborn Life* 17–18.
[258] Karnein *A Theory of Unborn Life* 22.
[259] Lupton's work clearly demonstrates this. See Lupton *Social Worlds of the Unborn*, generally.
[260] Lupton *Social Worlds of the Unborn*.
[261] Karnein *A Theory of Unborn Life* 23. Karnein notes that while newborns are dependent beings, they are not 'structurally' in a position to be denied life support. That is, other third parties can care for a newborn's needs in cases where its mother refuses to do so. Whereas, in the case of a pregnancy, if a woman denies her support, the unborn's life will be extinguished.
[262] Karnein *A Theory of Unborn Life* 23. Karnein founds her position on the work of Thomson. See JJ Thomson 'A defense of abortion' (1971) 1 *Philosophy & Public Affairs* 47. Thomson justifie termination of pregnancies on the grounds that pregnant women do not have a moral responsibility towards the unborn; they cannot be forced to give up the use of their bodies for the benefi of others, whether born or unborn.
[263] Karnein *A Theory of Unborn Life* 25.
[264] Karnein *A Theory of Unborn Life* 18.
[265] Karnein *A Theory of Unborn Life* 28.

of the embryos that may have a harmful consequence for the persons who develop in due course.[266]

Essentially Karnein is arguing that those embryos that have a chance of developing into persons should be attributed moral value, which is her 'Personhood Dependent Principle'.[267] Having a 'chance' indicates that there is a viable embryo and that there is a woman willing to carry the pregnancy to term.[268] Karnein's theory therefore does not extend value to all human embryos; embryos' status is contingent upon their prospects of development into living persons.

Determining which embryos have that prospect leads to Karnein's 'Principle of Precaution'.[269] This principle requires us to err on the side of caution, meaning that all embryos should be treated as if they will become persons.[270] The author explains that this position should stand for as long as we can say irrevocably that there is no possibility that the unborn can develop into persons.[271] This will be the case in respect of the termination of pregnancies or biologically rendering stem cells unable to develop into viable embryos.[272]

Karnein's attribution of special status does not fin experimentation with human embryos problematic, provided that a particular embryo does not go on to develop into a person.[273] Furthermore, where experimentation does occur and that embryo goes on to progress through development, the process of experimentation is not seen to violate the intrinsic worth of the embryo, but rather violates or 'affects the past-directed interests' of the person it develops into.[274] Karnein's theory is more concerned with the controversy surrounding the disposition of viable human embryos. She argues that we fin value in the creation of persons and this requires that we allow development to occur, especially where there is no important reason to stop it.[275] Consequently she argues that where there are viable embryos, they

[266] Karnein *A Theory of Unborn Life* 34. In this respect, Karnein views living persons as respectful 'safe-keepers' of later persons' biological possessions, being the physical, mental, genetic attributes inherent in their biological make-up.

[267] Karnein *A Theory of Unborn Life* 28.

[268] Karnein *A Theory of Unborn Life* 34. The author's (39) reliance on 'willingness' makes sense because 'embryos inside women's bodies have as little potential to become persons if women do not want to continue their assistance as do embryos by themselves without women wanting to carry them to term in the firs place'.

[269] Karnein *A Theory of Unborn Life* 28. See TF Murphy 'Adoption first The disposition of human embryos' (2014) 40 *Journal of Medical Ethics* 392. To date, Murphy is the only known author to cite Karnein's work discussed here. He refers to her 'Principle of Precaution' as 'presumption of expected personhood' in that we should respect embryos as if they are presumptive persons.

[270] Karnein *A Theory of Unborn Life* 29.

[271] Karnein *A Theory of Unborn Life* 29.

[272] Karnein *A Theory of Unborn Life* 29. Karnein understands that women are entitled to terminate their pregnancies; she views us as being under no obligation to treat embryos as if they are already persons. She argues (29) that our obligation arises retrospectively: 'They are applied in a forward-looking manner only via speculation (as to an embryo's future) and as a matter of caution so that we avoid violating our (retrospective) obligations.' Further, she states that we are also under no obligation to realise our speculations.

[273] Karnein *A Theory of Unborn Life* 33.

[274] Karnein *A Theory of Unborn Life* 33.

[275] Karnein *A Theory of Unborn Life* 37.

should not be readily disposed of.[276] Rather, they should be made available to willing women regardless of the biological origins of the embryos.[277]

Karnein's work is very new to the pool of theories dedicated to valuing the unborn, and as a result there is little by way of published criticism of her work. Murphy does offer some criticism, but his contribution relates to the practical application of Karnein's theory in respect of allowing women to 'adopt' biologically unrelated embryos.[278]

3.5.6 Significance of birth?

Special status consists of two elements. First, it captures a negative element in that there is something in or of the unborn that prevents them from having full status. Secondly, special status also has a positive element, namely that there is something in or of the unborn that demands something from us, or to be considered of value in one form or another. While all the above-considered theories offer legitimate grounds for justifying the special status of the unborn to some extent, it is suggested that, individually, each theory holds limited effect. This is particularly evident when one considers Morgan's position:[279]

> Social and biological birth have become uncoupled in the United States over the last two decades. As a result of reproductive imaging technologies, the commodificatio of babies, the attribution of personhood (what I call 'social birth') can now precede biological birth. The result is a new unprecedented category of fetal persons. . . . It is my contention that those who set off to prove the 'natural' importance of birth forgot to keep an eye on the weather. Their rhetoric of birth as the moral dividing line between persons and nonpersons is simply unconvincing in an era when ever greater social value is being attached to fetuses.

One is left questioning how theories on special status detract from the significanc of birth, thus rendering the law's approach to the unborn meaningless or 'out of sync' with prevailing theories. The answer stems from the fact that, generally, the theories and scientificall based arguments have failed (some more so than others) to emphasise the embodied nature of pregnancy: 'Pregnancy' involves an intrinsically unique connection between a woman and the unborn, whereby prenatal life is wholly dependent on women's bodies.[280] It is for this reason that the special status of the unborn should be viewed through the lens of re-embodied prenatal life, and this construction should be used as an informative tool for the purposes of extending special status.

Pregnancy must be brought back into context. To start, re-embodiment is necessary because a woman's body is a *sine qua non* for pregnancy (gestation and prenatal development). Biologically, pregnancy takes place in a woman's body, thus requiring that the unborn be understood as part and parcel of the body of a

---

276 Karnein *A Theory of Unborn Life* 37.

277 Karnein *A Theory of Unborn Life* 37. In this respect Karnein encourages us to take an affirmative approach towards the creation of persons and this approach demands that we allow women to become pregnant with embryos left over from other persons' fertility procedures.

278 Murphy 2014 *Journal of Medical Ethics* 392.

279 Morgan (1996) *Hypatia* 59–60.

280 For more on the nature of pregnancy see Lupton *Social Worlds of the Unborn* 52–69.

pregnant woman. The 'part and parcel' does not mean that the unborn are mere organs of a woman's body, but indicates that it is a woman's body that ensures continued gestation and development. Consequently, any discussion about status prior to birth requires the recognition that the unborn be considered in relation to the contextual setting of pregnancy and women too.[281]

With prenatal development placed back into its 'bodily context', it is necessary to turn to the different theories. A common feature gleaned from the discussed theories is the fact that each tends to emphasise that the process of human development negates the full status of the unborn. For instance, as a result of their partial development, the unborn cannot directly relate; they have an under-developed or undeveloped mental capacity, self-awareness and rationality or they lack consciousness for the purposes of having their own interests.[282]

While all these theoretical assertions bear an obvious element of truth (varying in degree), they are somewhat incomplete. This is so because even extremely premature neonates, full-term babies, toddlers and schoolchildren go through the processes of human development on a daily basis, but we do not attach less value to them in law on the grounds of continued development.[283] Instead, it is suggested that we limit the status of the unborn because they are going through a process of development which does not take place in an independent space, but rather within and dependent on another's body.[284] So while prenatal development signifie a process of the most basic form of human development, it is the additional fact that this development takes place in women's bodies that concretises the grounds of limiting the status of the unborn. As long as the limiting element of embodiment

[281] This is where the value of foetal viability comes in and the even further valuable occasion of biological birth.

[282] The only exception is that of Karnein *A Theory of Unborn Life* 22–6; she terms this limiting factor a 'symbiotic connection to the body of a woman'. It must be noted that Steinbock (*Life before Birth* 81) does attempt to follow an embodied approach to pregnancy because after arguing that foetal sentience is sufficient for moral standing and similar to neonates in respect of development, the unborn are entitled to less 'protection' because 'they are located inside the pregnant woman's body'. While this does fall in line with the concept of an embodied foetus, Steinbock (58), seems to have forgotten the embodied nature of pregnancy when under the discussion of 'the right to life' she states that there is no 'conceptual bar to ascribing a right to life to the nearly born fetus. A late-gestation fetus is conscious and sentient. It is very likely that it can experience pain, and presumably, it has pleasurable experiences, an interest that can be protected by a right to life.' However, understanding the foetus as being 'embodied' offers a conceptual bar to extending the right to life to the unborn.

[283] Admittedly, prenatal development is the most basic form of human development for purposes of sustaining life and this can be distinguished from non-life-sustaining forms of development that take place after foetal viability and birth.

[284] 'Independent space for development' needs some expansion and qualificatio here. 'Independent space' does not denote isolated existence but rather refers to the occupation of a space that does not include another person's body for purposes of advancement of one's life. Concerning development of a child, it is accepted that children cannot develop independently; children are dependent on caregivers for survival, but that survival does not include continued access to the use of another's bodily functions. It is necessary to point out that breastfeeding does not fall within this category because it is not comparable to the bodily resources needed to gestate a foetus. External means of nourishment can be differentiated from internally sustaining all functionalities of life for purposes of an individual's advancement.

persists, the foetus will lack full status. It is this embodied understanding of pregnancy and prenatal development that makes the significanc of biological birth more apparent. Concerning Morgan's argument that 'social birth' (linked to foetal imagery and assisted reproductive technologies) has replaced the significance of 'biological birth', Roth responds directly to Morgan and convincingly argues that:

> Most pregnant women probably do desire and create personhood by imagining the person their fetus will become, whom it will resemble, and so on, whether or not they consume such services as genetic testing and ultrasound. Women's personal actions and attempts to make meaning, and broader social efforts are not the same as political decisions to award personhood to the fetus through [full] legal status. These efforts can create pressure to recognise a fetus as an autonomous person, but they tell us little about *whether we ought to*. (Emphasis added.)

Roth's 'whether we ought to' is tied to the significanc of biological birth. Warren succinctly argues that it is 'impossible to treat fetuses *in utero* as if they were persons without treating women as if they were something less than persons'.[285] The key to full status is not linked to our social and clinical knowledge of the foetus and their processes of development. Rather, the key to full status lies in the physical biological detachment of a foetus from a woman's body at any point after clinical foetal viability.[286] This approach explains why extremely premature neonates, despite being in an underdeveloped state, or the fact that one was not given nine months to socially or clinically get to 'know' them, will still receive all of the law's protective reach and medical attention where resources permit.

The significanc of birth has also been argued on more abstract grounds and deserves some consideration here. One way to explain the significanc of birth is to demonstrate that there is a difference in moral worth between a foetus and a neonate, thus justifying why a neonate deserves full status and a foetus does not.[287] Warren defends the significanc of birth in relational terms based on the inherent social nature of human beings.[288] She considers social interaction as one of the fundamental parts of personhood and argues that the difference between a late-term foetus and a neonate is the ability of a neonate to socially interact. While accepting that sentience offers a good criterion for extending some moral value to the foetus, she argues that sentience is insufficient for full moral worth because it

---

[285] MA Warren 'The moral significanc of birth' (1989) 4 *Hypatia* 46 59.

[286] Justifying the significanc of foetal viability will be considered below when discussing the positive elements of special status.

[287] Currently, there is an ethical debate about the significanc of birth with respect to the permissibility of infanticide on the one hand or the impermissibility of termination of pregnancies. It is argued that since a late-term foetus and a neonate are intrinsically the same in terms of human development and personhood capacities or attributes they should be treated the same way. This approach rests on the fact that birth is merely a change in location and not a change in intrinsic properties. Whether one argues for permissible infanticide (Giubilini & Minerva (2013) *Journal of Medical Ethics* 261) or extending full status to the unborn (Morgan (1996) *Hypatia* 47) depends on how personhood is constructed. Also see Levy (2013) *Journal of Medical Ethics* 326.

[288] Warren (1989) *Hypatia* 55.

does not bring with it social interaction.[289] Warren explains that at birth, the neonate enters the human social world, where it lives and becomes enmeshed in social relationships which bring about social responsiveness from the child itself.[290]

Levy takes Warren's argument further.[291] Levy's relational account holds that the neonate's worth depends on its actual capacities (present at birth) but that the full realisation of these capacities are partly dependent on the neonate's relationship with others and its environment.[292] Thus, he advocates a combined relational account to justify the increased moral value of neonates based on relational facts about them which includes a 'relational account of worth' and a 'relational account of capacities'.[293]

Concerning Levy's account of relational worth, he argues that birth is a neonate's entrance into 'full sociality', as opposed to his or her limited entry prior to birth via imagery technologies.[294] Existence in 'full sociality' denotes the fact that there is the opportunity to interact (socially, clinically and legally) with the neonate independently and the neonate can engage in a wide range of interactions with a number of people who see or identify the neonate as an individual.[295] Ultimately, Levy asserts, we do not *give* the neonate value, rather, value *accrues* through the process of birth and identificatio via the child's social relations, thus obligating society to recognise his or her value.[296]

On the notion that neonates lack certain capacities for full moral worth, Levy turns to a relational account of capacities which is tied to the notion of 'scaffolding actions'.[297] Scaffolding actions are those actions that are made possible only because some form of external support is available to complete the action.[298] Levy suggests that neonates should be seen as having 'scaffolding capacities', in that their independent capacity is there, but in order to realise it to its fullest, the neonate relies on support structures (his or her relations to others and the environment) to actualise the capacity.[299] While neonates form part of a 'carer–child dyad', their lack of independence will not detract from their moral

[289] Warren (1989) *Hypatia* 55. Warren (55) states that 'it is doubtful that a child reared in total isolation from other sentient (or apparently sentient) beings could develop the capacities for self-awareness and social interaction that are essential to personhood'.
[290] Warren (1989) *Hypatia* 56.
[291] Levy (2013) *Journal of Medical Ethics* 326.
[292] Levy (2013) *Journal of Medical Ethics* 328.
[293] Levy (2013) *Journal of Medical Ethics* 327–8.
[294] Levy (2013) *Journal of Medical Ethics* 328.
[295] Levy (2013) *Journal of Medical Ethics* 328.
[296] Levy (2013) *Journal of Medical Ethics* 328.
[297] Levy (2013) *Journal of Medical Ethics* 328.
[298] Levy (2013) *Journal of Medical Ethics* 328.
[299] Levy (2013) *Journal of Medical Ethics* 328. For instance, Levy explains that support is needed to help develop certain 'onboard capacity' and once that capacity has developed, the support (scaffold) can be dispensed of. An example would be the training wheels on a bicycle. The training wheels are only there for as long as the child needs them to develop his or her riding capacity. Once that capacity is fully realised, the training wheels can be dispensed with.

worth, because their moral worth also stems in part from their availability (after birth) to form part of the dyad that supports his or her capacities.[300]

Arguments that call for anything more than special status prior to birth, and postulate the significanc of biological birth as merely signifying a change of location, are founded on a disembodied approach to pregnancy. Disembodying the unborn leaves such arguments with 'missing links' because, for as long as pregnancy takes place within a woman's body, no foetus can exist without the presence of another's body. All arguments that involve continued unborn life must be steered by the existence of female bodies. So while prenatal development justifie something more than no status at all (special status), whether it be on the grounds of dignity, interests, relationality or potentiality, prenatal life must firs and foremost be understood as a process that takes place in women's bodies and that very fact reinforces the grounds for limiting the status of the unborn.[301] Ignoring the significanc of women and their lived bodily experiences of pregnancy renders the pregnancy environment ripe for tensions to arise.

3.6 CONCLUDING REMARKS

This chapter demonstrates how far women have come and how much has changed in terms of women working towards attaining self-define direction in respect of social and political standing, education, career paths, reproduction and parenthood. An understanding of feminism's achievements and aims is necessary because it highlights what is at stake if women are denied their equality and reproductive freedom, especially when the ends they seek are not predominantly procreative in character or undermine individuated foetal interests. We run the risk of repeating history if these aims are frustrated, because, without sufficient freedom to make reproductive decisions, women's agency would be negated and they would face the possibility of forced domestication and reproduction in terms of externally define roles. In this respect, reproductive freedom is pivotal in the achievement of feminist aims for equality.

Prior to the emergence of technologically informed prenatal care, pregnancy fell in women's domain and it was pregnant women who would convey internal developments to outsider third parties. This is not to say that the unborn were not known of, obviously they were, but only through the existence of female experiences. With the need to know more about prenatal development in medicine and science, the maternal body was sidelined and female bodily experience began to be replaced by expert knowledge.

The unborn were located and identifie within the maternal body with the use of visualising technologies and they became independent objects to observe, study and eventually treat. Consequently, the foetus moved from identificatio to individuation followed by a trail of individuating terms such as foetal patient, foetal personality, foetal distress and foetal indications, to name a few. Non-clinical interpretations of the lifelike presentations of the unborn fed into the

---

[300] Levy (2013) *Journal of Medical Ethics* 329.

[301] That is until medical technology advances to the stage of introducing external means of gestating the unborn, through external uterine technologies, for instance.

politics advocating foetal rights, arguments concerning the right to life and the extension of full legal status (personhood) to the unborn. These developments proved problematic since third parties laid claim to women's pregnant bodies which hold the unborn and in which broader society have an interest. This approach disembodies the unborn from the pregnant women who carry them and removes women from their own reproductive processes.

Going further, while the different special status theories offered a certain degree of valuable insight pertaining to the use of technology to theorise on the value of the unborn, they too fell into the contemporary trap of sidelining the women who carry the unborn. This is because most of the theories failed to fully appreciate the embodied nature of pregnancy in their deliberations, with the exception of the relational approach and personhood dependency principle. The proper functioning of special status as a means of according justifiabl consideration of the unborn cannot adequately be applied in the context of a disembodied approach to pregnancy. Without considering the unborn in the real context of their existence, any argument concerning status would be flawed

Pregnancy is a particularly vulnerable area for women and girls of reproductive age because reproductive freedom is a relational experience. Women rely on others to help realise their reproductive decisions and this can be problematic in cases where women rely on people who are not aligned with the feminist agenda of reproductive freedom and equality. It is within this context that the flawe disembodied identification individuation and theorising on the value of the unborn contributes to readying the ground for an adversarial pregnancy environment.

Pregnancy adversarialism becomes a possibility because the experience of pregnancy no longer includes only women and the unborn, but includes other third parties such as medical professionals, state officials, fathers-to-be and other members of society. Technology offers these parties the opportunity of experiencing the unborn, in terms of monitoring their movements, watching facial expressions and tracking their growth, all prior to birth. These very real experiences prompt a sense of relativity, responsibility and interest in the unborn to the exclusion of pregnant women. With third parties experiencing this sense of connection to the unborn, there will inevitably be occasions where others view certain circumstances as necessitating actions for the benefi of the unborn (for its own good), beyond pregnant women's health indications, wellbeing and rights generally. With women concerned about advancing their rights to substantive equality and autonomy on the one hand, and third parties advancing their interests in the unborn as if slicing through an invisible female body on the other hand, an adversarial pregnancy environment is inevitable.

PART TWO

PREGNANCY UNDER SOUTH AFRICAN LAW

Chapter 4

THE LEGAL STATUS OF PREGNANT WOMEN IN SOUTH AFRICA

4.1 INTRODUCTION

This chapter explores the concepts of legal subjectivity and autonomy as they are elucidated in case law, and particularises these concepts to pregnant women. The chapter demonstrates that, despite the presence of a pregnancy, pregnant women remain legal subjects and, as such, they are entitled to regulate the course of their lives during pregnancy and birth. These concepts of legal subjectivity and autonomy are used in the very specifi context of reproductive decision-making processes that some pregnant women may face when confronted with a pregnancy and imminent birth. In this respect, the notion of reproductive autonomy, as a constitutive part of the general construct of autonomy, is drawn on and a number of constitutional rights that ensure that pregnant women can safely realise their reproductive autonomy while pregnant are also discussed.

In the context of this chapter, reproductive decisions and actions (as manifestations of reproductive autonomy) are broadly construed as including decisions that will take place once a pregnancy has already commenced. As such, reproductive decisions move beyond the limited scope of termination of pregnancy. Reproductive decisions must be understood to include decisions to continue with a pregnancy, lifestyle choices during pregnancy, and decisions pertaining to antenatal care and birth. These forms of decisions have not received enough attention in the context of South African reproductive rights discourse, to the extent that the current reproductive rights discourse tends to focus on the rights of women to terminate pregnancies. This chapter not only argues that reproductive rights discourse should extend to decisions made when pregnant and birthing, but shows how to apply the law to those decisions. Increased attention must be given to pregnant and birthing women's rights and this should fall under reproductive rights more specificall .[1]

Ultimately, this chapter shows that pregnant women, who constitute one part of the pregnancy, hold a solid position in law and this position is enriched by the Constitution's values and the Bill of Rights.[2] This protective legal framework creates the constitutional space to make, and meaningfully experience, reproductive decisions and it serves as a defence against challenges to women's reproductive autonomy and rights via the courts or legislative reform efforts. This contextual setting should be kept in mind when considering the various suggestions for law reform explored later in this book.

[1] RA Spence 'Abandoning women to their rights: What happens when feminist jurisprudence ignores birthing rights' (2012) 19 *Cardozo Journal of Law & Gender* 75.

[2] Constitution of the Republic of South Africa, 1996.

4.2 PREGNANT WOMEN AS AUTONOMOUS AND UNQUALIFIED LEGAL SUBJECTS

Pregnancy is seen to involve the process of women gestating the unborn. However, while the term pregnancy hints at an image of connection or unity between a woman and a foetus, there is a core distinguishing feature between pregnant women and the unborn under South African law, which lies in the issue of legal subjectivity. In law, a person is one who is born alive and legal subjectivity only vests at this moment.[3] Boezaart define a legal subject as 'any entity that can have rights, duties and competencies'.[4] It is this distinguishing feature of legal subjectivity that sets very different legal paths for pregnant women and the unborn during pregnancy under South African law, even though they may share the common connection of pregnancy.

All pregnant women, like other persons, have rights, and like those of any other person, their rights can be limited under justifiabl circumstances in terms of s 36 of the Constitution. Equal access to and enjoyment of all rights is secured under s 9 of the Bill of Rights, which states that everyone is equal before the law and that individuals also have the right to equal protection of the law. Further, equality includes the right to full and equal enjoyment of all rights and freedoms. The equality clause also prohibits unfair discrimination on a number of grounds and this specificall includes pregnancy.[5] Therefore the benefi of all rights, laws and freedoms vests in pregnant women, despite the fact that they are pregnant. This establishes the principle that pregnant women are unqualifie legal subjects.

Pregnant women's full and equal enjoyment of all the rights and freedoms secured in the Constitution requires that they are equipped to engage their sense of autonomy especially when determining how they plan to live their lives as procreative subjects. However, the Constitution does not specificall grant anyone the *right* to autonomy and findin a working legal definitio of autonomy has proved a challenge. Constitutional case law does not provide a once-off define principle; instead, a number of separate decisions have to be drawn on in order to decipher a workable concept. The Constitutional Court has made reference to the autonomy of individuals but has not necessarily looked at the content of the term in any substantive way.[6] This is in spite of the fact that autonomy (along with

---

[3] *Christian Lawyers Association of SA v Minister of Health* 1998 (4) SA 1113 (T) (*Christian Lawyers* (1998)); *Friedman v Glicksman* 1996 (1) SA 1134 (W); and *Christian League of Southern Africa v Rall* 1981 (2) SA 821 (O). Also see T Boezaart 'Child law, the child and South African private law' in T Boezaart (ed) *Child Law in South Africa* (2009) 4.

[4] Boezaart 'Child law, the child and South African private law' 4.

[5] Section 9(3) of the Constitution.

[6] For instance, in *Masiya v Director of Public Prosecutions* 2007 (5) SA 30 (CC) (*Masiya*) (concerning the constitutionality of the common-law definitio of rape in that it excludes anal penetration and is gender specific Nkabinde J (para 37), giving majority judgment, found that rape violates a woman's sexual autonomy. Also, Langa J (para 80), in his dissent in the same decision, found that the crime of rape violates the constitutional value of freedom since it negates a person's bodily autonomy and this negation transcends the parameters of gender specificit . In *Bernstein v Bester* 1996 (2) SA 751 (CC) (*Bernstein*) (dealing with constitutionality of ss 417 and 418 of the now-repealed Companies Act 61 of 1973) O'Regan J (para 150) held that the right to freedom should include within it the understanding that society is characteristically interdependent, but that this

dignity) is understood to be a constitutionally prized value.[7] Nonetheless, there are a number of decisions that contribute to developing a clear picture of autonomy.

To start, the Constitutional Court seems to have accepted an umbrella concept of autonomy. In *Barkhuizen*, Ngcobo J referred to autonomy as the 'ability to regulate one's own affairs, even to one's detriment' and this was seen as the very 'essence of freedom and a vital part of dignity'. Self-regulation can be seen as the core of autonomy.[8] In *NM v Smith*, O'Regan J recognised that underlying the constitutional rights to freedom of expression, human dignity, privacy and freedom 'is the constitutional celebration of possibility of morally autonomous human beings independently able to form opinions and act on them'.[9] In *Volks v Robinson*,[10] Sachs J in his minority judgment asserted that respect for human autonomy implies that the law must honour the choices that people make and it must give weight to those decisions, even if their decisions are seen as unconventional. In her minority judgment in *AB v Minister of Social Development*[11] (*AB* 2), Khampepe J had the following to say regarding the notion of autonomy:

> [A]utonomy is a concept that bears many conceptions, encompassing 'a tangled net of intuitions, conceptual and empirical issues, and normative claims'. Recent academic trends—which echo the lessons of our own past—point to the inherently relational character of the term: to be autonomous is to be socially and politically connected, rather than an agent of unfettered individual choice. This Court's repeated endorsement of *ubuntu* underscores this point. In *Pillay*, Langa CJ explained that 'an individual human person cannot develop and achieve the fullness of his/her potential without the

---

understanding should not deny the value of autonomy. Going further, O'Regan (para 150) recognised that the state plays an important role in enhancing autonomy among other rights in the Constitution. In *MM v MN* 2013 (4) SA 415 (CC) (*MM*) (dealing with the validity of a customary marriage where the firs wife's consent is lacking), Froneman J, Khampepe J and Skweyiya J (para 73) found that 'autonomy and control over one's personal circumstances are a fundamental aspect of human dignity'. These are some of many references without any substantive consideration as to what autonomy stands to mean in law and what one should do with it in a legal setting.

[7] *Barkhuizen v Napier* 2007 (5) SA 323 (CC) (*Barkhuizen*) para 150. (In this case the court had to decide on the constitutionality of a time-limitation clause in a short-term insurance policy in that such a clause violates a person's right to approach a court for redress.) While Sachs J was providing his minority decision in the context of contract law, it is asserted that if one accepts that people enjoy autonomy while engaging in contractual relations, autonomy must be constitutionally prized even more so in the context of pursuing one's life course.

[8] *Barkhuizen* para 57.

[9] 2007 (5) SA 250 (CC) para 145.

[10] *Volks v Robinson* 2005 (5) BCLR 446 (CC) paras 154 and 156. This case concerned the constitutionality of s 2(1) of the Maintenance of Surviving Spouses Act 27 of 1990 to the extent that the Act does not make provision for a permanent life partner's claim for maintenance from their partner's deceased estate.

[11] [2016] ZACC 43. Section 294 of the Children's Act 38 of 2005 regulates surrogacy agreements and provides that no surrogate agreement will be valid in law unless one or both parents make use of their own gametes for purposes of conception. The Constitutional Court found that this requirment does not violate the rights of infertile commissioning parents who are unable to provide their own gametes for purposes of conception and therefore cannot make use ofsurrogacy as a means of becoming parents.

concrete act of relating to other individual persons'. Autonomy is a necessary, but socially embedded, part of the value of freedom.[12] (Footnotes omitted.)

In order to experience this construction of autonomy, Ackermann J in *Bernstein* recognised that 'rights, like the rights to privacy, are not based on notions of the unencumbered self, but on the notion of what is necessary to have one's own autonomous identity'.[13] While this quote draws on the relational nature of rights and the scope of the right to privacy, it also shows that, although autonomy is not explicitly recognised in the Constitution as a human right, a number of rights give credence to a person's sense and possibility of an autonomous existence. For instance, one cannot fully enjoy autonomy where one's rights to freedom or privacy do not prevail.[14] Further, a person's experience of autonomy can also be justifiabl limited through a rights approach, because not all rights are absolute. This can be achieved by applying the limitation clause,[15] which thereby serves as a regulatory mechanism regarding the extent of one's autonomy.

Adding to a more informed picture of autonomy, in *National Coalition for Gay and Lesbian Equality*, in the context of the right to privacy, Sachs J referred to Ackermann J's decision in *Bernstein* and advanced the notion that autonomy does not mean the right to occupy a specifi space in which a 'socially detached individual can act freely from interference by the state'.[16] Sachs J understands that individuals are in a lived state of social connectedness and explains that what is important for autonomy is the nature of the activity and not where the activity takes place.[17] Therefore, autonomy takes on a relational tone[18] and in this context, the more an activity relates to a person's inner sanctum the more pressing the need for advancement and protection from conflictin rights of the community or the state. Without a contextual understanding of the different relationships at play, advancement and protection will not materialise.

[12] *AB* 2 para 51.

[13] *Bernstein* para 65. Ackermann J approvingly relied on R Forst 'How (not) to speak about identity: The concept of the Person in a theory of justice' (1992) 18 *Philosophy & Social Criticism* 293.

[14] See *Ferreira v Levin*; *Vryenhoek v Powell* 1996 (1) SA 984 (CC) (*Ferreira*). This case concerns the validity of s 417(2)*(b)* of Companies Act 61 of 1973 and an accused's right to a fair trial. Sachs J (para 251) stated that one needs to protect human autonomy in order to achieve freedom and personal security. Also, in *National Coalition for Gay and Lesbian Equality v Minister of Justice* 1999 (1) SA 6 (CC) (*National Coalition for Gay and Lesbian Equality*) (dealing with the constitutionality of the common-law crime of sodomy) para 32, Ackermann J stated that privacy recognises that we have a right to a sphere of intimacy and autonomy.

[15] Section 36 of the Constitution.

[16] *National Coalition for Gay and Lesbian Equality* para 117.

[17] *National Coalition for Gay and Lesbian Equality* para 117.

[18] Sachs J seems firml committed to understanding autonomy in relational terms. In fact, in two of his judgments Sachs J refers to Jennifer Nedelsky who is well known for her relational stance on autonomy. See *Ferreira* fn 11 and *S v Baloyi* 2000 (2) SA 425 (CC) (*Baloyi*) (dealing with aspects of the Prevention of Family Violence Act 133 of 1993) para 16 fn 40. The relational character of autonomy was recently confirmen by the minority in *AB*, see para 51.

Interestingly, in *S v Jordan*,[19] the appellants attempted to cluster the rights to dignity, privacy and freedom of the person under the concept of autonomy and base their litigation on that concept, but Sachs J and O'Regan J rejected this approach and found that, as autonomy is not explicitly included in the Constitution, the appellants would have to work with constitutionally recognised human rights that were argued to have been infringed. Justice O'Regan stated:

> While we accept that there is manifest overlap between the rights to dignity, freedom and privacy, and each reinforces the other, we do not believe that it is useful for the purposes of constitutional analysis to posit an independent right to autonomy. There can be no doubt that the ambit of each of the protected rights is to be determined in part by the underlying purport and values of the Bill of Rights as a whole and that the rights intersect and overlap one another. It does not follow from this, however, that it is appropriate to base our constitutional analysis on a right not expressly included within the Constitution.[20]

This demonstrates that in order to advance a person's autonomy in law or litigation, one must be aware of the rights that give weight to autonomy.[21] However, determining which rights are relevant to the specifi task of advancing a person's autonomy can be complicated, as any right in the Bill of Rights will inevitably advance a person's autonomous character.

In the context of the umbrella concept of human autonomy, case law originating from the Constitutional Court indicates that the rights to freedom, privacy and dignity all give credence to this wide understanding of autonomy.[22] Yet, in a number of decisions, one find references to sexual autonomy,[23] bodily autonomy,[24] personal autonomy[25] and patient autonomy,[26] to name a few. These references give an indication of which branch of the umbrella concept of autonomy is at play. Linked to that, when these branches of autonomy are relied on, it requires a focused application of rights in a very specifi way, and these rights are applied in addition to the rights relevant to the umbrella concept of human autonomy. Further, because each branch of autonomy stems from the umbrella concept, it can be accepted that asserting a particular branch inevitably

---

[19] *S v Jordan* 2002 (2) SACR 499 (CC) (*Jordan*) para 52. This case dealt with the constitutionality of criminalising brothel-keeping and sex for reward in terms of the Sexual Offences Act 23 of 1957.

[20] *Jordan* para 53.

[21] The Hight Court adopted this approach in *AB v Minister of Social Development* 2016 (2) SA 27 (GP) (*AB* 1).

[22] For instance, see the following two cases generally: *Jordan*; *MM*; *Barkhuizen*; *Bernstein*; *Minister of Home Affairs v Fourie; Lesbian and Gay Equality Project v Minister of Home Affairs* 2006 (1) SA 524 (CC) (*Fourie*); and *MEC for Education, KwaZulu-Natal v Pillay* 2008 (1) SA 474 (CC).

[23] *Masiya* para 37.

[24] *Masiya* para 80.

[25] *Baloyi* para 16.

[26] *Castell v De Greef* 1994 (4) SA 408 (C) (*Castell*). This case concerned medical negligence of an attending physician in that the physician failed to obtain his patient's informed consent. While *Castell* is not a Constitutional Court decision, it does enforce what is recognised today as a constitutional right to self-determination as found in s 12 of the Constitution. This case was decided by Ackermann J who later became a Constitutional Court judge.

assists in realising the umbrella concept of autonomy,[27] namely to pursue one's own envisaged ends without interference. However, neither of the branches should be conceived of as an isolated capsule of a particular form of autonomy. Rather, each branch of autonomy should be seen as being formed by permeable boundaries allowing for principles to transcend the wide array of autonomy branches and allow for each branch to complement and support the others.[28]

It is understood that each branch of autonomy is relative to specifi areas of human interaction and existence, and can therefore assist in identifying what rights are involved when it comes to protecting or advancing a person's autonomy in that area of interaction or existence. In the case where the same rights are relied on in respect of advancing different branches of autonomy, it is the particular branch of autonomy that will determine *how* the rights will be relied on. This construction frames autonomy as a flui concept which is influence by relationships and the context of those relationships.[29]

Linking these finding on autonomy to the theme of female[30] autonomy during pregnancy requires one to determine which branch of autonomy becomes relevant during a pregnancy. This approach will assist in identifying those constitutional rights that support pregnant women's experience of autonomy as legal subjects. Reproductive autonomy seems to fi this task well, as pregnancy and decision-making during pregnancy can be grouped as reproductive decisions leading to reproductive actions.[31] Reproductive actions will include those actions that lead to both having and not having children, and all the decision-making processes that are taken in order to realise those outcomes. It must be noted that reproductive actions are therefore not limited to decisions on terminating a pregnancy, but also include those decisions where women decide to continue with a pregnancy. Therefore, reproductive actions include those issues relating to how pregnant women decide to progress through pregnancies in respect of health-care and lifestyle choices.[32]

---

[27] For instance, if one's bodily autonomy were to be infringed through rape, one's wider experience of autonomy will also be negatively impacted upon.

[28] For example, in an act of embracing autonomy, a woman decides to bear a child. The process of bearing a child engages her reproductive autonomy as well has her autonomy as a medical patient. Both these branches of autonomy feed off of and bolster one another in the ultimate goal of realising and experiencing her human autonomy.

[29] If autonomy was a concept that could be considered in isolation, our courts surely would have provided a concrete definitio to work with by now. For more on context-related autonomy, see T Glennon 'Regulation of reproductive decision-making' in SD Sclater, F Ebtehaj, E Jackson et al (eds) *Regulating Autonomy: Sex, Reproduction and Family* (2009) 149–68.

[30] 'Female' autonomy includes girls and women. Further, female autonomy is not distinguished from human autonomy in an arbitrary sense but rather to highlight that female experiences of autonomy will invariably differ to that of men, particularly during pregnancy because pregnancy and having the capacity to be pregnant is unique to women and girls of reproductive age.

[31] While bodily, sexual and patient autonomy also have a role to play here, these concepts can be included under the broader label of reproductive autonomy in that bodily, sexual and patient autonomy all impact on pregnant women's overall experience of reproductive autonomy.

[32] The Preamble of Choice on Termination of Pregnancy Act 92 of 1996 lists a number of reproductive health-care services including access to contraception, sexual education, family planning, counselling programmes and termination-of-pregnancy services. This list gives an

Nonetheless, the term 'reproductive autonomy' seems problematic because this term does not appear in any South African legislation. It recently made its debut in *AB* 1,[33] but the High Court did not explicitly engage the concept and it did not clarify its meaning in a constitutional setting. The court merely used the phrase as a heading to its discussion of how s 12(2)*(a)* of the Constitution includes the right to procreate via the use of a surrogate. The majority in *AB* 2 did not go on to clarify the conceptual scope of reproductive autonomy and the Constitutional Court set the High Court's decision aside.[34] This makes it difficult to determine the position of women's reproductive autonomy generally and more specificall during pregnancy. Terms such as 'reproductive health care',[35] 'reproductive health',[36] 'reproductive choice'[37] and 'reproductive self-determination'[38] do make their appearances but, as seen earlier, rights such as these are not the experience of autonomy in themselves but represent what is necessary for autonomy to be experienced and they assist in offering protection in law.[39] The use of 'reproduction' as a qualifying word is understood to be an indication of the context in which the right is being applied.

If human autonomy is broadly understood as the process of self-regulation, then reproductive autonomy will be the process of self-regulation in the context of reproduction. This methodology falls in line with Mojapelo J's statement in *Christian Lawyers* (2005),[40] where the judge confirme that a woman's autonomy to determine the fate of her pregnancy can be protected through the application of a number of constitutional rights.[41] Identifying the relevant rights to achieve the aim of reproductive autonomy is much less complicated from this perspective. Further, considering how certain rights support reproductive autonomy assists with linking reproductive autonomy to broader concerns such as women's substantive equality, reproductive health and socio-economic issues. This will help

indication of what actions can be recognised as reproductive actions. The definitio of 'reproductive decisions' or 'reproductive actions' adopted in this book is in line with the approach adopted by the minority in *AB* 2. Khampepe J define decisions 'concerning reproduction' narrowly in so far as she found that reproductive decisions include decisions regarding the process of procreation and this is because procreation has a reproductive outcome; see para 75. The approach implies that if a decision has a reproductive outcome, it will be considered a reproductive decision.

[33] Paras 90–3.

[34] *AB* 2 para 330. However, the minority in *AB* 2 found that the freedom protected in s 12(2)*(a)* of the Constitution was not as broad as autonomy; Khampepe J held (at para 53) that even though s 12(2)*(a)* protects the ability to make decisions, '[t]he freedom protected by the right is not, however, coextensive with autonomy. The ambit of section 12(2)*(a)* is narrower and more specific.

[35] Section 27(1)*(a)* of the Constitution.

[36] Preamble to the Choice Act.

[37] *Stewart v Botha* 2007 (6) SA 247 (C) 247H. Also see *Christian Lawyers Association v Minister of Health* 2005 (1) SA 509 (T) (*Christian Lawyers* (2005)) 529E. In this case the Transvaal Provincial Division had to decide whether minors were able to consent to the termination of their pregnancies in terms of the provisions of the Choice Act, without the involvement of parents or guardians.

[38] *Christian Lawyers* (2005) 524I.

[39] *Bernstein* para 65.

[40] *Christian Lawyers* (2005) 527F.

[41] This case will be discussed in more detail below, with specifi reference to the rights relied on.

clarify how certain conditions negatively impact on the realisation of women's reproductive autonomy, and what needs to be done to counter these negative effects.

4.3 REPRODUCTIVE RIGHTS AND REPRODUCTIVE AUTONOMY

While a legal construction of reproductive autonomy is not available, a number of rights have been identifie as 'reproductive rights'. According to Albertyn, ss 12(2) and 27 of the Constitution 'was one of the earliest statements of reproductive rights in a national constitution.'[42] Also, the Preamble to the Choice on Termination of Pregnancy Act (Choice Act) makes specifi reference to promoting 'reproductive rights'. While it does not explicitly defin the term, the Act does recognise a number of rights as important for women's freedom of choice in reproduction. These include the rights to dignity, freedom, equality, security of the person, reproductive health and health care. These rights pooled together can be understood as reproductive rights.

In *Constitutional Law of South Africa*, O'Sullivan's chapter deals extensively with reproductive rights but primarily in the context of termination of pregnancy.[43] She also goes on to identify a number of rights, such as those recognised in the Choice Act, and she define reproductive rights as follows:[44]

> Even under the narrowest of constructions, reproductive rights demand respect for women's bodily integrity and an environment for decision making free from fear of abuse, violence and intimidation. Viewed more broadly, reproductive rights require the provision of information about access to voluntary and adequate reproductive and sexual services and may even command the provision of such basic necessities as food, shelter, childcare and education.

It is noticeable that in the South African context, searches relating to female reproductive decision-making during pregnancy all tend to result in information on the termination of pregnancy. Yet, deciding not to bear a child is only one element of reproductive decision-making and action.[45] The discussion of reproductive rights must therefore also go beyond the termination of pregnancy, otherwise only one element of reproductive autonomy would be covered here and

---

[42] C Albertyn 'Claiming and defending abortion rights in South Africa' (2015) *Revista Direito GV* 429 435.

[43] M O'Sullivan 'Reproductive rights' in S Woolman & M Bishop (eds) *Constitutional Law of South Africa* 2 ed (Service 2) ch 37. Also see C Albertyn, L Artz, H Combrinck et al 'Women's freedom and security of the person' in E Bonthuys & C Albertyn (eds) *Gender, Law and Justice* (2007) 363–74. The authors (368) also indicate that reproductive autonomy includes a wide range of rights, such as dignity, privacy, opinion and belief, bodily integrity and personal security and freedom. Later in the chapter (374), Albertyn, Artz, Combrinck et al recognise these rights and the rights to life and health care as reproductive rights. However, Albertyn, Artz, Combrinck et al tend to use reproductive freedom and reproductive autonomy interchangeably as if to mean the same thing. However, it must be emphasised that the right to freedom is something distinct from autonomy in that rights are what is necessary for autonomy or an autonomous identity.

[44] O'Sullivan 'Reproductive rights' 37-1.

[45] Also see C Pickles *S v Mshumpa: A Time for Law Reform* (unpublished LLM dissertation, University of Pretoria, 2010) 116 where reproductive rights were identifie as more than the right to terminate a pregnancy.

such a limited approach would not take the wider issue of tensions during pregnancy any further. Therefore, while most of the discussion to follow on rights stems from case law and literature relevant to the termination of pregnancy, it will be seen that this discourse can be extended to include the situation where women plan to continue with their pregnancies, and how identifie reproductive rights can also be used to ensure healthy pregnancies and healthy pregnancy outcomes.

As mentioned, O'Sullivan identifie a number of constitutional rights as being relevant to reproductive decision-making. She does so by applying the identifie rights in a reproductive context.[46] Her approach is very helpful and the same approach is adopted here with regard to structure. Further, the discussion draws on previous research linked to the right to terminate of pregnancy under the South African Constitution.[47] Unfortunately, there is very little case law dealing with the rights of pregnant women as a specifi group of rights-holders. However, general principles pertaining to human rights can be adapted for particular application to pregnant women.

4.3.1 Equality

Section 9 of the Constitution provides that everyone is equal before the law and has equal protection by the law. This right includes full and equal enjoyment of all rights and freedoms. Further, neither the state nor any person may unfairly discriminate directly or indirectly against any person on a number of grounds, including, among other grounds, gender, sex and pregnancy. Discrimination on any one of the listed grounds is unfair unless a party can establish otherwise.

In *Fourie*, Sachs J described equality as the right to be different, and explains that equality demands equal concern and respect across differences.[48] At the very least, equality insists that difference should not be the basis for exclusion, marginalisation or stigmatisation.[49] In view of our differences, the Bill of Rights is committed to a substantive understanding of equality.[50]

Birenbaum explains that formal equality involves treating individuals with similar characteristics equally, but this proves problematic because it could still lead to further inequality.[51] According to Albertyn, substantive equality essentially draws on the notion that people should be able to fully realise their human potential by participating in society and developing necessary relationships,

---

[46] O'Sullivan identifie many rights as being reproductive in nature, however not all of those rights will be considered here. Thus, only those rights understood to constitute fundamental building blocks to fostering an environment of respect towards reproductive autonomy will be considered. See O'Sullivan 'Reproductive rights' 37-18; 37-21; 37-24; 37-25 for her discussion of the children's rights and the rights to religion, information and freedom of expression respectively, as other examples of reproductive rights.

[47] C Pickles 'Termination-of-pregnancy rights and foetal interests in continued existence in South Africa: The Choice on Termination of Pregnancy Act 92 of 1996' (2012) 15 *PER* 403.

[48] *Fourie* para 60.

[49] *Fourie* para 60.

[50] J Birenbaum 'Contextualising choice: Abortion, equality and the right to make decisions concerning reproduction' (1996) 12 *SAJHR* 485 488.

[51] Birenbaum (1996) *SAJHR* 488.

despite the presence of difference.[52] In order for people to meaningfully engage their potential, arbitrary and systemic barriers to social participation must be removed, and conditions should be created where human potential can be realised and healthy relationships developed.[53] Fredman explains that a substantive approach to equality requires reconceptualising the right on the basis of gender.[54] She goes further to state that substantive equality highlights power struggles and gender roles in those struggles, it necessitates differential treatment in order to achieve equal outcome, and requires the transformation of social institutions as opposed to expecting individuals to conform and, lastly, it advances individuals rather than the notion of consistency.[55]

Narrowing the application of equality to the context of pregnancy, O'Sullivan[56] states that the explicit inclusion of pregnancy, sex and gender in s 9(3) is a constitutional acknowledgment that pregnant women form part of a systemically disadvantaged group and therefore are in need of greater judicial attentiveness. Birenbaum argues that a substantive approach 'addresses the forces of systemic discrimination which, in the case of gender discrimination, often result in "neutral" or "equally applied" rules having an adverse impact on women'.[57] This is problematic because the biological fact of pregnancy and its consequences are not considered when a formal approach to equality is adopted.[58] Substantive equality in the context of reproductive rights makes the connection between systemic discrimination against women and women's reproductive role.[59] O'Sullivan states that, from a substantive perspective, the right to equality requires the state to intervene positively and to provide the minimum resources necessary for the enjoyment of certain rights.[60]

In respect of termination of pregnancies, both the Choice Act and the National Health Act[61] aid in realising the aims of substantive equality. The Preamble to the Choice Act recognises that, in order to achieve equality, women must be able to decide whether to terminate a pregnancy or not, because they are best placed to make decisions of that nature. Their better placement stems from the fact that childbearing is physically, psychologically and economically[62] owned by women

[52] C Albertyn 'Equality' in E Bonthuys & C Albertyn (eds) *Gender, Law, and Justice* (2007) 95.

[53] Albertyn 'Equality' 95.

[54] S Fredman 'Engendering social and economic rights' in B Goldblatt & K McLean (eds) *Women's Social and Economic Rights: Developments in South Africa* (2011) 4–33.

[55] Fredman 'Engendering social and economic rights' 12–13.

[56] 'Reproductive rights' 37-14. Interestingly, pregnancy was not included in the equality clause found in the Interim Constitution of the Republic of South Africa, 1993.

[57] Birenbaum (1996) *SAJHR* 488.

[58] Birenbaum (1996) *SAJHR* 488.

[59] O'Sullivan 'Reproductive rights' 37-14.

[60] O'Sullivan 'Reproductive rights' 37-12. Equality provides women with the freedom to choose whether to have intercourse or how many children to have and when, and permissive termination-of-pregnancy legislation is an issue of social justice and sexual equality.

[61] Act 61 of 2003.

[62] In the sense that pregnant women bear the burden of uncertainty with respect to paid maternity leave or related benefits The unfortunate fact is that physicality of pregnancy limits women's earning capacity and this is despite the fact that run-of-the-mill household expenses continue to accrue throughout the existence of a pregnancy and during and after birth. In fact, expenses may even

and they shoulder it disproportionally in both the economic and social sense.[63] These consequences are increasingly detrimental when poverty and race intersect the issue.[64] Drawing on context shows that these circumstances all impact on women's ability to meaningfully develop their envisaged potential, particularly in cases where their inner direction does not include bearing children, having too many children, or having children too closely spaced. In recognising this, the Choice Act allows for the termination of a pregnancy on demand during the firs 12 weeks of gestation,[65] and from 13 to 20 weeks for socio-economic reasons.[66] Most importantly, the only required consent is that of the woman or girl who is seeking the health-care service,[67] and interference with access to termination-of-pregnancy services is an offence.[68]

On its own, the Choice Act will not realise equality for women; more is necessary.[69] For there to be substantive equality, even the poorest of women of any race or economic and social background should be able to have access to the Act's benefits [70] The state has realised this and in terms of s 4(3)*(c)* of the National Health Act, health-care centres funded by the state must provide women with free termination-of-pregnancy services. However, the National Health Act does not extend to 'abortion-related expenses' that some women have to cover; these include transport costs, loss of income due to absence from work, child care while

---

increase due to medical expenses, increased need for transport to and from ante- and post-natal care facilities and as the household prepares for the arrival of their new family member.

[63] O'Sullivan 'Reproductive rights' 37-13. Also see *President of the Republic of South Africa v Hugo* 1997 (4) SA 1 (CC) (*Hugo*). In this case the Constitutional Court was called on to decide whether granting special remission of sentence to mothers of children below the age of 12 years was unfair discrimination in respect of fathers with children of the same age. Goldstone J (para 37) recognised that generally women bear more responsibilities for child-rearing than fathers do. Further, Goldstone J explicitly recognised women's unequal social footing when the judge stated as follows (para 38): '[T]here can be no doubt that the task of rearing children is a burdensome one. It requires time, money and emotional energy. For women without skills or financia resources, its challenges are particularly acute. For many South African women, the difficulties of being responsible for the social and economic burdens of child rearing, in circumstances where they have few skills and scant financia resources, are immense. The failure of fathers to shoulder their share of the financia and social burden of child rearing is a primary cause of this hardship. The result of being responsible for children makes it more difficult for women to compete in the labour market and it is one of the causes of deep inequalities experienced by women in employment.' (Footnotes excluded.) The majority's position on women's roles does not come without debate; see the decisions of Kriegler J (paras 82–3); Mokgoro J (paras 92–3); and O'Regan J (para 113).

[64] O'Sullivan 'Reproductive rights' 37-13 and *Hugo*.

[65] Section 2(1)*(a)*.

[66] Section 2(1)*(b)*. Once a pregnancy has progressed passed 20 weeks' gestation, s 2(1)*(c)* provides that such pregnancy may only be terminated on therapeutic grounds. Therapeutic grounds are listed as maternal life endangerment, severe foetal malformation, or there is risk of injury to the foetus.

[67] Section 5 of the Choice Act.

[68] Section 10(1)*(c)* of the Choice Act.

[69] C Ngwena 'Accessing abortion services under the Choice on Termination of Pregnancy Act: Realising substantive equality' (2000) 25 *Journal for Juridical Science* 19 29. Ngwena points out that for substantive equality to be realised, merely legalising termination of pregnancies is not enough, and the state must make access available for those who cannot afford the service.

[70] Ngwena (2000) *Journal for Juridical Science* 29.

accessing termination-of-pregnancy services, pregnancy tests and sanitary pads.[71] Lince-Deroche, Constant, Harries et al emphasise that these costs may act as barriers to termination-of-pregnancy services.[72]

While s 4(3)*(c)* assists in ensuring that the benefi of the Choice Act permeates differences, the fact remains that public provision of termination-of-pregnancy services has not met its full potential even after years of implementation.[73] In fact, Albertyn demonstrates that there is a decline in the provision of termination-of-pregnancy services and states; 'the early gains of the 1990s have been eroded and the state has failed to progressively realise women's right of access to reproductive health-care in general and safe abortion in particular'.[74]

If equality means that all people should be able to fulfi their inner potential by moving beyond barriers linked to pregnancy, sex, gender, race, class and so on, then its reach must include the scenario in which women plan to continue with their pregnancies. Here, the right to equality requires that, while women are gestating, they still have the same access to rights and freedoms contained in the Constitution and the law generally. The existence of continued pregnancy should not nullify their opportunities for self-fulfilment On the substantive level, the right to equality requires that pregnancy is recognised as a biological process which has the effect of increasing women's needs[75] for more specialised attention regarding health care, obstetric care, education, and economic assistance, to name a few examples. If these context-related measures are not in place, women are at risk of being denied the opportunity of safely progressing through pregnancy and later resuming their non-reproductive activities.

[71] N Lince-Deroche, D Constant, J Harries et al 'The costs of accessing abortion in South Africa: Women's cost associated with second-trimester abortion services in Western Cape province' (2015) 92 *Contraception* 339.

[72] Lince-Deroche, Constant, Harries et al (2015) *Contraception* 343.

[73] For instance, see C Pickles 'Lived experiences of the Choice on Termination of Pregnancy Act 92 of 1996: Bridging the gap for women in need' (2013) 29 *SAJHR* 515. Also see Albertyn (2015) *Revista Direito GV* 430; R Hodes 'The culture of illegal abortion in South Africa' (2016) 42 *Journal of Southern African Studies* 79; J Harries, N Lince, D Constant, et al 'The challenges of offering public second trimester abortion services in South Africa: Health care providers' perspectives' (2012) 44 *Journal of Biosocial Science* 197; and J Harries, K Stinson & P Orner 'Health care providers' attitudes towards termination of pregnancy: A qualitative study in South Africa' (2009) 9 *BioMed Central Public Health* 296. Each article demonstrates that, although South Africa has this policy in place, the demand for termination-of-pregnancy services is rarely adequately met as a result of stigma, poor infrastructure, and a lack of physical space and personnel. The lack of personnel is linked to provider opposition to termination of pregnancies and unwilling care providers. The shortage of termination-of-pregnancy providers undermines the availability of termination services. These are some of the same issues raised by Ngwena more than 10 years ago; see Ngwena (2000) *Journal for Juridical Science* 19.

[74] Albertyn (2015) *Revista Direito GV* 443–6; 448.

[75] Here, 'increasing women's needs' is used to indicate that pregnancy brings with it very specifi issues, for instance, general basic health care will not be sufficient for pregnant women. The existence of a gestating foetus places women's bodies under very unique demands that require increased resources such as prenatal vitamins, folic acid, proper general nutrition, and access to obstetric care providers who can monitor pregnant women and foetal development. Most importantly, birth is understood to have the potential to be one of the most life-threatening instances in women's lives and this requires a unique form of health care.

There are a number of examples where special provision has been made for pregnant women which has the effect of securing space for women to experience reproductive autonomy on the basis of substantive equality. One such example is s 4(3)*(a)* of the National Health Act which states that the Minister, state clinics and community health-care centres funded by the state must provide pregnant women, among other listed recipients, with free health services if they are not beneficiarie of medical aid schemes.[76] The Act's definitio of health-care services specificall includes reproductive health care. This provision has the potential[77] to ensure that pregnant women can safely progress through pregnancy despite differences in race, class, gender, and so on. Further, having this sort of provision in place indicates that the state is engaging with the notion that, regardless of a woman's social standing, reproduction will not be a ground to deny women their chance of a healthy existence during the process of reproduction and beyond reproduction. In this sense, s 4(3)*(a)* aids in overcoming maternal morbidity and mortality.[78] By preventing the negative consequences associated with pregnancy and childbirth, in principle, women should be able to continue to work towards the path they envisage for themselves and not be physically hampered by the reproductive process.

Another example of reinforcing reproductive autonomy through the prism of reproductive rights stems from *Head of Department, Department of Education, Free State Province v Welkom High School*.[79] Here, the Constitutional Court dealt with pregnant learner policies that automatically excluded female learners from school if they became pregnant.[80] The court found that excluding learners from school on the grounds of their being pregnant was a *prima facie* violation of their

[76] Other examples of legislative support mechanisms relevant to economic security of pregnant women can briefl be identified In terms of s 25(1) of the Basic Conditions of Employment Act 75 of 1997 women are entitled to four consecutive months' maternity leave. However, the Act does not mandate paid maternity leave. In the case where the woman concerned contributed to the Unemployment Insurance Fund, s 24(1) of the Unemployment Insurance Act 63 of 2001 provides that she will be entitled to maternity leave benefits Also, in terms of s 5 of the Employment Equity Act 55 of 1998 every employer is mandated to take steps to promote equal opportunity in the workplace by eliminating unfair discrimination as specifie in terms of the equality clause. Additionally, s 187(1)*(e)* of the Labour Relations Act 66 of 1995 provides that dismissal on the grounds of pregnancy, intended pregnancy, or for any reasons related to pregnancy is automatically an unfair dismissal.

[77] Since this is a socio-economic right, the state's obligation to realise this right only goes so far as resources permit. See s 27(1)*(b)* and (2) of the Constitution. This right will be discussed below.

[78] See generally Human Rights Watch 'Stop making excuses: Accountability for maternal health care in South Africa' available at http://www.hrw.org/reports/2011/08/08/stop-making-excuses-0 (accessed on 23 March 2016).

[79] 2014 (2) SA 228 (CC) (*Welkom High School*).

[80] It should be noted that this was not the primary issue before the court. The primary issue to be decided related to the question of which body, being the provincial authorities or the school's governing bodies, had the authority to develop learner pregnancy policies, and what processes should be followed where the policy is seen as unconstitutional. However, a serious issue became apparent because regardless of who is vested with the authority in terms of legislation, the fact remained that the schools concerned were implementing a *prima facie* unconstitutional policy and the court took it upon itself to delve into that issue.

right to equality.[81] For substantive equality to be realised, a school's learner pregnancy policy should include aspects that advance these learners' equal benefi of the right to education by accommodating the unique position that pregnancy creates for girl learners. Therefore, the policies should rather include aspects such as the following: exemptions from mandatory sporting activities, procedures regarding maternity leave, adequate availability of medical and counselling services at the school, and special accommodation of babies within the school environment.[82]

Welkom High School is ground-breaking for two reasons. First, this case serves as an example of equality as a reproductive right beyond the realm of termination of pregnancy. It demonstrates how our rights system can be relied on to foster a healthy and supportive environment for women or girls to realise their reproductive autonomy where the realisation of autonomy includes the continuation of pregnancy. Secondly, the *Welkom High School* case emphasises that the decision to continue with a pregnancy should not come at such a high price that it could cost girls their educational advancement and thereby place them at a disadvantaged starting point when entering the economy or attempting to gain access to tertiary education. Expanding on that, this case explicitly recognises that girls do not have to be torn between advancing ambitions beyond motherhood and motherhood itself. Society and the state have to accommodate female reproductive capacity as a *norm* rather than as an exception to the norm, thus placing women and girls centre stage. This decision is a progressive move towards substantive equality. If having to make a choice between education and pregnancy continuation were to be imposed and the girl concerned chose to have an education instead, thereby requiring her to terminate her pregnancy, it could hardly be accepted that the termination decision was a voluntary act based on autonomy. In fact, a termination of pregnancy under those circumstances could be framed as a forced termination of pregnancy which violates the right to bodily and psychological integrity and the right to make reproductive decisions in terms of s 12(2) of the Constitution.

4.3.2 Dignity

The Constitution expressly protects a person's dignity. In this respect, s 10 states that everyone has inherent dignity and the right to have their dignity respected and protected. According to *National Coalition for Gay and Lesbian Equality*,[83] dignity, at the very least, requires us to acknowledge the value and worth of all individuals as members of society.[84] Building on that, in *Teddy Bear Clinic for*

[81] *Welkom High School* paras 111–14. While the reader is referred to paragraphs of the majority decision provided by Khampepe J, the decisions of both Froneman J and Zondo J are also aligned to this position. Further, the court recognised that such exclusionary policies also violate a female learner's rights to privacy, dignity, bodily and psychological integrity and education. These rights, in the context of their application to pregnancy, will be considered below.

[82] *Welkom High School* para 64.

[83] *National Coalition for Gay and Lesbian Equality* para 28.

[84] This is in line with Ackermann's approach to dignity, in that he understands dignity to mean human worth and this inestimable worth vests in all human beings by the very fact that they form

Abused Children v Minister of Justice and Constitutional Development,[85] Khampepe J reiterated[86] that dignity recognises the value of the choices individuals make, and this right also includes 'the deeply personal understanding we have of ourselves, our worth as individuals and our worth in our material and social context'. Later on Khampepe J expands on this and explains that a person's dignity embraces how that person values him or herself and how others value the person concerned.[87] Further, according to *S v Makwanyane*,[88] dignity and the right to life are the most important of all human rights. Therefore, as one of the most important rights, dignity is a constitutional acknowledgment that human beings are entitled to be treated as worthy of respect and concern.[89]

Applying this right in a reproductive context leads to O'Sullivan's work on termination of pregnancy. She asserts that '[d]enying a woman the freedom to make and to act upon a decision concerning reproduction treats her as a means to an end and strips her of her dignity'.[90] In terms of being an individual as an end in herself, a woman should not be treated as a mere instrument necessary to achieving the will of others, and approaching dignity in this way sets the standards at a level below which ethical and legal behaviour may not fall.[91]

Not only has dignity secured the space for reproductive decision-making in terms of termination of pregnancy, but, according to Woolman, this right has revolutionised the body of law that deals with the state regulation of termination of pregnancies.[92] He states that the courts[93] have expressly recognised that the right to dignity encapsulates two definition specificall relevant to women in relation

---

part of the human race. See L Ackermann *Human Dignity: Lodestar for Equality in South Africa* (2012) 86–114.

[85] 2014 (2) SA 168 (CC) (*Teddy Bear Clinic*) para 52.

[86] The judge relied on *Khumalo v Holomisa* 2002 (5) SA 401 (CC) para 27.

[87] *Teddy Bear Clinic* para 56.

[88] 1995 (3) SA 391 (CC) (*Makwanyane*) para 144. In this case the Constitutional Court had to decide on the constitutionality of the death sentence.

[89] *Makwanyane* para 328.

[90] O'Sullivan 'Reproductive rights' 37-23.

[91] S Woolman 'Dignity' in S Woolman & M Bishop (eds) *Constitutional Law of South Africa* 2 ed (Revised Service 3) 36-9. However, there are others who do not fin value in dignity and view it as merely requiring respect for autonomy or persons. See R Macklin 'Dignity is a useless concept: It means no more than respect for persons or their autonomy' (2003) 327 *British Medical Journal* 1419. Macklin views dignity as being so useless in medical ethics that it can be 'eliminated without any loss of content' to medical ethics.

[92] Woolman 'Dignity' 36-31.

[93] *Christian Lawyers* (2005) and *Christian Lawyers* (1998). While South African courts have adopted dignity as a means to secure their protection during reproductive decision-making, other jurisdictions have used dignity in a way that it must be balanced so as to protect the unborn as well as women seeking termination of pregnancies. See RB Siegel 'Dignity and the duty to protect unborn life' in C McCrudden (ed) *Understanding Human Dignity* (2013) 30. Siegel demonstrates how the German Constitutional Court adopted dignity in such a way that dignity of women is in competition with the dignity of the unborn and the right therefore must be balanced between the two claimants. The German 'duty-to-protect' approach was later accepted in other European countries including Spain, Columbia, Argentina and Portugal. To date, the South African Constitutional Court has not decided on the issue of termination of pregnancy.

to reproductive rights: 'equal concern and equal respect' and 'self-actualization'.[94] 'Equal concern and equal respect' is a negative obligation in the sense that one cannot treat another merely as a means, but should rather recognise in the other person the ability to act as an autonomous moral agent and to self-actualise.[95] This approach formulates dignity as a formal entitlement to equal concern and equal respect.[96] Viewing dignity as securing the space for self-actualisation, women's dignity is entitled to respect, since they hold the capacity to create meaning for themselves and pursue their own set of ends.[97]

While Woolman and O'Sullivan explain the role of dignity in the context of termination of pregnancy, it is asserted that those principles will also fin application where women plan to continue with their pregnancies. If dignity is seen as a formal entitlement to respect and concern regarding the space for self-actualisation, then continuation of pregnancy has to be included, because continuing with a pregnancy forms part of the process of self-actualisation. If not, one would be diminishing a pregnant woman's human worth. Consequently, the decision to continue with a pregnancy demands respect, and decisions made on how to progress through pregnancy when it comes to health care and lifestyle also demand respect, as women have the capacity to make decisions, create meaning for themselves and pursue their own ends.

The only known case dealing with the application of dignity in respect of pregnancy continuation is the *Welkom High School* case. In this instance, Khampepe J found that requiring girls to 'report' their pregnancies to school authorities, and further requiring other learners to report suspected pregnant girls to school authorities amounted to a violation of their dignity, especially because reporting was required for maintaining the quality of the learning environment and not to support the pregnant learners.[98] Khampepe J found that these reporting requirements may end up stigmatising learner pregnancy, thereby possibly creating an environment where pregnant learners hide the existence of a pregnancy.[99] This is a fairly clear lack of respect for self-actualisation, and a violation of the space required for self-actualisation. There is an air of punishment permeating the schools' reporting requirements and girls should not be punished for following through with the decision to continue with a pregnancy. Punishment for engaging in one of the body's biological processes will not foster a person's dignity, nor will it result in healthy progression through pregnancy because it may compromise healthy pregnancy outcomes. Further, the existence of a pregnancy may be hidden.

---

[94] Woolman 'Dignity' 36-34.

[95] Woolman 'Dignity' 36-10.

[96] Woolman 'Dignity' 36-10.

[97] Woolman 'Dignity' 36-11.

[98] *Welkom High School* para 115. According to the judge, these requirements also violate pregnant girls' rights to privacy and bodily and psychological integrity.

[99] *Welkom High School* para 115.

4.3.3 Life

Section 11 of the Bill of Rights provides that everyone has the right to life. In *Makwanyane,* the Constitutional Court found that the right to life is an unqualifie right.[100] O'Regan J stated that the right to life goes beyond mere existence; it includes the right to live as a human being with human dignity, to be part of a broader community, and to share in the experience of humanity.[101]

According to O'Sullivan,[102] s 11 of the Constitution is supported by the Choice Act in that its less restrictive provisions[103] provide women with access to reproductive health-care services that will or should prevent or reduce deaths associated with the illegal and unsafe termination of pregnancies. Ngwena demonstrates how the Choice Act is moving in the right direction concerning securing women's right to life.[104] He states that, during the implementation of the Abortion and Sterilization Act, it was estimated that 40 000 women accessed unsafe and illegal termination-of-pregnancy services, and that only an average of 1 200 women qualifie for legal terminations.[105] However, in the firs year of the Choice Act's implementation, 26 000 women had access to safe and legal termination-of-pregnancy services.[106] These figure suggest a gradual realisation of the value of women's lives in South Africa. Unfortunately, these gains are being lost as a result of an over-burdened health system, termination-of-pregnancy stigma, poor political will and inactive civil mobilisation aimed at protecting women's rights in this area.[107] Where inactivity prevails, women will continue to access unsafe and illegal services. In 2008, the World Health Organization estimated that 42 million pregnancies were terminated world wide, and, of these, 20 million were terminated by unskilled service providers using dangerous techniques, under unsanitary conditions, or were self-induced terminations.[108] While these figure do not represent only the South African experience, they do demonstrate extensive reliance on illegal termination-of-pregnancy services, which is something that plagues the South African reproductive health-care industry.[109]

---

[100] *Welkom High School* para 47.

[101] *Makwanyane* para 326.

[102] O'Sullivan 'Reproductive rights' 37-7.

[103] The Choice Act's provisions should be compared to the now-repealed Abortion and Sterilization Act 2 of 1975, where, in terms of s 3(1)*(a)–(d)*, a pregnancy could be terminated only in cases of rape, incest, or if the pregnancy constituted a serious threat to the woman's life, or physical or mental health. Two medical practitioners were required to certify that abortion was necessary in the circumstances indicated. Section 3(1) was further qualifie by s 3(2), which required that the medical practitioner who certifie the necessity of the termination could not be the practitioner to perform the termination procedure, or even fall under the same partnership or employer.

[104] C Ngwena 'An appraisal of abortion laws in southern Africa from a reproductive health rights perspective' (2004) 32 *Journal of Law, Medicine & Ethics* 708 715

[105] Ngwena (2004) *Journal of Law, Medicine & Ethics* 715

[106] Ngwena (2004) *Journal of Law, Medicine & Ethics* 715.

[107] Albertyn (2015) *Revista Direito GV* 430.

[108] World Health Organization 'Unsafe abortion: Global and regional estimates of the incidence of unsafe abortion and associated mortality in 2008' at 2, available at http://whqlibdoc.who.int/publications/2011/9789241501118_eng.pdf?ua=1 (accessed on 1 April 2016).

[109] Hodes (2016) *Journal of Southern African Studies* 73.

Going beyond termination of pregnancy, it must be accepted that the right to life also demands that the decision to continue with a pregnancy should not equate to a decision to risk one's life in order to realise that reproductive decision. Also, if the right to life is more than organic life and refers to a certain quality of life directed by dignity, then the right to life demands that, as women progress through pregnancy and birth generally, they are treated in a way that enhances their lives in a dignifie manner. Thus, women cannot be forced to forsake themselves and their inner-define direction solely for the purpose of procreation and/or ensuring the live birth of a child. A demand such as this extends to family members, partners, the community, the medical profession, and the state. This approach is supported by O'Regan J's findin in *Makwanyane*:[110] 'The right to life . . . incorporates the right to dignity. So the rights to human dignity and life are entwined. The right to life is more than existence—it is a right to be treated as a human being with dignity: without dignity, human life is substantially diminished. Without life, there cannot be dignity.'

4.3.4 Freedom and security of the person

The Bill of Rights ensures freedom and security of the person. Section 12(2)*(a)* and *(b)* provides that everyone has the right to bodily and psychological integrity and this right includes the right to make reproductive decisions and the right to security and control of their body.

O'Sullivan,[111] reflectin on Ackermann J's minority decision in *Ferreira*, explains that 'freedom' (as found in the title to the right) should not be construed too narrowly. A narrow construction views freedom as housing the right to not have obstacles to choices and activities placed on one's path by the state.[112] This overly narrow approach will effectively prevent positive claims against the state for the realisation of s 12(2) rights.[113] Again, O'Sullivan approvingly refers to Ackermann J, and emphasises that the experience of freedom and security is closely linked to the conditions in which it is exercised; therefore any meaningful experience of s 12 is dependent on the presence of other rights.[114] In a reproductive context, this means that freedom and security cannot be effectively developed or sustained where women do not have access to reproductive health-care services and other rights which support access to reproductive health care.[115]

Bishop and Woolman explain that s 12(2) recognises that 'each *physical body* is of equal worth and is entitled to equal respect'.[116] (Emphasis in original.) Further,

[110] *Makwanyane* para 327.
[111] O'Sullivan 'Reproductive rights' 37-16.
[112] *Ferreira* para 54, as cited by O'Sullivan 'Reproductive rights' 37-16.
[113] O'Sullivan 'Reproductive rights' 37-16.
[114] O'Sullivan 'Reproductive rights' 37-18.
[115] O'Sullivan 'Reproductive rights' 37-18. It should be remembered that O'Sullivan is specificall focusing on termination-of-pregnancy rights. However, the core principles of her argument can transcend the parameters of termination of pregnancies and be applied widely to include instances of pregnancy continuation.
[116] M Bishop & S Woolman 'Freedom and security of the person' in S Woolman & M Bishop (eds) *Constitutional Law of South Africa* 2 ed (Original Service 6) 40-77.

this right demands tolerance of diverse bodies and the authors construe s 12(2) as obliging the state to ensure that every 'body' can participate equally in society despite the presence of diversity.[117] This is the same approach adopted by the majority in *AB* 2. Writing for the majority, Nkabinde J found that '[t]he right to reproductive autonomy in section 12(2)*(a)* confronts directly the fact that many women do not enjoy security in and control over their own bodies. To that end, the focus is on the individual woman's own body.'[118] In the context of surrogacy, this means that a commissioning parent cannot rely on s 12(2)*(a)* because surrogacy requires the use of another woman's body. Alarmingly, the majority failed to consider 'psychological integrity' of the commissioning parent, which is explicitly protected in s 12(2).[119] Considering the meaning of 'psychological integrity', Bishop and Woolman suggest that this means protection from undue stress or shock, and as such it offers protection from insults and privacy violations.[120] However, Khampepe J states that s 12(2) should be interpreted to include all instances where the 'bodily *or* psychological integrity' of a person may be harmed.[121] In this respect, the minority recognised that intrusion on the ability to make a decision may amount to psychological harm (as something separate from bodily harm) and thus may constitute a violation of a person's psychological integrity.[122]

According to Bishop and Woolman,[123] 'security in' in terms of s 12(2)*(b)* refers to those bodily invasions that are more than 'trivial'. The invasion would move beyond trivial where it was not preceded by a hearing, established procedures were not followed, and there was an inflictio of unnecessary pain and anxiety, or the invasion ran the risk of causing disfiguremen or was detrimental to one's health.[124] The Constitution's recognition of the right to enjoy control over one's body is ultimately an acknowledgment that individuals are cable of making decisions for themselves and acting accordingly.[125] Bishop and Woolman argue that any action that infringes on this form of control is a *prima facia* violation of s 12(2)*(b)*.[126]

---

[117] Bishop & Woolman 'Freedom and security of the person' 40-77.

[118] *AB* 2 para 313 (footnote omitted).

[119] The minority took exception to the majority's position; see paras 63–72. The minority found the inclusion of 'psychological integrity' in s 12 recognises that a person's psychological integrity can be harmed, independently of their body; see paras 67–8. The minority found that '[a] stiflin of the ability to make a [reproductive] decision can therefore be a violation of psychological integrity, provided the consequences are of an invidious nature'; see para 69.]]

[120] Bishop & Woolman 'Freedom and security of the person' 40-78 to 40-79.

[121] *AB* 2 para 66 (emphasis added).

[122] *AB* 2 para 69.

[123] 'Freedom and security of the person' 40-86. The authors refer to the following as trivial invasions: finge -printing or breathalyser testing.

[124] Bishop & Woolman 'Freedom and security of the person' 40-87.

[125] Bishop & Woolman 'Freedom and security of the person' 40-88.

[126] Bishop & Woolman 'Freedom and security of the person' 40-88. Specifi to psychological wellbeing, Khampepe J found that s 12(2)*(b)* protects the right to make decisions and 'a person relying on this right need only show that their inability to make that decision—resultant upon some law or conduct—has caused (at least) psychological harm'. See *AB* 2 para 70. In this respect, Khampepe J devised a three-stage inquiry: 1. Does the impugned law or conduct prevent or inhibit a person from making a decision? 2. If yes, does the decision concern reproduction? 3. If yes, does

Section 12(2) plays a vital role in the context of voluntary parenthood avoidance. Albertyn, Artz, Combrinck et al view s 12(2) as essential to bodily autonomy and the source of reproductive freedom.[127] Bishop and Woolman[128] also understand s 12(2)*(a)* as protecting reproductive freedom,[129] and argue that the recognition of reproductive freedom was probably intended to prevent courts from prohibiting the termination of pregnancies. This argument stands firm especially when one considers that *Christian Lawyers* (2005) is the last case to challenge the Choice Act before a court and the unsuccessful challenge was never taken on appeal to the Constitutional Court.[130] The authors go on to assert that this section gives recognition of socially entrenched forms of physical oppression and exploitation related to women's reproduction and sexuality.[131] According to O'Sullivan, s 12(2) directly confronts the fact that women do not enjoy security in, and control over, their own bodies, taking into account the high rates of sexual violence against women, and the fact that circumstances in which women become pregnant are often beyond their control.[132] Further, O'Sullivan[133] states that the Choice Act promotes a woman's right to freedom and the security of her body by affording her the right to choose to terminate her pregnancy safely, and that only the women concerned are in the best position to make that decision; hence only their consent is needed.

The firs case to deal with s 12(2) of the Constitution in a reproductive context[134] was *Christian Lawyers* (1998). In this case the plaintiffs sought an order to declare the Choice Act to be unconstitutional and to strike it down in its entirety. The plaintiffs argued that the Act infringed on the unborn's right to life and was therefore unconstitutional. McCreath J rejected the argument that the Constitution applied to the unborn and went on to focus on the role of s 12(2) of the Constitution.[135] McCreath J recognised that, in order to overcome broad and deep-rooted forms of domination and disadvantage based on numerous grounds of

preventing or inhibiting the decision detrimentally affect the psychological integrity of the person concerned? See para 72.

[127] Albertyn, Artz, Combrinck et al 'Women's freedom and security of the person' 297; 364.

[128] Bishop & Woolman 'Freedom and security of the person' 40-80.

[129] Interestingly, the authors do not defin what they consider to be reproductive freedom.

[130] On an even more meaningful level, *Christian Lawyers* (2005) did not challenge the entire Act but only those portions that allowed for minors to consent to their own pregnancy terminations. That may be related to the fact that in 1998 an unsuccessful application was made to declare the Act unconstitutional in its entirety; see *Christian Lawyers* (1998).

[131] Bishop & Woolman 'Freedom and security of the person' 40-80.

[132] O'Sullivan 'Reproductive rights' 37-17. Also see Albertyn, Artz, Combrinck et al 'Women's freedom and security of the person' 295.

[133] 'Reproductive rights' 37-18.

[134] According to O'Sullivan ('Reproductive rights' 37-16), *Ferreira* was the firs Constitutional Court case to deal with s 12's equivalent in the Interim Constitution, and this was done so in the context of unlawful detention and the prohibition on cruel, inhumane and degrading punishment. Research reveals that it is mainly s 12(1) that makes its way through the judicial system, whereas the application of s 12(2)*(a)* and *(b)* rarely comes before the courts. In 2016 s 12(2)*(a)* came before the Constitutional Court in *AB* 2 but the majority did not meaningfully delve into the crux of the section. This is despite the fact that the applicant's case was premised on the notion of 'reproductive autonomy'.

[135] More about the court's approach to the unborn will be considered later.

discrimination, proper consideration must be given to women's rights, which include their right to make decisions concerning reproduction and control over their bodies, among other rights recognised by the court.[136] Also, in respect of reproductive autonomy or autonomy as a whole, the court confirme that s 12(2) of the Constitution is not explicitly qualifie for the benefi of the unborn.[137] Where a limitation of rights is sought, one must turn to the limitation clause found in s 36 of the Constitution, and, on this basis, the court accepted that the state may regulate the termination of pregnancies.[138]

Christian Lawyers (1998) did not really go to the core of what s 12(2)*(a)* and *(b)* of the Constitution means for women. However, *Christian Lawyers* (2005) did.[139] Also in the context of termination of pregnancy, *Christian Lawyers* (2005) brought the concept of 'reproductive self-determination' to the fore. The court found that the 'fundamental right to self-determination' is founded on a number of rights such as the rights to dignity, privacy, access to reproductive health care and bodily and psychological integrity, including the right to make decisions concerning reproduction and the security of one's own body.[140] These rights were found to provide the foundation for the right to terminate a pregnancy in South Africa.[141] Interestingly, Mojapelo J did not include the right to equality while building a rights-based foundation. This is strange because, without equal benefi of the listed rights, the effective reach of each right is substantially diminished. In any case, further in the judgment the judge found that, comparatively,[142] South Africa has the most explicit right concerning the termination of pregnancy and that this right is reinforced by the rights to life, equality,[143] dignity, privacy, and reproductive health care. Most importantly, the court emphasised that s 12(2)*(a)* and *(b)* were clearly designed to protect women's right to reproductive self-determination.[144]

Accepting that s 12 of the Constitution sets down the ambit for freedom and self-determination generally, and s 12(2)*(a)* and *(b)* read together recognise reproductive self-determination, there is certainly more to this section than the right to terminate a pregnancy. '[D]ecisions concerning reproduction', as used in s 12(2)*(a)*, must be construed more widely, and should include the decisions to continue with a pregnancy,[145] on how one envisages living through a pregnancy,

---

[136] *Christian Lawyers* (1998) 1123D–F.

[137] *Christian Lawyers* (1998) 1121I.

[138] *Christian Lawyers* (1998) 1121J–1122A.

[139] Briefl , this case concerned the right of a minor to consent to the termination of her pregnancy without the consent of her parents or guardian.

[140] *Christian Lawyers* (2005) 518A–D. See ss 10, 14, 27(1)*(a)* and 12(2)*(a)* and *(b)* respectively.

[141] *Christian Lawyers* (2005) 518D.

[142] The court compared the right to terminate a pregnancy in respect of the United States, Canada and Germany.

[143] It should be noted that the court did not consider equality to form part of the foundation to the right to terminate a pregnancy but it is seen as a right that strengthens a woman's right to terminate her pregnancy. This does not fall in line with the Preamble of the Choice Act.

[144] *Christian Lawyers* (2005) 524I.

[145] Obviously, reproductive decisions come into play before the existence of a pregnancy, and can include who to procreate with, when and how, contraceptive decisions or even sterilisation. However, these considerations fall beyond the scope of this book, since the topic is narrowly focused on reproductive autonomy during pregnancy.

and concerning patient-centred and person-specifi birthing needs. Reproductive decisions should be seen as encompassing those decisions that result in reproductive outcomes in one form or another. Furthermore, while progressing through gestation, birth and related decision-making processes, women's control over their bodies should not be diminished but ensured and promoted. Therefore, if we understand s 12(2)*(a)* as protecting reproductive freedom, then all discussions of this right should include those issues that are related to pregnancy continuation.[146]

In respect of pregnancy continuation, it is necessary to determine how s 12(2)*(a)* and *(b)* aid in realising female reproductive autonomy when that autonomous action involves pregnancy continuation. No South African case law has dealt with the application of s 12(2)*(a)* and *(b)* in this context. This is a discomforting judicial silence, especially because pregnancy is a common occurrence in women's lives and it would be naïve to accept that every woman's decision concerning pregnancy continuation and related health and lifestyle decisions have been unquestionably respected.

A fittin example of a violation of female reproductive self-determination can be found in *S v Mshumpa*.[147] In this case a pregnant woman was shot in the stomach with the aim of terminating her pregnancy without her consent. The victim's boyfriend and father-to-be of the unborn did not wish to have a child with the victim and chose this method to avoid parenthood.[148] The shots to the victim's abdomen successfully terminated the pregnancy, which the victim wanted.[149] The case came before the Eastern Cape Division as a criminal case of murder of the foetus,[150] rather than a violation of the victim's right to reproductive freedom and self-determination per s 12(2).[151]

In all the hype about prenatal life in law,[152] the woman, who lost the opportunity to fulfi her expectation of being a parent and having a child, was sidelined. The court refused to extend the definitio of murder to include a foetus for a number of reasons.[153] One reason being that developing the law to accommodate the unborn in the meaning of 'person', for purposes of the crime of murder, would violate

[146] In the beginning of their section on reproductive freedom, Albertyn, Artz, Combrinck et al ('Women's freedom and security of the person' 363) defin reproductive freedom as including 'claims to decision-making and control over their fertility, the freedom to decide when and whether to have children, and the information and the means to act on these decisions'. Most of the discussion that follows, in the context of pregnancy, relates to termination of pregnancy. Bishop and Woolman do not go on to develop a definitio of reproductive freedom.

[147] 2008 (1) SACR 126 (E) (*Mshumpa*). A more detailed analysis of this case will follow when discussing the position of the unborn under South African law.

[148] *Mshumpa* para 6.

[149] *Mshumpa* paras 1; 3.

[150] *Mshumpa* para 5.

[151] Froneman J (para 64) did recognise that the assault on the victim was a violation of s 12(2)*(a)* and *(b)* but not in respect of the right to freely and safely continue a pregnancy. Rather, the judge's focus was on the impact an assault has on a pregnant woman, and since the pregnant woman and foetus share a unique connection, an assault on the foetus is effectively an assault on the pregnant women. In that respect, her s 12 bodily security rights were violated.

[152] *Mshumpa* paras 49–50.

[153] *Mshumpa* paras 55–62.

women's right to terminate their pregnancies, ironically being a self-determination right itself.[154] The outcome of this case cannot be faulted; one cannot murder an entity which is not a person in law. However, there is an issue with the way the case was formulated and brought before the Eastern Cape Division. In effect, this case results in a situation where, since the law recognises the right to terminate a pregnancy, it cannot recognise the right to continue with a pregnancy because this recognition is framed as valuing the unborn and this approach will nullify women's claims to freely terminate early pregnancies.

Contrary to the *Mshumpa* outcome, *Minister of Health v Treatment Action Campaign*[155] serves as an example of a decision where the Constitutional Court supportively embraced pregnant women's reproductive decision to continue with a pregnancy and indirectly reinforced their s 12(2) rights to self-determination through applying their socio-economic rights to health-care services.[156]

In *Treatment Action Campaign*, the applicants sought to enforce HIV positive pregnant women's s 27 socio-economic rights to health-care services in the public sector and claim access to antiretroviral treatment, being Nevirapine. The relevant treatment was made available to the state without charge and would assist in preventing or materially reducing mother-to-child transmission of HIV, which is known to take place during pregnancy or at birth. While the treatment was made available at a select few research and training centres throughout the country,[157] the applicants successfully argued that this restrictive access was unreasonable on a number of grounds and was a breach of the state's duties in terms s 27(2).[158] In effect, the court not only supported these women's decisions to continue with their pregnancies by ordering the state to provide the necessary antiretroviral treatment, but also supported the notion that when reproductive decisions are made, there is an obligation to ensure meaningful realisation of those decisions.[159] In this instance, women wanted to gestate healthy foetuses and give birth to healthy children. This included the need to reduce the risk of transmitting HIV during pregnancy or at birth. Without the obligation on the state to provide the necessary treatment, reproductive freedom and self-determination in the context of pregnancy continuation would be left meaningless, a mere paper-right.[160]

[154] *Mshumpa* para 59.

[155] (No 2) 2002 (5) SA 721 (CC) (*Treatment Action Campaign*).

[156] In fact, this case serves as a perfect example of O'Sullivan's ('Reproductive rights' 37-18) assertion that freedom is bound up in the context in which it is experienced.

[157] These centres only catered for 10% of all births in the public sector; see *Treatment Action Campaign* para 62.

[158] The socio-economic right to reproductive health care is discussed in more detail below. However, it should be noted that *Treatment Action Campaign* was not brought before the Constitutional Court as an issue of access to reproductive health care but was based on the more general right to health-care services.

[159] See M Pieterse *Can Rights Cure? The Impact of Human Rights Litigation on South Africa's Health System* (2014) 68–70 and Amnesty International 'Struggle for maternal health: Barriers to antenatal care in South Africa' at 10, available at https://www.health-e.org.za/wp-content/uploads/2014/10/Struggle-for-Maternal-Health-.pdf (accessed on 1 April 2016).

[160] Also, from an equality perspective, the realisation of a woman's reproductive freedom cannot be denied on the grounds of ill-health.

It is also necessary to contemplate reproductive self-determination in the context of the right to make a decision to refuse medical treatment during the existence of a pregnancy. In *Treatment Action Campaign* women were enforcing their rights to treatment, but there is also a converse right to not submit to treatment. The motivation for whichever decision is taken lies at the heart of what 'healthy pregnancy' and 'healthy pregnancy outcomes' mean for the particular woman concerned, rather than a public policy on maternal and neonatal health.[161] For instance, a healthy pregnancy may not mean that one gives birth to a healthy child at *all* costs. Instead, some women may place increased value on how they perceive their bodies' physical integrity or healthy psychological progression through pregnancy and birth. Therefore, some women may wish to refrain from a medicalised birth, excessive ultrasound scans and physical examinations, or they may prefer to avoid foetal surgery, vaginal deliveries[162] or assisted deliveries in the form of caesarean-section deliveries or episiotomy incisions. In these instances, pregnant women may wish to continue with a pregnancy and birth but on personally define terms as determined according to their own lived contexts and experiences.

There is no known South African case law in which pregnant women have been forced to submit themselves for treatment by health-care providers to ensure healthy pregnancies or healthy pregnancy outcomes. This position may stem from the fact that South African law specificall recognises a competent person's right to refuse treatment. However, that position is void of the fact that many women are

---

[161] The right to dignity requires this shift. Women cannot be treated as a means for the state to meet its own policy criteria.

[162] In this instance, women may elect to undergo a caesarean-section delivery. This is known as elective caesarean delivery. According to Lurie, vaginal delivery is recognised as being potentially traumatic to the pelvic floo and the cause of anal and urinary incontinence. He also explains that there is an increased rate of post-traumatic psychological stress associated with vaginal and emergency caesarean-section deliveries. Lurie then goes on to question whether vaginal delivery can be classifie as medical treatment and suggests that if it so defined then women have the right to make a choice between vaginal or caesarean deliveries. Also, if vaginal deliveries were to be considered medical treatment, then refusing to provide women with caesarean-section services would amount to a scenario of 'forced vaginal deliveries'. See S Lurie 'The changing motives of cesarean section: From the ancient world to the twenty-firs century' (2005) 271 *Archives of Gynecology and Obstetrics* 281 284. Section 12(2)*(a)* and *(b)* may support this approach. As long as delivery takes place in a medical facility and medical personnel are attending to the pregnant woman, vaginal delivery could be construed as a medical procedure in that context. As such, s 12(2) secures the freedom to refuse vaginal delivery. This would obviously be qualifie in circumstances where the attending facilities do not have the necessary equipment or skilled physicians to provide the alternative treatment of caesarean-section delivery. It is due to the fact that caesarean-section deliveries place high demands on resources and increase health risks during birth that vaginal deliveries are preferred at public facilities in South Africa. Caesarean-section deliveries are only performed when medically indicated. Technically, that should be the case in private facilities. However, it is well known that private patients can get access to their preferred method of delivery. In this respect see S Basu, J Andrews, S Kishore et al 'Comparative performance of private and public healthcare systems in low- and middle-income countries: A systemic review' (2012) 9 *PLOS Medicine* e1001244.

susceptible to abuse and rights violations during pregnancy and birth,[163] and may not be aware that their rights have been violated, or may not know how to, or have the means to, seek legal redress.

There are two glaring examples where women's right to refuse medical treatment or intervention have been violated and to date there is no case law directed at redressing this issue. In 2014, Amnesty International released a report which highlights some of the struggles pregnant women face when accessing or attempting to access antenatal care in South Africa.[164] Amnesty International demonstrates, through a number of interviews, that pregnant women underwent HIV testing without voluntary consent and the majority of interviewees expressed their belief that they were not allowed to refuse to undergo HIV testing.[165] Further, reports are surfacing of involuntary sterilisation of women living with HIV in South Africa.[166] In these instances, some women reported that they perceived themselves as being unable to refuse consent for sterilisation.[167]

Therefore, it would be naïve to accept that women's rights to bodily and psychological integrity during pregnancy and birth are so readily respected. Medical paternalism still remains a contentious issue in South Africa; Carstens and Pearmain[168] point out that health-care professionals do not always align themselves to the principle of patient autonomy. The relationship between patients and health-care providers can be characterised as being hierarchical and authoritarian.[169] Castro and Erviti argue that there is an 'imbalance of power within the physician–patient relationship, in which one actor is invested with power/knowledge and the other is "only a patient"'.[170] Doctors' and nurses' position of power and superior knowledge is further entrenched and bolstered when the patients being treated are indigent, have little education, cannot speak the language being used by health-care providers or are marginalised individuals

---

[163] R Castro & J Erviti 'Violations of reproductive rights during hospital births in Mexico' (2003) 7 *Health and Human Rights* 90; AA Veleda & TE Gerardt 'About humanly giving birth: The insertion of the nursing in the humanization of birth movement' (2014) 1 *Journal of Nursing and Socioenvironmental Health* 47; AFPL d'Oliveria, SG Diniz & LB Schraiber 'Violence against women in health-care institutions: An emerging problem' (2002) 359 *The Lancet* 1681; and R Jewkes & L Penn-Kekana 'Mistreatment of women in childbirth: Time for action on this important dimension of violence against women' (2015) 12 *PLOS Medicine* e1001849 1.

[164] Amnesty International 'Struggle for maternal health'. This report also reveals third-party intervention for the benefi of the unborn but there is no law that sanctions such coercive conduct in South Africa.

[165] Amnesty International 'Struggle for maternal health' 24–6 and 28.

[166] A Strode, S Mthembu & Z Essack '"She made up a choice for me": 22 HIV-positive women's experiences of involuntary sterilization in two South African provinces' (2012) 20 *Reproductive Health Matters* 61; and South African National Aids Council 'The People living with HIV stigma index, South Africa: Summary report 2014' (May 2015) available at http://www.stigmaindex.org/sites/default/files/reports/Summary-Booklet-on-Stigma-Index-Survey%20South%20Africa.pd (accessed on 28 January 2016).

[167] See generally Strode, Mthembu & Essack (2012) *Reproductive Health Matters* 61.

[168] P Carstens & D Pearmain *Foundational Principles of South African Medical Law* (2007) 877.

[169] See generally Castro & Erviti (2003) *Health and Human Rights* 90; Veleda & Gerardt (2014) *Journal of Nursing and Socioenvironmental Health* 47; D'Oliveria, Diniz & Schraiber (2002) *The Lancet* 1681; and Jewkes & Penn-Kekana (2015) *PLOS Medicine* e1001849.

[170] Castro & Erviti (2003) *Health and Human Rights* 94.

as a result of their gender, socio-economic or health status.[171] According to Castro and Erviti, this hierarchical relationship 'is even greater during gynaecological or obstetrical procedures because of a woman's physical and emotional vulnerability during pregnancy and labor'.[172] Furthermore, the position of authority over patients has been naturalised[173] through health professions' training and practice and broader societal trends where women are viewed as having lower social status and are seen as 'needing discipline and control for their own good'.[174]

In the context of reproductive health care, medical paternalism can result in coerced or forced procedures. A procedure is deemed forced when the patient's consent is lacking.[175] A procedure will be coerced when there is a measure of manipulation, where patients are intentionally misinformed or offered incentives to consent to a particular treatment.[176] Coercion can be subtle, such as asserting medical authority in a forceful way or by making decisional space within a hospital setting inflexibl or hostile. At times coercion can be blatant, patients can be refused access to other needed health care unless consent is given for another procedure or patients are abused or face threats of abuse if consent is not provided.

Given that s 9 of the Constitution makes provision for equal benefi and protection of the law, the right to bodily and psychological integrity, including the right to make reproductive decisions (and refuse care) is to the equal benefi of pregnant women too. In the context of informed refusal to submit to medical procedures, *Castell* held the following:[177]

---

[171] See generally R Jewkes, N Abrahams & Z Mvo 'Why do nurses abuse patients? Reflection from South African obstetric services' (1998) 47 *Social Science & Medicine* 1781.

[172] Castro & Erviti (2003) *Health and Human Rights* 94.

[173] Castro & Erviti (2003) *Health and Human Rights* 97.

[174] D'Oliveria, Diniz & Schraiber (2002) *The Lancet* 1681.

[175] A procedure will be forced if it is performed without the consent of a patient, either because the patient is not informed that the procedure will take place, the procedure is performed on the basis of a court order, or when spousal consent is provided despite being contrary to the wishes of the patient.

[176] Glennon 'Regulation of reproductive decision-making' 152–55. Glennon explains that a patient's decision-making process can be manipulated so as to give the impression that patient autonomy is being realised. For instance, she explains that people, while making decisions, are influence by context which is never truly neutral. She refers to a number of different contexts, one being 'decisional context'. Decisional context includes the application of default rules which patients very rarely contest. As discussed above, vaginal delivery is a default rule and, as such, women accessing public services may simply accept that method because it is presented as a rule. Also linked to context is the use of 'starting points' as influencin what the patient will construe as reasonable. For instance, Glennon explains that artificia reproduction clinics concerned with high success rates will be enticed to encourage patients to implant more embryos than what may be necessary. Consequently, the clinic, when presenting information to a patient, would say that most other patients implant three or four embryos. These numbers then become the patient's analytic starting point and they will rarely stray from that. Glennon offers further examples and explanations on how patient autonomy can be subtly curbed, but what has been mentioned here helps demonstrate why there may be no case law on this issue: Women may very well be under the impression that informed consent is provided concerning their treatment while pregnant. Also see BM Dickens & RJ Cook 'Types of consent in reproductive health care' (2015) 128 *International Journal of Gynecology & Obstetrics* 181 182.

[177] *Castell* 409A–B.

> It is clearly for the patient, in the exercise of his or her fundamental right to self-determination, to decide whether he or she wishes to undergo an operation, and it is in principle wholly irrelevant that the patient's attitude is grossly unreasonable in the eyes of the medical profession: the patient's right to bodily integrity and autonomous moral agency entitles him or her to refuse medical treatment.

Furthermore, according to *Castell*, the right to refuse remains in place even if respect for one's refusal is going to result in that person's death.[178] However, s 6(1)*(d)* of the National Health Act prescribes that the decision to refuse should be informed.[179] Thus, informed consent ensures respect for patient autonomy and secures the space for bodily and psychological integrity. In this respect the Act stipulates that the decision will be informed if, when exercising the right to refuse, the patient is informed of the implications, risks and obligations of such a refusal.[180] However, Nelson suggests that in order to better protect autonomy during reproductive decision-making, the context in which decisions are made should be properly considered.[181] This should be in addition to the notion of consent being informed.

Since pregnancy itself does not render a woman mentally incompetent, any decision-making processes undertaken in respect of medical treatment must be honoured and respected.[182] Failure to do so would result in a violation of her sense of autonomy, implicating her rights to make reproductive decisions, and to ensure security in and control over her body and dignity.[183]

---

[178] *Castell* 421A.

[179] All decisions-making concerning whether to undergo or to refrain from medical treatment must be informed. See Carstens & Pearmain *Foundational Principles of South African Medical Law* 875–79 for a discussion of the role of consent in medical treatment. At the core of the requirement for consent is that it must be informed, which indicates that the patient knows and appreciates what he or she is consenting to.

[180] Informed decision-making, concerning whether to consent to or refuse medical treatment, is a topic that inspires wide debate, particularly with respect to the level of disclosure each requires; see LJ van Bogaert 'Rights of and duties to non-consenting patients—informed refusal in the developing world' (2006) 6 *Developing World Bioethics* 13 and K Boyd 'The impossibility of informed consent?' (2015) 41 *Journal of Medical Ethics* 44. According to Carstens and Pearmain (*Foundational Principles of South African Medical Law* 887), in the case where a patient refuses to undergo a necessary medical intervention, there is an obligation of the attending physician to 'impress upon him [or her] the necessity to undergo it'. Therefore, there is a different standard applied when one compares requirements for consent and refusal.

[181] E Nelson *Law, Policy and Reproductive Autonomy* (2013) 43–6.

[182] However, see *Government of the Republic of Namibia v LM* [2014] NASC 19. The Supreme Court of Namibia found that women who are in the throes of advanced labour and who face labour complications, have diminished capacity to provide informed consent. This case concerned involuntary sterilisation of pregnant women living with HIV. While this decision may seem to support the protection of reproductive autonomy, in that attending health-care providers must obtain informed consent for sterilisations well before the onset of labour, this decision may serve as a mechanism to pierce women's autonomy during labour and delivery. This is because it essentially denies women their capacity to consent or refuse consent as a result of labour pains. It will be interesting to see how this decision will impact women's s 12 rights, especially because South African courts may consider foreign law when interpreting the Bill of Rights; see s 39(1)*(c)*.

[183] Dignity is implicated because overriding women's decision-making capacity concerning their bodies, in order for an attending physician to provide what he or she thinks is best in terms of health care, reduces women to being a means to another's end.

The topic of pregnant women's rights to make decisions concerning reproduction, to enjoy bodily and psychological integrity, and maintain control over their pregnant bodies can go on and on. The principles discussed in this section serve to show that s 12(2)*(a)* and *(b)* cover the right not to continue with a pregnancy, as well as the right to continue with a pregnancy, and in exercising both avenues of reproduction, the process has to be on terms suitable for the particular woman concerned as it is her body that bears the consequences of her decisions.

4.3.5 Privacy

Section 14 of the Bill of Rights affords everyone the right to privacy. Ackermann J explains that the right to privacy is closely related to a person's identity in that it is what is necessary if someone is to have an autonomous identity.[184] The right to privacy recognises that all persons have the right to a sphere of private intimacy which relates to our inner sanctum.[185] The inner sanctum includes features such as family life, sexual preferences and the home environment,[186] and all those issues that can be considered closely linked to the development of one's personal identity. Concerning the scope of the right to privacy, the right is not location specifi (that is, in the private sphere of the home), but rather the right to privacy is protected so long as the activity or decision being made is linked to a core area of a person's inner sanctum. Thus, a person's privacy will be protected even in cases where he or she has left the sanctum of the home and is in engaging with the state or the community.

Sachs J[187] states that the right to privacy has been interpreted as the right to be left alone and exist free of state interference,[188] but he explains there is more to this right. First, it encompasses the right to 'get on with your life', express your personality and make intimate decisions about relationships.[189] Secondly, the right to privacy also places some responsibility on the state to promote conditions in which personal self-actualisation can take place.[190]

McQuoid-Mason understands the right to privacy as protecting personal autonomy, and when it is used in this way one refers to this as personal-autonomy privacy rights.[191] These are substantive privacy rights which permit individuals to make decisions about their lives without state interference, ultimately empowering them to exercise control over issues such as marriage, procreation, contraception and child-rearing.[192]

---

[184] *Bernstein* para 65.
[185] *National Coalition for Gay and Lesbian Equality* para 32, per Ackermann J.
[186] *Bernstein* para 67.
[187] *National Coalition for Gay and Lesbian Equality* para 116.
[188] O'Sullivan 'Reproductive rights' 37-8. Also see D McQuoid-Mason 'Privacy' in S Woolman & M Bishop (eds) *Constitutional Law of South Africa* 2 ed (Original Service 12) 38-1. He states that 'at the very least, the right to privacy embraces the right to be free from intrusions and interference by the state and others in one's personal life'.
[189] *National Coalition for Gay and Lesbian Equality* para 116.
[190] *National Coalition for Gay and Lesbian Equality* para 116.
[191] 'Privacy' 38-22 to 38-23.
[192] McQuoid-Mason 'Privacy' 38-22 to 38-23.

The right to privacy has direct application to reproductive decisions in that that sort of decision can be identifie as one of the core areas of a person's identity and links to their family and home environment. It is therefore clear that those decisions to either terminate or continue with a pregnancy should be protected by the right to privacy, in that the state or the wider community cannot dictate to women how to go about engaging reproductive decisions.

In the context of the termination of pregnancy, O'Sullivan[193] cautions that the right to privacy should be used in conjunction with equality rights, since relying on privacy rights in isolation has a number of drawbacks. In this respect, she argues that it is easier to justify limiting women's access to termination-of-pregnancy services, because the termination of a pregnancy is considered to fall within a woman's private sphere, thus ultimately removing a duty on the state's part to provide public funding or to intervene and protect women.[194] Her argument can be applied equally to cases of pregnancy continuation, in that maternity services should be made readily available as a state duty to all pregnant women for the safe realisation of the decision to bear children.

It should be noted that O'Sullivan's concern about the drawbacks to relying on the right to privacy as a ground for reproductive autonomy stems from her study of the Unites States' position concerning the basis of their termination-of-pregnancy laws. In the United States, a woman's right to terminate her pregnancy is founded on her right to privacy and states have used this approach as a ground to deny the allocation of state funding for the realisation and protection of the 'private issue' of abortion.[195] However, this is not the situation in South Africa. Sachs J, in the context of the right to privacy, explicitly states that rights cannot be viewed in isolation or compartmentalised.[196] He states: 'Human rights are better approached and defended in an integrated rather than a disparate fashion. The rights must fi the people, not the people the rights. This requires looking at rights and their violations from a persons-centred rather than a formula-based position, and analysing them contextually rather than abstractly.'[197] Also, as mentioned earlier, the state is recognised as having an obligation to promote the conditions necessary for the actualisation of one's identity. Thus, while having or not having children is considered a private issue, the state must promote conditions supportive to that end.

Privacy, as a reproductive right, therefore has an important role to play in the realisation of reproductive autonomy, since it not only creates the space to make decisions concerning reproduction but also creates an obligation to develop means to achieve meaningful reproductive outcomes.

4.3.6 Reproductive health care

Section 27(1)*(a)* of the Constitution provides that everyone has the right of access to health-care services including reproductive health care. However, these rights

[193] 'Reproductive rights' 37-12.
[194] O'Sullivan 'Reproductive rights' 37-12.
[195] O'Sullivan 'Reproductive rights' 37-11.
[196] *National Coalition for Gay and Lesbian Equality* para 112.
[197] *National Coalition for Gay and Lesbian Equality* para 112.

do not embrace an individual entitlement to the immediate provision of any service or resource.[198] Section 27(2) obliges the state to take reasonable legislative and other measures, within its available resources, to achieve the progressive realisation of this right. This places a positive obligation on the state to devise a comprehensive and workable plan to meet its obligations to progressively realise socio-economic rights within available resources.[199]

In *Soobramoney v Minister of Health*[200] the Constitutional Court held that the obligations imposed on the state to progressively realise socio-economic rights are dependent upon the resources available for such purposes and socio-economic rights are limited by reason of the lack of resources. In *Grootboom* the same court held that this limitation means that both the content of the obligation in relation to the rate at which realisation of rights is achieved, as well as the reasonableness of the measures employed to achieve the result, are governed by the availability of resources.[201]

Bilchitz explains that socio-economic rights require the state to develop a systematic and comprehensive programme that is designed to realise these rights progressively.[202] *Grootboom* found that progressive realisation means that 'accessibility should be progressively facilitated: legal, administrative, operational and financia hurdles should be examined and, where possible, lowered over time.'[203]

Whether the state has discharged its duty to progressively realise any particular socio-economic right will be evaluated by the courts in terms of the 'reasonableness' of the programme concerned.[204] This requires a contextual evaluation of the circumstances.[205] In respect of understanding the nature of the obligations imposed by socio-economic rights, *Treatment Action Campaign* is identifie as having gone further than any of the other socio-economic cases in pushing the state to realise pregnant women's right to health care.[206] However, while the decision's reach was extensive, the court did not create the right to receive treatment on demand; instead, it focused on the reasonableness of the challenged policy.[207]

---

[198] D Bilchitz 'Health' in S Woolman & M Bishop (eds) *Constitutional Law of South Africa* 2 ed (Revised Service 4) 56A–i.

[199] *Government of the Republic of South Africa v Grootboom* 2001 (1) SA 46 (CC) (*Grootboom*) para 39. This case concerned the constitutional right to housing.

[200] 1998 (1) SA 765 (CC) para 11. Here the court had to consider the constitutional right to have access to emergency medical treatment.

[201] *Grootboom* para 46.

[202] Bilchitz 'Health' 56A–i.

[203] *Grootboom* para 45.

[204] *Grootboom* para 42.

[205] Bilchitz 'Health' 56A–i. Bilchitz identifie criteria previously used by the Constitutional Court when evaluating a state programme: the programme must ensure that appropriate financia and human resources are available; it must be capable of facilitating the realisation of the right concerned; it must be flexibl and attend to 'crises'; it must not exclude a significan segment of the affected population; and it must balance short, medium and long-term needs.

[206] See *Treatment Action Campaign* and Pieterse *Can Rights Cure?* 67.

[207] Pieterse *Can Rights Cure?* 68.

In *Mazibuko v City of Johannesburg*[208] the Constitutional Court held that the positive obligations imposed on government will be enforced by courts in at least two of the following instances: If government takes no steps to realise rights at all or in the case where government adopts measures that are unreasonable, the court will require that the measure be revised.[209] The court identifie three instances of unreasonableness: the adopted measures make no provision for those in desperate need; the government adopts a policy with unreasonable exclusions or limitations; or where government fails to continually review its policies to ensure that socio-economic rights are progressively realised.[210]

Concerning the third example of unreasonableness, the court in *Grootboom* found that legislative measures on their own are not enough to constitute constitutional compliance with s 27 obligations.[211] The state is obliged to act to achieve the intended result; legislative measures must be supported by appropriate, well-directed policies and programmes.[212] These policies and programmes must also be reasonably implemented.[213] Further, the state must be aware that conditions do not remain static, thus requiring continuous review of devised programmes and policies.[214]

Having set the scene for the basic premise of socio-economic rights,[215] it is necessary to determine what the concept of 'reproductive health' denotes and its role for women in South Africa.[216] Carstens and Pearmain explain the role of reproductive health rights in the context of the South African constitutional setting. The authors argue that this right is specificall relevant to women of reproductive age, as their research indicates that these women disproportionately suffer with reproductive health problems and that these problems are found to account for 60% of the burden of disease for women in Africa.[217] They conclude that 'the reference to reproductive health care is an acknowledgment of the

[208] 2010 (4) SA 1 (CC) (*Mazibuko*) para 67. This case involved the constitutional right to have access to sufficient water.

[209] *Mazibuko* para 67.

[210] *Mazibuko* para 67.

[211] *Grootboom* para 42.

[212] *Grootboom* para 42.

[213] *Grootboom* para 42.

[214] *Grootboom* para 43 and *Mazibuko* para 40. For a critical review of the Constitutional Court's approach to adjudicating socio-economic rights disputes, see D Brand 'Judicial deference and democracy in socio-economic rights cases in South Africa' (2011) 3 *Stell LR* 614; G Quinot & S Liebenberg 'Narrowing the band: Reasonableness review in administrative justice and socio-economic rights jurisprudence in South Africa' (2011) 22 *Stell LR* 639; S Wilson & J Dugard 'Taking poverty seriously: The South African Constitutional Court and socio-economic rights' (2011) 22 *Stell LR* 664; and M Pieterse 'Legislative and executive translation of the right to have access to health care services' (2010) 14 *Law, Democracy & Development* 1.

[215] Bilchitz identifie *Grootboom* as providing the most extensive discussion of reasonableness, and views *Treatment Action Campaign* as fleshin out a better understanding of this criterion; see Bilchitz 'Health' 56A–12.

[216] Neither the Constitution nor the National Health Act define reproductive health.

[217] Carstens & Pearmain *Foundational Principles of South African Medical Law* 176–7.

prejudice suffered by women in this area and constitutes an express undertaking to remedy the situation'.[218]

Ngwena[219] states that reproductive health is a state of complete mental, physical and social wellbeing in all matters linked to the reproductive system. Further, reproductive health encompasses the right to a satisfying and safe sex-life, the ability to reproduce and the freedom to make decisions on procreation.[220] O'Sullivan[221] states that reproductive health therefore implies that people have the ability to engage in safe sexual relationships and that women can safely progress through their pregnancies.

Carstens and Pearmain understand the reach of the right to reproductive health as moving beyond a termination-of-pregnancy issue to include a wide range of other services.[222] These services include those relating to conception, contraception, fertility, infertility, prenatal, perinatal and postnatal care, gynaecological services, and advice and treatment regarding sexually transmitted diseases.[223]

For the purposes of understanding how reproductive health care contributes towards advancing female autonomy during pregnancy and birth it is necessary to consider what mechanisms are in place to achieve the aim of autonomy in this sphere. In this respect, both access to termination-of-pregnancy services and maternity care have received legislative attention. The Choice Act and the National Health Act address these concerns. However, as indicated above in the discussion on state obligations to progressively realise socio-economic rights, enacting legislation is not enough. The state must constantly review its policies and make necessary adjustments in order to gradually reach all women in need.

O'Sullivan understands that access to safe termination services contributes to reproductive health through the reduction of maternal morbidity and mortality.[224] The same can be said for those women who are pregnant and in need of health care while pregnant, during labour and after delivery. However, both these areas of reproductive health service face a number of issues and maternal mortality rates are still worrisome.

In 2011, Human Rights Watch finalise a report that focused on the public provision of maternal health-care services in South Africa, specificall focusing on the Eastern Cape.[225] Human Rights Watch emphasised that since the end of apartheid, South Africa has passed important sexual and reproductive health-related laws that, if implemented successfully, have the potential to improve

---

[218] Carstens & Pearmain *Foundational Principles of South African Medical Law* 176–7.

[219] Ngwena (2004) *Journal of Law, Medicine & Ethics* 708. Ngwena relies on the United Nations Programme of Action Adopted at the International Conference on Population and Development (Cairo, 1994). See specificall Chapter Seven of the Programme of Action.

[220] Ngwena (2004) *Journal of Law, Medicine & Ethics* 708. Also see Beijing Declaration and Platform for Action endorsed by the Fourth World Conference on Women (4–15 September 1995) paras 94–7 and United Nations Programme of Action.

[221] 'Reproductive rights' 37-24.

[222] Carstens & Pearmain *Foundational Principles of South African Medical Law* 176–7.

[223] Carstens & Pearmain *Foundational Principles of South African Medical Law* 176–7.

[224] Carstens & Pearmain *Foundational Principles of South African Medical Law* 176–7.

[225] Human Rights Watch 'Stop making excuses'.

maternal health care greatly.[226] They found that South Africa has the highest per capita spending on health in sub-Saharan Africa, and is recognised as having a strong legal and policy framework, which includes a constitutional guarantee of the right to health. Maternity care is free (per the National Health Act) and, as a result, 92% of women attend antenatal care and 87% give birth in health facilities.[227]

Despite these positive projections, pregnant women will benefi from these laws only *if* the reproductive health laws are implemented properly. At the release of its report, Human Rights Watch reported that South Africa was one of six sub-Saharan African countries that made no progress in reducing maternal mortality rates and actually reported an increase in deaths.[228] This increase amounted to an estimated 80% increase in maternal deaths. The reason for this increase is linked to appalling conditions that pregnant women are sometimes left to endure, especially when turning to public health-care facilities while in labour. The report describes circumstances where women have endured verbal or physical abuse by attending hospital staff, general neglect, refusal of urgent medical treatment, or have been turned away when presenting themselves at a hospital for delivery.[229] The report recognises that, even with the state's progressive framework in place, women's reproductive health rights are still being undermined, and the tragic fact is that many women who eventually die from pregnancy or birth-related causes have been in contact with the health-care system, meaning that some of the deaths could have been prevented.[230]

It is hopeful to note that South Africa's maternal mortality rate was drastically reduced from 311 deaths per 100 000 live births in 2010 to 141 deaths per 100 000 live births in 2013.[231] Nevertheless, South Africa failed to meet the Millennium Development Goal of reducing maternal mortality rate to 38 deaths per 100 000 live births.[232] One of the factors identifie as contributing to maternal mortality rates in South Africa is poor obstetric care,[233] and a number of publications have emerged which describe the unfortunate and deep-rooted presence of abusive and

[226] Human Rights Watch 'Stop making excuses' 15.

[227] Human Rights Watch 'Stop making excuses' 15.

[228] Human Rights Watch 'Stop making excuses' 15. These reporting requirements were linked to developing countries' efforts to reach a number of Millennium Development Goals. These goals are described as 'anti-poverty goals' and improving maternal health is one such goal. All countries had until 2015 to achieve the Millennium Development Goals. These goals have now been replaced with Sustainable Development Goals. See United Nations 'Sustainable development goals: 17 goals to transform our world' available at http://www.un.org/sustainabledevelopment/sustainable-development-goals/ (accessed on 4 April 2016).

[229] See generally Chapter Two of the report, 'Maternity care failures and patient abuse'.

[230] Human Rights Watch 'Stop making excuses', Chapter Two.

[231] Statistics South Africa 'Millennium development goals: Country report 2015' at 77–9, available at http://www.statssa.gov.za/MDG/MDG_Country%20Report_Final30Sep2015.pdf (accessed on 31 March 2016). However, see RJ Chadwick, D Cooper & J Harries 'Narratives of distress about birth in South African public maternity settings: A qualitative study' (2014) 30 *Midwifery* 862. The authors demonstrate how different organisations report rates of maternal mortality in South Africa.

[232] Statistics South Africa 'Millennium development goals: Country report 2015' 77.

[233] Statistics South Africa 'Millennium development goals: Country report 2015' 78.

disrespectful maternity care in South Africa.[234] Terms such as birth violence and obstetric violence are being used to describe these issues.[235] These are barriers to the realisation of the right to reproductive health care. What is important to recognise is that the problem is not the South African legal framework failing women, but rather a lack of individual and state accountability in the health-care system.[236]

Similar conditions have been found when pregnant women make use of public termination-of-pregnancy services in South Africa.[237] In 2008, the World Health Organization reported that an estimated 120 000 women in Southern Africa had accessed unsafe termination-of-pregnancy services, resulting in 500 maternal deaths.[238] Alarmingly, the report cautioned that these figure should be considered the 'tip of the iceberg', since the incidence of accessing unsafe services, as well as associated mortality rates, tended to be underreported in surveys, and unreported or underreported in hospital records.[239]

The World Health Organization figure indicate that the relevant provisions of the Choice Act are not being fully implemented in the South African context. This claim is substantiated by a previous study which looked at a number of recently published studies stemming from the medical profession in the context of the public provision of termination-of-pregnancy services.[240] Despite the fact that the Choice Act holds very liberal ideals, the study found that women face extensive access barriers combined with systematic failures within the public health-care system, such as ill-equipped facilities and over-burdened, uncompromising and hostile staff.[241] These failures become access barriers that place numerous women

---

[234] For instance, see S Honikman, S Fawcus & I Meintjes 'Abuse in South African maternity settings is a disgrace: potential solutions to the problem' (2015) 105 *South African Medical Journal* 284; Chadwick, Cooper & Harries (2014) *Midwifery* 862; LM Kruger & C Schoombee 'The other side of caring: Abuse in a South African maternity ward' (2010) 28 *Journal of Reproductive and Infant Psychology* 84; Jewkes, Abrahams & Mvo (1998) *Social Science & Medicine* 1781; and Jewkes & Penn-Kekana (2015) *PLOS Medicine* e1001849.

[235] See RJ Chadwick 'Obstetric violence in South Africa' (2016) 106 *South African Medical Journal* 423; C Pickles 'Eliminating abusive "care": A criminal law response to obstetric violence in South Africa' (2015) 54 *South African Crime Quarterly* 5; R Chadwick & M Stevens 'Confronting birth violence in South Africa' available at http://mothersandbirthmatter.co.za/Confronting-Obstetric-Violence-in-South-Africa.php (accessed on 31 March 2016); and R Chadwick 'Obstetric violence—starting a conversation' (6 March 2016) available at http://mothersandbirthmatter.co.za/Obstetric-Violence–Starting-A-Conversation.php (accessed on 31 March 2016).

[236] Human Rights Watch 'Stop making excuses' 3. One possible example of the state being held accountable in the context of health care is *Treatment Action Campaign*. However, as mentioned earlier, this case was not heard in the context of access to reproductive health care, but in terms of the broader right to access to health care generally.

[237] See Pickles (2013) *SAJHR* 515 and authority cited therein.

[238] World Health Organization 'Unsafe abortion' 19; 28. The report (2) define an 'unsafe' termination of pregnancy as a termination performed by a provider who lacks the necessary skills and qualification to perform an induced termination of pregnancy. This definitio also includes a self-induced termination of pregnancy. These practices fail to meet officially prescribed circumstances and safeguards.

[239] World Health Organization 'Unsafe abortion' 15.

[240] As demonstrated in Pickles (2013) *SAJHR* 515.

[241] See Pickles (2013) *SAJHR* 518–22 and authority cited therein.

at increased risk, either because they have to terminate their pregnancies later in the gestation period or are obliged to turn to illegal and unsafe termination-of-pregnancy providers.[242]

Perpetuating the issue is the fact that, despite the same complaints arising through the years of the Choice Act's implementation, the state is found to be inactive in terms of its s 27 obligations.[243] The research indicates that the state has failed to regularly review its current policy concerning the free provision of termination-of-pregnancy services as required in terms of s 27 of the Constitution.[244] Consequently, the state cannot progressively lower access barriers to termination-of-pregnancy services, since it lacks an adequate understanding of the lived experiences of women.[245] The state is thus ill-equipped to implement any meaningful reforms.

Going further, it can be argued that the state is failing to meet its obligations in terms of the Protocol to the African Charter on Human Rights and People's Rights on the Rights of Women in Africa.[246] Article 14(2)*(c)* requires states to take appropriate measures to protect women's reproductive rights by authorising access to termination-of-pregnancy services in cases of risk of health of the pregnant woman or the foetus, and where a pregnancy is a result of rape, sexual assault or incest. Article 26 obligates states to ensure the implementation of the Protocol and adopt all necessary measures within the available resources. Ngwena argues that the Protocol not only requires states to enact legislation that legalises termination of pregnancy but also requires states to facilitate meaningful enjoyment of the relevant termination-of-pregnancy provisions through policies, practice guides and regulations.[247] Meaningful access requires states to '*operationalize* the law'.[248] (Emphasis in original.) Thus, merely enacting liberal termination-of-pregnancy laws in South Africa is not enough. The state has a regionally imposed obligation to ensure that impediments to access are removed, and in this respect the state has much to do.

Both these reports and related studies linked to the socio-economic right to reproductive health care for pregnant women indicate that the mechanisms are there for pregnant women so that they can realise their reproductive autonomy. However, ineffective implementation at times renders these rights as mere paper rights. Interestingly, neither of these issues has been the subject of public interest litigation despite the obvious violation of these rights.

4.4 CONCLUDING REMARKS

Women and girls of reproductive age enjoy extensive protection under the law. This stems from the fact that they are legal subjects with vested constitutional

[242] Pickles (2013) *SAJHR* 518–22.
[243] Pickles (2013) *SAJHR* 525–29.
[244] Pickles (2013) *SAJHR* 525–29.
[245] Pickles (2013) *SAJHR* 525–29.
[246] Adopted by the second Ordinary Session of the Assembly of the Union (Maputo, 11 July 2003).
[247] CG Ngwena 'Inscribing abortion as a human right: Significanc of the Protocol on the Rights of Women in Africa' (2010) 32 *Human Rights Quarterly* 783 815.
[248] Ngwena (2010) *Human Rights Quarterly* 815.

rights and being pregnant does not serve as a ground to diminish women's worth as legal subjects. The protective reach of all rights remain intact for the duration of a pregnancy. These rights secure a safe space for self-realisation and autonomous existence, being aspects that this chapter identifie as intrinsic to legal subjectivity.

Autonomy is broadly understood to encompass the freedom and ability to self-regulate, and this concept gains its weight from the rights encapsulated in the Bill of Rights. Also, autonomy can be seen to be made up of a number of subdivisions, such as bodily autonomy or reproductive autonomy, to name two examples, all of which contribute to the greater experiences of the ability to self-regulate. In order for autonomy to be advanced, one is required to look at the context in which protection or advancement is needed. Context refers to particular areas of human interaction and relations, and this will identify the relevant subdivision of autonomy that is at play and aid in determining how to best apply the relevant constitutional rights.

Reproductive autonomy (being a subdivision of autonomy generally) is relevant to the context of pregnant women when they decide to continue their pregnancies and when they determine how to progress through pregnancy. The process of reproductive self-regulation requires a certain amount of reliance on external aid for its facilitation and realisation. External aid includes aspects such as the increased need for state funding, increased medical attention and general communal respect for decisions reached pertaining to the pregnancy at hand. The chapter has identifie a number of constitutional rights that enable pregnant women to entrench their claims to these external aids and protect and advance their reproductive autonomy against third parties such as the state and the community, while engaging in relations with them in order to get access to the needed aid.

Reproductive rights, being the rights identifie as giving weight to a woman's claim to reproductive autonomy, include the rights to life, equality, dignity, privacy, bodily and psychological integrity and access to reproductive health care. The reproductive context in which these rights are engaged and applied allow for them to be understood as reproductive rights. Currently, reproductive rights place extensive protective barriers around pregnant women. It is expressly noted that a woman's reproductive rights are not qualifie in the Constitution for the benefi of a foetus. This is not to say that their reproductive rights cannot be limited in terms of s 36 of the Constitution, but that the law does not qualify the value of women's legal existence based on the presence of a pregnancy.

Unfortunately, there are a number of areas where enforcement of reproductive rights is lacking. Such cases include the loss of wanted pregnancies through violence against pregnant women, abusive and coercive obstetric treatment and the poor provision of public termination-of-pregnancy services. As a result of these areas of inactivity, pregnant women's reproductive autonomy is compromised and they are left vulnerable to human rights infringements. Interestingly, while these areas deserve increased academic debates and state attention, this book will demonstrate that they do not form part of the calls for law reform on issues related to pregnancy under the law.

Chapter 5

THE LEGAL STATUS OF THE UNBORN

5.1 INTRODUCTION

This chapter explores the contentious issue of the legal position of the foetus in South African law. The legal status of the foetus is important because it is one of the entities involved in the tension between female autonomy rights and foetal interests, and this discussion goes on to demonstrate the scope of their legal existence in the context of that possible tension. Consequently, this chapter lays the foundation to properly consider the calls for law reform discussed in Chapter Six and provides context of the legal framework which these calls for reform seek to amend.

The foetus currently holds a curious position in South African law. While the Constitutional Court is yet to hear a case dealing with the legal status of the unborn,[1] the common law, legislation and decisions of the lower courts provide some insight into how South African law views the unborn. These sources demonstrate that despite not having legal subjectivity, the unborn's existence is sometimes recognised, while at other times it is denied any recognised existence. Accordingly, both instances are considered and compared here with reference to case law, legislation and relevant legal principles.

In this respect, this chapter looks at the born-alive rule as a pre-constitutional principle and its current role as a legal principle under the Constitution of the Republic of South Africa, 1996. The born-alive rule effectively informs the notion that pregnant women are viewed as embodying a single entity in law (single-entity approach), and case law validating this claim is considered. However, there is an emerging approach to pregnancy which has been taking hold in South Africa since the introduction of the Constitution, namely, the not-one-but-not-two approach (not-one/not-two). This concept is explored and principles stemming from case law and legislation relevant to termination of pregnancy and constitutional values are found to support its recent rooting in South Africa. One of the implications of following the single-entity and not-one/not-two approaches is that there is no room for a tension between female reproductive autonomy and foetal interests, and the chapter demonstrates why.

5.2 THE BORN-ALIVE RULE AND THE SINGLE-ENTITY APPROACH

There is no legislation that explicitly recognises the unborn as an independent entity in South African law. In most instances a child is define as a person below the age of majority without specifying when that age begins. A fittin example of this approach is s 28(3) of the Constitution, which states that a 'child', for the

[1] However, see *H v Fetal Assessment Centre* 2015 (2) SA 193 (CC) (*Fetal Assessment Centre*) para 50 where the court found that rights do not apply until birth.

purposes of s 28, means a person under the age of 18 years.[2] Neither 'age' nor 'person' has a definition particularly in respect of when either begins or comes into being.

This somewhat open-ended approach may be a subtle indication that the common-law position is approvingly adopted by the legislature for the time being.[3] While legislation does not expressly deny independent status, the common law does. Presently, the common-law born-alive rule denies the unborn legal status and the title of person.[4] Unless legislation specificall trumps the common-law position or it is developed through judicial precedent, any law applicable to persons excludes those not yet born.[5] This position has far-reaching implications in the context of the legal status of a foetus.

The requirement of live birth in South Africa features in criminal law for purposes of proving murder[6] and in the law of persons as the moment when legal subjectivity originates.[7] The common-law born-alive rule was developed as a result of a lack of advanced medical technology and because of a primitive understanding of the female body during pregnancy.[8] During these less technologically advanced eras, pregnancies could not be monitored with any certainty.[9]

[2] The Children's Act 38 of 2005 takes the same approach; see s 1(1), Definitions

[3] Although, it is noted that where a term is not define in a piece of legislation, its ordinary grammatical meaning should be applied. But, it is noteworthy that in cases where the literal meaning would lead to an ambiguous outcome and secondary interpretive aids, such as its long title, headings and other sections prove ineffective, the interpreter can have recourse to other interpretive aids such as common-law presumptions. See C Botha *Statutory Interpretation: An Introduction for Students* 5 ed (2012) 91. Botha does give examples of other methods of statutory interpretation, but this falls beyond the purpose of the topic.

[4] Here 'person' is being referred to in terms of its legal construction, rather than its social construction. The distinction between the two constructions can be found in D Lupton *The Social Worlds of the Unborn* (2013).

[5] Botha explains that it is presumed that legislation does not alter the common law more than is necessary; where it does, legislation will trump the common law. However, where there is no legislation dealing with the issue specificall , the common-law position stands. See Botha *Statutory Interpretation* 43.

[6] CR Snyman *Criminal Law* 5 ed (2008) 448 and JM Burchell *Principles of Criminal Law* 3 ed (2005) 671.

[7] T Boezaart *Law of Persons* 5 ed (2010) 11.

[8] R Pillay 'The beginning of human personhood: Is South African law outdated?' (2010) 21 *Stell LR* 230 231.

[9] Pillay (2010) *Stell LR* 231. Also see A Oakley *The Captured Womb: A History of the Medical Care of Women* (1986) 11–12. According to Oakley, in the eighteenth and nineteenth centuries antenatal care did not exist. Pregnant women and health-care providers did not consider routine medical supervision necessary. There were no clinics or hospital departments available to pregnant women. The general rule was that pregnancy did not constitute a medical phenomenon; in fact, there was no professional body claiming expert knowledge on the treatment of pregnant women.

Prior to the twentieth century and the discovery of foetal viability,[10] quickening[11] was considered the most important point in pregnancy in both law and medicine.[12] In medicine, it was assumed that the foetus became alive at quickening.[13] At common law, quickening was legally significan because it was the only objective proof that a woman was pregnant in an era where medical knowledge about pregnancy was very underdeveloped.[14] On the other hand, live birth offered the opportunity of providing an objective, clinical observation that the foetus, once born, was alive.[15] Further, the health of the foetus could not be established until born.[16] Consequently, until birth, proving the cause of termination of a pregnancy or injury to a foetus was impossible.[17] The born-alive rule was later extended to the law of persons, and it is now the only criterion used to determine whether there is an entitlement to personhood.[18]

Accordingly, the common-law crime of murder is applicable only when the victim has been born alive.[19] Section 239(1) of the Criminal Procedure Act 51 of 1977 assists in determining when one is born alive for purposes of murder and provides that if it is proved that a child breathed after separation it will be deemed to have been born alive. For purposes of legal subjectivity, the common law requires that the foetus must be separate from the mother's body and must have lived independently.[20] Boezaart states that any sign of life is evidence that the foetus survived after separation.[21] Foetal viability is not recognised as a qualifying element in either of these constructions of live birth.[22]

5.2.1 Conceptualising the single-entity approach to pregnancy

The extent of the non-existent status of a foetus is significantl obvious when one considers the recent criminal law decision of *S v Makhakha*.[23] In this case, a woman who was approximately seven months pregnant was one of the victims of a brutal rape and murder. While the accused was found guilty of the pregnant victim's rape and murder, the fact that a viable foetus was lost during the

[10] In his discussion of the development of the born-alive rule, Forsythe points out that foetal viability, as emphasised in American law today, did not actually play a role in the development of the common law concerning foetal life; see CD Forsythe 'Homicide of the unborn child: The born alive rule and other legal anachronisms' (1987) 21 *Valparaiso University LR* 563 569.

[11] 'Quickening' is define as the firs time a pregnant woman feels foetal movement within her uterus, usually in the second trimester of her pregnancy; see Forsythe (1987) *Valparaiso University LR* 567.

[12] Forsythe (1987) *Valparaiso University LR* 568.

[13] Forsythe (1987) *Valparaiso University LR* 568.

[14] Forsythe (1987) *Valparaiso University LR* 568.

[15] Forsythe (1987) *Valparaiso University LR* 568.

[16] Forsythe (1987) *Valparaiso University LR* 575.

[17] Forsythe (1987) *Valparaiso University LR* 575.

[18] Pillay (2010) *Stell LR* 232.

[19] Snyman *Criminal Law* 448 and Burchell *Principles of Criminal Law* 671.

[20] Boezaart *Law of Persons* 12.

[21] Boezaart *Law of Persons* 12.

[22] However, see Boezaart *Law of Persons* 12, where she points out that some authors specify an additional requirement of foetal viability for purposes of legal subjectivity.

[23] 2013 JDR 1934 (WCC) (*Makhakha*).

commission of the crime was not regarded as an issue before the Western Cape High Court. The judgment does not include the sentence imposed and it is therefore not clear if the loss of foetal life even contributed towards an increased sentence as a possible aggravating factor.

Makhakha is noteworthy because it demonstrates how deep-rooted South African law's perception of pregnancy is. That is, the law views pregnancy as a representation of a pregnant woman being a single entity.[24] Seymour explains that this is the 'body-part model' of pregnancy under law.[25] The single-entity approach means that 'the fetus is simply part of the woman's body', and denies the foetus its 'distinctiveness'.[26] The foetus is seen to be part of a woman's body in the same way a room is part of a house, or it can be interpreted as suggesting that the foetus is merely something like an organ which belongs to the body of a pregnant woman.[27] Consequently, the single-entity approach withholds any vested and protectable interests or rights for as long as the foetus remains unborn. Further, when a pregnancy comes to an end, it must result in a live birth before the law's protective reach can take hold.

The single-entity approach can be contrasted with the separate-entities approach. Seymour explains that the separate-entities approach views a woman and her foetus as though they are separate individuals and with distinctive needs.[28] In their separate existence, each is seen to hold a range of enforceable rights,[29] ultimately leading to the understanding that the foetus is a legal subject engaging in legal relations on its own account. Seymour argues that this is typically the modern medical profession's view of pregnancy because of their constant individualised interaction with the unborn as a result of medical technology.[30] Clearly, the born-alive rule does not encompass this approach.[31]

5.2.2 Single-entity approach in the pre-constitutional era

There are a number of private law cases that speak to the unborn's general lack of legal distinction. Usually, these cases come before courts as attempts to challenge the appropriateness of the single-entity approach in that it fails to acknowledge foetal life, and generally seeks to bring about reform in respect of the born-alive

---

[24] There is one exception to this; see *AP v S* (1895) 2 Off Rep 103. In this case it was held that according to Roman-Dutch law the crime of infanticide can be committed against a foetus. Hoctor considers the role of this case in South Africa and asserts that the decision has never been followed in South Africa. See S Hoctor 'Specifi crimes' (2008) 21 *SACJ* 99 212. He further alludes to Milton's argument that the decision originates from a lack of distinction between 'abortion' and infanticide. See JRL Milton *South African Criminal Law and Procedure: Common-Law Crimes* 3 ed (1996) 357.

[25] J Seymour *Childbirth and the Law* (2000) 189.

[26] Seymour *Childbirth and the Law* 190.

[27] Seymour *Childbirth and the Law* 190.

[28] Seymour *Childbirth and the Law* 190; 194.

[29] Seymour *Childbirth and the Law* 194. Seymour's assertion is in line with the finding of Part One.

[30] Seymour *Childbirth and the Law* 194.

[31] See Chapter Six for more on the separate-entities approach. Its resulting implications will be highlighted in the context of the United States' approach to pregnancy, as discussed in Part Three.

rule. Prior to the Interim Constitution, 1993[32] and Final Constitution, 1996,[33] the influenc of the born-alive rule as a legal principle enforcing the single-entity approach was consistently accepted in the context of civil law.

In the ambit of status and succession, the *nasciturus* fictio allowed for interest accruing to the unborn to be held in abeyance until its live birth.[34] There are a number of conditions attached to this fiction There should be some advantage or benefi for the unborn; the benefi must accrue after the unborn's conception; and the unborn must later be born alive in the legal sense of the word.[35] Consequently, this fictio does not in itself overcome the non-existence of the unborn; it remains a nonentity for as long as the fina condition of live birth is not realised.[36] It could be argued that, if anything, the *nasciturus* fictio portrays a foetus as a conditional entity of sorts, which still does not afford it an individualised protected space because the condition of live birth must still be realised.

In *Pinchin v Santam Insurance*,[37] the court took the application of the *nasciturus* fictio beyond property law and found it had a role to play with regard to delict. Hiemstra J found that, if causation could be proved, the fictio could be applied for the purposes of recovering damages for injuries sustained while *in utero*, provided the unborn was later born alive. This decision was later rejected by

[32] The Interim Constitution came into operation on 27 April 1994.

[33] The Final Constitution came into operation on 4 February 1997.

[34] This fictio stems from the Roman and Roman-Dutch law principle, '*nasciturus pro iam nato habetur quotiens de commodo eius agitur*'. Boezaart explains that, translated, this means that the unborn can be regarded as already having been born when it is in their interests; see T Boezaart 'Child law, the child and South African private law' in T Boezaart (ed) *Child Law in South Africa* (2009) 5–6. This fictio has been statutorily incorporated in s 2D(1)*(c)* of the Wills Act 7 of 1953. In terms of this provision, if the testator or testatrix does not provide otherwise, those already conceived will be included in the devolution of a benefit provided they are later born alive.

[35] Boezaart 'Child law, the child and South African private law' 6.

[36] There is a dispute as to whether this doctrine is a fictio or a legal rule; however, it is accepted that this doctrine encompasses a fiction It is a fictio in so far as the doctrine is viewed as not extending legal subjectivity, whereas if it were conceived as a rule, legal subjectivity would vest prior to birth. In this respect, see C Pickles *S v Mshumpa: A Time for Law Reform* (unpublished LLM dissertation, University of Pretoria, 2010) 51–2 and Seymour *Childbirth and the Law* 136–7. Also, see case law as discussed below, which indicates that the *nasciturus* doctrine is applied as a fictio in South Africa. It should also be noted that Du Plessis views the *nasciturus* doctrine as an example of *direct* protection of foetal interests; see GA du Plessis 'Feticide: Creating a statutory crime in South African law' (2013) 24 *Stell LR* 73 78. However, Seymour (*Childbirth and the Law* 135) suggests otherwise. Seymour explains that while the law recognises the unborn's claim to property in a deceased estate, the right to the property only vested after birth; he argues: 'The law on the inheritance rights of the unborn did not, however, necessarily reflec a desire to protect the welfare of the fetus: "[I]t was the testator's intent, not the personhood of the fetus, that was the common law's primary concern." ' The fact that birth is required in order for there to be a valid ground to transfer property indicates that there is no direct protection of the unborn, protection only realises after birth, thus providing direct protection of a born person. Further, this doctrine is aimed at protecting the testator's wishes rather than the unborn's interests.

[37] 1963 (2) SA 254 (W) (*Pinchin*). In this case, a pregnant woman was injured in a vehicle collision, and after her child's birth it became apparent that the child suffered from cerebral paralysis and brain damage.

the Supreme Court of Appeal in 2005.[38] However, the point to be taken is that for as long as there is no live birth, the reach of the fictio has limited effect.

This limited effect of the *nasciturus* fictio on the legal status of the unborn was confirme in *Christian League of Southern Africa v Rall*.[39] In this case the respondents attempted to use the *nasciturus* fictio as a mechanism for preventing the lawful termination of a pregnancy in terms of the now repealed Abortion and Sterilization Act 2 of 1975. Steyn J confirme that the *nasciturus* fictio 'does not clothe the unborn child with any legal personality'. Going further, the judge held that, where a stillbirth occurred, all rights or interests being held in abeyance died with the unborn. The *nasciturus* fictio therefore cannot be applied as a means of protection from conduct that may cause a termination of pregnancy because that very act prevents live birth.

Van Heerden v Joubert[40] and *Friedman v Glicksman*[41] will be discussed under pre-constitutional cases, even though both cases were heard within months of the Interim Constitution coming into operation on 27 April 1994.[42]

In *Van Heerden* the court had to determine whether, in terms of the Inquest Act 58 of 1959, an inquest could be conducted into the cause of a stillbirth, particularly when it is alleged that the stillbirth was a result of medical negligence, rather than

[38] See *Road Accident Fund v Mtati* 2005 (6) SA 215 (SCA). This case also concerned prenatal injuries that the plaintiff suffered as a result of a vehicle collision. The Supreme Court of Appeal rejected the *Pinchin* position and found that the application of the *nasciturus* fictio was not necessary in prenatal injury cases since the ordinary principles relevant to the law of delict could be applied. In this instance it was held, '[t]he damage is suffered by the plaintiff at the moment that, in law, the plaintiff achieves personality and inherits the damaged body for which the defendants are responsible for. The events prior to birth are mere links in the chain of causation between the defendants' assumed lack of skill and care and the consequential damage to the plaintiff.' This is the same approach adopted by the Constitutional Court in *Fetal Assessment Centre* regarding wrongful life claims.

[39] 1981 (2) SA 821 (O) (*Rall*).

[40] 1994 (4) SA 793 (A) (*Van Heerden*). While this case was heard after the Interim Constitution came into operation, the case must have been heard in terms of the law that was in place at the time this issue came to life because neither the Interim nor the Final Constitutions operate retroactively.

[41] 1996 (1) SA 1134 (W) (*Friedman*).

[42] This approach is adopted for a number of reasons. There is a common-law presumption that legislation is prospective unless the contrary is explicitly provided for. See Botha *Statutory Interpretation* 55–62. In respect of the principle against retrospectivity and the Constitution, see B Bekink *Principles of South African Constitutional Law* (2012) 408–9. Nothing is mentioned in the Interim Constitution with regard to its retrospective application. Therefore, since the facts in *Friedman* came about prior to the Interim Constitution, it is taken that its constitutional provisions and values did not come into play. The defendant did bring up s 9 of the Interim Constitution (right to life), but the court rejected their argument and did not refer to the Interim Constitution thereafter, 1138D. The *Van Heerden* case was an appeal from proceedings that took place in 1992. In terms of s 241(8) of the Interim Constitution, any pending proceedings in place when the Interim Constitution commences shall be dealt with as if the Constitution had not been passed, except where, in terms of those proceedings an appeal is noted after the commencement of the Interim Constitution, then its provisions are applicable. Since the decision appealed against was heard in 1992 it is assumed that the appeal was noted during the course of 1992 and not after the Interim Constitution came into operation. Further, both cases were decided so soon after the commencement of the Interim Constitution that it is questionable whether its provisions and values could have been meaningfully engaged and applied in any case.

an unfortunate natural occurrence. In this case, it was alleged that prenatal life was terminated during the course of birth as a result of the attending medical staff failing to apply adequate care. The would-be parents sought recourse by requiring an investigation into the cause of the stillbirth through the application of the Inquest Act.[43] However, the attending medical staff challenged the soundness of this approach and successfully argued that the Inquest Act applied only to persons and because the foetus was stillborn, no person came into existence in terms of the law. In this respect, Grosskopf JA, applying the literal meaning of 'person', found that this term did not include a stillborn child, unborn child, viable unborn child, unborn human beings, or a living foetus.

McCreath J, in *Christian Lawyers Association of SA v Minister of Health*[44] interprets the *Van Heerden* decision as leaving the common-law status of the unborn open, since the court was concerned only with the term 'person' in the narrow context of the Inquest Act and not so much with external legal developments. The common-law status of the unborn was never really 'open' to begin with. The undeveloped existence of the common-law born-alive rule speaks to this fact. Further, *Van Heerden* feeds into the body of law that views the unborn as nonentities, meaning that pregnant women and the unborn are considered to be a single entity. As such, this case removes any means in law to investigate conduct which may make a substantive contribution to causing a stillbirth, be it medical negligence or even violence against pregnant women.

In *Friedman* the court was confronted with a wrongful life claim.[45] A wrongful life claim is define as an action brought on behalf of a child on the basis that a physician negligently failed to inform his or her parents of the risk of being born a disabled child.[46] The argument goes that had the physician not acted negligently, the pregnancy would have been terminated and he or she would not have been born disabled.[47] The court was left with the question of whether a physician held a duty (in terms of the laws of contract or delict) towards a potentially disabled foetus to inform its would-be-parents that there is a risk of disability, thereby allowing its would-be parents to terminate the pregnancy.

The claim was rejected for a number of reasons[48] but, regarding the legal status of a foetus, the court found that would-be parents cannot contract or make

[43] According to Grosskopf JA, the main purpose of the Act is to determine the cause of death, circumstances surrounding the death, whether any person is responsible for death, and whether death can be attributed to the commission of any offence.

[44] 1998 (4) SA 1113 (T) (*Christian Lawyers* (1998)) 1120D–E.

[45] The court also had to decide on a wrongful birth claim, which is a claim brought by parents who assert that they would have terminated their pregnancy had they been properly informed of the risk of birth defects in the foetus. Where the claim is successful, the attending physician would face liability for damages suffered as a result of having to support a child with special needs, 1138A.

[46] *Friedman* 1138C.

[47] *Friedman* 1138C.

[48] *Friedman* 1124I–1123C. First, it is contrary to public morals to fin that a person would be better off not living than having to live a marred life. Secondly, allowing the action may open the doors for parents to be held liable for allowing a potentially disabled foetus to be born into a disabled life despite being aware of the risk of pain and suffering. Third, the court found that one cannot hold a physician liable for a child being born with disabilities that he or she is not responsible for causing. Also, the court (1143A–B) conceded that if a wrongful birth action were to be allowed, the principles of delict require that the person be put in the position he or she would have been had the negligent

elections on behalf of their foetus.[49] This is based on the legal premise that an agent cannot act on behalf of a 'non-existent principal', and in this case the foetus was considered non-existent because it had not yet been born.[50] Consequently, it is taken from this decision that, generally, no contractual obligation can be brought about in respect of those not yet born. This approach eliminates the notion that a foetus can be considered a second patient and protected as such within a medical setting.

Goldblatt J, after having approvingly cited English and American case law, found that in delict a physician does not owe a foetus the duty of ensuring its termination in the case of a less-than-desirable disabled life after its birth; only the pregnant woman can lay claim to the right to be informed.[51] The court rejected this duty to the unborn on the grounds of the sanctity of life, since it would mean viewing disabled life as less valuable than non-disabled life.[52] No child is seen to have the right to be born a whole, functional human being, and it is not for the law to determine whether it is preferable to have no life instead of a disabled one.[53] Instead, the court must be governed by the sanctity of life, and that approach calls for the preservation of all life.[54]

The approach adopted in the *Friedman* case is ambiguous. At firs glance, this case can be interpreted as the court attaching value to prenatal life generally, because all life in any form is something to value and to allow a wrongful life claim would strike to the core of that value. Additionally, it could be seen that this value remains intact despite there being no legal basis for one to owe a duty to the unborn.

On further reflection however, it must be pointed out that the essence of the sanctity of life argument is hollow if the court accepts that a physician owes a pregnant woman the duty of informing her of any potential disabilities, thereby providing the foundation for her to terminate a pregnancy that will gestate a potentially disabled foetus. It is not clear how providing the duty to women and not the unborn infringes less on the sanctity of life.[55] Termination of pregnancy on the grounds of foetal abnormalities (or disabilities) is statutorily provided for. It was available under s 3*(c)* of the repealed Abortion and Sterilization Act, and is presently available under s 2 of the Choice on Termination of Pregnancy Act 92 of

---

conduct not occurred. In essence this would require the court to determine the extent of damage as being the difference between disabled life and no life at all, because if the physician was not negligent, the pregnancy would have been terminated and no such person would have come to life. In this respect, there is no criterion in law that assists in establishing this difference.

[49] *Friedman* 1140F–H.

[50] *Friedman* 1140F–H.

[51] *Friedman* 1142A–F.

[52] *Friedman* 1142A–F.

[53] *Friedman* 1141E.

[54] *Friedman* 1142E.

[55] The fact that the court affirmed women's right to terminate a pregnancy on the grounds of foetal abnormality leaves the court's concept of sanctity of life in a questionable position. Whether it is in the interest of the foetus to be terminated on the grounds of potential disability or whether a woman feels it is necessary to terminate foetal life on the grounds of potential disability, the fact remains that there is a termination of prenatal life specially justifie by the potential of disability.

1996 (Choice Act). However, the court never took on the task of addressing this anomaly in its application of the sanctity of life approach. A more nuanced reading of *Friedman* could indicate that the court was leaning towards, or *wanting* to value the unborn in their own right but the uncertain legal terrain of such a move led to an ambiguous outcome. Either way, the court's sanctity of life approach is seen to have failed.

The same point was critically highlighted in *Stewart v Botha*.[56] In *Stewart*, the court also found that wrongful life actions do not disclose a cause of action in law but on different grounds to those of *Friedman*. Rejecting the sanctity of life argument, Louw J emphasised that the question under wrongful life actions is whether the disabled child concerned suffered any damage, and concluded that the child had not because the only life possible is the disabled one to which the child was born.[57] Consequently there is no delict and the negligent conduct of the attending physician, being the failure to inform the child's mother of potential disabilities, is legally irrelevant.[58] The court asserted that if medicine had advanced to the point where genetic disabilities could be treated prenatally, and the physician failed to act under those circumstances, then one may have a claim.[59]

It must be noted that the current position of wrongful life claims may change soon but not because the judiciary's position in relation to the foetus has changed. In *Fetal Assessment Centre*, the Constitutional Court criticised the *Stewart* case and found that the common law may need to be developed to allow for claims in cases where children are born with disabilities. The court found that claims such as these may need to be developed because the best interests of the child dictate development in this direction.[60] The court referred the case back to the High Court for it to decide on how to develop the common law so as to give effect to constitutional values and rights, particularly the best interests of the child.[61] However, Froneman J emphasised that any claim in the context of wrongful birth becomes relevant only upon birth.[62] It must be noted that the court did not explicitly recognise the validity of wrongful life claims and, for the time being, there is no development of the common law since the High Court has yet to hand down judgment on this issue.

The *Friedman* case takes the position that the unborn are nonentities, since one does not have any legal obligation to them and the prenatal life is sanctifie only in so far as pregnant women are prepared to continue gestating potentially disabled foetuses. This case, along with *Pinchin*, *Rall*, and *Van Heerden*, provides a clear demonstration that the single-entity approach is well rooted in South African law.

[56] 2007 (6) SA 247 (C) (*Stewart*) paras 20–1. In fact, Louw J is critical of the *Friedman* decision in a number of respects, see paras 22–8. These additional critiques fall beyond the scope of this discussion.

[57] *Stewart* para 29.

[58] *Stewart* para 30.

[59] *Stewart* para 30.

[60] *Fetal Assessment Centre* para 54.

[61] *Fetal Assessment Centre* para 81.

[62] *Fetal Assessment Centre* para 50. For more on the possible implications of this decision, see T Boezaart '"Wrongful life"—The Constitutional Court paved the way for law reform' (2015) 26 *Stell LR* 399.

It is now necessary to consider whether the introduction of the Interim Constitution and later the Final Constitution impacted on this approach in any meaningful way.

5.2.3 Single-entity approach under the constitutional dispensation

All pre-constitutional cases are unequivocally aligned to the born-alive rule and by implication pregnant women are viewed simply as embodying no more than themselves during the existence of a pregnancy. It was demonstrated that, when an attempt was made to bring about a change in the perception that pregnancy embodies a single entity, the cases inadvertently deepened and refine the single-entity perception even further. With the introduction of the Interim Constitution and later the Final Constitution, the curious position of the unborn comes to the fore because some cases go on to reaffirm the non-existence of foetal life, while another case linked to the interpretation of the Choice Act gives a glimmer of legal recognition. What is noticeable is that, in those instances where the unborn are ever so slightly recognised, it occurs in the context of constitutionally informed values. Only those cases that provide constitutional affirmation of the single-entity approach will be considered here, while those instances where prenatal life is recognised under the law will be discussed under paragraph 5.3 below.

Although it is not the firs foetal-related decision heard under our constitutionally informed judicial system, *Christian Lawyers* (1998) sets the scene for how prenatal life fit in with the Constitution and the provisions of the Bill of Rights. In this case, the plaintiffs argued that the right to life, in terms of s 11 of the Bill of Rights, also applied to the unborn, and on this basis the Choice Act was unconstitutional. They contended that life starts at conception, so the right to life vests then.[63] In response to this, the defendants raised an exception, arguing that the plaintiffs' summons did not disclose a cause of action, since a foetus does not bear any rights.[64]

The court found that the use of the terms 'everyone' and 'every person' are synonymously applied throughout the Constitution, and went on to question whether the unborn fell within the ambit of those terms.[65] This question was seen to relate to principles of legal interpretation, and the court found it unnecessary to have regard for medical or scientifi evidence concerning the beginnings of human biological life, or religious and philosophical arguments, since these features are not part of the process of interpreting the law.[66] The question is whether, despite medical knowledge or religious positions at the time of its drafting, the Constitution accorded the unborn the benefi of its provisions.

To clarify the court's approach to this issue, McCreath J[67] approvingly quoted the writing of Williams[68] in that the question before the court was not one of

[63] *Christian Lawyers* (1998) 1116B–I.
[64] *Christian Lawyers* (1998) 1117A.
[65] *Christian Lawyers* (1998) 1117H–1118B.
[66] *Christian Lawyers* (1998) 1118B–I.
[67] *Christian Lawyers* (1998) 1120H.
[68] As quoted, G Williams 'The foetus and the "right to life"' (1994) 53 *CLJ* 71 78.

whether the foetus is human, but whether it should be given the same legal protection as those already born. In that respect, the court found that there was no express provision in the Constitution that afforded the unborn either legal personality or protection.[69] Also, the court found that the wording of some subsections of s 28 were such that they could be applied to the unborn, for example, those rights pertaining to work,[70] detention[71] and armed conflict [72] and the court therefore decided all the other subsections of s 28 exist to the exclusion of the unborn.[73] Section 28 of the Constitution, pertaining to children's rights, is specificall applicable to those persons under 18 years of age, and the court found that age begins only at birth, thereby excluding the unborn.[74]

Since the specialist children's rights provision of s 28 of the Bill of Rights does not apply to the unborn, it being the section where one would expect express protection to stem from, the court found that none of the other provisions of the Constitution have application either.[75] In this respect, the court found that the term 'everyone', as used in a number of constitutional rights, cannot logically be applied to the unborn. The court listed a number of rights including the rights to privacy; freedom and control over one's body; freedom of conscience, religion, thought, opinion, expression, assembly, association and movement; and specifi cally the right to life.[76] 'To include the foetus in the meaning of that term in s 11 would ascribe to it a meaning different from that which it bears everywhere else in the bill of rights . . . that is clearly untenable.'[77] The judge found that as far as the Constitution is concerned, the foetus is not a legal person.[78]

Looking at the relationship between pregnant women and the unborn, the court recognised that women's reproductive rights as per s 12(2) of the Constitution are not limited for the benefi of the unborn.[79] While the court did recognise that women's reproductive choices can be limited in terms of s 36 of the Constitution, it did not expressly recognise the grounds to limit their rights within a foetal-interests framework, but rather according to state interests.[80] Unfortunately, the court did not explain what was meant by 'state interest'. One can speculate that the state has an interest in the preservation of prenatal life, but given the direction of this decision as leaning against the recognition of independently valued prenatal life, it can also be argued that the state has an interest in reducing the high levels of

69 *Christian Lawyers* (1998) 1121G.
70 Section 28(1)*(e)* and *(f)*.
71 Section 28(1)*(g)*.
72 Section 28(1)*(i)*.
73 *Christian Lawyers* (1998) 1122A–D.
74 *Christian Lawyers* (1998) 1122C. McCreath J does not cite authority for understanding age to begin at birth.
75 *Christian Lawyers* (1998) 1122E–H.
76 *Christian Lawyers* (1998) 1122E–H.
77 *Christian Lawyers* (1998) 1122I.
78 *Christian Lawyers* (1998) 1123B.
79 *Christian Lawyers* (1998) 1121I.
80 *Christian Lawyers* (1998) 1122A.

maternal mortality rates associated with illegal or unsafe pregnancy terminations and therefore sees the need to regulate the industry accordingly.[81]

This decision sets the tone concerning foetal life under the Constitution. Not only does the single-entity approach get constitutional 'endorsement' from the Provincial Division but the court goes further and rejects the separate-entities approach. Rejection of the separate-entities approach is apparent when one considers McCreath J's hypothetical application of s 11 to the unborn. According to McCreath J, if s 11 were to be interpreted as applying to the unborn, they would have separate claims to life and lawful termination of pregnancies would ultimately constitute murder, even if the terminations of pregnancies were medically indicated.[82] The judge find this to be an invalid approach and states, 'the drafters of the Constitution could not have contemplated such far-reaching results without expressing themselves in no uncertain terms'.[83] As a side note, the court's conclusion in respect of the outcome of the separate-entities approach is perceived as legally unsound, since if the unborn were granted the right to life, the defence of necessity would allow pregnant women to terminate their pregnancies in cases where their own lives are at risk.[84] Further, McCreath is labouring under the impression that the foetus, if accepted as a separate person, would have an enforceable claim to the use of a woman's body,[85] which would be stronger than a woman's claim to her own body: there is no such right in law.[86]

The Constitutional Court seems supportive of this approach. In the context of 'wrongful life' claims, Froneman J specificall emphasised that children's rights to equality, dignity and the paramount importance of their best interests, which may support developing the common law to permit wrongful life claims in South Africa, only become applicable at birth. This findin arguably serves as a constitutional endorsement of the single-entity approach because it emphasises that no rights apply prior to birth; the court specificall rejected arguments that a doctor owes the foetus a duty regarding testing for disabilities during gestation.

[81] Concerning high maternal morbidity and mortality rates associated to illegal and unsafe termination-of-pregnancy procedures, see generally, World Health Organization 'Unsafe abortion: Global and regional estimates of the incidence of unsafe abortion and associated mortality in 2008' available at http://whqlibdoc.who.int/publications/2011/9789241501118_eng.pdf?ua=1 (accessed on 1 April 2016).

[82] *Christian Lawyers* (1998) 1122I.

[83] *Christian Lawyers* (1998) 1123B.

[84] In respect of necessity, see Snyman *Criminal Law* 115–23. Necessity is define as an act directed at the protection of the victim's or someone else's 'life, bodily integrity, property or other legally protected interest which is endangered by a threat of harm which has commenced or is imminent and which cannot be averted in any other way'.

[85] This issue was specificall addressed and shown to be wrong in C Pickles 'Approaches to pregnancy under the law: A relational response to the current South African position and recent academic trends' (2014) 47 *De Jure* 20. More on issues linked to perceived implications of the separate-entities approach will be considered in Chapter Six.

[86] It is necessary to point out that McCreath J's position can be viewed as somewhat patriarchal in that it almost insists that women should be self-sacrificin and are under an obligation to give up their lives in order to save the unborn. This sort of self-sacrificin obligation is not imposed on anyone and it is not clear why the judge would fin that to be the case during pregnancy.

Looking at the criminal law perspective of the legal position of the unborn, s 239(1) of the Criminal Procedure Act is still in force, which requires the proof of live birth before a case of killing a new born child can be put forward. Further, while *Makhakha* did not delve into foetal existence under South African criminal law in the context of murder, *S v Mshumpa*[87] did. As far as research indicates, *Mshumpa* was the first and to date, the last-known case that deals with violence which results in the termination of a pregnancy. As briefl mentioned in Chapter Four, this case concerned the non-consensual termination of a woman's pregnancy (Shelver) by shooting her in the abdomen twice. The harm was inflicte on her with the intention of terminating her pregnancy. As a result of the gun shot wounds, the victim gave birth to a stillborn girl who had reached 38 weeks' gestation.[88] The state tried Mshumpa and Best (his co-accused) for the murder of the foetus and attempted murder of Shelver, the pregnant victim.

In an attempt to succeed with a murder conviction for the death of the foetus, the state used medical evidence to show that a 38-week foetus, verging on birth, is no different from a born child, in that their level of development and experience of and reaction to pain are the same.[89] Further, the medical expert attested to the fact that the foetus had attempted to breathe while still *in utero* and this is a comparable reaction to any born person in the case of severe loss of blood.[90] After their endeavour to blur the differential lines between a late-term (or viable) foetus and a born person, the state argued that the court should declare that 'killing of an unborn child in circumstances such as the present constituted the crime of murder'.[91] The state urged that a declaration of this sort would allow for law to properly reflec medical advancements and community convictions.[92] Ultimately, the state argued that the common-law crime of murder, the unlawful and intentional killing of another person, should be extended to include the unborn.[93] This extension is necessary, because 'person' means those who are already born and this definitio therefore excludes the unborn from the ambit of the crime of murder.[94]

When considering whether to develop the common law to include the unborn within the ambit of murder, the court looked at the status of the unborn generally and reiterated that constitutional rights did not extend to them.[95] Froneman J stated that as far as he was aware 'no South African court has ever held that an unborn child that was not born alive holds any right in its unborn state'.[96] Further, Froneman J found that, in other countries where feticide laws are in place, foetal

[87] 2008 (1) SACR 126 (E) (*Mshumpa*). *Mshumpa*'s outcome may be the reason why the prosecuting authority in *Makhakha* did not pursue the loss of prenatal life under criminal law.

[88] *Mshumpa* paras 1–3.

[89] *Mshumpa* para 48.

[90] *Mshumpa* para 48.

[91] *Mshumpa* para 50.

[92] *Mshumpa* para 50.

[93] *Mshumpa* para 53.

[94] *Mshumpa* para 53. Snyman (*Criminal Law* 448) confirm this and explains that to 'kill' a foetus and separate it from a pregnant woman's body is 'abortion' and not murder.

[95] *Mshumpa* paras 56; 64.

[96] *Mshumpa* paras 56; 64.

protection is not the result of the born-alive rule being done away with but is rather because statutory provisions were enacted to work around the rule.[97] Recognising the difficulties associated with formulating a reasonably precise extended definitio of murder, the court found that the legislature was best positioned to bring about this sort of reform.[98]

Ultimately, the court refused to extend the common-law crime of murder and found that the act must be punished as part of the offence committed against Shelver and that the aggravation of the act, in the form of harm to the foetus, could be taken into consideration at the sentencing stage.[99] The court found it acceptable to treat the harm caused to the foetus as a crime against the pregnant woman for two reasons. First, women are vested with constitutional rights. In particular, s 12(2)*(a)* and *(b)* provide that they have the right to bodily and psychological integrity, which includes the right to make reproductive decisions, thus terminating her pregnancy through assault is a violation of her rights.[100] Secondly, assaulting a pregnant woman with the intention of harming the foetus is construed as an assault on both the pregnant woman and the foetus, owing to their 'unique togetherness'.[101] Froneman J explained that '[a]n assault by an outsider on one is at the same time an assault on both, in their togetherness'.[102]

Given the boundaries within which the court had to work regarding current legal principles, such as the limited scope of the Constitution in respect of the unborn, the born-alive rule, the principle of legality, and requirement to incrementally develop the common law, the outcome of the case was unfortunate[103] but is perceived as legally sound. It should be noted that the court confirme that the born-alive rule is still a functioning principle of our legal

[97] *Mshumpa* para 57. This will be confirme in Part Three, when the United States is considered.

[98] *Mshumpa* paras 59; 65. Issues such as whether the crime should include maternal conduct during pregnancy, the role of foetal viability, and how the extended crime will fi in with illegal termination of pregnancies in respect of the Choice Act.

[99] *Mshumpa* para 58.

[100] *Mshumpa* para 64.

[101] C Pickles 'The introduction of a statutory crime to address third-party foetal violence' (2011) 74 *THRHR* 546.

[102] *Mshumpa* para 64.

[103] The outcome is viewed as unfortunate because Shelver's loss of pregnancy went unrecognised in law; she understood her loss as more than a mere bodily experience and there is no legally labelled crime validating and recognising her sense of loss. To the extent that Shelver had no legal recourse for her loss see MC Buthelezi & M Reddi 'Killing with impunity: The story of an unborn child' (2008) 41 *De Jure* 429. The authors argue that the state should have advanced the charge of common-law abortion or contravention of the Choice Act. In HJ Kruuse 'Fetal "rights"? The need for a unifie approach to the fetus in the context of feticide' (2009) 72 *THRHR* 126, Kruuse effectively discredits the application of the common-law crime of abortion to the extent that it is no longer in force in South Africa. Furthermore, in Pickles *S v Mshumpa: A Time for Law Reform* 46–8 it is demonstrated that the Choice Act is not applicable to the *Mshumpa* facts in so far as the provisions of the Act only become relevant when a woman has voluntarily decided to terminate her pregnancy and then actively seeks to give effect to that decision. In this respect, the Act regulates when she can terminate her pregnancy, where the services must be rendered and who is lawfully permitted to terminate the pregnancy. Furthermore, an alternative charge of assault would do little to bridge the gap between Shelver's sense of loss and the law's inadequate response to the wrong committed against her pregnancy.

system and that the Constitution does not extend to the unborn for as long as there is no live birth. Thus, this portion of *Mshumpa* confirm the single-entity approach.

Nevertheless, the use of 'unique togetherness' introduces a very subtle indication that the court recognises more in pregnant women than women as the only entity involved in a pregnancy. This is because a woman cannot be uniquely together with herself; there must be something more in order for there to be a 'together' element.[104] However, the court applied the 'unique togetherness' as a means to deny the unborn a recognised position in law, thus affirming a single-entity approach to pregnancy. This is so because the harm was punished as essentially being a physical harm only to the pregnant woman, while the other entity with which the woman was understood to be together was merely subsumed into one. What happened in *Mshumpa* was more than just harm to the body of a pregnant woman, but was the termination of a wanted late-term prenatal life, which was obviously something more than an assault on Shelver. This case demonstrates that recognising the 'extra-ness' in pregnancy is not necessarily the end of the single-entity approach, because the very fact that the foetus was seen as intrinsically connected to the woman served as a ground for denying its meaningful recognition in law.

Both *Christian Lawyers* (1998) and *Mshumpa* offer a view of how the single-entity approach is applied in both private and criminal law. In both instances it was established that the Constitution denies the unborn separate existence until live birth. Moving for a wider view, the discussion of case law here shows that, despite confirmin the born-alive rule and the resulting single-entity approach, there are elusive indications of attempts to recognise pregnancy as something more than embodying a single entity. This is seen in *Friedman*'s unsuccessful application of the sanctity of life, *Christian Lawyers* (1998) vague interest in regulating women's reproductive decisions and *Mshumpa*'s 'unique togetherness'. *Christian Lawyers Association v Minister of Health*[105] and the Choice Act, under the direction of the Constitution's founding value of dignity, expand on these curious references and will be discussed next.

5.3 THE NOT-ONE-BUT-NOT-TWO APPROACH

Accepting that the born-alive rule and the resulting single-entity approach is an entrenched principle in South African law, one nevertheless find instances where foetal life is acknowledged and the interests of the unborn are accounted for despite their not having been born. This is a recognition that, in some instances, the unborn are more than nothing. This section looks at the intersection of constitutional values (as opposed to rights), the limiting provisions of the Choice Act and the decision of *Christian Lawyers* (2005), where the court clarifie the state's interest as being an interest in prenatal life. This intersection changes the dynamics of prenatal life under law in that the born-alive rule remains intact but a

[104] This is especially the case if 'together' is understood as companionship or close association. It implies there is something to be in close association with.

[105] 2005 (1) SA 509 (T) (*Christian Lawyers* (2005)).

different perspective is introduced. This perspective ultimately goes beyond the single-entity approach. While functioning within the legal framework of the born-alive rule, the intersection of these three spheres of law introduces the notion that pregnancy can be seen as embodying more than one entity, but also not two completely separate entities.

5.3.1 Conceptualising the not-one-but-not-two approach

The not-one/not-two approach to pregnancy is seen to rest between the two extremes of the single-entity and the separate-entities approaches to pregnancy,[106] offering a middle ground.[107] The not-one/not-two approach is define as a female view of pregnancy.[108] MacKinnon explains that the legal system has failed to adequately conceptualise pregnancy and the maternal/foetal relationship because the interests, perceptions and experiences that have shaped the law on this topic are those of men and development has occurred to the exclusion of women.[109] This is problematic because pregnancy is a female experience, thus resulting in the development of principles from an uninformed outsider perspective. MacKinnon provides a description of the unborn from a female perspective as follows:[110]

> More than a body part but less than a person, where it is, is largely what it is. From the standpoint of pregnant women, it is both me and not me. It 'is' the pregnant woman, in the sense that it is in her and of her and is hers more than anyone's. It is 'not her' in the sense that she is not all that is there. In a legal system that views the individual as a unitary self, and that self as a bundle of rights, it is no wonder that the pregnant woman has eluded legal grasp, and her fetus with her. (Footnotes omitted.)

Lupton's studies support MacKinnon's position. Lupton recognises that some women do understand their pregnancies as embodying a separate individual.[111] However, even within the perception of foetal individuation, all the women

[106] While the concerns relating to the separate-entities approach will be considered in more detail in Part Three, it is necessary to mention that the not-one/not-two approach originally came about as a response to the ineffective outcomes of the separate-entities approach. In this respect, see I Karpin 'Legislating the female body: Reproductive technology and the reconstructed woman' (1992) 3 *Columbia Journal of Gender and Law* 325. Research indicates that she is the firs to have adopted this term and advanced it as an approach to pregnancy. Karpin (329) is critical of the separate-entities approach which she sees as being a means to gain political control over women through legal interventions during pregnancy. She asks why not view a pregnant woman and foetus as not one but not two. She argues that the separate-entities approach already does this in that legal action is taken on behalf of the unborn (as a separate entity) in cases where maternal conduct is seen as dangerous. However, that very action must acknowledge, for purposes of a successful claim against a woman, that there is a shared connection between a pregnant woman and foetus, it must acknowledge their inseparability. It is their inseparability that makes maternal conduct problematic for the unborn which separate-entities advocates wish it to address.

[107] Seymour *Childbirth and the Law* 190; 202.

[108] Seymour *Childbirth and the Law* 199 and CA MacKinnon 'Reflection on sex equality under law' (1991) 100 *Yale LJ* 1281 1309; 1313–14.

[109] MacKinnon (1991) *Yale LJ* 1281 1309; 1313–14.

[110] MacKinnon (1991) *Yale LJ* 1316.

[111] Lupton *Social World of the Unborn* 53–6.

understood the foetus to be in and somewhat part of their bodies, thus not completely apart from them.[112]

Focus on relationship allows for the recognition of the following elements as stemming from the existence of a pregnancy: united needs; interconnectedness; mutuality; and reciprocity.[113] Essentially, it advocates a view and embeds an understanding that a pregnant woman and foetus cannot be viewed in isolation. The not-one/not-two approach allows a foetus to be recognised as a distinct entity but it also expresses an unequivocal reminder of the relationship shared between a pregnant woman and her foetus.[114] Therefore, this approach acknowledges that a foetus has interests but that these interests must be promoted in such a way that a woman's rights are acknowledged.[115]

In order to achieve the aim of advancing foetal interests in such a way that women's rights are promoted, the not-one/not-two approach to pregnancy is context-driven, meaning that the maternal/foetal relationship must be understood in respect of the context in which that relationship exists. It is only through the process of including context that one can determine whether intervention in pregnancy is necessary, and whether such intervention should be a legal intervention or not. Where legal intervention is found to be necessary, context would assist in determining whether such an intervention would amount to an acknowledgment or infringement of women's rights.[116]

Seymour understands this approach as being flexible [117] First it acknowledges value in the unborn but denies them their separateness.[118] Secondly, it enables women's rights to be included and considered.[119] Third, it sets the scene for the protection of the unborn when their interests are threatened by a third party, but may produce different results when the unborn's interests are 'threatened' by the pregnant women carrying them.[120]

On the issue of harm caused by pregnant women, Seymour argues that this approach does not provide absolute legal immunity for pregnant women.[121] While he goes on to assert that female autonomy plays a crucial role in determining their

---

[112] Lupton *Social World of the Unborn* 53–6.

[113] Seymour *Childbirth and the Law* 190.

[114] Seymour *Childbirth and the Law* 200. This approach echoes the very principles of relational feminism thus supporting MacKinnon's premise that the not-one/not-two approach is a female perspective on pregnancy. See Chapter Three for a discussion of relational feminism. This topic will be discussed and further developed in Part Four. For examples of the practical application of relational feminism, see JE McConnell 'Relational and liberal feminism: The "ethic of care," fetal personhood and autonomy' (1996) 99 *West Virginia LR* 291; E Ordolis 'Maternal substance abuse and the limits of law: A relational challenge' (2008) 46 *Alberta LR* 119; and P Laufer-Ukeles 'Reproductive choices and informed consent: Fetal interests, women's identity, and relational autonomy' (2011) 37 *American Journal of Law & Medicine* 567.

[115] Seymour *Childbirth and the Law* 200.

[116] Seymour *Childbirth and the Law* 200.

[117] Seymour *Childbirth and the Law* 201–2.

[118] Seymour *Childbirth and the Law* 201–2.

[119] Seymour *Childbirth and the Law* 201–2.

[120] Seymour *Childbirth and the Law* 201–2.

[121] Seymour *Childbirth and the Law* 202.

immunity,[122] it is suggested that absolute freedom during pregnancy may never be in place because this approach demands that the value of the unborn will always play a part (not the central part, but certainly an important contributory one) in determining a way forward.[123]

Seymour recognised that there are very few cases that give any attention to this approach, but *Christian Lawyers* (2005) does, together with the Choice Act. As discussed earlier, in 1998, the Choice Act came under constitutional scrutiny in *Christian Lawyers Association* (1998), and it was clearly demonstrated that a foetus is not a bearer of constitutional rights. Also, the judge vaguely mentioned that the state has an interest in regulating women's reproductive decisions. Years later, in *Christian Lawyers* (2005), also in the context of the Choice Act, the court found that the right to terminate a pregnancy is not absolute and went on to clarify the state's interest in respect of reproductive decision-making processes.

While *Christian Lawyers* (2005) recognised the importance of women having a right to terminate their pregnancies,[124] the court also found that the right to terminate a pregnancy, like all constitutional rights, is subject to the limitation clause.[125] Focusing on state interest, Mojapelo J explicitly recognised '[t]he state has a legitimate role in the protection of pre-natal life as an important value in our society, to regulate and limit the woman's right to choose in that regard'.[126] Since the right to terminate a pregnancy is a fundamental constitutional right, state regulation cannot amount to a denial of the freedom to exercise the right.[127] Thus, the limitation must be reasonable and justifiabl in an open and democratic society based on human dignity, equality and freedom as required in terms of s 36 of the Constitution.[128]

This case fit squarely in line with the not-one/not-two approach to pregnancy because the value in prenatal life is acknowledged in its own light, indicating that pregnancy embodies more than one entity.[129] However, the acknowledgement does not go as far as to confer on the unborn an entire separate status and enforceable rights.[130] Rather, this judicial acknowledgment views the foetus in relation to the pregnant woman and her existing rights.[131] *Christian Lawyers* (2005) can also be distinguished from the cases discussed under the single-entity approach in that the court not only acknowledges the existence of prenatal life but also attaches value thereto, which value is understood to demand state action for

---

[122] His discussion of autonomy (in the context of Canada and the United States of America) goes beyond the scope of this chapter. Briefl he suggests that women will benefi from immunity where harm caused to the unborn is a result of women exercising their right to withhold consent to invasive bodily infringements. However, he refrains from answering the question of whether a woman can be held legally accountable where harm is caused to the unborn in the case where the woman engages in harmful conduct such as drug abuse or alcoholism.

[123] This was argued elsewhere; see Pickles (2014) *De Jure* 20.

[124] For a discussion of this portion of the *Christian Lawyers* (2005) decision, see Chapter Four, para 4.3.4.

[125] 527D.

[126] *Christian Lawyers* (2005) 527D.

[127] *Christian Lawyers* (2005) 527E.

[128] *Christian Lawyers* (2005) 527E.

[129] Pickles (2014) *De Jure* 20.

[130] Pickles (2014) *De Jure* 20.

[131] Pickles (2014) *De Jure* 20.

the benefi of prenatal life in a qualifie way that is respectful of women's rights.[132] Finally, *Christian Lawyers* (2005) demonstrates that the not-one/not-two approach has a strong chance of surviving constitutional muster.[133]

The state and society's interest in prenatal life and the value attached thereto has found legislative translation. The Choice Act sets out the circumstances and the conditions that allow for the termination of a pregnancy in terms of s 2(1)*(a)*, which states that a pregnancy may be terminated upon the request of a woman during the firs 12 weeks of gestation. Section (2)(1)*(b)* provides that, from 13 weeks' up to and including 20 weeks' gestation, a pregnancy may be terminated only once a woman has consulted with a medical practitioner and that medical practitioner is of the opinion that: continued pregnancy would pose a risk to the mother's physical or mental health; there is a substantial risk that the foetus will suffer from severe physical or mental abnormality; the pregnancy is a result of rape or incest; or the continued pregnancy will severely affect the woman's social or economic circumstances. Section 2(1)*(c)* provides that a pregnancy that has reached 21 weeks' gestation may be terminated only if a medical practitioner, after consulting with another medical practitioner, is of the opinion that the continued pregnancy would endanger the woman's life, would result in severe malformation of the foetus, or would pose a risk of injury to a foetus.

These provisions clearly demonstrate that, as the pregnancy progresses, women's freedom of choice is curtailed and the decision is shared with a medical practitioner and must fall within one of the stipulated grounds. Although *Christian Lawyers* (1998) set the scene of a rather grim legal framework concerning the advancement of foetal interests in that the Constitution does not extend to the unborn, *Christian Lawyers* (2005), read together with the Choice Act, introduced a different dimension concerning their protection. The restrictions contained in the Choice Act reveal a legislative commitment to the increasingly compelling interests of the foetus (at and after viability) but within the context of women's reproductive rights,[134] and this position feeds into the not-one/not-two approach, since a foetus is recognised but in the context of the pregnant woman carrying it.

A number of academics have contributed to creating an understanding of where this interest in foetal life is derived from. While it is accepted that a foetus is not a bearer of constitutional rights, Meyerson convincingly points out that this does not finalis the matter concerning foetal interests.[135] She argues that if that were the case, the state would pass laws permitting late terminations of pregnancies for any reason whatsoever.[136]

There is an obstacle to treating a foetus in such an arbitrary fashion. O'Sullivan[137]

---

[132] Pickles (2014) *De Jure* 20.

[133] Pickles (2014) *De Jure* 20.

[134] M O'Sullivan 'Reproductive rights' in S Woolman & M Bishop (eds) *Constitutional Law of South Africa* 2 ed (Original Service 2) 37-27. The issue of foetal viability is discussed below.

[135] D Meyerson 'Abortion: The constitutional issues' (1999) 116 *SALJ* 50 55.

[136] Meyerson (1999) *SALJ* 50 55.

[137] See O'Sullivan 'Reproductive rights' 37-6.

relies on Ronald Dworkin's[138] view that arguments about termination of pregnancies should not revolve round whether a foetus is the bearer of constitutional rights. This would be a flawe approach, because any argument that affords a foetus constitutional rights merely grants the state a derivative interest in prohibiting or regulating the termination of pregnancies.[139]

It is Dworkin's assertion that the argument is not whether we object to the termination of pregnancies because we believe that a foetus is a bearer of constitutional rights, but whether we attach some intrinsic value to life and the potential for human life.[140] Accordingly, the interest of the state in potential life derives from the state's interest in protecting the sanctity of human life in all its forms, therefore justifying the regulation of termination laws on grounds that are independent of the rights-bearing capacity of the foetus itself.[141] Dworkin argues that the state has a detached interest in regulating termination of pregnancies.[142] This argument falls in line with *Christian Lawyers* (2005) where the court describes prenatal life as an important value in our society.[143] This value is so important that it justifie limiting women's rights to terminate their pregnancies.[144]

The value of prenatal life, being a ground for justifying the limitation of women's rights, is informed by our constitutional values.[145] The Constitution includes a number of provisions that make specifi reference to values, such as ss 1, 7(2), 36(1), and 39(1) and (2). First, the Constitution recognises that human dignity, the achievement of equality, and the advancements of rights and freedoms are some of the specifie values on which the Republic of South Africa is founded.[146] Further, the Bill of Rights affirms the democratic values of human dignity, equality and freedom,[147] and thus any limitations of rights contained in the Bill of Rights must be reasonable and justifiabl in light of the founding values.[148] These founding values also play a central role when interpreting the Bill of Rights and legislation, or when developing the common and customary law.[149] Meyerson states that there is more to the Constitution than granting and protecting the rights, since it explicitly distinguishes between rights and freedoms on the one hand, and

[138] As provided for in RM Dworkin *Life's Dominion: An Argument about Abortion, Euthanasia, and Individual Freedom* (1993). Further authors relying on Dworkin are Meyerson (1999) *SALJ* 53 and Kruuse (2009) *THRHR* 134.

[139] A derivative interest is an interest based on the presumption that the entity involved is a person with rights and interests, and the state's interest in protecting it stems from the fact that it is a bearer of rights. See Dworkin *Life's Dominion* 11.

[140] Dworkin *Life's Dominion* 11.

[141] Dworkin *Life's Dominion* 11.

[142] A detached interest is an interest based on the fact that human life is itself intrinsically valuable, regardless of the status of the person. See Dworkin *Life's Dominion* 11 and Kruuse (2009) *THRHR* 135.

[143] *Christian Lawyers* (2005) 527D. Also see C Albertyn, L Artz, H Combrink, et al 'Women's freedom and security of the person' in E Bonthuys & C Albertyn (eds) *Gender, Law and Justice* (2007) 370; the authors recognise that the Choice Act reflect Dworkin's approach concerning the state's interest in later gestation foetuses.

[144] *Christian Lawyers* (2005) 527D.

[145] Meyerson (1999) *SALJ* 55.

[146] Section 1*(a)* of the Constitution.

[147] Section 7(2) of the Constitution.

[148] Section 36(1) of the Constitution.

[149] Section 39(1)*(a)* of the Constitution.

the values of human dignity, equality and freedom on the other.[150] Meyerson argues that, even if there are no human rights protected prior to birth, it is necessary to consider whether the value of human dignity might operate as a constitutional constraint on legislation governing the termination of pregnancies.[151]

Meyerson states that it is the value of human dignity that is under threat, because it is hard to deny that the destruction of foetal life, although it violates no constitutionally protected subject's right to life, undermines human dignity.[152] A foetus is not mere maternal tissue; she considers it to be a living organism, whose destruction is not a morally trivial matter but something to be regretted.[153] Meyerson published her work in 1999, and her position still stands today. Ackermann expressly took on this approach to dignity in his recent publication *Human Dignity: Lodestar for Equality in South Africa.*[154] Ackermann understands dignity (being synonymous with human worth) to vest in all who form part of the human species and asserts that, in order to protect the dignity of all, it may be required that dignity be protected even before birth.[155] Therefore, value in prenatal life, as something forming part of the human species, is ever present.

Since an interest in foetal life has been established on the basis of the value of dignity, it is now necessary to determine when one can act towards the preservation of that value. Ackermann argues that, since the very act of conception brings about a member of the human race, what conception produces joins in on the worth (dignity) of the species.[156] Accepting that the value of dignity serves as the ground for the state to limit female reproductive rights in terms of the Choice Act, and Ackermann understands it to vest at the moment of conception, a vexed question is raised: How can the Choice Act legitimately permit elective

---

150 Meyerson (1999) *SALJ* 55. Also see *Dawood v Minister of Home Affairs*; *Shalabi v Minister of Home Affairs*; *Thomas v Minister of Home Affairs* 2000 (3) SA 936 (CC) para 35.

151 Meyerson (1999) *SALJ* 56. Also see S Woolman 'Dignity' in S Woolman & M Bishop (eds) *Constitutional Law of South Africa* 2 ed (Revised Service 3) 36-19; 36-22 to 36-25. He states that the value of dignity can be invoked in three cases: where the value of dignity guides the interpretation of the right and, by doing so, shapes the ambit of the right; where the value of dignity can be used to justify the limitation of a right; and where the value of dignity can be used in those cases where the Bill of Rights does not directly apply to the circumstances, and, in this case, the value of dignity will inform the development of the common law or the interpretation of the statute (36-24).

152 Meyerson (1999) *SALJ* 59. In fact, when understanding dignity from this perspective it can be argued that the process of terminating pregnancies undermines dignity in all instances. In cases where necessity demands a termination because a pregnancy jeopardises a woman's health or life, there is a sense that one is not necessarily undermining dignity per se. One should not take the position that pregnant women are violating the unborn's inherent worth when a termination procedure is requested or performed without therapeutic justification Terminating a pregnancy is a response to broader issues and it is the very presence and persistence of those broader social issues that undermine human dignity of the unborn and the pregnant woman concerned.

153 Meyerson (1999) *SALJ* 59.

154 L Ackermann *Human Dignity: Lodestar for Equality in South Africa* (2012).

155 Ackermann *Human Dignity* 51.

156 Ackermann *Human Dignity* 52.

terminations of first and second-trimester pregnancies, since it can be claimed that these terminations also offend the value of human dignity?[157]

In respect of the above question, Meyerson asserts that early non-therapeutic pregnancy terminations are too controversial for the state to regulate, as the unborn are usually very underdeveloped when such terminations are permitted.[158] Further, the limitation clause prevents the state from limiting rights for intractably disputed reasons, since a person's own moral judgments do not justify legal interference by the state when a woman decides to exercise her choice to terminate her pregnancy.[159] Sarkin-Hughes states that:[160]

> [D]espite the fact that not every woman's decision will be in accordance with another's individual sense of morality, society's interest must only be an advisory one. Otherwise we will be left with the dangerous and oppressive situation of the state imposing a preconceived moral stance, which has been created in part from stereotypes of women's intellectual and physiological capabilities.

However, beyond early prenatal life, and once the foetus becomes more developed and approaches viability,[161] its destruction becomes less tied to intractably disputed views and the weight to be afforded to human dignity in relation to female reproductive rights becomes less controversial.[162] This is because, theoretically, it is at the point of viability that a foetus should be capable of living independently of the pregnant woman if it is born alive, since all its vital organs are developed and are able to perform their functions sufficiently.[163]

Accepting the above arguments as constitutionally valid, a concern remains regarding termination of pregnancies for socio-economic reasons in the second trimester.[164] The authors mentioned above[165] describe 'early pregnancy' as including first and second-trimester pregnancies. However, it is difficult to accept that a pregnancy that has developed into the second trimester can still be described

[157] C Pickles 'Termination-of-pregnancy rights and foetal interests in continued existence in South Africa: The Choice on Termination of Pregnancy Act 92 of 1996' (2012) 15 *PER* 403 420.

[158] (1999) *SALJ* 57.

[159] Meyerson (1999) *SALJ* 57–8.

[160] J Sarkin-Hughes 'A perspective on abortion legislation in South Africa's bill of rights era' (1993) 56 *THRHR* 83 89.

[161] Foetal viability is said to occur at around 22 weeks' gestation; see Sarkin-Hughes (1993) *THRHR* 89 and Pickles (2013) *Stell LR* 146.

[162] Meyerson (1999) *SALJ* 58.

[163] See generally IG Cohen & S Sayeed 'Fetal pain, abortion, viability and the Constitution' (2011) 39 *Journal of Law, Medicine & Ethics* 235. Cohen and Sayeed point out that there are normative societal tendencies, as expressed by the courts, to assign a particular point in development for foetal viability based on the estimation of gestational age. However, there are other factors that affect the probabilities of long-term neonatal survival, such as sex, birth weight, maternal exposure to steroids, and resource allocations. It must be noted that understanding viability as significan enough to justify increased protection under the law is seen as arbitrary by some, since it is argued that regardless of the point in development of the unborn, the fact remains that it represents human life. This issue will be addressed in more detail in Chapter Six.

[164] In terms of s 2(1)*(b)*(iv) of the Choice Act, a woman can terminate a pregnancy from 13 to 20 weeks' gestation if the continued pregnancy will significantl affect the social or economic circumstances of the woman.

[165] Meyerson (1999) *SALJ* 58 and Sarkin-Hughes (1993) *THRHR* 89.

as an 'early pregnancy'.[166] At this point, as a pregnancy develops through the weeks of the second trimester, the foetus begins to take the form of an infant and moves indisputably closer to viability. According to Myburgh, provisions that allow termination of pregnancies for socio-economic reasons are an 'irrational and arbitrary exclusion of the unborn and [create] an imbalance in liberal abortion jurisprudence', because only the rights of women are advanced.[167] By contrast, Ngwena has praised South African termination-of-pregnancy laws as radically liberal in comparison with those of our African neighbours, as South Africa is one of the very few African countries that permit termination of pregnancies for socio-economic reasons.[168]

Through the lens of foetal interests, and at firs glance, the socio-economic reason provision is arbitrary.[169] However, taking a closer contextual look into second-trimester terminations in South Africa, as the not-one/not-two approach calls for, it is argued that this provision fill a very important role for women in South Africa. Of the total number of pregnancies that were terminated in 2009, 13% took place in the second trimester (after 12 weeks' gestation).[170] These statistics lead one to question why second-trimester terminations are taking place (if not for therapeutic reasons) at a time when South African legislation permits first-trimeste termination of pregnancies on demand.[171] Going further into the inquiry, are these decisions infused with a sense of arbitrariness and tactless conduct on the part of women seeking second-trimester termination-of-pregnancy services?

A number of studies have provided an answer to this. Research stemming from the medical field where the provisions of the Choice Act are implemented, demonstrates that accessing the service later in pregnancy is not necessarily an indication of arbitrary decision-making but rather an indication of a system failing pregnant women, in that it is unable to effectively meet their reproductive

[166] Pickles (2012) *PER* 421.

[167] GA Myburgh *Humanity and the Protection of the Unborn: A Jurisprudential Rationale for the Furtherance of the Anthropological Paradigm of International Law* (unpublished LLM dissertation, University of the Free State, 2008) 60. Also see F van Oosten 'The Choice on Termination of Pregnancy Act: Some comments' (1999) 116 *SALJ* 60 64. He argues that the Choice Act merely grants a woman the freedom to terminate a pregnancy for whatever reason she considers fi since the Act simply views the foetus as a 'member of the pregnant woman's body, which includes the right to have her embryo killed'. Van Oosten (76) is very critical of the Choice Act and describes it as being plagued with 'lacunae, contradictions, inconsistencies and incomprehensibilities, and demonstrates a stunning ignorance of basic principles of criminal law and an inexplicable ambivalence on the issue of abortion, and a surprising insensitivity to the meaning of words on the legislature's part'.

[168] C Ngwena 'An appraisal of abortion laws in southern Africa from a reproductive health rights perspective' (2004) 32 *Journal of Law, Medicine & Ethics* 708 715.

[169] Pickles (2012) *PER* 422.

[170] Health Systems Trust 'TOPs by gestational age' available at http://indicators.hst.org.za/healthstats/88/data/gedo (accessed on 13 April 2016). Unfortunately, the only statistics available to date are those for 2009. Health Systems Trust is yet to update their termination-of-pregnancy statistics. Also, these statistics do not differentiate between elective or therapeutic termination-of-pregnancy procedures.

[171] Especially since first-trimeste terminations are free at public health care facilities; see s 4(3)*(c)* of the National Health Act 61 of 2003.

demands.[172] Having regard to the contextual reality in which women fin themselves when seeking to terminate their pregnancies,[173] elective, second-trimester termination of pregnancy fulfil a crucial role in South Africa.[174] It is not only the rights of pregnant women that are being advanced, but also the rights of those with whom these women already share a relationship and have a responsibility of care towards (children and dependent family members).[175] These women would fin themselves in dire circumstances if termination-of-pregnancy legislation prohibited second-trimester terminations, especially where delays in terminations are the result of external factors linked to financia resources, staff attitudes and poor referral systems.[176] Although the studies referred to here were limited to termination-of-pregnancy services in the public sector, the studies do give an indication of the hardship that the majority of women in South Africa may face in general. It can hardly be concluded that second-trimester termination of pregnancies is generally arbitrarily and irresponsibly sought after or relied on by pregnant women.[177]

O'Sullivan states that there are good reasons for the state to progressively limit the termination of a pregnancy after viability. First, foetal brain development may be sufficient for the foetus to feel pain,[178] which indicates that the foetus has

[172] C Morroni & J Moodley 'Characteristics of women booking for firs and second trimester abortions at public sector clinics in Cape Town' (2006) 12 *South African Journal of Obstetrics and Gynaecology* 81; J Harries, P Orner, M Gabriel et al 'Delays in seeking an abortion until the second trimester: A qualitative study in South Africa' (2007) 4 *Reproductive Health* 13; D Grossman, D Constant, N Lince, et al 'Surgical and medical second trimester abortion in South Africa: A cross-sectional study' (2011) 11 *BMC Health Services Research* 224; and J Harries, N Lince, D Constant et al 'The challenges of offering public second trimester abortion services in South Africa: Health care providers' perspectives' (2012) 44 *Journal of Biosocial Science* 197.

[173] Morroni and Moodley ((2006) *South African Journal of Obstetrics and Gynaecology* 81) explain that the women forming part of their study who were seeking second-trimester termination of pregnancy were all faced with unplanned pregnancies: 20 of the 82 women were teenagers, just over one-quarter were self-supporting, while 38 were still in school. Women are not terminating pregnancies for reckless reasons. At times the termination of a pregnancy is a response to social 'evils', including poor access to reproductive control measures, coercive sexual practices, a change in circumstances which leaves some women vulnerable to the burden of rearing a child alone, sexual violence or simply experiencing an unplanned pregnancy. If the aim is to better serve the interests of the foetus, in line with the value society vests in them, then these social evils need to be adequately addressed. In fact, not doing so can be labelled irrational, irresponsible and arbitrary on the side of the state and wider community.

[174] This conclusion was drawn in a previous study, see Pickles (2012) *PER* 424.

[175] See finding in Pickles (2012) *PER* 424.

[176] Pickles (2012) *PER* 424.

[177] See C Pickles 'Lived experiences of the Choice on Termination of Pregnancy Act 92 of 1996: Bridging the gap for women in need' (2013) 29 *SAJHR* 515 and authority cited therein.

[178] The ability to feel pain is a contested issue. See M Ford 'Nothing and not-nothing: Law's ambivalent response to transformation and transgression at the beginning of life' in SW Smith & R Deazley (eds) *The Legal, Medical and Cultural Regulation of the Body: Transformation and Transgression* (2009) 27. Ford argues that scientists disagree about the gestational age at which a foetus becomes sentient. Some have argued that sentience is present in the firs trimester, and there are those who doubt that a foetus is sentient at all. Ford states that there is a majority view that sentience emerges late in the third trimester. This argument is based on the fact that no sentience is possible without any cortical structures in place, which only fully develop between 30 and 35 weeks'

protectable interests of its own.[179] Secondly, by the time the pregnancy has reached that stage of development, the woman concerned has had ample time to decide whether termination is the best option for her.[180] Furthermore, at the stage of viability, the termination of a pregnancy becomes more problematic, because, as the foetus develops towards being an infant, the difference between being a foetus and a child becomes only a matter of location of the unborn in the womb rather than its development.[181] These arguments fall squarely in line with the provisions of the Choice Act. Section 2(1)*(c)* requires the life of the pregnant woman or foetus to be at risk before a termination may be granted where the pregnancy has advanced past 20 weeks' gestation.[182]

Examination of the *Christian Lawyers* (2005) decision regarding state interest and the provisions of the Choice Act indicate that female reproductive rights are the state's firs and foremost concern.[183] However, having given women the opportunity to exercise their rights during 'early pregnancy', the state's interest in female reproductive rights wanes in favour of acting on the value in prenatal life.[184] Subsequently, the state's detached interest, based on the value of human dignity, serves as a reasonable and justifiabl ground to limit female reproductive rights without diminishing the legal significanc of birth or bringing constitutional rights into play regarding the unborn.[185] All of this takes place despite the fact that the born-alive rule is still a functioning principle under South African law. The intersection of constitutional values, the Choice Act and state interest all give credence to the not-one/not-two approach to pregnancy in South Africa, as neither entity is entirely forsaken for the other, but both entities are nevertheless recognised as existing in law.

---

gestation. Also see generally SJ Lee, HJ Ralston, EA Drey et al 'Fetal pain: A systematic multidisciplinary review of the evidence' (2005) 294 *Journal of the American Medical Association* 947 and Cohen & Sayeed (2011) *Journal of Law, Medicine & Ethics* 235.

[179] See Steinbock's arguments concerning foetal interests based on sentience in B Steinbock *Life before Birth: The Moral and Legal Status of Embryos and Fetuses* 2 ed (2011). Her position was discussed in Chapter Three, para 3.5.3.

[180] O'Sullivan 'Reproductive rights' 37-9. However, this statement must be accepted cautiously since Chapter Four demonstrated that women in need tend to have a difficult time accessing termination-of-pregnancy services. This difficulty is known to cause delays in getting the termination-of-pregnancy procedure performed and these delays may even cause women to miss out on the opportunity to lawfully terminate a pregnancy because the pregnancy progressed into the third trimester. The third trimester is the point in pregnancy when women's rights to terminate a pregnancy are severely limited to serious health risks.

[181] O'Sullivan 'Reproductive rights' 37-10.

[182] Sarkin-Hughes ((1993) *THRHR* 89) states that it is preferred to set the cut-off line at 20 weeks rather than 22 weeks, because estimates of gestational age have an approximate two-week margin of error. Even though Sarkin-Hughes's work was published in 1993, to date there still remain gestation estimation difficulties; see Pickles (2013) *Stell LR* 156–7.

[183] Pickles (2012) *PER* 425.

[184] Pickles (2012) *PER* 425.

[185] Pickles (2012) *PER* 425.

5.4 ARE THERE CONTEMPORARY TENSIONS BETWEEN FEMALE AUTONOMY RIGHTS AND FOETAL INTERESTS DURING PREGNANCY?

Having completed the discussions of pregnant women's autonomy and foetal interests under South African law, it is necessary to consider how these two spheres intersect and whether this intersection gives rise to any tensions during pregnancy.

From the single-entity perspective, only women exist and the presence of a foetus, as forming part of the pregnancy, does not count for much in law.[186] Under this construction, pregnant women's autonomy rights cannot be viewed as being in tension with their own realisation. The single-entity approach, as is currently applied in South Africa, effectively prevents third parties from using the law to act for the benefi of the unborn.[187] Therefore, no third party has any legal foundation to interfere with a woman's pregnancy for the benefi of a foetus or its interests. This is pertinently clear, since, as indicated in Chapter Four, in the context of women's rights, there is no case law indicating that pregnant women can be forced to progress through pregnancy in accordance with others pursuing their own conceptions of healthy pregnancies or pregnancy outcomes. In this chapter it was also demonstrated that all litigation initiated with the aim of protecting the foetus or its interests has failed.

Even from the not-one/not-two approach there is no room for an adversarial pregnancy environment. This stems from the fact that, in cases where the value of foetal life is recognised, it is done in a qualifie manner: A foetus is recognised only in relation to the pregnant woman who carries it and its value is advanced so far as this sort of advancement is respectful of the woman and her rights. This expresses a scenario of 'meeting in the middle': Recognition is given to the existence of a foetus, while taking a little from female autonomy, and there is no space for absolute or extensive claims against either entity constituting a pregnancy. With its currently limited application in South Africa, the not-one/not-two approach offers a compromise in a situation that could have easily resulted in the rise of an environment for tensions during pregnancy.

Drawing from Chapter Four's discussion on pregnant women and their rights and what was demonstrated thus far in this chapter, there is sufficient authority indicating that, as South African law stands, there are no tensions between pregnant women's rights and foetal interests, so there is no adversarial pregnancy

[186] From the perspective of pregnant women, the presence of a pregnancy allows for women to lay increased claims against the state for the realisation of their reproductive autonomy.

[187] From a more traditional perspective in respect of the Abortion and Sterilization Act, research indicates that foetal interests were not the driving concern behind the commencement of the Act. In this respect see R Rebouché 'The limits of reproductive rights in improving women's health' (2011) 63 *Alabama LR* 1 4–8. Rebouché explains that in the regulation of termination of pregnancies during Apartheid the state was more concerned about preventing white women from terminating pregnancies in order to increase the white population. A further indication that the Act was not in place to serve the interests of the unborn rests on the fact that a woman could have her pregnancy terminated in the case of rape or incest. If the state was being driven by the desire to protect the unborn, the conditions leading to conception would be irrelevant.

environment.[188] However, the issue does not stop here because Chapters Four and Five clearly demonstrate the need for law reform in certain areas of pregnancy so as to enhance women's reproductive autonomy and create a safe space to offer improved consideration of the unborn. Chapter Six will demonstrate that, when suggested law reform proposals are advanced, the risk of a tension will come to the fore.

5.5 CONCLUDING REMARKS

The born-alive rule is deeply rooted in South Africa and has far-reaching implications. The rule gives rise to the single-entity approach, and this is currently the most prominent approach to the unborn in South Africa. The more traditional and pre-constitutional implications of the born-alive rule are that the unborn are essentially non-existent under the law and no one can, in legal technical terms, act for their benefit no one owes them a legal duty of any sort; and they cannot be considered victims of crime. Despite the law's denialist approach to prenatal life, there are examples where the courts have inched towards recognising the value of prenatal life. These attempts have been based on principles such as the sanctity of life and tentatively recognising pregnancy as resembling a 'unique togetherness'. However, neither of these attempts transformed into any concrete principles leading to the legal recognition of prenatal life. This result may stem from the fact that there was no obvious legal basis for authorising or justifying these attempts. However, this changed after the introduction of the Constitution, which brought the value of dignity within the parameters of the law.

The Constitution shifts the way the unborn are perceived, and this takes place in the context of the Choice Act. Despite the fact that the born-alive rule is still in force, the value of dignity, as one of the founding values in the Constitution, prescribes that all life is of value. This value informs how legislation should be interpreted and applied in respect of certain rights, and thus it encourages an interpretation of the Choice Act that accords value to the unborn, which ultimately serves to legitimately limit female reproductive autonomy from viability onwards. The approach adopted in this context fit the description of the not-one/not-two approach in that it recognises the existence of prenatal life, not as something wholly distinct from women but as something intrinsically related to them. Consequently, this approach does not extend legal subjectivity; rather it opens a window for limited legal recognition of the unborn, but only in the contextual setting of women and their rights.

The discussion of the Choice Act teaches us that prenatal life will always be valued, but whether we can act on that value, and how we go about protecting it, must be determined in the context in which the unborn exist, being through women and their rights. Despite the single-entity approach being the better-known approach, we are seeing the emergence of a new approach taking root in South Africa and it will be interesting to see whether the courts attempt to apply it to

[188] This findin is contrary to Pillay's assertion that without affording the unborn full legal subjectivity, our courts are not equipped to address 'maternal–foetal conflicts' see Pillay (2010) *Stell LR* 236.

other aspects beyond the termination-of-pregnancy laws.[189] However, it is questionable whether the wider legal community is even aware that such an approach exists.

Pooling the finding of Chapters Four and Five together establishes that neither of the two approaches applied in South Africa encourages tensions between female autonomy rights and foetal interests. However, this is not to say that there are no concerns with the application of these approaches. All of the scholarly opinions raised against the South African approach to prenatal life concern the single-entity approach. Generally, these concerns relate to the fact that this approach is irreconcilable with the scientifi fact that the unborn are biologically and genetically distinct from pregnant women.[190] Chapter Six will consider this matter and related calls for the reform of South African law relevant to pregnancy.

[189] Chapter 11 demonstrates how this might occur should the approach be accepted.

[190] Pickles (2014) *De Jure* 20.

Chapter 6

CALLS FOR REFORM OF SOUTH AFRICAN LAW: THE SEPARATE-ENTITIES APPROACH

6.1 INTRODUCTION

Chapters Four and Five laid the foundation for Chapter Six in so far as this chapter looks at South African[1] academic responses to the scenario presented in Chapters Four and Five. South African academics question whether the single-entity approach can effectively secure healthy pregnancies and healthy pregnancy outcomes, and have come to question the legal validity of this position as a whole. The single-entity approach is seen to pose a number of problems in securing healthy progression through pregnancy and birth because one 'entity' who contributes towards the make-up of a pregnancy, being the unborn, is not fully recognised in law.

A study of these scholarly contributions identifie a common thread, namely that the law is viewed as being ill-equipped to tackle harmful impediments to healthy pregnancies or healthy pregnancy outcomes, caused by either third parties or pregnant women themselves. While delving into different areas of law, each of the authors' arguments go on to express the common aim of introducing a separate-entities approach to pregnancy in South African law and this chapter looks at all these assertions in detail. All advocate for the reform of specifi aspects pertaining to pregnancy, such as third-party violence that terminates prenatal life, substance abuse during pregnancy, women's right to terminate their pregnancies, and the extension of personhood to the unborn. In each of these areas of law, it is generally asserted by South African scholars that viewing pregnant women and the unborn as two separate entities creates the necessary space for securing healthy foetal outcomes, since legal intervention can be justifie in cases where pregnant women's or third parties' conduct is seen as detrimental to ideal foetal health, development and eventual live birth. Thus, while many more areas were identifie in Chapters Four and Five as being in need of reform, this chapter focuses only on select issues as highlighted by current academic debates.[2]

[1] South African authors of particular interest include Kruuse, Pillay, De Freitas, Du Plessis (previously Myburgh), and Ovens. It is necessary to indicate who will be considered because other authors from foreign jurisdictions will also be included in this chapter, to provide clarity on certain concepts and support for some arguments.

[2] Only current suggestions for reform are considered in this chapter, 'current' indicating South African scholarly publications dating back to no later than 2008, since it was in 2008 that a South African court heard its firs criminal law case which confirme that the unborn lack legal status and cannot be victims of criminal conduct; see *S v Mshumpa* 2008 (1) SACR 126 (E) (*Mshumpa*). This case seems to have sparked academic debates concerning pregnant women, pregnancy more generally, and the unborn.

Chapter Six starts with determining what informs the authors' positions regarding their perception that South African law relevant to pregnancy requires reform, and then looks at how these motivations for reform commonly translate into legal arguments that support the separate-entities approach to pregnancy. After laying this foundation, the chapter contemplates each author's suggested area of reform by firs looking at the crux of their response to an identifie issue in pregnancy and then by critically considering the quality of their contribution to the end goal of effective law reform. Engaging in a critique of each of the authors' suggestions at this point has the added benefi of clarifying a number of South African legal principles that will aid the overall purpose of developing an effective approach to the tension that can arise between female reproductive autonomy and foetal interests during pregnancy.

6.2 UNDERLYING MOTIVATIONS FOR LAW REFORM

Since South African law primarily adopts a single-entity approach to pregnant women, thereby making the unborn nonentities, there is a perception that little room is left to allow for the law to be used as a mechanism to ensure healthy foetal-related outcomes during gestation and birth. Thus, if the law does not recognise the existence of a foetus, it cannot be called on for its protection and this is the focus of all the calls for law reform. All the South African authors aim to extend direct legal protection to the unborn, as legal subjects or quasi-legal subjects,[3] but in different spheres of the law.

All the South African authors advocating reform rightly emphasise that there is more to a pregnant woman than just the woman alone and they essentially argue that the unborn be recognised as more than nothing. In this respect, the law is seen to be out of sync with medicine, in that medical science has proven life before birth and, despite this evidence, the law is still labouring under the construct of viewing a pregnant woman as embodying only one life—her own.[4] It is on this basis that the law is viewed as being flawed and all the authors rely on and make reference to knowledge developed from science and medical technology which demonstrates that a foetus is more than mere maternal tissue.[5] The actual scientifi

[3] 'Quasi-legal subject' is used here because, even though some authors denounce a rights approach to protecting the unborn, they still argue for direct application of legal principles to the unborn. If one considers the meaning of legal subjectivity as including an element of legal interaction with a subject, these authors can be interpreted as advancing arguments for a subcategory of legal subjectivity. Boezaart define a legal subject as 'any entity that can have rights, duties and competencies'. Further, 'legal subjectivity' is define as 'the characteristic of being a legal subject in legal interaction'. See T Boezaart 'Child law, the child and South African private law' in T Boezaart (ed) *Child Law in South Africa* (2009) 4 and H Kruger & A Skelton (eds) *The Law of Persons in South Africa* (2010) 13 respectively.

[4] For instance, Pillay explicitly takes this route. See R Pillay 'The beginning of human personhood: Is South African law outdated?' (2010) 21 *Stell LR* 230 232.

[5] GA Du Plessis 'Feticide: Creating a statutory crime in South African law' (2013) 24 *Stell LR* 73 77–8; S De Freitas 'The South African Constitutional Court and the unborn' (2012) 5 *International Journal of Religious Freedom* 51 56; Pillay (2010) *Stell LR* 232; SA De Freitas & GA Myburgh 'The relevance of science for the protection of the unborn' (2009) 45 *Journal for Christian Scholarship* 61 70–4; 76; and HJ Kruuse 'Fetal "rights"? The need for a unifie approach to the

and medical advancements relied on will not be considered here because this was sufficiently covered earlier.[6] Generally, these sorts of arguments focus on medical knowledge pertaining to the biological aspects of foetal development, what the foetus looks like at varying stages of development and the medical understanding of foetal-genetic make-up, all of which point to the individuality of a foetus as a human being.[7] It is at this stage that we see those facets which contribute to creating an adversarial pregnancy environment seep into legal arguments, thus readying the ground for possible pregnancy adversarialism.

An example of how these arguments play out is worth noting. Kruuse, discussing the notion of feticide in South Africa, makes reference to the fact that our 'knowledge' of prenatal development is more developed than that of the Stoic notions of the unborn and we now understand and accept that foetal body parts belong to the foetus alone.[8] This means that we have come to agree that foetal body parts are not those of pregnant women's bodies, as that would mean that pregnant women have eight or more limbs, with two or more hearts, and some may even have penises, depending on the sex and number of foetuses being gestated at one time.[9] This knowledge is therefore interpreted as not only highlighting that a foetus is a distinct entity, but also as demonstrating the extent of its distinctness, namely, that a foetus is a biologically whole individual. Kruuse argues that any legal policy that does not accord with medical knowledge of foetal individuality is founded on 'one fictio too far',[10] the fictio being that the foetus has no independent existence because it is part of the woman who carries it.

Also, De Freitas and Myburgh[11] state that science, driven by principles of objectivity, provides evidence of life before birth and that this life starts at conception, thus justifying extending protection of the unborn from abortion from the moment of conception.[12] The authors then go on to 'clarify' the unborn through scientifi evidence by looking at what science tells us about fertilisation, implantation and foetal development from implantation in the uterus and

fetus in the context of feticide' (2009) 72 *THRHR* 126 132. This trend is also found in case law. In *Mshumpa* the state used the expert evidence of a neonatal surgeon to prove that later in gestation the unborn are very much the same as children, the only difference being that they are located in women's bodies. On this basis, the state argued for the extension of the crime of murder to the unborn.

[6] See Chapter Three, para 3.4 in this regard.

[7] Some do so more explicitly than others.

[8] Kruuse (2009) *THRHR* 131. See Chapter Two concerning the topic of how the unborn were perceived during antiquity and the Middle Ages.

[9] Kruuse (2009) *THRHR* 131. While Kruuse does not make specifi reference to science and medical technologies, her position must be founded on medical technology because these are the areas that led to the development of technologies that opened up living pregnant women's bodies for public scrutiny.

[10] Kruuse (2009) *THRHR* 132.

[11] De Freitas & Myburgh (2009) *Journal for Christian Scholarship* 69.

[12] The authors seem to be referring to conception as a synonym for fertilisation, which is not the case if one were to follow the Inter-American Court of Human Rights findin in *Case of Artavia Murillo et al ('in vitro fertilization') v Costa Rica* (2012) (*Case of Artavia Murillo et al*). It explains, with reference to extensive scientifi evidence, that fertilisation and conception are not synonymous but represent two different but mutual processes. See paras 186–7.

onwards.[13] The authors conclude their scientifi analysis of the unborn with the following:[14]

> When all the above [scientific information is considered it is clear that according to science there is enough data available to make a fir case for the protection of the human being from the zygote stage and given what is presently known in embryology, we can do no less. (Reference omitted.)

In fact, De Freitas is so convinced of the role of scientifi knowledge in identifying the unborn as distinct live entities that he asserts that, when issues related to termination of pregnancy reach the Constitutional Court, the court will have no choice but to consider what science has to say when making a findin on the legal status of the unborn.[15] It is his position that, if the court considers science, it will be impossible not to extend legal protection to the unborn.[16]

There are many more examples, but not all will be mentioned here, because each author adopts the same method of justifying the recognition of more in pregnant women, namely using science to identify and distinguish the unborn from the pregnant women carrying them. Thus far, what all the arguments rightly present to us is that South African law is not in line with the scientifi knowledge of prenatal life, in that there is certainly more to a pregnant woman than just a pregnant woman. A foetus is understood to be biologically alive before birth, and even though it is in the process of development, it is genetically unique.[17] There is consequently an obvious need for reform.

With this changed, scientificall informed image of pregnant women, the existing trend in South Africa is to favour the separate-entities approach to pregnancy over the currently applied single-entity approach.[18] The separate-entities approach to pregnancy views a woman and her foetus as though they are separate individuals of distinctive value with separable needs.[19] In their separate existence, the pregnant woman and the foetus are seen to hold a range of mutually exclusive enforceable rights or interests,[20] ultimately leading to an understanding that the foetus is able to directly engage in legal relations on its own account or for its own benefit obviously not in its personal capacity but through that of others.[21]

There are a number of key pointers indicating that the authors are adopting the separate-entities approach, despite none of them explicitly acknowledging this or using this exact term. Commonly these indicators relate to the use of terminology

---

13 De Freitas & Myburgh (2009) *Journal for Christian Scholarship* 70–4. In fact, the authors go on to refer to the unborn as 'children' and the women who carry them as 'mothers'. Having regard to *Case of Artavia Murillo et al* paras 186–7, one can argue that life existed prior to conception and even before fertilisation since sperm and ova can technically be considered alive. Thus, conception does not necessarily create 'life' per se.

14 De Freitas & Myburgh (2009) *Journal for Christian Scholarship* 74.

15 De Freitas (2012) *International Journal of Religious Freedom* 56.

16 De Freitas (2012) *International Journal of Religious Freedom* 56.

17 C Pickles 'Approaches to pregnancy under the law: A relational response to the current South African position and recent academic trends' (2014) 47 *De Jure* 20.

18 Pickles (2014) *De Jure* 20.

19 J Seymour *Childbirth and the Law* (2000) 190; 194.

20 Seymour *Childbirth and the Law* 190; 194.

21 Pickles (2014) *De Jure* 20.

or phrases which instil an image in the reader's mind of foetal separateness and independence.

Jordaan[22] contemplates the appropriateness of respecting a woman's advance medical directive that prohibits treatment should she be rendered unconscious and pregnant at the time that treatment is needed in order to sustain her life. Jordaan argues that the interests of a late-term foetus 'should at least be considered and balanced against the interests of the incompetent [unconscious] mother who made the advance directive refusing medical treatment'.[23] The process of balancing of interests signifie two competing entities and this understanding is strengthened by the use of the term 'mother'.

'Mother' indicates that one of those entities is already a parent. Kruuse also makes reference to 'mother' and uses the terms 'unborn child' and 'child' when describing the relationship between a pregnant woman and her foetus.[24] In fact, in *Mshumpa*, Froneman J makes several references to 'mother' and at times 'mother and baby' in respect of a pregnant woman.[25]

Understanding pregnant women as mothers goes to the core of the separate-entities approach. Generally, one is only understood to become a parent once birth has occurred. Thus, the use of the term 'mother' in relation to a foetus (where birth has not yet occurred) encourages an image of a relationship of parent and child, which image is representative of two separate persons. Roth, writing on the position in the United States, suggests that describing pregnant women as 'mothers' before they have even given birth turns the unborn into children and cultural expectations and legal standards pertaining to parental duty begin to influenc the image of pregnant women.[26] Roth argues that viewing a pregnant woman as a mother ends with identifying the foetus as independent from her thus enabling the foetus to engage in 'conflict with the pregnant woman.[27] This stands

[22] L Jordaan 'The legal validity of an advance refusal of medical treatment in South African law (Part 1)' (2011) 44 *De Jure* 32 45. While Jordaan's arguments are not being considered, her use of specifi terminology is a fittin example of the trend currently taking root in South Africa.

[23] Jordaan (Part 1) (2011) *De Jure* 44. Most of the South African authors considered in this chapter use the term 'mother' to refer to pregnant women, including Du Plessis (2013) *Stell LR* 73; De Freitas & Myburgh (2009) *Journal for Christian Scholarship* 73; and M Ovens 'A criminological perspective of prenatal abuse of substances during pregnancy and the link to child abuse in South Africa' (2010) 11 *Child Abuse Research in South Africa* 38.

[24] Kruuse (2009) *THRHR* 131.

[25] See paras 1–5; 10; 41; 48; 49; 57; 58; 64; 67. This is strange because, as already discussed in Chapter Five, the *Mshumpa* decision actually represents the single-entity approach in that the 'unique togetherness' of a pregnant woman and foetus was interpreted as not being sufficient enough, in a legal sense, to recognise the unborn in law (at least in the way that Froneman J interpreted the relationship that exists during a pregnancy). Froneman J did, however, suggest that even though the law, as it currently stands, cannot accommodate the unborn, the legislature is better equipped to deal with the issue of violence against pregnant women which terminates their pregnancies (para 65). One can speculate that the terminology preferred by Froneman J can be interpreted as the judge being personally swayed to viewing the unborn as something separate from pregnant women but the legal atmosphere prohibits such an approach. Since Froneman J is currently sitting as a Constitutional Court judge his position is important to note, especially given that no case law has yet reached the Constitutional Court pertaining to the status of the unborn in South Africa.

[26] See R Roth *Making Women Pay: The Hidden Cost of Fetal Rights* (2000) 6.

[27] Roth *Making Women Pay* 6.

as true when we consider Jordaan's suggestion of balancing foetal interests against those of pregnant women refusing medical treatment.

Apart from using terminology that characterises the relationship between a pregnant woman and her foetus as one of separateness, there are further terminological references which are distinctive to the separate-entities approach. For instance, Kruuse states:[28]

> [T]he fetus is a *distinct organism* from the mother and cannot be treated as a bit of human tissue comparable to her kidney, one of her appendages or her appendix. It is a *separate living organism*, whose destruction is something to be regretted in itself regardless of what happened to the mother carrying it. (Emphasis added.)

Further, De Freitas approvingly cites foreign sources to indicate that a foetus represents 'another person'.[29] Pillay states that allowing for the introduction of foetal rights 'would give expression to the legal convictions of the community which demand *separate* protection of the foetus through laws proscribing murder and assault of the foetus'.[30] (Emphasis in the original.) Du Plessis calls for the protection of the unborn 'irrespective and independent of its location or relationship to the mother'.[31] Pillay's and Du Plessis' suggestions imply that violent conduct directed at the unborn is something distinct from that directed at pregnant women, while in reality any conduct against the foetus will be experienced by a pregnant woman and conduct against a pregnant woman will have an impact on the foetus she carries.

All the authors' positions considered thus far adopt an approach to pregnancy that clearly follows the separate-entities approach, thereby highlighting a trend for preferring this approach to the single-entity approach.[32] The unborn are identifie and individuated from pregnant women based on scientifi understanding of prenatal development and this understanding transforms into language infused with legal undertones that feed into the notion that the unborn are entirely separate in their prenatal existence. References to notions such as 'balanced against', 'separate protection', 'irrespective of relationship', 'irrespective of location' and 'another person' all disconnect the unborn from pregnant women and the only time women are understood in the context of the unborn is when they are seen to be mothers.

6.3 SUGGESTED LAW REFORM: SEPARATE-ENTITIES APPROACH IN ACTION

Four themes have been identifie as being in need of reform, namely, status law pertaining to personhood, third-party violence that terminates a pregnancy (commonly referred to as feticide by South African scholars), substance abuse during pregnancy and the right to terminate a pregnancy. Each South African author considered here will be categorised according to one of these themes of reform; their suggestions are considered and critiqued.

---

[28] Kruuse (2009) *THRHR* 131.
[29] (2012) *International Journal of Religious Freedom* 56.
[30] Pillay (2010) *Stell LR* 237.
[31] Du Plessis (2013) *Stell LR* 77.
[32] See Pickles (2014) *De Jure* 20.

6.3.1 Extending personhood to a viable foetus

Pillay's argument for reform is considered firs because it is the most extreme and far-reaching of all the calls for reform. This is also the only argument that explicitly adopts a rights-based approach to the unborn.

Pillay states that the born-alive rule's purpose was evidentiary in nature. She explains that, at the time of the development of the rule, information about prenatal life was rudimentary and thus live birth was considered to be the only objective proof of the existence of life.[33] This rule then became the established criterion for personhood in law.[34] However, since the advancements in medical science, Pillay argues that we now have sufficient proof of life before birth to have removed the evidentiary difficulties the born-alive rule sought to remedy.[35] She argues that our current knowledge of foetal development also assists in determining the extent of any harm caused to the unborn in the case of violence against pregnant women.[36] It is on this basis that Pillay is critical of the common law and its approach to legal subjectivity, and also the fact that our courts have never questioned the continued relevance of the born-alive rule despite there having been opportunities to do so.[37]

Pillay goes on to argue that we should consider non-legal factors such as medical science when assigning status to the unborn, and she calls for the legal concept of personhood to be extended to include, at the very least, a viable foetus.[38] Consequently, she argues for the creation of foetal rights and she understands the attribution of rights as the appropriate mode to address those areas where foetal interests remain invisible to the law. She states:[39]

> In the abortion context, the attribution of foetal rights would constitute a radical departure from the prevailing legal position which focuses solely on the rights of pregnant women. As this unequal power relationship is challenged, both the judiciary and the medical profession will have the opportunity to adopt a more transparent, principled and balanced approach in resolving maternal-foetal conflicts In the non-abortion context relating to third party criminal acts directed against pregnant women, the attribution of foetal rights would give expression to the legal convictions of the community which demand *separate* protection for the foetus through laws proscribing murder and assault of the foetus. In delict, attributing foetal rights would facilitate wrongful death claims based on a stillbirth caused by the negligent conduct of another. . . . In each of these contexts, the attribution of foetal rights would facilitate judicial decision-making by enabling fictio and expediency to be replaced by fact, justice and reason. (Emphasis in original and footnotes omitted.)

Pillay's adoption of the separate-entities approach leads to the notion that a foetus is a separate legal subject with vested constitutional rights. She understands this application as being necessary to adequately protect a foetus from the pregnant woman who carries it and third parties such as perpetrators of assault or

[33] Pillay (2010) *Stell LR* 231.
[34] Pillay (2010) *Stell LR* 231.
[35] Pillay (2010) *Stell LR* 232.
[36] Pillay (2010) *Stell LR* 232.
[37] Pillay (2010) *Stell LR* 232–6.
[38] Pillay (2010) *Stell LR* 236.
[39] Pillay (2010) *Stell LR* 236–7.

murder and negligent medical professionals. However, there are a number of flaw in Pillay's argument.

As demonstrated in Chapter Five,[40] there are no 'maternal-foetal conflicts at present in South Africa, since we have yet to accept pregnant women as representing two separate entities.[41] Furthermore, it is only when the separate-entities approach is applied in a way that extends rights to a foetus that the true extent of 'conflict is observable. The discussion to follow demonstrates this point.[42]

For a start, Pillay's depiction of the relationship between a pregnant woman and her foetus as one being characteristically unequal in the context of termination of pregnancies cannot be supported. Academic commentary on the Choice on Termination of Pregnancy Act[43] (Choice Act) and the decision of *Christian Lawyers Association v Minister of Health*[44] (*Christian Lawyers* 2005) demonstrates that this is certainly not the case.[45] We would only fin an unequal power relationship if the Choice Act was not in place and termination of pregnancies was severely restricted[46] or if there was no law limiting the right to terminate a pregnancy, thus permitting women to terminate right up the moment of birth. In these instances, the unequal power relationship would exist because those preventing terminations for the benefi of the unborn would have greater say over women and their bodies than the women would have for themselves or, alternatively, women would have greater say over their bodies to the detriment of foetal life.

Concerning the notion of foetal rights providing legal leverage for the protection of the unborn, both Kruuse and McCreath J take the stance that granting rights to a foetus can certainly offer protection, particularly against unfavourable conduct during pregnancy.[47] In *Christian Lawyers Association of SA v Minister of Health*[48] (*Christian Lawyers* 1998) per McCreath J, it was found that *if* the right to life in s 11 of the Constitution of the Republic of South Africa, 1996 were to be interpreted as applying to a foetus, a foetus would have a separate claim to life and the lawful termination of a pregnancy would ultimately constitute murder, even if the termination of a pregnancy were medically indicated to preserve the life of the pregnant woman concerned.[49] Kruuse takes a more nuanced approach and asserts

---

[40] At para 5.4.

[41] At most it can be argued that a conflic exists in the mind of a person personally observing a pregnant woman engage in conduct that the viewer find offensive towards prenatal life. The pregnant woman's conduct might be viewed as offensive based on the viewer's subjective perceptions of what is or is not appropriate behaviour during pregnancy, but this subjective view has not been translated into legal conflict

[42] See Pickles (2014) *De Jure* 20.

[43] Act 92 of 1996.

[44] 2005 (1) SA 509 (T).

[45] This was discussed extensively in Chapter Five, para 5.2.

[46] As was the case under the Abortion and Sterilization Act 2 of 1975.

[47] Although, it must be noted that both suggest not taking a rights-based approach.

[48] 1998 (4) SA 1113 (T).

[49] *Christian Lawyers* (1998) 1122I. Here, the court understands that where a foetus is granted rights it could use those rights as a means to protect itself from termination of pregnancy for any reason

that if a foetus is vested with legal subjectivity and thus the right to life, it would mean that the right to terminate a pregnancy would be impossible to justify, except where the pregnant woman's life was in danger.[50] Later on, Kruuse explains that the unborn's right to life is a right that is not capable of being outweighed by a woman's rights generally, meaning that the unborn's right to life will always take precedence over women's rights (aside from her right to life).[51]

The separate-entities approach, applied in this way, seems to create a situation where Pillay's 'maternal-foetal conflicts are done away with because the right to life will always hold more weight than rights vested in others, including that of pregnant women (as emphasised by Kruuse and McCreath J).[52] All three of these positions therefore complement the premise that a rights-based approach could possibly serve as a workable method for the protection of a viable foetus.[53] However, further reflectio on this issue brings a different perspective to the fore, especially in the context of Thomson's article 'A defense of abortion'.[54]

Writing from the United States, Thomson offers a thought-provoking, if extreme, counter-argument to the above-described position, and her work is so well known[55] that it is surprising that her publication was not considered by those contemplating the consequences of foetal rights.[56] Thomson uses the example of waking up to fin that a violinist has been attached to your body in order to gain the benefi of the function of your kidneys, and this attachment was necessary for purposes of keeping the violinist alive.[57] The crux of the issue is that the violinist

whatsoever. However, it must be recognised that this position is unfounded, since principles of private defence (if a fatal pregnancy is construed as an attack on a woman's body) or necessity justify the termination of a pregnancy in cases where continued pregnancy poses a threat to a woman's life. See CR Snyman *Criminal Law* 5 ed (2009) 103–23 for a detailed discussion of private defence and necessity as grounds of justification

[50] Kruuse (2009) *THRHR* 133.

[51] Kruuse (2009) *THRHR* 135.

[52] Pickles (2014) *De Jure* 20.

[53] Pickles (2014) *De Jure* 20.

[54] JJ Thomson 'A defense of abortion' (1971) 1 *Philosophy & Public Affairs* 47. While this chapter is not focused on justifying termination of pregnancies, Thomson's argument transcends the abortion debate and has application in any argument that attempts to accord rights to the unborn.

[55] According to Google Scholar, and as at 5 May 2016, Thomson's article has been cited 1 499 times. See scholar.google.co.za/scholar?q=JJ+Thomson+%E2%80%98A+defense+of+abortion%E2%80%99+%281971%29+1+Philosophy+%26+Public+Affairs+47&btnG=&hl=en&as_sdt=0%2C5 (accessed on 5 May 2016). Also see C Kaczor *The Ethics of Abortion: Women's Rights, Human Life, and the Question of Justice* (2010) 145 who cites Thomson's article as 'the most famous article ever written about the subject of abortion'. This is not to say that her work is unquestionably accepted, for instance see D Boonin *A Defense of Abortion* (2003) 133–276. Boonin, while defending Thomson's position, cites and discusses 16 different objections to Thomson's argument.

[56] The only authors cited in the chapter that refer to Thomson are De Freitas & Myburgh (2009) *Journal for Christian Scholarship* 69–70 and Du Plessis (2013) *Stell LR* 88. However, these authors only cite authority that takes a stand against Thomson's position. The authors are in opposition to Thomson because they are attempting to justify protection of the unborn without adopting a rights-based approach. Their approach could have possibly been motivated by Thomson's convincing argument in that a rights-based approach may be legally problematic and overly complex for anyone seeking to protect the unborn on that basis.

[57] Thomson (1971) *Philosophy & Public Affairs* 48–9.

was attached to your body without your consent.[58] Her entire article revolves around this hypothetical anecdote and she raises challenging questions as to whether anything can be done to remove the attachment, even though removal will result in the violinist's death.[59]

In this context, Thomson goes on to suggest that we imagine the unborn as legal persons with the right to life (like the violinist) and further suggests that, generally, the right to life includes the right to be given at least the bare minimum one needs for continued life.[60] Thomson then poses the following challenge: What would the case be where the bare minimum one needs to sustain life turns out to be something that one does not have a right to?[61]

This question becomes relevant when, for the purposes of sustaining life, one needs continued use of another's body. The problem is that the mere presence of need does not create an enforceable right against another. Thomson contends:[62]

> [N]obody has the right to use your kidneys unless you give him such a right; and nobody has the right against you that you shall give him this right—if you do allow him to go on using your kidneys, this is a kindness on your part, and not something he can claim from you as his due. Nor has he any right against anybody else that *they* should give him continued use of your kidneys. (Emphasis in the original.)

Ultimately, Thomson's argument is that having the right to life does not guarantee the use of that right.[63] Where the right of use is provided, it is done because one is a 'Good Samaritan'.[64] Thomson views continued pregnancy as women acting as Good Samaritans in that they have no legal obligation to make the sacrifice that are necessary in order for the unborn to sustain prenatal life.[65] In this respect, Thomson questions whether engaging in voluntary sexual intercourse is an indication of consent to a resulting pregnancy, thus giving rise to an obligation, and she answers this in the negative.[66] Thomson states:[67]

> If the room is stuffy, and I therefore open a window to air it, and a burglar climbs in, it would be absurd to say, 'Ah, now he can stay, she's given him a right to the use of her house—for she is partially responsible for his presence there, having voluntarily done what enabled him to get in, in full knowledge that there are such things as burglars, and that burglars burgle.'

Similarly, Karnein suggests that, although women may be partly responsible for conception, given that contraception is arguably readily available these days, there is a limit to the amount of responsibility that can accrue for something that women

[58] Thomson (1971) *Philosophy & Public Affairs* 48–9.
[59] Thomson (1971) *Philosophy & Public Affairs* 47–50.
[60] Thomson (1971) *Philosophy & Public Affairs* 55.
[61] Thomson (1971) *Philosophy & Public Affairs* 55.
[62] Thomson (1971) *Philosophy & Public Affairs* 55.
[63] Thomson (1971) *Philosophy & Public Affairs* 56.
[64] Generally, Thomson's argument is cited as the 'Good Samaritan Argument'; see Boonin *A Defense of Abortion* 133.
[65] Thomson (1971) *Philosophy & Public Affairs* 63.
[66] Thomson (1971) *Philosophy & Public Affairs* 57–8.
[67] Thomson (1971) *Philosophy & Public Affairs* 58–9.

would have to go out of their way to prevent, especially if what is being prevented is a natural process of reproduction.[68] She explains:[69]

> [W]hile persons can be asked to make significan sacrifice to save those they have deliberately pushed into the water, women cannot be asked to provide a substantial amount of assistance to someone who came into existence because they did not prevent a 'natural' process from occurring.

Thomson's argument holds true in South Africa *if* legal personhood were to be extended to include a viable foetus. There is no known South African case law or legislation that compels someone to forsake their body, or portions thereof, in order for another to sustain his or her life. Drawing from laws regulating medical donation,[70] generally, no one has a claim to another's body without that person's informed consent, and this is a well-established principle under South African law.[71] This principle acts to the detriment of any intentions to protect the unborn as legal persons.[72]

Since the unborn live off the bodies of pregnant women and gain the benefi of pregnant women's bodily functions, a pregnancy can be understood as representing a relationship of donation because one person is using another person's body to sustain life.[73] Accordingly, if the unborn were persons, they would need pregnant women's informed consent to continue gestating.[74] The principle of informed consent requires that, in order for the consent to be informed, the person must have knowledge of and appreciation for what is being consented to prior to the

[68] AJ Karnein *A Theory of Unborn Life: From Abortion to Genetic Manipulation* (2012) 24.

[69] Karnein *A Theory of Unborn Life* 24.

[70] Specificall , the National Health Act 61 of 2003, case law and common-law principles relevant to informed consent.

[71] C Pickles & D Labuschagne 'Pregnancy, foetal individuation, and claims to another's body: Some relational issues in a South African context' (2014) unpublished paper presented at a conference of the Society of Law Teachers of Southern Africa hosted by the Oliver Schreiner Law School at the University of Witwatersrand, 15 January 2014 (copy on fil with the author). The argument presented here stems from research conducted by Labuschagne. She was commissioned to research the topics of donation and use of another's body, and assisted in linking these concepts to continued pregnancy.

[72] Pickles & Labuschagne 'Pregnancy, foetal individuation, and claims to another's body: Some relational issues in a South African context' (2014). One of the most worrying consequences of this approach is that it creates the space to voluntarily terminate viable but pre-term pregnancies, and this cannot be seen as serving important developmental needs of foetuses. Pre-term deliveries pose a number of health issues, and long-term medical and social risks. See MS Pignotti & G Donzelli 'Perinatal care at the threshold of viability: An international comparison of practical guidelines for the treatment of extremely preterm births' (2008) 121 *Pediatrics* e193; and D Moster, RT Lie & T Markestad 'Long-term medical and social consequences of preterm birth' (2008) 359 *New England Journal of Medicine* 262. This can hardly be seen as a positive outcome associated with foetal rights.

[73] Pickles & Labuschagne 'Pregnancy, foetal individuation, and claims to another's body: Some relational issues in a South African context' (2014). See s 56 of the National Health Act which makes provision for the donation and use of living persons' tissue, being blood, blood products and gametes.

[74] As required in terms of ss 6 and 7, read together with ss 55 and 66 of the National Health Act.

donation.[75] Given that pregnancy is fairly unpredictable in terms of what resulting procedures may be necessitated by deciding to be pregnant, Pickles and Labuschagne contend that no true informed consent can ever actually be obtained.[76] This leads to the very extreme position that, where informed consent is lacking,[77] as would be the case for all pregnancies, even planned ones, the person whose body is being used is essentially being assaulted.[78]

It is not worthwhile to adopt this extreme approach. However, it does demonstrate how far Pillay's proposal extends the potential for conflic between the unborn and pregnant women, if it were to be adopted and current South African principles were to be applied as if the unborn were legal persons. Thompson's work exposes the extreme implications of Pillay's proposal. These far-reaching implications serve as the very reason why Pillay's argument should be rejected—it fails to advance both pregnant women and the interests of the unborn.

This discussion shows that Pillay's rights-based argument is problematic when it comes to offering protection to a viable foetus, as vesting of rights does not always offer any tangible guarantees for the realisation of those rights.[79] A separate-entities approach applied in this way manifestly introduces conflic and creates an environment for head-on adversarialism between a pregnant woman and her foetus.[80] What becomes obviously clear is that an adversarial pregnancy environment, which encourages tensions during pregnancy, is in sight when viewing pregnancy through the lens of the separate-entities approach as the basis for extending rights to the unborn.

6.3.2 Feticide

The calls for reform considered under feticide are all in reaction to the *Mshumpa* decision and the perceived injustice stemming from the outcome of that case, in that the law failed to recognise the loss of prenatal life as a result of unlawful violent conduct inflicte on a pregnant woman. Basically, this case highlights that, as the law stands in South Africa, there is no crime to address the termination of a

[75] Pickles & Labuschagne 'Pregnancy, foetal individuation, and claims to another's body: Some relational issues in a South African context' (2014).

[76] Pickles & Labuschagne 'Pregnancy, foetal individuation, and claims to another's body: Some relational issues in a South African context' (2014).

[77] For consequences of having not obtained informed consent, see P Carstens & D Pearmain *Foundational Principles of South African Medical Law* (2007) 890–91.

[78] Here, Pickles and Labuschagne refer to *Palmer v Palmer* 1955 (3) SA 56 (O); *S v Goliath* 1972 (3) SA 1 (A); and *Castell v de Greef* 1994 (4) SA 408 (C). Viewing pregnancy as an assault is typical of older-generation pro-choice feminists; see BA Manninen 'The value of choice and the choice to value: Expanding the discussion about fetal life within prochoice advocacy' (2013) 28 *Hypatia* 663. Manninen identifie Thomson as one of these sorts of feminists (664) and she explains that older-generation pro-choice feminists have equated the unborn to an 'aggressive intruder' (664) and cites one pro-choice feminist as arguing that 'all cases of compelled pregnancy are morally akin to rape and kidnaping, since the fetus intrudes upon the body of the woman without her consent'. However, Manninen points out there is now a move away from such extreme oppositional standpoints.

[79] Pickles (2014) *De Jure* 20.

[80] Pickles (2014) *De Jure* 20.

pregnancy without the pregnant woman's consent. Kruuse and Du Plessis both adopt the separate-entities approach in their contribution to the discourse of reform in this area of law but each offers different possible avenues to address the *Mshumpa* outcome.

Du Plessis interprets *Mshumpa* as offering indirect protection to the unborn and rejects that approach as being insufficient.[81] Indirect protection is seen to be insufficient because the crimes of assault and attempted murder[82] recognise that such violent conduct constitutes a violation of only the woman's rights to bodily integrity and life.[83] Merely considering the termination of prenatal life as an aggravating factor during the sentencing phase obscures the loss of prenatal life. Du Plessis argues that, given that the purpose of criminalising certain conduct is to protect and maintain public order, approaching circumstances similar to those of *Mshumpa* as merely being assault or attempted murder of the pregnant woman is not sufficient where 'the mother and the unborn are [both] injured or killed'.[84]

For purposes of protection, Du Plessis understands the requirement of live birth to constitute a mere 'technicality', as 'birth is only a change of place and relationship to the mother and surrounding world'.[85] She understands birth to be a technicality because if a 38-week foetus died prior to birth as a result of the inflictio of grave harm, there would be no wrong-doing,[86] whereas if the same foetus was seriously harmed, delivered alive and later died of the same injuries, the crime of murder would come into play.[87] In both instances we would be dealing with the same entities in respect of their developmental attributes but one would be protected and the other would not, and this difference is linked to birth. Du Plessis also disagrees that foetal viability is relevant for protection, and she states: 'There is no rational reason why the fact that the unborn is able to survive outside the mother's womb should be a determining factor for protection of the unborn.'[88] She argues that protection from feticide from fertilisation onwards offers more sensitivity to the position of the unborn as human beings; Du Plessis rejects birth and viability as being irrational indicators of the humanness of the unborn.[89]

Contrary to Pillay's approach to protecting the unborn, Du Plessis argues that we should move beyond using the concept of personhood as a means of

[81] Du Plessis (2013) *Stell LR* 74–5.
[82] Attempted murder being one of the crimes that Mshumpa and Best were convicted of; see *Mshumpa* para 67.
[83] Du Plessis (2013) *Stell LR* 75.
[84] Du Plessis (2013) *Stell LR* 75.
[85] Du Plessis (2013) *Stell LR* 76.
[86] Du Plessis (2013) *Stell LR* 76.
[87] Du Plessis (2013) *Stell LR* 76. However, it must be noted that there is no case law to support this assertion.
[88] Du Plessis (2013) *Stell LR* 78. While this discussion is not concerned with issues arising prior to pregnancy, it should be noted that Du Plessis' approach, if accepted, would result in planned or anticipated embryo wastage from *in vitro* fertilisation processes constituting murder. The Inter-American court of Human Rights applauded *in vitro* fertilisation as a means to give life rather than amounting to murder or waste of life; see *Case of Artavia Murillo et al* para 310.
[89] Du Plessis (2013) *Stell LR* 78.

understanding the unborn as human beings in law, but she qualifie this, stating that this sort of move should not be understood as advocating the extension of the right to life to the unborn generally.[90] She understands that the avoidance of a rights approach aids in overcoming any possible confrontation with women's termination-of-pregnancy rights granted under the Choice Act.[91] However, Du Plessis leaves her argument there. While she encourages us to adopt an approach to the unborn beyond the bounds of our Constitution and its rights, she does not suggest what legal mechanisms we should use to justify the protection of the unborn or how to implement this.[92] She suggests that 'to be inclusive and rational regarding feticide arguments, it is necessary to expand the argument to more than human rights' and include considerations such as science, public interests, the protection of pregnant women from violence and the protection of 'sentient beings', among other possible considerations.[93]

---

[90] Du Plessis (2013) *Stell LR* 76. As with Pillay, she also discredits the application of the born-alive rule to determinine personhood.

[91] Du Plessis (2013) *Stell LR* 76. This is very surprising coming from Du Plessis because in 2009 Du Plessis co-authored an article with De Freitas under her maiden name Myburgh (De Freitas & G Myburgh (2009) *Journal for Christian Scholarship* 61) where she and De Freitas argue for the protection of the unborn from termination of pregnancy. (They both argue for protection from the moment of conception. Their arguments on termination-of-pregnancy law reform are discussed below.) This may indicate that Du Plessis has developed her position to take a more nuanced approach towards pregnancy-related concerns. If that is not the case, her arguments can be interpreted as being ambiguous. In one area of law she argues that there is a need to protect the unborn from third-party violence in a way that keeps pregnant women's termination-of-pregnancy rights intact, while in another area of law she argues for the protection of the unborn from termination of pregnancy from the moment of their conception. While this ambiguity might seem strange at first this is also a well-known tactical approach adopted by pro-life advocates in the United States. Pro-lifers, while working on rendering termination of pregnancy illegal, advocate for reform in all other areas of law in order to extend the status of the unborn in every possible avenue; this is discussed in more detail in Chapter Seven. In personal communication with Du Plessis via electronic mail (5 July 2014), Du Plessis clarifie her position in this regard. She emphasises that her argument for the introduction of a crime of feticide is not being used as a means to protect the unborn in this area of law for later protection against liberal termination-of-pregnancy laws in South Africa. She explains that in the context of feticide, a pregnant women's interests and that of the unborn are aligned, 'the rights and interests of both are not placed in tension with each other and an emphasis on the one-sided protection of the mother to the exclusion of the unborn is not needed'. Concerning issues with the 'alignment of interests' argument, see Chapter Eight. She explains that her primary position is focused on securing the right to life for the unborn but that she adopted the argument for her feticide position in order to 'stay away from the personhood argument since it creates such a deadlock position that one will struggle to have any rights for the unborn. Also, attempting to move away from the right to life argument is actually an attempt to provide the unborn and mother some protection because the right to life argument has not been helping thus far. Therefore, I am looking at alternative arguments to the right to life issue—however, this does not mean that I do not believe that the unborn should have the right to life.' There is a sense of uncertainty in her position and it seems to relate to the difficulty one faces when discussing the unborn in a women's rights arena. The difficulty links to the fact that the unborn have been individuated from the women carrying them which is a poor representation of the reality of pregnancy.

[92] Du Plessis (2013) *Stell LR* 87–90.

[93] Du Plessis (2013) *Stell LR* 90.

Du Plessis argues, '[i]t will be best to provide protection to the unborn irrespective and independent of its location and relationship to the mother'.[94] She argues that this could be achieved through the creation of a statutory crime of feticide allowing for the direct protection of the unborn, thus calling for the recognition of the unborn (from conception onwards) as separate victims of violent crime in their own right.[95] Du Plessis goes on to defin feticide as the 'unlawful and intentional or negligent causing of the death of an unborn by a third party and without the consent of the pregnant woman bearing the unborn'.[96] (Footnotes omitted.) This construction of feticide focuses on the lack of consent on the part of the pregnant woman concerned and emphasises third-party conduct, thereby exempting pregnant women as possible perpetrators.

There are a number of issues with Du Plessis' call for reform. From a practical criminal law perspective, protection from fertilisation presumes that one will know of the existence of a fertilised egg prior to implantation. However, according to *Case of Artavia Murillo et al,* this is impossible. The Inter-American Court of Human Rights found that:[97]

> [I]t is only possible to establish whether or not a pregnancy has occurred once the fertilized egg has been implanted in the uterus, when the hormone known as 'chorionic gonadotropin' is produced, which can only be detected when a woman has an embryo implanted in her. Prior to this it is impossible to determine whether the union between the egg and a spermatozoid occurred within the body or whether this union was lost prior to implantation. (Footnotes omitted.)

This findin implicates proof of causation of harm prior to implantation. Of further significanc is the fact that the Inter-American Court of Human Rights accepted expert evidence indicating that, of every 10 embryos naturally produced, no more than two or three will survive natural selection, with the rest dying in the genital tract without the knowledge of the woman concerned.[98] Frustrating this process is the fact that the cause of the loss is not readily known.[99]

Du Plessis' discontent with the Constitution and constitutional rights in the context of the unborn leaves her position vulnerable because the Constitution is the supreme law.[100] It provides the framework in which our entire legal system functions. Therefore, from a practical perspective, it is uncertain how one would effectively provide for the legal protection of the unborn outside of the reach of the Constitution.

Furthermore, Du Plessis understands it to be important to avoid a rights-based approach to protecting the unborn so as to prevent pregnant women and the unborn being placed in conflic with each another.[101] At firs glance, this seems to be the

---

[94] Du Plessis (2013) *Stell LR* 76–7.
[95] Du Plessis (2013) *Stell LR* 74–5.
[96] Du Plessis (2013) *Stell LR* 74–5.
[97] *Case of Artavia Murillo et al* para 187.
[98] *Case of Artavia Murillo et al* para 310.
[99] *Case of Artavia Murillo et al* para 308.
[100] Section 2 of the Constitution states: 'This Constitution is the supreme law of the Republic; law or conduct inconsistent with it is invalid, and the obligations imposed by it must be fulfilled.
[101] Du Plessis (2013) *Stell LR* 76.

right step towards avoiding an adversarial pregnancy environment. However, the very fact that she adopts the separate-entities approach to pregnancy could lead to the demise of her argument. This is because the separate-entities approach opens the door for women to be perpetrators when it comes to the unborn since the unborn and pregnant women are regarded as separate entities in relation to one another, each with individualised legal protection. This is especially true because Du Plessis argues for the protection of the unborn, *irrespective* of their relationship to pregnant women and *independent* of women as well.[102] Thus if the biological relationship or embodied connectedness is not considered relevant when understanding harm caused to the unborn, there is nothing preventing a woman from being a perpetrator in relation to her own foetus.

There is some ambiguity in Du Plessis' approach. It seems that the basis for Du Plessis' exclusion of women from the ambit of the crime of feticide lies in the fact that the unborn are located within their bodies, which then allows them to terminate pregnancies. She thus relies on the relationship between pregnant women and the unborn as the mode of exclusion of women. This exclusion contradicts Du Plessis' original arguments concerning viewing the unborn as a distinct entity worthy of separate legal consideration. Thus, in order to prevent 'creating a dichotomy with regard to South African laws concerning voluntary abortion',[103] Du Plessis would not only have to avoid extending rights to the unborn but would also have to understand the unborn as being something intrinsically linked to the essence of pregnant bodies belonging to women. Essentially, she would have to deny the separate status of the unborn. It is necessary to take this stance because, if the unborn are still, to some degree, seen to be part of pregnant women's bodies, only then will women still be entitled to terminate their pregnancies, because that action would be a form of women's exercise of bodily autonomy.

Taking this further, it is not clear how and on what justifiabl ground only third parties could be held liable for harm caused to the unborn and not pregnant women when they terminate a pregnancy, especially when the same outcomes are experienced by the unborn. If harm to the unborn serves as the foundation for reform, then the fact remains that it does not matter *who* commits the act that harms an entity but rather it is the fact that harm is inflicte when certain conduct takes place. It is understood that protecting and maintaining public order refers to conduct that is perceived to be harmful, and not specificall who conducts themselves in a harmful manner. Also, it is not clear what Du Plessis proposes the case would be where women consent to the termination of their pregnancies by a third party but outside the bounds of the Choice Act. The same ends are achieved, namely harm to the unborn, but the crime of feticide would not be applicable because the woman concerned consented.

Du Plessis offers an intriguing and thought-provoking perspective on violence that terminates prenatal life, but her suggestions leave the reader with a sense of uncertainty. While advocating protection of the unborn she has inadvertently

[102] Du Plessis (2013) *Stell LR* 77.
[103] Du Plessis (2013) *Stell LR* 76.

offered a contradictory response. If the reason for protecting the unborn lies in the fact that they are separate human beings (but not legal persons with rights) and should not be harmed on that basis, then it should not matter who harms the unborn—it is the mere fact of harming them that is of grave concern. Aside from this issue, her publication assists in highlighting how complex this issue can be and how many facets come into play when attempting to go forward.

Kruuse, writing in 2009, suggests that before we look at how to best protect the unborn, it is firs necessary to develop a 'unifie approach' to how we view the unborn in law.[104] She was not referring to Du Plessis' arguments, but to the state's actions after the *Mshumpa* decision had been reached.[105] However, her suggestion does impact on Du Plessis, who seems to have her roots in the separate-entities approach but is at odds with its possible far-reaching implications, thus falling short of translating her suggestion into a workable solution.

Kruuse, also dissatisfie with the indirect foetal protection stemming from *Mshumpa*, rejects the single-entity approach and calls for the introduction of the crime of feticide, being a crime that can be perpetrated against the unborn only.[106] She justifie this approach on the grounds that the unborn are distinct from the pregnant women who carry them. Kruuse is critical of Froneman J's use of the unique relationship shared between a pregnant woman and the foetus she carries, since this 'unique togetherness' is used as a ground for denying the opportunity for direct legal protection of the unborn.[107] She argues that this approach is 'inadequate', since, 'if we recognise, as most of us do, that the fetus is a potential life; a separate organism which will, all things being equal, in due course become a life, and that we value life' then we are obligated to provide direct protection.[108]

Kruuse rejects constitutional rights as being necessary for the protection of the unborn and turns to the value of human dignity (symbolising inherent human worth) as warranting her call for direct separate protection.[109] As Du Plessis does, Kruuse avoids a rights-based approach for the protection of the unborn because she understands it to create an environment where women's rights to terminate their pregnancies would be in competition with those of the unborn's right to life.[110]

Approvingly relying on Meyerson's comments on the Choice Act,[111] Kruuse argues that human life is intrinsically valuable, and this value remains intact

[104] Kruuse (2009) *THRHR* 128.

[105] Kruuse (2009) *THRHR* 128. Kruuse explains that, after Froneman J found that the crime of murder was not applicable to the unborn, the state planned to challenge the correctness of Froneman J's finding implying that they understood a viable foetus to be a legal subject. However, the state then approached the South African Law Reform Commission instead, seeking to develop a statutory crime to address circumstances similar to that of *Mshumpa* implying that a viable foetus is not a legal subject but still represents something in need of protection.

[106] Kruuse (2009) *THRHR* 126.

[107] Kruuse (2009) *THRHR* 132. It was Froneman J's findin that harm caused to a foetus can be adequately addressed as crime inflicte on the pregnant woman carrying the foetus since the foetus will also suffer the harm as a result of their 'unique togetherness'.

[108] Kruuse (2009) *THRHR* 132.

[109] Kruuse (2009) *THRHR* 134–6.

[110] Kruuse (2009) *THRHR* 133.

[111] See generally, D Meyerson 'Abortion: The constitutional issues' (1999) 116 *SALJ* 50.

despite an entity, such as the unborn, lacking legal subjectivity or rights.[112] Kruuse identifie the constitutional value of dignity as accommodating this principle in a legal context.[113] Thus, when one terminates a pregnancy it is a violation of the value of human dignity. Kruuse contends that valuing the unborn because they are representatives of human life avoids the 'inevitable clash between the rights of the mother and fetus', because '[w]hen it is not the fetus's right to life which is at stake, but the value of human dignity, this value (unlike the right to life) is capable of being weighed against—and outweighed by—the pregnant woman's rights'.[114] Kruuse is satisfie with this approach since it does not deny women their rights and at the same time it still allows us to recognise and protect the unborn.[115]

Having identifie the value of human dignity as the reason why the law should directly protect the unborn (as opposed to Froneman J's indirect approach), Kruuse stops there. She leaves the 'practicality' of formulating a definitio of the crime of feticide to the legislature. This makes it difficult to critique her contribution. Nevertheless, some reservations as to her argument can be noted. These reservations relate to her adoption of principles arising from the Choice Act and the use of the value of dignity generally.

Kruuse[116] relies on Meyerson's commentary on the Choice Act and her construction of the role of the value of dignity in the context of the Act,[117] to develop what Kruuse understands to be the necessary structure which will ensure that, when we approach the topic of the unborn in South Africa, we do so in a manner that is consistent across the board, whether it be lawful terminations of pregnancies or feticide. However, this aim for consistency is frustrated at the start as a result of her interpretation of the Choice Act.

As already demonstrated, the Choice Act views pregnant women as embodying not only one entity but not two completely separate entities either.[118] Thus, with Kruuse moving away from connectedness as a source of protection of the unborn, she interrupts consistency when she advocates for understanding the unborn as something separate from pregnant women, and, in that separateness, she advocates for direct protection of the unborn on the basis of the value of dignity. The Choice Act does not take that approach: the unborn are recognised but the influenc of this recognition is limited by the unborn's relationship to pregnant women and their right to terminate their pregnancies. Kruuse, therefore, cannot rely on Meyerson's arguments regarding termination-of-pregnancy laws in South Africa because her approach is in direct opposition to that understanding of how the Choice Act functions.

[112] Kruuse (2009) *THRHR* 135.

[113] Kruuse relied on Meyerson (1999) *SALJ* 50 and cites s 39(1) of the Constitution, which provides that when interpreting the Bill of Rights, one must do so in a way that promotes the value of dignity, among other values. See Chapter Five, para 5.3.1.

[114] Kruuse (2009) *THRHR* 135.

[115] Kruuse (2009) *THRHR* 135.

[116] Kruuse (2009) *THRHR* 134.

[117] See Meyerson (1999) *SALJ* 50.

[118] See Chapter Five.

Furthermore, Kruuse's application of the value of dignity as the primary source for direct protection of a separate, non-constitutional entity is questionable. Using the value of dignity as the only basis for the enactment of legislation leads to the understanding that Kruuse is adopting the value of dignity as a means to create enforceable claims in law. According to Kruuse's adopted position, if the value of dignity can be used to protect the interests of the unborn in the context of lawful termination of pregnancies, then it can also be used in the context of a statutory crime of feticide.

While the value of dignity is relevant, it is questionable whether constitutional values on their own lead to enforceable claims and on this basis it is also doubtful that the value of dignity as applied in the Choice Act is being applied in the same way that Kruuse is attempting to use it in feticide. However, this position is not arguing that the value of dignity does have a role to play in the protection of pregnancies from violence, but it is the *method of application* that is in question here. In order to distinguish between the use of the value of dignity in the context of termination of pregnancies and its use in the context of feticide, it is necessary to briefl go back to the basics concerning dignity as a constitutional value.

As a value, human dignity is described as one of the founding values of the Republic of South Africa.[119] The rights contained in the Bill of Rights affirm dignity as a democratic value.[120] Dignity serves as part of the process of justifying the limitation of rights in the Bill of Rights,[121] and it also aids in interpreting these rights.[122] When looking at the role that the constitutional value of dignity plays, Woolman[123] directs us to Chaskalson CJ's findin in *Minister of Home Affairs v National Institute for Crime Prevention and Reintegration of Offenders*.[124] Chaskalson CJ, responding to the applicants' argument that the values mentioned in the founding clause of the Constitution are absolute and not subject to limitation, stated:[125]

> The values enunciated in s 1 of the Constitution are of fundamental importance. They inform and give substance to all the provisions of the Constitution. *They do not, however, give rise to discrete and enforceable rights in themselves.* This is clear not only from the language of s 1 itself, but also from the way the Constitution is structured and in particular the provisions of ch 2 which contains the Bill of Rights. (Emphasis added.)

Woolman interprets this quote as meaning: values are one thing; rights are another. The difference between the two lies in what each provides.[126] Woolman

[119] Section 1*(a)* of the Constitution.

[120] Section 7(1) of the Constitution.

[121] Section 36 of the Constitution.

[122] Section 39 of the Constitution.

[123] S Woolman 'Dignity' in S Woolman & M Bishop (eds) *Constitutional Law of South Africa* 2 ed (Revised Service 3) 36–23.

[124] 2005 (3) SA 280 (CC) (*National Institute for Crime Prevention and Reintegration of Offenders*). This case concerns the right to vote and the application of this right to those who are imprisoned and serving a sentence of imprisonment without the option of a fine The Electoral Act 73 of 1998 was amended in such a way that it excluded prisoners from voting and the court had to address the constitutionality of such exclusion.

[125] *National Institute for Crime Prevention and Reintegration of Offenders* para 21.

[126] Woolman 'Dignity' 36–23.

explains that, while values shape the rules expressed in the Constitution, and those very rules will also shape our understanding of constitutional values, the difference between the two is that rights give rise to rules and enforceable claims, while values do not.[127]

From the above, the following can be extracted regarding the value of dignity as per the South African Constitution: dignity as a right will give rise to enforceable claims but dignity as a value cannot. As a constitutional value,[128] dignity comes into play when constitutional rights are involved, usually when they are being interpreted or limited. Thus, in order for the constitutional value of dignity to have a part to play in shaping the law, the presence of constitutional rights (a rights element) is necessary. A rights element is necessary because without a right to interpret or limit, the value of dignity has no footing.

Bringing these finding into the context of the unborn in law, the value of dignity offers us a device to recognise the value of the unborn in law generally, since the concept of dignity is synonymous with human worth, which attaches to all human life.[129] However, the Constitutional Court's application of the value does not allow for the value we vest in prenatal life generally[130] to be translated into enforceable legal claims. More specificall , on its own, the value of dignity does not provide the unborn with an individuated legal claim to protection from another's conduct.

Consequently, Kruuse's argument that the value of dignity is an adequate ground for the introduction of a statutory crime to allow for the independent protection of the unborn is difficult to accept. Even though dignity does inform the way forward, it will have the desired impact in law only if we engage with women as rights bearers. By focusing on the separateness of the unborn, Kruuse removed the only relevant rights-bearing agents in relation to the unborn, being pregnant women. She effectively removed the rights element required by the Constitutional Court. It is only once we have established that there are rights involved in a particular scenario that the value of dignity can become relevant and have any legal influence Consequently, there is a strong argument that feticide legislation based on the value of dignity alone, as applied in the separate-entities approach, may not stand.

The Choice Act can be seen as being in contrast with Kruuse's feticide approach in that the Choice Act is based on women's rights. It thus has a rights element embedded. The Act is seen to adopt a (not-one-but-not-two) approach, because there is recognition of the unborn, meaning that pregnant women are more than one entity but not two completely separate entities. This stance is supported by the

[127] Woolman 'Dignity' 36–23.

[128] As opposed to a general theory of human dignity.

[129] L Ackermann *Human Dignity: Lodestar for Equality in South Africa* (2012); see discussion in para 3.5.2.

[130] Another way of explaining this is to distinguish the constitutional value of dignity from the general philosophy of dignity. From a philosophical perspective, we value the unborn because they are part of humanity. The constitutional value of dignity then serves as a mechanism to translate that philosophy into a means of articulating that value in law which has legal weight. Kruuse seems to be relying on the philosophy of dignity and not so much the legal principle of the value of dignity as set out in the Constitution.

fact that recognising the unborn does not lead to absolute prohibition against termination of pregnancies for the benefi of the unborn. In determining the scope of women's rights to terminate their pregnancies, the value of dignity comes in as an interpretive tool, thus providing the opportunity to give legal credence to the value vested in the unborn through the application of the constitutional value of dignity. Therefore, the value of dignity will only fin application in a relational context where at least one agent to the relationship is vested with constitutional rights.

This discussion demonstrates that violence against pregnant women that causes the termination of their pregnancies is more complex than merely arguing that the unborn are separate entities because they are recognisable human beings and we can therefore protect them individually. As demonstrated when considering Du Plessis' position, limiting the scope of the crime to third parties only is flawed especially if the motivation for reform lies in the prevention of harm to the unborn. Women who terminate their pregnancies and third parties who assault women both bring about the same results, so this limited application of the crime to third parties is hard to justify as legitimate. Also, Kruuse's position is problematic because the value of dignity needs constitutional rights in order for it to be an active, functional and influentia legal principle, particularly in the context of the unborn.[131] Despite this, Kruuse does raise an important factor to consider, namely that when this issue is addressed it should be addressed in a unifie manner. However, in both instances, the authors' refusals to recognise the fundamental role of pregnant women in securing the legitimacy of the unborn's protection impedes the development of workable solutions.

6.3.3 Substance abuse during pregnancy as constituting child abuse

Ovens is the only known South African author to suggest law reform concerning protection of the unborn from the possible harms associated with substance abuse during pregnancy.[132] In the context of this discussion, substance abuse concerns the excessive use of legal and illegal substances which have the effect of changing the user's moods, feelings and perceptions, such as alcohol, prescription medication and other illegal psychoactive substances.[133] Further, Ovens explains that there are two different approaches to addressing substance abuse during pregnancy: the harm-reduction approach (treatment approach) and the punitive approach.[134] The harm-reduction or treatment approach views substance abuse

[131] The unborn are distinguished here from other legal subjects with vested constitutional rights because where a legal person find the value of their human worth (dignity) being diminished by certain conduct, their constitutional rights will aid in determining whether there was in fact any infringement of primary rights (dignity, equality, and so on) and these rights will also justify the development of the common law or the enactment of certain legislation aimed at preventing further conduct that has the effect of diminishing their human worth. The same cannot be said for the unborn, because despite the fact that the constitutional value of dignity informs how we view the unborn in law, they are not vested with constitutional rights and therefore cannot enforce or protect their human worth through the application of other primary rights.

[132] M Ovens 'Maternal substance abuse in South Africa: An area for concern?' (2008) 1 *Acta Criminologica* 77 and Ovens (2010) *Child Abuse Research in South Africa* 38.

[133] Ovens (2008) *Acta Criminologica* 78.

[134] Ovens (2008) *Acta Criminologica* 77.

during pregnancy as a social welfare issue, while the punitive approach views it as a crime.[135] The crime element of the punitive approach appears to lie in the fact that harm is caused to another and it is therefore submitted that the punitive approach follows the separate-entities approach.

Ovens points out that this area of pregnancy is problematic in that there is no information available concerning the incidence of substance abuse by pregnant women in South Africa.[136] However, relying on statistical data on substance abuse generally, she indicates that there is a noticeable increase in demand for substance-abuse treatment and goes on to assume that this increase could probably also be an indication of an increase in substance abuse during pregnancy.[137] Furthermore, while research is available indicating the harmful effects of alcohol abuse on the unborn, there is no conclusive evidence signifying that drug abuse during pregnancy has harmful effects on those children born from drug-dependent women.[138] It seems that harms are present but the nature and extent of the harms are still the subject of further research.

Concerning known harms caused to the unborn as a result of substance abuse, Ovens highlights that those children who were excessively exposed to substances prenatally are smaller in body size, have low birth weight, are at increased risk of Sudden Infant Death Syndrome and suffer withdrawal symptoms.[139] However, there are also indications of longer lasting harms linked to behavioural problems, such as learning disabilities, school failure, criminal activity among the youth and homelessness.[140] In line with Ovens' findings Häefele also notes that prenatal exposure to methamphetamine can result in abnormal infant behaviour, birth defects, noticeable change in brain structure, poor social adjustment and language defects.[141]

Unfortunately, many women are found to be unaware of the possible dangers or health-implications associated with substance abuse on the unborn.[142] Additionally, despite there being indications of possible harmful consequences associated with substance abuse during pregnancy, very little research exists on this topic in South Africa. Ovens states that currently, no treatment exists for pregnant women living with an addiction and that many in-patient centres do not accept them.[143] She explains that most treatment programmes are unable to provide the specialised

---

[135] Ovens (2008) *Acta Criminologica* 77.
[136] Ovens (2008) *Acta Criminologica* 80.
[137] Ovens (2008) *Acta Criminologica* 77.
[138] Ovens (2008) *Acta Criminologica* 77–8. Research on the position in the United States also indicates that there is insufficient evidence proving that abusing certain substances is factually the cause of adverse pregnancy outcomes. Despite this dearth of evidence, and as counter-intuitive as this might seem to be for purposes of assigning criminal liability, women still face criminal prosecution in the United States for 'harms' caused to their born babies who were exposed to illegal substances prenatally. This is discussed in detail in Chapter Nine.
[139] Ovens (2008) *Acta Criminologica* 88.
[140] Ovens (2008) *Acta Criminologica* 88.
[141] BW Häefele 'An explorative study on the impact of prenatal methamphetamine (TIK) abuse on early child and school behaviour' (2012) 1 *Acta Criminologica* 56 60.
[142] Ovens (2008) *Acta Criminologica* 80.
[143] Ovens (2008) *Acta Criminologica* 90.

medical services or support required by pregnant women as necessitated by the presence of a pregnancy.[144] She also explains that some women may not seek help because of their lack of access to transport, inadequate financia resources or lack of alternative care services for dependent children.[145] Further, some women may be concerned about the repercussions of seeking help, namely they fear domestic violence, criminal prosecution or losing their children to the foster-care system.[146] Ovens' research shows that some pregnant women are found to take personal responsibility, attempting to stop or reduce their substance abuse for the sake of the unborn.[147]

This stance on substance abuse by pregnant women is unnerving, because drug dependency is understood to involve a biochemical process.[148] This means that drug dependency impedes a person's efforts to successfully stop abusing substances, thus necessitating the inclusion of medical assistance and proper rehabilitation programmes in order to effectively overcome dependency.[149] Aside from the issue relating to access to supportive drug-addiction treatment, self-reliance in overcoming addiction is problematic, because substance-abusing pregnant women are seen to have extensive treatment needs, in that they require training on effective parenting, they need to learn how to deal with pregnancy, must come to understand the impact that substance abuse has on themselves and the unborn, and they need training in how to develop the necessary skills to provide for themselves and their children.[150]

Ovens' contribution indicates that substance abuse during pregnancy runs the risk of raising serious health concerns for pregnant women and the unborn, and this issue therefore requires increased attention. It seems that the state is aware of the need to address concerns associated with addiction more generally and at the time of Ovens' contribution, the Prevention of and Treatment for Substance Abuse Bill was before Parliament to tackle this concern. The Bill has now been assented to, and commenced in March 2013 under the title of Prevention of and Treatment for Substance Abuse Act[151] (Substance Abuse Act). Unfortunately, the Act does not address substance abuse during pregnancy.

The Substance Abuse Act takes on a harm-reduction or treatment approach towards substance abuse,[152] and sets out a number of guiding principles pertaining to the provision of treatment services. Section 4 of the Act requires that treatment

---

[144] Ovens (2008) *Acta Criminologica* 91.
[145] Ovens (2008) *Acta Criminologica* 82.
[146] Ovens (2008) *Acta Criminologica* 82.
[147] Ovens (2008) *Acta Criminologica* 91.
[148] Ovens (2008) *Acta Criminologica* 82.
[149] Ovens (2008) *Acta Criminologica* 82.
[150] Ovens (2008) *Acta Criminologica* 91.
[151] Act 70 of 2008.
[152] Section 1 of the Substance Abuse Act define treatment as the 'provision of specialised social, psychological and medical services to service users and to persons affected by substance abuse with the view to addressing the social and health consequences associated therewith'. 'Service users' refers to those persons abusing or dependent on substances and 'persons affected by substance abuse' refers to any family or community member not abusing substances but requiring services related to substance abuse.

services serve the best interests of those living with addiction and those persons affected by substance abuse and the Act provides a number of measures to ensure this. Included in the listed measures is the obligation to respect the rights of human dignity and privacy, and those living with addiction must be understood as human beings in need, with the potential to change.[153] Ovens interprets s 4 as meaning that any intervention must be approached in a way that is conducive to conciliation and problem-solving, and confrontational approaches should be avoided.[154] This interpretation is supported by s 9 of the Substance Abuse Act, which states that prevention programmes must preserve the family structure, develop appropriate parenting skills and create awareness about the dangers associated with substance abuse, among other listed purposes.

Ovens is critical of the Act's ability to protect the unborn from exposure to harmful substances.[155] She interprets the Act as being too broad, because it does not deal specificall with the consequences of substance abuse by pregnant women.[156] Ovens understands this Act as serving only the rights of women generally and views its provisions as failing in the protection of the unborn, as they are not considered persons in law until birth.[157] This lack of recognition of the unborn therefore impedes our ability to take their best interests into account, despite the fact that, according to Ovens, the unborn can technically be classifie as being affected by substance abuse, seeing that they are being gestated in bodies that are exposed to the substances.[158] Furthermore, she understands the requirement to avoid confrontation as being another impediment to the protection of the unborn.[159]

Ovens is concerned about the fact that there is no legislation providing a legal basis for intervention in pregnancies in order to prevent harm caused to the unborn by substance-abusing pregnant women.[160] She argues that, while child abuse attracts criminal prosecution, the Children's Act[161] does not consider the abuse of drugs by pregnant women as a crime and therefore no protection is offered to the unborn.[162] Looking to offer better protection to the unborn, Ovens advocates for a punitive approach to substance abuse during pregnancy by calling for the definitio of child abuse to be extended to include harms caused to the unborn by pregnant women's substance abuse.[163]

---

153 Section 4*(d)* and *(i)*.
154 Ovens (2008) *Acta Criminologica* 85.
155 Ovens (2008) *Acta Criminologica* 85.
156 Ovens (2008) *Acta Criminologica* 85. The Act's silence on substance abuse by pregnant women may stem from the fact that this specifi area of substance abuse has not been the subject of sufficient research.
157 Ovens (2008) *Acta Criminologica* 85. In a later publication on the same topic, Ovens ((2010) *Child Abuse Research in South Africa* 45) states that in this scenario 'the rights of the drug-using mother are upheld by legislation and the rights of the fetus [are] not taken into account'.
158 Ovens (2008) *Acta Criminologica* 85.
159 Ovens (2008) *Acta Criminologica* 85.
160 Ovens (2008) *Acta Criminologica* 92.
161 Act 38 of 2005.
162 Ovens (2010) *Child Abuse Research in South Africa* 38.
163 Ovens (2008) *Acta Criminologica* 92.

Before applying Ovens' suggested inclusion of the unborn in the definitio of child abuse, it is necessary to contemplate how she define child abuse in the firs place. She define child abuse as 'the deliberate or unintended physical and/or emotional abuse and/or neglect of a child by a parent'.[164] This is contrary to the definitio provided in the Children's Act. Section 1 of the Act define abuse as 'any form of harm or ill-treatment deliberately inflicte on a child'. The provision then goes on to list certain conduct included in this definition such as assault, sexual abuse, exploitative labour practices and exposing the child to conduct that may harm him or her psychologically or emotionally.

It must be noted that Ovens' work derives from a criminological perspective, and she therefore does not engage with the legal meaning of rights. She only briefl mentions applicable legal principles and it is therefore not clear whether her intention is to extend personhood and advocate for foetal rights generally. While Ovens does use the term 'rights' in respect of the unborn, it is not obviously clear whether she is using that term in a technical legal sense. However, her arguments can be interpreted as bestowing on the unborn an enforceable right against the pregnant women carrying them to be born in a healthy (specificall , non-drug exposed) condition. Where this right is not respected, Ovens proposes that the women concerned be held criminally liable, since their conduct would amount to child abuse.

While there is an unquestionable need to address substance abuse during pregnancy in South Africa, a number of reservations can be stated against Ovens' proposal for law reform in this area.

To start with, it is noticeable that Ovens understands child abuse as constituting unintentional conduct as well as intentional conduct. However, as mentioned above, s 1 of the Children's Act define 'abuse' in relation to children as any form of harm or ill-treatment deliberately inflicte on a child. Furthermore, in common law, child abuse in itself is not a crime but a generic term for the possible offences that a perpetrator may be charged with.[165] It is pertinent to note the fault requirements linked to those underlying offences. Carstens and Du Plessis[166] identify a number of common-law and statutory crimes as being relevant to the general realms of child abuse, all of which require the element of intent.[167]

[164] Ovens (2008) *Acta Criminologica* 78.

[165] However, aside from the common-law position, s 305(3) of the Children's Act provides for the statutory crime of child abuse. The section provides that any person (parent, guardian, care-giver, or otherwise) will be guilty of an offence if that person abuses or deliberately neglects a child in his or her care. Since the Act define abuse as intentional conduct, the same issue concerning intention is relevant with the statutory crime of child abuse as with the common-law position.

[166] P Carstens & R Du Plessis 'Medico-legal aspects pertaining to children' in T Boezaart (ed) *Child Law in South Africa* (2009) 601–13.

[167] In terms of the common law, the following crimes were identified Assault, assault with intent to cause grievous bodily harm, indecent assault, rape, sodomy, incest, murder and culpable homicide. The only crime listed here that does not require intention is that of culpable homicide, which requires negligence on part of the perpetrator. The statutory crimes identifie by Carstens and Du Plessis stem from s 14 of the Sexual Offences Act 23 of 1957 and the Criminal Law (Sexual Offences and Related Matters) Amendment Act 32 of 2007.

Focusing on the subject matter at hand, substance abuse during pregnancy as a possible form of child abuse would amount to physical abuse, since Carstens and Du Plessis identify 'chemical substance abuse' as a form of physical abuse against a child.[168] Chemical substance abuse is define as 'poisoning resulting from the deliberate, concealed administration of a toxin to a child'.[169] The relevant common-law crime is the crime of administering poison or another noxious substance.[170] Snyman explains that the perpetrator must have unlawfully and intentionally administered a poison or noxious substance to another person.[171] Intention here refers to the fact that the perpetrator 'must have been aware of the fact that the substance he [or she] was dealing with was or contained poison or some other noxious substance, and he [or she] must have foreseen the possibility that someone might consume it'.[172]

This discussion highlights a number of concerns pertaining to Ovens' approach. First, the perusal of South African criminal law principles pertaining to child abuse emphasise intention as being an essential element for criminal liability. Ovens' very research indicates a lack of intention on the part of substance-abusing pregnant women. Secondly, all of the crimes relevant to child abuse are applicable only to legal persons. Extending the scope of the general term of child abuse to include the unborn would thus require a complete overhaul of the entrenched legal principles applicable to criminal law, which goes far beyond merely rephrasing the definitio of 'child abuse'.

Ovens' proposal links to women's conduct during pregnancy and poses a particularly difficult position in respect of criminal liability: from a technical perspective there can never really be a crime of child abuse against a foetus. There must be a born child for the purposes of identifying harm and proving that the woman's conduct was the factual and legal cause of that particular harm. Until birth, harm is merely 'theoretical'.

Going back to the foundational principles of criminal law, Snyman explains that the firs requirement for criminal liability is that there must be conduct in the form of an act or an omission that falls within the definitiona elements of a particular crime.[173] Thus, if child abuse were define to include prenatal substance abuse, which causes adverse foetal health implications, abusing substances while

[168] Carstens & Du Plessis 'Medico-legal aspects pertaining to children' 594.

[169] Carstens & Du Plessis 'Medico-legal aspects pertaining to children' 599.

[170] Snyman *Criminal Law* 453.

[171] Snyman *Criminal Law* 453. While this crime is still in place, Burchell and Milton (in JM Burchell *Principles of Criminal Law* 3 ed (2005) 691) explain that there may no longer be a need for a separate crime of poisoning because the common-law crimes of assault, assault with intent to do grievous bodily harm, murder, and attempted murder overlap with this crime and the crime of poisoning therefore does not offer any greater protection to society. In the case where the crime of poisoning does not come into play concerning substance abuse during pregnancy then the other mentioned common-law crimes become applicable and each requires intention on the part of the perpetrator.

[172] Snyman *Criminal Law* 453.

[173] Snyman *Criminal Law* 51.

pregnant would amount to 'conduct' within the definitiona scope[174] of that crime. However, aside from conduct, there is a requirement that the conduct must have been the cause of the outcome proscribed by the crime.[175] Causation involves factual and legal causation and factual causation must be established first thereafter, if factual causation is established, legal causation must be determined.[176] A pregnant woman will have factually caused the adverse foetal-health implication if her conduct cannot be thought away without the adverse outcome disappearing at the same time.[177] This is where Ovens' suggestion falls short. Adverse health implications cannot be assessed while the foetus remains *in utero*. Birth is required in order to assess whether harm occurred while *in utero* and then substance abuse must be factually linked to the child's adverse health. As soon as birth occurs, the issue is no longer that of abuse of the foetus.

However, if, as Ovens argues, the unborn are children, then it is possible to still consider it child abuse but the crime can be detected only after birth. This still poses a problem, because Ovens' aim is to prevent harm to the unborn, yet criminal law will not act unless there is evidence of factual and legal cause of harm. This can only be established after birth, thus frustrating her aim of preventing harm during gestation.

It is odd that Ovens takes a punitive approach to substance abuse during pregnancy, especially given that she recognises serious inadequacies currently plaguing the treatment of drug-dependent pregnant women, their general inability to gain access to effective treatment, and the fact that she explicitly recognises that drug-dependency involves a biochemical process which requires medical attention. It is also concerning that criminalisation is her preferred method of reform even though the extent of substance abuse among pregnant women and resulting harms are not conclusively established yet,[178] either in South Africa or abroad.[179] It appears as though her position against the treatment approach lies in the fact that this approach will be less effective in South Africa owing to the limited availability

[174] See Snyman *Criminal Law* 71 for a discussion of the legal requirements pertaining to definitiona elements. Since this discussion is working off a hypothetical application of the crime of child abuse against a foetus, this element for criminal liability will not be discussed.

[175] Snyman *Criminal Law* 79.

[176] Snyman *Criminal Law* 79.

[177] Snyman *Criminal Law* 79. This is the *conditio sine qua non* test.

[178] Something that stands out here is the unanswered issue of harm caused to the unborn as a result of excessive exposure to harmful substances, and whether it can be said with any certainty that the harm is only caused by pregnant women after fertilisation. It may be worthwhile to research the impact of substance abuse on the gametes of both men and women (prior to any fertilisation), and to further research the potential consequences on the biological quality of resulting foetuses. It is a critical question in respect of criminalising harm caused to the unborn because it may be found that men are also causing harm to the unborn and their prospective children, and applying Ovens' approach would require that they be held criminally liable in cases where they father children from their drug-exposed gametes. This point may impact on the prosecution's ability to prove causation beyond a reasonable doubt.

[179] The extent of the dearth of available scientifi data indicating harm becomes obviously clear when the United States is considered; see Part Three.

of treatment resources.[180] In this respect *S v Williams*[181] must be noted. In this case, the state argued that whipping was an appropriate sentence to impose on children given that South Africa suffers shortages of resources and infrastructure, thus impeding the implementation of any alternative sentencing options.[182] Langa J rejected this argument as 'untenable' and found that 'state unreadiness' should not be the price for children to pay.[183] He further emphasised that 'resources should be made available and that they should be utilised properly, so that the values in the Constitution may be upheld and maintained'.[184] Thus, recognising that overcoming addiction includes aspects of medical treatment clearly points to the inappropriateness of criminal sanctions, and the lack of resources will not come to the aid of Ovens' approach.

Furthermore, Ovens fails to demonstrate how convicting pregnant women of crimes associated with child abuse would prevent the recurrence of substance-abuse-related issues when further pregnancies are encountered by the same women. Ovens' resulting recommendation of criminalising substance abuse stands out as incongruous because in the abstract for her contribution she states: 'This article explores areas which need to be researched in order to develop a policy that would be beneficia to pregnant substances (sic) abusers and also protect the unborn foetuses.'[185]

6.3.4 Reform of termination-of-pregnancy laws

The call for reform under the context of the Choice Act is for the repeal of the Act for the benefi of the unborn from the moment of fertilisation. In 'The relevance of science for the protection of the unborn', De Freitas and Myburgh attempt to demonstrate the value of science when striving to clarify the status of the unborn, which clarificatio will serve to better protect the unborn from termination of pregnancies.[186] They explain that science is traditionally used as the basis for when protection should set in, and this currently stands at the point of viability, as science shows that it is at this point that the unborn may be able to survive independently and may also be able to feel pain.[187] De Freitas and Myburgh then turn to the 'science of the unborn' to clarify 'just what sort of being the unborn is

[180] Ovens (2008) *Acta Criminologica* 79. Ovens (87) also considers the adequacy of available treatment resources when approaching the issue of how to address substance abuse during pregnancy in a South African context. She states: 'A further area of interest is to ascertain whether a treatment or harm reduction approach used in other developed countries to deal with the pregnant drug dependent, will be less effective in South Africa due to limited treatment resources available to . . . drug dependent mother.'

[181] 1995 (3) SA 632 (CC) (*Williams*) paras 61; 63. In this case the Constitutional Court found whipping, as a sentence option, constitutes a violation of children's rights to dignity, and that their right to be protected from cruel, inhumane and degrading treatment or punishment prohibits this course of sentencing.

[182] *Williams* paras 61; 63.

[183] *Williams* para 63.

[184] *Williams* para 64.

[185] Ovens (2008) *Acta Criminologica* 79.

[186] De Freitas & Myburgh (2009) *Journal for Christian Scholarship* 63.

[187] De Freitas & Myburgh (2009) *Journal for Christian Scholarship* 63.

during the course of coming into being' because, if the purpose of the law is to protect 'people', it can do so only with accurate scientifi data.[188] In fact, it is their contention that new medical technologies will 'solve the abortion problem'.[189]

De Freitas and Myburgh advocate a non-rights approach, arguing that it is not purely the attribution of rights that makes it wrong to kill another, and on that notion they conclude that a right-to-life argument is not necessary when seeking to develop grounds for justifying legal protection of the unborn from the women who carry them.[190] They contend that other measures can be used for protection and turn to science to work towards the determination of 'life' and whether the unborn require legal protection or not.[191] In this respect the authors unequivocally draw on the separate-entities approach by using science to demonstrate that the unborn are more than mere maternal 'tissue' and embody a distinct human life which has independent value and characteristics that are present from the moment of conception.[192] De Freitas and Myburgh go on to conclude that, since human life begins at conception, law is under an obligation to protect it and limiting women's rights to terminate their pregnancies only once the foetus is viable is 'logically and biologically flawe and unworkable'.[193]

Most of De Freitas and Myburgh's[194] critique is directed against the United States, concerning its adoption of the foetal viability criterion to limit women's rights to terminate a pregnancy in *Roe v Wade*.[195] They are critical of *Roe* in respect of the court's explicit refusal to consider science to determine the status of unborn life as 'human life', but then it contradictorily relied on viability, which is a scientificall informed concept, to be the identifie point in development to confer protection.[196] The crux of their contribution ties into the use of viability as a determinative marker for protection of the unborn because, if one understands there to be human life from fertilisation, it is not clear why survivability should be accepted as the only point requiring protection.

While the authors' critique is focused on *Roe*, the implications of their arguments also extend to a South African context. First, these are both South African-based academics and in South Africa it is accepted that the Choice Act limits access to termination-of-pregnancy services once foetal viability sets in.[197] Secondly, in a later 2012 publication pertaining to the status of the unborn in a

[188] De Freitas & Myburgh (2009) *Journal for Christian Scholarship* 64.
[189] De Freitas & Myburgh (2009) *Journal for Christian Scholarship* 66.
[190] De Freitas & Myburgh (2009) *Journal for Christian Scholarship* 65–70.
[191] De Freitas & Myburgh (2009) *Journal for Christian Scholarship* 70.
[192] De Freitas & Myburgh (2009) *Journal for Christian Scholarship* 70–81.
[193] De Freitas & Myburgh (2009) *Journal for Christian Scholarship* 80. These flaw lie in the fact that viability is a relative term, where despite the advanced development of a foetus, external non-biological factors can negatively impact on survivability levels. The authors argue that viability does not 'measure the universal human characteristics shared by the foetus and the larger community and species, rather it focuses on the potential ability of the foetus to breathe air. Therefore, clearly, the viability standard makes little sense from a human development perspective.' (References omitted.)
[194] De Freitas & Myburgh (2009) *Journal for Christian Scholarship* 81.
[195] 93 S Ct 705 (1973).
[196] De Freitas & Myburgh (2009) *Journal for Christian Scholarship* 78.
[197] See para 5.3.1 and authority cited therein.

South African context,[198] De Freitas relies on the very same scientific-base arguments as presented in his co-authored 2009 publication. In his 2012 publication he argues that when the issue of the legal status of the unborn eventually has its day in the Constitutional Court, the court will have to consider science in developing an understanding of the unborn.[199] It is his contention that this understanding 'should assist in supporting the South African Constitutional Court in coming to a findin that recognises the protection of the unborn to some or other degree'.[200]

In the context of presenting discussions in 'preparation' for the Constitutional Court's deliberations on the imminent issue of the legal status of the unborn, De Freitas states:[201]

> This article calls for having the Constitutional Court assist in gaining more clarity on the legal status of the unborn against the background of a more improved degree of legal recognition. In this regard, support is given to the role of the South African Constitutional Court in approaching the legal status of the unborn from a more nuanced and sensitive point of view, bearing in mind that the woman's right to have an abortion should be qualifie against the background of the interests of the unborn as well.

There are a number of issues with the two contributions considered here. Following the technical terminology adopted in *Case of Artavia Murillo et al* by the Inter-American Court of Human Rights, there is no pregnancy prior to implantation.[202] Consequently, the Choice Act will not necessarily be applicable in cases where a fertilised egg is prevented from implantation, since such conduct would not amount to a pregnancy termination. However, this covers only one of the issues that the authors raise.

Going further, it is in the very context of the Choice Act that we have come to see that the unborn *are* valued. Chapter Five shows that this is the only piece of legislation that does this. As has already been established, in South Africa the value we vest in the unborn in law stems from the constitutional value of dignity.[203] Ackermann find that this value vests in all of those who are representatives of humanity: the unborn, the born and the deceased.[204] Theoretically, that which is just conceived is vested with the value of human dignity because even in its unborn state it is recognised as being part of the essence of what it means to be human. It can be argued further that dignity is present even before conception, especially if one understands reproductive gametes or other cells used in reproductive or regenerative procedures[205] as constituting foundational representatives of the human race. What is important to note is that it can therefore be argued that we value the unborn regardless of their viability.

[198] De Freitas (2012) *International Journal of Religious Freedom* 51.
[199] De Freitas (2012) *International Journal of Religious Freedom* 51.
[200] De Freitas (2012) *International Journal of Religious Freedom* 59.
[201] De Freitas (2012) *International Journal of Religious Freedom* 52.
[202] Para 186.
[203] Chapter 5, para 5.3.1.
[204] Ackermann *Human Dignity* 51–2.
[205] I Wilmut, AE Schnieke, J McWhir et al 'Viable offspring derived from fetal and adult mammalian cells' (2007) 9 *Cloning & Stem Cells* 3 and P Mali & L Cheng 'Concise review: Human cell engineering: Cellular reprogramming and genome editing' (2012) 30 *Stem Cells* 75.

Concerning the status of the unborn in law, they are unborn human beings and as such the value of dignity vests in them. Contrary to the picture presented by De Freitas and Myburgh, the mechanism for valuing the unborn in a legal framework is already in place in South African law. Science can tell us whether what is developing is human enough to accrue some form of value, but it cannot direct us on how to respond in law.

The issue remaining links to when it is acceptable to act on this value with legal force. The question of the acceptability of any action that seeks to protect the unborn demands the consideration of context, and the context of the unborn directly links to the pregnant women carrying them. This essential and inseparable link serves as an impediment when looking to directly protect the unborn. Thus, if one seeks to protect the unborn it must be done through its very life-support, namely pregnant women. It is strongly emphasised that one cannot identify termination of pregnancy as the 'problem' that needs to be addressed in order to protect the unborn. Context of pregnancies tells us that one must understand that the action of turning to termination-of-pregnancy services is a response to underlying social issues, and in this respect Albertyn, Artz, Combrinck et al state that:[206]

> [F]ew feminists argue for abortion on demand in the third trimester, no feminists support sex selection as a reason for abortion and all desire a world in which women do not have to resort to terminations, because they have real control over their fertility and because they do not have to worry about the social and economic factors that make it difficult to carry the pregnancy to term and raise a child.

Of further concern is the fact that, at times, women do not have control over the circumstances of conception owing to coercive sexual pressures, sexual violence against women and limited access to contraception.[207]

Consequently, if De Freitas and Myburgh's concern is for the protection of the unborn, it is argued that they will be better placed to tackle the issue by moving beyond science as the answer to protecting the unborn and focusing more on eradicating those factors that feed the demand for termination-of-pregnancy services. In order to do so, they would have to look at the context of pregnancies generally. Merely removing permissible termination-of-pregnancy laws will not resolve the issue of harming the unborn, because if their position were to be adopted we would more than likely fin an increase in unsafe illegal terminations[208] and possibly an increase in concealed births and neonatal abandonment, simply because the underlying social issues that feed the need to curb having too

---

[206] C Albertyn, L Artz, H Combrinck et al 'Women's freedom and security of the person' in E Bonthuys & C Albertyn (eds) *Gender, Law and Justice* (2007) 295 365.

[207] Albertyn, Artz, Combrinck et al 'Women's freedom and security of the person' 364 and RJ Cook & BM Dickens 'The injustice of unsafe motherhood' (2002) 2 *Developing World Bioethics* 64.

[208] See Center for Reproductive Rights 'Whose right to life? Women's rights and prenatal protections under human rights comparative law' *Center for Reproductive Rights* (20 March 2012) at 12, available at http://reproductiverights.org/sites/crr.civicactions.net/files/documents/ TL_3%2014%2012.pdf (accessed on 3 July 2014). The organisation indicates that the legal status of termination of pregnancy does not impact on the incidence of termination of pregnancies but does impact on incidence of maternal mortality and morbidity rates.

many children will still be present. Neither of these scenarios can be seen as protecting anyone.

Manninen asserts a similar argument.[209] She emphasises that financia difficulty or poverty is one of the leading reasons for women to terminate their pregnancies, and, where pregnancies are terminated on these grounds, these decisions are not based on choice but 'coercion', since free choice is removed.[210] She argues further that implementation of and access to socio-economic rights will alleviate the demand for termination of pregnancies, since supportive services such as access to housing, health care and reproductive services are found to reduce the termination-of-pregnancy rate.[211] In fact, Manninen cites a pro-life advocate from a Catholic organisation as making this connection between poor socio-economic status and the termination of pregnancy.[212] Manninen highlights that even though this particular Catholic organisation argued for restrictive termination-of-pregnancy laws, it nevertheless recognised that criminalising termination of pregnancies would be ineffective if social support were not offered simultaneously.[213]

It is obviously a utopian stance to think that the demands for termination-of-pregnancy services could be completely removed, since there will always be instances where women feel that they may have to turn to those services, especially regarding therapeutic terminations and in cases of unexpected turns of events. However, as already indicated in Chapters Four and Five, the Choice Act effectively reaches a middle ground between women's autonomy and the value we vest in foetal life as a society. The middle ground is reached in so far as the Act recognises the value of the unborn, but in a qualifie manner which is informed by context of the unborn's existence.[214] The Act's provisions indicate that protection must be afforded prior to birth but that protection cannot be in place from the moment of conception because that would absolutely tip the scales in favour of the unborn and may result in serious violations of women's rights and ultimately dehumanise them to primarily reproductive tools.

The meeting in the middle is in place through the application of foetal viability, this being the point at which protection can be legitimately enforced. Therefore, capability for independent life is not the reason why we value the unborn. It is, however, the reason why we act on the value we vest in the unborn. Even though

[209] Manninen (2013) *Hypatia* 663.
[210] Manninen (2013) *Hypatia* 676.
[211] Manninen (2013) *Hypatia* 677.
[212] Manninen (2013) *Hypatia* 677.
[213] Manninen (2013) *Hypatia* 677. However, Fredman emphasises that socio-economic rights will do little unless those rights reflec 'the specificitie of gender'. This means that women's experience of poverty is a different experience to that of men and merely making these rights available on the basis of formal equality (as opposed to substantive equality) will not address the unique position of women faced with poverty. See S Fredman 'Engendering social and economic rights' in B Goldblatt & K McLean (eds) *Women's Social and Economic Rights: Developments in South Africa* (2011) 4–33.
[214] In this respect, see s 2 of the Choice Act generally where the subsections recognise a number of circumstances as impacting on women's experiences of pregnancy, namely their socio-economic circumstances, mental and physical health, and whether the pregnancy was a result of rape or incest, to name a few circumstances.

De Freitas and Myburgh are critical of viability as a justifiabl point for protection, this point in foetal development cannot too easily be dismissed as insignificant

There are well-established concerns regarding the translation of the clinical construction of foetal viability into a legally applicable principle.[215] Generally, foetal viability is not a fixe term, since the determination of a foetus as viable includes the consideration of a number of clinical and biological factors.[216] All of these factors have been found to vary in relation to the socio-economic elements associated with the pregnant woman concerned, and thus require that the viability of any given foetus be considered on a case-by-case basis.[217] This uncertainty poses a problem in law because law, by its very nature, requires certainty. However, the concept of foetal viability is firs and foremost centred on there being a certain degree of foetal development, and this degree of development indicates that the most basic necessities for independent life are in place.[218] This point in development is absolutely significan as this is the firs time that third parties can begin to consider how they can best act for the benefi of the unborn should birth be necessary at this point. Only once this development is present can one go on to determine whether adequate external factors are available to provide any necessary support to the viable foetus if born.

Understanding that there is a biological developmental element to the concept of foetal viability (indicating a core minimum in foetal development), the Choice Act specificall attaches to the biological aspect of the concept instead of external factors, such as those relative to a woman's economic standing. This approach extends the 'benefi of the doubt' to the unborn, meaning that, regardless of unequal access to qualitative external factors such as attending health-care facilities, the interests of all those unborn that have reached 20 weeks' gestation will receive the Act's protective reach and women will no longer be able to terminate pregnancies on demand or for socio-economic reasons.[219] Foetal viability in the context of the Choice Act is crucial to our respect for human life because any termination of a pregnancy from that point on *may* end with the live birth of a child who is capable of independent life, thus obliging us to act for its independent benefit [220]

Reading the 2012[221] and 2009[222] contributions together, the two authors considered here can be interpreted as demanding that women's rights be qualifie against the backdrop of the interests of the unborn and this qualificatio should

[215] C Pickles 'Personhood: Proving the significanc of the born-alive rule with reference to medical knowledge of foetal viability' (2013) 24 *Stell LR* 146.

[216] Pickles (2013) *Stell LR* 146.

[217] Pickles (2013) *Stell LR* 146. The implication of this is that those extremely premature neonates born in private facilities have a better chance of survival than those born in public facilities.

[218] See para 3.5.3 and authority cited therein.

[219] See s 2(1)*(c)* of the Choice Act.

[220] Should a termination procedure result in the live delivery on a non-viable child nothing can be done to secure any kind of life for it, but the same cannot be said for the live delivery of a viable child during a termination procedure.

[221] De Freitas (2012) *International Journal of Religious Freedom* 56.

[222] De Freitas & Myburgh (2009) *Journal for Christian Scholarship* 61.

stand from the moment of conception.[223] The Choice Act has already achieved the process of legitimately limiting women's rights for the benefi of the unborn. However, the separatist approach calling for direct protection from the moment of conception introduces the scenario wherein the carefully balanced provisions become unjustifiabl uneven. It is not clear how De Freitas and Myburgh can legitimately justify valuing one entity more than the other when both are accepted as representatives of the human race and each are vested with intrinsic worth. Thus, the very same ground for demanding uncompromised respect for the unborn serves as the very basis for nullifying women's legal status.

From this perspective, it is clear that no law reform in respect of the Choice Act is necessary to better protect the unborn. Improving women's control over the conditions in which they become pregnant through reform of social policies and better provision of reproductive health measures better serve women of reproductive age, pregnant women and the unborn.[224]

6.4 READYING THE GROUND FOR PREGNANCY ADVERSARIALISM

All these calls for reform can be characterised as third-party intervention during pregnancy and such intervention is arguably necessitated by the need for securing healthy foetal development. The grounds advanced for justificatio for intervention relates to third-parties' interests in prenatal life, as an important value in society, which is informed by our advanced knowledge of the development of prenatal life generally. The primary focus of these authors' submissions relates to the a contextual consideration of the unborn as entities separate from the pregnant women carrying them.

If each of these suggested reform measures is acceded to, pregnant women will suffer broad limitations in respect of their autonomy linked to legal subjectivity. They face forced third-party interventions and possible criminal liability for conduct described as harmful to the unborn, thus placing them under strict societal and state surveillance for the duration of the pregnancy.[225] These sorts of reforms would change the dynamics of the doctor–patient relationship, since attending health physicians will in all likelihood be the firs persons to notice or suspect that

[223] Concerning the extent of the qualificatio of women's rights, Du Plessis explains, in personal communication via electronic mail (5 July 2014), that the authors 'do not argue that women's rights to her body should not be considered—in fact—this is very important. What is argued [is] that the over-emphasis on women's rights to the exclusion of considering other factors is arbitrary and contrary to a reasonable approach where all relevant factors are considered. Therefore, the argument is for a balanced approach concerning the unborn.' She explains further that as the position stands concerning the 'abortion debate' women's rights are being over-emphasised to the point that their rights are considered the sole criterion in the debate.

[224] The Center for Reproductive Rights supports this view; see Center for Reproductive Rights 'Whose right to life?'

[225] This position stands for both Du Plessis' and Kruuse's construction of feticide because, as already indicated above, it is not clear how the authors can justifiabl limit criminal liability to third parties only when the focus of the issue is on harm caused the unborn. It cannot be denied that pregnant women harm the foetus through termination of pregnancy or other 'harmful' conduct, which is exactly what third parties do when assaulting or attempting to murder pregnant women.

intervention is necessary, and use their relationship with pregnant women to effect intervention. While Chapters Four and Five have highlighted the need for reform concerning pregnancy and related issues, reform on the grounds suggested by South African academics would promote pregnancy adversarialism which might negatively impact our ability to ensure healthy outcomes for both pregnant women and the unborn.

Part One has shown that pregnancy adversarialism comes about when the existence of a pregnancy, which usually symbolises a physical and metaphysical bond, is turned into a relationship characterised by tension between three opposing 'parties' with diverging interests. In this instance one party's rights or interests are being advanced to the detriment of the other party's interests or rights. The parties involved in this sort of adversarialist environment include pregnant women, the unborn and third parties, who all have an interest in the pregnancy concerned. These third parties include other persons such as the father-to-be, family members and members of wider society, as well as established institutions such as the medical profession and the state.

The South African authors' separatist approach to pregnancy sets the foundation for adversarialism in South Africa. On the one hand, we have women, with their vested rights with the autonomy to do as they please with their own bodies, such as refuse medical treatment, prevent conception, terminate pregnancies and engage in what can be perceived by others as 'dangerous conduct'. On the other hand, we have the unborn, portrayed as distinct and individuated entities, as well as third parties who attempt to 'speak for' the interests of the unborn as valued entities in society. What is noticeable in respect of the authors' contributions is that the pregnancy environment they create tends to nullify women's claims to their rights as human beings and overlooks the fact that pregnant women also have an interest in their unborn and the goal of progressing through pregnancy and birth healthily.[226] Instead, all emphasise the humanness of the unborn and primarily focus on society's interest in the unborn.

A tension is seen to arise because in order for third parties to act for the benefi of the unborn's interests, they will have to overcome female autonomy, especially when society's perceived method of foetal protection goes against what a woman envisages as acceptable actions on her body. However, autonomy is not something anyone will be prepared to give up too readily: hence, a tension arises between female autonomy rights and foetal interests.

It can therefore be concluded that the authors considered here are effectively readying the ground for pregnancy adversarialism in South Africa, which could very well be realised if their contributions are taken seriously. However, it is questionable whether this approach to pregnancy will, in fact, secure healthy foetal outcomes. Part Three will investigate whether approaching these areas of pregnancy with a separatist view will, in fact, bring about the results envisaged by the authors considered in this chapter.

---

[226] That is, aside from Kruuse, because she specificall refers to a pregnant woman's need to see justice be done for the non-consensual and violent termination of a wanted pregnancy.

6.5 CONCLUDING REMARKS

Pregnant women certainly do embody more than merely themselves. While this has been demonstrated in science for quite some time now, South African law has failed to articulate this 'extra-ness' in its legal principles pertaining to pregnancy. Science and advancements in technology have rendered the single-entity approach redundant and it now serves as a legal obstruction when attempting to secure healthy pregnancies and healthy pregnancy outcomes through the application of legal principles.

The South African academics use science as the basis for identifying the 'extra-ness' in pregnant women and to individualise the unborn as entities separate from pregnant women. Further, they commonly hold that, since the unborn are distinct in their existence and representative of humanity, there is a legal obligation to act for their direct benefi and to offer protection from harmful consequences stemming from the conduct of pregnant women and third parties. This foundation then serves as the basis for arguments for extending personhood to the unborn, to protect them from violence and from substance abuse during pregnancy or termination of pregnancy.

It is clear that the law's approach to particular areas in pregnancy must be reformed in South Africa. However, each of the recommended proposals for reform is questionable. There are a number of flaw in respect of each contribution. Pillay's application of principles pertaining to human rights is viewed as unreliable. Du Plessis adopts a somewhat ambiguous construction of the unborn by portraying them as separate entities worthy of direct protection while still subjecting them to the limitations of their biological links to pregnant women and their rights. Kruuse compares and links a separate-entities-based feticide law to the principles of the Choice Act and the constitutional value of dignity, which draw mutually on the connection between the unborn and pregnant women. Ovens extends the scope of criminal-law principles to include unintended conduct of substance-abusing pregnant women and justifie this approach on the basis of a lack of resources to provide the more acceptable option of treatment. De Freitas and Myburgh misplace their emphasis on termination of pregnancies as the primary cause of harm to the unborn and effectively use the humanity argument regarding the unborn as grounds for dehumanising pregnant women.

Aside from these ambiguously formulated responses to the inadequacies of the single-entity approach, the authors are collectively laying the foundation for tensions to arise between pregnant women's autonomy rights and foetal interests. The opportunity for tension or adversarialism arises because the unborn are 'disembodied' from pregnant women and presented as separate entities with interests in need of individualised protection, and there are attempts to protect these interests to the detriment of pregnant women's autonomous existence. Legal tensions during pregnancies will not result in healthy pregnancies or optimal foetal outcomes generally.

This is where the value of a comparative study comes to the aid of the dilemma currently encountered. To elucidate: there seems to be general consensus that the single-entity approach is irreconcilable with scientifi fact, since it denies the 'extra-ness' that the foetus embodies during a continued pregnancy. The law is therefore unable to respond to areas of concern when pregnancies are deemed to be at risk. South African scholars are actively advocating a preference to adopt a separate-entities approach, rectifying the identifie areas of concern, yet no one is able to test the strength of these claims in a South African context. One can only really theorise on the consequences of giving heed to the recommendations for the reform covered in this chapter. Thus, a comparative study with the United States, where the separate-entities approach is applied to the same areas of pregnancy discussed in this chapter, will clarify whether these recommended calls for reform are legally sound. It will further establish whether each offers protection for the unborn, as envisaged by South African academics, and whether women's autonomy rights and foetal interests are both advanced in each scenario.

PART THREE

PREGNANCY UNDER UNITED STATES' LAW

Chapter 7

THE LEGAL STATUS OF PREGNANT WOMEN AND THE UNBORN IN THE UNITED STATES

7.1 INTRODUCTION

This chapter contemplates the legal status of pregnant women and the unborn, and it discusses the concept of 'personhood' and its application in United States' law, particularly in the contextual setting of pregnancy. The legal construction of personhood is the preferred point of departure, because the term provides an indication of an entity's legal status under federal and state laws. Writing on the concept of personhood in the United States, Fagundes[1] states that, broadly, personhood 'raises the fundamental question of who counts for purposes of law'. We can accept that if a person is counted for, they can be protected and their interests can be advanced and promoted.

In determining who counts or who should count for the purposes of United States' law, this chapter looks at the born-alive rule and the concepts of 'constitutional personhood' and 'foetal personhood'. Also, in the United States, pregnancy is construed as embodying two separate entities and the chapter delves into the reasons why this view was adopted. With this contextual setting in place, the chapter goes on to consider attempts at furthering the recognition of foetal interests in law, which are currently being advanced via personhood measures. Personhood measures focus on extending full legal status to the unborn on the basis that they are human beings, thus removing the relevance of the born-alive rule altogether. The chapter concludes by considering the implications of the United States' experience for South Africa and calls for reform in South Africa, specificall in respect of reform suggestions by Pillay,[2] De Freitas and Myburgh.[3]

[1] D Fagundes 'What we talk about when we talk about persons: The language of a legal fiction (2001) 114 *Harvard LR* 1745 1746.

[2] R Pillay 'The beginning of human personhood: Is South African law outdated?' (2010) 21 *Stell LR* 230. For an extensive discussion of Pillay's position, see Chapter Six. In short, it is Pillay's contention that if the unborn were vested with rights the legal system would be better placed to protect them from termination of pregnancies and third-party violence that terminates prenatal life. Pillay asserts further that law reform of this nature would make wrongful death claims permissible in the case of negligently causing stillbirth.

[3] SA De Freitas & GA Myburgh 'The relevance of science for the protection of the unborn' (2009) 45 *Journal for Christian Scholarship* 61; S De Freitas 'The South African Constitutional Court and the unborn' (2012) 5 *International Journal of Religious Freedom* 51; and the discussion in Chapter Six. Even though De Freitas and Myburgh advocate an approach that is not founded on the notion of rights or personhood, they none the less call for the repeal of termination-of-pregnancy legislation in South Africa on the basis that the unborn are human beings and are in need of protection, which is the same premise being used by personhood advocates in the United States. As will become evident

7.2 THE BORN-ALIVE RULE AND 'PERSONHOOD' IN THE UNITED STATES

As with South Africa, in the United States the common-law born-alive rule determines that only those who are born alive constitute legal subjects or persons.[4] The rule thus determines whether an entity is a legal person and whether an entity has vested rights protectable under law. In this respect, a pregnant woman is a legal subject but a foetus is not. However, there has been considerable development away from the common-law position and this has taken place through the enactment of legislation at both the federal and state levels. As will be discussed below, 'personhood' or 'person' can be define in legislation or case law in a way that expands its definitiona reach to the unborn.

Generally, where there is no legislation in place, or the interpretation of legislation does not justify a move away from the common-law position, the born-alive rule remains in force.[5] However, this principle is not followed universally. For instance, Fagundes explains that, in a number of cases where the term 'person' was not define in state homicide legislation, the state courts have excluded the unborn out of 'deference' to the common-law born-alive rule,[6] whereas some courts have assumed that all the unborn are human for purposes of the law.[7] As an example of this approach, Fagundes cites a decision reached by the Massachusetts Supreme Judicial Court as stating that if all human beings are legal persons and the unborn are human, then the unborn are also legal subjects, thus

---

from the discussion below, these personhood measures are advanced on the basis that the unborn are human beings from the moment of conception, thus justifying the call that federal and state constitutions should protect them as they do any other person. It should be noted that termination-of-pregnancy laws in the United States will not be extensively considered. This issue has received sufficient attention. See R Rebouché 'The limits of reproductive rights in improving women's health' (2011) 63 *Alabama LR* 1. She explains that the South African approach to termination of pregnancy was adopted in the wake of the United States' experience and that the United States served as an 'anti-model' on how to deal effectively with termination of pregnancy in law (22). Also worthy of notice is that some view the United States as having little to add to the current South African position on termination of pregnancy, De Freitas and Myburgh argue this from a pro-life perspective, see De Freitas & Myburgh (2009) *Journal for Christian Scholarship* 81. Rebouché, who takes a pro-choice position, also expresses dissatisfaction with the position of termination-of-pregnancy laws in the United States, see generally Rebouché (2011) *Alabama LR* 1.

[4] J Seymour *Childbirth and the Law* (2000) 137; *Roe v Wade* 93 S Ct 705 (1973) (*Roe*) 716–21; Z Ives 'Feticide and criminal law: Is there an acceptable approach?' (1998) at 4–5, available at http://repository.unm.edu/bitstream/handle/1928/2402/IvesZachary.pdf?sequence=1&isAllowed=y (accessed on 9 May 2016); and A Tsao 'Fetal homicide laws: A shield against domestic violence or sword to pierce abortion rights?' (1998) 25 *Hastings Constitutional Law Quarterly* 457 460–1.

[5] Seymour *Childbirth and the Law* (2000) 137; *Roe* 716–21; Ives (1998) 4–5; and Tsao (1998) *Hastings Constitutional Law Quarterly* 460–1. Also see Fagundes (2001) *Harvard LR* 1757. In the context of the unborn and criminal law principles, Seymour (*Childbirth and the Law* 140) explains that these scenarios where the common law prevails are generally not concerned with the legal nature of the unborn, but rather the proper function of the judiciary. Namely, it is not the function of the courts to create new crimes for the protection of the unborn.

[6] Fagundes (2001) *Harvard LR* 1757.

[7] Fagundes (2001) *Harvard LR* 1757.

granting them legal personhood.[8] Furthermore, there is no trans-substantive application of the legal concept of 'personhood', in that what establishes the unborn as persons in one area of law does not necessarily render the unborn persons in other areas of law.[9]

Consequently, these approaches indicate that there is personhood in the traditional, common-law sense. This concept is narrowly construed and applies to those human beings who are born alive. Traditional personhood is the form of personhood that attaches to pregnant women, while, on the other hand, there is a broad construction of personhood that extends to the unborn by virtue of the fact that they are of human origin. This construction of personhood can be understood as a wide construction of personhood and generally comes about through legislative enactments or via judicial precedents which develop the law beyond the born-alive rule. The scope of these two concepts of personhood varies according to federal and state jurisdictions.

7.2.1 Personhood at the federal level

The United States Constitution is one of the three identifie supreme laws in the United States, and it governs both federal and state laws.[10] In doing so, it guarantees certain benefit and protection for all persons in the Unites States, among other national governmental aims.[11] The term 'person' features frequently in the Constitution but it is not defined [12] The provisions most relevant to the protection of a person are the Fifth and Fourteenth Amendments, known as the Due Process Clause and Equal Protection Clause respectively. Specificall , the Fifth Amendment states: 'No person . . . shall be compelled in any criminal case to be a witness against himself; nor be deprived of life, liberty, or property without due process of the law.' Section 1 of the Fourteenth Amendment stipulates that no

> state shall make or enforce any law which shall abridge the privileges and immunities of citizens of the United States; nor shall any state deprive any person of life, liberty, or property, without due process of law; nor to deny any person within its jurisdiction the equal protection of the laws.

[8] Fagundes (2001) *Harvard LR* 1757–8. Aljalian also refers to a number of examples; see NN Aljalian 'Fourteenth Amendment personhood: Fact or fiction? (1999) 73 *St John's L Rev* 495 533.

[9] Fagundes (2001) *Harvard LR* 1758. Also see TS Jost 'Rights of embryo and foetus in private law' (2002) 50 *American Journal of Comparative Law* 633.

[10] Article 6, cl 2 provides that the Constitution, federal statutes and United States treaties are the supreme laws of the United States.

[11] The preamble to the Constitution states a number of purposes, such as the aim to create a 'more perfect union', secure freedom and achieve justice. For further information, see DP Kommers, JE Finn & GJ Jacobsohn *American Constitutional Law: Essays, Cases, and Comparative Notes* 3 ed (2009) 31–3; 1093–102.

[12] This was noted in *Roe*, 729. The term 'person' appears in the listing of requisite qualification for Representatives and Senators (art 1, s 2, cl 2), in the Apportionment Clause (art 1, s 2, cl 3), in the immigration and importation provision (art 1, s 9, cl 1), in the Emolument Clause (art 1, s 9, cl 8), the election provisions (art 2, s 1, cl 2), in the provision specifying qualification for the office of President (art 2, s 1, cl 5), and in the extradition provisions (art 4, s 2, cl 2). 'Person' also appears in the Fifth, Twelfth, and Twenty-second Amendments, and in ss 2 and 3 of the Fourteenth Amendment.

Consequently, for the purposes of constitutional law at the federal level, the concept of 'person' plays an integral role when determining who gains the benefi of the Constitution's protective reach, particularly when it comes to the protection of one's life.

Roe offers some clarity on what entities do not constitute persons regarding the United States Constitution. In this case the United States Supreme Court decriminalised the termination of pregnancies and found that women have a right to choose whether to terminate a pregnancy or not, and that this right is founded on their right to privacy.[13] However, the court found that the right to privacy is not absolute and that states can justifiabl limit a woman's right to terminate a pregnancy once the foetus has reached viability.[14] The court found that once a foetus is viable the state has a 'compelling interest' in protecting potential life.[15] Thus, states can proscribe the termination of pregnancies from viability onwards, but not in cases where pregnant women's health or lives are at risk.[16]

In *Roe*, Wade and some *amici* argued that the termination of pregnancies should be proscribed from the moment of conception, because the unborn are persons for the purposes of the Fourteenth Amendment.[17] The argument goes: if an entity constitutes a 'person', then the Fourteenth Amendment guarantees that the unborn's right to life will be protected and they will receive equal protection of the law generally.[18] The court found that, in the majority of the constitutional provisions where 'person' appears, it appears as a 'postnatal' concept.[19] The court found that the unborn are therefore not included in the constitutional concept of 'person'.[20] Later the court states: 'In short, the unborn have never been recognised in the law as persons in the whole sense.'[21] Reference to 'postnatal' persons indicates that the court requires live birth for the purposes of constitutional protection at the federal level. Kommers, Finn and Jacobsohn state that, as a result of *Roe,* a 'fetus is not a "person" in a *constitutional sense*'.[22] (Emphasis added.) Accordingly, the Supreme Court's findin in *Roe* adopted a narrow construction of

[13] *Roe* 728.

[14] The court stated (727), 'the right of personal privacy includes the abortion decision, but that this right is not unqualifie and must be considered against important state interests in regulation'. Viability is understood to be significan because it is at this point that the unborn can survive independently if born, thus justifying state regulation.

[15] *Roe* 732.

[16] *Roe* 732. This approach has since been developed in later judgments; see L Greenhouse & RB Siegel '*Casey* and the clinic closings: When "protecting health" obstructs choice' (2016) 125 *Yale LJ* 1428. However, *Roe* is still relevant in respect of determining who a 'person' is for purposes of the United States Constitution.

[17] *Roe* 728.

[18] *Roe* 728.

[19] *Roe* 729.

[20] *Roe* 729. For a critique of the Supreme Court's interpretation of the Fourteenth Amendment, see MS Paulsen 'The plausibility of personhood' (2012) 74 *Ohio State LJ* 13 and Aljalian (1999) *St John's LR* 495. There are many more criticisms raised against the court's construction of 'person' but these two articles are sufficient for purposes of demonstrating that the *Roe* decision is not unanimously accepted.

[21] *Roe* 731.

[22] *American Constitutional Law* 624.

personhood, and in relation to pregnancy this means that a pregnant woman will receive constitutional protection while a foetus will not, and this difference relates to the fact that one entity is born and the other is not.

Another example of a narrow construction of personhood can be found in the United States Code Annotated (1 USCA).[23] Section 8(a) stipulates that any references to 'child', 'person', 'human being' and 'individual' in Acts of Congress, rulings or regulations of various administrative bureaus and agencies of the United States means 'a member of the species homo sapiens who is born alive at any stage of development'. Section 8(b) define live birth as the complete expulsion or extraction of a foetus at any stage of development and after delivery the child breathes, has a heartbeat, the umbilical cord pulsates, or there is definit voluntary muscular movement. This definitio of live birth does not require that the umbilical cord be cut and it is irrelevant that expulsion or extraction is a result of natural or induced labour, caesarean section or 'induced abortion'.[24] However, s 8(c) states that s 8 must not be interpreted as affirming, denying, expanding or contracting any legal status or right applicable to any member of *Homo sapiens* at any point prior to live birth.

Section 8(c) of 1 USCA seems to ensure that, despite the unborn not being identifie as persons in a constitutional sense, protection can still accrue to 'homo sapiens' prior to live birth. Thus, not being recognised as a constitutional person does not bring the issue to an end regarding the status of the unborn in the United States at the federal level. Section 8(c) of 1 USCA indicates that the unborn are not persons for the purposes of the United States Constitution. However, they receive protection or beneficia consideration as human beings generally or as persons widely construed.

It is at this stage that another form of legal subjectivity comes to light at the federal level. Section 8(c) of 1 USCA acknowledges the unborn as somewhat separate subjects of law, since they are considered in the section without reference to the fact that they are embodied in other persons' bodies. In fact, by preventing s 8(c) from being interpreted as neither expanding nor contracting any 'legal status' or 'legal rights' vested in the unborn, this section constitutes a legislative acknowledgment that the unborn themselves may have a particular status under certain laws and possibly individuated rights as well. If the unborn are not persons in the narrow sense, then it can be argued that this section creates independent subjects of the unborn in law in a wider sense.[25] That is, they are granted 'foetal personhood'.

The concept of 'foetal personhood' is taken to be a form of personhood that is distinct from the Supreme Court's construction of constitutional personhood in

---

[23] This section came into effect August 2002 and serves to guide the interpretation of federal legislation, rulings and regulations.

[24] The inclusion of 'induced abortion' more than likely indicates that those viable foetuses delivered alive as a result of a failed termination-of-pregnancy procedure will be considered 'born alive' and thus constitute persons and will therefore be entitled to all of the law's protective reach.

[25] This must be distinguished from the position in *Roe*, in that *Roe* is interpreted as considering the value of the unborn in relation to pregnant women carrying them whereas this section considers the unborn as individuated entities worthy of legislative attention.

Roe. It denotes a wider construction of personhood status which demands legal recognition and protection of the unborn on the basis that they are members of the human species. This legal acknowledgment of the unborn allows for them to be considered separately from pregnant women and demands that certain laws attach for the benefi of the unborn individually. Foetal personhood is present in two instances: where an enactment goes as far as definin the unborn as persons for the purposes of that particular Act or where such definitio is not extended but the implication of an Act is that the unborn directly benefit from its provisions as separate subjects of its law. Essentially, foetal personhood creates a different class of legal subjects which allows the unborn to exist as independent subjects of law.[26]

The federal Unborn Victims of Violence Act of 2004[27] (Unborn Victims Act) demonstrates that foetal personhood is in place at the federal level. Also, the Act serves as an example of how s 8(c) of 1 USCA find practical application to the unborn regarding the notion of foetal personhood. The Unborn Victims Act specificall aims to address those circumstances wherein a third party,[28] while committing a federal crime,[29] also causes or attempts to cause harm to or the death of an unborn. In such an instance that person faces an additional criminal charge of murder or attempted murder.[30] Essentially, the Unborn Victims Act renders the foetus concerned a separate victim of criminal conduct.

The Act does not defin the unborn as persons. Instead, it define the unborn as a 'child in utero, and the term "child in utero" or "child, who is in utero" means a member of the species homo sapiens, at any stage of development, who is carried in the womb'.[31] Thus, while the Unborn Victims Act does not extend constitutional or narrow personhood,[32] it does nevertheless extend extra-constitutional protection to the unborn on the basis that they are members of the human species. This Act applies directly to the unborn as separate subjects of federal law,[33] and the unborn have subsequently been viewed as 'unique legal victim[s]'.[34] In *Montgomery*, the court held that the Unborn Victims Act recognised the unborn as a 'special class of victims not previously recognised under federal law'.[35]

---

[26] This is what the South African authors were aiming to achieve while arguing for law reform; see Chapter Six in this regard.

[27] 18 USCA s 1841.

[28] The Act specificall excludes women and their conduct from its ambit; see s 1841(c).

[29] The Act lists 68 relevant federal crimes; see s 1841(a).

[30] Section 1841(a)(2)(C).

[31] Section 1841(d).

[32] This was recently confirme in *US v Montgomery* 635 F 3d 1074 (8th Cir 2011) 1086 (*Montgomery*). In this case the United States Court of Appeals had to decide whether kidnapping that results in the death of a person constitutes felony murder. In this case, the accused attacked a pregnant woman in order to forcibly remove the foetus from the pregnant woman's uterus and then kidnap the child once born. The process of removing the foetus led to the pregnant woman's death.

[33] See WD Malcolm 'The Unborn Victims of Violence Act: Addressing moral intuition and the right to choose' (2004) 1 *Tennessee Journal of Law & Policy* 277 282.

[34] See E Falk *Privacy, Due Process, and Morality: A Legal Analysis of Federal Fetal Personhood* (unpublished Honours capstone, American University, 2013) 46.

[35] *Montgomery* 1086.

It is obvious that two concepts of personhood exist at the federal level: Constitutional personhood (narrow personhood) and foetal personhood (wide personhood). Section 8(a) and (b) of 1 USCA and the *Roe* decision indicate that the born-alive rule still plays an active role in the United States, at least as far as the United States Constitution and some federal legislation are concerned.[36] However, despite those legislative provisions and judicial holdings, there are examples wherein the unborn receive legal recognition at the federal level in spite of not being born.

7.2.2 Personhood at the state level

The federal position concerning constitutional personhood implicates every state in the United States. According to the supremacy clause of the United States Constitution, the Constitution and the federal laws are supreme.[37] Consequently, state laws pertaining to the unborn and their recognition cannot interfere with women's termination-of-pregnancy rights as developed through *Roe,* and states cannot grant the unborn any enforceable right to life. However, Linton explains that, notwithstanding the *Roe* decision, states are free to extend legal status to the unborn, albeit limitedly.[38] He argues that

> neither *Roe* nor *Casey* purported to address the State's authority to defin the legal status of the unborn child outside the context of abortion or to confer legal rights upon the unborn child that do not interfere with the exercise of the 'abortion liberty'.[39]

While the federal legal system imposes some limitation on states, states can and do extend protection to the unborn in other areas, such as in respect of foetal homicide and foetal pain laws.[40] Bird understands these laws as legislative enactments of foetal personhood.[41] Regarding foetal homicide laws at the state level, the National Conference of State Legislation reports that at least 38 states in

---

[36] This position was challenged. In 2013 a Bill was introduced to Congress titled Sanctity of Human Life Act. The Bill aimed to guarantee the right to life of all human beings and provided that life begins at 'fertilization, cloning, or its equivalent'. The Bill failed; see Govtrack.us 'H.R. 23 (113th): Sanctity of Human Life Act' available at https://www.govtrack.us/congress/bills/113/hr23 (accessed on 10 May 2016).

[37] Article 6 cl 2 of the United States Constitution. This means that states cannot enact laws that contradict federal laws. Thus the supremacy clause creates a hierarchy with state law falling under federal law.

[38] PB Linton 'The legal status of the unborn child under state law' (2011) 6 *St Thomas Journal of Law & Public Policy* 141 143; 155.

[39] Linton (2011) *St Thomas Journal of Law & Public Policy* 143; 155.

[40] Foetal pain laws are laws generally linked to the regulation of termination of pregnancies. These laws aim to limit women's access to termination-of-pregnancy services on the basis that the unborn can feel pain. An example of a 'foetal pain law' is the Alabama Pain-Capable Child Protection Act. This Act declares that the state has a compelling state interest in the unborn from the moment that they can experience pain (s 12) and the legislature has established (s 13) that this compelling interest is separate and independent from the state's compelling interest regarding foetal viability and the Act declares that neither of these compelling interests are intended to replace the other.

[41] See B Bird 'Fetal personhood laws as limits to maternal personhood at any stage of pregnancy: Balancing fetal and maternal interests at post-viability among fetal pain and fetal homicide laws' (2014) 25 *Hastings Women's LJ* 39.

the United States have enacted foetal homicide laws.[42] Linton points out that, while some states require foetal viability or quickening, the majority of states criminalise violent third-party pregnancy terminations from the moment of conception.[43] The Guttmacher Institute reports that, as of 1 May 2016, 12 states implement foetal pain laws.[44] In fact, Linton's research highlights that foetal interests are recognised as interests separable from the women carrying them in numerous areas of law at the state level; these areas include the law of delict, health-care laws, property law and 'guardianship laws'.[45]

There are more explicit examples of foetal personhood emerging at the state level. These take the form of legislatively definin the unborn as persons under state law or through enacted statements of intent regarding a particular state's policy on the unborn. Concerning the extension of the definitio of person to include the unborn, s 43.1 of the California Civil Code states that the unborn are deemed to be existing persons in so far as it is necessary to give effect to their interests after birth.[46] A legislated statement of intent can be found in s 2 of Amendment 68 to the Arkansas Constitution. Amendment 68 concerns the state's 'abortion policy' and s 2 states: 'The policy of Arkansas is to protect the life of every unborn child from conception until birth, to the extent permitted by the Federal Constitution'.

The United States, through various state actions, has a long history of encouraging a view of the unborn as a 'person' in law.[47] This historical perspective has now culminated in attempted state constitutional amendments, where the unborn are define as persons from the moment of conception. Scott discusses this topic as 'personhood amendments' and points out that, to date, those attempts to extend full legal personhood to the unborn have failed.[48] The main premise behind the notion of 'personhood amendments' is for states to demonstrate what they perceive to be 'persons' on a factual and scientifi basis, and from there force the

[42] National Conference of State Legislation 'Fetal homicide state laws' (March 2015) available at http://www.ncsl.org/research/health/fetal-homicide-state-laws.aspx (accessed on 14 July 2016).

[43] Linton (2011) *St Thomas Journal of Law & Public Policy* 144.

[44] Guttmacher Institute 'State laws and and policies: An overview of abortion laws' (2016) available at https://www.guttmacher.org/state-policy/explore/overview-abortion-laws (accessed on 10 May 2016).

[45] See generally Linton (2011) *St Thomas Journal of Law & Public Policy* 141. Also see Jost (2002) *American Journal of Comparative Law* 646. Some of these areas will be considered later in the chapter.

[46] Also see s 1.07 of the Texas Penal Code. For purposes of the penal code, s 1.07 define an individual as a 'human being who is alive, including an unborn child at every stage of gestation from fertilization until birth'.

[47] See generally R Roth *Making Women Pay: The Hidden Costs of Fetal Rights* (2000) 37–183. Roth describes numerous attempts to place foetal interests above women's rights. Also see Bird (2014) *Hastings Women's LJ* 50 fn 93. Bird indicates that the United States has viewed the unborn as persons from as early as the 1970s. As authority she cites *Keeler v Superior Court* 2 Cal 3d 619 (1970); in this Californian case, the born-alive rule was rejected in order for the crime of murder to be extended to protect the unborn.

[48] TJ Scott 'Why state personhood amendments should be part of the profil agenda' (2011) 6 *University of St Thomas Journal of Law & Public Policy* 222. Also see LR Collins & SL Crockin 'Fighting "personhood" initiatives in the United States' (2012) 24 *Reproductive Biomedicine Online* 689 690.

federal government via the Supreme Court to re-examine *Roe*.[49] Taking note that personhood amendments may be futile, Scott argues that, even though the unborn are not constitutionally protected persons at the federal level, state constitutional amendments could secure the unborn's 'rights' to the extent permissible under current federal law.[50] Further, he argues that a state 'would recognize its right and duty to protect the unborn, a subset of persons, under the rights and privileges available in its constitution'.[51]

As with the federal system, there are certainly two forms of personhood at the state level. Aside from federally sanctioned constitutional personhood, there is also a form of quasi-legal subjectivity at play. This limited form of legal subjectivity which vests in the unborn is being stretched to the absolute limits of what federal law permits, thus extending foetal protection wherever possible, even at the constitutional level. In fact, Jost indicates that a number of states still have termination-of-pregnancy laws which are in contravention of the Constitution as per *Roe*.[52] He explains that, while these laws are not being enforced, they are being kept in place in the hope that the Supreme Court will at some point reconsider its position in *Roe* and extend constitutional personhood to the unborn.[53]

7.2.3 Foetal personhood creates a multi-party pregnancy

The extension of a lesser degree of legal personhood to the unborn has implications on how pregnancy is perceived in the United States. Fagundes considers a number of state codes that criminalise the termination of pregnancies through third-party violence, and he argues that, whether legal status is bestowed on the unborn via judicial interpretations of the common law or statutory enactments,

> these laws can still send a strong message about the personhood status of fetuses . . . the act of criminalizing feticide, regardless of method, sends a message about the state's regard for fetal life and thereby implicitly grants fetuses limited personhood status.[54]

---

[49] Scott (2011) *University of St Thomas Journal of Law & Public Policy* 224. Scott explains (230) that this is linked to the 'Blackmun Hole'. The 'Blackmun Hole' refers to Justice Blackmun's decision in *Roe* where he stated (728) that if the unborn are established as persons within the meaning assigned to personhood as per the Fourteenth Amendment then the unborn's right to life would be guaranteed.

[50] Scott (2011) *University of St Thomas Journal of Law & Public Policy* 233.

[51] Scott (2011) *University of St Thomas Journal of Law & Public Policy* 233. However, see PB Linton 'A fool's errand: State "personhood" proposals' (2009) 35 *Human Life Review* 61. Linton is very critical of 'personhood amendments' generally.

[52] Jost (2002) *American Journal of Comparative Law* 635.

[53] Jost (2002) *American Journal of Comparative Law* 635.

[54] Fagundes (2001) *Harvard LR* 1756. Regarding the Unborn Victims Act, Fagundes' argument concerning the limited character of foetal personhood stands true. Malcolm ((2004) *Tennessee Journal of Law & Policy* 295), a supporter of the Act, points out that the unborn are not extended full status since women who terminate their pregnancies are excluded from the ambit of the Act and the Act is limited to 68 federal crimes. If full status were afforded to the unborn, women would not be excluded and the Act would inevitably not be limited to only 68 federal crimes. However, one might argue that merely offering protection does not in itself accrue personhood status, since the aim of criminalising conduct is to prevent public or collective harm. In similar vein, animals are not afforded personhood status merely because the state prohibits cruelty to animals.

Also, Scott identifie 'personhood amendments' as an explicit expression of a state's theoretical belief in the personhood of the unborn.[55] Along similar lines, Karnein states:[56]

> If all states are allowed to create a set of cases that make the treatment of embryos as persons into precedents, a new reality may be created. This may be a reality in which people have grown used to thinking of embryos as persons and thus change their attitudes about abortion.

These strong messages and theoretical beliefs embedded in federal and state laws pertaining to foetal personhood without a doubt shape peoples' perceptions on how pregnancy is viewed in the United States. The United States is identifie as primarily adopting the separate-entities approach to pregnancy in that the unborn are viewed as entities distinct from the pregnant women carrying them. Further, since the unborn are part of the human species they are seen to be entitled to certain rights and legal protections.

Karnein points out that the firs official recognition of the unborn as separate entities came about in 1946.[57] In *Bonbrest v Kotz*[58] the court had to determine whether a delictual claim for injuries sustained prenatally should stand. In previous cases these claims were rejected because the unborn were understood to form part of the pregnant women carrying them.[59] In *Bonbrest*, McGuire J rejected the historical notion that the unborn are part of pregnant women's bodies and stated:[60]

> As to a viable child being 'part' of its mother—this argument seems to me to be a contradiction in terms. True, it is in the womb, but it is capable now of extra-uterine life—and while dependent for its continued development on sustenance derived from its peculiar relationship to its mother, it is not a 'part' of the mother in the sense of a constituent element—as that term is generally understood. Modern medicine is replete with cases of living children being taken from dead mothers. Indeed, apart from viability, a non-viable fetus is not a part of its mother.

The judge went on to assert that, if viable, the unborn has 'its own bodily form and members, manifests all of the anatomical characteristics of individuality, possesses its own circulatory, vascular and excretory systems and is capable *now* of being ushered into the visible world'.[61] (Emphasis in original.) Karnein notes that a number of cases followed the separate-entities position found in *Bonbrest* and a new theory of the unborn came to the fore in the United States.[62] While *Bonbrest* concerns the law of delict, the discussion above indicates that the

[55] Scott (2011) *University of St Thomas Journal of Law & Public Policy* 235.

[56] AJ Karnein *A Theory of Unborn Life: From Abortion to Genetic Manipulation* (2012) 72. In the context of foetal homicide laws, Karnein (73) understands treating the unborn as separate victims may 'habituate' people into thinking that the termination of prenatal life is the same as killing a person.

[57] Karnein *A Theory of Unborn Life* 69.

[58] 65 F supp 138 (DDC 1946) (*Bonbrest*).

[59] Karnein *A Theory of Unborn Life* 68.

[60] *Bonbrest* 141.

[61] *Bonbrest* 142.

[62] Karnein *A Theory of Unborn Life* 69–70.

separate-entities approach is clearly present in other contemporary areas of law which concern protection of the unborn as distinctive entities.

These arguments reveal that, if a pregnancy embodies a woman and the unborn as separate entities, then one is dealing with the notion that a pregnancy may involve multiple 'parties'.

7.3 ORIGINS OF A SEPARATIST APPROACH TO PREGNANCY IN LAW

The discussion above reveals that, despite the presence of the born-alive rule, the United States has gone on to assign the unborn separate status in law and this leads to the question: why was separate status established? The answer will assist in understanding the legal milieu of pregnancy in the United States.

Seymour explains that a separatist view of pregnancy exists as a result of the United States adopting a 'definitiona approach' to determining the legal nature of a foetus.[63] A definitiona approach considers how the law should classify the unborn by considering its essential characteristics.[64] The underlying issue is to determine whether the unborn's characteristics inform us as to whether they are human beings, persons or body parts.[65] This approach is founded on the assumption that the unborn cannot possess rights or be owed any duty of care unless their nature is identifie as being distinctive (one complete entity on its own) but also in that distinctive existence they share characteristics similar to those of the human race.[66] Seymour states that once the nature of the unborn has been determined, certain conclusions follow concerning the legal recognition to which the unborn are entitled.[67] He explains:[68]

> A particularly clear example of the operation of this process is seen in the United States cases dealing with claims under wrongful death statutes in respect of stillbirths. These have frequently been decided on the basis that, since the relevant statutes refer to 'persons', they must be applied in the case of a still-birth if the fetus can be categorized as a 'person'.[69]

Consequently, how the nature of the foetus is define impacts on whether or not a pregnancy will be viewed as embodying a single entity or two separate entities.

In determining whether to defin the foetus as a separate human being or merely part of the body of the pregnant woman carrying it, reference is generally made to the medical knowledge of prenatal development. This is evident in *Bonbrest*, the

[63] Seymour *Childbirth and the Law* 185.
[64] Seymour *Childbirth and the Law* 185.
[65] Seymour *Childbirth and the Law* 185. Seymour identifie this approach as problematic, because what it means to be a person differs from context to context, and this is very true if one considers that different forms of personhood have developed in American law, each with different consequences attaching.
[66] Seymour *Childbirth and the Law* 159; 170; 185.
[67] Seymour *Childbirth and the Law* 185.
[68] Seymour *Childbirth and the Law* 185.
[69] Seymour's contribution was published in 2000 and there have been substantial developments in American law pertaining to the unborn since then. The discussion to follow in this part will demonstrate that the definitiona approach is being applied beyond wrongful death claims, thus also indicating wide acceptance of the separate-entities approach to pregnancy.

firs case to individuate the foetus, and this knowledge is still being advanced as a ground for justifying separate recognition of the unborn.[70] However, it must be noted that the development of foetal personhood in the United States did not come about simply as a result of considering what science has demonstrated. If that were true, one uniform concept of foetal personhood would attach to the unborn regardless of which area of law is relevant and one would expect there to be uniformity across the United States, yet this is not the case.

Roth points out that there are other forces at play, and explains that in the United States it is the context in which medical technology is being used that gives rise to foetal personhood, or foetal 'rights', as she puts it.[71] She urges that one should understand the social context and political setting of technology rather than the technology itself and argues:[72]

> Though technological capabilities are not all together irrelevant, if the United States was not at a place where struggles over gender equality and abortion in particular were so intense, longstanding, and seemingly intractable, then new medical technologies might not have been put to use in a campaign to achieve fetal rights.

She argues that technology gave the highly politicised anti-abortion lobby in the United States the leverage to support their claims that the unborn are separate human beings who are in need of protection, which then translated into legal arguments for rights or personhood.[73] Roth explains that foetal personhood claims are layered on older moral claims pertaining to women's duty to fulfi their 'feminine destiny by bearing children' thus increasing cultural demands, and this all takes place in a context where pregnancy is highly medicalised, ultimately leading to increased professional and state authority over women.[74]

To prove the validity of her argument that foetal personhood is not purely a result of advances in technology but also of political climate, Roth compares the United States with other countries where prenatal technology is also present.[75] She argues that Australia, Britain, and Canada all have the same access to prenatal technology as found in the United States, but none of these jurisdictions recognise foetal rights which allow for women to be held criminally liable in respect of adverse pregnancy outcomes and forced medical interventions during pregnancies are few and far between.[76] This position stands despite the firs 'test-tube baby' being born in England in 1978, or the fact that Scotland was the firs country to use ultrasonography, or that Australia was a pioneer in the research and development

[70] See the general discussion in Chapter Two. Also, as the discussion develops in Part Three the reader should note how often medical technology crops up in the debates concerning the foetus and pregnancy-related issues.
[71] Roth *Making Women Pay* 30–3.
[72] Roth *Making Women Pay* 32.
[73] Roth *Making Women Pay* 33.
[74] Roth *Making Women Pay* 32; 34. It is here that we can see the tension during pregnancy, where women are fightin to advance beyond their historical disadvantage while others are using their pregnancies as means to keep women in their subordinate and reproductive positions. This is achieved by using technology to speak for the unborn. It is in this context that we fin forced medical interventions and the criminalisation of certain conduct during pregnancy.
[75] Roth *Making Women Pay* 34.
[76] Roth *Making Women Pay* 34.

of reproductive technologies.[77] Roth's[78] arguments demonstrate that foetal personhood is uniquely American and her discussion convincingly shows that 'something besides the simple availability of technology must account for the degree of fetal rights activity in the United States: the heightened intensity of reproductive politics'.[79]

Roth[80] identifie the foetal-rights movement (or the extension of foetal personhood) as stemming directly from the *Roe* decision, in the form of a 'backlash'[81] to the reproductive autonomy that the decision created for all women. According to Solinger,[82] the backlash was based on a 'values crisis', meaning that women were seen to be given 'an excess of equality', in that by enjoying the reproductive autonomy established through *Roe* 'women were grabbing social power from men and challenging social stability in part by claiming reproductive rights'. Those concerned with the implications of *Roe* on social stability turned to religion for answers and these organisations became the foundation for organising resistance against liberal access to the termination of pregnancies. Roth[83] explains that *Roe* provided a framework for thinking of the unborn from a legal perspective. Within *Roe*'s framework women focused on advancing their rights to reproductive autonomy while third parties sought to advance their interest in preserving social order based on gender roles and this was achieved by 'protecting' the lives of the unborn (as entities that the state has a compelling interest in) and advances in medical technology assisted in legitimising anti-abortion arguments.[84]

Resistance to the freedom to terminate a pregnancy unfolds in the political arena.[85] Meredith explains that anti-abortion lobby groups work together to enact

---

[77] Roth *Making Women Pay* 34.

[78] Roth *Making Women Pay* 34–5.

[79] According to Solinger 'reproductive politics' is a term that developed during second-wave feminism (see Chapter Two) in the United States and concerns issues related to contraception, termination of pregnancy, sterilisation, adoption and sexuality among other reproductive-related topics. Solinger states that this term demonstrates how politics is at the centre of reproductive-related issues and uses the following questions to illustrate this: '[W]ho has the power to make decisions about keeping or ending a pregnancy: the pregnant woman, a physician, or a member of Congress? Who has the power to defin a *legitimate* mother, that is, a woman who has the right to raise her own child: a city welfare official, an adoption agency and its client, a judge, or the mother herself?' (Emphasis in the original.) Going further, Solinger explains that all reproductive decisions are influence by law and policy and this ultimately creates a power struggle between the public and private spheres. Solinger, in very basic terms, explains that many follow the notion that the decision on whether to have a child or not is a private matter which should be governed by a woman's choice. While, on the other hand, there are many who believe that reproductive issues are public concerns that should be governed by legislation and these laws generally reflec underlying values that society attaches to childbearing women and the unborn. See R Solinger *Reproductive Politics: What Everyone Needs to Know* (2013) 1–2.

[80] *Making Women Pay* 17.

[81] Although she identifie that foetal personhood did not come to life in a vacuum, she argues that it is the historical political climate of subordinating women through controlling their reproduction that enabled the foetal personhood movement to take hold.

[82] *Reproductive Politics* 15.

[83] *Making Women Pay* 17.

[84] Roth *Making Women Pay* 17.

[85] Hence the notion of 'reproductive politics': public regulation via 'anti-abortion politics' of private spheres of women's lives being the 'politics of choice'.

federal and state laws; they garner political support and promote anti-abortion candidates, seek out test cases and tie their campaigns to intersect with the decisions.[86] The fundamental aim of these organisations is to render the termination of pregnancies illegal in the United States.[87] First and foremost, they focus on extending full constitutional personhood to the unborn.[88] While constitutional amendments are being advocated, anti-abortion groups employ backdoor tactics to slowly chip away at the right to terminate a pregnancy.[89] This is done through advocating law reform in other areas of law that would result in enhancing the legal status of the unborn more generally.[90] Most alarmingly, while *Roe* concerned advancing women's autonomy rights concerning reproduction, it is *Roe*'s compelling state interest in protecting prenatal life that serves the foundation for justifying wider reforms for the legal status of the unborn.[91] Ultimately, *Roe*'s use of compelling interest in prenatal life serves as the basis for its demise.

Discussing the intersection of the anti-abortion movement and the drive to develop the legal status of the unborn, Meredith states:

> Pressures for more fetal rights legislation are unlikely to subside in the US, and the anti-abortion agenda views any attempt to give the fetus 'personhood', even through legislation with entirely different aims, as positive progress towards its own goals.[92]

Consequently, where measures to extend full legal subjectivity fail, lobby groups adopt substitutive efforts, such as promoting foetal homicide laws and

---

[86] S Meredith *Policing Pregnancy: The Law and Ethics of Obstetric Conflict* (2005) 182. While Meredith was specificall focusing on the issue of forced medical interventions, she equated forced medical intervention tactics to that adopted by the anti-abortion lobbyists. Also see Solinger *Reproductive Politics* 16. Roth (*Making Women Pay* 21) gives a brief exposé of how even the various Unites States presidents were involved in either the pro-life or pro-choice movement. Their affiliation to any side either resulting in diminished access to termination of pregnancy or increased access to termination of pregnancy.

[87] Roth *Making Women Pay* 20.

[88] Roth *Making Women Pay* 20.

[89] Meredith *Policing Pregnancy* 182. See also Greenhouse & Siegel (2016) *Yale LJ* 1428 and LM Paltrow 'How Indiana is making it possible to jail women for having abortions' *Political Research Associates* (29 March 2015) available at http://www.politicalresearch.org/2015/03/29/how-indiana-is-making-it-possible-to-jail-women-for-having-abortions/#sthash.9lp9ETVr.dpbs (accessed on 11 May 2016).

[90] Meredith *Policing Pregnancy* 182.

[91] See BA Burkstrand-Reid 'From sex for pleasure to sex for parenthood: How the law manufactures mothers' (2013) 65 *Hastings LJ* 211 221. In addition to the state's interest in prenatal life, Burkstrand-Reid explains that grounds justifying the regulation of all women of reproductive capacity are also linked to the state's interest in maternal health. She argues that using the term 'maternal health' instead of 'women's health' renders women 'mothers' in law and thereby justifie state regulation over women in order to secure the realisation of 'good mothers'. Applying references such as 'maternal health' to women who are not pregnant or women who are pregnant but do not wish to continue with their pregnancies opens the door to increased regulation. The use of *Roe* and subsequent termination-of-pregnancy case law in this way becomes more apparent in the chapters to follow concerning the United States' position on the identifie areas of concern regarding pregnancy in law.

[92] Meredith *Policing Pregnancy* 182.

'drug mother' laws, and keeping 'uncooperative "mothers"' in check for the purposes of protecting the unborn.[93]

The theorised separateness of the unborn sets the scene for pregnancy, pregnant women, and the unborn in the United States. This setting is what Part One identifie as creating an environment for adversarialism during pregnancy and fostering tensions. It is the intersection of diverging approaches tied together by pregnancy. Women are on one side responding to their historical subordination by advocating an autonomous and substantively equal existence, and on the other side, third parties are using technology and a history of gender inequality to secure 'healthy pregnancy outcomes' and advance control over women to achieve that end. This three-party approach sets out fertile ground for an adversarial pregnancy environment. This tension comes at the price of preventing the law from adequately addressing those issues that implicate the realisation of women's reproductive autonomy and advancing foetal interests at the same time. Under adversarialism, instead of advancing both entities' needs, only one 'party's' interests are being advanced to the detriment of the other 'party' and the law is used to sanction this.

7.4 PERSONHOOD MEASURES: EXTENDING FULL LEGAL SUBJECTIVITY TO THE UNBORN

The following discussion serves to evaluate the strength of Pillay's suggestion that reforming South African status law by extending full legal subjectivity to the unborn from viability onwards will serve to adequately protect them.[94] Aside from responding to Pillay's proposal, this discussion also inadvertently responds to De Freitas and Myburgh's proposals for repealing termination-of-pregnancy laws in South Africa.[95]

In the United States, the fact that the unborn are vested with only foetal personhood is not accepted by some and the issue of extending full legal status to the unborn has received extensive attention through the process of attempted legislative enactments or constitutional amendments. These enactments or amendments were briefl introduced above as 'personhood amendments'[96] or 'personhood initiatives'.[97] The collective activity driving these initiatives is referred to as the 'personhood movement', which has been define as a branch of the pro-life movement in the United States.[98]

As already mentioned above, the provisions of the United States Constitution do not apply to the unborn, since they are not considered persons in a constitutional

[93] Meredith *Policing Pregnancy* 182. Also see JR Schroedel, P Fiber & BD Snyder 'Women's rights and fetal personhood in criminal law' (2000) 7 *Duke Journal of Gender Law & Policy* 89 who support the position set out by Roth and Meredith.

[94] Pillay (2010) *Stell LR* 230.

[95] De Freitas & Myburgh (2009) *Journal for Christian Scholarship* 61; De Freitas (2012) *International Journal of Religious Freedom* 56; and the discussion in Chapter Six.

[96] Scott (2011) *University of St Thomas Journal of Law & Public Policy* 222.

[97] Collins & Crockin (2012) *Reproductive Biomedicine Online* 689.

[98] A Armstrong & D Hsieh 'The "personhood" movement is anti-life: Why it matters that rights begin at birth, not conception' (31 August 2010) available at http://www.seculargovernment.us/docs/a62.pdf (accessed on 10 May 2016).

sense. This was established by *Roe* in 1973 and the position remains today.[99] Collins and Crockin confir that personhood measures are pro-lifers' response to the *Roe* decision.[100] The authors explain that most of the bills or personhood initiatives stem from an organisation called Personhood USA.[101] The organisation primarily focuses on developing a concept of personhood that includes the unborn, thereby rendering the termination of pregnancy unlawful, as it would constitute the crime of murder.[102] Personhood USA's position of viewing the unborn as persons stems from the premise that science has revealed that the unborn are human beings and should thus be understood as persons in law and culture.[103] The ultimate aim of these measures is to extend constitutional rights to the unborn,

[99] Kommers, Finn & Jacobsohn *American Constitutional Law* 624. However, it must be noted that it is only really the crux of *Roe* that remains today, being that the Constitution does not apply to the unborn. The anti-abortion lobbyists and sympathising state officials have successfully chipped away at what *Roe* originally stood for. For a brief summary see Kommers, Finn & Jacobsohn *American Constitutional Law* 626–30. The authors summarise United States Supreme Court litigation that took place after the *Roe* decision; all these cases are indications that there are regular disputes linked to a woman's right to terminate her pregnancy and there is a constant move towards limiting this right in one respect or another. See *Planned Parenthood of Central Missouri v Danforth* 96 S Ct 1976 (1976); *Bellotti v Baird* 99 S Ct 3035 (1979); *Planned Parenthood v Ashcroft* 103 S Ct 2517 (1983); *Akron v Akron Centre for Reproductive Health* 103 S Ct 2481 (1983); *Webster v Reproductive Health Services* 109 S Ct 3040 (1989); *Planned Parenthood of Southeastern Pennsylvania v Casey* 112 S Ct 2719 (1992); *Stenberg v Carhart* 120 S Ct 2597 (2000); and *Gonzales v Carhart* 127 S Ct 1610 (2007). For the position at state level see Guttmacher Institute 'State laws and policies: An overview of abortion laws'. The Institute tabulates extensive restrictive measures which include mandated (pro-life) counselling, extensive physician and hospital resource requirements, limited public funding, mandated waiting period of 24 hours, and mandated parental involvement in cases of teenage related pregnancy termination. Hospital resource requirements are currently before the United States Supreme Court. Texas passed legislation under the guise of protecting women's health which requires termination-of-pregnancy clinics to effectively function as ambulatory surgical centres (mini hospitals). The Supreme Court in *Whole Woman's Health v Hellerstedt* 579 US (2016) found this regulatory approach to be medically unnecessary and places the reproductive health care sector under such an extreme burden that clinics will be forced to close down and women will be denied access to termination-of-pregnancy services. It ultimately creates an undue burden for women of reproductive age. See also Center for Reproductive Rights 'Whole Women's Health v Hellerstedt' available at http://www.reproductiverights.org/case/whole-womans-health-v-hellerstedt (accessed on 10 May 2016). There is a plethora of criticism of the United States' position concerning the legal protection of a woman's right to decide to terminate a pregnancy, too much to consider here. However, this discussion demonstrates that *Roe*'s position is being diluted and anti-abortion efforts are unlikely to subside. For more on this issue, see generally BA Burkstrand-Reid 'The invisible woman: Availability and culpability in reproductive health jurisprudence' (2010) 81 *University of Colorado LR* 97.

[100] Kommers, Finn & Jacobsohn *American Constitutional Law* 624.

[101] Collins & Crockin (2012) *Reproductive Biomedicine Online* 689. Falk's research supports Collins and Crockin's assertion in this regard; see Falk *Privacy, Due Process, and Morality: A Legal Analysis of Federal Fetal Personhood* 10–1.

[102] See Personhood USA 'About us' available at http://www.personhood.com/about (accessed on 11 May 2016).

[103] Personhood USA 'Education' available at http://www.personhood.com/education (accessed on 11 May 2016).

which enables the law to fully protect them at the federal level, thereby allowing states to do so too.[104]

Personhood measures have been taking place in the United States for a number of years, since 1995 at the federal level and since 2008 at the state level.[105] As an example, in 2013, a federal Bill (HR 23) was introduced during the 113th Congress titled the Sanctity of Human Life Act. Section 2(1)(A) of the Bill provided that the constitutional right to life is the 'most fundamental right of a person' and sub-s (B) stated:

> [T]he life of each human being begins with fertilisation, cloning, or its functional equivalent, irrespective of sex, health, function or disability, defect, stage of biological development, or condition of dependency, at which time every human being shall have all the legal and constitutional attributes and privileges of personhood.

Section 3(3) of the Bill define the concepts 'human' and 'human being' as including 'every member of the species homo sapiens at all stages of life, beginning with the earliest stage of development'.

Commentators suggested that the Bill only had a 4% chance of being enacted and, in line with those expectations, the Bill failed to muster enough support.[106] This is unsurprising given that there is a long history of attempts to render *Roe* unconstitutional through various federal bills. These date as far back as 1995 and none have garnered sufficient support to make it past the House Committee.[107]

These failed attempts are also apparent at state level, where similar personhood endeavours have taken place. Collins and Crockin[108] state that while various states' initiatives have adopted different language and forms[109] the essential and common characteristic found in every initiative is to redefin 'person' so as to include the unborn from the moment of fertilisation and thereby extending full legal status and rights to them.[110] To date all personhood measures have failed and Collins and Crockin provide a glimpse into these failures: in 2008 Colorado citizens voted down a personhood initiative; in 2009 a Virginia personhood bill

---

[104] Personhood USA 'Become a citizen co-sponsor of the Life at Conception Act' available at http://www.personhood.com/become_a_citizen_co_sponsor_of_the_life_at_conception_act (accessed on 11 May 2016). As discussed above, Scott ((2011) *University of St Thomas Journal of Law & Public Policy* 224) explains that if states, through legislative expression, defin the unborn as humans, the Supreme Court may be forced to revisit *Roe* and reconsider its position on excluding the unborn from constitutional personhood.

[105] Collins & Crockin (2012) *Reproductive Biomedicine Online* 689 and Falk *Privacy, Due Process, and Morality: A Legal Analysis of Federal Fetal Personhood* 9.

[106] See generally Govtrack.us 'H.R. 23 (113th): Sanctity of Human Life Act'.

[107] Falk *Privacy, Due Process, and Morality: A Legal Analysis of Federal Fetal Personhood* 9.

[108] M Manian 'Lessons from personhood's defeat: Abortion restrictions and side effects on women's health' (2013) 74 *Ohio State LJ* 75 77; JF Will 'Beyond abortion: Why the personhood movement implicates reproductive choice' (2013) 39 *American Journal of Law & Medicine* 573 576; and Collins & Crockin (2012) *Reproductive Biomedicine Online* 690.

[109] Manian ((2013) *Ohio State LJ* 79–82) explains that personhood proposals can take the form of ballot initiatives or legislative proposals. Ballot initiatives must generally gather sufficient support by way of signatories. Once enough signatures have been obtained, a relevant personhood measure can be placed on a particular year's state ballot where state citizens can vote on whether they approve or not. Majority approval would allow for the adoption of the personhood initiative.

[110] Collins & Crockin (2012) *Reproductive Biomedicine Online* 689.

failed; during 2010–2011 personhood measures were defeated in Alabama, Arizona, Kansas, Oklahoma, Mississippi, North Dakota and South Carolina.[111] However, these defeats seemed to have fuelled efforts and in 2012 11 states introduced personhood bills,[112] and Manian points out that all failed.[113] Yet, the drive to extend personhood is unrelenting and, as of May 2016, eight personhood bills have been introduced in a number of state legislatures.[114]

After perusing commentary on various positions taken in a number of states, it seems that personhood initiatives are unsuccessful because they fail to attract sufficient support at the grass roots level.[115] There is very little research available indicating what it is about personhood measures that shuns public support generally. In fact, at firs glance, this wholesale resistance is viewed as a peculiar response. Manian explains that, given that the United States has a strong anti-termination-of-pregnancy climate, one would expect personhood measures to succeed, especially since the collective purpose of the movement is focused on outlawing the termination of pregnancies.[116]

Manian[117] theorises[118] that the concern over personhood initiatives lies in the fact that these initiatives have far-reaching implications that go far beyond the issue of termination of pregnancies. She concedes that any enacted personhood measures are likely to result in non-therapeutic pregnancy termination being rendered criminal,[119] but she argues that 'the likely reason for the failure of personhood proposals, even in states extremely hostile to abortion rights, lies in this link between personhood legislation and healthcare'.[120] If enacted, personhood laws could hold implications for women's wider reproductive health concerns by negating their lawful access to contraception[121] and infertility

[111] Collins & Crockin (2012) *Reproductive Biomedicine Online* 690.

[112] Collins & Crockin (2012) *Reproductive Biomedicine Online* 690.

[113] Manian (2013) *Ohio State LJ* 82. However, see Personhood USA 'North Dakota Measure 1' available at http://www.personhoodusa.com/campaigns/north-dakota-measure-1-2014 (accessed on 22 April 2014) where the organisation claimed victory in North Dakota because the state legislature was the firs of all states to pass a personhood amendment allowing for the unborn to be considered persons in that state. The sense of victory did not last long because North Dakota's citizens voted on this amendment in November 2014 and it was defeated.

[114] See Resolve 'Personhood legislation: Personhood bills and ballot initiatives' available at http://www.resolve.org/get-involved/the-center-for-infertility-justice/personhood-legislation/?referrer=https://www.google.co.za/ (accessed on 11 May 2016).

[115] Collins & Crockin (2012) *Reproductive Biomedicine Online* 690 and Armstrong & Hsieh 'The "personhood" movement is anti-life' 5–7.

[116] Manian (2013) *Ohio State LJ* 77. Manian (83) points out that in 2011, 1 100 reproductive health-related provisions were introduced to state legislatures, of that 68% related to restricting access to termination-of-pregnancy services. The 'anti-abortion' sentiment led to a record-breaking 92 termination-of-pregnancy restrictions being enacted.

[117] Manian (2013) *Ohio State LJ* 86.

[118] The term 'theorises' is used because even Manian ((2013) *Ohio State LJ* 99) admits that one cannot conclusively list the reasons why personhood measures have failed to the extent that they have.

[119] Manian (2013) *Ohio State LJ* 87–9.

[120] Manian (2013) *Ohio State LJ* 86.

[121] Manian (2013) *Ohio State LJ* 89. Contraceptive methods such as intrauterine devices, the conventional pill and 'morning after' pill all prevent fertilised eggs from attaching to the uterus wall.

treatments, especially in respect of *in vitro* fertilisation.[122] Manian[123] points out that women's decision-making powers while pregnant, in respect of lifestyle choices and medical treatment options, may be substantially curbed by consideration of what is best for prenatal persons. Also, all miscarriages would have to be investigated[124] and pregnant women may face increased forced detention as a means of curtailing unfavourable behaviour during pregnancy.[125] Manian argues that personhood laws could also have implications for family-law principles to the extent that partners would be entitled to legitimately exert significan control over their pregnant partners, and women's bodies may possibly become material to parental rights disputes in divorce proceedings.[126] She goes so far as to implicate employers in the aftermath of personhood laws:

> Given the risk of substantial tort liability under a legal regime granting personhood to embryos, employers may argue that the embryo-protection policies are justifie to ensure that female workers do not cause injury to their future children while performing the functions of their jobs.[127]

Thus, where personhood is define from the moment of fertilisation these contraceptive methods will be viewed as being the cause of death of a person. In this respect also see Will (2013) *American Journal of Law & Medicine* 592–3, whose contribution supports this contention. Will goes into more detail about the impracticality of these laws. He explains (596–7) that it will be impossible to implement these sorts of laws in respect of contraceptive intake because hormonal contraceptives use multiple methods to prevent conception. These methods include preventing ovulation, altering cervical mucus or uterine environments to prevent sperm penetration or travel or altering the uterus in such a way that it makes implantation of a fertilised egg impossible. Will (597) concludes that a women making use of contraceptives will never be able to conclusively determine which one of these methods prevented conception.

122 Will (2013) *American Journal of Law & Medicine* 592–3; 610–14 and Manian (2013) *Ohio State LJ* 89–2. Manian (91) explains that the very nature of *in vitro* fertilisation (the various processes involved) could lead to a number of criminal charges such as murder, abandonment and neglect. Criminal liability of this kind is highly probable because Manian explains (91) that *in vitro* fertilisation centres perform a number of processes such as implanting, donating, or discarding freshly retrieved and fertilised eggs, at times eggs are frozen for later use, donated to other patients or used for research purposes, or the eggs are eventually discarded. The concern over the impact of personhood measures on access to assisted reproduction is a deeply entrenched concern; Collins and Crockin ((2012) *Reproductive Biomedicine Online* 690–1) attribute Virginia's 2011 personhood initiative's failure to the fact that assisted reproduction patients and doctors fought the initiative on the basis that such provisions are harmful to patients receiving reproductive care. This 'health-care approach' might have proved successful because the personhood initiative failed.

123 Manian (2013) *Ohio State LJ* 93–9.

124 Will (2013) *American Journal of Law & Medicine* 590–1. Will explains that since personhood laws render fertilised eggs persons then all miscarriages would have to be investigated since it involves the death of a person.

125 Manian (2013) *Ohio State LJ* 95–6. Manian suggests that these concerns cannot be overstated; she argues that the United States already has a history of detaining pregnant women for unfavourable conduct during pregnancy and personhood laws would exacerbate the issue even further.

126 Manian (2013) *Ohio State LJ* 98.

127 Manian (2013) *Ohio State LJ* 98. It can also be argued that where 'embryo-protection policies' are not put in place, employers could face criminal liability should the work environment be hazardous enough to cause a miscarriage. However, see *International Union, Union Automobile, Aerospace and Agricultural Implement Workers of America v Johnson Controls* 499 US 187 where the Supreme Court of the United States found that excluding fertile women of reproductive age from

From the above considerations, it can be accepted that a reason for these personhood initiatives' widespread failures lies in the fact that these measures have far-reaching implications. Personhood measures directly and adversely impact on women and their families, health-care providers and employers in cases where women are employed. Going further, the above discussed implications cannot be viewed as a closed list. Only if, or once, personhood laws take root can one begin to determine the full extent of the measures' reach into the lives of a community and the personal spheres of women and girls of reproductive age. Suffice it to say the potential foreseeable consequences seem to provide a sufficiently frightening view, resulting in the extension of personhood's defeat.

7.5 IMPLICATIONS OF PERSONHOOD MEASURES FOR EXTENDING PERSONHOOD IN SOUTH AFRICA

Relating finding on the United States' experience to Pillay's suggestion of extending personhood to the unborn, it is noticeable that, even in a jurisdiction where foetal personhood exists, there is still a very persistent avoidance of extending full legal subjectivity to the unborn at any point prior to birth. Drawing on De Freitas and Myburgh's arguments, even with the presence of scientifi evidence that the unborn are human beings, the complete removal of permissive termination-of-pregnancy laws is unlikely in the foreseeable future.

What this chapter demonstrates is that extending full legal status to the unborn on the grounds that they are human cannot be legitimately limited to rendering the termination of pregnancy illegal or protecting the unborn from termination-of-pregnancy decisions. It will inevitably render the unborn 'super-persons' with more rights than born persons and no existing obligations to others. The unborn are rendered super-persons because the duties to the unborn are not like any other person's duties in that the unborn can lay claim to another's body for necessary development. This arguably permits third-party access to ensure optimal foetal development and law would sanction this. Also, in all the hype surrounding the personhood measures, there is no discourse on holding the unborn liable for threatening the life or health of the women who carry them, or rendering the unborn liable for their contribution to necessitating caesarean-section deliveries or emergency invasive treatments, thus demonstrating the one-sidedness of these measures.[128] These are absurd potential outcomes which ignite adversarialism and correspond with Pillay, De Freitas and Myburgh's extension of protection of the unborn as persons or as human beings.

To date, the personhood movement has failed in its endeavour to be considered an effective means of protecting the unborn, because obtaining such protection comes at an invasively high cost. This failure may be an indication that there is consensus that there are less extreme means of achieving the ends of prenatal

employment on the grounds that exposure to certain chemicals might prove hazardous to future children was discriminatory and such a policy was found indefensible.

[128] Interestingly, none of the authors considered in this discussion engage with Thomson's notion that granting rights to the unborn will not necessarily guarantee the use of those rights; see generally JJ Thomson 'A defense of abortion' (1971) 1 *Philosophy & Public Affairs* 47 and Chapter Six for an extensive discussion of Thomson's position.

protection or optimal foetal development. The question of whether personhood initiatives will secure healthy pregnancies or healthy pregnancy outcomes cannot be answered here because none of the initiatives have taken root. However, the wholesale rejection of the movement may be an indication that personhood measures will not effectively achieve that end.

Linking personhood initiative finding to the broader project of addressing the tension between pregnant women's reproductive autonomy and foetal interests to continued development, Manian recognises that 'personhood laws seem likely to instigate increased investigation, prosecution, and control over pregnant women's autonomy for the sake of protecting her fetus'.[129] Manian considers these measures as increasingly adversarialist because, as the situation in the United States currently stands, women are facing these issues without the application of personhood measures.[130] This is discussed in the chapters that follow. These finding specificall support the argument that a separate-entities approach to pregnancy introduces pregnancy adversarialism or intensifie already existing tensions, rather than addressing pregnancy-related issues in a way that supports the notion of pregnancy being a shared experience between two inseparable entities, both with interests that need advancing.[131] These finding contradict Pillay's notion that extending legal subjectivity assists in resolving conflicts [132]

7.6 CONCLUDING REMARKS

Using *Roe* and the common-law born-alive rule as the starting point, full legal subjectivity in the United States vests in those who are born alive and these persons are constitutionally protected. This is a fairly clear position but, when pregnancy is brought into the equation, a number of issues arise. Status law during pregnancy is a contested issue in the United States. This position is linked to the influentia role of reproductive politics and its characteristically polarised constituency, made up of anti-abortion lobby groups arguing for full legal subjectivity for

[129] Manian (2013) *Ohio State LJ* 97–6. Also see generally, VE Beetly 'Mississippi Initiative 26: Personhood and the criminalization of intentional and unintentional acts by pregnant women' (2011) 81 *Supra* 55.

[130] See LM Paltrow & J Flavin 'Arrests of and forced interventions on pregnant women in the United States, 1973–2005: Implications for women's legal status and public health' (2013) 38 *Journal of Health Politics, Policy and Law* 299.

[131] There are a number of supportive structures available that assist in ensuring healthy pregnancies and pregnancy outcomes which are being employed and do not render the pregnancy relationship adversarialist. See LM Sagrestano & R Finerman 'Pregnancy and prenatal care: A reproductive justice perspective' in JC Chrisler (ed) *Reproductive Justice: A Global Concern* (2012) 201–30. The authors highlight increased access to health insurance for low income families, improved access to preconception health which involves consumer awareness, preventive visits, interventions for any identifie risks, interconception care, increased public health programmes and strategies and regular monitoring of improvements. These efforts improve knowledge about nutrition and healthy lifestyle options before, during and after pregnancy and birth. Women get increased access to diagnostic tests during prenatal checkups which aim at identifying and addressing any serious risks to the pregnant woman or foetus. The authors conclude their chapter by emphasising that access to services will do little unless women have choices concerning preferred health-care models and service providers.

[132] Pillay (2010) *Stell LR* 236.

the unborn on the one hand, and women-centred organisations pushing forward to preserve reproductive autonomy and the right to terminate pregnancies on the other.

Anti-abortion efforts focus on reversing *Roe,* while at the same time using *Roe* to advance their aims of extending legal subjectivity to the unborn. Substantial effort is invested in bringing the unborn to the law's attention via personhood measures and other legal developments that contribute to extending the status of the unborn. While personhood measures have failed, the anti-abortion lobbyists' efforts have paid off to a certain extent, when one considers the diminished role of the born-alive rule. The born-alive rule was the sole criterion for determining who counted for the purposes of law, particularly with regard to the protection of life. However, the intersection of advances in science and medical technology and reproductive politics diluted birth as being relevant and turned to the 'human being' criterion as a driving factor for extending status to the unborn.

As a result of this development, the concept of foetal personhood comes into the picture, as a form of personhood which is not constitutionally informed but still attracting independent legal consideration. The fact that different forms of personhood are at play in one pregnant body indicates that the separate-entities approach to pregnancy is applied. This is evident at both the federal and the state levels.

Drawing on all these findings legal status may thus be described as being stratifie in the United States. Those who are already born are vested with constitutional personhood and these individuals receive constitutional rights and protection, while those already conceived but yet to be born are vested with foetal personhood, which attracts only extra-constitutional protection. Also, the extent of the personhood strata varies, because the unborn's status is fluid [133] in that it depends on the state and the statute involved. However, the chapters to follow will show that it is not only the unborn's status that is flui but also pregnant women's, because they are pregnant. Fluidity creates uncertainty and uncertainty opens the doors to adversarialism.

Also, concluding on Pillay, De Freitas and Myburgh's proposals for extending the fullest possible protection to the unborn as a separate entity, there may be a preference for adopting less extreme means of achieving the ends of foetal protection than definin the unborn as full legal subjects, whether from the moment of conception or of viability. Understanding the unborn as human beings or persons in law has implications for more than mere termination-of-pregnancy issues, and even in a highly charged foetal rights arena such measures are consistently avoided. This notion of less extreme means will be built on in Part Four, where pregnancy, as a whole, is contextualised. Contextualising a pregnancy requires us to take note of the embodied relationship between women and the unborn, and this approach shows that by advancing women's rights the unborn's interests will be advanced too; therefore, according full legal status to the unborn is not necessary.

[133] See Meredith *Policing Pregnancy* 181, who specificall uses this term to describe the status of the unborn in the United States.

An environment for pregnancy adversarialism is already established in the United States despite avoiding the extension of full status to the unborn. This is evidenced by the fact that the unborn are granted foetal personhood and third parties are using this form of personhood to navigate women's rights and autonomy ambitions. The chapters that follow look at how this construction of status works out in the identifie areas of concern, being violence against pregnant women or the unborn and substance abuse during pregnancy constituting child abuse.

Chapter 8

FETICIDE AND FOETAL HOMICIDE

8.1 INTRODUCTION

Du Plessis[1] and Kruuse[2] both suggest enacting South African legislation to criminalise violence that terminates prenatal life. While each author proposes different strategies to achieve that end, both propose strongly that the unborn be considered separate victims of crime under feticide, thereby advancing the separate-entities approach.[3] This discussion evaluates whether Du Plessis and Kruuse offer sound legal responses to violence that terminates prenatal life by looking at the position in the United States, where measures are already in place to address this area of concern. Not all measures in the United States adopt a separate-entities approach to addressing violence that terminates prenatal life.[4] However, in order to test the effectiveness of Kruuse and Du Plessis's feticide proposals, only those states that adopt the separate-entities approach will be considered.

First, this chapter will look at how the United States has approached the issue of violence that terminates prenatal life, the theoretical soundness of the adopted approaches and whether these approaches achieve the ends of healthy pregnancies and healthy pregnancy outcomes. Violence that terminates prenatal life has received attention at both the federal and state levels. However, neither legislature has adopted a unifie approach to the issue. Perusal of various codes across the United States reveals that individuated prenatal protection from violence varies according to jurisdiction.[5]

8.2 APPROACHES TO VIOLENCE THAT TERMINATES PRENATAL LIFE

To start, there is no uniform title allocated to the crime of terminating prenatal life through violent third-party conduct. Some refer to the termination of prenatal life

[1] GA Du Plessis 'Feticide: Creating a statutory crime in South African law' (2013) 24 *Stell LR* 73.

[2] HJ Kruuse 'Fetal "rights"? The need for a unifie approach to the fetus in the context of feticide' (2009) 72 *THRHR* 126.

[3] See Chapter Six, para 6.3.2 for a detailed discussion.

[4] See AS Murphy 'A survey of state fetal homicide laws and their potential applicability to pregnant women who harm their own fetuses' (2014) 89 *Indiana LJ* 847 896; Murphy explains that both the states of Colorado and Connecticut do not recognise the unborn as separate victims of violent crimes. However, see J Flavin *Our Bodies, Our Crimes: The Policing of Women's Reproduction in America* (2009) 100, who states that 'dozens' of states adopt this approach which generally imposes harsher penalties rather than creating two separate victims. The fact that a separate-entities approach is not unanimously adopted might be an indication that it does not adequately respond to violence against pregnant women. More on this is discussed below.

[5] This is in line with the fact that, as pointed out in Chapter Seven, the unborn's status is flui depending on the state involved.

as murder, feticide or 'fetal homicide'. For instance, s 187(a) of the Californian Penal Code define murder as 'the unlawful killing of a human being, or a fetus, with malice aforethought'. Indiana uses the term 'feticide'; according to s 35-42-1-6 of the Indiana Code, if a person knowingly or intentionally terminates a human pregnancy other than to produce a live birth or to remove a dead foetus, that person commits feticide. The Kentucky Penal Code uses the term 'fetal homicide' and makes provision for 'fetal homicide' in the first second, third and fourth degrees.[6] At the federal level, the Unborn Victims of Violence Act of 2004 does not designate any title to the crime of terminating prenatal life through violence. The Act merely states that where a person, while committing a federal crime, causes the death of or injury to an unborn, that person is 'guilty of a separate offence under this section', in addition to the offence applicable to the original federal crime.[7]

Aside from the issue of allocating different titles, there is no uniform approach concerning when protection of the unborn vests. Some states offer protection from the moment of conception,[8] while others refer to protection from the moment of quickening[9]

[6] See ss 507A.020; 507A.030; 507A.040; and 507A.050 of the Kentucky Statutes respectively.

[7] Section (a)(1). Another method of extending penal provisions to include the unborn is to include them in the definitio of 'person' for purposes of criminal law provisions thus making it possible to commit a number of criminal offenses against the unborn. An example of this can be found in 'Alexa's Law' of the state of Kansas (see s 21-5419 of the Kansas Criminal Code). Alexa's Law amends the statutory definitio of 'person' or 'human being' to include the unborn for purposes of capital murder, murder, murder in the second degree, vehicular homicide, culpable homicide and battery in its various forms (see s 21-5419(c) of the Kansas Criminal Code).

[8] Section 16-5-80(a) of the Code of Georgia Annotated provides that for purposes of this section pertaining to feticide, 'the term "unborn child" means a member of the species homo sapiens at any stage of development who is carried in the womb'.

[9] Section 782.09(1) of Florida Statutes Annotated provides that the unborn must be 'quick' in order for a charge of murder to stand against an accused. However, there is no consensus among states concerning the definitio of 'quick child'. For instance, in Florida 'quick child' is deemed synonymous with 'viable child', see s 782.071(2) of Florida Statutes Annotated which provides that 'a fetus is viable when it becomes capable of meaningful life outside the womb through standard medical measures'. Generally, quickening occurs before viability. Quickening refers to the point in foetal development when a pregnant woman can feel the unborn stir, this can occur as early as 16 weeks' gestation, see Begin before Birth 'Fetal development' available at http://www.beginbeforebirth.org/in-the-womb/fetal-development (accessed on 19 May 2016). Yet, a foetus reaches viability from roughly 20 weeks' gestation (depending on social and economic circumstances of the pregnant woman concerned), see C Pickles 'Personhood: Proving the significanc of the born-alive rule with reference to medical knowledge of foetal viability' (2013) 24 *Stell LR* 146 for a discussion of the difficulties faced when attempting to pinpoint foetal viability. Contrary to Florida, Michigan follows the traditional understanding of quickening, according to s 750.322 the 'wilful killing of an unborn quick child' is prohibited. The section does not provide a definitio for 'quick child' but the Court of Appeals of Michigan in *People v Nixon* 42 Mich App 332 (1972) 335 fn 3, van Valkenburg J, following the common-law position, found that a quick child is one that 'indicates signs of life by way of fetal movements which can be felt by the mother' during the fourth or possibly as late as the fift month of pregnancy. Rhode Island also uses the 'quick child' criterion but attaches a different definitio to that term. Section 11-23-3(a) of the General Laws of Rhode Island Annotated prohibits the wilful killing of an unborn quick child and sub-s (c) states that '[f]or the purposes of this section, "quick child" means an unborn child whose heart is beating, who is experiencing electronically measurable brain waves, who is discernibly moving, and who is so far developed and matured as to be capable of surviving the trauma of birth with the aid of usual medical care and facilities

or viability.[10] It is noteworthy that protection tends to correlate with the point in gestation that the unborn is considered to be a human being or person for purposes of that particular criminal provision. Despite the divergent positions, the most popular approach is to offer protection from the moment of conception, and at least 23 states currently do so.[11]

Also, most states have explicitly excluded the lawful termination of pregnancies from the ambit of crimes against the unborn.[12] It should be noted that state legislation does not have to explicitly exempt the lawful termination of pregnancies, since the right to terminate a pregnancy is constitutionally protected in terms of *Roe v Wade*.[13] Any legislation infringing that right cannot be enforced, since the constitutional position as set out in *Roe* stands supreme in this instance.[14]

There are also divergent legislative approaches pertaining to whether pregnant women can be held liable for conduct that causes the termination of a prenatal life, aside from those instances of lawful termination of pregnancies. The federal Unborn Victims of Violence Act excludes a woman as a possible perpetrator of violence against her own foetus. Subsection (c)(1) of the Act simply states that the Act will not be 'construed to permit the prosecution . . . of any woman with respect to her unborn child'. This Act can be interpreted as providing the comprehensive exemption of pregnant women for any harmful conduct towards their pregnancies. Murphy terms these exemptions 'maternal exceptions'.[15] However, not all states have followed the federal example of including an explicit all-encompassing 'maternal exception', and Murphy[16] explains that the state legislative silence on the issue allows for the inclusion of a woman as a perpetrator against her own foetus via broad interpretation of the relevant statutes.[17]

---

available in this state'. This definitio seems to have meshed quickening with viability by requiring movement and survivability.

[10] For instance, s 2-103(b) of the Maryland Code, Criminal Law provides that 'a prosecution may be instituted for murder or manslaughter of a viable fetus'. Section 20-209 of the Maryland Code, Health—General define viability as that stage when, 'in the best medical judgment of the attending physician based on the particular facts of the case before the physician, there is a reasonable likelihood of the fetus's sustained survival outside the womb'. It should be noted though, that the term 'viability' differs from state to state, see Pickles (2013) *Stell LR* 146 for a discussion of these diverging approaches.

[11] See National Conference of State Legislatures 'Fetal homicide state laws' (March 2015) available at http://www.ncsl.org/research/health/fetal-homicide-state-laws.aspx (accessed on 14 July 2016).

[12] For those states which explicitly exclude lawful termination of pregnancies see National Conference of State Legislatures 'Fetal homicide state laws'. The federal Unborn Victims of Violence Act of 2004 also excludes lawful termination of pregnancies from the its ambit, see s 919a(c)(1).

[13] 93 S Ct 705 (1973) (*Roe*).

[14] See Chapter Seven, para 7.2 for a discussion on the hierarchy of laws in the United States.

[15] Murphy (2014) *Indiana LJ* 850.

[16] See generally Murphy (2014) *Indiana LJ* 847.

[17] In fact, Paltrow and Flavin, from National Advocates for Pregnant Women, studied the incidence of women facing criminal charges and prosecution in respect of their own pregnancies and report 413 cases of pregnant women being criminally charged for certain conduct during pregnancy. The authors found that in most of these cases women were facing this treatment despite the fact that there was no legislative authority for it. Further, their study highlights 200 more reported cases since 2005.

Two such examples are the states of Utah and Oklahoma. Utah only exempts certain conduct of pregnant women when it comes to specifi aspects relevant to pregnancy. According to s 76-5-20(3) of the Utah Criminal Code, a person will not be held criminally responsible for causing the death of an unborn child in cases where the death is a result of a refusal to consent to medical treatment or caesarean-section delivery, or the death is a result of failing to follow medical advice. Subsection (4)(a) also exempts women in cases where the death of the unborn is a result of a 'criminally negligent or reckless act of the woman'. However, sub-s (4)(b), read together with sub-s (1)(b), provides that a woman can be found guilty of criminal homicide 'of her own unborn child' in cases where she intentionally terminates the pregnancy beyond the realm of the lawful termination-of-pregnancy laws in Utah.[18] In Oklahoma a different approach is adopted, for purposes of homicide. Section 691.D of the Oklahoma Statutes provides: 'Under no circumstances shall the mother of the unborn child be prosecuted for causing the death of the unborn child unless the mother has committed a crime that caused the death of the unborn child'. Thus, aside from intentional conduct against prenatal life, in Oklahoma a woman can be held criminally liable in cases where her conduct is regarded as criminally negligent.[19]

8.3 THE UNITED STATES APPROACH IS THEORETICALLY UNSOUND

On the face of it, the notion of criminal liability for terminating prenatal life through violence can be understood as a legislative commitment to valuing and preserving the intrinsic worth of the unborn in so far as they are understood to be human beings. Also, leaving the right to terminate a pregnancy intact and available to women, despite foetal protection measures being in place, gives the *impression* that there is a commitment to securing the advancement of reproductive autonomy not to bear children.[20] Further, it gives the *impression* that women's rights to

---

See LM Paltrow & J Flavin 'Arrests of and forced interventions on pregnant women in the United States, 1973–2005: Implications for women's legal status and public health' (2013) 38 *Journal of Health Politics, Policy and Law* 299 320; 335. The 413 cases are not limited to instances where women have been charged for homicide in relation to their foetuses but include various charges linked to child abuse, dealing in drugs and so on. The authors state (321), 'our study documents hundreds of arrests or equivalent deprivations of liberty, with the majority relying on interpretations and applications of criminal laws that were never intended to be used to punish women in relationship to their own pregnancies'. Though most of these cases relate to child abuse or endangerment (Paltrow & Flavin (2013) *Journal of Health Politics, Policy and Law* 321) they prove Murphy's point that explicit exceptions need to be made where the unborn are considered separate entities in law.

[18] This provision is identifie as a legislative development of the common-law position regarding a woman's criminal liability in instances where she unlawfully terminates her pregnancy; see generally S Visser 'Prosecuting women for participating in illegal abortions: Undermining gender equality and the effectiveness of state police power' (2011) 13 *Journal of Law & Family Studies* 171.

[19] Also see Murphy (2014) *Indiana LJ* 862, where Murphy reaches the same conclusion.

[20] Although it must be noted that these protection measures are being encouraged by groups which seek to eventually render termination of pregnancy illegal, thus the underlying motives make the realisation of reproductive autonomy unachievable. This being the case, the impression is purposefully created to reduce resistance to these sorts of protective laws.

continue through pregnancy without interference are also being protected. This is what Kruuse and Du Plessis argue will be the case.[21] However, looking at how these commitments translate into lived experiences of pregnant women and looking at these two commitments in relation to one another highlights inherent flaws which emerge as a direct result of disembodying the unborn from pregnant women.

8.3.1 Termination-of-pregnancy provisions

Contradictions are apparent in relation to the termination-of-pregnancy laws. The most obvious fla relates to those legislative provisions that protect the unborn from fatal violence from the moment of conception or earlier, while *Roe*, which also regulates the termination of a pregnancy, only allows states to act on their compelling interests in the unborn from the moment of viability.[22] If each area of law is being driven by the same underlying motive (being the value or the humanity that the unborn represent) it is not clear how protection can vest at different times in gestation when both acts can be viewed as factually violating that value.[23] Ultimately, there is no cohesive, theoretical basis for adopting this approach. This very issue was highlighted when discussing Du Plessis[24] and it seems to remain an unaddressed issue in the United States.

The only theoretical basis for permitting protection from the moment of conception that comes to mind is to understand that pregnant women have the right to determine the fate of their own pregnancies while third parties do not, thus rendering the issue of gestation irrelevant. The issue of gestation would be considered irrelevant because the harm inflicte would be viewed as a violation of the pregnant woman's choice in relation to her pregnancy and not in relation to the unborn's individuated interests. Adopting this approach requires that the relevant statutory crime move away from viewing the unborn as separate from pregnant women. This would result in denying the unborn the status of separate victims and would require the unborn to be re-embodied into the concept of pregnancy. However, this is not the case under these foetal protection measures.

The fla of extending protection to any point in a pregnancy becomes particularly contradictory in cases where women can be held criminally liable for the termination of their own pre-viable pregnancies. Liability persists despite the fact that the right to terminate a pregnancy still stands and the United States Constitution demands the availability of pregnancy terminations at the request of a

[21] See the discussion in Chapter Six, para 6.3.2.

[22] *Roe* 732.

[23] For instance, in *State v Merrill* 450 NW 2d 318 (Minn 1990) (*Merrill*) Merrill murdered a woman who was one month pregnant and he was charged for committing foetal homicide since the crime was define in a way that included non-viable pregnancies. The court (322) went on to recognise that *Roe* identifie a compelling state interest in the potentiality of human life that the unborn represent and use this interest to justify providing statutory protection to the unborn from the moment of conception in the form of foetal homicide statutes. The court found that as long as these provisions do not negatively implicate women's privacy rights then the legitimacy of the foetal protection measures stand.

[24] See Chapter Six, para 6.3.2.

woman provided that the termination relates to a pre-viable foetus or embryo.[25] Under these instances, the perceived commitment to advancing female reproductive autonomy is no longer present and foetal interests take centre stage, even at the cost of women's rights. *Roe* held that the regulation of termination of pregnancy in the United States is premised on the state's interest in preserving and protecting women's health (in addition to that of protecting prenatal life),[26] thus termination-of-pregnancy regulations do not aim to punish those women who function outside the accepted regulations.[27] This is in line with the fact that there is no common-law precedent for women being held criminally liable for adverse pregnancy outcomes as a result of prenatal conduct.[28] However, despite this, the State of Utah has passed what Visser has termed the 'self-abortion homicide provision'.[29]

According to s 76-5-201(1)(a) of the Utah Criminal Code, a person commits criminal homicide if he or she causes the death of another human being, including an 'unborn child, at any stage of development'. Subsection (1)(b) provides that this crime will not stand in the case of lawful termination of pregnancies and sub-s 4(b) attributes criminal liability to women who intentionally terminate their pregnancies outside the bounds of the lawful termination-of-pregnancy provisions. Consequently, these provisions effectively render unlawful pregnancy terminations performed by women on themselves as the crime of homicide from the moment of fertilisation.[30] Oddly, the lawful termination of a pregnancy is not termed justifiabl homicide nor is it considered a defence against a homicide charge. This scenario creates the impression that women's punishment relates more to the fact that they fail to conform to the law's regulation over them rather than by their failure to respect prenatal life. This impression is created because the termination-of-pregnancy laws remain in place.

Visser understands this provision to be an attack on women living in Utah and views it as one of many attempts to outlaw the termination of pregnancies.[31] Visser argues further that provisions such as these overlook 'the Supreme Court's decisions in *Roe v Wade* and *Planned Parenthood v Casey*, which deal expressly with women's autonomy and place a high value on protecting this autonomy, at

[25] *Roe* 732.

[26] *Roe* 732.

[27] See J Seymour *Childbirth and the Law* (2000) 147–8 who argues that from an historical perspective, self-induced termination of pregnancies were not crimes and women were never held criminally liable for making use of illegal termination-of-pregnancy services. In this respect, Seymour explains that the legal regulation of termination of pregnancies was aimed at illegal service providers whose dangerous methods were likely to place vulnerable women at increased risk. Also see Visser (2011) *Journal of Law & Family Studies* 175–6 whose study confirm this position.

[28] See G Brown 'Bei Bei Shuai: Pregnancy, murder, and mayhem in Indiana' (2014) 17 *Journal of Gender, Race & Justice* 221 240–5.

[29] See generally Visser (2011) *Journal of Law & Family Studies* 171.

[30] Bearing in mind that a pregnancy only constitutes such when implantation occurs, technically this crime cannot apply to every stage of development, especially in respect of mere fertilised eggs. Technically, there is no termination of a pregnancy. See the Inter-American Court of Human Rights in *Case of Artavia Murillo et al ('in vitro fertilization') v Costa Rica* (2012).

[31] Visser (2011) *Journal of Law & Family Studies* 185.

least prior to fetal viability'.[32] In fact, Visser argues that these sorts of provisions manipulate the judiciary into placing prenatal life at any stage of development before that of women.[33] Women's criminal liability in relation to their own pregnancies will be discussed further below. The point of this discussion is to highlight the flaw inherent in offering protection from the moment of conception in relation to termination-of-pregnancy rights generally.

Flaws remain even in those cases where legislation extends protection to the unborn from the moment of viability onwards. On the face of it, these foetal protection measures are in line with the state's compelling interest in viable prenatal life as identifie in *Roe*.[34] However, a contradiction exists in relation to the diverging approaches each adopts: Foetal protection measures render the unborn separate victims of crime, thus employing the separate-entities approach to pregnancy,[35] while *Roe* can be interpreted as representing the not-one-but-not-two approach[36] (not-one/not-two approach) to pregnancy.[37]

The root of the issue lies in the misinterpretation of *Roe* as creating separate entities of the unborn during gestation.[38] Paltrow and Flavin argue that the underlying legal theory being advanced for justifying the protection of the unborn stems from the fact that the unborn are viewed as separate entities from viability onwards and the purported authority for this lies in a misinterpretation of *Roe*.[39] After examining a number of cases,[40] Paltrow and Flavin argue that prosecutors, hospital attorneys and even judges hold or present understandings that *Roe* 'established that viable fetuses must be treated as legal persons fully separate from the pregnant woman'.[41] (Footnotes omitted.)

The principles stemming from *Roe* cannot be relied on for protection from fatal criminal conduct from the moment of viability if the basis for that position is

---

[32] Visser (2011) *Journal of Law & Family Studies* 185.

[33] Visser (2011) *Journal of Law & Family Studies* 184.

[34] According to *Roe*, the state has a compelling interest that can only be acted on once the unborn is viable, 727.

[35] Seymour (*Childbirth in Law* 198) disagrees with this assertion, however the basis for him taking that position has changed since his 2000 publication. It is Seymour's contention that the judiciary reluctantly viewed pregnant women as separate entities in the context of prenatal homicide laws but since 2000, however, as described above, legislation specificall regards the unborn separate victims of crime thus explicitly following the notion that the unborn are separate entities from the pregnant women carrying them.

[36] See Chapter Five, para 5.3.1 for an extensive discussion of the concept of the not-one/not-two approach to pregnancy. Briefl , this approach recognises the unborn as distinctive entities but maintains the embodied nature of pregnancy by recognising the relationship the unborn share with pregnant women carrying them. This approach views a pregnancy as embodying two entities but the special relationship also renders a foetus and pregnant woman one entity. Also see Seymour *Childbirth and the Law* 199–202.

[37] The same conundrum presents itself in Kruuse's proposal for the crime of feticide in South Africa where the author used principles stemming from the Choice on Termination of Pregnancy Act 92 of 1996 to justify separate victimhood for the unborn. See Chapter Six, para 6.3.2.

[38] Paltrow & Flavin (2013) *Journal of Health Politics, Policy and Law* 322.

[39] Paltrow & Flavin (2013) *Journal of Health Politics, Policy and Law* 325.

[40] The authors cite roughly 10 cases to illustrate their point; see Paltrow & Flavin (2013) *Journal of Health Politics, Policy and Law* 325.

[41] Paltrow & Flavin (2013) *Journal of Health Politics, Policy and Law* 325.

founded on the separate-entities approach. To start with, the court explicitly found that the unborn are not persons under the United States Constitution,[42] thus plainly rejecting the notion that a pregnant woman represents two separate legal entities for the duration of a pregnancy. However, the court went on to recognise value in the potential that prenatal life represents at the point of viability onwards, and on that basis limited women's rights to terminate their pregnancies.[43] This limitation does not serve as an absolute limitation on women's rights, since the court found that a woman cannot be prevented from terminating a viable pregnancy in the case where her life or health is at risk.[44] This serves as recognition of the need to protect the potential that a viable foetus represents, but in relation to the pregnant woman carrying it, thus adopting the not-one/not-two approach.[45] This is comparable to the South African position regarding the Choice on Termination of Pregnancy Act[46] (Choice Act).

8.3.2 Women's criminal liability regarding their own pregnancies

Another fla identifie in legislative provisions that seek to protect pregnancies from violence relates to the comprehensive exemption of pregnant women from the ambit of criminal liability, despite identifying the unborn as entities separate from the women carrying them. If the purpose of feticide, foetal homicide or homicide is to protect prenatal life as an important state interest (whether from the moment of conception, quickening or viability), then it is unclear how pregnant women's intentional or negligent conduct can be justifiabl excluded in the context of the separate-entities approach.[47]

Comprehensive exemption of women can be viewed as violating the value vested in the unborn as the separate entities created by these criminal provisions. Most of these provisions defin the unborn as persons or human beings, and it is on this basis that they are protected under the particular homicide, feticide or foetal homicide statute.[48] However, exempting a woman in relation to her own foetus leads to the position that the foetus is not valued solely because it is a person or human being but rather the value of the foetus is determined by considering which party is asserting some form of relationship with the foetus. For instance, if the scenario involves a woman's violent conduct in relation to her own foetus, despite the fact that the unborn is a human being or person, no criminal liability will vest. This suggests that the unborn, in relation to the woman carrying it, is vested with very little, if any, value at all, thereby creating a category of

---

[42] *Roe* 729.

[43] *Roe* 732.

[44] *Roe* 732.

[45] For a contrary view see JR Schroedel, P Fiber & BD Snyder 'Women's rights and fetal personhood in criminal law' (2000) 7 *Duke Journal of Gender Law & Policy* 89 91–2. They identify *Roe* as treating pregnant women and the unborn as separate entities, whereas Paltrow and Flavin (2013) *Journal of Health Politics, Policy and Law* 325 and Seymour *Childbirth and the Law* 177 support the notion that *Roe* does not create separate entities of pregnant women.

[46] Also see the discussion in Chapter Five, para 5.3.1.

[47] This too was identifie as an issue when considering Du Plessis' proposal for feticide laws in South Africa. See Chapter Six, para 6.3.2.

[48] See discussion in para 8.2.

human being that is valueless. This is not viewed as an application of the not-one/not-two approach, because the value of the unborn is wholly overlooked when considered in relation to pregnant women and the not-one/not-two approach sees more in a pregnant woman than just the woman concerned. If the scenario involves a third-party's violent conduct in relation to the unborn, criminal liability will vest. This suggests that the foetus, in relation to a third party, is comprehensively valued as a human being or person in the context of the homicide laws.

A consequence of this anomaly is that the value of the foetus as a person or human being is being determined only by the fact that a woman intends to continue with a pregnancy.[49] Thus, only where continuation of pregnancy is intended does the fact that the foetus represents a person or human become an influentia or definin factor in determining another's criminal liability. A further consequence leads to the position that, despite the foetal homicide laws expressing a separate-entities approach to pregnancy, in reality the separate-entities approach is applicable only to third parties, while the single-entity approach[50] is applied to pregnant women. This is quite contradictory to the premise of valuing the unborn on the basis of their humanity.

The stance described above is problematic. The unborn are not valued because they represent a wanted pregnancy, but they are valued because they represent humanity or, as per *Roe,*[51] 'potential human life'.[52] This statement is supported by the fact that women cannot simply elect to terminate late pregnancies because they no longer intend to be pregnant. Restrictions are placed on women's freedom in this regard, and these restrictions are identifie as relating to the value the unborn represent.[53] Thus, termination-of-pregnancy laws still extend protection to the unborn, regardless of women's intentions during late pregnancy. This suggests that the unborn are valued in and of themselves once they have reached a certain point in gestation. Nevertheless, as a result of applying the separate-entities approach in the context of violence that terminates pregnancies there has been a failure to adequately articulate this value into a legal principle that can be soundly applied.

Seymour discusses the issue of excluding women from feticide or foetal homicide provisions at length and considers a number of cases decided across the

[49] For instance, if a woman decides not to continue with a pregnancy, she can terminate her pregnancy legally or inflic trauma upon herself to terminate her pregnancy, and this does not receive the attention of foetal protection measures. However, where she continues a pregnancy (by not having her pregnancy legally terminated or causing a self-induced termination) then the foetus is valued and others cannot interfere with the pregnancy continuation without attracting attention under foetal protection measures.

[50] The single-entity approach can be define as viewing a foetus as a non-existent entity, thus taking the view that pregnancy represents a single entity, being the woman only. For a detailed discussion, see Chapter Five, para 5.2.1 and Seymour *Childbirth and the Law* 182.

[51] 731.

[52] For a detailed discussion of the argument that unborn life represents a worth of its own see Chapter Three, para 3.5.2.

[53] In the context of the United States, *Roe* (732) placed this limitation on women from the moment of foetal viability since it is at this point that the unborn can survive independently.

United States which justify this stance.[54] He takes the position that, as long as women's interests are aligned with the state's interest in preserving prenatal life, there is no reason why third-party violence that terminates pregnancies should not be criminalised, regardless of when protection is extended in gestation.[55] Under this position it is argued that liberal termination-of-pregnancy laws should not be used as a ground for third parties to evade prosecution for harm inflicte against pregnant women which causes the termination of their pregnancies.[56] Seymour[57] explains that this approach allows for flexibilit according to context; in the case of a termination of pregnancy, the woman concerned is asserting her right not to bear children and the state has an interest in securing the healthy and unburdened realisation of that right. Whereas, in the context of protection from third-party violence, she is asserting her right to bear children and the state vests value in the unborn she carries.[58]

While the 'alignment of interests' argument offers a compelling view, it does not resolve the issue of the devalued position of the unborn when they are considered in relation to pregnant women. Also, if the focus is on the alignment of interests between women and the state, then the definitio of the crime should regard women as victims since their interests in the unborn are infringed but not those of the unborn.

Murphy views 'maternal exceptions' as the source of legitimacy for any legislation seeking to prohibit violent termination of prenatal life.[59] However, this discussion shows otherwise. Under the construction of the separate-entities approach, which expresses independent value in the unborn, the source of illegitimacy stems from 'maternal exceptions', since it should not matter who causes harm to the unborn in order to secure their protection as separate valued

[54] Seymour *Childbirth and the Law* 178–86. One such example is *Merrill.* In this case Merrill murdered a woman who was roughly a month into her pregnancy and was charged for the murder of both the pregnant woman and her embryo. It should be noted that at the time of this decision the State of Minnesota criminalised third-party violence that terminates a pregnancy at any point in gestation; such conduct was define as murder. Merrill argued that limiting criminal liability to third parties and not pregnant women or their attending physicians when performing termination of pregnancies is differential treatment. In essence he argued that similarly situated persons are treated dissimilarly. In response, the court held (321–2): 'The situations are not similar. The defendant who assaults a pregnant woman causing the death of the fetus she is carrying destroys the fetus without the consent of the woman. This is not the same as a woman who elects to have her pregnancy terminated by a person who is legally authorized to perform the act. In the case of abortion, the woman's choice and the doctor's actions are based on the woman's constitutionally protected right to privacy. This right encompasses the woman's decision whether to terminate or continue the pregnancy without interference from the state, at least until such time as the state's important interest in protecting the potentiality of human life predominates over the right to privacy, which is usually at viability. *Roe v Wade* protects the woman's right of choice; it does not protect, much less confer on an assailant, a third-party unilateral right to destroy the fetus.' (Reference omitted.) The court found (322) that the relevant statutory provisions are aimed at protecting the potentiality of human life without impinging directly or indirectly on a woman's right to privacy.

[55] Seymour *Childbirth and the Law* 182.

[56] Seymour *Childbirth and the Law* 182.

[57] Seymour *Childbirth and the Law* 180.

[58] Seymour *Childbirth and the Law* 180.

[59] Murphy (2014) *Indiana LJ* 850.

entities. The root cause of all the inconsistencies discussed here stem from the compulsion to provide *independent legal recognition* of the unborn via the notion of foetal personhood, while at the same time arguing that these efforts advance the protection of women's *autonomous* existence during pregnancy.[60] Splitting a pregnancy in this way inevitably leads to irreconcilable contradictions.

8.3.3 Advancing the notion of foetal protection

The above-described inconsistency pertaining to the translation of the value of the unborn into a workable legal principle can be seen to be addressed in cases where states hold women criminally liable either explicitly in terms of legislative provisions[61] or through wide interpretation of foetal protection measures.[62] Paltrow and Flavin[63] point out that it is the result of adopting a separate-entities approach that there is now a trend in the United States of holding or attempting to hold women criminally liable in relation to their own unsuccessful pregnancies.

Proehl[64] discusses three very well-documented incidences of holding or attempting to hold women criminally liable in terms of homicide laws for stillbirths or adverse pregnancy outcomes resulting in the death of a born child,[65] namely, that of Regina McKnight,[66] Melissa Rowland[67] and Bei Bei Shuai.[68] However, while only three incidents will be discussed here, Paltrow and Flavin point out that during the time spanning 1973–2005 there were 68 cases of women being charged and involved in criminal proceedings because they experienced

60 Foetal personhood is understood to be at play here because the unborn are granted legal leverage over others in their individuated capacities.

61 Such as that found in the State of Oklahoma. According to s 691D of the Oklahoma Statutes Annotated, a woman can be held criminally liable for conduct that causes the termination of her pregnancy in cases where the conduct concerned constitutes a crime in Oklahoma.

62 Concerning the issue of wide statutory interpretation of prenatal homicide laws, see Murphy (2014) *Indiana LJ* 863.

63 (2013) *Journal of Health Politics, Policy and Law* 322–6.

64 K Proehl 'Pregnancy crimes: New worries to expect when you're expecting' (2013) 52 *Santa Clara LR* 661 664–72. In fact, many authors have covered numerous cases including these; there are so many contributions that not all can be included here.

65 These cases cover criminal liability for conduct not generally considered criminal but for the fact that these women were pregnant and Proehl ((2013) *Santa Clara LR* 663) identifie these instances as involving a new form of status crime. By this Proehl means that these sorts of crimes against the foetus only apply to a very particular subset of the population, being pregnant women.

66 *State v McKnight* 576 SE 2d 168 (SC 2003) (*McKnight* (2003)) and the appeal decision *McKnight v State* 661 SE 2d 354 (SC 2008) (*McKnight* (2008)).

67 The record of the court's decision cannot be sourced in the form of a reported case and most of what is discussed here stems from academic publications. Some information from Rowland's case fil was obtained from J Flavin, a Professor of Sociology and President of the Board of Directors of National Advocates for Pregnant Women via electronic mail on 27 May 2014.

68 *Shuai v State* 966 NE 2d 619 (Ind App 2012) (*Shuai*).

miscarriages, stillbirths, or infant deaths.[69] In 48 of these cases women were charged under variations of state homicide laws in the form of feticide, manslaughter, reckless homicide, homicide by child abuse and first-degre murder.[70] They further point out that, in four cases where women's conduct constituted 'self-abortion', they were charged under murder or manslaughter statutes.[71] Paltrow and Flavin argue that the number of cases their study identifie represents a 'substantial undercount' in that many cases may be unaccounted for because not all the charges were properly documented or else did not result in published court opinions.[72]

While the true extent of women's criminal exposure is somewhat uncertain, Paltrow and Flavin's comprehensive study does identify that a substantial number of women face criminal charges for adverse pregnancy outcomes. The authors argue that despite these laws being passed in the wake of extreme violence against pregnant women, they are now being used as grounds for arresting pregnant women themselves.[73] However, as with Murphy's cautionary note urging explicit 'maternal exceptions',[74] Paltrow and Flavin[75] explain that:

> Even when women are not charged under feticide laws, such laws are used to support the argument that generally worded murder statutes, child endangerment laws, drug delivery laws, and other laws should be interpreted to permit the arrest and prosecution of pregnant women in relationship to the embryos or fetuses they carry.

Going back to the three identifie cases specificall , in the State of South Carolina, McKnight[76] was the firs woman to be charged with and successfully convicted of homicide by way of child abuse[77] for experiencing the stillbirth of her viable foetus.[78] In May 1999, McKnight experienced a stillbirth and the autopsy revealed that prenatal life terminated an estimated three days before delivery and that the foetus had been exposed to cocaine.[79] On this basis, McKnight was

[69] Paltrow & Flavin (2013) *Journal of Health Politics, Policy and Law* 321. It must be noted that their study covers only traceable cases spanning this time period. Since some time has passed there may be more cases on the books. In fact, in their conclusion the authors state that they have 'identifie more than 200 cases initiated against pregnant women since 2005 that also overwhelmingly rest on the claim of separate rights for fertilized eggs, embryos and fetuses'. (References omitted.) However, the authors do not indicate whether these cases are related to homicide charges or not.

[70] Paltrow & Flavin (2013) *Journal of Health Politics, Policy and Law* 321.

[71] Paltrow & Flavin (2013) *Journal of Health Politics, Policy and Law* 322.

[72] Paltrow & Flavin (2013) *Journal of Health Politics, Policy and Law* 303–4.

[73] Paltrow & Flavin (2013) *Journal of Health Politics, Policy and Law* 323.

[74] Murphy (2014) *Indiana LJ* 849–50.

[75] Paltrow & Flavin (2013) *Journal of Health Politics, Policy and Law* 323.

[76] *McKnight* (2003).

[77] This crime is identifie as being unique to South Carolina and is understood to be crime developed in line with the state's tough-on-drugs approach; see Proehl (2013) *Santa Clara LR* 665–6.

[78] While this case involves child abuse it is discussed here because of the fact that McKnight faced a homicide charge in relation to her own foetus; other cases regarding child abuse that did not result in terminated prenatal life will be discussed in Chapter Nine.

[79] *McKnight* (2003) 171. McKnight admitted to using cocaine and consented to drug testing (*McKnight* (2003) 178–9). However, Page offers the compelling argument that her consent was

charged and convicted of homicide by child abuse,[80] and sentenced to 20 years' imprisonment in the Circuit Court.[81] This was later confirme by the majority in the Supreme Court of South Carolina.[82] The Supreme Court found that the crime of homicide by child abuse was applicable to a pregnant woman in relation to her viable foetus[83] and since 'it is public knowledge that use of cocaine is potentially fatal, we fin the fact that McKnight took cocaine knowing she was pregnant was sufficient evidence to submit to the jury on whether she acted with extreme indifference to her child's life'.[84]

In 2008, McKnight's conviction was overturned as a result of post-conviction relief proceedings, where the Supreme Court of South Carolina found that McKnight received ineffective assistance from her counsel at trial.[85] The court found that the prosecution's research concerning the effects of cocaine on prenatal development was outdated.[86] In fact the court accepted that recent studies show that the harm suffered as a result of prenatal exposure to cocaine is comparable to harms associated with exposure to nicotine, poor nutrition and inadequate prenatal care, meaning that a causal link had not been established beyond a reasonable doubt.[87] McKnight went on to plead guilty to manslaughter and was released from prison.[88] She allegedly pleaded guilty to avoid being retried and possibly sentenced to a longer term.[89] Murphy explains that, while McKnight got some relief, the court did not address the constitutionality of holding women criminally liable for adverse pregnancy outcomes despite the fact that substance abuse during pregnancy is now understood to be a lot less harmful than previously believed.[90]

---

uninformed since the nurse who obtained McKnight's consent for urine testing did not understand the legal implications of obtaining such tests so she was not in the position to relay the legal implications of those tests to McKnight; see D Page 'The homicide by child abuse conviction of Regina McKnight' (2003) 46 *Howard LJ* 363 366.

[80] The crime of homicide by child abuse is governed by s 16-3-85(A) of the South Carolina Code Annotated, which provides that a person is guilty of homicide by child abuse if that person causes the death of a child under the age of 7 while committing child abuse or neglect and death occurs as a result of the person's 'extreme indifference to human life'.

[81] *McKnight* (2003) 179.

[82] *McKnight* (2003) 179.

[83] *McKnight* (2003) 173. However, dissenting with the majority, Moore J found that at most McKnight's conduct constituted a violation of the state's termination-of-pregnancy statute which imposed less severe punishment being a fin of 1000 USD or two years' imprisonment for 'feticide by its mother'. Moore J explained that this provision took due account of the special relationship between the unborn and women carrying them and was thus unconvinced that homicide statutes are applicable against pregnant women, 179–89.

[84] *McKnight* (2003) 173.

[85] *McKnight* (2008).

[86] *McKnight* (2008) 360–1.

[87] *McKnight* (2008) 358 fn 2.

[88] Paltrow & Flavin (2013) *Journal of Health Politics, Policy and Law* 306 and B Steinbock *Life before Birth: The Moral and Legal Status of Embryos and Fetuses* 2 ed (2011) 173.

[89] Paltrow & Flavin (2013) *Journal of Health Politics, Policy and Law* 306 and Steinbock *Life before Birth* 173.

[90] Murphy (2014) *Indiana LJ* 862.

Page[91] gives some background information on McKnight that demonstrates the tragedy of this case. McKnight was an African-American woman who was homeless, unemployed, 'educably mentally handicapped' and a mother of three, who at the time of the 2003 case had been using drugs for three years.[92] While she repeatedly sought treatment for her addiction, she was turned away.[93] In fact, she was only admitted for treatment to overcome her addiction after her firs trial ended in a mistrial and while receiving treatment, she became pregnant once again as a result of a relationship with her treatment counsellor.[94] Page points out that holding McKnight criminally responsible diverted attention from the state failing to take responsibility for wider social concerns such as poverty, racism[95] and a misguided national health policy.[96] This is a compelling argument because, if McKnight had received treatment when she originally attempted to obtain it, her addiction would have been addressed and her entire ordeal in the criminal justice system could possibly have been averted.[97] Page concludes that it is unfair to punish people who are sick because they cannot get well, while, at the same time, refusing to provide the means to get better.[98] More on the effectiveness of these criminal policies will be discussed below. The discussion here is to point out the theoretical inconsistencies pertaining to holding women liable in order to protect the wellbeing of the unborn.

In December 2010 in Indiana, Bei Bei Shuai was in her third trimester when her partner broke off their relationship.[99] Feeling distraught, she attempted suicide by ingesting rat poison.[100] She informed the father-to-be of her actions telephonically.[101] In addition to verbally communicating her intentions she wrote a suicide note indicating that she intended to end her life as well as that of the foetus.[102] Soon after she spoke to her partner, the police arrived to check on her, however she

---

[91] Page (2003) *Howard LJ* 368–9.
[92] Page (2003) *Howard LJ* 368–9.
[93] Page (2003) *Howard LJ* 368–9.
[94] Page (2003) *Howard LJ* 368–9.
[95] Racism is relevant here because non-white women, being those who represent the minority in the Unites States are over represented in cases dealing with holding women criminally responsible for adverse pregnancy outcomes, see Paltrow & Flavin (2013) *Journal of Health Politics, Policy and Law* 311. Their study highlights that aside from race, the indigent are overly represented and so too are African-American women in the South. This is where McKnight was tried, in South Carolina. Page argues that it is the intersectionality of McKnight's circumstances that left her vulnerable to limited protection by the United States Constitution, this intersectionality includes the meeting points of disadvantages associated with race, class and gender. For a detailed discussion see Page (2003) *Howard LJ* 397–9.
[96] Page (2003) *Howard LJ* 364.
[97] One might be inclined to argue that McKnight might not have experienced an adverse pregnancy outcome had she received treatment. However, as will be demonstrated below, there are many factors that influenc the increased risk of adverse pregnancy outcomes, and substance abuse increases it. Merely removing substance abuse as a risk factor therefore may not have saved McKnight's pregnancy.
[98] Page (2003) *Howard LJ* 403. More on adequate state response will be discussed below.
[99] *Shuai* 622.
[100] *Shuai* 622.
[101] *Shuai* 622.
[102] *Shuai* 622.

sent them away.[103] Shuai then went to a friend who suspected that something was amiss; after a while, she told her friend what she had done, and they went to the hospital.[104] Shuai received treatment to stabilise her condition. However, a few days later complications occurred which necessitated an emergency caesarean-section delivery.[105] After delivery, Shuai's child's condition worsened, requiring that the child be placed on life support. Unfortunately, when the life support was removed, the child passed away.[106] An autopsy revealed that the child had died of an intra-cerebral haemorrhage, which was purportedly a result of the toxins in the rat poison ingested by Shuai during her prenatal suicide attempt.[107]

Shuai[108] was charged with murder[109] and attempted feticide[110] and was jailed. At trial, Shuai's motion to dismiss the charges and her petition for bail were both denied. On appeal a number of issues were raised regarding her right to bail and the applicability of the charges to Shuai in relation to her own foetus. Despite the fact that women's liability in respect of their own pregnancies was not explicitly provided for in either of the charges against Shuai, the Court of Appeals of Indiana found these crimes to be applicable, nonetheless.[111] 'Shuai is a "person," the State alleged she intended to kill A.S. [the foetus] by virtue of Shuai's mention of the fetus in the suicide note, and the victim was an entity protected under the murder statute, be it a "viable fetus" or "human being," [that] died'.[112] Feticide was found to be applicable on the basis of Shuai's suicide note, because it undisputedly demonstrated that Shuai intended to end her pregnancy and the fact that she did so with rat poison indicated the intention to ensure a live birth did not ensue.[113] Furthermore, even though the Appeals Court found suicide did not constitute a crime in the United States, the court accepted the state's argument that the charges Shuai faced were not in relation to the harm she caused to herself but linked to her conduct towards the unborn and once again Shuai's suicide note served as the basis for this since she expressly indicated that she intended to kill herself and the

[103] *Shuai* 622.
[104] *Shuai* 622.
[105] *Shuai* 623.
[106] *Shuai* 623.
[107] *Shuai* 623.
[108] *Shuai* 623.
[109] According to s 35-42-1-1(4) of the Indiana Code, murder is define as knowingly and intentionally killing a viable foetus. Despite the fact that the child was born alive, the court (627) held that this charge stands because the harm inflicte occurred while the baby was a foetus. The court (627) found that removing the charge simply because medical staff effected birth in an attempt to save the child's life should not be used as a ground for Shuai to avoid liability.
[110] Section 35-42-1-6 of the Indiana Code define feticide as the termination of a human pregnancy with the intent to procure a non-live birth.
[111] *Shuai* 629.
[112] *Shuai* 629.
[113] *Shuai* 629.

foetus.[114] Litigation in this matter finall ceased when Shuai pleaded guilty to criminal recklessness and did not have to serve any additional jail time.[115]

The significanc of this case relates to the fact that pregnant women can now possibly be held criminally liable for 'self-harm' in Indiana, which if it were not for the existence of a pregnancy, no crime could be committed. Pollitt cites Linda Pence (Shuai's attorney) as stating that '[t]hese laws say there's one law for pregnant women and another for everyone else. . . . For everyone else suicide is a mental health issue. For a pregnant woman, it's a crime'.[116] Ultimately, this sort of scenario leads to the puzzling position that pregnant women are legally required to 'stay sane' until they give birth.[117] Shuai's case is another unfortunate example of taking the easy route away from state responsibility especially because suicide is a response to wider social issues such as health concerns, being an illness of depression.[118] Pillott rightly points out that pregnant women in crisis need compassion and treatment.[119]

Through a study on homicide and suicide during pregnancy, Palladino, Singh, Campbell et al demonstrate that in the United States the maternal mortality rate from suicide is greater than many other obstetric complications that are understood to be the traditional causes of maternal mortality.[120] While the authors identify a number of limitations, they confidentl assert that the study's finding 'suggest that effective methods aimed at perinatal psychological health are imperative'.[121] However, suggesting help implies that women would be able to ask for it in circumstances where they are experiencing suicidal ideation. Shuai's ordeal impedes the opportunity for seeking help in Indiana because a cry for help could very well be interpreted as an indication of the intention to commit murder or feticide. Foetal interests are being placed before the needs of pregnant women

---

[114] *Shuai* 630.

[115] JM Pieklo 'Plea deal reached in Bei Bei Shuai prosecution' *Rewire* 2 August 2013, available at http://rhrealitycheck.org/article/2013/08/02/plea-deal-reached-in-bei-bei-shuai-prosecution/ (accessed on 19 May 2016).

[116] K Pollitt 'Protect pregnant women: Free Bei Bei Shuai' *The Nation* 7 March 2012 available at http://www.thenation.com/article/166664/protect-pregnant-women-free-bei-bei-shuai (accessed on 19 May 2016).

[117] Pollitt 'Protect pregnant women: Free Bei Bei Shuai'.

[118] See the *amici curiae* brief of American Association of Suicideology, American College of Obstetricians and Gynecologists, American Congress of Obstetricians and Gynecologists et al in the matter of *Shuai v State* 966 NE 2d 619 (Ind App 2012) 19. The *amici curiae* argue that charging women for attempted suicide is in effect punishing them for their health status.

[119] Pollitt 'Protect pregnant women: Free Bei Bei Shuai'.

[120] CL Palladino, V Singh, J Campbell et al 'Homicide and suicide during prenatal period: Findings from the National Violent Death Reporting System' (2011) *Obstetrics & Gynecology* 1056 1059; 1061. Traditional causes of mortality are identifie as including eclampsia, preeclampsia, haemorrhage, placenta previa or amniotic flui embolism.

[121] Palladino, Singh, Campbell et al (2011) *Obstetrics & Gynecology* 1062. This suggestion is problematic because according to JH Perlow & H Lesmes 'Homicide and suicide during the perinatal period: Findings from the National Violent Death Reporting System: To the Editor' (2012) 119 *Obstetrics & Gynecology* 1275 1276, the American College of Obstetricians and Gynecologists decided against universal depression screening being made available to pregnant women in the health-care system. The authors argue that this would assist with identifying cases in need of intervention and thus aid in reducing suicide rates during pregnancy.

and, if pregnant women's needs are not properly addressed, a successful suicide would come at the high price of two valued lives.[122]

Melissa Rowland from Utah is another example of homicide charges being brought against a pregnant woman. In this case, one of Rowland's twins was stillborn while the other was born alive.[123] The live-born twin tested positive for exposure to alcohol and cocaine,[124] and it was estimated that the stillborn twin died two days prior to delivery.[125] Rowland faced one charge of child endangerment in relation to her born-alive twin and was charged with criminal homicide in respect of her stillborn twin.[126]

Rowland's murder charge was based on the fact that she refused to follow medical recommendations to undergo a caesarean-section delivery at an earlier point during her pregnancy.[127] According to National Advocates for Pregnant Women, this case faced an 'unexpected storm of controversy', but instead of the state dropping all charges against Rowland, she pleaded guilty to two counts of

---

[122] A chilling report emphasises this point; see DL Dell & BW O'Brien 'Suicide in pregnancy' (2003) 102 *Obstetrics & Gynecology* 1306. The authors report on a case where a young woman suffered with bipolar disorder for which she was receiving treatment. She unexpectedly became pregnant and the relationship with her partner ended. However, terminating the pregnancy was not an option for her and she opted to have the child adopted once born. Her caregivers discontinued her psychiatric medication out of fear that the medication she was taking could cause foetal anomalies and complicate labour and delivery. As a result of suddenly stopping her medication the pregnant woman experienced a relapse, sought help a number of times at a psychiatric crisis centre and eventually she was admitted as an in-patient at a psychiatric unit. She was stabilised and released; within two days after being discharged she shot and killed herself. This case is an example of treatment being in reach but the separately construed interests of the foetus were placed above that of the pregnant woman carrying it, and this approach led to the demise of both the pregnant woman and the foetus. This is a tragic example of the extreme results that the separate-entities approach invokes. In fact, had the foetus been understood in relation to the pregnant woman one would undoubtedly see some benefi in allowing adequate treatment of the pregnant woman concerned or demanding state action and investment to fin treatment appropriate for pregnant women suffering with mental health issues. The unity that pregnancy represents means foetal interests will be advanced where the interests of the pregnant woman are advanced too, and this is particularly obvious in this case.

[123] National Advocates for Pregnant Women 'Lessons from the U.S. experience with unborn victims of violence laws' (13 January 2004) at 6, available at http://www.arcc-cdac.ca/action/Lessonsfrom US.pdf (accessed on 23 May 2016). No case law can be cited here because the case has not been reported. Thus, anecdotal accounts of Rowland's legal ordeal will be relied on.

[124] National Advocates for Pregnant Women 'Lessons from the U.S. experience with unborn victims of violence laws' 6.

[125] See MK Miller 'Refusal to undergo a cesarean section: A woman's right or a criminal act?' (2005) 15 *Health Matrix* 383.

[126] National Advocates for Pregnant Women 'Lessons from the U.S. experience with unborn victims of violence laws' 6.

[127] National Advocates for Pregnant Women 'Lessons from the U.S. experience with unborn victims of violence laws' 6. Miller ((2005) *Health Matrix* 383) explains that Rowland sought medical attention several times during the third trimester and each time she was advised to undergo an emergency caesarean-section delivery because the unborn were understood to be in danger that may either result in stillbirth or serious injury. Further, on 2 January 2004, Rowland signed a document acknowledging that her refusal to submit to treatment might cause adverse pregnancy outcomes including stillbirth.

third-degree felony child endangerment.[128] As a result of the charges being brought against Rowland, she spent 105 days in jail before reaching a plea agreement and being released.[129] According to Miller, this case represents the firs reported case of a woman being prosecuted for refusing to deliver a foetus via caesarean-section surgery.[130] The ground for dropping the murder charge did not relate to the fact that Utah's homicide laws did not explicitly exclude pregnant women, but because of Rowland's history of mental illness.[131] This leaves the door open for the possibility that other women may face homicide charges under similar circumstances. However, no such cases can be sourced.

While actual homicide convictions seem to be rare in the United States, that does not mean that women do not face these charges when they experience stillbirths, miscarriages[132] or the death of a child soon after delivery. Charging women for these adverse pregnancy outcomes is widespread across the United States.[133] Generally women are charged with murder, homicide or feticide in relation to their own pregnancies but they end up pleading to lesser offences through plea agreements with the prosecution.[134] Alternatively, courts at times reject the idea that women can be held liable in respect of their own pregnancies and dismiss the cases. However, in these instances, women still have had to spend time in prison awaiting trial and secure representation which are both high prices to pay.[135]

From a theoretical perspective, holding women criminally liable in respect of their own adverse pregnancy outcome seems more in line with the direction of the

---

[128] National Advocates for Pregnant Women 'Lessons from the U.S. experience with unborn victims of violence laws' 6.

[129] National Advocates for Pregnant Women 'Lessons from the U.S. experience with unborn victims of violence laws' 6.

[130] Miller (2005) *Health Matrix* 384.

[131] National Advocates for Pregnant Women 'Lessons from the U.S. experience with unborn victims of violence laws' 6. With mental illness being a concern, it is not clear how Rowland's child endangerment conviction stands.

[132] In this chapter focus is placed on stillbirth and perinatal death since the cases considered herein revolve around the occurrence of these two forms of pregnancy outcomes. However, the discussion concerning stillbirths is equally applicable to the experience of a miscarriage. Flavin *Our Bodies, Our Crimes* 106 define miscarriage as the loss of a pre-viable pregnancy while stillbirth constitutes the loss of a viable pregnancy. She indicates that miscarriage is more common than stillbirth and the uncertainty plaguing the causes of stillbirth are also applicable to the causes of miscarriages. These uncertainties are discussed below in para 8.4.

[133] See generally LM Paltrow '*Roe v Wade* and the new Jane Crow: Reproductive rights in the age of mass incarceration' (2013) 103 *American Journal of Public Health* 17 and Paltrow & Flavin (2013) *Journal of Health Politics, Policy and Law* 299.

[134] For instance, see B Bird 'Fetal personhood laws as limits to maternal personhood at any stage of pregnancy: Balancing fetal and maternal interests at post-viability among fetal pain and fetal homicide laws' (2014) 25 *Hastings Women's LJ* 39 51. This stems from the fact that women are represented by inadequate counsel or do not have counsel at all, see Paltrow (2013) *American Journal of Public Health* 17.

[135] For instance, see Paltrow (2013) *American Journal of Public Health* 18. Also see Center for Reproductive Rights 'Punishing women for their behavior during pregnancy: An approach that undermines women's health and children's interests' (September 2000) at 11–15, available at http://reproductiverights.org/sites/default/files/documents/pub_bp_punishingwomen.pd (accessed on 23 June 2016).

separate-entities approach in respect of consistency. It is more in line because if the unborn and pregnant women are rendered two separate entities and the unborn are valued as human beings or persons in law, then an exemption cannot logically be extended to women because the issue at hand is the harm caused to the unborn and not who causes the harm.

However, this approach is also flawe to a certain degree. Substance abuse, attempted suicide and refusal to undergo a caesarean section all rely on the embodied connectedness of pregnancy for the purposes of harm. Without there being a pregnancy, none of these scenarios is a crime in itself. Thus, it is the combination of the physical biological relationship between pregnant women and women's self-harm that creates a 'fatal environment' for prenatal life. Yet, the separate-entities approach is applied in a way that renders the relational aspect of pregnancy irrelevant despite the fact that, but for the relational aspect, no adverse outcome would have ensued, essentially nullifying the causal connection giving rise to the 'offence'.

Going further, criminal sanctions for these women's experiences of stillbirth or perinatal death can be viewed as responsive actions rather than preventive. It can be argued that responsive actions can never lead to healthy pregnancies or pregnancy outcomes if applied in a particular case, because these actions only become applicable once prenatal life is lost. Thus, applying homicide laws will never really address those actions that are argued to cause stillbirths or perinatal deaths as adverse pregnancy outcomes. One can argue that, if prenatal life was truly valued, emphasis should be on preventive rather than responsive actions. This stance would demand research and meaningful access to state resources, allowing for a better understanding of the causes of stillbirth or miscarriages and the ability to prevent its occurrence. Ultimately, these provisions do give weight to the value that the unborn represent and demonstrate that the loss of prenatal life is something that should not go unnoticed in law, but they fail to prevent the loss.

Also discrediting the notion that these measures are being employed to protect the unborn is the fact that it is mainly poor women of colour (representing the minority in the United States) who bear the brunt of criminal charges for experiencing stillbirths or perinatal deaths. In Paltrow and Flavin's study, which identifie 416 cases of women's facing charges that threaten their freedom on the grounds of pregnancy-related issues, the authors found that, regardless of race, the majority of women in the system were 'economically disadvantaged', indicating that poor women bear the brunt of these foetal protection measures.[136] Of the women identifie in the study, in 368 cases the women's race could be identifie and of these, 59% of the women involved were women of colour, of that, 52% were black.[137] The authors found that black women are overrepresented in their study, despite the fact that these women constitute a minority group. The majority

[136] Paltrow & Flavin (2013) *Journal of Health Politics, Policy and Law* 311.

[137] Paltrow & Flavin (2013) *Journal of Health Politics, Policy and Law* 311. However, the authors (332–3) emphasise that while these statistics demonstrate some women are more susceptible to state intervention, pregnant women as a whole group and across the United States all suffer from these sorts of state actions.

of these liberty violations take place in the South.[138] While the authors are presenting data on all forms of state intervention during pregnancy, based on numerous grounds (not only in respect of criminal charges for stillbirth or perinatal death), their study does demonstrate that the intersection of poverty and race intensifie state action and women who fall into this category are particularly vulnerable.[139] The authors cite a number of studies supporting their findings and submit that racial disparity is not a result of ' "colour-blind" decisions' but is linked to a 'history of devaluing African-American mothers'.[140]

Page explains this history of devaluing black women in the context of her discussion of the *McKnight* case, and argues that 'criminalization of poor black women's conduct during pregnancy is part of a larger continuum of the devaluation of black women as mothers that began during slavery and continues in numerous forms today'.[141] By criminalising their conduct, the state lays the cause of stillbirth or perinatal deaths squarely on their shoulders, thus rendering their actions during pregnancy as 'bad acts of individual mothers'.[142] However, these 'bad acts' (such as addiction to controlled substances), are linked to and exacerbated by poverty and associated social issues, and by attributing personal responsibility, the state has removed itself from the obligation to address these concerns.[143] This issue raises a unique situation for black women: black women experience significantl more stillbirths each year than white women which renders them vulnerable to increased prosecutions, and this position will persist if the state fails to address the underlying issues giving rise to stillbirth as a pregnancy outcome. Page argues: 'The comments made by those involved [in the prosecution of women] indicate that these prosecutions are solely about punishing these women for their "bad" mothering and have little to do with actually protecting the health of children.'[144] The fact that these measures do not result in healthy 'children' will become even more obvious when this chapter considers the fact that criminalising stillbirths is founded on flawe assumptions of who factually causes harm to pregnancies.[145]

From a theoretical perspective, the separate-entities approach to pregnancy in the context of feticide or foetal homicide is rendered unsound and leads to ambiguous outcomes. Understanding that these protective measures are infused with anti-abortion sentiments in the United States, a clash must be expected between the right to terminate a pregnancy and the protection from violence that terminates prenatal life.

---

[138] Paltrow & Flavin (2013) *Journal of Health Politics, Policy and Law* 311.
[139] Paltrow & Flavin (2013) *Journal of Health Politics, Policy and Law* 333.
[140] Paltrow & Flavin (2013) *Journal of Health Politics, Policy and Law* 333–4.
[141] Page (2003) *Howard LJ* 364.
[142] Page (2003) *Howard LJ* 364.
[143] Page (2003) *Howard LJ* 364.
[144] Page (2003) *Howard LJ* 401.
[145] See para 8.4 below.

8.4 CRIMINAL LIABILITY FOR ADVERSE PREGNANCY OUTCOMES: FLAWED ASSUMPTIONS

Despite the theoretical inconsistencies described above, there are practical concerns that point to the inadequacy of these measures, which are generally linked to proving factual causation in cases that involve pre-viable pregnancies, whether it is a woman or a third party being charged. Also, proving intention is problematic in cases of pre-viability, since it can be convincingly argued that the perpetrator was unaware of the existence of a pregnancy at the time he or she inflicte violence against a particular woman, thereby making intention difficult to prove. These issues have been covered elsewhere and have generally been criticised and debated at length, so will not be the focus of this discussion.[146] The primary focus of this portion is to determine whether adopting a separate-entities approach to addressing violence that terminates pregnancies is an appropriate means of addressing tensions in a way that secures optimal pregnancy-related outcomes.

Here, the discussion will focus on the fact that these criminal actions are based on flawe assumptions concerning causation, namely, by holding women criminally liable in respect of adverse pregnancy outcomes, these women are being designated as the sole cause of harm. This implies that these women alone could have prevented stillbirth or death soon after delivery. It must be conceded that women's conduct (self-agency) during pregnancy will sometimes have a role to play pertaining to a pregnancy outcome. However, the fact remains that these women exist in wider social settings that also contribute to the experience of adverse pregnancy outcomes and this issue is so complex that the designation of responsibility becomes rather problematic. Daniels contemplates the issue of attributing individual responsibility to women who experience adverse pregnancy outcomes and argues that 'it is clear the responsibility for fetal harm is so deeply shared with men, with public institutions, and with social structures, that it makes little sense to try teasing out individual from collective responsibility for fetal harm'.[147]

Concerning men's contribution to foetal harms, Daniels argues that men's physical distance from pregnancy and gestation tends to create the illusion that they have less of a connection to foetal harm, and she convincingly demonstrates otherwise.[148] Daniels explains that contemporary studies have linked paternal use of alcohol and drugs and toxic exposures to viruses and chemicals to adverse

[146] See the discussions in C Pickles *S v Mshumpa: A Time for Law Reform* (unpublished LLM dissertation, University of Pretoria, 2010) 103–8 and C Pickles 'The introduction of a statutory crime to address third-party foetal violence' (2011) 74 *THRHR* 546 559–61. These sources argue that proving causation and intention is problematic in cases that involve pre-viable pregnancies. However, for a contrary view, see Du Plessis (2013) *Stell LR* 87, who argues that medical technology has developed enough to be able to prove the cause of very early pregnancy terminations. This argument should be treated with caution because, as this portion of the chapter demonstrates, many adverse pregnancy outcomes cannot be explained despite advances in medical technology.

[147] CR Daniels 'Fathers, mothers, and fetal harm: Rethinking gender difference and reproductive responsibility' in LM Morgan & MW Michaels (eds) *Fetal Subjects, Feminist Positions* (1999) 83–4.

[148] Daniels 'Fathers, mothers, and fetal harm' 83–4.

pregnancy outcomes such as miscarriage, low birth weight, congenital abnormalities, cancers, neurological disorders and other health problems.[149] While there are biological links to poor pregnancy outcomes, Daniels also highlights men's social contribution to adverse pregnancy outcomes and explains that men who abuse substances may not only produce damaged sperm but may also create a social environment that has implications for the health of pregnant women.[150] For instance, they may encourage substance abuse by pregnant partners or physically abuse women, and studies demonstrate that pregnant women are susceptible to increased partner violence in respect of severity and frequency.[151] She urges that, if there is a serious drive to address foetal harm, we are required to recognise the role of men in a biological and social sense.[152]

Looking at 'collective responsibility' for foetal harm, Daniels argues that 'risky' behaviour by a woman during pregnancy on its own may not necessarily result in an adverse pregnancy outcome.[153] Referring to the issue of alcohol abuse and foetal-alcohol syndrome, Daniels looks at a study that indicates that women of low socio-economic status experience higher rates of foetal-alcohol syndrome compared with those women of higher socio-economic status, despite the fact that all the women in the study drank the same amount of alcohol per day during their pregnancies.[154] The diverging results were found to be linked to poor socio-economic status.[155] The study concluded that poverty and risky behaviour work together to produce increased adverse pregnancy outcomes.[156] She argues: 'When we widen the lens to include social structures we can clearly see the ways in which we share collective responsibility for fetal harm' and further states that women's responsibility must therefore be shared.[157]

Linking this thought process to the issue of criminal liability for stillbirth or perinatal death leads one to question whether women can shoulder the sole responsibility on the basis that they themselves are responsible for that harm.

[149] Daniels 'Fathers, mothers, and fetal harm' 85; 87–8. Daniels acknowledges that some of the studies she relies on to demonstrate paternal responsibility for foetal harms have certain limitations. She nevertheless persuasively argues that science has demonstrated that men certainly have a role to play when considering a particular pregnancy outcome.

[150] Daniels 'Fathers, mothers, and fetal harm' 85; 87–8.

[151] Daniels 'Fathers, mothers, and fetal harm' 89. However, see LE Saltzman, CH Johnson, BC Gilbert et al 'Physical abuse around the time of pregnancy: An examination of prevalence and risk factors in 16 states' (2003) 7 *Maternal and Child Health Journal* 31. This study demonstrates that the prevalence of domestic violence does not necessarily increase during pregnancy and that women should not be presumed to be at greater risk of violence when pregnant. Instead, the increased statistics of violence might be attributed to the fact that women access medical care more frequently during pregnancy which allows for domestic violence to be more readily detected. For instance, see RJ Cook & BM Dickens 'Dilemmas in intimate partner violence' (2009) 106 *International Journal of Gynecology & Obstetrics* 72.

[152] Daniels 'Fathers, mothers, and fetal harm' 89.

[153] Daniels 'Fathers, mothers, and fetal harm' 91.

[154] Daniels 'Fathers, mothers, and fetal harm' 91.

[155] Particularly, poorer women had poorer eating habits which was linked to their socio-economic status.

[156] Daniels 'Fathers, mothers, and fetal harm' 91.

[157] Daniels 'Fathers, mothers, and fetal harm' 92.

Paltrow and Flavin point out that, in their study of cases brought against women for adverse outcomes, including charges related to experiencing stillbirth, they found a number of instances where 'cases proceeded without any evidence, much less scientifi evidence, establishing a causal link between the harm and the pregnant woman's alleged action or inaction'.[158] This might be the case because, despite the presence of self-destructive behaviour or the inflictio of self-harm, the cause of a stillbirth remains the subject of uncertainty and it is really a medical game of speculation based on probabilities and possibilities.[159] This is not to suggest that women do not make a contribution to that specifi outcome, but it is argued that their conduct is not the sole factor leading to that outcome, meaning that responsibility must be shared and not carried by women alone.[160]

Turning back to the *Shuai* case, the *amici curiae* brief of Legal Voice and Perinatal Loss Support Organizations and Experts deals with this topic extensively.[161] The *amici curiae* indicate that each year in the United States an estimated 26 000 pregnancies end in stillbirths and 19 000 neonates die very soon after delivery as well, with the loss being unexplained in the majority of instances.[162] The *amici curiae* assert that some factors associated with pregnant women's conduct (such as smoking) have links to stillbirth and infant death as pregnancy outcomes. However, 'an association, and even a *likelihood* of causation, does not prove *actual* causation in any particular case'.[163] (Emphasis in original.)

There are a number of factors that contribute to pregnancy loss, which include genetic disposition, poor nutrition, environmental hazards, intimate partner violence, paternal factors and lack of access to adequate health care.[164] However, despite identifying certain risk factors that contribute to stillbirth, the Stillbirth

---

[158] Paltrow & Flavin (2013) *Journal of Health Politics, Policy and Law* 318. This issue of proving causation was obviously clear in the cases discussed above; see para 8.3.3.

[159] For instance, see Stillbirth Collaborative Research Network Writing Group 'Association between stillbirth and risk factors known at pregnancy confirmation (2011) 306 *Journal of the American Medical Association* 2469 and Stillbirth Collaborative Research Network Writing Group 'Causes of death among stillbirths' (2011) 306 *Journal of the American Medical Association* 2459.

[160] Flavin urges that risk factors should be distinguished from causes, and explains that while risk factors for stillbirth may be present, they are not necessarily the actual cause of stillbirth in and of themselves; see Flavin *Our Bodies, Our Crimes* 106.

[161] *Amici curiae* brief of Legal Voice and Perinatal Loss Support Organizations and Experts in the matter of *Shuai v State* NE 2d 619 (Ind App 2012). Interestingly, Daniels, who argues for shared responsibility in respect of foetal harm, is one of the listed *amici curiae* in the *Shuai* case which indicates that her arguments are relevant to sharing the responsibility of the experience of a stillbirth as well as general adverse pregnancy outcomes.

[162] *Amici curiae* brief of Legal Voice and Perinatal Loss Support Organizations and Experts in *Shuai* 8.

[163] *Amici curiae* brief of Legal Voice and Perinatal Loss Support Organizations and Experts in *Shuai* 9.

[164] *Amici curiae* brief of Legal Voice and Perinatal Loss Support Organizations and Experts in *Shuai* 9. Regarding access to adequate health care, the *amici curiae* brief of Legal Voice and Perinatal Loss Support Organizations and Experts in *Shuai* 12 refers to a number of contemporary studies indicating that income and race have the potential to adversely impact a woman's health and pregnancy. Drawing on Daniels' ('Fathers, mothers, and fetal harm' 83) notion of shared responsibility, it can be argued that if poor pregnancy outcomes are associated to social issues linked

Collaborative Research Network Writing Group indicates that black women experience substantially higher rates of stillbirth and this racial disparity with white women's pregnancy outcomes cannot be explained, even with today's access to advances in medical science.[165] Where contributory risk factors have been identified Dudley, Goldenberg, Conway et al indicate that assigning one particular factor as the cause of death can only be done in a relatively small portion of the cases; one of these cases is 'catastrophic fetal trauma'.[166] Concerning the allocation of causation, they go on to explain:[167]

> Given the degree of uncertainty in the majority of cases regarding the event or condition that led directly to fetal death, we adopted a hierarchical system wherein a condition that was a potential cause of fetal death was graded as being a present condition, a possible cause of death, or a probable cause of death.

On account of the difficulty of allocating one particular factor as the cause of foetal death, the *amici curiae* persuasively argue that prosecuting women for experiencing a stillbirth is factually and socially wrong.[168] The *amici curiae* argue that from a social perspective, mental-health concerns need adequate attention and constant treatment.[169] This is especially true given the high incidence of suicide during pregnancy, and the failure to provide care must be viewed as contributing to foetal harm.[170] The *amici curiae* go on to also implicate men's contribution to the experience of stillbirth, particularly those men who procreate at an advanced age, who have smoked, drunk alcohol, used drugs, consumed caffeine, have genetic disorders or been exposed to workplace or wartime exposures, all of which can adversely impact the potential for live birth.[171] While the *amici curiae* are not advocating for men to be prosecuted for contributing towards a stillbirth, they are arguing that 'prosecuting women in these circumstances ignores the contribution

---

to race and poverty and inaction on the part of the state to alleviate these influences then the state is partly liable for the incidence of stillbirth as well.

165 See generally Stillbirth Collaborative Research Network Writing Group (2011) *Journal of the American Medical Association* 2469 and Stillbirth Collaborative Research Network Writing Group (2011) *Journal of the American Medical Association* 2459.

166 DJ Dudley, R Goldenberg, D Conway et al 'A new system for determining the causes of stillbirth' (2011) 116 *Obstetrics & Gynecology* 254 255.

167 Dudley, Goldenberg, Conway et al (2011) *Obstetrics & Gynecology* 255.

168 *Amici curiae* brief of Legal Voice and Perinatal Loss Support Organizations and Experts in *Shuai* 9.

169 *Amici curiae* brief of Legal Voice and Perinatal Loss Support Organizations and Experts in *Shuai* 10.

170 For instance, see Palladino, Singh, Campbell et al (2011) *Obstetrics & Gynecology* 1059. The authors highlight that homicide and suicide are two of the leading causes of death of pregnant women, higher than mortality rates associated to placenta praevia, eclampsia, preeclampsia and amniotic flui embolism. Also see ME Wallace, D Hoyert, C Williams et al 'Pregnancy-associated homicide and suicide in 37 US states with enhanced pregnancy surveillance' (2016) 215 *American Journal of Obstetrics & Gynecology* 364.e1.

171 *Amici curiae* brief of Legal Voice and Perinatal Loss Support Organizations and Experts in *Shuai* 11.

of sperm and paternal acts, and assumes that all aspects of fetal development rest entirely with the pregnant woman and her behaviour during pregnancy'.[172]

Ultimately, prosecuting a woman for delivering a stillborn child or a live-born child that dies soon after delivery renders her a criminal for experiencing outcomes that fall beyond her control.[173] In fact, the attribution of criminal liability for the experience of a stillbirth is widely opposed in the medical community. In supporting McKnight's Petition for writ of *certiorari*,[174] 26 separate institutions joined together to argue against adopting this approach to stillbirth and argued that medical science did not claim that the use of cocaine was the cause of McKnight's stillbirth and that 'it is exceedingly difficult to reliably isolate, beyond a reasonable doubt, any one factor (or group of factors) as having caused the stillbirth'.[175] Compounding the injustice of prosecution is the fact that, generally, addiction, suicide and refusal to undergo medical treatment are themselves not crimes in the United States and the United States approach demonstrates that the experience of a stillbirth for any possible conduct opens the door to criminal liability.[176]

8.5 IMPLICATIONS OF ADOPTING A SEPARATE-ENTITIES APPROACH

The separate-entities approach is perceived as being necessary to 'protect' the unborn on the basis of their being human beings, despite the fact that they are still in the process of gestation. This notion requires that, if the separate-entities approach is going to be advocated for and adopted as the means of protecting the

---

[172] *Amici curiae* brief of Legal Voice and Perinatal Loss Support Organizations and Experts in *Shuai* 11.

[173] *Amici curiae* brief of Legal Voice and Perinatal Loss Support Organizations and Experts in *Shuai* 11.

[174] *McKnight* (2003). According to EA Farnsworth *An Introduction to the Legal System of the United States* 4 ed (2010) 49–50, a writ of *certiorari* is the primary method of review by the United States Supreme Court, and it is essentially a command issued by the Supreme Court to a lower federal or state court of last resort requiring it to certify and return the record of proceedings. The command may be granted on the petition of either party to the case but a *certiorari* will only be granted for 'special and important reasons' and the fact that the decision concerned is 'erroneous' is not reason enough.

[175] *Amici curiae* brief of American Public Health Association, American Nurses Association, American Psychiatric Association et al in the matter of *McKnight v South Carolina* 540 US 819 (2003) 3. Even though this *amici curiae* brief was drafted in 2003 and relied on sources relevant to the state of medical technology at the time, the fact that the *amici curiae* brief for *Shuai* echoes the same issues demonstrates the inherent difficulty of providing an effective explanation of the cause of stillbirths.

[176] In fact, Burkstrand-Reid indicates that women were charged for involuntary manslaughter when their preferred birth method (home births) resulted in stillbirths; see BA Burkstrand-Reid 'From sex for pleasure to sex for parenthood: How the law manufactures mothers' (2013) 65 *Hastings LJ* 211 249. See *Commonwealth v Pugh* 969 NE 2d 672 (Mass 2012) (the Supreme Judicial Court of Massachusetts reversed Pugh's conviction of involuntary manslaughter based on the fact that she decided to have a home birth) and *United States v Jumper* 3 Fed Appx (4th Cir 2001) (In this case, Jumper decided against a hospital birth and after delivery of her child at her father's house, the neonate stopped breathing. Jumper did not call for assistance and concealed the child's corpse. On her admission of guilt, she was convicted of involuntary manslaughter.)

unborn as victims of violent crimes, then a woman cannot be excluded in relation to her own pregnancy, since it is the harm inflicte against the foetus which is of concern. The fact that the crimes of feticide, foetal homicide and murder of a foetus are being attributed to women (whether expressly in legislation or via imaginative interpretations) indicates that parties involved in or advocating for prosecutions have identifie the theoretical fla of exempting women.[177] This discussion will show that, while exempting women does not protect the unborn as human beings, including women within the ambit of 'perpetrator' renders some pregnancies at increased risk, and this leads to the emergence of tensions, which prevent healthy pregnancy outcomes.

By following a separate-entities approach to pregnancy the parties involved in prosecuting women for stillbirths have lost sight of the very obvious fact that ensuring a healthy woman is expected to increase the likelihood of a healthy birth outcome, genetics permitting. Bringing this perspective back into the context demonstrates that the threat of criminal prosecution for self-harm or 'risky' conduct during pregnancy would not encourage women to turn to the state and health-care system to get help but would rather cause them to avoid those institutions altogether, ultimately avoiding seeking prenatal care, drug and alcohol-related treatment and assistance during suicide ideation. This has received widespread recognition by the health-care community, who regularly co-operate and draft *amici curiae* briefs or release statements opposing the prosecution of women in respect of stillbirths or perinatal deaths.[178] Paltrow and Flavin identify 250 different organisations and experts opposed to the approach of criminalising adverse pregnancy outcomes.[179]

This approach negatively impacts on women's reproductive autonomy, in that these women are pregnant and in need of help and advancing punitive tactics against them deters them from seeking care or even communicating openly with care providers.[180] This places women at risk and consequently also fails to serve the aim of securing optimal foetal development and healthy birth outcomes.

Proehl explains that criminal liability 'creates perverse incentives', such as opting to terminate pregnancies instead of facing the possibility of prosecution.[181] Proehl asserts that there has already been one recorded incidence of this taking

[177] See Flavin *Our Crimes, Our Bodies* 100–3 for a neat summary of how this has taken place.

[178] For instance, see Bird (2014) *Hastings Women's LJ* 51; Paltrow & Flavin (2013) *Journal of Health Politics, Policy and Law* 331; Proehl (2013) *Santa Clara LR* 687–9; *amici curiae* brief of American Public Health Association, American Nurses Association, American Psychiatric Association et al in *McKnight* (2003) 16; and *amici curiae* brief of American Association of Suicideology, American College of Obstetricians and Gynecologists, American Congress of Obstetricians and Gynecologists et al in *Shuai*.

[179] Paltrow & Flavin (2013) *Journal of Health Politics, Policy and Law* 331.

[180] Paltrow & Flavin (2013) *Journal of Health Politics, Policy and Law* 332. The *amici curiae* brief of American Public Health Association, American Nurses Association, American Psychiatric Association et al in *McKnight* (2003) 16–8 explains the importance of developing a safe place within medical settings for women to openly relay information. This allows for attending health-care providers to assist in developing the most effective treatment for that particular woman. However, criminalising this area turns health care into an evidence-collection activity for purposes of prosecution, ultimately violating the 'sanctity of [the] health care provider–patient relationship'.

[181] Proehl (2013) *Santa Clara LR* 689.

place, when a pregnant woman terminated her pregnancy to avoid being charged with child endangerment.[182] Proehl argues that the threat of criminal sanction 'creates a strong incentive against carrying a pregnancy to term. A state's goal of raising healthy babies is seriously undermined by resorting to the criminal system to regulate pregnancy.'[183] However, this approach not only impacts negatively on the aim of securing healthy live births but also undermines women's reproductive autonomy because the threat of prosecution could drive women to terminate wanted pregnancies—thus removing choice.[184]

The application of criminal provisions against women in relation to their failed pregnancies is a poor response. If the aim is to protect pregnancies from harm, then pregnant women must be understood contextually in order for there to be responsible and effective practical translation of the state's goal of advancing prenatal life and women's health during pregnancy. Context requires that underlying risk factors of stillbirth are addressed,[185] those broadly associated with poverty, addiction, mental illness, inadequate access to respectful prenatal care, education, domestic violence, and so on. Removing women from their contextual setting and assigning sole criminal responsibility effectively draws attention away from the collective and multifaceted causes of stillbirth. In fact, it may even make the identificatio of these contributors impossible. Ultimately, this renders addressing the issue of stillbirth an absolute failure for women and their pregnancies. Going further, failure to address the wider social issues essentially ensures repeated adverse pregnancy outcomes.

Also, failing to understand pregnant women's context means that even those feticide measures that are limited to third parties may possibly be failing to protect women and thus the unborn as well. The original incentive[186] for advancing feticide or foetal homicide laws was to tackle domestic violence against pregnant women by their partners which resulted in adverse pregnancy outcomes.[187] However, interest in men's contribution to poor pregnancy outcomes seems to be a non-issue.[188] Schroedel, Fiber and Snyder advanced this argument in 2000.[189] A

[182] Proehl (2013) *Santa Clara LR* 689. She cites the case as *State v Greywind*; however, no reference is provided and a reported version of this case cannot be sourced.

[183] Proehl (2013) *Santa Clara LR* 690. American Public Health Association, American Nurses Association, American Psychiatric Association et al argue the same: 'The criminal investigation and possible prosecution of women like Ms McKnight sends a perilous message to pregnant addicts not to seek prenatal care or drug treatment, not to confid their addiction to health care professionals, and not to give birth in hospitals—or not to carry the fetus to term.' See *amici curiae* brief of American Public Health Association, American Nurses Association, American Psychiatric Association et al in *McKnight* (2003) 20.

[184] *Amici curiae* brief of American Association of Suicideology, American College of Obstetricians and Gynecologists, American Congress of Obstetricians and Gynecologists et al in *Shuai* 22.

[185] *Amici curiae* brief of American Association of Suicideology, American College of Obstetricians and Gynecologists, American Congress of Obstetricians and Gynecologists et al in *Shuai* 19.

[186] Bird (2014) *Hastings Women's LJ* 50 and Paltrow & Flavin (2013) *Journal of Health Politics, Policy and Law* 323.

[187] Obviously the fact that women can be prosecuted under these laws indicates that protecting women may not be of concern any longer.

[188] Schroedel, Fiber & Snyder (2000) *Duke Journal of Gender Law & Policy* 111–2.

[189] Schroedel, Fiber & Snyder (2000) *Duke Journal of Gender Law & Policy* 111–2.

2011 study of the causes of maternal mortality indicates that, aside from suicide, homicide is a leading cause of maternal mortality and Palladino, Singh, Campbell et al demonstrate that homicide rates have increased compared with those indicated in 1999 studies.[190] This can be interpreted as indicating that the threat of criminal prosecution and the development of the foetus as a separate victim of crime have done little to protect women and the foetus because the context of a pregnancy has been removed. In fact, the context of pregnancy is so far removed that these feticide measures which render the unborn separate victims of violence have essentially removed women as victims as well.[191] Interestingly, Palladino, Singh, Campbell et al do not suggest increasing criminal prosecutions but rather suggest that the underlying social concerns that foster abusive conduct receive attention.[192] Failing to do so flie in the face of women's reproductive autonomy since the decision to bear a child is interfered with, and this not only costs her her life, but also takes prenatal life with it. These are extreme cases of poor pregnancy outcomes.

The separate-entities approach fails to produce positive pregnancy outcomes, because it encourages pregnancy adversarialism and because this approach renders the unborn separate victims of violent conduct and makes pregnant women potential wrongdoers. Further, third parties intercept and speak for the unborn. Adversarialism in the United States is generally referred to as 'maternal–foetal conflicts' which creates the impression that women's interests are in conflic with the interests of the unborn. This in turn creates the situation where one party is pitted against the other, and, as in all adversarial conflicts only one party can succeed.[193] The 'conflict is deemed to arise in cases where a pregnant woman engages in 'risky' behaviour as an autonomous agent (as her personal interests generally permit),[194] and this behaviour is judged by others to be in contravention of the unborn's interest for optimal development and eventual live birth. In reality, the 'conflict is not between women and the unborn but between others and the pregnant women, since others perceive her conduct as infringing on the unborn as a separate entity and attempt to act to prevent it, as 'foetal guardians' through policing and regulating women.[195]

---

[190] Palladino, Singh, Campbell et al (2011) *Obstetrics & Gynecology* 1056–7; 1061.

[191] See Flavin *Our Bodies, Our Crimes* 101.

[192] Palladino, Singh, Campbell et al (2011) *Obstetrics & Gynecology* 1062. Their summarised conclusion provides (1056): 'Our results indicate that pregnancy-associated homicide and suicide are important contributors to maternal mortality and confir the need to evaluate the relationships between sociodemographic disparities and intimate-partner violence with pregnancy-associated violent death.'

[193] Steinbock *Life before Birth* 155; 156.

[194] However, it is noted that conduct associated with addiction and mental illness impacts negatively on women's ability to act autonomously since these conditions have the effect of removing or substantially reducing the experience of freedom in the 'decision'-making processes.

[195] R Roth *Making Women Pay: The Hidden Cost of Fetal Rights* (2000) 6–7. See S Meredith *Policing Pregnancy: The Law and Ethics of Obstetric Conflict* (2005) 170–5 who, aside from discussing the conflic between pregnant women and health-care providers seeking to secure healthy pregnancies and live births, also discusses other areas where conflic arises between third parties and pregnant women. She effectively demonstrates that efforts to act for foetal interests diminish

Roth[196] provides a fittin example of the above 'foetal guardian' construction: in a Californian case concerning the attempted prosecution of a woman for experiencing a stillbirth which was allegedly a result of her substance abuse during pregnancy, the deputy district attorney is quoted as arguing that under *Roe*:[197]

> [T]hat baby that isn't born that happens to be over the age of twenty-four to twenty-eight weeks gestation has Constitutional rights, and somebody has to listen to that voice. Even though no one else can hear it, we hear it, and we intend to protect that child's Constitutional rights.

Essentially, the situation of speaking for the unborn against the women who gestated them aids in removing context (being those wider social issues that have a role to play in creating adverse pregnancy outcomes) and thus renders women exclusively liable for ensuring foetal health without providing them the means of doing so. The implications of adopting a separate-entities approach to addressing violence that terminates pregnancies encourages pregnancy adversarialism and fails to ensure healthy pregnancies or outcomes where both female reproductive autonomy and foetal interests are advanced.

8.6 IMPLICATIONS FOR REFORM PROPOSALS IN SOUTH AFRICA

Both Kruuse[198] and Du Plessis[199] refer to the United States as an example of a possible avenue for South Africa to consider regarding law reform. In this respect, the lack of conformity in the United States concerning how best to address the issue of violent termination of pregnancies offers valuable insight on the range of possibilities available in dealing with this concern within the parameters of the separate-entities approach. Du Plessis' position is not too far off from the general position in the United States, in that she proposes protection from the moment of conception while still advocating that lawful termination of pregnancies remain in place.[200] Most importantly for feticide proposals in South Africa as advanced by Du Plessis[201] and Kruuse,[202] both the federal and the state codes have extended prenatal protection outside the realms of constitutional provisions. This is important because it is both Kruuse's[203] and Du Plessis'[204] contention that

---

women's autonomy during pregnancy, thus highlighting the notion that viewing the unborn as separate entities opens the door for one 'party' to lose something for the benefi of the other 'party'.

196 Roth *Making Women Pay* 135.

197 Roth cites *People v Jaurigue*; see Roth *Making Women Pay* 135. This case cannot be sourced and a full citation cannot be provided.

198 Kruuse (2009) *THRHR* 134–5. While Kruuse does not specificall rely on particular statutes in place in the United States, she does rely on Dworkin's position. Dworkin's commentary focuses on the United States' approach to this specifi topic.

199 Du Plessis (2013) *Stell LR* 80–4.

200 Du Plessis (2013) *Stell LR* 91.

201 Du Plessis (2013) *Stell LR* 76–8; 87–90. Generally, Du Plessis argues against the position that advancing the right to life to the unborn or designating the attribution of 'personhood' is not necessary for protecting the unborn from third-party violence that terminates prenatal life.

202 Kruuse (2009) *THRHR* 133.

203 Kruuse (2009) *THRHR* 133.

204 (2013) *Stell LR* 91.

working outside the parameters of constitutionally informed foetal rights prevents a clash with women's rights or prevents the scenario in which women will be denied access to termination-of-pregnancy services.

After reviewing the theoretical soundness of the various approaches, a number of flaw emerged and these flaw are found to negate the value of Kruuse's and Du Plessis' proposals for South Africa. Du Plessis' and Kruuse's positions, that avoiding foetal rights or personhood will allow for termination-of-pregnancy laws and feticide to co-exist, is theoretically unsound, purely on the basis that the unborn are individuated as separate entities. In cases where pregnant women are excluded, those proposed exclusionary provisions attribute contradictory values to the unborn, and if one is dealing with the same entity across all the spheres of law and relationships it is not clear what basis is being relied on for the attribution of different values. Further, where one asserts a uniform value in the unborn for purposes of law, feticide or foetal homicide measures are used against pregnant women in respect of their adverse pregnancy outcomes via imaginative statutory interpretations. This proves problematic because, theoretically, these measures do not ensure healthy births but merely respond to the adverse outcome. The measures do nothing to actually protect prenatal life while it exists.

Also, a deeper consideration of how the United States employs and applies these provisions indicates that its primary concern is to oust the lawful termination of pregnancy and impose 'good mother' laws on those who are socially constructed as being 'bad mothers'.[205]

8.7 CONCLUDING REMARKS

The value of Du Plessis and Kruuse's position of arguing for direct protection of the unborn as separate victims of violence that terminates prenatal life can be critically reviewed in the wake of the United States' experience. The United States demonstrates that there are various definitiona methods that can be adopted to extend direct protection to the unborn under the separate-entities umbrella. Similar to the arguments promoted by Kruuse and Du Plessis, the basis for direct protection stems from the foundation that the unborn are part of humanity and thus require consideration in law. The Unites States was able to do this under *Roe,* which prevents the allocation of constitutional rights to the unborn. On the surface, this creates a welcoming impression that the same methods pertaining to protection from violence can be adopted in South Africa and this will protect women who plan to continue with their pregnancies and also protect the unborn

[205] Concerning the 'good mother' versus 'bad mother' rhetoric in the United States, see Flavin *Our Bodies, Our Crimes* 102–3. Flavin argues that the practice of prosecuting women for pregnancy continuation is based on society's beliefs about who is fi to procreate and who is not. In this respect, society expresses what it views as constituting a good mother. A good mother is one who provides and secures healthy foetal development. Flavin explains that those women who cannot secure these requirements are regarded as bad mothers. The allocation of this title removes attention from the real causes of poor pregnancy outcomes, such as poor access to health care and a lack of policies that that support parenting and pregnant women. Flavin views the prosecution of women for issues related to their pregnancies or pregnancy outcomes as a mechanism to normalise and standardise the notion of a 'good mother'.

even though they lack constitutional recognition. However, further consideration highlights contradictory outcomes and the root cause of this lies in the application of the separate-entities approach to pregnancy.

The United States' experience has shown that limiting potential perpetrators to only third parties violates the founding notion that the unborn are human beings and are in need of protection on that basis. This consequently leads to questionable outcomes concerning the actual protection of the unborn. Further, laws directed at protecting the unborn as separate victims seem to have made little impact on violence against pregnant women and thus have failed to prevent harm to both subjects that constitute a pregnancy.

While this leaves Kruuse's and Du Plessis' proposals in a questionable position, one could argue for the extension of protection measures to include pregnant women. The chapter tested the credibility of this approach and it highlighted further concerns. It could be argued that including women as potential perpetrators is more in line with the premise that the unborn are being protected because they are human beings. However, this chapter shows that it also fails to extend any meaningful protection from stillbirth.

The wholesale failure of feticide or foetal homicide measures is linked to the fact that the separate-entities approach is being employed. The unborn are viewed as separate from the women who gestate them and are vested with individuated and distinguished needs. This has led to women's needs being ignored, but they are also identifie as the sole cause of foetal demise. This fails to understand that an unhealthy woman leads to unhealthy pregnancies and unhealthy birth outcomes. With this realisation, context can be considered and wider social-related risk factors can be included when considering how to develop an effective way forward to address issues associated with violence against pregnant women. Instead of addressing pregnancy-related concerns, the separate-entities approach is the epitome of pregnancy adversarialism and as a result it fails to advance women's reproductive autonomy *or* foetal interests.

Further, the fact that *Roe* remains in place despite these foetal protections being enacted should not be interpreted as rendering foetal protection measures valid in respect of women's rights generally. Pregnancy and all pregnancy-related issues in the United States are plagued by the undercurrents of hostile reproductive politics, and foetal protection measures such as feticide or foetal homicide laws are used to weaken *Roe* and its legitimacy.[206] This means that, if the unborn were extended legal status in all areas of law excluding termination of pregnancy, there would no longer be a basis on which *Roe* could be saved. What is evident is that *Roe* is being relied on to advance protection, that decision is interpreted as providing a judicially sanctioned discourse of the unborn in law, and it is being used in a way which leads to its own demise.[207] In fact, Flavin argues that 'champions of

[206] See Chapter Seven, para 7.4.

[207] Interestingly, Kruuse (2009) *THRHR* 126 is interpreted as adopting the same approach, however, maybe without the intended consequence of rendering termination of pregnancies illegal in South Africa. Kruuse turns to the Choice Act as an indication that, in South Africa, there is a vested interest in the unborn since we limit women's access to termination procedures as the pregnancy progresses. She then goes on to use this to justify protecting the unborn from third-party violence. This

fetus-centred laws have co-opted the language of the women's movement to garner support for their position and arguably mask their intent'.[208]

Even if all of what has been argued here concerning the application of feticide to pregnant women can be removed by imaginative legislative provisions in South Africa, the next chapter will demonstrate how feticide measures, which are applicable only to third parties, are now being relied on to justify charging women with child abuse as a result of their use of and addiction to substances during pregnancies. This is yet another indicator that a separate-entities approach to pregnancy generally fosters pregnancy adversarialism.

---

highlights the relevance of studying the United States; it demonstrates the consequences of developing the law in this way. Should Kruuse's approach be adopted, anti-termination-of-pregnancy lobby groups may fin this the perfect opportunity to deny women the right to terminate a pregnancy, similar to what is happening in the United States.

[208] Flavin *Our Bodies, Our Crimes* 101.

Chapter 9

PRENATAL SUBSTANCE ABUSE AS CHILD ABUSE

9.1 INTRODUCTION

Ovens demonstrates a legitimate concern surrounding the issue of substance abuse during pregnancy and the need to address its occurrence.[1] Briefl , Ovens[2] advocates for the extension of child abuse to include the unborn in order to protect them from the perceived harmful consequences of prenatal substance abuse.[3] This chapter tests whether substance abuse during pregnancy should constitute child abuse against the unborn and discusses how the United States has approached the issue. This will prove beneficia to the overall purpose of advancing women's reproductive autonomy and foetal interests in South Africa.

When discussing Ovens' position in Chapter Six, it was argued that, from a practical perspective, there can never be a crime of foetal abuse, since birth is necessary to witness harm and then prove causation.[4] Until birth, harm is purely theoretical and this is evident when considering the United States' position, because child abuse or endangerment charges are brought against women only after they have given birth. While the United States has grappled with the issue of substance abuse during pregnancy for a number of years now,[5] to date no pregnant woman has been charged with the crime of child abuse of a foetus,[6] meaning that no woman has been charged or convicted of child abuse while still pregnant. Rather, child abuse charges have been brought against women after they have given birth and the children have tested positive for exposure to certain substances.

Consequently, Ovens' recommendation is different from the United States' approach. She calls for substance abuse during pregnancy to constitute child abuse in respect of a foetus, while the United States renders prenatal substance abuse as child abuse in respect of a neonate born alive and testing positive for exposure to certain substances prenatally. Despite these differences, the common ground

---

[1] M Ovens 'Maternal substance abuse in South Africa: An area for concern?' (2008) 1 *Acta Criminologica* 77 and M Ovens 'A criminological perspective of prenatal abuse of substances during pregnancy and the link to child abuse in South Africa' (2010) 11 *Child Abuse Research in South Africa* 38. See the discussion in Chapter Six, para 6.3.3.

[2] Ovens (2010) *Child Abuse Research in South Africa* 38. She titles this 'prenatal substance abuse'.

[3] Substance abuse is taken to include addiction and use, and concerns the abuse or use of illegal substances.

[4] See Chapter Six, para 6.3.3 for a full discussion of Ovens' proposal for reform.

[5] Guttmacher Institute 'State laws and policies: Substance abuse during pregnancy' (1 March 2016) available at http://www.guttmacher.org/statecenter/spibs/spib_SADP.pdf (accessed on 23 June 2016). According to the Guttmacher Institute policymakers have been debating the best way forward since the 1980s.

[6] Guttmacher Institute 'State laws and policies: Substance abuse during pregnancy'.

between the two is that there is a move towards criminalising prenatal substance abuse and each adopts a separate-entities approach to pregnancy in order to do so.[7]

This chapter discusses how the United States has opted to address issues related to substance abuse or use during pregnancy that results in the live birth of a neonate who tests positive for drug exposure as a result of prenatal substance abuse or use. Thereafter the discussion turns to identifying a number of inconsistencies related to those approaches and the chapter demonstrates that adopting a separate-entities approach as advocated by Ovens may fail to achieve healthy pregnancies and pregnancy outcomes.

It is noteworthy that Chapter Nine draws on similar arguments presented in Chapter Eight in relation to the notion of holding women criminally liable in respect of adverse pregnancy outcomes. However, this chapter covers those instances where there is live birth and considers possible child abuse charges as a result of prenatal exposure to certain substances. Chapter Eight, on the other hand, looks at cases of stillbirth and consequential murder charges against women as a result of a wide range of conduct during pregnancy.

9.2 SUBSTANCE ABUSE DURING PREGNANCY IN THE UNITED STATES

Until fairly recently, no state had explicitly criminalised the conduct of substance abuse during pregnancy as any particular crime.[8] According to Harris, Arbor and Paltrow, avoiding criminalisation is in line with two United States Supreme Court decisions which established that addiction is not a crime but rather an illness that requires treatment and not punishment.[9] Instead of using criminal law, 18 states have expanded civil child-welfare requirements to include substance abuse during pregnancy, thus detecting drug-exposure in neonates serves as a ground for terminating parental rights on the basis of child abuse or neglect.[10] Only a few states consider prenatal substance abuse to be the criminal child abuse of born neonates.[11] Despite this focus on civil regulation,[12] the Guttmacher Institute points

---

[7] LM Paltrow & J Flavin 'Arrests of and forced interventions on pregnant women in the United States, 1973–2005: Implications for women's legal status and public health' (2013) 38 *Journal of Health Politics, Policy and Law* 299 identify all criminal actions against pregnant women in relation to their own pregnancies as being based on the separate-entities approach to pregnancy.

[8] Guttmacher Institute 'State laws and policies: Substance abuse during pregnancy' and LH Harris, A Arbor & L Paltrow 'The status of pregnant women and fetuses in US criminal law' (2003) 289 *Journal of the American Medical Association* 1697.

[9] Harris, Arbor & Paltrow (2003) *Journal of the American Medical Association* 1697. In this respect, see *Linder v United States* 268 US 5 (1925) and *Robinson v California* 370 US 660 (1962).

[10] See Guttmacher Institute 'State laws and policies: Substance abuse during pregnancy'. Harris, Arbor and Paltrow explain that in some states civil child abuse laws involve establishing women's parenting abilities while in other states substance abuse serves as a basis of 'presumptive neglect'. The authors emphasise that these laws are aimed at protecting children and not punishing women on the grounds of foetal rights. See Harris, Arbor & Paltrow (2003) *Journal of the American Medical Association* 1698.

[11] These states will be discussed in more detail below.

[12] For instance, some states make provision for civil commitment of pregnant women who use drugs and these commitments can later be used in child-welfare proceedings after birth. Also, a number of states have taken a different route and made treating drug-addicted pregnant women a

out that prosecutors have nevertheless attempted to attack prenatal substance abuse by relying on other criminal laws not related to the specifi issue of substance abuse.[13] In this context Harris, Arbor and Paltrow[14] indicate that women are generally charged with one of three types of crime in relation to their pregnancies: child abuse or endangerment, foetal murder or manslaughter,[15] or illegal delivery of drugs[16] to a minor. Paltrow and Flavin report that feticide laws are commonly used to support the argument that generally worded legislation regulating child endangerment or drug delivery to a minor should be interpreted to

---

priority, allowing for treatment to be more readily accessible. See Guttmacher Institute 'State laws and policies: Substance abuse during pregnancy'. However, these sorts of provisions render questionable outcomes; see Paltrow & Flavin (2013) *Journal of Health Politics, Policy and Law* 307. The authors discuss Rachael Louw's case. When Louw voluntarily sought treatment for her addiction while pregnant, she was reported under Wisconsin's 'cocaine mom' statute which allows for a pregnant woman to be kept in custody if she is known to 'habitually lack self-control' in respect of alcohol or controlled substances. Paltrow and Flavin report that while Louw was involuntarily detained in a psychiatric ward she did not receive prenatal care, she was prescribed numerous medications including Xanax, and while her foetus was assigned a guardian *ad litem*, Louw did not receive any counselling until 12 days after being detained. Even after a doctor testifie that Louw's substance usage posed no material risk to her pregnancy and the court ordered her release, she remained in detention for several days after the court order and remained under state surveillance until she gave birth.

[13] Guttmacher Institute 'State laws and policies: Substance abuse during pregnancy'.

[14] Harris, Arbor & Paltrow (2003) *Journal of the American Medical Association* 1697. Also see J Flavin & LM Paltrow 'Punishing pregnant drug-using women: Defying law, medicine, and common sense' (2010) 29 *Journal of Addictive Diseases* 231 233 for more recent figures The authors state that their study identifie hundreds of cases across 40 states where pregnant women are identifie as drug-users and arrested and during the period spanning 2005 and 2006 dozens of cases came to the attention of National Advocates for Pregnant Women.

[15] See discussion in Chapter Eight, para 8.3.3 concerning Regina Knight.

[16] Under these charges women are accused of delivering drugs to the unborn via the umbilical cord. In this respect Harris, Arbor and Paltrow ((2003) *Journal of the American Medical Association* 1697) state that at times prosecutors have accepted that the unborn is not a person but continue with the charges on the basis that a woman arguably delivers drugs through the umbilical cord just after birth but before the cord is clamped and cut. For instance, see *Johnson v State* 578 So 2d 419 (Fla App 5 Dist 1991). The District Court of Appeal of Florida confirme two counts of delivering a controlled substance to neonates through the umbilical cord after birth. In this case Johnson used cocaine while pregnant and very soon before the delivery of each of her two children. The court held (420): 'Appellant voluntarily took cocaine into her body, knowing it would pass to her fetus and knowing (or should have known) that birth was imminent. She is deemed to know that an infant at birth is a person, and a minor, and that delivery of cocaine to the infant is illegal. We can reach no other conclusion logically.' Sharp J, dissenting with the majority (421–5), raised a number of issues. Relevant to this discussion, the judge dissented on the basis that the legislation criminalising the delivery of a controlled substance by an adult to a minor is not meant be applied to a woman in relation to her just-born child since there was no legislative indication of this intent. Further, Sharp J found that there was insufficient evidence before the court to prove that delivery of the controlled substance took place after birth, being the only time relevant for the crime. However, in *Johnson v State* 602 So 2d 1288 (Fla 1992) the Supreme Court of Florida quashed the District Court's finding The court (1290) followed Sharp J's position concerning lack of legislative intent to allow for the crime to be applicable to a woman and her just-delivered child, and that 'delivery' does not include the method of delivery of a controlled substance via the umbilical cord. This closed down the avenues of charging women for dealing in a controlled substance to their babies just after birth but before the umbilical cord is cut.

allow for the arrest and prosecution of pregnant women in relation to their own pregnancy outcomes.[17]

Aside from criminal charges there are also documented incidences of 'preventive detention'. This involves incidents when pregnant women are charged with a particular crime which is unrelated to pregnancy or substance use, but because they tested positive and were pregnant at the time of being brought before the court, they were sentenced to detention instead of probation, which would be the usual course of action.[18]

Given that this chapter is concerned with testing the validity of Ovens' calls for changes to the law, only those instances where women have been held criminally liable in terms of criminal child abuse charges will be considered here.[19] It is noteworthy that there is no federal legislation or case law that holds prenatal substance abuse to be criminal child abuse. However, at the state level there is a hive of activity.

Schroedel, Fiber and Snyder point out that earlier attempts at protecting the unborn from substance exposure took the form of applying existing child abuse legislation, which, technically, was relevant only to those children who had already been born.[20] Harris, Arbor and Paltrow explain that, in these instances, prosecutors attempted to equate a viable foetus with a child and argued that, by using drugs or suffering from addiction, a pregnant woman was committing child abuse.[21] However, in all the cases examined in the study conducted by Harris, Arbor and Paltrow, the courts refused to extend the child abuse provisions to include the unborn on the basis that no such legislative intent was apparent from the legislation as drafted.[22] Otherwise, the courts found that the extension of these

---

[17] Paltrow & Flavin (2013) *Journal of Health Politics, Policy and Law* 323.

[18] For instance, see Flavin & Paltrow (2010) *Journal of Addictive Diseases* 235. The authors refer to a case concerning Brenda Vaughan who pleaded guilty to forgery charges and the prosecution recommended probation instead of being sentenced to a term of imprisonment. After the judge found out that Vaughan was pregnant and tested positive for cocaine, the judge sentenced her to 30 days' imprisonment pending a decision as to whether she could be admitted to a special intensive probation programme. It turned out that she was not a resident of the state and therefore did not qualify for the intensive probation programme and the judge sentenced her to a further six months' imprisonment. The authors quote the judge as saying: 'I'm going to keep her locked up until the baby is born because she'd tested positive for cocaine when she came before me. . . . She's apparently an addictive personality and I'll be darned if I am going to have a baby born that way.' Flavin and Paltrow point out that there was no trial or conviction of any charge relating to possession or use of illegal substances. It is not clear how this sort of judicial discretion has any legal force as it offends the principle of legality.

[19] However, given the fact that there is a strong civil law presence concerning substance abuse or use during pregnancy, it may be an indication that there is a majority view that criminal law responses are inappropriate.

[20] JR Schroedel, P Fiber & BD Snyder 'Women's rights and fetal personhood in criminal law' (2000) 7 *Duke Journal of Gender Law & Policy* 89 103.

[21] Harris, Arbor & Paltrow (2003) *Journal of the American Medical Association* 1697.

[22] Harris, Arbor & Paltrow (2003) *Journal of the American Medical Association* 1698. Further Schroedel, Fiber and Snyder ((2000) *Duke Journal of Gender Law & Policy* 103) explain that where prosecutors did obtain convictions in lower courts, their manipulation of legal terms adopted in legislation made reversal more likely in higher courts. For some examples, see *State v Gethers* 585

laws would render the statute constitutionally invalid on the basis of vagueness.[23] These statutes would be vague in the sense that women could be held criminally liable for an endless array of scenarios, such as smoking or taking up employment in a hazardous working environment, thus making it difficult to determine beforehand whether any particular conduct was criminal or not.[24] Thus, in the context of child abuse, the courts have generally refused to extend the definitio of a child to include a foetus, or the definitio of a parent to include a pregnant woman in relation to her foetus or that the term 'delivery' to include the transfer of drug-contaminated blood via the umbilical cord.[25]

9.3 CHILD ABUSE CONVICTIONS

Writing more recently on substance abuse during pregnancy in the context of criminal law, Flavin and Paltrow[26] state that when women challenge the imposition of criminal sanctions brought against them for substance abuse during pregnancy, the appellate courts have almost consistently dismissed or overturned the charges or convictions. However, some exceptions stand.

In 1992 in the state of South Carolina, Cornelia Whitner pleaded guilty[27] to criminal child neglect[28] due to her using cocaine during her third trimester, thus causing her child to be born with traces of cocaine in his system. She was sentenced to eight years' imprisonment by the Circuit Court and she did not appeal her conviction.[29] Whitner later file a petition for post-conviction relief[30] on the basis that the court *a quo* lacked the jurisdiction to accept her guilty plea, since she pleaded guilty to a non-existent crime.[31] Additionally, she argued that she was represented by ineffective counsel in that her attorney failed to advise her that the crime she was being prosecuted for might not apply to prenatal drug use.[32] Her petition was granted, but the state appealed and the case went before the South Carolina Supreme Court, with the same questions to be addressed.[33]

So 2d 1140 (Fla App 4 Dist 1991); *Reinesto v Superior Court* 894 P 2d 733 (Ariz App Div 1 1995); and *Herron v State* 729 NE 2d 1008 (Ind App 2000).

[23] Harris, Arbor & Paltrow (2003) *Journal of the American Medical Association* 1697.

[24] Harris, Arbor & Paltrow (2003) *Journal of the American Medical Association* 1697.

[25] Harris, Arbor & Paltrow (2003) *Journal of the American Medical Association* 1697.

[26] Flavin & Paltrow (2010) *Journal of Addictive Diseases* 235.

[27] *Whitner v State* 492 SE 2d 777 (SC 1997) (*Whitner*) 778. The history of previous proceedings was obtained from the Supreme Court's decision as it recounted how the case ended up before it.

[28] The Supreme Court of South Carolina (779) provides the following definitio for criminal child neglect (as per South Carolina Code Annotated s 20-7-50): 'Any person having the legal custody of any *child* or helpless person, who shall, without lawful excuse, refuse or neglect to provide . . . the proper care and attention for such *child* or helpless person, so that the life, health or comfort of such *child* or helpless person is endangered or likely to be endangered, shall be guilty of a misdemeanour and shall be punished within the discretion of the circuit court.' (Emphasis in the original.)

[29] *Whitner* 779.

[30] *Whitner* 779.

[31] *Whitner* 779.

[32] The court dismissed this notion (784) because, as will be evident from the discussion that follows, the court found that the crime of child endangerment is applicable to a viable foetus.

[33] *Whitner* 777.

Concerning whether Whitner pleaded guilty to a non-existent crime, the state argued that the criminal child endangerment statute encompasses acts by a pregnant woman that endanger the life, health or comfort of her viable foetus.[34] The Supreme Court[35] then went on to state that the question before the court was therefore whether a viable foetus is a 'person' as per the definitio of child being 'a person under the age of eighteen'.[36] To answer this question the court emphasised that it must determine the intention of the legislature, which could be ascertained by reference to the language adopted and the context of that language within the entire construct of the statute and policy of the law generally.[37] After referring to the fact that a viable foetus is a person in respect of wrongful death actions and feticide, the court stated:[38]

> [W]e do not see any rational basis for findin a viable fetus is not a 'person' in the present context. Indeed it would be absurd to recognize the viable fetus as a person for purposes of homicide laws and wrongful death statutes but not for the purpose of statutes proscribing child abuse. Our holding in Hall that a viable fetus is a person rested primarily on the plain meaning of the word 'person' in light of existing medical knowledge concerning fetal development. We do not believe that the plain and ordinary meaning of the word 'person' has changed in any way that would deny viable fetuses status as persons.

Whitner argued against the inclusion of a viable foetus within the ambit of 'person' on a number of grounds, but what stands out is the fact that including a viable foetus in a child endangerment statute would lead to the incongruous result that 'every action by a pregnant woman that endangers or is likely to endanger a fetus, whether otherwise legal or illegal, would constitute unlawful neglect'.[39] Even smoking or drinking during pregnancy might lead to women being prosecuted under the statute.[40] The court rejected this argument and asserted that the alcoholic parents of born children can be found guilty of child neglect or endangerment, even though the act of drinking alcohol is legal in itself.[41]

The court went on to express its lack of interest in the implications of extending criminal child endangerment provisions to a viable foetus when it stated that it did not need to address 'this potential parade of horribles advanced by Whitner'.[42] The court emphasised that it was concerned only with the particular case before it, being that Whitner admitted to using drugs in the third trimester which caused her child to be born with traces of the drug in his system.[43] The court found Whitner's conduct to have endangered the life, health and comfort of her child, despite the fact that 'the precise effects of maternal crack use during pregnancy *are somewhat*

---

[34] *Whitner* 779.

[35] *Whitner* 779.

[36] This is the definitio provided in the South Carolina Children's Code, s 20-7-30(1) (1985).

[37] *Whitner* 779.

[38] *Whitner* 780. The court found the South Carolina Children's Code supported their position of including a viable foetus within the ambit of the term 'child'.

[39] *Whitner* 781.

[40] *Whitner* 781.

[41] *Whitner* 781.

[42] *Whitner* 782.

[43] *Whitner* 782.

unclear, [however] it is well documented and within the realm of public knowledge that such use can cause serious harm to the viable unborn child'.[44] (Emphasis added.)

The South Carolina Supreme Court also rejected Whitner's argument that she had not been provided with sufficient notice that her conduct constituted a crime,[45] since the plain meaning of 'child' includes a viable foetus and that it is 'common knowledge' that drug use can cause harm to the unborn.[46] Whitner also advanced the argument that prosecuting her violated her right to carry her pregnancy to term, which right is founded on the right to privacy.[47] She asserted that the United States Constitution 'protects women from measures penalizing them for choosing to carry their pregnancies to term'.[48] The court accepted that it is true that women have a constitutional right to continue with a pregnancy. However, the court was critical of this argument in the context of Whitner's case, findin that none of Whitner's rights are implicated (privacy or otherwise) because no one has the right to use cocaine.[49] The court found that the state has a compelling interest (as provided for in *Roe v Wade*)[50] in protecting the life and health of a viable foetus and that the

> State's imposition of an additional penalty when a pregnant woman with a viable fetus engages in the already proscribed behavior does not burden a woman's right to carry her pregnancy to term; rather, the additional penalty recognizes that a third party (the viable fetus or newborn child) is harmed by the behaviour.

The South Carolina Supreme Court reversed the decision by the Circuit Court concerning Whitner's post-conviction relief motion and the United States Supreme Court denied her petition for a writ of *certiorari*.[51] Accordingly, in South Carolina, the position stands that a pregnant woman can commit the crime of child endangerment and abuse against her own foetus via substance abuse or even by using a substance on a once-off basis, and this also may involve legal or illegal substances.

---

[44] *Whitner* 782.

[45] This being a question of legality in South African terms.

[46] *Whitner* 785.

[47] *Whitner* 785.

[48] This argument is based on the premise that women who engage in conduct perceived to be harmful must either terminate their pregnancies or face criminal prosecution and imprisonment which places them in a position to have to choose. This imposition of choice violates their right to continue with a pregnancy. The threat of imprisonment is a great burden on women's freedom to carry a pregnancy to term. In this respect, the defence referred to a number of United States Supreme Court decisions relating to pregnant women's procreative rights; *Whitner* 785.

[49] *Whitner* 786.

[50] *Roe v Wade* 93 S Ct 705 (1973) (*Roe*) 732.

[51] *Whitner v South Carolina* 523 US 1145 (1998). According to EA Farnsworth *An Introduction to the Legal System of the United States* 4 ed (2010) 49–50, a writ of *certiorari* is the primary method of review by the United States Supreme Court, and it is essentially a command issued by the court to the lower federal or state courts of last resort requiring it to certify and return the record of proceedings. The command may be granted on the petition of either party to the case but a *certiorari* will only be granted for 'special and important reasons' and the fact that the decision concerned is 'erroneous' is not reason enough. Thus, it should be kept in mind that just because the United States Supreme Court denied a writ of *certiorari* it does not confir or deny the correctness of the South Carolina Supreme Court finding in the least.

A number of issues need to be raised concerning *Whitner*. It is not clear how the court can impose criminal liability without sufficient evidence pertaining to the fact that there was even a possibility of harm to the viable foetus as a result of exposure to cocaine. There must be harm or a possibility of harm, and substance abuse must be the factual and legal cause of that. The court's reference to 'public knowledge' of harm is questionable. Thus it is debatable whether any endangerment to life, health or comfort was proved at all. In all fairness, harm or possibility thereof must be founded on objective evidence, conceivably from the medical profession, of any harm. Public knowledge itself is not an indication that harm or the possibility of harm factually exists.

Going further, it is noteworthy that this stance towards pregnant drug-dependent women not only equates pregnant women with parents of born children, but possibly extends far more onerous parental obligations and legal duties regarding the prenatal relationship. This is the case because the prenatal relationship involves women's bodies and requires that their bodies are kept in an optimal condition for purposes of gestation. On the other hand, the body of a female parent of a born child is somewhat irrelevant to the wellbeing of the child concerned, aside from cases of breastfeeding. Thus, this case creates a heavier obligation on pregnant women as 'parents' of the unborn, while parents of born children are allocated a lesser degree of responsibility regarding the healthy upkeep of their bodies. Also, it is only pregnant women who carry this responsibility because it is only conduct during gestation that is viewed as relevant rather than harmful conduct by men who contribute to conception. Consequently, paternal contributors bear no responsibility for ensuring healthy foetal development. Taking this argument to extremes, focusing on women's obligations to their bodies during pregnancy could render living in poverty a crime, because poor nutrition and lack of financia resources to secure qualitative health care implicate the condition of pregnant women's bodies. Focus on female responsibility removes the focus on the state too.

However, the resulting implications do not stop there. *Whitner* presumptively allocates the title of 'parent' to a woman who may not intend to be a parent at all. It presumes that pregnancy continuation is an indication of the assumption of parental responsibilities, and this is flawed Not all pregnant women who continue with their pregnancies plan to be parents after birth. This may be particularly true regarding unplanned pregnancies or those pregnancies that exist as a result of rape, incest or coercive sexual relationships. It might be due to personal moral direction that a woman chooses to avoid the option of terminating her pregnancy and rather puts the child up for adoption once born. However, the existence of addiction at the time of falling pregnant inhibits women's ability to secure an environment optimal for foetal development and prenatal health, and punishment ensues on this basis.

From a purely technical perspective, pregnancies might be unplanned, but the burden of ensuring that the unborn's 'life, health or comfort' is not endangered rests with the pregnant woman alone, and not with the paternal contributor to the pregnancy or even the state at large. This creates an unsettling scenario, particularly when the pregnancy is the result of rape. Not only is the woman pregnant, but she bears the sole burden of child abuse provisions concerning her conduct for nine months. Although it is the state's obligation to protect the unborn via its compelling interest, women are left with the bill.

Another example of extending criminal child abuse laws to pregnant women who use or abuse substances during pregnancy relates to child abuse provisions in Alabama. These pertain to 'chemical endangerment of exposing a child to an environment in which controlled substances are produced or distributed' in terms of s 26-15-3.2 of the Code of Alabama (Chemical Endangerment Statute). According to this provision, a person commits the crime of chemical endangerment when that person knowingly, recklessly, or intentionally causes a child to be exposed to, ingest, inhale, or have contact with a controlled substance, chemical substance or drug paraphernalia.[52]

'Child' is not define in chapter 15 of the Code of Alabama, which is the chapter that deals with child abuse generally. Nevertheless, in 2009 when Hope Ankrom gave birth to a child that tested positive for exposure to cocaine, she was arrested and charged with the chemical endangerment of a child a month later.[53] Later that year, Ankrom was formally indicted by a grand jury, whereafter she file a motion to dismiss the charges on the grounds that the Chemical Endangerment Statute was not intended to be applied to the unborn. Her motion was denied, and in 2010 Ankrom pleaded guilty to chemical endangerment charges but stipulated that she reserved an issue, namely that the facts of her case did not assert an offence in the law under which she was charged. This was the issue that the Court of Criminal Appeals of Alabama had to determine after the trial court noted her reservation.

The court found that the ordinary meaning of 'child' includes the unborn, and, to justify its position, the court referred to the fact that the Alabama wrongful death statute includes a viable foetus within its provisions, and the court also went on to cite a number of dictionaries which all include the unborn in their definition of 'child'. Going further, the court approvingly cited *Whitner*'s definitio of 'person' as including a foetus. The court found that a viable foetus is included in the definitio of 'child' and stated that referring to the unborn as children was so common that:

> Unless the legislature specificall states otherwise, the term 'child' is simply a more general term that encompasses the more specifi term 'viable fetus'. If the legislature desires to proscribe conduct against only a 'viable fetus' it is necessary to use that specifi term. However, if the legislature desires to proscribe conduct against a viable fetus and all other persons under a certain age, the term child is sufficient to convey that meaning.

Also, Ankrom argued that allowing these charges and consequent conviction would encourage an endless string of possible criminal charges against women for day-to-day conduct during pregnancy. However, the court found that since this

---

[52] The seriousness of the offence increases in relation to the harm caused to the child, that is, either causing serious physical injury or death.

[53] *Ankrom v State* 2011 WL 3781258 (Ala Crim App). At the time of writing, this decision is unreported thus page numbers cannot be referenced.

statutory provision is limited to chemical endangerment and not general endangerment the issue of 'endless extensions' is removed.[54]

On appeal to the Supreme Court of Alabama, the court confirme the Criminal Appeal Court's findin that the Chemical Endangerment Statute is intended to include a pregnant woman's conduct in relation to her foetus.[55] The court also went further and expanded the reach of the statute to protect all foetuses and not just viable ones.[56] Consequently, abuse of a controlled substance at any point during pregnancy is a criminal offence in Alabama via the Chemical Endangerment Statute.

The Alabama Supreme Court decision was written by Parker J who, while concurring with the majority, expressed the necessity of drafting a separate decision, where the judge concurs 'specially' with the majority. Parker J found that '*Roe* has sometimes been misread as holding that those unborn children are not persons and do not have the same fundamental rights as does every other person, which rights must be protected by the law . . . nothing could be further from the truth'.[57] To demonstrate how far from the truth such a statement is, Parker J cited fiv other areas of law (property law, criminal law, law of delict, guardianship law and health care law) as recognising the unborn as persons with 'legally enforceable rights'. The judge concluded by reiterating that the decision reached by the court was in line with widespread legal recognition of the unborn as persons and went on to point out that the only area in law where the unborn lacked protection was in respect of the termination of pregnancy and this was purely on the basis of the *Roe* decision. Should this be the ultimate guiding light for the court taking this approach, it is intrinsically flawe because *Roe* is not legal authority for viewing the unborn as a separate entity in law, let alone victims of pregnancy-related conduct.[58]

The judge's position concerning the status of the unborn in the United States can be interpreted as demonstrating the practical successes of the anti-abortion lobby

[54] The court pointed out that cigarettes and alcohol do not fall within the ambit of 'controlled substances', although it must be noted that the definitio of this term is not provided for in the statute.

[55] *Ex parte Ankrom; Ex parte Kimbrough* 2013 WL 135748 (Ala) (*Ex parte Ankrom*). This decision is also unreported and consequently page numbers cannot be cited. Amanda Kimbrough was also charged, convicted and sentenced to imprisonment for chemically exposing her foetus to a controlled substance. In this case Kimbrough went into premature labour (at 25 weeks' gestation) three days after smoking methamphetamine and the child died very soon after delivery. The court recited the evidence as indicating that Kimbrough presented at hospital with 'occult cord prolapse' which is a condition where the umbilical cord descends down the birth canal before the foetus and causes a cut in the blood supply to the foetus. However, a medical examiner provided testimony that the child's autopsy results indicates that he died from 'acute methamphetamine intoxication' while the paediatrician who treated the child after birth indicated that the cause of death was a result of 'respiratory arrest secondary to prematurity'. In fact, after delivery the child was not breathing at all, and it was only after intervention that he recovered to a point, but his condition rapidly declined to his ultimate death. He only lived for an estimated 19 minutes.

[56] *Ex parte Ankrom.*

[57] *Ex parte Ankrom.*

[58] This was argued in Chapter Eight, para 8.3.1; see authority cited therein.

groups in the United States. Chapter Seven[59] demonstrated that, while working towards securing full personhood for the unborn, the anti-abortion lobby groups adopt alternative 'backdoor' tactics to attack the validity of *Roe*'s standing. In this respect, the lobby groups work towards extending status to the unborn in all other areas of law. This approach is adopted with the aim of rendering *Roe* at odds with other developed areas of law which provide the unborn with increased status, thus rendering *Roe* illogical, since it would be the only area of law denying the unborn proper status.[60]

Suppé states that Alabama experienced a drastic increase in methamphetamine production during 2002 and 2006 and the Chemical Endangerment Statute was intended to protect children from exposure to harmful production processes.[61] However, at last count 60 women have been charged under this law for giving birth to babies testing positive for drug exposure during gestation.[62] Steele cites state authorities involved in prosecuting these women as viewing this law as an effective means of protecting women and their babies, since the threat of punishment will deter the use of drugs while pregnant, and arresting the women offers them 'rehabilitation opportunities'.[63]

Another example where substance addiction or use constitutes child abuse brings the discussion to Tennessee. Aside from the above exceptions, most of the cases against pregnant substance-dependent women were dismissed on the grounds of there being a lack of legislative intent to include pregnant women within the ambit of a particular child abuse statute. Focus on legislative intent leaves open the possibility of merely enacting legislation with the explicit intent of definin criminal child abuse as including the unborn in relation to the pregnant women carrying them. In 2003 Harris, Arbor and Paltrow suggested that there was no support for holding women criminally liable in relation to their adverse pregnancy outcomes, but conceded that statutory proposals might be made to address issues the courts avoided.[64] In line with that prediction, on 16 May 2014 the Tennessee Senate passed Senate Bill (SB) 1391, which renders the use of illegal substances during a pregnancy an assault if the child is born addicted to or harmed by the illegal substance used prenatally.[65] The legislation expired on 1 July 2016 and no action was taken to extend the law,[66] but women have been adversely affected by its implementation.

The Bill amended the Tennessee Code regulating offences against the person regarding 'assaultive offenses'. Section 39-13-107(a) provides that, for purposes

---

[59] Chapter Seven, para 7.4.

[60] See Chapter Seven, para 7.4 where the aims of the anti-abortion lobby were discussed.

[61] R Suppé 'Pregnancy on trial: The Alabama Supreme Court's erroneous application of Alabama's Chemical Endangerment Law in *Ex parte Ankrom*' (2014) 7 *Health Law & Policy Brief* 49 50.

[62] Suppé (2014) *Health Law & Policy Brief* 50. This is according to National Advocates for Pregnant Women, as reported by C Steele 'DA to begin prosecution of mothers who use drugs' (1 October 2012) available at http://newsok.com/article/feed/441574 (accessed on 26 June 2016).

[63] Steele 'DA to begin prosecution of mothers who use drugs'.

[64] Harris, Arbor & Paltrow (2003) *Journal of the American Medical Association* 1698.

[65] See Legi Scan 'Tennessee Senate Bill 1391' available at http://legiscan.com/TN/bill/SB1391/2013 (accessed on 23 June 2016).

[66] See s 3 of the Bill.

of assault, 'another', 'individuals' and 'another person' include the unborn at any point in gestation when those terms refer to the victim of any act made criminal by this provision. Subsection (c) originally stated that nothing in sub-s (a) 'shall apply to any act or omission by a pregnant woman with respect to an embryo or fetus with which she is pregnant, or to any lawful medical or surgical procedure to which a pregnant woman consents, performed by a health care professional'. The Bill added a new sentence to the end of this provision, stating:

> However, nothing in this section shall preclude prosecution of a woman for an assaultive offense for the illegal use of a narcotic drug while pregnant, if her child is born addicted to or harmed by the narcotic drug or for criminal homicide if her child dies as a result of her illegal use of a narcotic drug taken while pregnant.

According to Cohen,[67] these measures were introduced after collecting data to determine the rates of neonates being born with Neonatal Abstinence Syndrome[68] and the data was interpreted as indicating that there was a sudden increase in cases of neonates being born with this syndrome.[69] While one arrest has been recorded,[70] the true implications of this legislation have yet to be determined. Smith points out that despite the introduction of this amendment, there continued to be an increase in reported cases of neonates being born with Neonatal Abstinence Syndrome, indicating that the law has had 'little effect'.[71]

There was some speculation concerning the implications of the Bill in the United States. There was widespread concern that those women who decide to continue with their pregnancies despite suffering with addiction will face criminal charges; these might even ensue in cases where these women are in active treatment.[72] In fact, this legislation has been dubbed the 'Pregnancy Criminalization Law'.[73] Flavin and Paltrow explain how these laws are seen to criminalise pregnancy:[74]

---

[67] R Cohen 'Will Tennessee legalize the New Jane Crow?' *Socialistworker.Org* (23 April 2014) available at https://socialistworker.org/2014/04/23/will-tennessee-legalize-new-jane-crow (accessed on 23 June 2016).

[68] Cohen explains that this condition is a medical condition found in neonates who were exposed to addictive substances prenatally, however the condition is treatable provided that attending health-care providers know there is a need to provide treatment; see Cohen 'Will Tennessee legalize the New Jane Crow?'

[69] See SE Smith 'No safe harbors: Examining the shift from voluntary treatment options to criminalization of maternal drug use in Tennessee' (2015) 45 *University of Memphis LR* 203 208–9 for a discussion of the increase in rates of neonates being born with Neonatal Abstinence Syndrome. Smith indicates that in 2000, there were only 57 reported cases of Neonatal Abstinence Syndrome. However, in 2008, Tennessee recorded 855 reported cases of neonatal abstinence syndrome.

[70] Smith (2015) *University of Memphis LR* 203–5. However, the charges were dismissed after the accused completed treatment for her addiction.

[71] Smith (2015) *University of Memphis LR* 209.

[72] American Civil Liberties Union 'Tenn. Governor singles out pregnant women for discrimination' (29 April 2014) available at https://www.aclu.org/reproductive-freedom-womens-rights/tenn-governor-singles-out-pregnant-women-discrimination (accessed on 23 June 2016).

[73] Angry Black Women Watch 'ABWW Signal Boost: Tennessee's pregnancy criminalization law will hit black women the hardest' (18 April 2014) available at https://abww.wordpress.com/tag/sb-1391/ (accessed on 23 June 2016).

[74] Flavin & Paltrow (2010) *Journal of Addictive Diseases* 234.

> If a woman who is already addicted to drugs becomes pregnant and is not able to completely abstain from using drugs, the only way she can be assured of avoiding criminal charges for such crimes as child abuse, drug delivery to minors, and homicide is to get an abortion. Even though proponents of arrests and prosecutions articulate the problem as one of a woman who uses drugs while she is pregnant, their perspective is more accurately characterized as an objection to a woman becoming and remaining pregnant.

Cohen views SB 1391 as another attack on termination-of-pregnancy rights in the United States, since it treats the unborn as a separate entity, because charging a woman for assaulting her own foetus implies that the foetus is independent, with separate interests.[75] This notion will then infuse the hotly contested debates concerning termination-of-pregnancy laws.[76]

These instances of child abuse laws in South Carolina, Alabama and Tennessee clearly demonstrate that a separate-entities approach is at play in the context of the issue of addressing prenatal substance abuse or use. On the surface, this method seems to highlight a commitment to aims of protecting the unborn as human beings, thus advancing their interests, and the fact that this is being done under *Roe*'s umbrella gives the impression that women's right to terminate a pregnancy remains intact, thus also serving her autonomy rights (being narrowly construed). However, there are a number of theoretical and practical flaw inherent in adopting the separate-entities approach to addressing the issue of prenatal exposure to drugs.

9.4 THEORETICAL FLAWS OF CHILD ABUSE CONVICTIONS

From a theoretical perspective, criminal child abuse or endangerment provisions that hold women liable in respect of their own prenatal conduct are more in line with the underlying premise of the separate-entities approach. That is, the unborn, identifie as human beings, are separate subjects under the law and on that basis deserve protection from whoever may cause harm, including women and their prenatal substance abuse.[77]

Despite this congruency, a number of flaw can be identified Some of these flaw are also present in the discussion concerning feticide, foetal homicide or murder of a foetus,[78] therefore this discussion will be brief. One aspect that will not be repeated here is the contradiction that these child-abuse provisions pose with *Roe*; this was discussed as length in Chapter Eight and the same flaw are applicable here.[79] Further, criminal charges for child abuse in relation to prenatal

[75] Cohen 'Will Tennessee legalize the New Jane Crow?'

[76] Cohen 'Will Tennessee legalize the New Jane Crow?'

[77] This can be juxtaposed to contradictory application of the separate-entities approach under feticide or foetal homicide as identifie in Chapter Eight, para 8.3.2, where women were exempted from criminal liability via 'maternal exemptions'.

[78] See Chapter Eight, para 8.3.

[79] See Chapter Eight, para 8.3.1 and all authority cited therein. Only that portion of the discussion that relates to holding a woman criminally liable for experiencing a stillbirth is relevant here. Very briefl , offering protection at any point in gestation (as Tennessee and Alabama have done) contradicts the notion that *Roe* offers protection only from the moment of viability and it can hardly be argued that these provisions protect pre-viable unborn for exposure to drugs since women can

substance abuse rely on the embodied connectedness of pregnancy, yet the crime separates a pregnancy, making the foetus a victim and the woman a perpetrator. This is a stark contradiction in the theoretical underpinnings of this crime.

Aside from contradicting *Roe*, another aspect threatening sound translation of the aim of the separate-entities approach is the fact that protection from prenatal exposure to drugs through the imposition of criminal sanctions after birth has occurred is reactive rather than preventive. Flavin argues that this approach will have no effect on improving pregnancy outcomes since 'arresting a pregnant woman after she gives birth will not have a retroactive impact on her pregnancy'.[80] She understands this line of action as missing out on a 'valuable opportunity' to provide women with access to supportive health care and drug treatment while pregnant and engaging in risky behaviour.[81] As argued in Chapter Eight,[82] if prenatal life was valued and in need of protection from harm, emphasis should be on preventive actions rather than responsive ones. Ultimately, these provisions do give weight to the value that the unborn represent as human beings and demonstrate the potential for adverse birth outcomes as something that should not go unnoticed in law, but these measures for foetal protection fail to prevent the possibility of an adverse outcome.

Flavin[83] and Goodwin[84] report that substance abuse is comparable across race and class. With that in mind, one would expect states to apply child abuse measures consistently across the board, regardless of race and class. However, and as already indicated in Chapter Eight,[85] poverty and race tend to indicate which women will face judicial attention regarding adverse pregnancy outcomes.[86]

---

simply terminate a pregnancy to avoid the possibility of criminal liability. Also, extending protection to viable foetuses (as South Carolina has done) is erroneously founded on the argument that *Roe* creates separate legal subjects of the unborn; the discussion in para 8.3.1 demonstrates that this is not the case.

[80] J Flavin *Our Bodies, Our Crimes: The Policing of Women's Reproduction in America* (2009) 113.

[81] Flavin *Our Bodies, Our Crimes* 113. In this respect, offering support during pregnancy to overcome addiction or instil grounded knowledge of the health risks linked to substance usage is viewed as preventive action rather than mere reaction. Flavin (*Our Bodies, Our Crimes* 113) warns that incarceration during pregnancy should not be viewed as an adequate prevention strategy, because prisons or jails are known for their poor living conditions generally, never mind considering the special needs of pregnant women. These environments are not seen as ideal for protecting the unborn from harm since these environments fail to offer quality prenatal care, nutritional diets and effective reproductive health care. Also see Suppé (2014) *Health Law & Policy Brief* 69–70, who cited authority that Alabama received an 'F' rating for the delivery of services to pregnant inmates, being one of the worst ratings in the United States.

[82] Para 8.3.3.

[83] *Our Bodies, Our Crimes* 109.

[84] M Goodwin 'Prosecuting the womb' (2008) 76 *George Washington LR* 1657. Goodwin (1679–81) points out that though all races abuse substances, poor women and particularly poor black women abuse illegal substance while more affluent white women tend to abuse legal substances. She argues that this approach is more about criminalising choice in substance rather than abuse of substance.

[85] Goodwin (2008) *George Washington LR* 1657.

[86] See Suppé (2014) *Health Law & Policy Brief* 71; Paltrow & Flavin (2013) *Journal of Health Politics, Policy and Law* 332–3; Schroedel, Fiber & Snyder (2000) *Duke Journal of Gender Law & Policy* 110; and R Roth *Making Women Pay: The Hidden Costs of Fetal Rights* (2000)146–9.

Suppé points out that in Alabama there is increased focus on 'hard' drugs, being cocaine and methamphetamine, which are the drugs that tend to be used more in poor communities, thus rendering women in these communities more vulnerable to prosecutions.[87] Also, Schroedel, Fiber and Snyder[88] attribute increased attention on poor women because of their reliance on the public health-care system, being the institutions at the forefront of testing and reporting women to authorities for their prenatal drug use.[89] Explaining the over-representation of poor women in the criminal system, Suppé suggests that not all women can afford termination-of-pregnancy services in order to avoid criminal charges, so poor women are more susceptible to facing criminal charges and convictions.[90] All of this shows how poor women, and particularly poor black women, are valued rather than how much the unborn are valued as separate entities and protected as such.[91]

The argument that there is lack of prevention of harm is especially obvious when one considers the fact that a woman still has the right to terminate a pregnancy. In the context of the separate-entities approach, a termination of pregnancy allows for the ultimate 'harm' being the complete termination of prenatal life. This means that only those women who do not terminate their pregnancies face criminal sanctions, leading to the likely conclusion that these laws are directed at punishing women for becoming mothers, since they are poor, or poor and black, and addicted. Thus they should not be creating or mothering children. This draws on Chapter Eight's 'bad mother' rhetoric, which is equally applicable to the context of prosecuting women for prenatal substance abuse or use.[92]

From a theoretical viewpoint, criminal child abuse laws do not offer the protection intended. Having these laws apply after birth fails to prevent exposure and the fact that *Roe* remains in force renders the unborn and born children unprotected from the potential harms and implications of substance abuse.

---

[87] Suppé (2014) *Health Law & Policy Brief* 71. However, Roth's (147) work points to the fact that this is not a new approach; crack cocaine has always been a drug that authorities have focused on. She argues that the fact that other substances which are used by white women or more affluent women (such as alcohol, powder cocaine or heroin) do not reach the attention of authorities is an indication of the social value of black women in American society. All substances have the potential to cause harm, yet they do not get equal attention from authorities. Also see D Page 'The homicide by child abuse conviction of Regina McKnight' (2003) 46 *How LJ* 363 370–2.

[88] Schroedel, Fiber & Snyder (2000) *Duke Journal of Gender Law & Policy* 110.

[89] Also see Roth *Making Women Pay* 143. However, Roth (147), drawing from a number of studies, highlights that black women, of all the women using public care facilities, are more likely to be tested and reported than white women. Page asserts a similar argument; see Page (2003) *Howard LJ* 372.

[90] Suppé (2014) *Health Law & Policy Brief* 72. Also see Flavin *Our Bodies, Our Crimes* 112, who explains that termination of pregnancy is 'frequently considered among pregnant women who use illicit drugs, but less frequently obtained'. She lists a number of reasons why pregnancy terminations were not obtained, being that women realised they were pregnant too late in gestation; lacked financia means to secure the service; or decided against terminating their pregnancies on moral or religious grounds.

[91] Many authors come to this conclusion, for an example see Goodwin (2008) *George Washington LR* 1657 generally.

[92] See para 8.3.3.

9.5 PRACTICAL FLAWS OF CHILD ABUSE CONVICTIONS

The use of drugs or other harmful substances during pregnancy, whether legal or illegal, is viewed in a disapproving light and the fact remains that this is a social concern that requires serious attention. Ovens and all those involved in the quest to adequately address this concern make this very clear. However, if criminal law is going to be the method of addressing these concerns, certain principles must be adhered to for the purposes of sound and legitimate application of the law.

Aside from the theoretical issues, there are also practical concerns relating to causation of harm and the underlying assumption that women are the sole contributors of harm in cases of adverse pregnancy outcomes. If harm from prenatal exposure cannot be established, or if a link between the harm and prenatal substance abuse cannot be established, then the attribution of criminal liability cannot be ascribed.[93] Further, criminal liability can attach only in the case of there being the intention to cause a particular harm, and substance abuse, if fuelled by addiction, removes intention to cause harm to the unborn, since addiction is not an intentional criminal act against others but an illness that requires adequate treatment.[94]

The firs issue is to determine whether substance abuse during pregnancy renders the unborn harmed as a result of exposure. In *Whitner*, the South Carolina Supreme Court asserted that it is 'well documented and within public knowledge' that the use of cocaine can seriously harm the unborn when ingested by women during pregnancy.[95] Also, that it is 'common knowledge' that drug use causes harm to the unborn.[96] To support this position, the court relied on two medical journal articles, one published in 1992 and another published in 1985.[97] However, after perusing both articles, a different conclusion was reached to that of the court. At most, these articles illustrate that there is a risk of harm in the case of intrauterine cocaine exposure but neither indicates that this highly technical, scientific-base knowledge is readily available to the general public and that the articles' finding are easily understood by those outside of medicine.[98] In fact,

[93] See generally CR Snyman *Criminal Law* 5 ed (2008) 79–94. Causation constitutes factual and legal causation. Even where the factual causation of harm can be established or is eventually established in the future, legal causation must also be established.

[94] Regarding intention, see Snyman *Criminal Law* 181–208. Concerning the nature of addiction as a disease and its consequential effect of removing 'choice' to use a particular drug, see American Society of Addiction Medicine 'Public policy statement: Definitio of addiction' (19 April 2011) available at http://www.asam.org/quality-practice/definition-of-addictio (accessed on 23 June 2016). This will be discussed in further detail below.

[95] *Whitner* 782.

[96] *Whitner* 785.

[97] *Whitner* 782. The court cites the following articles as authority of public knowledge of harm: JJ Volpe 'Effect of cocaine use on the fetus' (1992) 327 *New England Journal of Medicine* 399 and IJ Chasnoff, WJ Burns, SH Schnoll et al 'Cocaine use in pregnancy' (1985) 313 *New England Journal of Medicine* 666. Roth *Making Women Pay* 142 identifie Chasnoff's publication as being the source of the 'crack baby' myth.

[98] In fact, access to these articles is limited by the fact that paid subscription is needed. This removes a large portion of the general population from gaining knowledge of the perceived potential risks associated with prenatal substance abuse. Further, it is questionable whether articles published in medical journals amount to common knowledge.

Volpe introduces his finding with something akin to a cautionary note, mentioning that '[d]elineating the effects of intrauterine exposure to cocaine on fetuses and newborn infants is difficult', and one such difficulty rests with the fact that the use of other drugs, smoking cigarettes or marijuana, poor nutrition or lack of prenatal care confounds the process of identifying whether cocaine is the actual cause of an adverse prenatal development or pregnancy outcome.[99] Referring to two articles does not seem sufficient to prove harm and knowledge of such harm.

Some years later, in 2003, the same court relied on the basis of public knowledge again and cited its decision in *Whitner* as authority: Regina McKnight was convicted of murder for experiencing a stillbirth on the basis that it was 'public knowledge the usage of cocaine is potentially fatal'.[100] Concerning the impact of cocaine, the court held:[101]

> The drug 'cocaine' has torn at the very fabric of our nation. Families have been ripped apart, minds have been ruined, and lives have been lost. It is common knowledge that the drug is highly addictive and potentially fatal. The addictive nature of the drug, combined with its expense, has caused our prisons to swell with those who have been motivated to support their drug habit through criminal acts. In some areas of the world, entire governments have been undermined by the cocaine industry.

In neither instance is any standard authority cited that supports the court's conclusion that foetal harm occurs directly as a result of prenatal substance abuse or that foetal harm was widely known to occur as a result of substance exposure. Paltrow and Flavin offer a compelling argument to explain the court's position and the general hype around legal action against women who used substances during pregnancy.[102] They explain[103] that during the 1980s and 1990s (when Whitner was charged and pleaded guilty)[104] a 'war on drugs' (particularly against the use of cocaine) took hold in the United States and using women were found at the centre of it: they were 'crack mothers'[105] creating 'crack babies'. According to Roth,[106] 'crack babies' are those who, as a result of prenatal exposure to crack cocaine, were portrayed as being destined to 'fail in school and grow up to be less than human, wreaking havoc on society'. She explains that these babies were characterised as the 'biological underclass' and expected to suffer with developmental defects.[107] These character traits stemmed from 'drug war propaganda' in

[99] Volpe (1992) *New England Journal of Medicine* 399.

[100] *State v McKnight* 576 SE 2d 168 (SC 2003) 173 (*McKnight* (2003)). See Chapter Eight, para 8.3.3 for a full discussion of the case.

[101] *McKnight* (2003) 173.

[102] Flavin & Paltrow (2010) *Journal of Addictive Diseases* 231. Although, it must be noted that these authors are not the only ones to offer this explanation, see Roth *Making Women Pay* 136.

[103] Flavin & Paltrow (2010) *Journal of Addictive Diseases* 232.

[104] Being 1992.

[105] According to Paltrow and Flavin ((2010) *Journal of Addictive Diseases* 232), 'crack mothers' were women portrayed as drug-using women and 'hypersexual, out-of-control women who would "do anything" for drugs. They were characterized as being completely indifferent to any harm they might cause to themselves or others, especially the children they would give birth to.'

[106] *Making Women Pay* 136.

[107] Roth *Making Women Pay* 142.

the media with 'grossly exaggerated claims about the risks posed by prenatal exposure to certain substances'.[108]

Paltrow and Flavin explain that this public moral panic concerning drug use during pregnancy implicated not only respectable media[109] houses but also universities. They cite Columbia University's Centre on Addiction and Substance Abuse as stating in their 1994 Annual Report that prenatal exposure results in 'a slaughter of innocents of biblical proportions'.[110] Academic publishing houses were also involved. Roth explains that those academic pieces that emphasised prenatal harm were more likely to be published than those that did not.[111] She argues: 'This skewed selection distorts the public's understanding of the problem and contributes to a climate of panic in which coercive intervention into pregnant women's lives seems acceptable.'[112]

The media successfully, via sensationalism, created a picture of the United States being in the grip of an 'epidemic which was destroying a generation of young people'.[113] This media coverage of 'medical misinformation' was uncritically and widely accepted, thus permeating the minds of all in society.[114] Aside from facing criminal prosecution,[115] Roth reports that some politicians went so far as to push for the implementation of very harsh policies, such as suggesting that addicted women should be sterilised, or face the forced imposition of contraception for the duration of their reproductive age.[116]

With judicial precedents in place concerning the prosecution of women for prenatal substance use in *Whitner*,[117] the panic eventually abated during the 1990s.[118] Nevertheless, it has resurfaced more recently, but not in relation to cocaine. Now the public moral panic is in relation to methamphetamine.[119] Paltrow and Flavin report that, in the United States, 'the public is still fed a regular diet of accounts that distort and misrepresent the effects of illicit drug use . . . rely

---

[108] Flavin & Paltrow (2010) *Journal of Addictive Diseases* 231.

[109] Flavin & Paltrow (2010) *Journal of Addictive Diseases* 231. Flavin and Paltrow cite *Time Magazine* and the *New York Times* as reporting on and feeding the panic of 'crack mothers' and 'crack babies'. However, for more on the media's hype concerning the 'crack crisis', see L Paltrow & K Jack 'Pregnant women, junk science, and zealous defense' (2010) *The Champion* 2 3.

[110] Flavin & Paltrow (2010) *Journal of Addictive Diseases* 232.

[111] Roth *Making Women Pay* 144.

[112] Roth *Making Women Pay* 144.

[113] Flavin & Paltrow (2010) *Journal of Addictive Diseases* 232.

[114] Flavin & Paltrow (2010) *Journal of Addictive Diseases* 233.

[115] Roth (*Making Women Pay* 146) gives a brief exposé of when prosecution against women started in relation to their substance use. She cites 1992 as holding the record for the number of women facing criminal charges.

[116] Roth *Making Women Pay* 142.

[117] Hence the *McKnight* (2003) decision relying on *Whitner*.

[118] Flavin & Paltrow (2010) *Journal of Addictive Diseases* 233.

[119] Flavin & Paltrow (2010) *Journal of Addictive Diseases* 233. Suppé's work supports this argument; she explains that Alabama's Chemical Endangerment Law was enacted in response to the rise in methamphetamine use; see Suppé (2013) *Health Law & Policy Brief* 51–8.

on non-experts, and demonize the people who use illicit drugs'.[120] (Footnotes omitted.)

Despite a change in focus regarding the drug of concern, the more recent panic surrounding drug use during pregnancy is taking place in a more informed context,[121] hence McKnight being granted post-conviction relief in 2008.[122] Briefl , the 2008 court found that the evidence the state originally relied on during the 2003 trial to prove that McKnight's prenatal substance use was the cause of her stillbirth was outdated.[123] The court accepted that the prenatal use of cocaine was no more harmful than smoking, poor nutrition and lack of prenatal care,[124] all of which have strong links to poverty.[125] This more informed position stems from the fact that health care professionals are more assertively open about what their finding reveal concerning studies pertaining to prenatal substance abuse. In this respect, Flavin and Paltrow[126] report that health care experts and researchers publicly denounce misinformed media coverage and urge that publications be founded on science as derived from fiel specialists rather than local sheriffs or paediatricians.

National Advocates for Pregnant Women compiled a 'fact sheet' concerning experts' positions of the consequences of prenatal substance abuse and looked at crack cocaine, methamphetamine, opiates, marijuana and alcohol.[127] Regarding crack cocaine, researchers are cited as findin that the effect of prenatal exposure to cocaine is less severe than prenatal exposure to alcohol, and the effects of cocaine exposure are similar to prenatal nicotine exposure.[128] Also, there is no convincing evidence that prenatal cocaine exposure is associated with developmental concerns, and that, if attending health care providers were not informed of women's cocaine use during pregnancy, those babies who were exposed could not be distinguished from the non-exposed neonates.[129] The organisation indicates that, in an open letter to the media during 2004, 30 leading researchers and doctors unanimously rejected the notion of there being a 'crack baby' syndrome, disorder

[120] Flavin & Paltrow (2010) *Journal of Addictive Diseases* 234. For an example, see B Lester 'Another "drug baby" media scare?' (12 March 2005) available at http://www.csdp.org/publicservice/dejavumeth.htm (accessed on 20 June 2014).

[121] Paltrow & Jack (2010) *The Champion* 2.

[122] *McKnight v State* 661 SE 2d 354 (SC 2008) (*McKnight* (2008)). See Chapter Eight, para 8.3.2 for a discussion of this case.

[123] *McKnight* (2008) 360–1. As reported, the *McKnight* (2003) decision does not cite what evidence was advanced but the fact that the *Whitner* case was cited as authority indicates that the underlying reasons for the state's position concerning prenatal substance abuse is outdated since the *Whitner* case relied on two articles, from the 1980s and the early 1990s respectively.

[124] *McKnight* (2008) 358 fn 2.

[125] Paltrow & Jack (2010) *The Champion* 2.

[126] Flavin & Paltrow (2010) *Journal of Addictive Diseases* 234.

[127] National Advocates for Pregnant Women 'Prenatal exposure to illegal drugs and alcohol: Media hype and enduring myths are not supported by science' (24 March 2010) available at http://advocatesforpregnantwomen.org/2010%20drugmyth%20factsheet%20v3.pdf (accessed on 23 June 2016).

[128] National Advocates for Pregnant Women 'Prenatal exposure to illegal drugs and alcohol' 1.

[129] National Advocates for Pregnant Women 'Prenatal exposure to illegal drugs and alcohol' 1.

or condition, and further went on to argue that neonates could not be born addicted to substances.[130]

On the topic of prenatal exposure to methamphetamine, the organisation indicates that further research is required for the purposes of determining the effects of prenatal exposure to methamphetamine in respect of developmental issues.[131] Further research is required because currently there is insufficient evidence to draw any substantive conclusions on the topic.[132] In 2005, more than 90 medical doctors, scientists, psychological researchers and treatment specialists released an open letter denouncing the use of the term 'meth babies', since it lacked scientifi basis and any such syndrome, disorder or condition could not be validated.[133] This issue rests on the fact that the effects of prenatal methamphetamine use cannot be separated from other factors.[134] Other factors include poor nutrition, lack of prenatal care, and the concurrent use of other legal and illegal substances such as nicotine, alcohol, cocaine and marijuana.[135]

Prenatal exposure to opiates (such as heroin and oxycodone) leads to some neonates being born with Neonatal Abstinence Syndrome,[136] but exposure is not associated with compromised birth defects or growth and development.[137] Also, the use of marijuana has resulted in concerns such as the weight or length of the baby being affected in high-risk pregnancies; however, after a few months, those effects subside.[138] It was also pointed out that prenatal exposure to alcohol and nicotine had a more pronounced effect on birth weight or growth, when compared with marijuana.[139] The National Institute on Drug Abuse indicates that exposure to nicotine increases the risk of stillbirth, infant mortality, Sudden Infant Death Syndrome, preterm birth, respiratory problems, slowed foetal growth and low birth weight.[140] Also important to note is the fact that second-hand exposure can increase the risk of harm by the above-described conditions.[141]

---

[130] National Advocates for Pregnant Women 'Prenatal exposure to illegal drugs and alcohol' 1. Also see K Sunderlin & L Huss 'The mythology of "addicted babies": Challenging media distortions, laws, and policies that fracture communities' (2014) 86 *Different Takes* 1.

[131] Sunderlin & Huss (2014) *Different Takes* 1

[132] National Advocates for Pregnant Women 'Prenatal exposure to illegal drugs and alcohol' 1.

[133] National Advocates for Pregnant Women 'Prenatal exposure to illegal drugs and alcohol' 2.

[134] National Advocates for Pregnant Women 'Prenatal exposure to illegal drugs and alcohol' 2.

[135] American College of Obstetricians and Gynecologists 'Information about methamphetamine use in pregnancy' (2006) available at http://vanilla47.com/Methamphetamine%20Pharmacology/Information%20about%20Methamphetamine%20Use%20in%20Pregnancy.pdf (accessed on 23 June 2016).

[136] This syndrome can be successfully treated. If the withdrawal symptoms are not too severe no medication is needed. However, in cases of severe withdrawal symptoms medication can be prescribed to alleviate the condition. See Substance Abuse and Mental Health Services Administration 'Methadone treatment for pregnant women' (March 2009).

[137] National Advocates for Pregnant Women 'Prenatal exposure to illegal drugs and alcohol' 2.

[138] National Advocates for Pregnant Women 'Prenatal exposure to illegal drugs and alcohol' 3.

[139] National Advocates for Pregnant Women 'Prenatal exposure to illegal drugs and alcohol' 3.

[140] National Institute on Drug Abuse 'Topics in brief: Prenatal exposure to drugs of abuse' (May 2011) available at http://www.drugabuse.gov/sites/default/files/prenatal.pd (accessed on 23 June 2016). However, the Institute highlights that low birth weight is 'dose-dependent' which means that the more a woman smokes during pregnancy, the more the infant's birth weight is reduced.

[141] National Institute on Drug Abuse 'Topics in brief: Prenatal exposure to drugs of abuse'.

The National Institute on Drug Abuse identifie alcohol as one of the widely abused substances during pregnancy in America,[142] and frequent or excessive exposure to alcohol during gestation is known to cause Foetal Alcohol Syndrome, which is a recognised disorder.[143] However, there are a number of issues associated with predicting an outcome with any certainty:

> [T]here is no medical certainty regarding the level of alcohol consumption during a particular pregnancy that will result in negative fetal outcomes. Even the exact mechanism that establishes a causal link between alcohol ingestion and the manifestation of harmful fetal symptoms has yet to be definitivel established.[144]

Nevertheless, a number of identifie risk factors indicate that some women are more susceptible to giving birth to children with the syndrome, which include age, socio-economic status, ethnicity, genetic factors, and maternal alcohol metabolism.[145] Even with this knowledge, experts are calling for further research.[146]

It is widely acknowledged in the medical fiel that proving factual causation in respect of adverse pregnancy outcomes is scientificall problematic.[147] In each of the cases mentioned in this chapter, the *amici curiae* have collectively asserted this point. For instance, the *amici curiae* in the *Whitner* matter collectively support the notion that as scientifi knowledge stood in 1997, the consequences of prenatal exposure are inconclusive and 'there remains a genuine scientifi dispute as to

[142] National Institute on Drug Abuse 'Topics in brief: Prenatal exposure to drugs of abuse'.
[143] National Advocates for Pregnant Women 'Prenatal exposure to illegal drugs and alcohol' 3.
[144] National Advocates for Pregnant Women 'Prenatal exposure to illegal drugs and alcohol' 3.
[145] National Advocates for Pregnant Women 'Prenatal exposure to illegal drugs and alcohol' 3.
[146] National Advocates for Pregnant Women 'Prenatal exposure to illegal drugs and alcohol' 3.
[147] See the following *amici curiae* briefs: *amici curiae* brief of the National Association of Alcoholism and Drug Abuse Counselors, South Carolina Association of Alcoholism and Drug Abuse Counselors, American College of Obstetricians and Gynecologists et al in the matter of *Whitner v State* 492 SE 2d 777 (SC 1997) (listing 21 *amici curiae*); *amici curiae* brief of American Public Health Association, American Nurses Association, American Psychiatric Association et al in the matter of *State v McKnight* 576 SE 2d 168 (SC 2003) (listing 26 *amici curiae*); *amici curiae* brief of South Carolina Medical Association, South Carolina Nurses Association, South Carolina Association of Alcoholism and Drug Abuse Counselors et al in the matter of *McKnight v State* 661 SE 2d 354 (SC 2008) (listing at least six *amici curiae*, however the exact number cannot be ascertained from the brief since the appendix listing the *amici* is not available); *amici curiae* brief of American Public Health Association, National Association of Social Workers, Alabama Women's Resource Network et al in the matter of *Kimbrough v State of Alabama* in the Court of Criminal Appeals of Alabama, criminal appeals number CR-09-0485 (2010) (listing 23 *amici curiae*); *amici curiae* brief of the Alabama Women's Resource Network, American Academy of Addiction Psychiatry, American Society of Addiction Medicine et al in the matter of *Ankrom v State* 2011 WL 3781258 (Ala Crim App) (listing 24 *amici curiae*); *amici curiae* brief of American Academy of Addiction Psychiatry, American College of Obstetricians and Gynecologists, American Psychiatric Association et al in the matter of *Ex parte Kimbrough* 2013 WL 135748 (Ala) (listing 44 *amici curiae*); and *amici curiae* brief of American Academy of Addiction Psychiatry, American College of Obstetrics and Gynecologists, American Psychiatric Association et al in the matter of *Ex parte Ankrom* 2013 WL 135748 (Ala) (listing 46 *amici curiae*). The *amici curiae* are generally made up of individuals or organisations linked to the provision of health care and social or legal services, either as practitioners, researchers, academics or theorists with expert knowledge in their field These listings represent vast opposition to criminalising prenatal substance abuse on the basis of there being a lack of established causation, among other areas of concern.

whether a causal link exists between cocaine and serious fetal harm'.[148] This was reiterated in 2003, when the *amici curiae* in *McKnight* (2003) emphasised that more research is needed concerning the potential causes of harm in respect of prenatal exposure to cocaine.[149] The *amici curiae* argued:

> While current studies are unable to link cocaine use to adverse fetal developments, neither do they exclude cocaine as a potential fetotoxin. Without a doubt, more research is needed. It is precisely this fact that exposes the injustice and irrationality of the *McKnight* decision.[150]

The same has been argued by *amici curiae* in respect of methamphetamine in 2010[151] and 2013.[152] While these arguments failed in these cases, they have succeeded in all others where the courts have assessed and recognised the value of scientifi research pertaining to the medical knowledge of prenatal exposure to certain substances.[153]

Evidence indicates that science has failed to prove that prenatal exposure to illegal drugs causes 'unique harms distinguishable from those caused by other uncontrollable factors'.[154] It also brings the legitimacy of these approaches into question because alcohol and nicotine, while legal, also negatively implicate pregnancy outcomes.

The National Institute on Drug Abuse warns that prenatal drug exposure is associated with the potential risk of harmful and possibly long-term effects on

[148] *Amici curiae* brief of the National Association of Alcoholism and Drug Abuse Counselors, South Carolina Association of Alcoholism and Drug Abuse Counselors, American College of Obstetricians and Gynecologists et al in *Whitner* 6–8. This remains an issue today; see National Institute on Drug Abuse 'Topics in brief: Prenatal exposure to drugs of abuse' whose work was updated in 2011.

[149] *Amici curiae* brief of National Association of Alcoholism and Drug Abuse Counselors, South Carolina Association of Alcoholism and American Public Health Association, American Nurses Association, American Psychiatric Association et al in *McKnight* (2003) 16.

[150] *Amici curiae* brief of National Association of Alcoholism and Drug Abuse Counselors, South Carolina Association of Alcoholism and American Public Health Association, American Nurses Association, American Psychiatric Association et al in *McKnight* (2003) 16. Also see the later brief file when the case went on appeal, *amici curiae* brief of South Carolina Medical Association, South Carolina Nurses Association, South Carolina Association of Alcoholism and Drug Abuse Counselors in *McKnight* (2008) 14–6.

[151] *Amici curiae* brief of American Public Health Association, National Association of Social Workers, Alabama Women's Resource Network et al in *Kimbrough* (2010) 22–5.

[152] *Amici curiae* brief of American Academy of Addiction Psychiatry, American College of Obstetricians and Gynecologists, American Psychiatric Association et al in *Kimbrough* (2013) 27–9.

[153] *Amici curiae* brief of American Academy of Addiction Psychiatry, American College of Obstetricians and Gynecologists, American Psychiatric Association et al in *Kimbrough* (2013) 27–9. The *amici curiae* are specificall referring to the *McKnight* (2008) decision where the court accepted that medical research showing that cocaine use during pregnancy does not cause as much harm as smoking, poor nutrition or lack of prenatal care. Also see *amici curiae* brief of the Alabama Women's Resource Network, American Academy of Addiction Psychiatry, American Society of Addiction Medicine et al in *Ankrom* (2011) 19–20 fns 53–7. In this brief, the *amici curiae* cite a number of cases, some refer to the fact that the courts refused to extend child endangerment laws to pregnant women because the unborn do not constitute 'children', however there are some examples where the courts have refused to convict women on the grounds that there was insufficient evidence that any harm was caused as a result of prenatal exposure to cocaine or other illegal substances.

[154] *Amici curiae* brief of American Academy of Addiction Psychiatry, American College of Obstetricians and Gynecologists, American Psychiatric Association et al in *Kimbrough* (2013) 33.

children who were exposed to substances prenatally.[155] However, ascertaining the full extent of the consequences of prenatal drug exposure is problematic because of the negative impact that many other factors have on pregnancy as well; these include: '[m]ultiple individual, family and environmental factors—such as, nutritional status, extent of prenatal care, neglect or abuse, socio-economic conditions, and many other variables'.[156] Other variables can include sexually transmitted diseases, genetic disease, chromosomal abnormalities, structural birth defects, health problems (such as high blood-pressure), uterine and cervical problems, maternal obesity, low maternal weight gain, and multiple gestations.[157] Further, Daniels highlights men's roles in contributing to poor pregnancy outcomes, in respect of their own addictive behaviours, genetic defects, environmental exposures and their role in domestic violence.[158] The *amici curiae* in *Kimbrough* (2013) assert that adverse pregnancy outcomes occur despite the best intentions of pregnant women or their attending physicians,[159] and identifie risks associated with adverse outcomes are not necessarily the direct cause of an outcome and thus can never be completely removed.

Aside from the issue of causation, the National Institute on Drug Abuse calls for a supportive home environment and promotion of quality parenting, since these factors are associated with reducing negative outcomes in exposed children.[160] The fact that wider issues contribute to adverse pregnancy outcomes brings Daniels' position on shared responsibility for foetal harm back into perspective.[161] It is her position that, since there is a wide range of contributors that impact on pregnancies in a negative way, which sometimes fall even beyond the control of the pregnant women concerned (such as poverty and genetic inclinations), it is unfair to hold them solely responsible for adverse pregnancy outcomes.[162] While this does not completely remove women's responsibility for self-destructive

---

[155] National Institute on Drug Abuse 'Topics in brief: Prenatal exposure to drugs of abuse'.

[156] National Institute on Drug Abuse 'Topics in brief: Prenatal exposure to drugs of abuse'.

[157] E Jackson *Regulating Reproduction: Law, Technology and Autonomy* (2001) 148; *amici curiae* brief of American Public Health Association, National Association of Social Workers, Alabama Women's Resource Network et al in *Kimbrough* (2010) 21; *amici curiae* brief of American Academy of Addiction Psychiatry, American College of Obstetricians and Gynecologists, American Psychiatric Association et al in *Kimbrough* (2013); and *amici curiae* brief of the National Association of Alcoholism and Drug Abuse Counselors, South Carolina Association of Alcoholism and Drug Abuse Counselors, American College of Obstetricians and Gynecologists et al in *Whitner* 11.

[158] CR Daniels 'Fathers, mothers, and fetal harm: Rethinking gender difference and reproductive responsibility' in LM Morgan & MW Michaels (eds) *Fetal Subjects, Feminist Positions* (1999) 85–8. In fact, Daniels (87) highlights that birth defects appear in respect of abuse of legal substances such as alcohol and nicotine. She (87) also points to studies highlighting that cocaine use by men is associated with increased abnormal sperm and sperm mortality. Further, cocaine is found (88) to bind to sperm making it transmittable to ova during fertilisation. However, it is uncertain whether this has led to birth defects.

[159] *Amici curiae* brief of American Academy of Addiction Psychiatry, American College of Obstetricians and Gynecologists, American Psychiatric Association et al in *Kimbrough* (2013) 25.

[160] National Institute on Drug Abuse 'Topics in brief: Prenatal exposure to drugs of abuse'.

[161] Daniels 'Fathers, mothers, and fetal harm' 83–98. See the discussion in Chapter Eight, para 8.4.

[162] Daniels 'Fathers, mothers, and fetal harm' 83–98.

behaviours, it does call for the attribution of diminished responsibility in the context of criminal law.

Roth explains that a 'war on drugs' stance focuses on law enforcement rather than prevention of drug use or treating drug users.[163] This position therefore removes attention from the state as a role-player in contributing to the cause of foetal harm and detracts from the social need for treatment.[164] Flavin demonstrates that the nature of addiction is such that it can remove the 'choice' or the 'intention' to continue use, and is define as 'a chronic relapsing brain disease that is characterized by compulsive drug seeking and use, despite harmful consequences'.[165] In 2011, the American Society of Addiction Medicine released a policy statement definin addiction as a chronic brain disorder.[166] The Society warns that, 'without treatment or engagement in recovery activities, addiction is progressive and can result in disability or even premature death'.[167] As such, the threat of criminal sanction will probably do very little to curb use of illegal substances.[168] Yet, despite the gripping effects of substance abuse, Flavin reports that pregnant women are motivated to cease using substances during pregnancy; however, complete cessation is very difficult and women are not likely to succeed without properly trained assistance.[169] Also, complete cessation places pregnancies at risk if done outside of a treatment facility, because withdrawal symptoms (particularly in respect of opiates and alcohol) can cause harm to the unborn or even terminate a pregnancy.[170] Nevertheless, with proper treatment, these risks can be substantially reduced.[171]

This indicates that adequate treatment for addiction needs to be available in order to address addiction and maintain healthy pregnancies. If the aim is to secure healthy birth outcomes, one would expect treatment to be readily available, allowing for as many healthy births as possible but, as the position stands, pregnant women's access to drug treatment facilities is lacking in the United

[163] *Making Women Pay* 139.

[164] In fact, adopting a criminal law response does very little to protect a child once born since he or she will be removed from his or her mother's care (while she is incarcerated), at times parental rights will be terminated, mother–child ties will be very difficult to maintain while the mother is incarcerated and the child might be placed in the foster care system if relatives are unable to care for the newborn. Concerning the implications of incarceration on the mother–child relationship, see Flavin *Our Bodies, Our Crimes* 139–63.

[165] Flavin *Our Bodies, Our Crimes* 111. She cites the definitio of addiction as provided by the National Institute on Drug Abuse.

[166] American Society of Addiction Medicine 'Public policy statement: Definitio of addiction'. According to Flavin *Our Bodies, Our Crimes* 111, this characteristic of addiction removes the notion of criminal intent.

[167] American Society of Addiction Medicine 'Public policy statement: Definitio of addiction'.

[168] This was pointed out in the *amici curiae* brief of American Academy of Addiction Psychiatry, American College of Obstetricians and Gynecologists, American Psychiatric Association et al in *Kimbrough* (2013) 36.

[169] Flavin *Our Bodies, Our Crimes* 111.

[170] Roth *Making Women Pay* 139; Jackson *Regulating Reproduction* 149; and Paltrow & Jack (2010) *The Champion* 4.

[171] Paltrow & Jack (2010) *The Champion* 4.

States.[172] Also, lack of access to treatment facilities impacts more on poor and rural women, placing them and their pregnancies at further risk.[173] Jackson builds on this issue and asserts that having treatment available is only one aspect of substance abuse, and argues that there should be increased focus on alleviating the triggers of addiction.[174] She highlights that drug-dependent people are 'often poor, undernourished, homeless, victims of violence and abuse' and unless these issues are addressed the benefit of treatment are likely to be minimal or to last only temporarily.[175] Jackson states 'concentrating on the harm caused by individual women both punitive and therapeutic strategies may obscure society's responsibility for the health and wellbeing of the next generation'.[176] Essentially, women are burdened with the responsibility of securing optimal foetal outcomes without being provided with the support or the means to achieve that aim.[177]

The above considerations implicate the state and wider society (in respect of violence and abuse) and highlights the shared responsibility towards poor pregnancy outcomes that stem from the failure to adequately tackle both the issues associated with poverty and health care generally, specificall drug-addiction treatment. This is not to argue that women do not have a role to play in ensuring that their own pregnancies result in healthy outcomes, but there should be wider recognition of all the facets affecting the experience of pregnancy, possible outcomes and everyone's obligations regarding human reproduction.

From this perspective, the grounds advanced for holding women liable are inherently flawe in respect of women's drug abuse during pregnancy. Proof of

---

[172] The lack of treatment facilities for pregnant women is widely documented; see Daniels 'Fathers, mothers, and fetal harm' 96–5; Center for Reproductive Rights 'Punishing women for their behavior during pregnancy: An approach that undermines women's health and children's interests' (September 2000) available at http://reproductiverights.org/sites/default/files/documents/pub_bp punishingwomen.pdf (accessed on 23 June 2016); Roth *Making Women Pay* 138–41; B Steinbock *Life Before Birth: The Moral and Legal status of Embryos and Fetuses* 2 ed (2011) 169; *amici curiae* brief of American Public Health Association, National Association of Social Workers, Alabama Women's Resource Network et al in *Kimbrough* (2010); *amici curiae* brief of South Carolina Medical Association, South Carolina Nurses Association, South Carolina Association of Alcoholism and Drug Abuse Counselors in *McKnight* (2008) 24–5; and *amici curiae* brief of American Academy of Addiction Psychiatry, American College of Obstetricians and Gynecologists, American Psychiatric Association et al in *Kimbrough* (2013) 37. Flavin *Our Bodies, Our Crimes* 110–1 explains that women do not enter treatment because they cannot afford to, there is not enough space to absorb them or the treatment centre does not offer childcare facilities to children already born and in their care. Also Flavin (112) points out that those facilities that do accommodate children or make provision for child care typically limit the number and ages of the children accepted.

[173] *Amici curiae* brief of South Carolina Medical Association, South Carolina Nurses Association, South Carolina Association of Alcoholism and Drug Abuse Counselors in *McKnight* (2008) 26.

[174] Jackson *Regulating Reproduction* 151.

[175] Jackson *Regulating Reproduction* 151; fn 199. This argument is supported by a study that demonstrates that women resume substance abuse after giving birth; see American Society of Addiction Medicine 'Survey find lower rates of substance use by pregnant women, but rapid resumption of use after pregnancy' (2009) 24 *American Society of Addiction Medicine News* 16.

[176] Jackson *Regulating Reproduction* 151.

[177] Roth *Making Women Pay* 177. In fact, she (163) argues that when the state regulates women's behaviour during pregnancy, it is effectively declaring that its goal is to increase healthy birth outcomes as cheaply as possible.

harm beyond a reasonable doubt is lacking, thus rendering causation questionable.[178] From a public policy perspective, addiction is not a crime but a health concern that generally attracts treatment, yet this standard is not applicable in the case of pregnant or birthing women. Despite the fact that some attending healthcare staff are at the forefront of reporting positive-testing neonates to state officials in order to charge the mothers, the wider medical community stands in strong opposition to the criminalisation of substance abuse during pregnancy and argues that using the legal system 'to address perinatal alcohol and substance abuse is inappropriate'[179] since it results in increasing the adverse consequences of prenatal substance abuse. Further, the state, men and the wider communities remain invisible concerning their contributions to creating unhealthy pregnancy environments and poor pregnancy outcomes.

9.6 IMPLICATIONS OF THE SEPARATE-ENTITIES APPROACH

Adopting a separate-entities approach to pregnancy in the context of substance abuse is being advanced in order to protect the unborn from the pregnant women who carry them. In this instance, protection from women's self-destructive prenatal behaviour is needed in order to secure optimal foetal development and healthy birth outcomes. From this perspective, pregnant women are constructed as perpetrators against the unborn they gestate and are implicitly perpetrators against their own bodies. This view of pregnancy fails to promote the aims of healthy pregnancies and pregnancy outcomes, since it fosters adversarialism by focusing on foetal interests as a primary concern for advancement, thus diluting female reproductive autonomy.[180]

It is the position of all *amici curiae* considered in this chapter that criminalising substance abuse and threatening criminal prosecution will serve as a barrier to realising healthy pregnancies and birth. This includes scores of interested organisations and relevant experts who have at certain times come together to denounce punitive state action. This has the impact of sending a very stern, well-supported message against adopting a punitive law in such an arbitrary fashion.[181] To start with, adopting a punitive approach fails to achieve healthy pregnancies and jeopardises pregnancy outcomes. Those women addicted to or

[178] For instance, see the arguments presented in the *amici curiae* brief of American Academy of Addiction Psychiatry, American College of Obstetrics and Gynecologists, American Psychiatric Association et al in *Ankrom* (2013) 29–30 where it is argued that charges will be brought against women who are known to have previously used an illegal substance and at birth her neonate tests positive: 'Drug tests, however, can only confir that someone took the drug or was exposed to it. Drug tests do not establish that a particular drug caused particular harms. Nor does the fact that a drug is an illegal controlled substance establish such a causal connection.'

[179] *Amici curiae* brief of American Academy of Addiction Psychiatry, American College of Obstetricians and Gynecologists, American Psychiatric Association et al in *Kimbrough* (2013) 7.

[180] Some of what is relevant to this discussion has already been covered in Chapter Eight, however, it is considered necessary to revisit these issue in the specifi context of prenatal substance abuse allegedly causing harm to neonates.

[181] Concerning this chapter alone, 180 *amici curiae* have been listed, however, there are many more cases with *amici curiae* filin briefs in opposition to criminal sanctions against women for prenatal substance abuse.

occasionally making use of substances will refrain from accessing prenatal care,[182] or will avoid hospital births altogether.[183] Further, if or when care is obtained, these women will be less likely to be honest regarding their addiction issues or to reliably divulge information critical for adequate treatment.[184] Criminalising prenatal substance abuse also affects effective drug treatment during pregnancy,[185] since women who actively seek treatment might face prosecution, despite wanting to overcome their addiction.[186]

This scenario presents a number of problems because prenatal care is identifie as improving pregnancy outcomes,[187] even among those women who are unable to completely stop drug use.[188] Also those who decide to overcome addiction without treatment may face increased complications as a result of potentially fatal

---

[182] K Proehl 'Pregnancy crimes: New worries to expect when you're expecting' (2013) 53 *Santa Clara LR* 661 687; SCM Roberts & C Pies 'Complex calculations: How drug use during pregnancy becomes a barrier to prenatal care' (2011) 15 *Maternal and Child Health Journal* 333; *amici curiae* brief of the National Association of Alcoholism and Drug Abuse Counselors, South Carolina Association of Alcoholism and Drug Abuse Counselors, American College of Obstetricians and Gynecologists et al in *Whitner* 12–4; *amici curiae* brief of National Association of Alcoholism and Drug Abuse Counselors, South Carolina Association of Alcoholism and American Public Health Association, American Nurses Association, American Psychiatric Association et al in *McKnight* (2003) 19; and *amici curiae* brief of South Carolina Medical Association, South Carolina Nurses Association, South Carolina Association of Alcoholism and Drug Abuse Counselors in *McKnight* (2008) 27.

[183] *Amici curiae* brief of American Public Health Association, American Nurses Association, American Psychiatric Association et al in *McKnight* (2003) 20.

[184] Proehl (2013) *Santa Clara LR* 687; *amici curiae* brief of American Academy of Addiction Psychiatry, American College of Obstetricians and Gynecologists, American Psychiatric Association et al in *Kimbrough* (2013) 12–13; *amici curiae* brief of the National Association of Alcoholism and Drug Abuse Counselors, South Carolina Association of Alcoholism and Drug Abuse Counselors, American College of Obstetricians and Gynecologists et al in *Whitner* 12–14; and *amici curiae* brief of National Association of Alcoholism and Drug Abuse Counselors, South Carolina Association of Alcoholism and American Public Health Association, American Nurses Association, American Psychiatric Association et al in *McKnight* (2003) 20.

[185] *Amici curiae* brief of the National Association of Alcoholism and Drug Abuse Counselors, South Carolina Association of Alcoholism and Drug Abuse Counselors, American College of Obstetricians and Gynecologists et al in *Whitner* 18.

[186] *Amici curiae* brief of South Carolina Medical Association, South Carolina Nurses Association, South Carolina Association of Alcoholism and Drug Abuse Counselors in *McKnight* (2008) 28. This is a likely situation because it is reported that pregnancy and motherhood serve as strong motivators to get treatment and overcome addiction for women; see Flavin *Our Bodies, Our Crimes* 111 and American Society of Addiction Medicine (2009) *American Society of Addiction Medicine News* 16.

[187] *Amici curiae* brief of American Academy of Addiction Psychiatry, American College of Obstetricians and Gynecologists, American Psychiatric Association et al in *Kimbrough* (2013) 8–9 and *amici curiae* brief of the National Association of Alcoholism and Drug Abuse Counselors, South Carolina Association of Alcoholism and Drug Abuse Counselors, American College of Obstetricians and Gynecologists et al in *Whitner* 16.

[188] *Amici curiae* brief of American Academy of Addiction Psychiatry, American College of Obstetricians and Gynecologists, American Psychiatric Association et al in *Kimbrough* (2013) 6. However, for a contrary view, see GA Richardson, SC Hamel, L Goldschmidt et al 'Growth of infants prenatally exposed to cocaine/crack: Comparison of a prenatal care and a no prenatal care sample' (1999) 104 *Pediatrics* 18. Regardless, Roberts and Pies indicate that lack of prenatal care places clear limits on opportunities for offering health-related interventions that assist in promoting healthier outcomes; see Roberts & Pies (2011) *Maternal and Child Health Journal* 333.

withdrawal symptoms.[189] Little, Snell, Van Beveren et al report that treatment for substance abuse while pregnant assists in increasing foetal growth, improving foetal wellbeing and reducing the risk of poor pregnancy outcomes; they suggest that these results possibly ensued as a result of attending health-care professionals' awareness of pregnant women's status regarding exposure to substances.[190] From this perspective, criminal sanctions compromise the health of pregnant women and the unborn and thus fail to offer any meaningful protection.

Fear of prosecution can be taken to absolute extremes and serves as motivation to terminate pregnancies.[191] Concerning the threat of terminating pregnancies, National Advocates for Pregnant Women report an incident in North Dakota, where Martina Greywind, who was approximately 12 weeks' pregnant, was charged with reckless endangerment of the unborn for allegedly inhaling paint fumes.[192] Greywind spent some time in prison and managed to arrange release for a medical appointment where she had her pregnancy terminated. She thereafter file for a motion to dismiss the charges on endangerment.[193] The prosecutor reportedly stated that the case of child endangerment was no longer worth the time or effort because Greywind had terminated her pregnancy.[194] The Greywind incident is at loggerheads with the notion that foetal protection measures are effective mechanisms for protecting the unborn.

Further, prosecuting and sentencing women for prenatal substance abuse is an acontextual approach to addressing the harm concerns related to substance abuse. As a result of removing pregnant and mothering women's context, criminal child-abuse laws fail to adequately translate into any meaningful protection and merely ensure the continuous cycle of destruction. Imprisonment will not serve the interests of the women concerned nor those of existing and future children. Concerning serving women's interests, sentencing women to imprisonment will not address the underlying issues associated with addiction, let alone provide the

---

189 Roth *Making Women Pay* 139; Jackson *Regulating Reproduction* 149; and Paltrow & Jack (2010) *The Champion* 4.

190 BB Little, LM Snell, TT Van Beveren et al 'Treatment of substance abuse during pregnancy and infant outcome' (2003) 20 *American Journal of Perinatology* 255 260. In fact, the authors' finding indicate that the longer pregnant women remain in treatment the more likely they will give birth to neonates who are comparable to those neonates born from women that did not abuse substances prenatally. Also see *amici curiae* brief of National Association of Alcoholism and Drug Abuse Counselors, South Carolina Association of Alcoholism and American Public Health Association, American Nurses Association, American Psychiatric Association et al in *McKnight* (2003) 18 and Center for Reproductive Rights 'Punishing women for their behavior during pregnancy' 7.

191 Proehl (2013) *Santa Clara LR* 687 and *amici curiae* brief of American Academy of Addiction Psychiatry, American College of Obstetricians and Gynecologists, American Psychiatric Association et al in *Kimbrough* (2013) 10–1. This was specificall recognised by the District Court of Appeal of Florida in *Johnson* (discussed above under para 9.2).

192 National Advocates for Pregnant Women 'NAPW documentation State v. Greywind' (14 April 2012) available at http://advocatesforpregnantwomen.org/issues/criminal_cases_and_issues/napw_documentation_state_v_greywind.php (accessed on 24 June 2016) and Paltrow & Flavin (2013) *Journal of Health Politics, Policy and Law* 308. This case cannot be sourced; consequently, secondary sources are being relied on.

193 National Advocates for Pregnant Women 'NAPW documentation State v. Greywind'.

194 National Advocates for Pregnant Women 'NAPW documentation State v. Greywind'.

specialist care needed to overcome drug addiction or parental training to assist in coping with parental responsibilities.[195] Further, illegal substances are known to be readily available in prisons.[196] This scenario proves problematic because women might remain addicts, and would still be able to bear more children in the future. They would also remain ill-equipped to face the issues that are present at the intersection of addiction, pregnancy and parenting.

Concerning the interests of existing children, the *amici curiae* in *Martinez* argue that separating a mother and child 'carries with it profound and well-documented dangers'.[197] These dangers include negative effects on emotional, behavioural and psychological development. Some children develop problems with aggression and withdrawal, criminal involvement and depression, and this may impact negatively on their ability to concentrate.[198] They argue further that arresting and incarcerating women who have recently given birth removes the chance to bond, which poses unique concerns, because the days following birth are argued to be one of the most crucial times of a newborn's life.[199] Bearing in mind that prenatal substance abuse is a non-violent 'crime', it is unsettling that this form of separation should occur. If the concerns of substance abuse were addressed, the family unit could remain intact and future children could be better received into this family unit.

Viewing the unborn as entities separate from pregnant women with distinguished and diverging interests and health needs is the core reason why the aim for foetal protection fails. This approach, in a foetal personhood environment, fosters adversarialism, Flavin asserts:[200]

> Singling out pregnant women and mothers for prosecution, court orders through family courts and drug treatment courts, and civil commitments contributes to a climate in

[195] These are some of the issues that were identifie by Daniels ('Fathers, mothers, and fetal harm' 94–6) as being important to address in order for women to overcome addiction, but given the poor condition of the prison system, it is unlikely that these issues will receive any meaningful attention. Concerning the poor conditions of prisons, see Flavin *Our Bodies, Our Crimes* 134. Also see *amici curiae* brief of Pegasus Legal Services for Children, New Mexico Section of the American College of Obstetricians and Gynecologists, New Mexico Public Health Association et al in the matter of *State v Martinez* 141 NM 763 (NM 2007) 16–7. In this case the Supreme Court of New Mexico struck down the state's attempt to convict Martinez for abusing substances prenatally. The state petitioned to the Supreme Court of New Mexico after the Court of Appeals ruled against its move to prosecute Martinez; see *State v Martinez* 137 P 3d 1195 (NM App 2006). Something to note further, if there is already a short supply of adequate drug treatment facilities outside of the prison system, it is not clear how treatment would be readily available in prisons.

[196] Jackson *Regulating Reproduction* 149.

[197] *Amici curiae* brief of Pegasus Legal Services for Children, New Mexico Section of the American College of Obstetricians and Gynecologists, New Mexico Public Health Association et al in *Martinez* 15.

[198] *Amici curiae* brief of Pegasus Legal Services for Children, New Mexico Section of the American College of Obstetricians and Gynecologists, New Mexico Public Health Association et al in *Martinez* 15–6.

[199] *Amici curiae* brief of Pegasus Legal Services for Children, New Mexico Section of the American College of Obstetricians and Gynecologists, New Mexico Public Health Association et al in *Martinez* 16.

[200] Flavin *Our Bodies, Our Crimes* 116.

which pregnant women are increasingly seen as adversaries of the fetuses they carry rather than people who have a stake in a healthy pregnancy and a positive outcome.

Those third parties who participate in the pregnancy relationship between women and the unborn and who fuel that adversarialist environment must be recognised. It must be emphasised that it is others' perception that women are in an adversarial position with the unborn they carry, and women do not hold this perception themselves. Roth points out that adversarialism does not exist between pregnant women and the unborn, but rather pregnant women are in an adversarial relationship with medical or state authority.[201] Roth's example of the prosecutor 'listening' to the voices of the unborn is relevant here.[202] Aside from state prosecutors, there is a wide range of other individuals speaking for the unborn through the actions of reporting women who are known to have abused substances prenatally. These include nurses, doctors, midwives, hospital social workers, hospital administrators, drug treatment counsellors, partners and other family members.[203] Paltrow and Flavin quote a doctor as saying that the health profession's goal, from the medical perspective, is to secure the best outcome for the infant, and, where substance abuse is detected, they have to report it to the Department of Human Services.[204]

This process of reporting women to protect the individuated foetus invites the prosecutorial process, which is, by its very nature, adversarial[205] and inevitably ends with one 'party's' interests being advanced over the other's. Instead of getting help, these women face prosecution.

With broader health concerns brought into perspective, a policy favouring criminalisation clearly fails to secure the best possible outcomes for the unborn, but also fails pregnant women and all women who have the potential to become pregnant. This approach brings pregnancy adversarialism to the fore, thus imposing tensions between female reproductive autonomy and foetal interests. In each of the cases discussed in this chapter, the women represent those who continued with a pregnancy. This is a reproductive decision and is an expression of reproductive autonomy. In order to effectively and meaningfully realise this decision, women need access to health care, particularly general health care, prenatal care and drug treatment.

Criminalising prenatal substance abuse makes it difficult for these women to realise their reproductive decision to bear a child and therefore violates their

---

[201] Roth *Making Women Pay* 90. However, Steinbock (*Life before Birth* 156) does refer to instances where she views pregnant women as being in an adversarial position with the unborn since there are times when pregnant women's interests conflic with foetal interests. For instance, she refers to the example where a pregnant woman has cancer and the only treatment available to secure the woman's survival may likely terminate the pregnancy. She states (156): 'It is wishful thinking to pretend that what is best for the pregnant woman is necessarily best for the fetus or future child, or what is best for the fetus always promotes the pregnant woman's interests. Moreover, it is possible that some pregnant women choose to engage in behaviors that are risky both for themselves and their future children.'

[202] Roth *Making Women Pay* 133–4. This is discussed in Chapter Eight, para 8.5.

[203] Paltrow & Flavin (2013) *Journal of Health Politics, Policy and Law* 326–7.

[204] Paltrow & Flavin (2013) *Journal of Health Politics, Policy and Law* 328.

[205] Schroedel, Fiber & Snyder (2000) *Duke Journal of Gender Law & Policy* 105.

reproductive autonomy. It impedes the realisation of a healthy outcome. This occurs in one of two ways. Women are forced either into the decision to terminate a wanted pregnancy or progress through pregnancy without any adequate care proportionate to their health risks; if neither of these two options is chosen, these women face prosecution.

When reproductive autonomy is threatened in this way, so are foetal interests. A healthy pregnant woman aids in securing the realisation of a healthy child. This emphasis on an inseparable link and the impact of that link between the unborn and pregnant women requires that women's environments be addressed. Understanding reproductive autonomy as including the right to have a child and safe progression through pregnancy with access to drug treatment and prenatal care opens the door to removing tensions and securing optimal pregnancy outcomes, thus serving both female reproductive autonomy and foetal interests.

9.7 REFLECTING ON OVENS' PROPOSAL

The United States' experience assists in substantiating the concerns raised in Chapter Six when discussing Ovens' proposal of extending child abuse laws to include prenatal substance abuse. The experiences in the United States demonstrate that criminalising prenatal substance abuse should not be considered an option for South Africa. Not only do the foundational principles of criminal laws prohibit the expansion of criminal law in this area of pregnancy but also such a move would fail to protect both women and the unborn.

Ovens[206] acknowledges that not only is the extent of prenatal substance abuse in South Africa unknown,[207] but there is no conclusive evidence demonstrating that a specifi harm is inflicte through prenatal exposure to abused substances. She recognises the potential for a number of harms possibly resulting from prenatal substance abuse (such as low birth weight or increased risk of Sudden Infant Death Syndrome),[208] but fails to locate those harms within the context of other factors associated with increasing the risks of adverse pregnancy outcomes. Ovens very briefl mentions that socio-economic factors affect pregnancy outcomes,[209] but she does not seem to link the significanc of those factors with attributing criminal responsibility solely to women. Additionally, Ovens recognises that addiction is a medical or health-related concern that requires treatment,[210] but nevertheless advocates a punitive approach[211] in circumstances where there are no known prenatal drug treatment facilities.[212] If prenatal substance abuse is to be taken seriously, it is required that the complexity of the issue be considered in the context in which it exists. Without that knowledge, no adequate policy can be developed and this issue will remain stagnant.

---

206 Ovens (2008) *Acta Criminologica* 80; 88.
207 This leads one to question to what extent intervention is even needed.
208 Ovens (2008) *Acta Criminologica* 88.
209 Ovens (2008) *Acta Criminologica* 88.
210 Ovens (2008) *Acta Criminologica* 91.
211 Ovens (2008) *Acta Criminologica* 92.
212 Ovens (2008) *Acta Criminologica* 90.

Ovens refers to the United States as having punitive legal measures in place to tackle prenatal substance abuse and views these measures as necessary, since without them the unborn are left unprotected.[213] However, as demonstrated here, since these measures have only been applied after birth, harm is not prevented because the 'harmful' conduct was present during gestation. Further, Ovens argues that the Choice on Termination of Pregnancy Act[214] (Choice Act) offers the unborn more protection than is currently afforded to the unborn being exposed to substances prenatally.[215] This assumption is unfounded when applied to the issue of criminalising prenatal substance abuse, because the Choice Act will serve as an opportunity to avoid prosecution by terminating pregnancies.[216] Consequently, framing the unborn as victims who suffer unique harms apart from women renders efforts for protection unsound from a theoretical and practical perspective.

In the abstract to her publication Ovens pointed out that she was seeking to develop a policy that would be beneficia to pregnant addicts and their unborn.[217] The United States' experience demonstrates that her suggestion of turning to criminal law failed to fulfi this aim. In fact, South Africa is on the right path, given that treatment-based legislation has been enacted. The Prevention of and Treatment for Substance Abuse Act[218] should remain in place, but should possibly be amended to make specifi provision for the treatment of pregnant women, with the aim of securing healthy pregnancies and training aimed at keeping the family unit together after birth. This approach recognises the value in pregnancy and acts on this value in such a way that tensions are avoided and all interests are advanced.

9.8 REVISITING LEGAL STATUS IN THE UNITED STATES

The implication of foetal personhood (as denoting a separate subject in law but not a constitutional person) is far-reaching: it allows for the increased limitation of termination-of-pregnancy rights, inspires calls for the extension of constitutional personhood, secures the development and implementation of feticide laws, foetal homicide or murder provisions, and serves as grounds for justifying the criminalisation of prenatal substance abuse. These measures are being applied against not only third parties but also the pregnant women who gestate the unborn.

Leeway for this sort of extensive protection is a result of the separate-entities approach being applied in one area of law and the notion of separatism then gaining momentum. It gains a life of its own, in that the application of the separate-entities approach in one area of law leads to establishing authority for the application of that approach more broadly in other areas of law, for instance, feticide provisions originally aimed at affording protection from third-party

213 Ovens (2008) *Acta Criminologica* 85 and Ovens (2010) *Child Abuse Research in South Africa* 40; 45.

214 Act 92 of 1996.

215 Ovens (2010) *Child Abuse Research in South Africa* 45.

216 The Choice Act is correctly being interpreted as offering protection to the unborn, but as already demonstrated, this protection takes place in a not-one-but-not-two approach to pregnancy as opposed to Ovens' separate-entities approach. See the discussion in Chapter Five.

217 Ovens (2008) *Acta Criminologica* 79.

218 Act 70 of 2008.

violence against pregnant women. However, logic demands that, if the unborn are separate victims of crime, then these provisions can be equally applicable to women who experience stillbirths or perinatal deaths as a result of self-harm or self-destructive behaviour. From there, feticide provisions are cited as justificatio for criminalising other conduct that does not necessarily result in pregnancy terminations, such as prenatal substance abuse.[219]

These are extensive protections in spite of the fact that the unborn lack constitutional personhood. Foetal personhood as a form of legal personhood vests the unborn with greater rights than born persons[220]—'super-rights'.[221] This expansive legal recognition of the unborn is geared towards rendering the vestment of constitutional personhood irrelevant.[222] Lupton emphasises that the unborn are unique, in that they are granted a range of rights but have no obligations, and that their rights span the legitimate expectation that pregnant women must submit all of themselves for the unborn's gestational benefi and prospects of a healthy birth outcome.[223]

Looking at the United States' experience in the context of separatism forces a reconsideration of the status of pregnant women in the United States. Flavin asserts that 'foetal protectionism' results in women being bystanders to their own bodies.[224] Foetal personhood predominates pregnant women's personhood, diminishing their status to what has been described as a 'special class of persons',[225] 'second-class citizen',[226] 'second-class status',[227] and 'unique category of persons',[228] whose existence can be bypassed in the name of foetal personhood. Women's diluted status during pregnancy makes them vulnerable to far-reaching state intrusions and 'effectively strip[s] them of their status as

[219] *Whitner* is a fittin example of this taking place.

[220] Schroedel, Fiber & Snyder (2000) *Duke Journal of Gender Law & Policy* 109.

[221] Roth *Making Women Pay* 134.

[222] Lupton argues that cadavers (in respect of the use of their organs) have more rights than pregnant women in the United States. See D Lupton *Social Worlds of the Unborn* (2013) 107–8. This argument is linked to the incidence of forced medical interventions in the United States and the trend of rendering women's advance directives null and void if they are unconscious while pregnant and in need of life-sustaining treatment. In this instance, if these women, in their advance directives, indicated the desire to not be resuscitated or kept alive artificiall , this directive will not be respected if resuscitation is needed when they are pregnant. Lupton refers to a study that highlights a number of incidences where pregnant women who were braindead were artificiall kept alive in order for their pregnancies to mature to the point when the unborn could be safely delivered alive. Bringing this back to cadavers, Lupton (108) argues that the state may not harvest any organ of a deceased person without that person's consent, which must have been given while still alive, yet pregnant women's wishes concerning what happens to their bodies after death are rendered irrelevant. Roth also asserts a similar argument; see Roth *Making Women Pay* 134.

[223] Lupton *Social Worlds of the Unborn* 108.

[224] Flavin *Our Bodies, Our Crimes* 118.

[225] B Bird 'Fetal personhood laws as limits to maternal personhood at any stage of pregnancy: Balancing fetal and maternal interests at post-viability among fetal pain and fetal homicide laws' (2014) 25 *Hastings Women's LJ* 39 54.

[226] Proehl (2013) *Santa Clara LR* 690.

[227] LM Paltrow '*Roe v Wade* and the New Jane Crow: Reproductive rights in the age of mass incarceration' (2013) 103 *American Journal of Public Health* 17.

[228] Paltrow (2013) *American Journal of Public Health* 19.

constitutional persons'.[229] Paltrow and Flavin's study highlights that there is one law for non-pregnant individuals, where addiction, attempted suicide, and refusal to undergo medical treatment are not criminal, and then there is another law for pregnant women, whereby these issues are criminal.[230] Criminal responsibility rests with women purely because the value vested in the unborn has been translated into foetal personhood, which is now a value that has more legal clout than the value vested in the women who carry them.

Focus turns now to Du Plessis and Kruuse's arguments that avoiding constitutional protection or rights avoids the implication of women's rights and freedoms: this discussion shows that developing the view that the unborn are separate entities in law will encroach on women's rights because they are the very people who gestate the unborn. The more protection afforded the unborn as individuated subjects, the more women fade out of law's protective reach, regardless of the constitutional status of the unborn. This demonstrates the fluidit of women's status as legal subjects: prior to pregnancy their bodies are their own and autonomy vests. Suicide, addiction and refusal to undergo medical intervention are not criminal and women are viewed as competent enough to progress through their lives as they deem fit However, once conception has occurred, depending on the state and relevant body of law, pregnancy removes women's autonomy and the state and others in authority take over, almost rendering women incompetent and untrustworthy to see pregnancies through without broader surveillance and intervention on behalf of the unborn. These invasions of autonomy do not take place in respect of any other person, being men and non-pregnant women, and this speaks volumes about pregnant women's status in the United States.

9.9 CONCLUDING REMARKS

Generally, substance abuse, in the form of addiction, is an important social concern that requires meaningful attention. The United States' experience concerning prenatal substance abuse as constituting child abuse has proved invaluable for the purposes of determining the way forward for South Africa. Ovens argues that the unborn are in need of protection from pregnant women's substance abuse, and she recommends that prenatal substance abuse should constitute child abuse. This chapter demonstrates the need for a more informed and multi-disciplinary approach to the issue of substance abuse and requires innovative thinking when looking at tackling this issue.

In the United States, few states have adopted an approach similar to Ovens' proposal and this is despite the fact that foetal personhood is well-established in a large number of states. The fact that so few states implement such child abuse or

---

[229] Paltrow (2013) *American Journal of Public Health* 17. Paltrow discusses extensive violations of pregnant women's rights as protected under the United States Constitution.

[230] See generally Paltrow & Flavin (2013) *Journal of Health Politics, Policy and Law* 299.

endangerment provisions indicates that this approach is not viewed in a favourable light and less extreme, more appropriate methods could be adopted to tackle prenatal substance abuse.

A number of concerns were raised about adopting a punitive approach to address addiction during pregnancy. The firs relates to causing harm to children born after being prenatally exposed to illegal substances. Expert arguments advanced by numerous *amici curiae* demonstrate that merely testing positive for drugs does not indicate the inflictio of harm. Further, if an adverse pregnancy outcome is experienced, the adverse outcome cannot always be linked directly to prenatal substance abuse as the cause. Furthermore, addiction is considered a disease which implicates the requirement of intent. It therefore cannot be accepted that a drug-dependent woman intentionally sets out to harm her foetus by abusing substances. Flavin points out that, in most cases, women in the system were firs addicts before becoming pregnant and did not become addicted to substances while pregnant with the intention of harming the unborn or compromising the healthy progression of their pregnancies.[231] This all speaks to the fact that foundational principles for intentional criminal responsibility are lacking, namely causation and intention.

Imposing criminal liability on women alone implies that women have control over their pregnancy outcomes, and therefore have the means of preventing adverse outcomes. However, in some instances no unique harm can be identifie as having been caused by the abuse of a particular illegal substance, and this indicates that other factors contribute to the risk of adverse outcomes. These factors are wide-ranging and include other role-players such as the state and the wider community. Factors identifie include violence, low socio-economic standing, poor health care, poor nutrition, genetic disorders, and lack of health care. More alarming is the fact that, while these factors are indicated risk factors for poor pregnancy outcomes, they are also identifie as driving addictive behaviour. Consequently, the responsibility for adverse pregnancy outcomes extends beyond pregnant women who abuse substances.

Separating the unborn from pregnant women for the purposes of better protection essentially leads to the increased risk of adverse outcomes. Criminalising prenatal substance abuse turns pregnancy into an adversarial zone, which perpetuates tensions, because third parties attempt to act for the best interests of the unborn and women are portrayed as perpetrators against their own pregnancies. This fails to advance women's reproductive autonomy and ultimately fails to advance the interests of the unborn. An unhealthy woman can do very little to ensure a healthy birth outcome, and to expect otherwise is to expect the impossible.

The United States' experience, in respect of the three states that criminalised prenatal substance abuse, demonstrates that this approach should not be adopted. In doing so, it has also demonstrated what should be done in order to address prenatal substance abuse, that is, focus on substance abuse as a health concern requiring treatment rather than a criminal act against 'others'. From this

[231] Flavin *Our Bodies, Our Crimes* 95–118.

perspective, South Africa has already made progress towards this in respect of the Prevention of and Treatment for Substance Abuse Act and now, if any law reform should follow, it should be focused on including pregnancy-specifi provisions concerning adequate treatment.

Reflectin on the United States discussion in its entirety, this study demonstrates that adopting a separate-entities approach to addressing pregnancy-related concerns fails to secure optimal foetal outcomes and healthy pregnancies for women, and almost guarantees poor pregnancy outcomes. This is largely because separatism fosters tensions between pregnant women's autonomy and foetal interests as advanced by third parties. In this respect the United States serves as an anti-model for addressing the tension between female autonomy rights and foetal interests during pregnancy and birth. As things stand, it seems as though the United States is moving backwards, leaning towards placing women in their historical role of reproductive vessels.[232] Those advocating law reform in South Africa should be critical of the United States model and approach it with caution.

Extending full legal subjectivity to the unborn, criminalising maternal conduct suspected of causing stillbirth or perinatal death, and criminalising prenatal substance abuse do not contribute to creating a supportive pregnancy environment. All those scenarios invite the inclusion of third parties into a very personal realm of reproductive experience and they tend to take over women's bodies in order to advance the interests of the unborn as separate entities in need of outside protection. This study has effectively shown that this approach fails to protect the unborn from harm, in that it renders women invisible despite the fact that it is their bodies that gestate the unborn, secure prenatal life and provide nourishment. Ultimately, this approach abuses the source of prenatal life.

The separate-entities approach does provide a medium in which to speak about pregnancy-related concerns, but the discourse is one of adversarialism and offends the embodied connection that pregnancy represents. Less extreme measures can be adopted that will reap increased protection. The separate-entities approach fails to grasp the notion that healthy women and healthy pregnancy environments offer better prospects for women to safely advance through pregnancies and secure healthy pregnancy outcomes. Understanding the context in which individual pregnant women exist highlights this. The single-entity and separate-entities approaches to pregnancy must be rejected, as both fail to adequately articulate a respectful discourse of pregnancy, female reproductive autonomy (as including the right to terminate or continue with pregnancies) and foetal interests based on unity of interests. The chapter to follow will discuss an alternative narrative of pregnancy in law based on relational theory in the form of the not-one-but-not-two approach to pregnancy.

---

[232] Women's historical position was discussed in Part One. It could even be argued that women are being placed in a further disadvantaged position. Historically women and the unborn were viewed as being equal under the head of the household, while today the unborn seem to be valued more than women.

PART FOUR

ADDRESSING PREGNANCY ADVERSARIALISM

Chapter 10

A RELATIONAL VIEW OF PREGNANCY

10.1 INTRODUCTION

The chapters in this book have highlighted a number of areas of concern regarding pregnancy, namely, the legal personhood of the unborn, violence against pregnant women that terminates prenatal life, termination of pregnancy and prenatal substance abuse. They have also considered what South African academics have suggested for a way forward regarding these issues and then tested these suggestions against the United States' experience. Up to this point, it is clear that, while there are areas in need of the law's attention, current proposals are not yielding the intended outcomes of healthy pregnancies or healthy pregnancy outcomes, because the method of addressing these issues ends in an adversarial pregnancy environment.

In the process of working through South African academics' suggestions for changes to the law and testing the appropriateness of these suggestions, a number of broader concerns have come to light. These concerns move beyond merely identifying which areas of pregnancy are in need of development in law, but include foundational aspects such as how to properly view pregnancy in law more generally and how to value the unborn in law and give effect to that value. It has come to light that, as things stand, the South African legal system is lacking an informed foundation from which to work, which includes the essential aspects of pregnancy, being the constitutive parts of a pregnancy (women *and* the unborn) and the context in which pregnancies exist. Without a proper foundation from which to work, any attempt to address issues arising from pregnancy cannot effectively be addressed, hence the questionable responses to pregnancy-related issues considered up to this point.

This chapter develops a framework in which to view pregnancy in law that provides space to consider the contexts in which pregnancy exists. This task draws on relational theory and is inspired by and adopts facets of Nedelsky's work in *Law's Relations*.[1] From there, a project is developed under the guidance of a number of identifie relational principles and feminist aims. This project aims to develop a view of pregnancy in law that is sensitive to both women's rights and foetal interests, while a number of aspects are clarifie and explained. Thereafter, identifie areas of concern are considered through a relational lens to demonstrate that it is possible to advance both female reproductive autonomy and foetal interests in a non-adversarial way. This chapter shows that a relational approach to pregnancy removes tensions, allowing for an adequate legal response to

[1] See J Nedelsky *Law's Relations: A Relational Theory of Self, Autonomy, and Law* (2011). Also see J Nedelsky 'Reconceiving autonomy: Sources, thoughts and possibilities' (1989) 1 *Yale Journal of Law & Feminism* 7.

pregnancy-related concerns.[2] It also indicates how the law can be used constructively to improve pregnancy experiences and outcomes.

While Nedelsky does not specificall tackle the issues raised in relation to pregnancy, her work does serve as a guide to pregnancy in law generally. A number of other authors rely on relational theory in respect of pregnancy-related matters and their work will be considered later when the chapter applies relational principles to the identifie areas of concern.

10.2 RELATIONAL THEORY AND FEMINISM

At the outset, this book emphasised the need to focus on 'context'. Context highlighted how certain laws or calls for changes to the law failed to have a contextual understanding of pregnant women's lives and how, as a result of their unique contexts, these women experienced very individual pregnancy experiences. Without context one would be left with flawe notions of pregnancy, pregnant women, and the unborn and, without proper consideration of context in law, the scene is set for disastrous or less than meaningful outcomes. Ultimately, contextualising pregnancy served as the leading facet in framing how to offer meaningful law reform, as opposed to what was being suggested.

Focusing on context has links to relational feminism in so far as it allows for the inclusion of context by focusing on the role of relationships.[3] This book is clearly lined up with feminist aims in a broad sense, but the aim of contextualising pregnancy is also theoretically backed by relational theory. Consequently, relational feminism forms part of the solution to addressing the tension between reproductive autonomy and foetal interests. There are very specifi arguments that have been presented throughout the book, which all tie into relational theory[4] and, since these arguments are advanced in the context of women and women's rights, they also tie into the broader feminist aims of advancing and securing women's rights. How these arguments tie into relational feminism will become apparent as the discussion develops.

The concept of relational feminism, as adopted herein, is founded on Nedelsky's work,[5] in which she reconceptualised autonomy in relational terms.[6]

---

[2] Herring identifie relational theory as primarily functioning on an 'abstract level' with little attempt being made to apply the theory to lived settings; see J Herring 'Relational autonomy and rape' in SD Sclater, F Ebtehaj, E Jackson et al (eds) *Regulating Autonomy: Sex, Reproduction and Family* (2009) 53. This chapter aims to not only theorise pregnancy as relational but also apply that view to concrete examples.

[3] More specificall , it was Professor Van Marle at the University of Pretoria, Faculty of Law who highlighted this point during a research focus group discussion on law and poverty early in 2012.

[4] For instance, throughout this book there have been concerns raised about how the context of the unborn is ignored, how their inseparable connection falls away when adopting a separate-entities approach to pregnancy and how third-party interventions impact poorly on pregnancies and pregnancy outcomes when an adversarialist stance is adopted.

[5] Nedelsky *Law's Relations* and Nedelsky (1989) *Yale Journal of Law & Feminism* 7.

[6] This is not to say that relational feminism goes uncriticised, for instance see J Christman 'Relational autonomy, liberal individualism, and the social constitution of selves' (2004) 117 *Philosophical Studies* 143. Also see JA Shields & S Serna 'The demise of feminist communitarianism' (2011) 40 *Perspectives on Political Science* 9. The authors explain that the most glaring

Her work serves as the theoretical framework for the solution to adversarialism. Nedelsky's work is valuable in four respects: her work provides a synopsis of relational feminism; she applies this theory to autonomy within the realms of context; Nedelsky also explains the role of interconnection in respect of persons and other life-forms and she demonstrates how to use the law as a mechanism to frame relationships in a way that fosters autonomy and respect for other life-forms.

As briefl mentioned in Chapter Three[7] relational feminism moves away from a liberalist construction of individuals as isolated beings with rights and the law being the employed mechanisms to protect such isolation.[8] Relational feminism focuses on the importance of relationships and context. Nedelsky identifie relationships as being central to people's lives, 'to who we are, to the capacities we are able to develop, to what we value, what we suffer, and what we are able to enjoy'.[9]

Focusing on this aspect of human existence recognises that human beings are inherently social, which means that we are constantly engaged in relationships and are fundamentally interconnected.[10] Nedelsky explains that every individual is engaged in relationships at various levels, from intimately personal relationships shared between parent and child, to wider relationships with teachers, employers, and state institutions.[11] Further, the context in which these relationships play out impacts on the relationships themselves.[12] For instance, Nedelsky demonstrates that wider societal and cultural practices can intersect the parent/child relationship and shape how parents care for their children.[13] This indicates that wider facets of

---

criticism against adopting a relational approach is the fact that adhering to an ethic of care denies women their right to terminate their pregnancies. Shields and Serna point out that this issue was one of the causes of the fall of relational feminism in the United States. The ethics of care was seen to place an obligation on women to be caring and maternal and terminating a pregnancy went against those inherent relational principles. However, this book moves away from this issue in so far as the chapter places an obligation on all role-players to foster healthy pregnancies and pregnancy outcomes. Nedelsky's work is not the only work to rely on relational theory in respect of autonomy, for instance see E Nelson *Law, Policy and Reproductive Autonomy* (2013) and J Downie & J Llewellyn 'Relational theory & health law policy' (2008) Special Edition *Health LJ* 193.

[7] Para 3.2.

[8] See Nedelsky (1989) *Yale Journal of Law & Feminism* 12. She explains that according to a liberalist notion of autonomy, the most isolated person is the most autonomous. Her work focuses primarily on revising the liberalist view of autonomy in relational terms. Her argument is based on the notion that autonomy cannot be experienced in isolation from others. Rather, she asserts that autonomy is experienced in relationships with others who provide support and guidance necessary for the development and experience of autonomy.

[9] Nedelsky *Law's Relations* 3.

[10] Nedelsky *Law's Relations* 19.

[11] Nedelsky *Law's Relations* 20.

[12] Nedelsky *Law's Relations* 20.

[13] Nedelsky *Law's Relations* 21. Nedelsky explains that while she views individuals as relational, she emphasises that relationships do not determine who an individual is, rather relationships are viewed as playing a constitutive role in an individual's life. Nedelsky (32) explains 'constitutive' by quoting from Steven Winter as stating: 'We are constituted because the situated quality of human existence means that both the physical and social environment with which we interact is already formed by the actions of those who have preceded us'. Also, we are not determined by our

life such as laws and long-standing social or cultural norms impact on relationships and how those relationships are experienced.[14] Nedelsky states: 'In short, every level is both shaped by and shapes those it intersects with. All human beings are both constituted by, and contribute to, changing or reinforcing the intersecting relationships of which they are part.'[15]

Understanding people as being relational rather than atomistic[16] shows that they are interdependent and dependent, and are not purely independent[17] by nature.[18] According to Nedelsky, interdependency and dependency run to the core of our existence in that we all rely on our social world to enable us to realise 'core capacities' such as love, reason, creativity and autonomy, to name a few capacities.[19] Therefore, part of the point of adopting a relational approach is to centralise relationships in our views on human existence and to then identify the relationships that foster or undermine core values, and determine how various laws and norms help to structure these relationships in the way that they do.[20]

With regard to the role of law and rights, Nedelsky argues that law and rights structure relationships and play a role in determining the quality of those relationships by either enhancing or undermining core values.[21] She advances that, when problems do arise, this is because law has structured relationships in ways that undermine certain core values.[22] The issue is therefore not that law permeates people's lives to the extent that it does, but rather *how* it does so.[23] This requires one to investigate whether the influenc of the law advances a person's core values or undermines it. Consequently, reform of the law is not necessarily advocated in order to increase the role of the state but rather to adjust the role of the state. This perspective is paramount given that everyone engages with the law, the state and collective power in their everyday relations and interconnectedness.[24]

Nedelsky understands a relational approach to take an 'evaluative' stance which is aimed primarily at transforming relationships in order to better secure certain core values.[25] Consequently, one needs to be aware of the central role of relationships and evaluate which ones are destructive in order to free oneself from

relationships because all human beings have an internal 'significan ability to make themselves who they are' through what Nedelsky terms 'creative capacity' in place of 'self-determination'. See Nedelsky *Law's Relations* 31; 167.

[14] Nedelsky *Law's Relations* 21.

[15] Nedelsky *Law's Relations* 22.

[16] Indicating the liberalist stance of a person, isolated from others and protected in their isolation.

[17] Nedelsky *Law's Relations* 3.

[18] Nedelsky *Law's Relations* 28.

[19] Nedelsky *Law's Relations* 28.

[20] Nedelsky *Law's Relations* 32.

[21] Nedelsky *Law's Relations* 66.

[22] Nedelsky *Law's Relations* 67. Nedelsky (39–41) refers to a number of examples of how structured relationships can either undermine or foster autonomy. Ultimately, it comes down to the issue of hierarchy and the way a power relation is allowed to be exercised over others in a position of dependency. Dependency can be viewed as graded and the more a person is dependent the more likely it is that the person's core value will be left vulnerable to the other's position of power.

[23] Nedelsky *Law's Relations* 67.

[24] See general discussion, Nedelsky *Law's Relations* 65–9.

[25] Nedelsky *Law's Relations* 67.

that relationship but also to transform the structures that shaped the destructive relationships to start with.

Nedelsky highlights a number of core values important to individuals and asserts that her relational model can be applied to any value.[26] However, her focus is on the value of autonomy. She views feminism as an 'emancipatory project' and identifie autonomy as being central to women's drive to self-defin their lives and make their lives their own.[27] However, she asserts that the current and prevailing view of autonomy, as derived from liberalism, is flawe because it overemphasises independence as the primary indication of autonomous existence.[28] She therefore argues that, since autonomy is important to feminist aims, it is necessary to keep the value but to reconceptualise it as a relational value.[29] She argues for 'relational autonomy', a concept that allows for the recognition that people are social by nature indicating that people are not 'self-made' but rather come about through the social relations that constitute us.[30]

Autonomy is presented by Nedelsky as a capacity. She views it as an ongoing process to fin 'one's own law' in the quest towards 'becoming' autonomous.[31] 'One's own law' denotes internally derived values, orders, limits and commands, and she asserts that how these values come about is through social interaction and spiritual consciousness.[32] According to Nedelsky, 'becoming' autonomous indicates that people are not born into autonomy; it is something that must be developed and this is done in relation to others.[33]

Nedelsky argues: 'If we ask ourselves what actually enables people to be autonomous, the answer is not isolation, but relationships—with parents, teachers, friends, loved ones—that provide support and guidance necessary for the development and experience of autonomy.'[34] Consequently, she views interdependence, as opposed to independence, as a constant component of autonomy.[35] With relationships drawn back into perspective, she establishes that it is easier to identify the role of relationships in realising autonomy, in that some relationships undermine autonomy while others foster it.[36]

Being understood as interconnected and dependent does not render people powerless to collective power.[37] Nedelsky encourages a move away from the traditional view of pitting individuals against the state, since this is a destructive

---

[26] Nedelsky *Law's Relations* 41.

[27] Nedelsky *Law's Relations* 43–4.

[28] Nedelsky (1989) *Yale Journal of Law & Feminism* 8.

[29] Nedelsky (1989) *Yale Journal of Law & Feminism* 7.

[30] Nedelsky (1989) *Yale Journal of Law & Feminism* 8.

[31] Nedelsky (1989) *Yale Journal of Law & Feminism* 10.

[32] Nedelsky (1989) *Yale Journal of Law & Feminism* 10.

[33] Nedelsky (1989) *Yale Journal of Law & Feminism* 10.

[34] Nedelsky (1989) *Yale Journal of Law & Feminism* 12.

[35] Nedelsky (1989) *Yale Journal of Law & Feminism* 12.

[36] Nedelsky *Law's Relations* 36. She (36) states that her claim 'is that autonomy requires constructive relationship[s] throughout a person's life. Autonomy can thrive or wither in adults depending on the structures of relationships they are embedded in.'

[37] Nedelsky (1989) *Yale Journal of Law & Feminism* 13.

outlook and ignores how much people actually rely on the state.[38] Taking this approach closes the door to findin ways to secure autonomy in spite of being part of the collective. Most people encounter the collective power of the state when having to rely on state services (such as public education, health care services or for social welfare in general) and when they fin themselves subject to state regulations (for instance mandatory licensing or health and safety regulations).[39] Therefore, there will always be some form of interdependence on the state at various levels.[40]

An individual's encounter with the state is an interaction between individual autonomy, interdependence (because of the need for state services) and collective power. In this context, Nedelsky argues that whenever a state takes on the responsibility for social welfare, it must do so in ways that foster an individual's own sense of competence, control and integrity.[41] Since autonomy can be experienced only in relation to others, the problem is not a question of how to keep the state away but how to ensure the autonomy of individuals when they are in a legitimate sphere of state power.[42] This requires a construction of autonomy that is compatible with the notions of interdependence, and a relational approach to autonomy does this, since it opens the space for more creative thinking on how to foster autonomy.

Nedelsky states that the force behind her desire to reconceive autonomy as relational was driven by the need to protect those who are already in a position of dependency on the state.[43] In fact, Nedelsky's position inspires a perspective that anyone in any form of hierarchical relationship requires protection from the imposition of power. Looking at ways in which to foster people's autonomy in these relationships, Nedelsky turns her attention to the role participants play within that relationship or the participants' subjective experiences of those relationships.[44] For instance, if participants in a relationship feel helpless or degraded, something is amiss,[45] especially if autonomy instils a sense of power to shape and direct one's life.[46]

According to Nedelsky, even in extreme cases of dependency, the law can structure relations in a way that fosters the autonomy of participants in a relationship, and this can be achieved through providing and maintaining channels

[38] Nedelsky (1989) *Yale Journal of Law & Feminism* 14–5. The traditional approach to an encounter to collective power is for individuals to shield themselves from the collective by setting up legal barriers which the collective may not cross. If the state crosses that barrier, autonomy is compromised but if the state is prevented from crossing, autonomy is secured. This means that if one were to rely on the state, he or she would have to accept diminished autonomy. Nedelsky highlights that this view breaks down any prospects of developing alternative options for securing autonomy.
[39] Nedelsky (1989) *Yale Journal of Law & Feminism* 13.
[40] Nedelsky (1989) *Yale Journal of Law & Feminism* 13.
[41] Nedelsky (1989) *Yale Journal of Law & Feminism* 13.
[42] Nedelsky (1989) *Yale Journal of Law & Feminism* 13.
[43] Nedelsky *Law's Relations* 84.
[44] Nedelsky *Law's Relations* 133.
[45] Nedelsky *Law's Relations* 136.
[46] Nedelsky *Law's Relations* 135.

for participation and inclusion.[47] Ultimately, inclusion is necessary because, if something has an impact on a person's life, it is important that they actively participate in the decision-making process.[48] This position obligates the design of a process that encourages participation in order to address power imbalances, and participation must take place at all levels.[49]

Up to this point, relationships between human beings (born individuals) have been considered as well as how the law has a role to play in that aspect. Next it is necessary to consider how Nedelsky's relational approach applies to other life-forms (animals or otherwise). On the topic of the equality of moral worth and the ordering rank of different life-forms' claims to moral consideration,[50] Nedelsky explains that a relational mode of thinking must be inclusive.[51] To be inclusive means that as human beings we are obligated to hold 'respectful and responsible relations' with 'other life-forms', because all life holds intrinsic worth.[52] This requires that we reduce any harmful impact thereon and structure our relations with other entities on the premise of reducing our negating impact on them.[53] She states that, in this respect, the relational project 'would be to discern how human action could have as positive (or minimal) an impact as possible, while fostering wise relations between human beings (both individuals and in the aggregate) and other entities broadly conceived'.[54]

Even though Nedelsky does not specificall address the position of the unborn, the unborn can be included here by interpreting 'other life-forms' widely. Her discussion emphasises that the relational project requires us to be considerate of other life-forms, which indicates the broad, inclusionary scope of the relational theory.

In an earlier article, Nedelsky discusses how to structure relationships with the unborn and gives a glimpse into the possible factors that need to be considered within the context of this chapter. In this article, she contemplates 'potential life' in the context of artificia reproductive technologies and presents a convincing argument against viewing potential life as property.[55] This article considers the assertion that the law of property can be used as a suitable means of protecting

---

[47] Nedelsky *Law's Relations* 139. Her focus is on administrative law, however, the argument she advances transcends administrative law and can aid any form of hierarchical relationship, between teachers and learners, parent and child, or even doctor and patient. Later in her book (153) Nedelsky recognises this.

[48] Nedelsky *Law's Relations* 139.

[49] Nedelsky *Law's Relations* 139. Nedelsky recognises that this may be easier said than done. She notes (155) that sometimes power imbalances are combined with established notions of fault, poverty, about who is deserving and who is not, and in these instances it is not only the relationship that needs transformation but the entire institution. This sort of reform cannot not take place overnight; it will be an incremental process of reform.

[50] See generally Nedelsky *Law's Relations* 194–199.

[51] Nedelsky *Law's Relations* 195.

[52] Nedelsky *Law's Relations* 195.

[53] Nedelsky *Law's Relations* 196.

[54] Nedelsky *Law's Relations* 196.

[55] J Nedelsky 'Property in potential life? A relational approach to choosing legal categories' (1993) 6 *Canadian Journal of Law & Jurisprudence* 343.

people's stake in their products of reproduction while making use of reproductive technologies.

Basically, Nedelsky argues against the use of property law because this law will structure relationships in a way that leaves women's equality and autonomy vulnerable and might result in disrespect for and depreciation of children generally.[56] She explains that this might possibly result because, as property law currently stands, it governs ownership, commodification exploitation and alienation, all of which, if used in the context of reproduction, offend women and the respect for and appreciation of children born from reproductive technologies.[57] She encourages that attention be given to context, meaning what sort of relationships are being fostered by adopting a property law approach: a relationship of commodity or a relationship that advances autonomy in women to reproduce and respect for the children that originate therefrom?[58] From this perspective it can be seen that the law of property fails to foster desirable relationships in relation to reproduction.

In the process of proving her point that it is preferable to avoid the use of property law in respect of reproduction-relation issues, Nedelsky contemplates other concerns beyond artificia reproductive technologies. Her discussion helps identify the role of relationships when considering the unborn and indicates the importance of context in determining how to interpret those relationships.

She explains that focusing on relationships helps to highlight a more constructive path. For instance, Nedelsky considers termination of pregnancy and explains that because a woman has a choice in pregnancy continuation (as a form of bodily freedom) she will not necessarily also have a choice in selling her reproductive capacities (as another form of bodily freedom).[59] The difference lies in the quality of the relationship each 'choice' fosters, Nedelsky argues:[60]

> [T]hese two forms of 'choice' will have completely different implications for the relationships between mothers and their children, and between people and children more generally. The effects on these relationships are likely to be undesirable in the case of selling and desirable in the case of ensuring that pregnancy is always a consensual relation for the mother. Similarly, if we look closely at how each form of 'choice' would affect relations of equality and conditions for autonomy, or would contribute to the relations that foster exploitation, commodification and alienation, the difference in impact on patterns of relationships renders the overlap of the term 'choice' trivial.

On the topic of unwanted pregnancy and the freedom of choice to terminate those pregnancies, Nedelsky identifie pregnancy as a relationship, and in the case of it being unwanted, she argues than no woman should be compelled into a

[56] Nedelsky (1993) *Canadian Journal of Law & Jurisprudence* 343–53. Her arguments are more detailed than what is presented here.

[57] Children are involved here because Nedelsky argues that if we understand the biological products of reproductive technologies to be products of ownership we would be violating the respect and appreciation we have towards the children they are born to become.

[58] Nedelsky (1993) *Canadian Journal of Law & Jurisprudence* 364.

[59] Nedelsky (1993) *Canadian Journal of Law & Jurisprudence* 364–5. Nedelsky explains that when pro-choice arguments are framed in property rights arguments (meaning that women's bodies are owned by women alone) this confusion arises.

[60] Nedelsky (1993) *Canadian Journal of Law & Jurisprudence* 365.

'nine-month relationship of pregnancy'.[61] However, she concedes that, as the pregnancy progresses through the months, the relationship changes and in the fina months 'respect and appreciation for children' may require that the pregnant woman who wishes to end her relationship, wait until birth to do so.[62]

This article, together with Nedelsky's insistence on inclusivity in *Law's Relations*,[63] gives some insight into how a relational approach might play out in respect of the unborn and the women who carry them, therefore demonstrating how to use the value of connection to resolve pregnancy adversarialism. The following is drawn from her work here: the unborn are entities that must be included in our considerations and by requiring this there is recognition that pregnant women share a relationship with the unborn. Further, how this relationship is experienced can be influence by the particular laws being adopted or applied in certain ways. This indicates that the law structures relationships in a way that fosters either desirable or undesirable relationships during pregnancy. Desirable relationships are those relationships that nurture women's autonomy (allowing for them to be driven by their own laws) and respect for other life forms, while undesirable relationships remove women as autonomous equal agents and disrespect other life-forms.[64]

Relational theory and Nedelsky's view thereof are not foreign to South Africa. This supports the use of this theory as a way forward in South Africa in relation to pregnancy in law. There may be many examples of how a relational approach ties in with the current South African legal milieu, but more specificall , Chapters Four

---

[61] Nedelsky (1993) *Canadian Journal of Law & Jurisprudence* 364. In fact, in the context of artificia reproductive technologies Nedelsky discusses feelings of 'attachment' and 'responsibility' towards the unborn, and when a couple's preserved embryo is destroyed without their consent, it is viewed as a violation of those feelings. While this is accepted, the arguments presented herein go much further and express an intrinsic value in products of human conception in addition to feelings of attachment. Thus destroying a couple's preserved embryo without their involvement also constitutes a violation against the intrinsic worth of the embryo over and above the couple's violation.

[62] Nedelsky (1993) *Canadian Journal of Law & Jurisprudence* 364.

[63] Nedelsky *Law's Relations* 196.

[64] Ultimately, according to Nedelsky, the law should foster relationships that secure respect and equality for women and respect and appreciation for children; see Nedelsky (1993) *Canadian Journal of Law & Jurisprudence* 364. Nedelsky is viewed as adopting a potentialities approach to valuing the unborn. The position of viewing the unborn as future children is a topic that will not be considered here; for a detailed discussion of this approach see Chapter Three, para 3.5.1. One might interpret Nedelsky as adopting a separate-entities approach to pregnancy but there are many different reasons why a person might value the unborn and merely attributing value to the unborn is not necessarily a separatist act. What renders a view of pregnancy as separatist is *how* an individual acts to protect the value of the unborn. The differentiating feature between the two approaches is whether actions for protection are founded on liberalism's separatist basis or whether action is taking place within a relational framework. Nedelsky accords value in prenatal life but does so within the framework of relational theory. Merely affording value to the unborn on the basis that they will become children is not in itself a separate-entities approach to pregnancy. A revised view of the unborn is offered in this chapter which does not take the stance that we act a certain way towards the unborn because they might become children later, but rather for other reasons. Despite this difference in opinion, it is viewed as important to recognise that pregnancy represents a relationship between a woman and the unborn she carries and law plays a role in determining the quality of that relationship.

and Five provide examples of relational theory taking root and even findin application in legislation.

In Chapter Four, the discussion of autonomy as per South African Constitutional Court decisions demonstrates established relational undertones.[65] While the decisions considered in that chapter do not employ an exact replica of Nedelsky's approach they do demonstrate that relational elements are currently present in judicial thinking. Furthermore, the presence of relational discourse hints at the notion that the current legal atmosphere might be more open to further development directed by relational perspectives. In Chapter Five, the Choice on Termination of Pregnancy Act[66] (Choice Act) was identifie as adopting a relational approach to pregnancy in that it adopts a not-one-but-not-two (not-one/not-two) approach.[67]

These two instances mentioned here confir that not only is the South African legal system open to relational thinking processes[68] but also that the relational approach is already legislatively established in an area of reproduction. The task now is to build on this and develop the notion of pregnancy in law as relational beyond termination of pregnancy to the broader project of pregnancy in law more generally.

10.3 THE PROJECT

The way in which pregnancy is articulated in law has far-reaching implications for women and girls. Chapter Two shows that, historically, reproduction has played a definin role regarding women's status. It is in this context that there is stern opposition from the women's movement when it comes to arguing for a view of pregnancy that allows the unborn to be recognised and their value articulated in law. This is justified given that whenever the unborn have been recognised it has mostly been done to the detriment of the women who carry them,[69] creating a sense of history repeating itself.

Manninen find it understandable that women were driven to dissociate themselves from the unborn.[70] A manifestation of this dissociation is found among a prominent branch of pro-choice feminists who advocate a view of the unborn as nothing more than a 'clump of cells' or mere 'tissue'.[71] That is, it could be argued that they adopt a single-entity view of pregnant women.[72] Michaels and Morgan indicate that talking of the unborn was viewed as surrendering to the pro-life

[65] See the discussion in para 4.2.

[66] Act 92 of 1996.

[67] Para 5.3. This aspect was covered extensively; it is therefore unnecessary to repeat the arguments and finding in para 5.3.

[68] Further, the fact that these relational aspects originate from the Constitutional Court speaks volumes to the acceptability of such an approach in South Africa.

[69] This is what Part Three reveals.

[70] BA Manninen 'The value of choice and the choice to value: Explaining the discussion about fetal life within prochoice advocacy' (2013) 28 *Hypatia* 663 665.

[71] Manninen (2013) *Hypatia* 665.

[72] This conclusion makes sense if one considers the separate-entities approach as deriving from a male-centred perspective of pregnancy; see I Karpin 'Legislating the female body: Reproductive technology and the reconstructed woman' (1992) 3 *Columbia Journal of Gender and Law* 325.

movement and thereby obstructing the movement's quest for reproductive freedom and equality.[73]

While feminist support for a single-entity approach can be appreciated, Manninen points out that there have been some developments away from this position while still remaining within a feminist framework.[74] There is a more contemporary, but not so popular, feminist view of pregnancy, which is not one of a single entity but one where there is a desire to fin an expression of the unborn as being more than 'tissue' or a 'clump of cells'.[75] These feminists characterise themselves as being 'pro-choice', but fin it necessary to articulate a value in the unborn in the modern pro-choice arena.[76] Manninen relates this shift in mind set to changes in social dynamics, in that the younger generation of feminists are 'far removed from the concerns and oppression suffered by the generations of women before them'.[77] She argues that women now feel more at ease about expressing value in the unborn, because the unborn no longer symbolise women's predetermined roles as mothers or homemakers.[78]

Manninen's arguments should be accepted with caution. The process of moving beyond the home is ongoing. For some women, the battle to develop economic value in care work or gain meaningful access to paid employment outside the home is still a very real struggle, and this process yields different results, depending on socio-economic status, race, class and gender.[79] However, women today, at least in South Africa, have better prospects than they had before the feminist movement,[80] and this has the potential to provide security when engaging discourses about prenatal life.

Manninen explains that, by denying value in the unborn, the feminist movement isolates those women who fin it difficult to undergo a termination-of-pregnancy procedure as a result of their opinions of the unborn as something to value.[81] Some

---

[73] MW Michaels & LM Morgan 'Introduction: The fetal imperative' in LM Morgan & MW Michaels (eds) *Fetal Subjects, Feminist Positions* (1999) 2.

[74] Manninen (2013) *Hypatia* 665.

[75] Manninen (2013) *Hypatia* 665.

[76] Manninen (2013) *Hypatia* 667.

[77] Manninen (2013) *Hypatia* 665. While younger generation feminists are emphasised here, there are some seasoned feminists that have called for an acknowledgement of the unborn as being 'respect-worthy', Manninen cites a number of them, 665 fn 1. Morgan and Michaels, publishing an edited piece in 1999, dedicated an entire collection of essays related to feminist positions of the subjectivity of the unborn. Therefore, this call for an inclusive feminist agenda is not new but Manninen's article demonstrates that it seems to have been gaining increased momentum more recently.

[78] Manninen (2013) *Hypatia* 665.

[79] Chapter Three demonstrates this.

[80] Initially, the agenda was to secure rights akin to that of men; now we have rights in terms of the Constitution (as covered in Chapter Four) and the agenda is to secure meaningful realisation and enjoyment of our rights.

[81] Manninen (2013) *Hypatia* 667. Manninen (664–5) explains that some women found that while they understood they had a right to terminate their pregnancies, actually going through the procedure was found to be a difficult experience because they felt that what was being terminated was something more than detached 'tissue' or 'cells'. She goes on to explain that these feelings are associated with the realisation, understanding and appreciation of the fact that 'gestation will not just yield *a* baby, rather it will yield their baby; gestation and birthing *turns one into a mother*'.

women view their general experiences of pregnancies, whether planned or unplanned, as being sidelined or ignored if that experience attaches value to the unborn.[82] Lupton's[83] work expands on Manninen's finding regarding the new generation of feminist scholars and provides a further account of women's experiences of pregnancy.

Generally, Lupton[84] shows that the unborn are certainly understood to be more than cells, but the process of giving expression to the value the unborn represent tends to be ambiguous. An ambiguous articulation transpires because not every foetus is equally valued. For instance, Lupton explains that women who are pregnant as a result of rape may view the unborn as 'monstrous, less than human, even as a kind of cancerous growth, and certainly not as an "innocent baby" '.[85] However, even when pregnancies are planned, Lupton points out that foetuses' value is relative to their biological quality. She explains that those unborn who have been diagnosed with genetic deformities are at times considered 'less worthy of life in the medical arena' and it is medical practice to encourage terminations over pregnancy continuation.[86] Furthermore, the value vested in one particular foetus varies according to a pregnant woman's different experiences during the course of her pregnancy.[87] These varying views generally relate to how women perceive themselves as pregnancy progresses and whether they attribute the responsibility for these perceptions to the existence of gestating life.[88] For instance, negative perceptions might render the unborn temporarily less valued, while positive perceptions increase the value of the unborn.

Support for the single-entity approach served women well. However, it serves a questionable role today. In order for feminism to legitimately claim the role of advancing women's concerns, it needs to adopt a stance towards pregnancy that is inclusive of the above positions of younger generation feminists who want to engage in discussions about the unborn and consider how to value them. It is this point that serves the reason for wanting to develop a revised view of pregnancy so as to allow for the space to include, discuss and recognise the unborn.

This proposal is not new to the feminist agenda. In 1999 Morgan and Michaels called for 'born again feminism', and advocated 'feminist recuperation' of the unborn.[89] A feminist 'recuperation' of the unborn is arguably a fundamental task for the movement, especially because pregnancy is a woman's lived concern. To

---

(Emphasis in the original.) This not only explains that there is more to the unborn but also illustrates that women are not terminating pregnancies because they do not value the unborn but might also represent that realisation that the continuation of a pregnancy has a profound impact on one's life in respect of motherhood and responsibility.

[82] Manninen (2013) *Hypatia* 667.

[83] D Lupton *The Social Worlds of the Unborn* (2013).

[84] Lupton *Social Worlds of the Unborn*.

[85] Lupton *Social Worlds of the Unborn* 58.

[86] Lupton *Social Worlds of the Unborn* 58.

[87] Lupton *Social Worlds of the Unborn* 56–9.

[88] Lupton *Social Worlds of the Unborn* 56–9.

[89] Michaels & Morgan 'Introduction: The fetal imperative' 3; 6. However, the two authors are not the firs to do so; they cite other works published as early as the 1980s which call attention to the need for feminist consideration of the unborn.

expand on the notion of 'recuperation' of the unborn: Morgan and Michaels[90] explain that, despite developments in science in respect of prenatal care and fertility treatment, feminist positions worked around the issue of the unborn rather than directly with them, and thus failed to develop a feminist discourse of the unborn. By contrast, third parties[91] worked with advances in science and went on to directly grapple with the issues of how to talk about the unborn generally, how best to express a value in them and how to apply that value in specifi contexts.[92] This allowed for third-party appropriation of the unborn to the exclusion of women in terms of their views and experiences.[93] Consequently, feminism is somewhat starved of a position regarding the unborn. Thus, there is clearly a need to develop a language of the unborn and recuperate the foetus in a way that is sensitive to the women's movement.

This discussion emphasises three guiding and delineating considerations for the project of developing a revised view of pregnancy that advances women *and* allows for consideration of the unborn. First, the revised view must be developed on the basis that women's history plays a significan role in women's lived experiences today and still impacts on their ability to secure and protect self-determination and reproductive freedom. Secondly, there are women in the pro-choice arena who are aiming to give weight to the existence of the unborn as entities 'worthy' of better consideration and this must be built on. Thirdly, in looking to add a perspective on the unborn, more attention should be given to women's varying attribution of value to the unborn instead of sidelining their perspectives.

It is noteworthy that a significan length of time has elapsed between Morgan and Michael's publication in 1999 and Manninen's article published in 2013, yet both contributions are essentially advocating the same things. This might suggest that the call for developing a discourse of pregnancy that is inclusive of valuing the unborn is not well supported or not worthy of being acted on, and this raises some concerns for the project being developed here. These authors are all from the United States, so their calls and those that they cite might be ignored because the United States is still divided in the context of termination of pregnancy. Part Three clearly demonstrated this, specificall in relation to reproductive politics and increasing invasive interventions taking place regarding pregnant women's bodies and lives. However, this is not the climate in South Africa, and thus the time is ripe for developing and advancing a project of this sort in respect of pregnancy under South African law.

90 Michaels & Morgan 'Introduction: The fetal imperative' 6.

91 These third parties include the medical profession and people generally associated to the pro-life movement.

92 Michaels & Morgan 'Introduction: The fetal imperative' 6.

93 Michaels & Morgan 'Introduction: The fetal imperative' 6. This topic was covered extensively in Chapter Three. Manninen points out that the primary face of feminism is the one that denies the value in the unborn, and this remains a problem to date. In fact, the point of her publication is to open feminism up to include those women who do fin value in the unborn and she advocates feminist respect for those positions. See generally Manninen (2013) *Hypatia* 663.

10.4 PARTICULARS OF THE PROJECT

A number of issues require specifi clarificatio so as to distinguish the relational approach from the single-entity and separate-entities approaches. Clarificatio will demonstrate how a relational approach addresses the criticisms raised when considering the single-entity and separate-entities approaches. First, the reasons for rejecting the single-entity and separate-entities approaches will be explained. Secondly, with arguing for the need to include a consideration of the unborn, this portion of the chapter will revisit and refin the notion that the unborn are vested with special status and thereafter see how this revised notion of special status can be absorbed into the South African legal system when dealing with pregnancy. Thirdly, after having established that the South African legal system can accord special status to the unborn, the chapter will clarify how to view pregnancy as a relationship between pregnant women and the unborn and advance a view of pregnancy that voids the notion of tension between reproductive autonomy and foetal interests.

10.4.1 Rejecting the single-entity and separate-entities approaches

All the South African authors[94] who call for changes to South African law regarding the unborn correctly reject the single-entity approach as irreconcilable with scientifi fact.[95] The single-entity approach denies the distinctive existence, the 'extra-ness' that the foetus embodies during a continued pregnancy. The unborn are biologically and genetically distinct from the pregnant women who carry them, and women are 'whole' with or without the presence of prenatal life.[96] MacKinnon, a feminist herself, also rejects the single-entity approach to pregnancy and describes the foetus as a separate organism comparable to a 'parasite'.[97] However she argues that the unborn's dependence does not go so far as to make it a body-part belonging to the pregnant woman.[98] In this respect, the current South African approach to pregnancy is flawed and the existence of the foetus cannot continue to be overlooked for much longer.[99]

---

[94] M Ovens 'Maternal substance abuse in South Africa: An area for concern?' (2008) 1 *Acta Criminologica* 77; SA de Freitas & GA Myburgh 'The relevance of science for the protection of the unborn' (2009) 45 *Journal for Christian Scholarship* 61; HJ Kruuse 'Fetal "rights"? The need for a unifie approach to the fetus in the context of feticide' (2009) 72 *THRHR* 126; M Ovens 'A criminological perspective of prenatal abuse of substances during pregnancy and the link to child abuse in South Africa' (2010) 11 *Child Abuse Research in South Africa* 38; S de Freitas 'The South African Constitutional Court and the unborn' (2012) 5 *International Journal of Religious Freedom* 51 56; GA Du Plessis 'Feticide: Creating a statutory crime in South African law' (2013) 24 *Stell LR* 73; and R Pillay 'The beginning of human personhood: Is South African law outdated?' (2010) 21 *Stell LR* 230.

[95] See Chapter Six.

[96] Seymour advances this argument, see J Seymour *Childbirth and the Law* (2000) 191. Seymour refers to, and quotes from, MacKinnon's work: See CA MacKinnon 'Reflection on sex equality under law' (1991) 100 *Yale LJ* 1281 1313–6.

[97] MacKinnon (1991) *Yale LJ* 1314.

[98] MacKinnon (1991) *Yale LJ* 1314.

[99] The arguments presented here have been argued elsewhere, see generally C Pickles 'Approaches to pregnancy under the law: A relational response to the current South African position and recent academic trends' (2014) 47 *De Jure* 20.

More importantly, flaw inherent in the single-entity approach must be understood beyond what science tells us. Seymour explains that some argue for the retention of this approach because it secures female autonomy during pregnancy. If the foetus is considered to merely constitute part of a body, women will still enjoy the space for freedom of choice—in other words, whether or not to terminate the pregnancy.[100] However, this is a very superficia and one-sided understanding of female autonomy during pregnancy and Chapter Four demonstrated this. Reproductive autonomy involves more than the issue of parenthood avoidance.

Female autonomy must also recognise women's vested interests in their unborn, or at the very least their experiences of valuing the unborn, however varied this might be. Therefore, female autonomy must be understood as including the decision to continue with a pregnancy, as well as decisions on *how* to progress through pregnancy and birth.[101] This manifestation of autonomy must be protected in law in order for it to have any meaningful effect for women who want children. Consequently, the single-entity approach speaks to only one side of female autonomy and fails to assist those women who plan to continue with their pregnancies and to adequately protect such decisions. For instance, Seymour refers to an example where a pregnant woman is unlawfully attacked and, as a result miscarries,[102] a situation similar to that in *S v Mshumpa*.[103] Here, the single-entity approach prevents the law from responding to her loss of a pregnancy, because the 'extra-ness' the foetus represents is not recognised in law as worthy of consideration.[104] Going further, it also fails to encourage an inclusive stance to women who do value the unborn but nevertheless terminate their pregnancies for reasons that outweigh the value they accord to the unborn.[105]

Ultimately, the single-entity approach must be rejected because it fails not only to speak to scientifi fact, but it also fails to comprehensively engage female experiences and expectations of pregnancy, feminine issues related to pregnancy continuation, and the resulting consequences of pregnancy for parenthood. It is

---

[100] Seymour *Childbirth and the Law* 193.

[101] See Chapter Four and Pickles (2014) *De Jure* 20.

[102] *Childbirth and the Law* 193–4.

[103] 2008 (1) SACR 126 (E) (*Mshumpa*).

[104] Through the inflictio of violence, a woman's decision to have a child was interfered with, but no one can be held accountable for that interference because, before birth, the foetus does not exist. The same issue arises in the case where, as a result of medical negligence, a woman who continues with a pregnancy and intends to give birth to a live child, delivers a stillborn child. The single-entity approach precludes any recourse, because the foetus, as a nonentity, never acquired legal personality owing to medical negligence preventing live birth. Also, if the existence of the unborn is denied in law, it is not clear how pregnant women can lay justifiabl claims to extra, more specialised medical attention or increase their claims for state support that is needed in order to progress safely through continued pregnancies.

[105] This does not mean that the value is something that has very little weight, but when considered contextually in relation to individual women's lives, affording too much weight to the value might come at an excessively high price. In this respect see JC Williams & SL Shames 'Mothers' dreams: Abortion and the high price of motherhood' (2004) 6 *University of Pennsylvania Journal of Constitutional Law* 818.

acontextual and void in the understanding of the connection women might share with the unborn when pregnant.

That said, South African authors' support for a separate-entities approach to pregnancy to allow the law to be true to scientifi revelations about prenatal life is just as problematic.[106] Seymour explains that, while the single-entity approach precludes the possibility of intervention on behalf of the unborn, the separate-entities approach invites intervention and conflict [107] Part Three demonstrated this when considering the United States' experience regarding the unborn in law.

Part Three established that the separate-entities approach, which accords rights or attributes quasi-legal subjectivity[108] to the unborn, in fact fails to protect the unborn. The separate-entities approach strikes at the core of the embodied reality of pregnancy. By directly engaging with the unborn through the application of legal principles, it denies pregnancy's very nature, which is one of relationship and factual connectedness. The central issue in the separate-entities approach is that it almost completely negates the significanc of the existence of women and also denies women their full legal status.[109] Women and their bodies cannot be bypassed, ignored or made invisible: they are essentially a *sine qua non* for the existence of prenatal life. Seymour points out that the more the separate-entities approach individuates the unborn, the less the individuality of women is recognised.[110]

Thus, while science does demonstrate the unique genetic character of the unborn, Karpin convincingly argues as follows:[111]

> There is no scientificall verifiabl 'fact' that designates woman and fetus as separate. There are only scientifi descriptions that hypothesize the notions of separateness, and certain descriptions are being privileged over others. For example, the scientifi 'fact' that the fetus and mother are genetically different does not answer the question of whether the description of them as separate is appropriate.[112]

---

[106] Ovens (2008) *Acta Criminologica* 77; De Freitas & Myburgh (2009) *Journal for Christian Scholarship* 61; Kruuse (2009) *THRHR* 126; Ovens (2010) *Child Abuse Research in South Africa* 38; De Freitas (2012) *International Journal of Religious Freedom* 56; Du Plessis (2013) *Stell LR* 73; and Pillay (2010) *Stell LR* 230.

[107] Seymour *Childbirth and the Law* 200. However, it should be remembered that the discussion of Thomson's 'good Samaritan' argument demonstrated that the extent of conflic will obviously depend on whether the separate-entities approach is adopted to justify personhood before birth or whether it is used to develop a quasi-legal subject for the unborn. See JJ Thomson 'A defense of abortion' (1971) 1 *Philosophy & Public Affairs* 47. For a discussion of Thomson see Chapter Six, para 6.3.1.

[108] For a discussion of how calls for changes to South African law, in respect of legally recognising the unborn, amount to attribution of quasi-legal subjectivity see Chapter Six, para 6.2.

[109] Karpin (1992) *Columbia Journal of Gender and Law* 325–7. Part Three also came to this conclusion.

[110] Seymour *Childbirth and the Law* 195.

[111] Karpin (1992) *Columbia Journal of Gender and Law* 326.

[112] To emphasise this point, it is worthwhile referring to J Herring & PL Chau 'My body, your body, our bodies' (2007) 15 *Medical LR* 34 45–7. The authors, in debating whether one owns one's body, turn to medical science to *prove* the interconnection of bodies. In fact, they start off with pregnancy and defin it as a relationship of shared space and fluids They justify their position by referring to scientifi studies pertaining to the development of the placenta and its role in ensuring optimal foetal development through its connection to the body of a pregnant woman.

Accordingly, the separate-entities approach to pregnancy can only ever be justifie in the abstract and in the context of hypothetical anecdotes. This is especially true when foetal separateness leads to direct engagement with the unborn in the context of law, being direct application of rights and legal doctrines or principles. Even Thomson, who goes to extremes to demonstrate the flaw inherent in the separate-entities approach, suggests that we should focus on the unique dependency of the unborn on pregnant women, and views this dependency as a source of a 'special kind of responsibility' a pregnant woman will have towards the unborn she carries.[113] She views this responsibility as special because it is not something that can be claimed by other independent persons.[114] This approach is founded on the relationship shared between the unborn and pregnant women.

Both the single-entity and separate-entities approaches fail the relational tone of the project: the single-entity approach denies intrinsic worth in the existence of prenatal life during pregnancy and also fails to realise fundamental aspects of women's reproductive autonomy. The separate-entities approach structures the pregnancy relationship very poorly, in that women's autonomy is compromised and, as a result of the connection between women and the unborn, when women's autonomy is compromised the unborn are not meaningfully protected either.

Accordingly, the not-one/not-two approach to pregnancy as found in terms of the Choice Act is adopted. The not-one/not-two approach is understood as relational in that it recognises the value of both participants to a pregnancy but understands their connection as inseparable. Before going on to discuss this approach in a little more detail it is firs required that a view of the unborn be developed in a way that allows for their value to be better considered, but also in a way that does not compromise women's position in society and law and fit in with the feminist agenda of advancing women.

10.4.2 The unborn in law and 'special status'

With the rejection of both the single-entity and separate-entities approaches, and the not-one/not-two approach being advanced,[115] it is necessary to clarify the suggested position of the unborn, since they are being recognised, but not in the same way the separate-entities approach recognises them. This is especially necessary if the aim of the project is to include an understanding of pregnancy that allows for the consideration of foetal interests. Accordingly, the discussion advances a theory of what it is about the unborn that denies them their complete separateness but simultaneously acknowledges their existences as more than the body parts of women.

Chapter Three discussed the notion of the unborn being afforded 'special status' and at this point it is necessary to provide the gist of that chapter's finding in order for the present arguments to make sense. In Chapter Three the phrase

[113] Thomson (1971) *Philosophy and Public Affairs* 58.

[114] Thomson (1971) *Philosophy and Public Affairs* 58.

[115] Thus, the approach being advanced here rests on the developmental approach of the Choice Act and *Roe v Wade* 93 S Ct 705 (1973) (*Roe*), being the trimester approach.

'special status'[116] was advanced as the phrase to relay the idea that, while the unborn are not ascribed legal status as persons, they still represent something that holds intrinsic value and therefore are worthy of our consideration or protection. 'Special status' therefore encompasses two elements: a 'negative element' denoting the denial of full status in law and a 'positive element', being the attribution of value despite the lack of personhood. In Chapter Three, a number of theories were considered,[117] and some reservations were raised generally, but more particularly the theories were identifie as failing (some more than others) to understand the embodied nature of the unborn as the reason to deny legal personhood.[118]

It was argued that it is not the fact that the unborn cannot relate or are in the process of development that denies them full status, but that they are 'embodied' and factually live off of another's body. The discussion in Chapter Three stopped there, and the purpose here is to expand on that position and consider what it is about the unborn that demands some status. Recognising the unborn as 'embodied' represents a process of re-contextualising the unborn as being held within the body of pregnant women and this identifie a special relationship between women and the unborn.[119]

While a foetus lacks personhood status, it nevertheless does have special status. Granting *some* status despite the lack of personhood is the 'positive element' in special status which identifie something in and of the unborn that demands consideration by society. The positive element of special status is aligned with Ackermann's[120] construction of human worth. His writing on human worth in respect of the unborn is not very detailed, but human dignity of the unborn can be contextualised via Dworkin's work.[121] Ackermann highlights that the unborn are afforded dignity and Dworkin helps identify what factors limit the unborn's dignity. Further, Steinbock's[122] interests approach and the medical construction of foetal viability are also employed to advance the argument that there is something in and of the unborn that supports the call for special status.

In Chapter Three some criticisms were raised against the various approaches used in the argument being advanced in this chapter.[123] However, working with these theories in combination with one another strengthens their position in

[116] As used by Ford; see M Ford 'Nothing and not-nothing: Law's ambivalent response to transformation and transgression at the beginning of life' in SW Smith & R Deazley (eds) *The Legal, Medical and Cultural Regulation of the Body: Transformation and Transgression* (2009) 22.

[117] See para 3.5; the theories discussed include potentiality; dignity and speciesism; foetal interests based on consciousness; relationality and the personhood dependent principle.

[118] See para 3.5.6.

[119] This move is viewed as necessary because, as Chapter Three demonstrated, technology had the effect of 'removing' the unborn from women's bodies allowing for others to not only identify the unborn but also individuate them from women too.

[120] See L Ackermann *Human Dignity: Lodestar for Equality in South Africa* (2012) and discussions in paras 3.5.2 and 6.3.2.

[121] RM Dworkin *Life's Dominion: An Argument about Abortion, Euthanasia, and Individual Freedom* (1993).

[122] B Steinbock *Life before Birth: The Moral and Legal Status of Embryos and Fetuses* 2 ed (2011).

[123] See Chapter Three, paras 3.5.2 and 3.5.3.

justifying valuing the unborn. Working with a combination of theories suggests that a layered approached is adopted: human dignity forms the foundation for the claim for special status, and foetal viability and interests feed into, support, and are bolstered by the notions of human dignity, thus building from dignity up. One layer builds on the other as the unborn near birth thus strengthening their stake in special status.

Since Ackermann and Dworkin's position on the value of the unborn was thoroughly covered in Chapter Three, it will be briefl said that Ackermann advances the argument that dignity is an expression of inherent human worth.[124] The mere fact of being part of humanity accords an individual worth and this accrues regardless of whether an individual is a perfect example of humanity or not.[125] He continues and extends human worth to those who are also just conceived.[126]

In line with Ackermann, this chapter's embodied approach to prenatal life accepts that any form of human life, at the very least, is deserving of our attention and consideration. Furthermore, there are times when 'consideration' takes the form of protection. However, the dynamics of a particular situation may not allow for *absolute* protection since absolute protection will only ever extend after biological birth.

Here, human dignity is seen as the foundational informative principle that sets down the parameters and directs how we should conduct ourselves when dealing with prenatal life. While dignity demands that the unborn always receive attention, how much attention they receive depends on the point of prenatal development and the context in which pregnant women fin themselves.[127] For instance, experimenting with products of human reproduction *ex utero* or stem cells[128] may be permissible, but the fact that they form part and parcel of humanity demands that such products receive our consideration, to which extent legislative regulation may be justified Moving beyond embryos, foetuses, as further developed entities, demand more intensifie consideration and the grounds to justify this turn on whether they are viable and have interests, as depicted by Steinbock.

While the process of development in another's body denies full status to the unborn, and dignity demands something more than 'nothing', foetal viability offers a worthwhile explanation as to how much more than 'nothing' the foetus will be. Essentially, the limiting effect of the embodied approach decreases as the foetus develops towards the 'clinical construction' of foetal viability. This view does not come without criticism, and the discussion to follow will firs explain the concept of 'clinical viability' and thereafter there will be an attempt to explain how

---

124 Ackermann *Human Dignity* 4.

125 Ackermann *Human Dignity* 52. Also see Dworkin *Life's Dominion* 70, whose position falls in line with Ackermann's approach.

126 Ackermann *Human Dignity* 52. Ackermann provides that only certain aspects of the value will be present before birth. He does not, however, indicate what those aspects are.

127 Relating this position to the context in which pregnant women fin themselves is in line with Dworkin; see Dworkin *Life's Dominion* 50–60. This was discussed in Chapter Three; see para 3.5.2.

128 Concerning stem cell research practices, see Steinbock *Life before Birth* 255–70.

this concept adds to the second layer that justifie affording increased special status to the foetus.

The clinical construction of viability is preferred because, when one considers the legal construction of viability, one is left with an incomplete and ambiguous definitio of foetal viability.[129] The legal construction of viability as found in case law and legislation is somewhat flawed because each tends merely to refer to gestational age as an indicator of foetal survivability.[130] Also, research shows that the specifie gestational age for viability varies between different judgments, and between case law and legislation.[131] Contrary to the legal construction of viability, the clinical definitio of foetal viability is understood as a grey-zone for survivability, and does not indicate an 'on-off switch', as generally depicted in law.[132] Determining foetal survivability involves the consideration of a wide range of medical and social factors,[133] and gestational age is only one relevant factor. While foetal survivability is a medically informed estimation that can be confirme only on physical examination after birth, it nevertheless represents an inevitable point in foetal development that will occur, unless the pregnancy is terminated or miscarried.

The biological significanc of viability lies in the fact that from the point of viability the foetus is no longer undergoing the process of the rudimentary development of a body that can sustain its life.[134] Rather, at the point of viability, all necessary functionalities are in place and as the foetus progresses through gestation closer to birth, it goes through a perfecting and strengthening process of bodily organs and functionalities.[135] The fact is that everything is developed for the purposes of sustaining life. But for the foetus' location it cannot sustain independent life. Foetal viability is a significan developmental milestone in prenatal life, because the unborn's stake in independent life gradually strengthens.

---

[129] See generally C Pickles 'Personhood: Proving the significanc of the born-alive rule with reference to medical knowledge of foetal viability' (2013) 24 *Stell LR* 146.

[130] Pickles (2013) *Stell LR* 148–55. A comparative study was conducted between the United States and South Africa and it was determined that, according to the legal construction of foetal viability, a foetus may be viable at any time from 19–28 weeks' gestation.

[131] Pickles (2013) *Stell LR* 148–55.

[132] Pickles (2013) *Stell LR* 156.

[133] These factors include gestational age, weight, antenatal exposure to corticosteroids, foetal sex, presence or absence of deformities, whether the pregnancy involves single or multiple gestations, resource availability, and socio-cultural factors. For a more detailed discussion of the role of these factors see Pickles (2013) *Stell LR* 155–60 and authority cited therein.

[134] However, see NK Rhoden 'Trimesters and technology: Revamping *Roe v Wade*' (1986) 95 *Yale LJ* 639 655–73. She approvingly cites a number of pro-choice authors who argue against the biological significanc of foetal viability. Their argument is that viability lacks significanc because to them, consciousness is understood to be significan and not merely the ability for independent survival.

[135] In this respect, see A Christoffersen-Deb 'Viability: A cultural calculus of personhood at the beginning of life' (2012) 26 *Medical Anthropology Quarterly* 575. Christoffersen-Deb (584–5) explains that in the case of imminent pre-term delivery, foetal viability is the dividing line between terminating the pregnancy or getting ready for a caesarean-section delivery and facilitating neonatal intensive care. He (585) indicates that increased gestation after viability will increase the chances for positive foetal outcomes.

At this point it is necessary to attach the significanc of clinical viability to the layered approach of justifying special status. Viewing viability through the informative lens of dignity (human worth), it is proposed that this somewhat more advanced stage of prenatal development justifie increased consideration or protection than that of embryos. This is so because viable foetuses are developing stronger connections to their eventual birth and the developmental process moves from being a biologically significan event to also being a socially significan event.[136] Foetal viability thus bolsters the foetus' stake in respect of securing special status. However, the limiting effect of embodied status is not done away with altogether once a foetus is viable, but the consequences of embodiment become ameliorated.[137]

To sum up, as a foetus reaches and passes the grey-zone of viability, its special status is strengthened. This strengthened status prevents arbitrary interferences with prenatal life.[138] A fittin practical example of this notion can be found in the South African Choice Act. In terms of s 2(1)*(a)*, pregnancy terminations are available on demand in South Africa up to 12 weeks' gestation. Reasons for a pregnancy termination need not be justified However, the procedure must be regulated for health concerns. After 12 weeks' gestation, s 2(1)*(b)* sets more stringent grounds for allowing a pregnancy termination. For instance, grounds that indicate that the pregnancy poses mental or physical maternal risk, foetal abnormalities, the pregnancy is a result of rape or incest, or continued pregnancy will significantl affect maternal social or economic circumstances will have to be demonstrated. After the stage of what is considered to be viability, from 20 weeks on, s 2(1)*(c)* completely narrows down the option of terminating a pregnancy to fatal pregnancy circumstances (maternal or foetal related) or severe foetal malformations.[139]

The fina sheet of the layered approach to special status is the adoption of Steinbock's foetal interests approach. Steinbock's basic premise is acceptable. She argues that a late-term foetus, through its ability to feel pain, has interests that are worthy of protection for its own sake.[140] Steinbock uses the foetus' ability to feel pain, as an indicator of rudimentary consciousness, to justify preferring the

[136] See generally D Meyerson 'Abortion: The constitutional issues' (1999) 116 *SALJ* 50.

[137] It should be noted that Steinbock cites a number of critiques against the significanc of viability (in the context of termination-of-pregnancy debates) as a ground to justify special status of foetuses. See Steinbock *Life before Birth* 99–101. Most criticisms seem to originate from the legal construction of viability and as indicted above, the embodied approach to pregnancy works off the clinical construction and therefore their critiques are more nuanced here.

[138] See Meyerson (1999) *SALJ* 57. This approach diverges somewhat from Meyerson to the extent that she argues that foetal viability and sentience tend to occur in tandem, however more recent clinical determinants suggest otherwise.

[139] One might be inclined to argue that the mere presence of regulation does not necessarily indicate a respect for prenatal life but rather respect for the life and health risks involved in terminating pregnancies in a haphazard fashion. However, the fact is, very specifi grounds are set down for pregnancy terminations. If there was no drive to protect prenatal life it would be possible to terminate a very late-term foetus for any reason with the only proviso being that it can be performed safely on the woman concerned. This is clearly not the case in South Africa.

[140] Steinbock *Life before Birth* 81.

sentience criterion over foetal viability criterion for purposes of special status.[141] For Steinbock, sentience is understood to signify a definitiv line in foetal development that makes a foetus more like a neonate, despite the fact that it cannot be said with any certainty whether a later-term foetus is factually conscious.[142]

The issue of foetal ability to feel pain needs to be considered. In Chapter Three it was argued that Steinbock's position of the unborn being able to feel pain was somewhat unfounded, since it is not possible to actually determine this factual aspect of foetal development.[143] However, the worth of the approach is not wholly removed, especially if one were to adopt a layered approach to special status which builds on the foundation of human dignity. The notions of human dignity enforce the need to err on the side of caution when it comes to the very likely possibility of foetal sentience being present.[144] Further, research indicates that foetal viability sets in prior to the possible experience of sentience and, while the possibility of conscious experience increases special status, a viable foetus should be included in the equation of when the benefit of special status vest, even if a viable foetus' stake in special status is weaker than that of a 'sentient' foetus.

The vestment of special status in the unborn that is being advanced in this chapter needs to be distinguished from the process of extending legal or quasi-legal legal subjectivity to the unborn.

In Chapter Six, a number of South African authors were considered and it was demonstrated that each called for changes to certain aspects of the law in order to offer better protection for prenatal life.[145] The authors were all identifie as advocating a separate-entities view of pregnancy and argued for the direct application of the law to the unborn as if the unborn are separate legal subjects of law.[146] It was consequently argued that the various authors were essentially extending legal or quasi-legal subjectivity to the unborn.[147] The relational approach adopted in this chapter moves away from the position that the unborn can be directly engaged through the law and asserts that they cannot have legal or quasi-legal subjectivity, as purported by the South African scholars.

The position of denying the unborn legal subjectivity originates from the insistence that the unborn are embodied in pregnant women.[148] A consequence of embodiment is that one cannot ever, regardless of the designation of foetal-separateness, directly engage with the unborn in any tangible way, since the

[141] Steinbock *Life before Birth* 99.

[142] Steinbock *Life before Birth* 46–50; 101.

[143] See para 3.5.3. In fact, it was pointed out that some argue that pain is something a person learns only after birth. See IG Cohen & S Sayeed 'Fetal pain, abortion, viability, and the Constitution' (2011) 39 *Journal of Law, Medicine & Ethics* 235; SJ Lee, HJ Ralston, EA Drey et al 'Fetal pain: A systematic multidisciplinary review of the evidence' (2005) 294 *Journal of the American Medical Association* 947; and EJ Lee 'The abortion debate today' in K Horsey & H Biggs (eds) *Human Fertilisation and Embryology: Reproducing Regulation* (2007) 238–9.

[144] This might be implied by Steinbock in her approach, but she does not explicitly allude to that fact, rendering her approach problematic.

[145] See the various arguments considered in para 6.3.

[146] Para 6.3.

[147] See Chapter Six, para 6.2. Footnote 3 explains how this conclusion is reached.

[148] In Chapter Three, para 3.5.6 this position was argued in detail.

unborn exist in a factually non-permeable[149] environment, that is, within the body of a woman. It is this embodied connection that must be acknowledged, since this connection prevents direct contact or interaction between the unborn and others.[150] Also, an embodied view or understanding of pregnancy should always inform the thinking processes whenever the unborn are considered, regardless of how much science identifie the unborn as genetically unique and individuates them from the women who carry them.

While it is conceded that 'special status' is a form of status in law, the status it accords to the unborn is not comparable with the status accorded to individuals who are already born, so there is no situation of foetal personhood or full personhood being extended. It is asserted that status is afforded to the unborn as participants of humanity and it is special because it does not go so far as to vest legal subjectivity yet it nevertheless demands acknowledgment. This acknowledgment is made possible via engagement with pregnant women, being the *sine qua non* for foetal existence. Consequently, all foetal-related concerns must be addressed through women: foetal-related concerns must be addressed because the unborn involve humanity and the further a pregnancy progresses the more can be demanded from the law's protective reach.

Having attributed special status to the unborn, the next step is to establish how to incorporate this view into the divergent social discourses and experiences of the unborn.

10.4.3 'Special status' and fluid perceptions of the unborn

In the process of developing a discourse of pregnancy that includes women, embodies the unborn and articulates a specifi value in the unborn, one is left with a glaring issue. This revised view of pregnancy can be seen as proposing a view that all foetuses are of equal value to everyone. However, it was earlier highlighted that each foetus is valued differently depending on the woman concerned, the circumstances that led to conception, the stage of foetal development, the public health policy or merely because personal preferences vary from one person to the next.[151] The task, therefore, is to reconcile a 'stable' principle of 'special status' of the unborn with the ambiguous and almost flui position of the unborn in respect

---

[149] Karpin (1992) *Columbia Journal of Gender and Law* 333 states that technology, for instance ultrasonography, has led to the impression that the female body is permeable and flexibl to outside curiosities, and argues that pregnant women are viewed as passive foetal containers in the sense that they are denied the capacity to carry the unborn and determine their boundaries. She understands this to be a technocultural phenomenon based on ultrasonography, with viewers of prenatal ultrasound scans coming to (mistakenly) understand the uterus as permeable as a result of being able to view the unborn before birth.

[150] Here, 'others' must be understood to include third parties, such as the outside community and the medical profession, the state and the law with its legal principles. An exception to direct connection with the unborn prior to birth is found in cases of foetal surgery which can take place *in utero* or allow for the unborn to be removed and returned to the uterus after the procedure. However, these processes also implicate women's bodies because one cannot gain access to the unborn without moving through women's bodies.

[151] See para 10.2.

of women's ever-changing and diverse subjective perspectives during pregnancy, as well as divergent social policies and society's responses to the unborn.

Valuing the unborn on the foundational principle that they form part of humanity demands that the value attached to the unborn attaches because the unborn themselves are entities worthy of value, even though they may be embodied. This value should therefore attach irrespective of the value any one individual might attach to them. This approach therefore requires that special status of the unborn (as representing a particular value in the unborn) must traverse differing values attributed to the unborn.

When a uniform value is being advanced in respect of the unborn, a problem arises, because there will be cases in which people value the same foetus differently. Consequently, there is a concern that if each foetus is provided with special status in law in spite of the subjective feelings of the pregnant woman concerned, there may be a situation in which women have a value externally imposed on them as a result of adopting a relational approach. The external imposition of the special status of the unborn onto pregnant women can ultimately result in the same experiences highlighted in the United States, where third parties intervene in pregnancies for the sake of 'foetal-wellbeing' but do so to the detriment of the women, thereby violating their autonomy, constitutional rights and bodily integrity more generally.[152]

On the other hand, if the special status of the unborn is not universally accorded to all foetuses regardless of a subjective sense of valuation or intentions pertaining to the unborn, the unborn might ultimately be valued merely on the basis of the particular relationship at play. This is what occurred in the United States regarding the application of feticide legislation that excludes pregnant women in respect of their own pregnancies, while at the same time legally sanctioning the termination of pregnancies.[153]

Briefl , in Chapter Eight it was demonstrated that in the United States some feticide provisions are aimed at protecting the unborn as victims of third-party violent conduct and that this protection is justifie on the grounds that the unborn are define as persons or human beings. However, it was pointed out that, by holding only third parties criminally liable for the violent termination of prenatal life and not pregnant women in respect of their own pregnancies, the provisions are articulating a contradictory value in the unborn. A contradictory value is being attached because both acts essentially terminate a 'person', but different consequences result, depending on the actor. Thus, the foetus is valued as a person in relation to a third party but not in relation to the pregnant woman carrying it. This leads to the conclusion that the unborn are not valued because they are 'persons' or 'human beings' but rather because they represented a wanted pregnancy.[154] Therefore, the unborn's value is determined by the relationships different people share with them rather than on the basis of their humanity.

[152] See Part Three generally.

[153] See Chapter Eight, para 8.3.2.

[154] Chapter Eight, para 8.3.2.

These contradictory positions can be attributed to the inconsistent adoption of the separate-entities approach to pregnancy. Recognising these challenges provides insight into possible issues that need to be considered when aiming to develop a revised view of pregnancy in law that includes a uniform value in the unborn. Consequently, it must be determined how to value the unborn in a uniform way, but such that it does not contradict our sense of humanity that the unborn are viewed as representing nor to serve as the basis for undermining women, and must therefore accord with the broader aims of feminism. Both these issues could be overcome if the unborn were re-embodied in the concept of pregnancy and their value was understood as intrinsically linked to the context of women and women's rights. This will become more apparent later in the chapter when special status is applied to the identifie areas of concern.

Even in the case where this conundrum can be addressed through a revised view of pregnancy, further issues arise in the form of resistance to adopting a uniform value for the unborn in law.

Advocating a universal value for the unborn in the form of special status is not readily supported.[155] Support is lacking for the very reason that such an approach might compromise flexibilit in the law. Flexibility is understood to be necessary when dealing with the unborn in law, either because not every foetus is equally valued by women, society and the state, or because a foetus does not have one particular value all through a pregnancy. Ultimately, the concern is that different contexts demand different responses, and if one uniform value is advanced, law's flexibilit will be sacrificed

Seymour is one such author who argues against assigning a uniform value to the unborn in law. While Seymour specificall argues against the separate-entities call for the vestment of personhood in the unborn, his arguments are also viewed as a broader argument against any set form of status for the unborn in law. This interpretation is advanced because Seymour does not advance any other form of uniform value in the place of personhood or legal subjectivity of the unborn. His position is therefore worthy of consideration because it assists in understanding why securing a uniform status for the unborn is something to avoid in law.

Before considering his argument, it is necessary to understand the context of Seymour's preferred position on pregnancy in law. Seymour suggests that he supports a relational account of pregnancy, being the not-one/not-two approach.[156] He adopts this approach because he argues that it is necessary to have consideration for the unborn, but only as far as women's rights allow.[157] It is his position that, because the unborn are not wholly one entity and pregnancy does not represent two completely separate entities, women's rights play a central role in determining the extent to which the unborn can be recognised in law. It is clear that he is pro-choice and is a women's-rights advocate who nonetheless find value in the unborn.

155 For instance, see Seymour *Childbirth and the Law* 186.
156 Seymour *Childbirth and the Law* 191–202.
157 Seymour *Childbirth and the Law* 191–202.

Seymour asserts that conferring a uniform status on the unborn is not possible primarily because there will never be consensus about the nature of the foetus.[158] He further asserts that the process of ascribing status is a normative task, and normative processes make certainty in law unattainable.[159] He emphasises that it is better to avoid pursuing any uniform status for the unborn, because such avoidance assists in allowing for flexibl responses to pregnancy-related concerns in law in a way that advances women.[160] His argument means that there will always be a measure of uncertainty when considering the status or position of the unborn in law more generally, and this approach provides leeway for lawmakers to respond differently to the various claims made for the unborn. The difference in response lies in the context in which the unborn are being considered.[161] Here, Seymour is stating that the law does not protect the unborn in a termination-of-pregnancy context in the way it would in the context of third-party violence, and that it is the context that determines whether or not the state will intervene. He views this approach as necessary in order to secure women's rights but does so in a way that does not overlook the unborn in any absolutist way.

Since Seymour advocates that the law should adopt the not-one/not-two approach, one can see that he recognises the unborn as having intrinsic worth. However, he seems to lose sight of that when advocating flexibilit in law. His focus on context, being the relevant relationships at play, gives the impression that it is relationships that determine whether or not the law will value the unborn, rather than the unborn having inherent worth in and of themselves, as he argues the not-one/not-two approach does. This can be gleaned from the following excerpt of his understanding of a relational approach to pregnancy and the role of different relationships in respect of the law's approach to the unborn:[162]

> While this approach accepts that a fetus is a distinctive entity with intrinsic worth, it recognises that in some contexts it is appropriate for the law to intervene to protect fetal interests, but not in others. Crucial to making this distinction is an examination of the relationships between the parties to proceedings involving fetal harm. For example, a doctor or midwife caring for a pregnant woman is in a particular relationship to that woman and her fetus. The practitioner can be seen as owing a duty of care to both and it is in the interests of both for there to be a possibility of damages claim if the duty is breached. Similarly, when an assailant attacks a pregnant woman and causes a stillbirth, there is (as some courts and legislatures have recognized) no reason why the assailant should not be found guilty of an offence in respect of the destruction of fetal life. In each of these illustrations, there is a particular relationship between the woman, her fetus, and a third party. From this perspective, it is a consideration of the nature of the *relationship*, rather than of the nature and characteristics of the fetus, which determines

---

[158] Seymour *Childbirth and the Law* 186.
[159] Seymour *Childbirth and the Law* 186.
[160] Seymour *Childbirth and the Law* 186.
[161] Seymour *Childbirth and the Law* 186. Essentially he asserts that context aids in determining whether it is appropriate for the state to act on its interest in prenatal life in one situation, while not do so in another situation. He argues that having a flexibl approach to the unborn in law allows for women to terminate their pregnancies while at the same time allowing for the protection of the unborn from third-party violence.
[162] Seymour *Childbirth and the Law* 185.

> whether it is appropriate for the law to acknowledge the existence of the fetus and the harm done to it. (Emphasis in the original and footnotes omitted.)

Seymour emphasises the appropriateness of the relational approach (not-one/not-two approach) to pregnancy because it creates space to include the consideration of the unborn as having intrinsic worth but then goes on to use the approach's reliance on context to deny intrinsic value. This leads to an ambiguous outcome, because worth that is 'intrinsic' is something understood to be inherent, derived from within, as opposed to being determined by external factors such as the contextual influence of relationships. In Seymour's quest for securing flexibilit in law he not only ensures a flui position for the unborn in law, but also renders the unborn's value as something less than intrinsic.[163] From this, it seems that flexibilit in law compromises value in the unborn, and, if one wants to establish a value in the unborn, such value will compromise flexibilit and any attempt to overcome this issue results in ambiguous outcomes.

Considering the outcomes of Seymour's relational position and the outcomes of the separate-entities approach in the United States, it is evident that ambiguous and inconsistent outcomes persist, despite both adopting different approaches to pregnancy. The common feature between Seymour and the United States' position is the fact that there is no foundational uniform view of the unborn. In both these contexts, the entire scenario of pregnancy in law becomes a complicated maze. Assigning flui value to the unborn in law makes it unclear whether one can express any value in the unborn at all. If possible, how should one go about valuing them, what is it about the unborn that is being valued, and how would one determine when it is appropriate to value the unborn? The entire task of working with pregnancy in law becomes lined with indeterminable or blurred boundaries. This leads to consequences that inadvertently prepare the ground for increased women's rights violations.

Contradictory,[164] ambiguous and inconsistent[165] outcomes must be expected if the law is required to be responsive to the ever-changing context in relation to a flui concept such as the unborn. When the drive for flexibilit leads to such inherent ambiguous or contradictory outcomes, something is amiss and injustices will ensue. Injustices are certainly possible when one recalls the United States' experience as recorded in Part Three and how the law was manipulated to advance one group's position over the rights of another group.

In Part Three it was demonstrated that the articulation of the value of the unborn in the United States (while under the umbrella of the separate-entities theory) was far from uniform. Some states enforce a value in the unborn through the application of certain laws, but the value accorded varies across different branches of law, thus impacting on the effect of the value generally. For instance, the expression of the value in the unborn in respect of termination-of-pregnancy laws differed from that expressed in respect of feticide or foetal homicide laws. This

[163] With this in mind, it is not clear why it would be necessary for Seymour to adopt an approach that provides the space to consider the intrinsic value of the unborn to start with.

[164] Referring to the United States' position.

[165] Referring to Seymour's position.

position allows for easy manipulation of principles by 'pro-life' groups to the detriment of women's rights.[166] While the vulnerability to manipulation is very much a product of the United States' history of reproductive politics, the patchy method of dealing with the unborn in law opens the legal system to abuse and can result in illegitimate outcomes. Avoiding a uniform value readies the ground for those with ulterior motives to make their way through the law and set unfavourable precedents for women's rights, because there is no uniform value guiding the various issues.

All the uncertainty and ambiguous outcomes originate from the fact that a crucial piece of the pregnancy puzzle is missing, namely, an objective foundational principle (or starting point) on how to deal with the unborn in law. This foundational principle indicates what it is about the unborn that needs to be considered or even overlooked when one attempts to deal with pregnancy-related concerns in law.

Vesting special status in the unborn (as a uniform value) will assist in drawing determinable lines indicating where the unborn stand in the general body of law. Special status merely indicates a starting point and does not serve the purposes of providing a fina say on the issue of the unborn in law. Special status as a starting point could guide and direct debates concerning pregnancy and could assist in maintaining consistency in respect of outcomes. Adopting this view is necessary because it removes the opportunities to manipulate existing legal principles relevant to pregnancy and curbs the use of backdoor tactics and substitutive methods to extend full status to the unborn.

While South Africa is not plagued by polarised reproductive politics comparable with those in the United States,[167] it is necessary to establish a 'South African' uniform value for the unborn, because the patchwork approach to dealing with the value of the unborn in law is already taking root in academic writing. For instance, Du Plessis'[168] call is for the introduction of the crime of feticide to be applicable from the moment of conception, yet her recommendation contains a termination-of-pregnancy exemption, which is an almost perfect reflectio of what is transpiring in the United States.[169] If her call for changes to the law is accepted, the value of the unborn would differ according to the different spheres of law, despite the fact that each law is dealing with the same entity across the board.[170]

---

[166] This manipulation of the law was sufficiently recorded throughout Part Three and will not be discussed here.

[167] R Roth *Making Women Pay: The Hidden Cost of Fetal Rights* (2000) and R Solinger *Reproductive Politics: What Everyone Needs to Know* (2013).

[168] Du Plessis (2013) *Stell LR* 73.

[169] Most importantly, those foetal homicide or feticide provisions that apply from the moment of conception are being used to justify the extension of child abuse laws to prenatal conduct; see the discussion in para 9.2 and LM Paltrow & J Flavin 'Arrests of and forced interventions on pregnant women in the United States, 1973–2005: Implications for women's legal status and public health' (2013) 38 *Journal of Health Politics, Policy and Law* 299 323. Although the ultimate aim is to render termination of pregnancies unlawful; see Chapter Seven, para 7.3.

[170] A similar argument can be advanced in respect of Kruuse's call for feticide, although she makes more of an attempt to reconcile termination-of-pregnancy laws with her proposed feticide laws; see generally Kruuse (2009) *THRHR* 126.

Furthermore, while Du Plessis has explained that her primary aim is to protect the unborn from third-party violence rather than employ backdoor tactics to advance personhood status for the unborn,[171] her position raises some concerns. The study of the United States' position indicates that there are certainly people or organisations with the intention of using backdoor personhood tactics and Du Plessis' position provides the perfect opportunity to advance certain alternative agendas. Aside from Du Plessis, Kruuse's publication on feticide expresses the need to adopt a unifie approach to the unborn in law more generally[172] and, while Kruuse's adopted method is questionable, her call for a unifie approach is legitimate and absolutely necessary.

Having demonstrated the risks inherent in allowing for a flui concept of the unborn and having substantiated the need for establishing a uniform view of the unborn, the following question now arises: will adopting a uniform value in the unborn compromise the ability of the law to respond flexibl to the plethora of contexts in which pregnancy exists and is experienced by pregnant women personally or by others via observations?

Seymour asserts that flexibilit , when it comes to the value the law vests in the unborn, is necessary to ensure that women's rights are respected. However, the above discussion demonstrates that, when a flexibl stance is adopted on the value of the unborn in law, women's rights are more easily violated, or violations are more likely. It is asserted that Seymour's emphasis on flexibilit might be misplaced. The law need not be flexibl in its view of the value of the unborn, but rather it should offer flexibilit in respect of *how* the law responds to the uniform value of the unborn in the various contexts and relationships in which it appears. Flexibility of the law should focus on allowing a respectful space for different responses to a set value. This perspective of flexibilit in law allows for special status to transcend all the different possible perspectives of the unborn. This argument will be explained further.

The approach of having a set value or principle in law but allowing for different responses to that particular value or principle is not foreign to South Africa, and what follows is rather obvious. For instance, s 31 of the Constitution of South Africa, 1996 provides that everyone has the right to participate in religion or culture. This section is expressing a value in religion and culture but does not obligate any one person to be religious or follow one particular religion or align themselves with one culture. In respect of reproduction, the Choice Act expresses a value in women's reproductive freedom. It does not make termination of pregnancy compulsory by its mere enactment into law.

While these principles or laws recognise a particular value, neither of them means that one precise result has to realise from the values they advance. Each seems to provide a 'respectful space' for different responses to life's circumstances within the realms of the particular value at hand. The value serves as the starting point (as a core minimum) and assists in determining the parameters within which one is functioning. It also demands that respect be accorded when working within

[171] Personal communication with G du Plessis via electronic mail (5 July 2014).

[172] Kruuse (2009) *THRHR* 126.

the parameters of the value. This respect links to the broader acknowledgment that people are unique in and of themselves and also that their individual responses to a value will differ according to community, race, sex, culture, country, and so on. This is an example of how expressing a uniform value on one particular aspect can be achieved even though there is a plethora of perspectives on the aspect at hand. How this plays out will be demonstrated below when applying the not-one/not-two approach to *capita selecta* areas of reform.

This discussion illustrates that establishing a uniform value for the unborn in law can be achieved through the application of this chapter's 'special status', because this status is founded on the fact that the unborn are embodied. Recognising the unborn as embodied brings women back into focus and allows for an informed, contextual understanding of pregnancy as experienced by women. Further, adopting a uniform value in the unborn assists in overcoming contradictions, inconsistencies and ambiguities currently plaguing debates about the unborn. In the process of securing special status, women's rights violations should be significantl reduced because the status proposed not only acknowledges the unique interconnection during pregnancy but also removes the opportunities for manipulating the law to advance laws contrary to women's rights.

10.4.4 Removing the notion of tension

Having rejected the current prevailing approaches to pregnancy and demonstrating how to advance a value of the unborn in law, it is now necessary to contemplate how to articulate pregnancy as involving relationships and how to construct those relationships in a way that removes the perception that pregnancy embodies a tension. Thereafter, these views will be reconciled with the not-one/not-two approach as found in the Choice Act.

In Chapter Six it was established that, currently, there is no tension espoused in South African law between female autonomy rights and foetal interests and this position rests on the fact that South Africa adopts a mainly single-entity approach to pregnancy.[173] However, it was also shown that, as a result of the application of this approach the law is ill-equipped to tackle pregnancy-related concerns, particularly those associated with pregnancy continuation.[174] While South African scholars have advanced suggestions on how to rectify the current position, each has adopted a separate-entities approach to pregnancy that renders pregnancy riddled with adversarialist positions. Further, the study of the United States' experience showed that, as long as adversarialism remains, any possible changes to the law will be laced with tensions and will be rendered fruitless.[175]

Without developing a view of pregnancy in law in a way that pregnancy is not premised on tension, the law will be poorly developed and those issues highlighted as being in need of reform will not be meaningfully addressed. The task is therefore to address the underlying notion that there is a tension between the autonomy rights of pregnant women and foetal interests before going on to

[173] Para 6.4.

[174] These concerns were raised in Chapters Four and Five.

[175] See Part Three generally.

suggest how to address any identifie areas of concern. Essentially this task requires a consideration of the relationships at play, an evaluation of how the law is structuring those relationships and then a determination of how to reform that structure so as to remove tension and secure healthy pregnancy outcomes.

Looking at the relationships at play, pregnancy represents a relationship which is a unique one shared between a woman (with associated autonomy rights) and the unborn (with associated interests) she carries. It is unique in that the connection cannot be removed without terminating the pregnancy (and possibly prenatal life) and no one else can relate to the unborn directly in the way that a pregnant woman does during the existence of a pregnancy because the unborn is wholly embodied in her. This point is in conflic with the South African authors' position since they postulate that the existence of a pregnancy gives rise to two separate entities, whereas here, the pregnancy relationship is postulated as including two entities which are inseparable thus also constituting one. In essence this is the not-one/not-two approach.

How the pregnancy relationship is interpreted impacts on how third parties' relationships (the state, intimate partners, medical staff, family) are construed in respect of a particular pregnancy. According to a relational construction of a pregnancy relationship, others cannot directly relate to the unborn without implicating the women who carry them. They are, in effect, relating to the pregnancy unit or relationship as constituted by both a woman and a foetus. Under this construction, focus should be on 'optimal pregnancy progression' and 'optimal pregnancy outcomes' and how third parties can secure this in their interaction with pregnancies. This demonstrates that, when the pregnancy relationship as a unit is cared for, more meaningful outcomes can be expected because both participants in the relationship are considered.

Construing the pregnancy as including two separate entities opens up the means for *theoretically* engaging with the unborn to the exclusion of the woman concerned, or vice versa. Since pregnancy embodies an entrenched connection, this view ignores the fact that what happens to one will inevitably happen to the other, thus diminishing the quality of the pregnancy relationship.[176] The quality of the relationship will be diminished because one participant's interests or rights are being overridden for the benefi of the other participant's rights, and this means one participant is being treated poorly, yet the connection implies that poor treatment will negatively impact both. Here, one will typically fin references to securing 'optimal foetal development' or 'optimal foetal outcomes', all of which are void of women who experience pregnancy progression and birth.

It is clear that one view of pregnancy encourages a tension, while the other does not. The tension being expressed here is not a tension between a woman and the unborn she carries, but a tension between two concepts as developed and structured in law. These structures result in arbitrary relationship outcomes and invasive interventions.

---

[176] Violence against a pregnant woman is violence against the woman and the unborn she carries; substance abuse and treatment thereof during pregnancy has implications for both a woman and her foetus; even termination of pregnancy involves both participants of a pregnancy relationship.

With this view, it becomes apparent that the concepts of pregnant woman and the unborn, as currently being used in law, do not adequately reflec the lived existence of pregnancy—being one of factual connection,[177] and the connection is biologically entrenched in that where autonomy is advanced, so are the interests of the unborn.[178] Focus should be squarely on the pregnancy relationship as expressing an inseparable unit between a woman and the unborn and this structure requires that when the law is applied to this relationship it should advance a healthy relationship which fosters female autonomy and foetal interests (special status).[179]

This view of pregnancy falls in line with the not-one/not-two approach of the Choice Act as discussed in Chapter Five.[180] That entire discussion will not be repeated here. However, for the purposes of guiding what follows below, a brief[181] overview of the not-one/not-two approach will be provided and it will also be shown how the Choice Act is a legislative incarnation of that approach. Basically the not-one/not-two approach centralises the pregnancy relationship and characterises it as recognising the interests of the unborn but instils the notion that these interests cannot be viewed in isolation. Thus foetal interests can only be advanced in a way that promotes women's rights.[182] In order to achieve this aim, the not-one/not-two approach is context-driven, which requires that the pregnancy relationship be considered in the context in which it exists. Focus on context helps detect what is required from others and even the pregnant woman concerned in order to secure a healthy pregnancy relationship or healthy relations with others generally.

This approach is applied in respect of the Choice Act, in that women do not have the absolute right to terminate their pregnancies and the limitation of this right is argued to originate from the value vested in the unborn by society.[183] This

---

[177] The notion of connection and its role in women's lives is a contested issue; see R West 'Jurisprudence and gender' (1988) 55 *University of Chicago LR* 1; PS Karlan & DR Ortiz 'In a different voice: Relational feminism, abortion rights, and the feminist legal agenda' (1993) 87 *Northwestern University LR* 858; and S Noonan 'Theorizing connection' (1992) 30 *Alberta LR* 719. This chapter will not delve into these issues. The point of 'connection' here is that pregnancy is a biological connection between a woman and the unborn she carries.

[178] Harris presents a similar argument in the context of medical treatment of pregnant women who through their own conduct are perceived as placing their pregnancies at risk. She states: 'Common sense tells us that if a fetus inhabits the body of a pregnant woman, they share a physiology, and so have many common needs. One could argue that the most important aspect of fetal wellbeing is maternal wellbeing'. See LH Harris 'Rethinking maternal–fetal conflict Gender and equality in perinatal ethics' (2000) 96 *Obstetrics & Gynecology* 786 788.

[179] In cases where special status is compromised, law should prevent such compromises on frivolous grounds because the unborn form part and parcel of humanity and that is the very least that is required. For instance, by gradually limiting women's right to terminate their pregnancy as the pregnancy progresses, it is the special status of the unborn that is being advanced.

[180] See para 5.3.

[181] A brief explanation is preferred because Chapter Five, para 5.3.1 provides a detailed conceptualisation of this approach as developed from considering MacKinnon (1991) *Yale LJ* 1316; Karpin (1992) *Columbia Journal of Gender and Law* 329; and Seymour *Childbirth and the Law* 190. This was further developed in Pickles (2014) *De Jure* 20.

[182] This means that the context of the unborn is informed by the women who carry them.

[183] See *Christian Lawyers Association v Minister of Health* 2005 (1) SA 509 (T) 527D.

indicates that value in prenatal life is acknowledged, which means that a pregnant woman embodies more than one entity. However, this acknowledgment does not go on to accord separate status to the unborn; rather, the unborn are understood in relation to pregnant women and their existing rights, thus meeting in the middle between women's rights and foetal interests.[184]

10.5 APPLICATION OF THE NOT-ONE/NOT-TWO APPROACH

This discussion is guided by the theoretical positions developed above. In this respect the not-one/not-two approach (as an incarnation of the relational approach) to pregnancy will be applied to the different areas of law identifie as being in need of reform. The aim is to secure meaningful pregnancy outcomes and optimal pregnancy progression. This discussion will demonstrate that these areas can be addressed in a way that is void of tensions between female reproductive autonomy rights and foetal interests, thus allowing for more effective proposals.

10.5.1 Reform of the Choice on Termination of Pregnancy Act

The idea behind advocating law reform in respect of the termination of pregnancy in South Africa is to afford better consideration of the unborn in law, since they are viewed as human beings and therefore deserving of better protection from elective pregnancy terminations.[185] After considering Du Plessis and De Freitas' work in Chapter Six, it was highlighted that the Choice Act is not in need of reform because it is the only piece of legislation that gives expression to the value in prenatal life and does so in a balanced fashion, which accords respect to female reproductive autonomy.[186] However, other aspects are relevant to this area and need some consideration.

When termination of pregnancy is discussed in a relational sense, some authors focus on how the services should be provided in order to better realise pregnant women's autonomy while functioning within the relationship between the service provider and pregnant woman. For instance, Riley and Furedi explain that a woman's autonomy is diminished unless the service is offered in an environment that respects women's self-determination by offering support for informed decision-making, secured confidentialit , and ensuring availability of the choice of treatment methods and access to treatment.[187] These concerns were highlighted in a South African context, too, in that the current public provision of termination-of-

[184] A meeting in the middle is viewed as being in place because neither entity receives absolute protection in law.

[185] De Freitas & Myburgh (2009) *Journal for Christian Scholarship* 63 and De Freitas (2012) *International Journal of Religious Freedom* 51.

[186] Para 6.3.4. In fact, it is the Choice Act that applied the not-one/not-two approach that serves as an example on how to advance other areas of pregnancy in law towards more improved outcomes.

[187] L Riley & A Furedi 'Autonomy and the UK's law on abortion: Current problems and future prospects' in SD Sclater, F Ebtehaj, E Jackson et al (eds) *Regulating Autonomy: Sex, Reproduction and Family* (2009) 241. Also see C Kaposy 'Improving abortion access in Canada' (2010) 18 *Health Care Analysis* 17 and Nelson *Law, Policy and Reproductive Autonomy* 133–50. There are many contributions focusing on how access to termination of pregnancy advances women's autonomy; not all can be considered here. These references merely serve as an example of some facets which need to be present in a patient–provider relationship in order for pregnant women's autonomy to be

pregnancy services does not line up with the liberating aims of the Choice Act and one of the identifie reasons for this lies in service providers' attitudes to women attempting to gain access to the services.[188]

While discussion of these issues highlights legitimate concerns regarding the quality of the relationship pregnant women share with service providers and that better policies need to be in place at grassroots level, it does not suggest how the area of parenthood avoidance can be better structured so as to ensure the realisation of healthy pregnancy relationships. Something more can be said on the issue, especially if the aim is to foster healthy pregnancies. In the critique raised against calls for more restrictive termination-of-pregnancy laws it was demonstrated that restricting access to the elective termination of pregnancy will not offer better protection for the unborn, but the focus should rather be placed on addressing those wider social factors that feed the demand for termination-of-pregnancy services.[189] This argument can be phrased in relational terms, which helps clarify what needs to be done in order to secure improved pregnancy outcomes.

Emphasis on securing a healthy pregnancy means that the existence of a pregnancy should be welcomed and this means that the pregnancy should be the result of a woman exercising her reproductive autonomy. Turning to termination of pregnancy is understood to be a responsive action which is deemed required because the woman concerned is trying to avoid parenthood. While the Choice Act serves a vital role in women's lives, more could be done in the area of parenthood avoidance. This requires expanding the contextual view to include existing relationships which were in place before the need to terminate a pregnancy became relevant. This means that one should be considerate of those conditions and relationships that were present at the time of and leading up to conception.

A broader contextual view seeks to answer why women are relying on termination of pregnancy to start with. Turning to the termination-of-pregnancy services could be an indication that their reproductive autonomy might have been compromised in one form or another through other relationships, such as through the poor provision of reproductive health-care services or coercive sexual relationships. This means that, where women's autonomy is respected concerning their reproductive decisions,[190] the need for termination of pregnancies should be diminished, thus securing more wanted pregnancies than unwanted.

This demonstrates that more needs to be done to foster better relationships between women and their partners, between women and the state in cases where women rely on the state for reproductive health services, and between women and

advanced. The discussion can go much deeper than this, but these examples are sufficient to serve the purpose of this discussion.

188 C Pickles 'Lived experiences of the Choice on Termination of Pregnancy Act 92 of 1996: Bridging the gap for women in need' (2013) 29 *SAJHR* 515 522–5.

189 Chapter Six, para 6.3.4.

190 Such as decisions regarding who to engage in sexual relationships with and when, contraception, reproductive health, and marriage, to name a few.

society.[191] Merely changing the termination-of-pregnancy laws will not secure better outcomes in terms of those relationships. Instead, more effective and constructive social policies need to be developed. This is particularly true in respect of health-care services, addressing the vulnerable position women and girls hold in society generally and specificall in sexual relationships, ensuring improved sex and reproductive health education, and working towards alleviating poverty and its impact on women. Taking these foundational steps helps ensure that more pregnancies are wanted than unwanted, which helps secure the realisation of healthy pregnancies in that the relationship between pregnant women and the unborn is welcomed.

10.5.2 Addressing violence during pregnancy that terminates prenatal life

Violence against pregnant women is a complex occurrence that is recognised as a health and human rights issue, and this topic needs increased attention in law.[192] However, not all aspects of this form of violence can be covered here. Instead, focus will be narrowed to Kruuse's and Du Plessis' suggestions of feticide in response to violence against pregnant women that terminates prenatal life and then focus will shift to the offer of an alternative view on feticide.

Both Kruuse[193] and Du Plessis[194] argue for the introduction of the crime of feticide in order to offer better and more direct protection of the unborn from the violence that terminates prenatal life. Ultimately this is violence against a pregnancy unit and the form of harm inflicte can be viewed as unique because it can be inflicte only at a time when a woman is pregnant.[195] Thus, an alternative

---

[191] This obligation has been recognised in the Convention on the Elimination of All Forms of Discrimination against Women (New York, 18 December 1979). In art 16(1)(e) the Convention obligates state parties to eliminate discrimination against women in all matters and to ensure women equally enjoy their right to decide freely and responsibly on reproduction.

[192] For instance, see S Shamu, N Abrahams, M Temerman et al 'A systematic review of African studies on intimate partner violence against pregnant women: Prevalence and risk factors' (2011) 6 *PLoS ONE* e17591 and A van Parys, A Verhamme, M Temmerman et al 'Intimate partner violence and pregnancy: A systematic review of interventions' (2014) 9 *PLoS ONE* e85084. However, not all violence against pregnant women constitutes intimate partner violence; a shocking example is the recent forced caesarean section on a woman by another women with the aim of kidnapping the new born: see South African Press Association 'Foetus theft may have been to keep boyfriend, court hears' *news24* 26 August 2014, available at http://www.news24.com/SouthAfrica/News/Alleged-foetus-thief-says-murder-was-to-keep-boyfriend-20140826 (accessed on 30 June 2016).

[193] Kruuse (2009) *THRHR* 126. For a full discussion of Kruuse's position and raised criticisms see Chapter Six, para 6.3.2.

[194] Du Plessis (2013) *Stell LR* 73. For a full discussion of Du Plessis' position and raised criticisms see Chapter Six, para 6.3.2.

[195] Violence against women who are not pregnant might render similar harms upon their bodies but violence during pregnancy involves the added element of the unborn and health complications specificall associated with pregnancy. Violence during pregnancy is a serious concern that requires proper reflectio of the factual issues at hand. The uniqueness of the harm goes beyond foetal-related concerns and implicates the entire pregnancy as a unit. The World Health Organization reports that murder and suicide are the most extreme health consequences of violence against pregnant women. The less extreme, but still concerning, consequences include poor foetal growth, preterm labour, increased risk of miscarriage (which occurs before viability) or abortion (which occurs after viability), poor bonding after birth, depression, and certain maternal physical impairments such as

approach to the issue needs to be adopted which recognises that harm against the foetus is harm against a woman.

While the essence of Kruuse's and Du Plessis' arguments are rejected on the basis that the authors adopt a separate-entities approach to pregnancy, each raised important issues that require consideration. First, both emphasise that when aiming to address the concern of violence against a pregnant woman that terminates prenatal life, women's rights must remain intact. However, the study of the United States' experience unquestionably demonstrated that, for as long as pregnancy is construed as including two separate entities, this aim will be frustrated.[196] Secondly, Kruuse suggests that a unifie approach to the value of the unborn be adopted, meaning that when introducing the crime of feticide it should be reflectiv of the provisions of the Choice Act.[197] However, it was revealed not only that the Choice Act does not adopt a separate-entities approach[198] but also that, as demonstrated when considering the United States,[199] employing a separate-entities approach in the context of feticide might serve as the demise of the Choice Act specificall and women's rights more generally.[200]

Suggestions for the introduction of feticide impose a number of problems on the pregnancy relationship, because women are removed from consideration and efforts are placed on advancing foetal interests in isolation. This can culminate in violating female reproductive autonomy rights because it opens the doors to maternal liability for the unborn women carry.[201] This is widely viewed as a poor reflectio of the pregnancy relationship.[202] Nevertheless, value can be drawn from these two aspects and both can be meaningfully realised if the view of pregnancy is revised and amended to a not-one/not-two view.

To start with, the not-one/not-two approach requires that pregnant women are viewed as more than one but do not constitute two, as a result of the interconnection between the pregnant woman and the unborn. Consequently, the issue of violence that terminates prenatal life is an issue of not only violence against the unborn but also of violence against pregnant women.[203] This means

---

broken maternal bones, cuts and bruises. See World Health Organization 'Information fact sheet: Intimate partner violence during pregnancy' (2011) at 2–3, available at http://apps.who.int/iris/bitstream/10665/70764/1/WHO_RHR_11.35_eng.pdf?ua=1 (accessed on 30 June 2016).

[196] See Chapter Eight generally.

[197] See generally Kruuse (2009) *THRHR* 126.

[198] See the arguments presented in Chapter Five, para 5.3 where an alternative interpretation was advanced.

[199] See Chapter Eight generally.

[200] See Chapter Nine generally which highlights how feticide measures implicate women's health rights while pregnant and addicted; also see quoted comments of Parker J as per *Ankrom v State* 2011 WL 3781258 (Ala Crim App) in para 9.3.

[201] These arguments were presented in detail in both Chapters Eight and Nine.

[202] For instance, see generally Roth *Making Women Pay* 135–83; E Jackson *Regulating Reproduction: Law, Technology and Autonomy* (2001) 140–51; J Flavin *Our Bodies, Our Crimes: The Policing of Women's Reproduction in America* (2009) 95–118; Steinbock *Life before Birth* 154–98; Lupton *Social Worlds of the Unborn* 104–9; and Nelson *Law, Policy and Reproductive Autonomy* 194–204.

[203] Even in the case where the sole intention for inflictin violence is to terminate a pregnancy, the intrinsic connection between a pregnant woman and the unborn means that a woman will be affected.

that a third party is interacting with the pregnancy relationship in a way that compromises the health of the pregnancy as a unit and if that conduct results in stillbirth, it also compromises a healthy pregnancy outcome.

It is necessary to understand the motivation behind the calls for feticide legislation. The crime of feticide in seen as necessary, because women have the crimes of assault or murder attached to the harms inflicte on them, but no crime is attached to the harm inflicte on the unborn.[204] Of further issue is the view that the loss of a pregnancy is considered merely an aggravating factor for the purposes of sentencing.[205] This is insufficient because something more is happening when one attacks a pregnant woman, something more than mere assault, attempted murder or murder of a woman. The fact is these are women who are pregnant and pregnancy indicates something more, this being the presence of the unborn with their vested special status. The unborn's special status obligates society to recognise the unborn when crimes are perpetrated against women during a pregnancy and, further, the obligation requires the development of a specialised statement of crime that acknowledges harms caused to pregnancies. As long as pregnancy is acknowledged as embodying women and the unborn in their unique interconnection, both participants to a pregnancy should receive the law's protective reach in respect of a crime against pregnancy.[206]

Concerning how violent crimes against pregnancy should be phrased, one may be inclined to suggest introducing a statutory crime akin to the unsuccessful United States Bill[207] titled the Motherhood Protection Act of 2004.[208] Arguing for provisions similar to the Motherhood Protection Act is motivated by the need to realign focus on pregnant women who are the recipients of violent conduct and use their reproductive rights to justify state intervention in cases where a pregnancy is terminated through violence by another.[209] Pregnant women's reproductive rights are relevant because a continued pregnancy constitutes a decision to bear a child and interference with the realisation of that decision is an infringement of a woman's reproductive rights.[210] In addition to women's reproductive rights, the state's interest in prenatal life may take on a supportive role (rather than a leading

---

204 Kruuse (2009) *THRHR* 132 and Du Plessis (2013) *Stell LR* 75.

205 This was the court's approach in *Mshumpa*.

206 This allows for harm inflicte on the unborn to remain in focus and therefore moves beyond the position in *Mshumpa* where harm to the unborn was merely an aggravating factor.

207 Instead of enacting the Motherhood Protection Act, the federal government enacted the Unborn Victims of Violence Act 2004. This Bill focused on harm caused to women and rendered women the sole victims of violence. However, the Unborn Victims of Violence Act created two separate victims of violence: the woman and the unborn. For a further discussion on this topic see C Pickles *S v Mshumpa: A Time for Law Reform* (unpublished LLM dissertation, University of Pretoria, 2010) 108–11.

208 C Pickles 'The introduction of a statutory crime to address third-party foetal violence' (2011) 74 *THRHR* 546 565.

209 Pickles (2011) *THRHR* 565.

210 Pickles (2011) *THRHR* 565. For more on this Bill see M Fitzpatrick 'Fetal personhood after the Unborn Victims of Violence Act' (2006) 58 *Rugters LR* 553 and MB Hickcox-Howard 'The case for pro-choice participation in drafting fetal homicide laws' (2008) 17 *Texas Journal of Women & the Law* 317.

one) in justifying the state's interest in protecting pregnant women from violence.[211]

This is a good starting point but some adjustments are required. First, since the aim of the project is to protect pregnancy in a way that advances both women's reproductive autonomy and foetal interests, a more fittin title might be 'Pregnancy Protection Act'. Requirements of foetal viability should remain intact (for purposes of proving causation)[212] but be open to amendment in cases where causation can eventually be proved through improved sciences, especially if human dignity serves as the foundation for protection. This should be approached cautiously, though, because such an amendment should not render crimes against pregnancies in contradiction to the Choice Act.[213] However, viewing pregnancy as embodying not-one/not-two might allow for such contradictions to be avoided, because women and their rights remain part of the primary focus.

Secondly, foetal interests should not offer a mere supportive role since that would detract from the intrinsic worth of the unborn. Their role in justifying a statutory crime against pregnancy must be central rather than supportive. Recognising the centrality of their interests does not necessarily make foetal interests a primary concern, but due to the fact that the unborn are embodied, their important role must always be recognised in relation to the women who carry them.

To use the Choice Act's adoption of the not-one/not-two approach to pregnancy as a guide to criminalising third-party violence during pregnancy offers more reliable benefit for pregnancies. It creates the space to address harms of third-party violence in law in uniformity with the Choice Act. As a result, women's termination-of-pregnancy rights are left intact while also securing special status of the unborn, effectively advancing healthy pregnancy relationships for those pregnancies that are continued.[214]

This discussion has merely provided a safe criminal law *response* to violence already inflicted If the aim is to realise female reproductive autonomy and respect for special status of the unborn, then *preventive* measures must also be in place or improved in order to secure healthy pregnancies and pregnancy outcomes. However, identifying appropriate preventive measures falls beyond the scope of

---

[211] Pickles (2011) *THRHR* 565.

[212] Regarding concerns associated with causation, see Pickles (2011) *THRHR* 559–60. It was highlighted that pre-viable pregnancies are incredibly fragile and spontaneously abort without apparent reasons. This makes proving causation beyond a reasonable doubt almost impossible.

[213] This means that South Africa should not be left in the same position as that in the United States where their feticide and foetal homicide laws are in direct contradiction with the *Roe* decision since one branch of law offers foetal protection from the moment of conception while another branch of law only offers protection from viability onwards.

[214] A response to violence that terminates pregnancies must be developed in law, because it is not possible to criminally charge perpetrators for the additional loss of prenatal life in the case of assault or murder of pregnant women; for instance, see South African Press Association 'Man in court for murderous rage' *IOL news* 28 August 2014 available at http://www.iol.co.za/news/crime-courts/man-in-court-for-murderous-rage-1.1742716#.U__OB8WIBXs (accessed on 20 June 2016). It is reported that the accused allegedly stabbed his pregnant girlfriend to death after an argument, and attempts to save the unborn failed. He was charged for murder in respect of his girlfriend's death.

this discussion, since the main purpose here is to consider an alternative approach to that adopted by Kruuse and Du Plessis. It is noted, though, that developing preventive measures will require a broader contextual lens which moves beyond mere consideration of the unborn, and this implies the adoption of a relational analysis.[215]

Having clarifie the position in respect of third parties relating to a pregnancy relationship, it is now necessary to contemplate the position where women harm themselves during pregnancy.

10.5.3 Addressing prenatal substance abuse

Ovens' publication demonstrated that prenatal substance abuse is a cause for concern in South Africa and needs addressing. She went on to recommend a punitive approach via application of child abuse laws instead of treatment.[216] However, the United States' experiences of prenatal substance abuse demonstrates that a punitive approach is not readily accepted and is too narrowly focused on women as wrongdoers.[217] Those states identifie as adopting a punitive approach to prenatal substance abuse face concerted opposition from the medical community and human rights organisations.[218] The position is that addiction is a

---

[215] It seems a relational analysis is already taking place; see generally World Health Organization 'Information fact sheet: Intimate partner violence during pregnancy'. For instance, see Shamu, Abrahams, Temerman et al (2011) *PLoS ONE* e17591 and World Health Organization 'Understanding and addressing violence against women: Intimate partner violence' (2012) available at http://apps.who.int/iris/bitstream/10665/77432/1/WHO_RHR_12.36_eng.pdf?ua=1 (accessed on 30 June 2016).

[216] See her arguments generally: Ovens (2008) *Acta Criminologica* 77; Ovens (2010) *Child Abuse Research in South Africa* 38 and para 6.3.3 herein. There are different theories of addiction, but these are too many to consider here. For further reading see R West 'Theories of addiction' (2001) 96 *Addiction* 3.

[217] See Part Three generally.

[218] This is particularly evident from the list of *amici curiae* briefs: *Amici curiae* brief of the National Association of Alcoholism and Drug Abuse Counselors, South Carolina Association of Alcoholism and Drug Abuse Counselors, American College of Obstetricians and Gynecologists et al in the matter of *Whitner v State* 492 SE 2d 777 (SC 1997); *amici curiae* brief of American Public Health Association, American Nurses Association, American Psychiatric Association et al in the matter of *McKnight v South Carolina* 540 US 819 (2003); *amici curiae* brief of American Public Health Association, American Nurses Association, American Psychiatric Association et al in the matter of *State v McKnight* 576 SE 2d 168 (SC 2003); *amici curiae* brief of Pegasus Legal Services for Children, New Mexico Section of the American College of Obstetricians and Gynecologists, New Mexico Public Health Association et al in the matter of *State v Martinez* 141 NM 763 (NM 2007); *amici curiae* brief of South Carolina Medical Association, South Carolina Nurses Association, South Carolina Association of Alcoholism and Drug Abuse Counselors et al in the matter of *McKnight v State* 661 SE 2d 354 (SC 2008); *amici curiae* brief of American Public Health Association, National Association of Social Workers, Alabama Women's Resource Network et al in the matter of *Kimbrough v State of Alabama* in the Court of Criminal Appeals of Alabama, criminal appeals number CR-09-0485 (2010); *amici curiae* brief of the Alabama Women's Resource Network, American Academy of Addiction Psychiatry, American Society of Addiction Medicine et al in the matter of *Ankrom v State* 2011 WL 3781258 (Ala Crim App); *amici curiae* brief of American Academy of Addiction Psychiatry, American College of Obstetricians and Gynecologists, American Psychiatric Association et al in the matter of *Ex parte Kimbrough* 2013 WL 135748 (Ala); and *amici curiae* brief of American Academy of Addiction Psychiatry, American College of Obstetrics and

health concern and should be treated as such.[219] This argument regards punitive intervention as an ineffective means of tackling a health concern such as addiction. In essence, the position is that criminal law has no role to play in this pregnancy-related concern.[220]

Drawing from the finding on the United States' position, this chapter approvingly adopts the treatment approach to prenatal drug abuse. Punitive third-party interventions fail to secure healthy pregnancy relationships between pregnant women and the unborn in that the state's actions are focused primarily on the advancement of the unborn's interests without consideration of the pregnant women who carry them.[221] Furthermore, this approach compromises optimal pregnancy outcomes, because the condition of addiction persists. At times, pregnancies are terminated (not because the pregnancy is unwanted but because of fear of prosecution), women are incarcerated and families are broken up.[222] The interconnection between women and the unborn means that punishment of pregnant women punishes the unborn too.[223] Overall, this approach is viewed as an inadequate response. A treatment-based approach, on the other hand, focuses on the pregnancy as a unit and seeks to advance the interests of both women and the unborn during pregnancy and maintains the family unit after birth.[224] This approach therefore secures and maintains relationships rather than undermining them.[225]

The discussion to follow will provide an alternative view of prenatal substance abuse and through that view will demonstrate that, while harmful conduct is taking place, interests can be constructively realigned. This realignment holds the potential to positively link pregnant women to their unborn, thus promoting a healthy pregnancy relationship and healthy pregnancy outcomes. It further assists in bringing a more positive note to the relationship shared between pregnant women and the state and medical profession based on the fact that all three parties are essentially aiming for the same results.

Gynecologists, American Psychiatric Association et al in the matter of *Ex parte Ankrom* 2013 WL 135748 (Ala). See further examples as posted on National Advocates for Pregnant Women's website, www.advocatesforpregnantwomen.org.

[219] Flavin *Our Bodies, Our Crimes* 111.

[220] This can be gleaned from the content of Chapter Nine, but also see M Horn 'Mothers versus babies: constitutional and policy problems with prosecutions for prenatal maternal substance abuse' (2008) 14 *William & Mary Journal of Women & the Law* 635; S Smith 'Criminalising prenatal substance abuse: Hurting women and their unborn children' (2012) 6 *Health Law Outlook* 14; and S Mohapatra 'Unshackling addiction: A public health approach to drug use during pregnancy' (2011) 26 *Wisconsin Journal of Law, Gender & Society* 241.

[221] These were the general finding originating from the study of the United States' position in respect of prenatal substance abuse; see Chapter Nine.

[222] Chapter Nine; Horn (2008) *William & Mary Journal of Women & the Law* 635; Smith (2012) *Health Law Outlook* 14; and Mohapatra (2011) *Wisconsin Journal of Law, Gender & Society* 241.

[223] KA Kellett 'Miscarriage of justice: Prenatal substance abusers need treatment, not confinemen under chemical endangerment laws' (2014) 40 *New England Journal on Criminal & Civil Confinement* 455 467.

[224] Kellett (2014) *New England Journal on Criminal & Civil Confinement* 467.

[225] Smith (2012) *Health Law Outlook* 14.

Prenatal substance abuse should be characterised as a form of 'self-harm'[226] instead of foetal abuse. The term 'self-harm' serves the tactical purpose of avoiding the argument that women are abusing drugs with the view to abusing the unborn. Further, the use of 'self-harm' in the context of prenatal substance abuse has the effect of stressing that, while the consequences of prenatal substance abuse on the unborn are somewhat unknown, it is nevertheless accepted that substance abuse is known to be harmful to the substance abuser. Since the substance abusers considered here are pregnant, the interconnection between women and the unborn during pregnancy must be noted. Therefore, self-harm in this context must also be understood as harming the pregnancy relationship and compromising healthy pregnancy progression, in that one participant in the pregnancy relationship is in an unhealthy state of addiction. It also allows for one to accept that, if the pregnant women, being the leading participants in pregnancy relationships,[227] are in an unhealthy state, foetal wellbeing must surely be susceptible to compromise too.[228]

However, focus on the issue of prenatal substance abuse as a form of self-harm does not mean that it is only pregnant women who are involved in imposing harm on themselves. As mentioned above, a relational approach requires that the context in which decisions are made or actions are taken must be considered, too. Moving away from the narrow perspective of child abuse[229] allows for a more informed

[226] Although, as a concept, self-harm can range from prenatal substance abuse (addictions) to instances of intentional and drastic inflictio of harm, such as suicide ideation, attempted suicide or personal inflictio of violence in order to terminate a pregnancy outside of the provisions of termination-of-pregnancy laws. Since this chapter is concerned with those suggestions for changes to the law as advanced by South African authors, the primary focus of this discussion will consider an alternative route to Ovens' proposal that prenatal substance abuse should constitute the crime of child abuse. It is pertinent to address this issue in a productive way because if women can be held liable for substance abuse during pregnancy then a precedent is set for liability in other respects of self-harm, whether this involves smoking, participation in sports, suicide ideation, unlawful termination of pregnancy and any other actions viewed as compromising a healthy pregnancy relationship and healthy pregnancy progression. This would be a concerning development because as already shown with reference to research on the United States' position, healthy pregnancies are compromised to the extent that health care was avoided or pregnancies were terminated. (See Chapter Nine generally.) However, it is also recognised that knowing how to respond to the notion of self-harm via prenatal substance abuse generally will assist in understanding how to use the law to address other areas of self-harm without opening the 'floodgates for criminal sanctions against pregnant women. It must be noted that 'self-harm' does not indicate that the process of harming oneself through addiction is void of the contextual understanding that addiction is a social issue that intersects with poverty, race, violence against women, gender discrimination, and poor nutrition and education. These influencin factors were generally highlighted in Chapter Nine. Also, see generally C MacIntosh 'Conceiving fetal abuse' (1998) 15 *Canadian Journal of Family Law* 178.

[227] Women are identifie as the leading participants in the pregnancy relationship because they are essentially a *sine qua non* for foetal existence. Identifying them as taking a leading position should not be seen to detract from the special status of the unborn, it is a result of the special status of the unborn that requires this issue to be addressed, because if addiction was purely an issue of self-harm that is not illegal in South Africa then there would be no real need to tackle the concern.

[228] See E Ordolis 'Maternal substance abuse and the limits of law: A relational challenge' (2008) 46 *Alberta LR* 119 121.

[229] It is viewed as narrow because it only focuses on harms to the unborn, whereas substance abuse harms the substance-abusing women too.

contextual view of pregnant women who are addicted to substances, because it keeps women and their lived experiences in clear view.

Johnsen points out that pregnant women are usually addicted to substances before falling pregnant, and prenatal addictive behaviours are not intentional acts to compromise the pregnancy or healthy outcomes.[230] Johnsen explains that at times women will go to great lengths to secure healthy pregnancies and babies and that it is not bad intentions but existing obstacles that prevent them from overcoming addiction.[231] This encourages one to consider the context in which women become addicted and contemplate why their addictions remain, despite being motivated to stop using.

A number of factors have been identifie as facilitating an environment conducive to self-harm,[232] such as sexual abuse and violence,[233] diminished economic standing, racial discrimination, poor education, and women's vulnerable position in society, to name a few relevant factors.[234] Once addiction has settled in, the most glaring factors that act as obstacles to overcoming addiction include poverty and as a result of poverty, there is a lack of access to health care in the form of drug addiction treatment as well as a lack of choice in respect of the treatments available.[235]

Viewing substance abuse as an act a woman commits against herself helps to clarify the context involved. Further, since pregnancy embodies not-one/not-two, the harm against oneself naturally implicates the unborn being carried. Relying on interconnection from the start helps to emphasise and centralise the health interests shared by pregnant women and the unborn they carry, while understanding the context of addiction helps to highlight what can be done to foster healthier pregnancies.

Having established the pregnancy relationship in the context of self-harm and highlighted the alignment of interests in the pregnancy relationship, it must be pointed out that there is also a shared interest between pregnant women and those third parties who want prenatal substance abuse to be addressed. Johnsen explains that the underlying motivation for state or collective action against drug abuse during pregnancy relates to the health risks associated with such behaviour and the possible wide-reaching implications for children born from women who abuse substances.[236] Advancing the view that pregnant women and the unborn are

[230] D Johnsen 'Shared interests: Promoting healthy births without sacrificin women's liberty' (1992) 43 *Hastings LJ* 569 571.

[231] Johnsen (1992) *Hastings LJ* 573; 575–6.

[232] Answering this question falls beyond the scope of this chapter but it must be recognised that if the underlying aim of addressing prenatal substance abuse is to protect the unborn and the unborn are inherently linked to the women who carry them, then focus should be on preventive measures.

[233] MacIntosh (1998) *Canadian Journal of Family Law* 193–4.

[234] See Ordolis (2008) *Alberta LR* 138.

[235] Johnsen (1992) *Hastings LJ* 157; Ordolis (2008) *Alberta LR* 137; and SE Smith 'No safe harbors: Examining the shift from voluntary treatment options to criminalization of maternal drug use in Tennessee' (2015) 46 *University of Memphis LR* 203.

[236] Johnsen (1992) *Hastings LJ* 601. Horn identifie these interests as originating from the resulting responsibilities that state will have to shoulder when more and more children are born exposed; see Horn (2008) *William & Mary Journal of Women & the Law* 652.

inseparable means that both women and third parties (the state and medical profession) share in the objective of realising healthy pregnancy outcomes and the interests are therefore aligned.

With interests aligned it becomes clearer that adversarial tactics are not necessary in order to achieve the aims of addressing addiction during pregnancy. This takes the issue to another level allowing for creative consideration of how to realise these aligned interests in a way conducive to the pregnancy relationship and the relationship between pregnant women and third parties.

Having revealed the interests shared by pregnant women and the unborn and by pregnant women and third parties, the task now is to determine how to realise these shared aims in a way that promotes both women's autonomy rights and foetal interests, thus fostering not only healthy pregnancy progression but also healthy pregnancy relationships between women and the unborn. At this point, one is required to contemplate the nature of the relationships at play and their existing structures. The pregnancy relationship between the unborn and pregnant women is already well established and will not be repeated here. However, it is necessary to consider how third parties would relate to pregnant women who are addicted to substances under Ovens' punitive approach and then to contemplate how they should relate to pregnancy relationships in the future.

Characterising prenatal substance abuse as a health concern indicates that assistance is required, not only for overcoming addiction but also sustaining a drug-free life, thus securing healthy pregnancies and eventual healthy family units.[237] In essence this emphasises the requirement of third-party intervention into a pregnancy relationship. Taking this standpoint provides a very clear view of how others are inherently intertwined in the issue of substance abuse and shows that these relationships each play an integral role: there are pregnant women in need of assistance, there is the state which passes laws regarding the issues of illegal drugs and prenatal health care and also adopts certain policies regarding the provision of health care, and there is the health-care profession, which provides the know-how and relevant care ultimately acting as the go-between for state resources and healthy outcomes. Also, women are viewed as being in a hierarchical relationship, as they are in a position of need but the know-how and resources to meet that need rests in the hands of the medical profession and the state.

The state is also viewed as the link between pregnant women and health-care providers in that its response to addiction via policies and laws will determine the quality of third-party interventions and the care provided to pregnant women. Laws and policies would indicate what would be permissible interventions and what types of care could be provided, if any at all. How these measures are developed and imposed will inevitably impact on the quality of the role players' relationships and the resulting outcomes stemming from those interactions. For instance, in the United States, which is essentially a replica of Ovens' approach, there is third-party intervention, but relationships are structured through criminal law provisions, which renders relationships adversarial in nature and this

---

[237] Mohapatra (2011) *Wisconsin Journal of Law, Gender & Society* 253.

adversarial stance infuses the pregnancy relationship and the relationship between third parties and the pregnancy relationship. This therefore also compromises women's autonomy and foetal interests. In this instance, the relationships are so poorly constructed that the shared aims and interests described above are left unrealised or severely compromised. Johnsen explains:[238]

> Policymakers who truly wish to foster healthy childbearing must understand that government, women, and their future children all have shared interests in taking the steps necessary to promote healthy births. They also must recognize that imposing special penalties that restrict the capacity of women to control their lives will not further these shared interests. Rather, the government must take positive steps to remove obstacles that prevent women from receiving the health services, treatment, and prenatal care they need.

With that in mind, characteristically, the assistance advanced by the state and health providers should be of such a nature that it provides the means of fostering a better pregnancy relationship, since a healthy foundational relationship between pregnant women and the unborn ensures better prospects for healthy pregnancy outcomes. Given that South Africa is already well-prepared for a relational approach it is further argued that a more fittin approach for the current South African climate is to turn to a relations-fostering approach to prenatal substance abuse.[239]

A treatment-based approach is understood as relational in that, according to Smith, 'it aims to balance the interests of women's autonomy and the state's interest in potential life resulting in policies that are more functional and just for women and their families'.[240] This emphasises the recognition of relationships and the need to maintain or foster them. Further, according to Mohapatra, the public health approach to drug addiction focuses on the broader context of a particular issue rather than isolating focus on individual actions or behaviour, and it considers how social determinants impact on the health of particular individuals.[241] She explains that it is useful to understand the social make-up of a particular concern, because such knowledge allows for public policies to be developed in a way that prevents and reduces harms rather than merely punishing them.[242] This approach more readily realises all parties' interests in a way that does not render them adversaries.

This discussion demonstrates that something more must be done in South Africa and that these efforts should take place outside of criminal law. In South Africa, women have justiciable socio-economic rights, such rights being the right to health care and the right to reproductive health care.[243] Further, in terms of s 4 of

[238] Johnsen (1992) *Hastings LJ* 613.
[239] See para 10.2 above.
[240] Smith (2012) *Health Law Outlook* 14.
[241] Mohapatra (2011) *Wisconsin Journal of Law, Gender & Society* 260.
[242] Mohapatra (2011) *Wisconsin Journal of Law, Gender & Society* 260.
[243] Section 27(1)*(a)* of the Constitution. Also see S Lutchman 'Insufficient access to substance abuse centres for illicit drug users and its potential effect on a foetus: A breach of the right to access to health care services' (2015) 19 *Law, Development & Democracy* 65.

the National Health Act,[244] women in need should receive free prenatal care at state-funded facilities. If they are suffering with substance-related concerns, treatment for this should be included within the ambit of prenatal care, because it assists in securing healthy pregnancy progression and outcomes. Additionally, even though the Prevention of and Treatment for Substance Abuse Act[245] does not make specifi mention of pregnant women's access to treatment, the equality clause (s 9 of the Constitution) explicitly prevents discrimination on the basis of pregnancy, thus obligating the treatment of pregnant women who suffer from addiction. Collectively these provisions should have more impetus regarding the issue of prenatal substance abuse, yet the issue seems to remain unaddressed.[246] The upside to this is that there are laws in South Africa that can be used to encourage values-fostering relationships. Additionally, these laws can simultaneously serve as a means of protecting women when relationships become structured in a way that compromises the values of female reproductive autonomy or foetal interests.[247]

The fina issue that needs to be considered is why it is appropriate to support criminal sanctions against third parties who inflic violence on pregnant women but not support criminal sanctions against pregnant women who self-harm during pregnancy. The distinction lies in the application of the not-one/not-two approach to pregnancy.

Applying the principles of criminal law to third parties who relate violently to pregnancy assists in fostering healthy pregnancies and pregnant relationships between the unborn and women. This is because both women's rights and the special status of the unborn are being advanced by the application of criminal law against others. However, doing the same in respect of pregnant women's conduct will compromise the pregnancy relationship and hamper efforts to secure healthy pregnancy outcomes altogether. This was clearly demonstrated in Chapters Eight and Nine regarding the United States' experiences.

Adopting this approach does not mean that pregnant women's self-harm must go unaddressed. If it were left unaddressed it would mean that the single-entities approach would be at play, since the unborn's special status would be rendered unrecognised and meaningless in law. However, the not-one/not-two approach

[244] Act 61 of 2003.

[245] Act 70 of 2008.

[246] According to Ovens there are no treatment facilities for pregnant women suffering with addiction, Ovens (2008) *Acta Criminologica* 90.

[247] Protection will certainly be required in cases where pregnant women exist in hierarchical relationships such as the doctor–patient or state–welfare recipient relationships, because as the United States' experience demonstrates in Chapter Nine, there are third parties who are not aligned with the treatment approach. In fact, Ovens is the South African example of that position. This view is necessitated by the realisation that while the medical profession in the United States argue against the use of criminal law to address addiction, it must be noted that they are the ones at the forefront of reporting women which serves to initiate criminal proceedings. Concerning health care providers reporting women who have used drugs prenatally, see Roth *Making Women Pay* 143; 147; JR Schroedel, P Fiber & BD Snyder 'Women's rights and fetal personhood in criminal law' (2000) 7 *Duke Journal of Gender Law & Policy* 89 110; and D Page 'The homicide by child abuse conviction of Regina McKnight' (2003) 46 *Howard LJ* 363 372.

demonstrates that, while women are harming themselves, the presence of the unborn intensifie the extent of harm and therefore justifie increased or improved state action. The adoption of the not-one/not-two approach further means that different legal measures must be applied—in place of criminal law principles—that will promote a healthy relationship, thus improving the prospects of healthy pregnancy outcomes.

To conclude, it is noted that this discussion has been focused on responding to substance abuse during pregnancy, based on the fact that it attempts to suggest more constructive alternatives to Ovens' suggestions. However, it should be mentioned, from a relational perspective, if the underlying concerns are to foster healthy pregnancy relationships and optimal pregnancy outcomes, more effort should be placed on the prevention[248] of substance abuse rather than on criminalisation or responding treatment regimes. Further, attention should be drawn to the role of the state and effort should be turned towards forcing the state into action to address those social concerns that facilitate drug use. Focusing on substance abuse as a crime against the unborn is far too narrowly focused to render any meaningful outcomes in both a responsive and preventive approach.

10.5.4 Extending personhood to the unborn

Briefl , Pillay argues for the extension of personhood and foetal rights to viable foetuses in order to better protect them from a wide range of possible harms such as third-party violence, termination of pregnancy, and civil wrongs, such as wrongful death issues.[249] Chapter Six[250] demonstrated how adopting such an approach would fail to realise the intended outcomes and it was revealed that, even in a country such as the United States, which is characterised by foetal protection measures, such sweeping protections are not in place.[251] The study on the United States' personhood measures aimed at extending full legal subjectivity to the unborn highlighted a hesitation to go so far as to extend personhood to the unborn because less extreme means are available for achieving protection for the unborn.[252]

This topic was strategically left for last. While Pillay's suggestion for law reform cannot be supported, her work does indicate a need for increased consideration of the unborn in law, particularly with regard to status. A relational approach has achieved this without necessitating full legal subjectivity or foetal rights.

The development of the special status of the unborn via a relational approach shows that full legal subjectivity is not necessary in order to create the space to consider the unborn in law. That development, together with the application of the not-one/not-two approach, demonstrates that the extension of full legal subjectiv-

[248] This falls beyond the scope of this discussion, however Mohapatra advances some compelling suggestions; see Mohapatra (2011) *Wisconsin Journal of Law, Gender & Society* 264–6.

[249] Pillay (2010) *Stell LR* 236–7. Also see the detailed discussion in Chapter Six, para 6.3.1.

[250] Para 6.3.1.

[251] See Chapter Seven, para 7.4.

[252] Chapter Seven and see generally M Manian 'Lessons from personhood's defeat: Abortion restrictions and side effects on women's health' (2013) 74 *Ohio State LJ* 75.

ity to the unborn is unnecessary to protect the unborn. Up to this point, this chapter has suggested alternative ways of effectively protecting the unborn without advancing any legal subjectivity akin to born persons. The relational stance adopted here clearly shows that advancing the unborn's interests in a way that removes the women who carry them creates an environment that compromises the unborn's wellbeing rather than fostering it.

10.6 CONCLUDING REMARKS

Throughout this book, criticisms were raised about the adoption of the law in a way that advances either women's reproductive autonomy or foetal interests, as if neither of the two interests could coexist. Yet, in reality, pregnant women and the unborn coexist and have done so for as long as human procreation has taken place. This lived reality clearly shows how the law is failing to articulate pregnancy correctly. This incorrect view originates from our emphasis on individuality and separateness and possibly removing women from participation in the development of law regarding pregnancy-related concerns.

Parts Two and Three show the flaw inherent in both the single-entity and separate-entities approaches to pregnancy in law. These flaw exist because each approach ignores the connection (the living coexistence) between pregnant women and the unborn. This acontextual view of pregnancy places these approaches in a poor position for addressing pregnancy-related concerns: both approaches either ignore the existence of the unborn altogether or, where the unborn are acknowledged, they are acknowledged in a way that renders pregnancy steeped in tensions, whereby female reproductive autonomy hinders advancement of the unborn or where foetal interests hinder the advancement of women's reproductive autonomy. For as long as one is adopting an adversarial approach, it will be difficult to reach effective changes to the law. Revising the view of pregnancy in law is clearly necessary. There must be another way of viewing pregnancy in law that is reconcilable with the lived realities of pregnant women.

Nedelsky's work on relational theory in law supports the argument for a better consideration of the context of pregnant women and the unborn and helps to emphasise the need to return the focus to the unique connection between women and the unborn. Her work provides a framework for simultaneously considering the unborn and women in relation to each other and also demonstrates that it is the way in which relationships are structured that tends to either foster or undermine certain values. Further, she demonstrates how to reflec on the law and its structuring mechanisms so as to highlight what needs changing in order to achieve desirable outcomes. In the context of pregnancy, desirable outcomes would be those that advance female reproductive autonomy and foetal interests, thus securing a respectful pregnancy relationship and optimal pregnancy outcomes because both participants in the pregnancy are cared for.

This newly created theoretical space which considers the unborn in relation to pregnant women ties into the Choice Act's not-one/not-two approach to pregnancy and suggests that the unborn be accorded special status. Since this special status is built on the unborn as embodied, it keeps women central to any considerations concerning pregnancy in law. Focus on pregnancy as a relationship even though the pregnant woman and the unborn are not on an equal footing in law offers a number of benefits It articulates a more fittin view of pregnancy based on female experiences of pregnancy. It allows for an expression of value of the unborn in law, while simultaneously serving as a constant reminder that the unborn can never be engaged in isolation from women. Leading on from that, understanding pregnancy as an inseparable connection provides guidance on how others may or may not relate to pregnant women when their primary focus relates to concerns about the unborn. Most importantly, understanding pregnancy as a connection recognises that what happens to one entity will involve the other, advancing one advances the other, and violating one violates the other.

Adopting this view facilitates an alternative view of pregnancy. It also allows those relating to pregnancy to develop in a non-adversarial way. Further, when adversarial positions begin to develop, this approach provides the evaluative mechanisms for addressing and reforming those structures which allow for tensions to develop. While theoretically this makes sense, this chapter went on to test this theory and apply it to the various pregnancy-related concerns pointed out by South African scholars.

The identifie areas of law in need of reform were all characteristically identifie as being steeped in tension, since each sought to protect the unborn while effectively sidelining women and their reproductive autonomy. A relational approach transformed those relationships, meaning that, instead of the relationships being based on separatism, they are now all based on entrenched connection. When using connection as the starting point, it naturally guides the parameters of what would constitute constructive or destructive interventions and helps identify which mechanisms would achieve constructive interventions. It also shows that, when relationships and shared interests are the elements of primary focus, the right role-players can be called on to effect the necessary change. Finally, it reveals that, while responsive actions are necessary, if our concerns are truly about realising healthy pregnancy relationships and healthy outcomes, better preventive measures need to be established.

Chapter 11

CONCLUDING REFLECTIONS

This book is driven by the central question: Can the value of connection serve as the basis for addressing the tension between foetal interests and female reproductive autonomy, ultimately allowing for both interests and rights to co-exist? As demonstrated, this can be achieved through the not-one-but-not-two approach to pregnancy (not-one/not-two approach). Further, it is clear that, for as long as laws develop views of pregnancy which are void of the connection between the unborn and pregnant women, a tension between female autonomy and foetal interests will persist. Without the value of connection, all efforts to address the pertinent issues of pregnancy in law will be unmanageable and remain stagnant in law.

The ambitious task of addressing the tension between female reproductive autonomy and foetal interests during pregnancy and birth is in fact a search for a suitable model for pregnancy in law. One might be inclined to assume that there are various tensions at play, depending on the particular aspect of law being applied to an issue in pregnancy. For instance, the tension that exists in criminal law regarding third-party violence involves a separate tension in pregnancy from that which appears in private law regarding the regulation of pregnancy terminations. However, the book reveals that one tension exists and it plagues all the branches of law, whenever one attempts to apply the law to a particular issue in pregnancy. The search for a solution to the tension between female autonomy rights and foetal interests during pregnancy and birth is, in fact, a search for a model of pregnancy in law which views pregnancy in a way that extinguishes the tension. Thus, if one model of pregnancy is developed which indicates what pregnancy is in law and how the law could be applied to it (as a form of framework), then this new model could transcend all the branches of law. This would remove the opportunity of pitting the unborn against the pregnant women who carry them and allow for consistent and effective application of the law or improved law reform.

The following is an overview of the substantive facets that motivated this book and contributed to establishing the contextual importance of this topic for the advancement of women and the unborn in law. Further, the overview reveals how a revised approach to pregnancy could fin suitable application to a broad spectrum of pregnancy-related concerns spanning termination of pregnancy, status of the unborn, criminal harms and self-imposed harms by pregnant women.

As female reproductive autonomy and foetal interests are currently understood or constructed in law they are oppositional and this gives the sense that reconciliation between the two notions is almost impossible. Having foetal interests and female reproductive autonomy pitted against one another in polarised positions has far-reaching implications regarding how law is equipped to tackle pregnancy-related concerns. Within this oppositional framework, the law cannot be used to protect those pregnancies that are continued without somehow reducing women's autonomy rights. Alternatively, reproductive autonomy rights are so narrowly construed that protecting these rights means that the value of the unborn will be diminished.

This points to the very broad premise that currently there is a tension between female autonomy rights and foetal interests during pregnancy and birth, and a number of areas have been identifie in law where the tension is present and is therefore hampering progression in law. Progression is hampered because neither of the two interests or rights can be simultaneously advanced. This position hinders women's progression in law and, if pregnant women are not being advanced, neither are the unborn. The aim therefore is to develop a view of pregnancy that allows for the law to address pregnancy-related concerns in such a way that a tension between female autonomy rights and foetal interests does not arise.

The tension between pregnant women and the unborn was found in arguments supporting the extension of legal personhood to the unborn[1] and making the unborn victims of crime when others commit violence against pregnant women.[2] This tension was also found to be present in arguments that regard prenatal substance abuse as child abuse against the unborn[3] and in calls for the repeal of the Choice on Termination of Pregnancy Act[4] (Choice Act).[5] While all these themes are associated with different pregnancy-related areas, they are all linked in their aim to offer better protection to the unborn in law. Ultimately, these identifie areas serve two roles. Each assists in identifying what areas are in need of increased legal attention and each demonstrates how the tension between female autonomy rights plays out, thus revealing what the resulting implications are of this ever-present tension.

---

[1] R Pillay 'The beginning of human personhood: Is South African law outdated?' (2010) 21 *Stell LR* 230. This call for reform highlights that the law needs to be developed so as to allow for a discourse of the unborn in law which advances better protection more generally.

[2] HJ Kruuse 'Fetal "rights"? The need for a unifie approach to the fetus in the context of feticide' (2009) 72 *THRHR* 126 and GA du Plessis 'Feticide: Creating a statutory crime in South African law' (2013) 24 *Stell LR* 73. Calling for a view of the unborn as victims of crime indicates that the law might need to be reformed in so far as it fails to acknowledge that when a pregnant woman is attacked, more than bodily injury occurs in that a pregnancy might be lost too. This needs recognition in law.

[3] M Ovens 'Maternal substance abuse in South Africa: An area for concern?' (2008) 1 *Acta Criminologica* 77 and M Ovens 'A criminological perspective of prenatal abuse of substances during pregnancy and the link to child abuse in South Africa' (2010) 11 *Child Abuse Research in South Africa* 38. Introducing criminal sanctions for prenatal substance abuse is an indication that too little is being done regarding drug use and abuse, and the resulting implication for children born from women who abused drugs prenatally and are born into families who continue to use drugs.

[4] Act 92 of 1996.

[5] S De Freitas 'The South African Constitutional Court and the unborn' (2012) 5 *International Journal of Religious Freedom* 51 and SA de Freitas & GA Myburgh 'The relevance of science for the protection of the unborn' (2009) 45 *Journal for Christian Scholarship* 61. Looking to repeal termination-of-pregnancy laws is viewed as an indication that more can be done regarding the prevention of termination of pregnancy and the question is how to do so without removing the right of women to choose what is best for them without the imposition of undue external restraints.

Having recognised that there is a tension during pregnancy, the next step is to consider what factors encouraged the rise of the notion of adversarialism in pregnancy. The identifie tension does not come about in a vacuum.

It is well known that women's history is characterised by roles associated with subordination, domestication and reproduction, but very little is known of the basic historical position of the unborn. Further, less is known about the significanc of pregnancy and how the position of the unborn and pregnant women intersected in history (how they were positioned in relation to each other). A number of aspects stand out from Part One.

It seems that from the period spanning Classical antiquity through to the Middle Ages, pregnant women and the unborn were one and in that oneness they usually resided under the head of the household in which the woman lived. As a result of this shared subordinate position, the unborn and women were not structured relationally to be in tension with each other, but maybe were in tension with only the head of the household. There are clear indications that women acted contrary to the head of the household, because scholars have referred to 'women's knowledge' and the use of magic potions and amulets to curb unwanted pregnancies and so forth. These actions did not seem to be labelled in legal terms as equivalent to reproductive autonomy as it is known today, but in retrospect they could certainly constitute underground attempts at securing bodily autonomy. Also, the unborn did receive attention, but articulating that consideration into any workable theory or policy was difficult, given the lack of knowledge of the invisible development of the unborn. With regard to the unborn, it seems there was no known legal term (such as foetal interests) that described what the unborn might mean and how that meaning could be imposed in law or otherwise, except in so far as the unborn represented heirs and connection to a particular household.

Eventually Christianity became widely adopted, and women's subordination under the household head was confirme and inculcated further while the unborn gradually became recognised as entities of inherent worth. Nevertheless, these developments do not in themselves give an indication of a specifi tension between women advancing an inner direction and the unborn as vested with distinct interests in law. The makings were there, however, because these teachings permeated the later development of laws.

With this historical perspective in place, what is gleaned from the chapter on feminism and the scientificall justifie individuation of the unborn is that the terms 'female autonomy rights' and 'foetal interests' are contemporary terms. These terms are expressions of the developments that took place during the rise of feminism and foetal individuation, and the environment in which the terms came to be developed seems to have played a significan role in positioning these terms as polarised.

The historical study brings home how negative women's history was in comparison with the freedoms presently being enjoyed.[6] Women's history must have been something inherently demeaning in many respects and ultimately it was

[6] This is not to say that the task is complete because the extent of freedoms enjoyed directly correlates with race, socio-economic status, gender, culture and so on.

not accepted by women because a focused social movement was born in response to it, which remains strong today. The fact that it took an entire social movement to bring about change over a vast span of time indicates an environment of entrenched opposition to women's emancipation. Furthermore, the fact that the movement is still active today can also be interpreted as indicating that opposition to further emancipation is ever-present in varying degrees.[7] Opposition to emancipation already sets an adversarial tone.

Furthermore, when one considers that women were aiming for emancipation from the constraints of reproduction, it is clear that the drive for freedom would clash with the newly discovered foetus with treatable defects. This is seen to result in numerous efforts to curb women's conduct during pregnancy for the benefi or treatment of the unborn.

In spite of feminism taking several and at times opposing positions, the uniting factor is that, as a movement, feminism must advance women. Since reproduction was one of the primary sources of subordination and women's position in domestic life, focus was on securing the freedom to choose in respect of reproductive matters. Given the very central role that reproduction plays in women's lives, it makes sense that feminism generally viewed securing reproductive freedom for women as a precondition for equality. These efforts must surely have been frustrated by the simultaneous opposition to emancipation and the increased discoveries regarding foetal development. These developments in reproductive health were supposedly meant to secure safe progression through pregnancies but the environment in which these developments took place allowed for the appropriation of science by some to individuate the unborn as separate entities and present them as being worthy of separate consideration and protection beyond the fiel of medicine.

Also, a central idea of feminism is to bring women back into the centre so as to deconstruct what is considered a 'norm'. This is achieved by increasing women's participation and rendering their experiences relevant to the development of better informed norms. One of the reasons why a comprehensive history of women in relation to the unborn could not be provided is because women as a group were not recorded, so their first-han accounts of how they lived and functioned within the various classes are missing. They were somewhat invisible from the records of history. However, the extent of their invisibility varied according to their class. This indicates a lack of participation, which means that many laws and policies were developed without female perspective and input. Thus as science develops and brings new issues to the fore regarding pregnancy, such as the unborn as separate entities, the law is poorly equipped to articulate workable solutions because of women's past exclusion. Consequently, principles are applied and enforced in pregnancy-related issues that do not really resonate with the lived realities of pregnancy and this can entrench tensions.

[7] The study of the United States in Part Three demonstrates this is certainly true, however the fact that South Africa does not share the same intensity of opposition comparable to the United States shows that opposition is common but the degree of severity differs from one jurisdiction to the next.

The simultaneous individuation of the unborn and the development of theories regarding the unborn with the use of science to justify those theories prove particularly problematic to a movement seeking to defin women beyond procreation and child bearing and rearing. On the one hand these developments are meant to secure safe progression through pregnancy and offer more choices concerning procreation, but, on the other hand, women are being sidelined once again because the focus is on the unborn as separate entities, even though women's bodies serve as the means of prenatal existence. This indicates that feminist aims are being frustrated in two respects: first women are possibly being rendered invisible again and this indicates that there is the potential for history to repeat itself. Secondly, the significanc of women and their experiences is being devalued, thus denying them participation.

As a whole, gaining an understanding of this context is incredibly valuable because it shows where women came from and where they are going, and it provides indications of how they plan to reach their desired ends. It also shows how the existence of a pregnancy has the potential to derail women's efforts for freedom and reproductive autonomy, especially in an environment infused with wider social tensions, which frustrate women's general efforts for advancement. It establishes that there is a lot at stake when developing an understanding of pregnancy in law, because women's history serves as a constant reminder of where the result of our reform efforts are not permitted to go. Women must remain central, their participation must be secured and maintained and their interests and rights should not be sacrifice for externally define motivations (being those developed by third parties and not pregnant women themselves). Part One also shows that there are flourishin debates about the unborn, some of which are being developed in ways that remove women from being significan role-players in pregnancies, and any move forward must rectify this. This position is premised on the fact that pregnancy is a woman's concern, more so than anyone else's, because it is something that occurs within her.

Finally, understanding the context demonstrates that pregnancy is complex and not simply a matter of theoretical definitio of the unborn. Pregnancy is a manifestation of reproduction, which can be either a source of liberation when it is wanted or a struggle for women when it is unwanted. Pregnancy is also a symbol of existing prenatal life, which is highly prized by different people who are situated differently across various contexts. Further, it is an embodied experience for women. These multidimensional perspectives in themselves increase opportunities for tensions between the concepts of reproductive autonomy and foetal interests. Regardless, foundational pointers bring home the importance of women's rights and the fact that the unborn do exist even if in an embodied form, and the remaining question is how to manoeuvre these complexities in a constructive way.

Part Two concerned current developments in South Africa regarding pregnancy in law and considerable attention was given to the legal positions of pregnant women and the unborn respectively. Ultimately, Part Two reveals that reproductive autonomy, as a concept, receives substantial support via constitutionally infused principles and rights, but its scope is very narrow. This narrow construction results in poor realisation of autonomy for a woman while she continues her pregnancy and blurs the boundaries when considering how to develop laws relevant to instances of pregnancy continuation.

When considering reproductive autonomy and the rights that support autonomous experience, most of the literature relevant to pregnancy focuses primarily on the right to terminate a pregnancy and the right of a woman not to be a parent. This is clearly an underdeveloped concept. Reproduction is not only avoiding parenthood but also securing it. The South African picture of reproductive autonomy is very constricted and obstructs the consideration of autonomy in the context of pregnancy continuation. This as an area in need of nurturing,[8] which allows for reproductive autonomy to be extended to include the consideration of pregnancy continuation and birth, and any action taken in relation to the pregnancy and birth has implications for women's autonomy in reproduction.[9]

Having argued for a more inclusive understanding of reproductive autonomy, another issue comes forward. On the one hand there are many supportive mechanisms in relation to parenthood avoidance in the form of constitutionally informed legislation[10] and case law[11] enhancing the reach of legislative and constitutional provisions. On the other hand, in the context of pregnancy continuation, there is clearly a lack of supportive mechanisms that are specificall relevant to the protection and advancement of women's rights during pregnancy continuation and birth.[12] For instance, the Choice Act does not have a correlating Act, something akin to the Choice on Continuation of Pregnancy Act,[13] which would regulate private or public relations between third parties and pregnant women for the duration of a pregnancy. Without recognising the 'extra-ness' that pregnancy represents for women and the unborn, the law will be unable to address the very unique concerns relevant to pregnancy, such as distinctive health care or treatment needs or the unique vulnerability pregnant women face in the context of criminal conduct.

---

[8] Nurturing is used because the research on constitutional rights showed that these rights are equally applicable to all issues relevant to pregnancy generally and not just termination of pregnancy.

[9] Looking at Parts One and Two together, the possible reason why this is in place is because feminists were firs and foremost seeking freedom of choice concerning reproduction, which would mean that where conception is unwanted or forced, mechanisms must be in place for women to rectify this, so it would make sense to firs secure the right not to be a parent and then move on to secure rights while pursuing the goal of parenthood.

[10] For instance, the Choice Act.

[11] For instance, see *Christian Lawyers Association v Minister of Health* 2005 (1) SA 509 (T) (*Christian Lawyers* (2005)); *Christian Lawyers Association of SA v Minister of Health* 1998 (4) SA 1113 (T); and *S v Mshumpa* 2008 (1) SACR 126 (E).

[12] This is not to say that nothing exists at all, but when comparing provisions relevant to the termination of a pregnancy in law and pregnancy continuation, there is a dearth of protective mechanisms for those women choosing to continue their pregnancies. The reason for this might relate to the fact that reproductive autonomy is not properly developed in South African law and therefore litigation on the topic will not take place nor will legislation be introduced.

[13] Schulman argues for similar legislation in the context of holding negligent medical professionals criminally accountable in cases where they cause a stillbirth; see generally M Schulman *The Nasciturus Non-Fiction, The Libby Gonen Story: Contemporary Reflections on the Status of the Nascitural Personhood in South African Law* (unpublished LLM dissertation, University of the Witwatersrand, 2014). (Although he adopts a separate-entities approach nonetheless.)

Understanding the position of pregnant women in law helps to identify how expansive their autonomy rights really are. It also provides a point of reference which specifie very clear parameters of which law reform efforts relevant to pregnancy secure rather than undermine their autonomy. It also demonstrates that something is missing in South African law. If women are continuing with pregnancies, there is some form of investment taking place in the unborn but the lack of legislation or case law on the matter points to the fact that this topic is not reaching law's full attention. With that note, our attention shifts to the unborn and their position in South African law. This brings 'approaches' to pregnancy to the fore in that the way the law approaches pregnancy is an indication of the position of the unborn.

Three approaches to pregnancy exist: the single-entity, the separate-entities and the not-one/not-two approaches. South Africa is recognised as adopting two of these approaches simultaneously. The single-entity approach is applied to all areas of the law, except in the context of the termination of pregnancy, where the not-one/not two approach is relevant. Under the single-entity approach, the unborn's interests are not recognised in law and pregnant women are viewed as the only relevant entities. This approach is a result of South Africa's adherence to the common-law born-alive rule, whereas the not-one/not-two approach recognises the existence and intrinsic worth of the unborn, but does so contextually, meaning that they are understood to be part and parcel of women and therefore their interests can be advanced only in relation to women and their rights.

The adoption of the single-entity approach is problematic in several respects. It denies the unborn's existence as entities with interests and it denies the lived reality of pregnancy as experienced by women who progress through pregnancy with the unborn gestating within them. Furthermore, it is removed from scientifi fact and it fails to resonate with contemporary knowledge and experiences of the unborn. Therefore, the application of the single-entity approach in law is no longer appropriate.

Further issues stand out as peculiar but resonate with what was highlighted regarding women's autonomy rights: the unborn's interests are not recognised in broader areas of law, such as those regulating health care, criminal law, status and so on and these are the laws relevant to the situation when a pregnancy is continued. Foetal interests are recognised when termination of pregnancy is at issue, in that women's rights to terminate a pregnancy are increasingly curbed as pregnancy progresses and this is viewed as being linked to the unborn's interests.[14] By adopting two different approaches to pregnancy, South African law is assuming contradictory positions regarding foetal interests because it recognises foetal interests when it comes to the termination of prenatal life by pregnant women but not when it comes to ensuring and maintaining optimal progression through gestation towards live birth. This is a contradictory position and it does not make sense for it to be maintained, so law reform is necessary in this regard.

---

[14] This resonates with the fact that pregnancy continuation in respect of women's rights has not been properly developed, and probably explains why foetal interests would not be recognised there because the extra-ness that pregnancy embodies is being overlooked. If pregnancy continuation is not receiving increased attention, the unborn would not either.

This is the firs research output to recognise South Africa as adopting two different approaches to foetal interests.[15] While a number of academics have recognised the Choice Act as advancing and limiting women's rights for the benefi of the unborn, none have understood this process as the product of relational thinking processes nor has a descriptor such as the not-one/not-two approach ever been assigned in South Africa. Instead, in South Africa, the majority of scholars have laboured under the erroneous view that the Choice Act applies the single-entity approach. This book shows otherwise. Arguing for an alternative view of the Choice Act creates the opportunity for the relationships between the unborn and pregnant women to be taken beyond the mere termination of pregnancy and infused into other debates involving pregnancy. This relational interpretation of the Choice Act is supported not only by case law[16] regarding the Choice Act but by the relational setting found in South African constitutional law.[17]

Part Two established that, as a result of applying the two approaches, there is no room for a tension to develop between female reproductive autonomy and foetal interests. This rests on the fact that, under the single-entity approach, the interests of the unborn are not recognised, while under the not-one/not-two approach both foetal interests and reproductive autonomy are advanced in relation to each other in a balanced way. However, there is clearly a need to reform the law away from the single-entity approach, and when considering how South African scholars suggested reform, a tension loomed. Furthermore, the study of the United States' position demonstrates that, as a result of this tension, their proposals for law reform would fail to advance pregnancy in law.

South African scholars have identifie a number of areas in need of reform and these are legitimate areas in need of increased consideration in the context of pregnancy.[18] However, their positions are worthy of support only in so far as they all reject the single-entity approach to pregnancy. The arguments presented in this book diverge from the commonly found positions among South African scholars in a number of respects. First, the reasons advanced for substantiating reform differ in that focus should be on protecting pregnancy as the representation of a unit between pregnant women and the unborn, thus allowing for a balanced consideration of female reproductive autonomy and foetal interests. On the other hand, South African academics argue for direct protection of the unborn to the exclusion of women. Secondly, their method of effecting reform takes place via the application of the separate-entities approach, whereas, here, a relational approach via the application of the not-one/not-two approach to pregnancy is adopted, which is already found to be in place in South Africa and its legitimacy is therefore already established.

---

[15] However, see C Pickles 'Approaches to pregnancy under the law: A relational response to the current South African position and recent academic trends' (2014) *De Jure* 20.

[16] *Christian Lawyers* (2005).

[17] As demonstrated in Chapter Four.

[18] Except in so far as it has been argued that the Choice Act should be repealed or access to termination of pregnancy should be increasingly curbed.

The diverging approach employed herein takes its cue from the concerning developments in the United States regarding pregnant women's rights in the context of the separate-entities approach. What the study of the United States reveals is the fact that too many complications and contradictory outcomes arise as a result of adopting a separate-entities approach to pregnancy. It shows that when the relationship between a woman and the foetus she carries is structured in a way that fosters tensions, poor pregnancy outcomes must be expected. Part Three demonstrates that these poor outcomes are a direct result of the fact that the separate-entities approach is a poor representation of the unborn in relation to pregnancy and, when the pregnancy unit is not properly represented, foetal interests and women's rights cannot be adequately advanced. Further, where women's rights are violated in order to secure foetal interests, the condition of pregnancy is compromised and this inevitability impacts negatively on the unborn, albeit indirectly. Given the expansive constitutional protections in place for women, this approach will not pass constitutional muster in South Africa. Women's rights are entrenched and, if one is aiming to address pregnancy-related concerns in South African law, it must be done in relation to those rights.

Feminist views on pregnancy are central when searching for a more effective and accurate articulation of pregnancy in law. Feminism is appropriate because it serves as an established voice for women (in spite of divergent approaches in it), and it makes sense to turn in that direction because pregnancy is a woman's concern in that only women experience the unique physicality of pregnancy. Further, when laws are developed around pregnancy, they will have a direct impact on women, either as part of a pregnancy unit or individually. Their participation is necessary so as to ensure that their views and experiences are included in broader considerations when developing the law.

Nedelsky's relational feminism categorically shapes the development of the way forward.[19] First, she highlights that everyone is involved in relationships and these relationships are central to who we are and the quality of life's experiences. Secondly, relationships exist not only between persons but also between persons and other entities such as the unborn, and a responsibility to lessen harm originates from that relationship. Thirdly, the quality of the various relationships is shaped by those forces that structure relationships, such as the law and wider contextual issues, being social and cultural norms. She explains that when relationships are not of a good quality in that capacities are not being developed or rights are being undermined, then one is required to restructure the relationship to allow for the proper realisation of rights, interests or capacities.

Her emphasis on constructing relationships in a way that builds and fosters capacities and rights reveals that if we are concerned with addressing the tension between women's rights and foetal interests, then it is necessary to reform the law, policies and general arguments in a way that removes the opportunity for tension between women and the unborn. What stands out after delving into Nedelsky's

[19] J Nedelsky 'Reconceiving autonomy: Sources, thoughts and possibilities' (1989) 1 *Yale Journal of Law & Feminism* 7; J Nedelsky 'Property in potential life? A relational approach to choosing legal categories' (1993) 6 *Canadian Journal of Law & Jurisprudence* 343; and J Nedelsky *Law's Relations: A Relational Theory of Self, Autonomy, and Law* (2011).

work is the fact that, in the context of the United States study, all the commentaries against the separate-entities approach were adopting a relational approach, in that they were all seeking to secure a healthy pregnancy unit for both pregnant women and the unborn. Collectively, their arguments demonstrated that, when a healthy relationship or unit is secured between pregnant women and the unborn, better pregnancy outcomes can be expected. This view supports the notion that women are not naturally (as a point of departure) in an adversarialist position with the unborn, but, rather, it is the way that pregnancy is being structured in law or by other third parties that creates the notion of there being a tension.

Building from Nedelsky, we can accept that pregnant women are in a relationship with the unborn they carry, and this constitutes a pregnancy relationship. Characteristically, this relationship is unlike any other in that it takes place in one body and the entities cannot be separated unless via birth, miscarriage or termination of the pregnancy. The uniqueness of this relationship therefore means that women and the unborn are two, but their inseparability makes them one. Further, since the unborn are embodied within women, others cannot relate to them directly but only to the unit of pregnancy being the pregnancy relationship. This position demonstrates that, when something needs to be done to 'protect' the unborn, it must be done via the women who carry them and must therefore be respectful of their rights as human beings. This forces a broadening of context; instead of merely asking how the foetus can be protected in law, the question grows into how the law can secure an environment that protects healthy pregnancy progression and outcomes as a 'unitary need' (being made up of foetal interests and women's autonomy rights).

The uniqueness of this relationship demands the development or use of a pregnancy-specifi approach rather than the mere application of existing legal positions of either the single-entity or separate-entities approaches generally applicable to individual born persons. The not-one/not-two approach falls neatly in line with this requirement. It meets the relational demands of acknowledging the unborn and, by identifying pregnancy as not constituting two separate entities, it positions the recognition of the unborn in direct relation to the pregnant women carrying them and their rights. Furthermore, this approach is already applied in a pregnancy-specifi context, being the South African Choice Act.

Identifying that the unborn are recognised in law begs the question of what it is about the unborn that is being recognised in law. Ultimately, the unborn should be recognised as forming part of humanity, which is in line with what science tells us. However, they are also embodied (thus also falling in line with the lived reality of pregnancy) and, as a result of their embodied nature, they are not legal subjects either. Instead, the unborn are vested with special status, which is a unique status in law devised specificall for the distinctive position of the unborn. This status demands that protective measures are increasingly made available as pregnancy progresses closer to birth to secure healthy pregnancies and pregnancy outcomes for both women and the unborn. Developing and working with this status and securing this status' connection to pregnant women's (by emphasising the embodied nature of the unborn), women's rights and foetal interests must mutually form part of securing a way forward.

In this respect there is space created in law to recognise the unborn in an appropriate way, while also acknowledging women's rights and their wider social and cultural experiences. This nullifie the necessity for going so far as to extend personhood to the unborn in order to acknowledge and protect their interests. Furthermore, Chapter Ten showed how this approach could be applied to other areas of pregnancy in law, thus allowing for reform without compromising either foetal interests or female autonomy rights. Most importantly, this approach allows for third parties to be held criminally liable when the pregnancy relationship is arbitrarily harmed but encourages more constructive approaches to be adopted when addressing issues of self-harm during pregnancy. This proves the transcendental character of this approach, which therefore reflect its appropriateness for its application to pregnancy in law.

The book establishes that neither the single-entity nor the separate-entities approach adequately recognises or engages the connected nature of pregnancy. The single-entity approach makes nonentities of the unborn and fails to give effective legal recognition to broader constructs of female reproductive autonomy. The application of the separate-entities approach to pregnancy goes on to make almost obscure nonentities of pregnant women and, where they are recognised, it is on a limited basis and focuses mainly on them as adversarial participants in a pregnancy. Furthermore, neither approach gives effective legal recognition to the values and interests of the unborn. In conclusion, both approaches to pregnancy fail as a result of the very fact that neither successfully grasps the lived experiences of pregnancy and therefore neither provides an adequate foundation for a tension-free model of pregnancy in law.

When considering pregnancy under the law, the value of the unborn must be recognised, but understood in relation to pregnant women. Understanding the togetherness that pregnancy represents allows the law to recognise both entities that constitute the pregnancy. Any calls for law reform regarding pregnancy, pregnant women or the unborn may essentially fail, because their foundational approaches tend to exclude one of the constituent 'parties' that form a pregnancy. Without women, no pregnancies would exist—and the same can be said of the unborn.

The not-one/not-two approach employs the embodied connectedness of pregnancy as a point of departure, and seeks to advance an inclusive approach to issues stemming from pregnancy. It uses the pregnancy relationship and its context as an interpretive tool in determining a way forward. While this approach may not always place the interests of the unborn above those of the pregnant women carrying them, it does require that their interests be considered with reference to the dictates of context. The very fact that South Africa already has the makings of this approach in the judicial interpretation of the Choice Act in *Christian Lawyers* (2005) speaks volumes regarding its appropriateness and constitutional soundness. The not-one/not-two approach should therefore receive proper consideration henceforth and, where reform is recommended, those recommendations should be tested against the demands of this model of pregnancy. This would ensure that tensions are avoided and the interests of both participants to the pregnancy are advanced.

Focusing on the value of connection between pregnant women and the unborn serves as the foundation for securing a tension-free way forward for law relating to pregnancy. It also indicates that the law plays an integral role in structuring relationships and can thus protect both women and the unborn from possible infringements through adversarialist interventions and environments.

INDEX

S

www.ingramcontent.com/pod-product-compliance
Lightning Source LLC
LaVergne TN
LVHW080528210926
848481LV00023B/3754
* 9 7 8 1 4 8 5 1 1 9 5 4 8 *